TRADITIONS & ENCOUNTERS

TRADITIONS & ENCOUNTERS

A GLOBAL PERSPECTIVE ON THE PAST
VOLUME II: FROM 1500 TO THE PRESENT

JERRY H. BENTLEY

University of Hawai`i

. . .

HERBERT F. ZIEGLER

University of Hawai`i

Boston   Burr Ridge, IL   Dubuque, IA   Madison, WI   New York   San Francisco   St. Louis
Bangkok   Bagotá   Caracas   Lisbon   London   Madrid
Mexico City   Milan   New Delhi   Seoul   Singapore   Sydney   Taipei   Toronto

McGraw-Hill Higher Education

A Division of The **McGraw-Hill** *Companies*

TRADITIONS & ENCOUNTERS: A GLOBAL PERSPECTIVE ON THE PAST, VOLUME II: FROM 1500 TO THE PRESENT

This book is printed on acid-free paper.

2 3 4 5 6 7 8 9 0 VNH/VNH 0 9 8 7 6 5 4 3 2 1 0

ISBN 0–07–004920–3

Editorial director: *Jane E. Vaicunas*
Senior sponsoring editor: *Lyn Uhl*
Developmental editors: *Donata Dettbarn/Jeannine Ciliotta*
Senior marketing manager: *Suzanne Daghlian*
Project manager: *Marilyn M. Sulzer*
Production supervisor: *Laura Fuller*
Designer: *Michael Warrell*
Senior photo research coordinator: *Carrie K. Burger*
Art editor: *Brenda A. Ernzen*
Senior supplement coordinator: *Candy M. Kuster*
Compositor: *Shepherd, Inc.*
Typeface: *10/12 Galliard*
Printer: *Von Hoffmann Press, Inc.*

Interior design: *Becky Lemma*
Cover photo: *Traveling Companion.* Zifen Qian/Superstock
Photo research: *Deborah Bull/PhotoSearch, Inc.*

The credits section for this book begins on page C–1 and is considered an extension of the copyright page.

Library of Congress has cataloged the combined edition as follows:

Bentley, Jerry H., 1949–
    Traditions & encounters : a global perspective on the past /
Jerry H. Bentley, Herbert F. Ziegler.
        p.   cm.
    Includes index.
    ISBN 0–07–004923–8
    1. World history.   2. Intercultural communication—History.
I. Ziegler, Herbert F.,   1949–   . II. Title.
D20.B42   2000
909—dc21   99–13503
                                                            CIP

www.mhhe.com

ABOUT THE AUTHORS

· · ·

Jerry H. Bentley is professor of history at the University of Hawai`i and editor of the *Journal of World History*. He has written extensively on the cultural history of early modern Europe and on cross-cultural interactions in world history. His research on the religious, moral, and political writings of Renaissance led to the publication of "Humanists and Holy Writ: New Testament Scholarship in the Renaissance" (1983) and "Politics and Culture in Renaissance Naples" (1987). His more recent research has concentrated on global history and particularly on processes of cross-cultural interaction. His book, *Old World Encounters: Cross-Cultural Contacts and Exchanges in Pre-Modern Times (1993)*, studies processes of cultural exchange and religious conversion before modern times, and his pamphlet, *Shapes of World History in Twentieth-Century Scholarship (1996)*, discusses the historiography of world history. His current interests include processes of cross-cultural interaction and cultural exchange in modern times.

· · ·

Herbert F. Ziegler is an associate professor of history at the University of Hawaii. He has taught courses on world history for the last 19 years and is currently the director of the world history program at the University of Hawaii. For several years he also served as the book review editor of the *Journal of World History*. His interest in twentieth-century European social and political history led to the publication of *Nazi Germany's New Aristocracy (1990)*. He is at present working on a study that explores uncharted aspects of German society, especially the cultural manifestations of humor and satire in the Nazi era. His other current research project focuses on the application of complexity theory to a comparative study of societies and their internal dynamics.

BRIEF CONTENTS

· · ·

DETAILED CONTENTS

. . .

PART V

THE ORIGINS OF GLOBAL INTERDEPENDENCE, 1500–1800   530

PART VI

AN AGE OF REVOLUTION, INDUSTRY, AND EMPIRE, 1750–1914 722

LIST OF MAPS

• • •

PREFACE

. . .

During the 1990s the term *globalization* entered the vocabulary of politicians, journalists, scholars, and others who commented on the increasingly tight connections linking the world's lands and peoples. By the late twentieth century, global transportation and communication networks had become more intricate than ever before, and they supported voluminous trade and systematic interaction among peoples throughout the world. Global links brought problems as well as opportunities: pollution, environmental change, ethnic tensions, political conflicts, and weapons of mass destruction loomed as potential threats to all peoples. Yet even though they are more prominent today than ever before, global interactions and global problems are by no means new features of world history. To the contrary, there is a long historical context for contemporary globalization, and only in the light of past experience is it possible to understand the contemporary world.

A GLOBAL PERSPECTIVE ON THE PAST

Our purpose in this book is to offer a global perspective on the past—a vision of history that is meaningful and appropriate for the interdependent world of contemporary times. During an era when peoples from all parts of the earth meet, mingle, interact, and do business with each other, a global perspective has become an essential tool for informed and responsible citizenship. Because global interactions profoundly influence the fortunes of peoples in all lands, it is impossible to understand the contemporary world by approaching it exclusively from the viewpoint of western Europe, the United States, Japan, or any other individual society. And it is equally impossible to understand the world's history by viewing it through the lenses of any particular society.

A global perspective on the past calls for analysis that respects the historical experiences of all the world's peoples—not just one or a few—and that examines the roles of all in the making of a world inhabited by all. A global perspective calls also for analysis that goes beyond the study of individual societies to examine their larger regional, continental, hemispheric, and global contexts and to explore the structures promoting interactions between peoples of different societies. By bringing this kind of global perspective to world history, we hope to offer an understanding of the past that places the contemporary world in meaningful historical context.

At first glance, *Traditions and Encounters* might look similar to several other books that survey the world's past. Like the others, *Traditions and Encounters* examines the historical development of societies in Asia, Europe, Africa, the Americas, and Oceania. But *Traditions and Encounters* differs from other works in two particularly important ways. First, in addition to charting the development of individual societies, it focuses attention systematically on interactions between peoples of different societies. And second, it organizes the human past into seven eras that represent distinct and coherent periods of global historical development.

THEMES: TRADITION AND ENCOUNTER

How is it possible to make sense of the entire human past? The study of world history is exhilarating, but given the range of human diversity, it also presents a daunting challenge. Human communities have adopted widely varying forms of political, social, and economic organization, and they have elaborated even more diverse cultural, religious, and philosophical legacies. Given the manifold diversity of human societies, it might seem that masses of unrelated detail threaten to swamp any effort to deal with all the world's history.

In this book we concentrate on two main themes—tradition and encounter—that help to bring order to world history. These two themes bring focus to some of the most important features of human experience on the earth. In combination, they account for much of the historical development of human societies.

The theme of tradition draws attention to the formation, maintenance, and sometimes collapse of individual societies. From their earliest days on earth, human groups have generated distinctive political, social, economic, and cultural traditions that have guided affairs in their own societies. Some of these traditions arose and disappeared relatively quickly, while others influenced human affairs over the centuries and millennia, sometimes up to the present day. Thus one of our principal concerns in this book is to examine the development of political, social, economic, and cultural traditions that have shaped the lives and experiences of the world's peoples. Individual chapters explore the traditions that different people relied on to organize and sustain societies in Asia, Europe, Africa, the Americas, and Oceania. Emphasis falls especially on the large, densely populated, complex, city-based societies that have most deeply influenced the course of history for the past six thousand years, but smaller and less powerful societies also receive their share of attention.

While elaborating distinctive political, social, economic, and cultural traditions to organize their own affairs, the world's peoples have also interacted regularly with one another since the earliest days of human history. The theme of encounter directs attention to communications, interactions, and exchanges that have linked individual societies to their neighbors and the larger world. By systematically examining encounters between peoples of different societies, we draw attention to processes of cross-cultural interaction that have been some of the most effective agents of change in all of world history. In the form of mass migrations, campaigns of imperial expansion, long-distance trade, diffusions of food crops, the spread of infectious and contagious diseases, transfers of technological skills, and the spread of religious and cultural traditions, these interactions have profoundly influenced the experiences of individual societies and the development of the world as a whole. Thus, while paying due attention to individual societies and their traditions, chapters of this book also discuss interactions that linked the fortunes of peoples from different societies. Many chapters also examine the large-scale structures of transportation, communication, and exchange that supported interactions among the world's peoples.

ORGANIZATION: SEVEN ERAS OF GLOBAL HISTORY

While focusing on the themes of tradition and encounter, we seek to bring additional clarity to the human past by organizing it into seven eras of global history. These eras, treated successively in the seven parts of this book, represent coherent epochs that form the larger architecture of world history as we see it. The seven eras do not reflect the particular experience of any single society so much as the common experience of societies engaged in cross-cultural interaction. Thus our seven epochs of global history owe their coherence particularly to networks of transportation, communication, and exchange that linked peoples of different societies at different times in the past. Even in ancient times these networks supported interactions that shaped the experiences of peoples from different lands, and with the development of increasingly effective means of transportation and communication, interactions grew more frequent, systematic, and intense. By situating the development of the world's peoples in the framework of the seven eras of global history, we seek to offer meaningful comparisons between different societies and also to highlight the role of cross-cultural interactions in shaping the experiences of individual societies and influencing the development of the world as a whole.

Thus from the beginning to the end of this book we focus on the twin themes of tradition and encounter, which in combination go a long way toward accounting for the historical development of the human species on planet earth, and we place the experiences of individual societies in their larger regional, continental, hemispheric, and global contexts. By bringing a global perspective to the study of humanity's common historical experience, we seek to offer a vision of the past that is both meaningful and appropriate for the interdependent world of contemporary times. We hope that *Traditions and Encounters* will enable readers to understand the development of world history and to place the modern world in its proper historical context.

A BRIEF NOTE ON USAGE

· · ·

This book qualifies dates as B.C.E. ("Before the Common Era") or C.E. ("Common Era"). In practice, B.C.E. refers to the same epoch as B.C. ("Before Christ"), and C.E. refers to the same epoch as A.D. (*Anno Domini,* a Latin term meaning "in the year of the Lord"). As historical study becomes a global, multicultural enterprise, however, scholars increasingly prefer terminology that does not apply the standards of one society to all the others. Thus reference in this book to B.C.E. and C.E. reflects emerging scholarly convention concerning the qualification of historical dates.

Measurements of length and distance appear here according to the metric system, followed by their English-system equivalents in parentheses.

The book transliterates Chinese names and terms into English according to the *pinyin* system, which is increasingly displacing the more cumbersome Wade-Giles system. Transliteration of names and terms from other languages follows contemporary scholarly conventions.

ACKNOWLEDGEMENTS

. . .

Many individuals have contributed to this book, and the authors take pleasure in recording deep thanks for all the comments, criticism, advice, and suggestions that helped to improve the work. The editorial team at McGraw-Hill did an outstanding job of keeping the authors focused on the project. Special thanks go to Leslye Jackson, Jeannine Ciliotta, Jane Vaicunas, Lyn Uhl, Amy Mack, and Donata Dettbarn, who provided crucial support by helping the authors work through difficult issues and solve the innumerable problems of content, style and organization that arise in any project to produce a history of the world. Many colleagues at the University of Hawai`i and elsewhere aided and advised the authors on matters of organization and composition. For her contributions that went far beyond the call of duty, recognition goes particularly to Mimi Henriksen of the University of Hawai`i. Elton L. Daniel and Louise McReynolds at the University of Hawai`i and Roger Adelson at Arizona State University also provided expert help. Timothy M. Sullivan and David A. Robyak prepared materials for the maps. Finally, we would like to express our appreciation for the advice of the following individuals who read and commented on the book's text as it went through its various drafts:

Roger Adelson
Arizona State University

Alfred Andrea
University of Vermont

Ed Anson
University of Arkansas at Little Rock

Maria Arbelaz
University of Nebraska–Omaha

Peter Arnade
University of California–San Marco

Karl Bahm
University of Southern Mississippi

Guy Beckwith
Auburn University

Lynda Bell
University of California–Riverside

Norman Bennett
Boston University

Robert Blackey
California State University–San Bernadino

Samuel Brunk
University of Texas–El Paso

Deborah Buffton
University of Wisconsin–LaCrosse

Sharon L. Bush
LeMoyne-Owen College

Antonio Calabria
University of Texas–San Antonio

Orazio Ciccarelli
University of Southern Mississippi

Hugh R. Clark
Ursinus College

Daniel Connerton
North Adams State

Bruce Cruikshank
Hastings College

Graciella Cruz-Tara
Florida Atlantic University

Ross Dunn
San Diego State University

Nancy Erickson
Erskine College

Edward Farmer
University of Minnesota

Lanny Fields
*California State University–
San Bernadino*

Robert Frankle
University of Memphis

Bonnie Frederick
Washington State University

Steve Gosch
University of Wisconsin, Eau Claire

Travis Hanes III
*University of North Carolina–
Wilmington*

Gerald Herman
Northeastern University

Udo Heyn
California State University–Los Angeles

Cheryl Johnson-Odim
Loyola University

Thomas Kay
Wheaton College

Winston Kinsey
Appalachian State University

Paul Knoll
University of Southern California

Zoltan Kramer
Central Washington University

Lisa Lane
Miracosta College

George Lankevich
Bronx Community College

Loyd Lee
SUNY–New Paltz

Richard Lewis
Saint Cloud State University

David Longfellow
Baylor University

Ben Lowe
Florida Atlantic University

Dorothea A. L. Martin
Appalachian State University

Ken Mason
Santa Monica College

Robert Mathews
Northshore Community College

Randall McGowen
University of Oregon

Pamela McVay
Ursuline College

John Mears
Southern Methodist University

Monserrat Miller
Marshall University

Peter Nayenga
Saint Cloud State University

Ruth Necheles-Jansyn
Long Island University

Marian Nelson
University of Nebraska

Veena Talwar Oldenburg
Baruch College

Patricia O'Neill
Central Oregon Community College

James Overfield
University of Vermont

Patrick Peebles
University of Missouri–Kansas City

Peter W. Petschauer
Appalachian State University

Clifton Potter
Lynchburg College

Douglas Reynolds
Georgia State University

Cheryl Riggs
*California State University–
San Bernadino*

William Schell
Murray State University

Gary Scudder
Georgia Perimeter College

Howard Shealy
Kennesaw State College

David Smith
*California State Polytechnic
University–Pomona*

Roland Spickerman
University of Detroit–Mercy

Robert Tignor
Princeton University

Jeff Wasserstrom
Indiana University–Bloomington

Robert Wenke
University of Washington

Sally West
Truman State University

Scott Wheeler
West Point

Joe Whitehorne
Lord Fairfax Community College

Richard Williams
Washington State University

John Woods
University of Chicago

C. K. Yoon
James Madison University

THE ORIGINS OF GLOBAL INTERDEPENDENCE, 1500–1800

. . .

By 1500 C.E. peoples throughout the world had built well-organized societies with distinctive cultural traditions. Powerful agricultural societies dominated most of Asia, the Mediterranean basin, Europe, much of sub-Saharan Africa, Mexico, and the central Andean region. Pastoral nomads thrived in the dry grassy regions of central Asia and Africa, and hunting and gathering societies with small populations survived in lands where cultivation and herding were not practical possibilities. The vast majority of the world's peoples, however, lived in agricultural societies that observed distinctive political, social, and cultural traditions.

By 1500 peoples of the world had also established intricate transportation networks that supported travel, communication, and exchange between their societies. For more than a millennium, merchants had traveled the silk roads that crossed central Asia to link lands from China to the Mediterranean basin, and mariners had plied the Indian Ocean and neighboring waters in connecting lands from Japan to east Africa. Caravan routes across the Sahara desert brought sub-Saharan west Africa into the larger economy of the eastern hemisphere. Although pioneered by merchants in the interests of trade, these transportation networks also supported cultural and biological exchanges. Several religious traditions—most notably Buddhism, Christianity, and Islam—traveled along the trade routes and attracted followers in distant lands. Similarly, food crops, animal stocks, and disease pathogens spread throughout much of the eastern hemisphere in premodern times. Transportation networks in the Americas and Oceania were not as extensive as those in the eastern hemisphere, but they also supported communication and exchange over long distances. Trade linked societies throughout North America, and seafarers routinely sailed between island groups especially in the central and western Pacific Ocean.

Commercial, cultural, and biological exchanges of premodern times prefigured much more intense cross-cultural interactions after 1500. These later interactions followed the establishment of new transportation networks in the form of sea-lanes linking the lands of the Indian, Atlantic, and Pacific Ocean basins. Beginning in the fifteenth century, European mariners sought new, all-sea routes to the markets of Asia. As a result of their exploratory voyages, they established trade routes throughout the world's oceans and entered into dealings with many of the world's peoples. The new sea-lanes not only fostered direct contact between Europeans and the peoples of sub-Saharan Africa and Asia but also facilitated the first sustained encounter between the peoples of the eastern hemisphere, the western hemisphere, and Oceania. In short, European mariners created globe-girdling networks of transportation, communication, and exchange that supported cross-cultural interactions much more systematic and intense than those of earlier times.

The establishment of links between all the world's regions and peoples gave rise to the early modern era of world history, approximately 1500 to 1800 C.E. The early modern era differed from the period from 1000 to 1500, when there were only a few sporadic contacts between peoples of the eastern hemisphere, the western hemisphere, and Oceania. It also differed from the modern era from 1800 to the present, when national states, heavy industry, powerful weapons, and efficient technologies of transportation and communication enabled peoples of European ancestry to achieve political and economic dominance in the world.

During the early modern era, several global processes touched peoples in all parts of the world and influenced the development of their societies. One involved biological exchange: plants, animals, diseases, and human communities crossed the world's oceans and established themselves in new lands where they dramatically affected both the natural environment and established societies. Another involved commercial exchange: merchants took advantage of newly established sea-lanes to inaugurate a genuinely global economy in which agricultural products, manufactured goods, and other commodities reached markets in distant lands. Yet another process involved the diffusion of technologies and cultural traditions: printing and gunpowder spread throughout the world, and Christianity and Islam attracted increasing numbers of converts in widely spread regions of the world.

These global processes had different effects for different peoples. The indigenous peoples of the Americas and Oceania experienced turmoil and disruption: diseases introduced from the eastern hemisphere ravaged their populations and sometimes led to the collapse of their societies. Europeans by contrast largely flourished during the early modern era: they traded profitably throughout the world and claimed vast stretches of land in the Americas, where they founded colonies and cultivated crops for sale on the open market. Africans benefited from the introduction of new food crops and the opportunity to obtain trade goods from abroad, but these benefits came at a terrible cost: millions of enslaved individuals from sub-Saharan Africa underwent a forced migration to the western hemisphere, where they performed hard labor, lived in poverty, and suffered both physical and psychological abuse. East Asian and Islamic peoples sought to limit the influence of global processes in their lands: they prospered from increased trade but sharply restricted the introduction of foreign ideas and technologies into their societies.

European peoples drew most benefit from global processes of the period 1500 to 1800, but by no means did they dominate world affairs in early modern times. They established large empires and settler colonies in the Americas, but most of the western hemisphere lay beyond their control until the nineteenth century. European peoples established a series of fortified trading posts and the colony of Angola in Africa, but mostly they traded in Africa at the sufferance of local authorities and rarely wielded direct influence beyond the coastlines. European peoples conquered the Philippines and many Indonesian islands but posed no threat at all to the powerful imperial states that ruled China, India, southwest Asia, and Anatolia, or even to the island state of Japan. Although they did not establish world hegemony in early modern times, European peoples nevertheless played a far more prominent role in world affairs than any of their ancestors, and their efforts fostered the development of an increasingly interdependent world.

ASIA	AFRICA	EUROPE	AMERICAS AND OCEANIA
1450	**1450**	**1450**	**1450**
Ottoman Sultan Mehmed II (1451–1481)	Songhay empire (1464–1591) Songhay ruler Sunni Ali (1464–1493) Portuguese slave trade to Iberian peninsula Trade between Kongo and Portugal (1482)	Russian Tsar Ivan III (1462–1505) Spanish reconquista complete (1492)	Christopher Columbus sails to the Caribbean (1492) Treaty of Tordesillas (1494)
1500	**1500**	**1500**	**1500**
Safavid empire (1501–1722) Shah Ismail (1501–1524) Battle of Chaldiran (1514) Ottoman Sultan Selim the Grim (1512–1520) Ottoman Sultan Süleyman the Magnificent (1520–1566) Mughal empire (1523–1763) Zahir al-din Muhammad; Mughal conquest of India (1523) Jesuit Francis Xavier in Japan (1549)	Portuguese fleet sacks Swahili city-states Kongo King Affonso I converts to Roman Catholicism (1506–1543) African slaves to Caribbean and Central and South America (1520s)	Ferdinand Magellan's circumnavigation of the world (1519–1522) Holy Roman Emperor Charles V (1519–1556) Martin Luther, John Calvin, and the Protestant Reformation Nicolaus Copernicus (1543)	Vasco Nuñez de Balboa sights the Pacific Ocean (1513) Aztec King Motecuzoma II (1502–1520) Inca Emperor Atahualpa Hernán Cortés conquers the Aztec empire (1519–1521) Epidemic smallpox in the Aztec and Inca empires (1519–1530s) Francisco Pizarro conquers the Inca empire (1532–1533) Establishment of encomiendas in the Americas
1550	**1550**	**1550**	**1550**
Mughal Emperor Akbar (1556–1605) Wanli and decline of the Ming dynasty (1572–1620) Jesuit Matteo Ricci in China (1582–1610) Safavid Shah Abbas the Great (1588–1629)	Timbuktu and Islamic university	Russian Tsar Ivan IV (1533–1584) Council of Trent (1545–1563), the Society of Jesus, and the Counter-Reformation Spanish King Philip II (1556–1598) English Queen Elizabeth (1558–1603)	Spaniard Miguel López de Legazpi conquers the Philippines (1575) Galleon trade between Manila and Acapulco
1600	**1600**	**1600**	**1600**
Tokugawa bakufu (1600–1867) Tokugawa Ieyasu and the unification of Japan (1600–1616) "Floating World" Ihara Saikaku Nurhaci and organization of the Manchus (1616–1626) Mughal Emperor Shah Jahan (1630s) Taj Mahal End of the Ming dynasty (1644) Qing dynasty (1644–1911) *The Romance of the Three Kingdoms, The Dream of the Red Chamber*	African slaves to North America (early 1600s) Queen Nzinga of Angola (1623–1663)	Thirty Years' War (1618–1648) Cardinal Richelieu (1624–1642) Johannes Kepler (1571–1630) and Galileo Galilei (1564–1642) English Civil War (1642–1649)	French found Port Royal (1604) and Quebec (1608) English found Jamestown (1607) and the Massachusetts Bay Colony (1630) Dutch found New Amsterdam (1633) First African slaves reach Virginia (1610) Dutch mariners sight Australia (1606) Dutchman Jan Pieterszoon Coen founds Batavia in Java (1619)

ASIA	AFRICA	EUROPE	AMERICAS AND OCEANIA
1650	**1650**	**1650**	**1650**
Mughal Emperor Aurangzeb (1659–1707) Qing Emperor Kangxi (1661–1722) *Collection of Books*	War between Kongo and Portugal (1665) Portugal conquers Angola Dutch conquer Khoikhoi in south Africa Fulani found Islamic states in Guinea, Senegal, Mali, and Nigeria (1680s)	French King Louis XIV (1643–1715) John Locke (1632–1704) and Isaac Newton (1642–1727) Glorious Revolution (1688) Schism in Russian church (1660s–1680s)	Epidemic smallpox in Guam (1688)
1700	**1700**	**1700**	**1700**
Qing Emperor Qianlong (1736–1795) *Complete Library of the Four Treasuries*	Dona Beatriz and Antonian movement (1704) Execution of Dona Beatriz (1706) High point in African slave trade Average of 55,000 Africans a year to Americas Rise of Asante, Dahomey, and Oyo societies	Russian Tsar Peter the Great (1682–1725) Baron de Montesquieu (1689–1755)	
1750	**1750**	**1750**	**1750**
	Olaudah Equiano (1745–1797)	Seven Years' War (1756–1763) Voltaire (1694–1778) Adam Smith (1723–1790) Russian Tsarina Catherine the Great (1762–1795) Partitions of Poland (1790s)	French and Indian War (1754–1763) James Cook's exploration of Australia, New Zealand, and Hawai`i Establishment of first European settlement in Australia (1788) Slave revolt in Saint-Domingue and creation of Haiti (1793)
1800	**1800**	**1800**	**1800**

TRANSOCEANIC ENCOUNTERS AND GLOBAL CONNECTIONS

· · ·

On 8 July 1497 the Portuguese mariner Vasco da Gama led a small fleet of four armed merchant vessels with 170 crewmen out of the harbor at Lisbon. His destination was India, which he planned to reach by sailing around the continent of Africa and through the Indian Ocean. He carried letters of introduction from the king of Portugal, as well as cargoes of gold, pearls, wool textiles, bronzeware, iron tools, and other goods that he hoped to exchange for pepper and spices in India.

Before there would be an opportunity to trade, however, da Gama and his crew had a prolonged voyage through two oceans. They sailed south from Portugal to the Cape Verde Islands off the west coast of Africa, where they took on water and fresh provisions. On 3 August they headed southeast into the Atlantic Ocean to take advantage of the prevailing winds. For the next ninety-five days, the fleet saw no land as it sailed through some six thousand nautical miles of open ocean. By October, da Gama had found westerly winds in the southern Atlantic, rounded the Cape of Good Hope, and entered the Indian Ocean. The fleet slowly worked its way up the east coast of Africa, engaging in hostilities with local authorities at Mozambique and Mombasa, as far as Malindi, where da Gama secured the services of an Indian Muslim pilot to guide his ships across the Arabian Sea. On 20 May 1498—more than ten months after its departure from Lisbon—the fleet anchored at Calicut in southern India.

In India the Portuguese fleet found a wealthy, cosmopolitan society. Upon its arrival local authorities in Calicut dispatched a pair of Tunisian merchants who spoke Spanish and Italian to serve as translators for the newly arrived party. The markets of Calicut offered not only pepper, ginger, cinnamon, and spices but also rubies, emeralds, gold jewelry, and fine cotton textiles. Alas, apart from gold and some striped cloth, the goods that da Gama had brought attracted little interest among merchants at Calicut. Nevertheless, da Gama managed to exchange gold for a cargo of pepper and cinnamon that turned a handsome profit when the fleet returned to Portugal in August 1499. Da Gama's expedition opened the door to maritime trade between European and Asian peoples and helped to establish permanent links between the world's various regions.

A recently discovered portrait of James Cook painted by William Hodges about 1775 depicts a determined man. • National Maritime Museum, Greenwich, London

Cross-cultural interactions have been a persistent feature of historical development. Even in ancient times mass migration, campaigns of imperial expansion, and long-distance trade deeply influenced societies throughout the world. As a result of these interactions, Buddhism, Islam, and Christianity spread from their places of birth to the distant corners of the eastern hemisphere. Long before modern times arteries of long-distance trade served also as the principal conduits for exchanges of plants, animals, and diseases.

After 1500 C.E. cross-cultural interactions took place on a much larger geographical scale, and encounters were often more disruptive than in earlier centuries. Equipped with advanced technologies and a powerful military arsenal, western European peoples began to cross the world's oceans in large numbers during the early modern era. The projection of European influence brought about a decisive shift in the global balance of power. During the millennium 500 to 1500 C.E., the world's most powerful societies were those organized by imperial states such as the Tang dynasty of China, the Abbasid dynasty in southwest Asia, the Byzantine empire in the eastern Mediterranean region, and the Mongol empires that embraced much of Eurasia. After 1500, however, western European peoples became much more prominent than before in the larger world, and they began to establish transoceanic empires that by the nineteenth century ruled most of the world.

The expansion of European influence also resulted in the establishment of global networks of transportation, communication, and exchange. A worldwide diffusion of plants, animals, diseases, and human communities followed European ventures across the oceans, and intricate trade networks gave birth to a global economy. Although epidemic diseases killed millions of people, the spread of food crops and domesticated animals led to a dramatic surge in global population. The establishment of global trade networks ensured that interactions between the world's peoples would continue and intensify.

THE EUROPEAN RECONNAISSANCE OF THE WORLD'S OCEANS

Between 1400 and 1800 European mariners launched a remarkable series of exploratory voyages that took them to all the earth's waters, with the exception of those in extreme polar regions. These voyages were very expensive affairs. Yet private investors and government authorities had strong motives to underwrite the expeditions and outfit them with advanced nautical technology. The voyages of exploration paid large dividends: they enabled European mariners to chart the world's ocean basins and develop an accurate understanding of world geography. On the basis of this knowledge, European merchants and mariners established global networks of communication, transportation, and exchange—and profited handsomely from their efforts.

Motives for Exploration

A complex combination of motives prompted Europeans to explore the world's oceans. Most important of them were the search for basic resources and lands suitable for the cultivation of cash crops, the desire to establish new trade routes to Asian markets, and the aspiration to expand the influence of Christianity.

Mariners from the relatively poor and hard-scrabble kingdom of Portugal were most prominent in the search for fresh resources to exploit and lands to cultivate. Beginning in the thirteenth century, Portuguese seamen ventured away from the coasts and into the open Atlantic Ocean. They originally sought fish, seals, whales, timber, and lands where they could grow wheat to supplement the meager resources of Portugal. By the early fourteenth century, they had discovered the uninhabited Azores and Madeiras Islands. They called frequently at the Canary Islands, inhabited by the indigenous Guanches, which Italian and Iberian mariners had visited since the early fourteenth century. Because European demand for sugar was strong and increasing, the prospect of establishing sugar plantations on the Atlantic islands was very tempting. Italian entrepreneurs had organized sugar plantations in Palestine and the Mediterranean islands since the twelfth century, and in the fifteenth century Italian investors worked with Portuguese mariners to establish plantations in the Atlantic islands. Continuing Portuguese voyages also led to the establishment of plantations on more southerly Atlantic islands, including the Cape Verde Islands, São Tomé, Principe, and Fernando Po.

Portuguese Exploration

Even more alluring than the exploitation of fresh lands and resources was the goal of establishing maritime trade routes to the markets of Asia. During the era of the Mongol empires, European merchants often traveled overland as far as China in order to trade in silk, spices, porcelain, and other Asian goods. In the fourteenth century, however, with the collapse of the Mongol empires and the spread of bubonic plague, travel on the silk roads became much less safe than before. Muslim mariners continued to bring Asian goods through the Indian Ocean and the Red Sea to Cairo, where Italian merchants purchased them for distribution in western Europe. But prices at Cairo were high, and Europeans sought ever-larger quantities of Asian goods, particularly spices.

The Lure of Trade

By the fourteenth century the wealthy classes of Europe regarded Indian pepper and Chinese ginger as expensive necessities, and they especially prized cloves and nutmeg from the spice islands of Maluku. Merchants and monarchs alike realized that by offering direct access to Asian markets and eliminating Muslim intermediaries, new maritime trade routes would increase the quantities of spices and other Asian goods available in Europe—and would also yield enormous profits.

African trade also beckoned to Europeans and called them to the sea. Since the twelfth century Europeans had purchased west African gold, ivory, and slaves delivered by the trans-Saharan camel caravans of Muslim merchants to north African ports. Gold was an especially important commodity because the precious metal from west Africa was their principal form of payment for Asian luxury goods. As in the case of Asian trade, maritime routes that eliminated Muslim intermediaries and offered more direct access to African markets would benefit European merchants.

Alongside material incentives, the goal of expanding the boundaries of Christianity also drove Europeans into the larger world. Like Buddhism and Islam, Christianity is a missionary religion. The New Testament specifically urged Christians to spread their faith throughout the world. Efforts to spread the faith often took peaceful forms. During the era of the Mongol empires, Franciscan and Dominican missionaries had traveled as far as India, central Asia, and China in search of converts. Yet the expansion of Christianity was by no means always a peaceful affair. Beginning in the eleventh century, western Europeans had launched a series of crusades and holy wars against Muslims in Palestine, the Mediterranean islands, and Iberia. Crusading zeal remained especially strong in Iberia, where the *reconquista* came to an end in 1492: the Muslim kingdom of Granada fell to Spanish Christian forces just

Missionary Efforts

A detail from the Catalan Atlas, a magnificent illustrated representation of the known world produced about 1375, depicts a camel caravan traveling from China to Europe across the silk roads. • Bibliothèque Nationale de France

weeks before Christopher Columbus set sail on his famous first voyage to the western hemisphere. Whether through persuasion or violence, overseas voyages offered fresh opportunities for western Europeans to spread their faith.

In practice, the various motives for exploration combined and reinforced each other. Dom Henrique of Portugal, often called Prince Henry the Navigator, promoted voyages of exploration in west Africa specifically to enter the gold trade, discover profitable new trade routes, gain intelligence about the extent of Muslim power, win converts to Christianity, and make alliances against the Muslims with any Christian rulers he might find. When the Portuguese mariner Vasco da Gama reached the Indian port of Calicut in 1498, local authorities asked him what he wanted there. His reply: "Christians and spices." The goal of spreading Christianity thus became a powerful justification and reinforcement for the more material motives for the voyages of exploration.

The Technology of Exploration

Without advanced nautical technology and navigational skills, even the strongest motives would not have enabled European mariners to reconnoiter the world's oceans. Embarking on voyages that would keep them out of the sight of land for weeks at a time, mariners needed sturdy ships, navigational equipment, and sailing techniques that would permit them to make their way across the seas and back again. They inherited much of their nautical technology from Mediterranean and northern European maritime traditions and combined it imaginatively with elements of Chinese or Arabic origin.

Ships and Sails

From their experiences in the coastal waters of the Atlantic, European sailors learned to construct ships strong enough to brave most adverse conditions. Beginning about the twelfth century, they increased the maneuverability of their craft by building a rudder onto the stern. (The sternpost rudder was a Chinese invention that had diffused across the Indian Ocean and probably became known to Europeans through Arab ships in the Mediterranean.) They outfitted their vessels with two main types of sail, both of which Mediterranean mariners had used since classical times. Square sails enabled them to take full advantage of a following wind (a wind blowing from behind), although they did not work well in crosswinds. Triangular "lateen" sails, on the other hand, were very maneuverable and could catch winds from the side as well as from behind. With a combination of square and lateen sails, European ships were able to use whatever winds arose. Their ability to tack—to advance against the wind by sailing across it—was crucial for the exploration of regions with uncooperative winds.

Navigational Instruments

The most important navigational equipment on board these vessels were magnetic compasses and astrolabes (soon replaced by cross staffs and back staffs). The compass was a Chinese invention of the Tang or Song dynasty that had diffused throughout the Indian Ocean basin in the eleventh century. By the mid-twelfth century European mariners used compasses to determine their heading in Mediterranean and Atlantic waters. The astrolabe was a simplified version of an instrument used by Greek and Persian astronomers to determine latitude by measuring the angle of the sun or the pole

By using cross staffs to measure the angle of the sun or pole star above the horizon, mariners could determine latitude.

star above the horizon. Portuguese mariners visiting the Indian Ocean in the late fifteenth century encountered Arab sailors using more serviceable instruments for determining latitude, which the Portuguese then used as models for the construction of cross staffs and back staffs.

Their ability to determine direction and latitude enabled European mariners to assemble a vast body of data about the earth's geography and to find their way around the world's oceans with tolerable accuracy and efficiency. (The measurement of longitude requires the ability to measure time precisely and so had to wait until the late eighteenth century, when dependable, spring-driven clocks became available.)

Knowledge of Winds and Currents

Equipped with advanced technological hardware, European mariners ventured into the oceans and gradually compiled a body of practical knowledge about the winds and currents that determined navigational possibilities in the age of sail. In both the Atlantic and Pacific Oceans, strong winds blow regularly to create giant

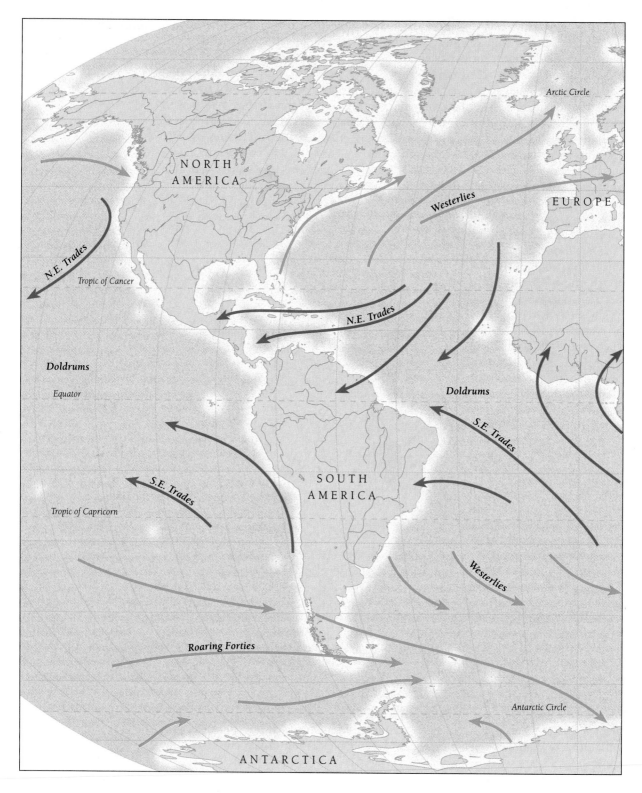

MAP [22.1]

Wind and current patterns in the world's oceans.

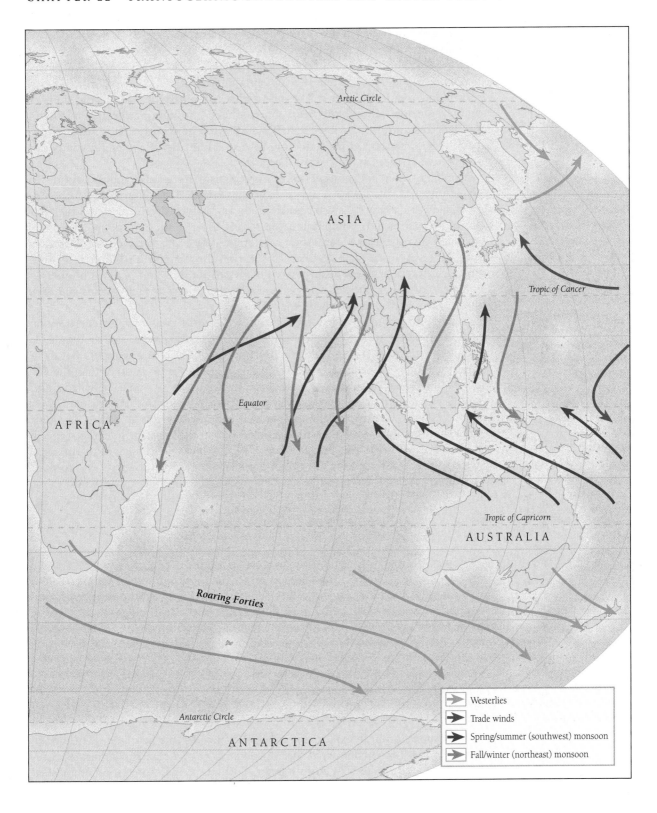

"wind wheels" both north and south of the equator, and ocean currents follow a similar pattern. Between about five and twenty-five degrees of latitude north and south of the equator, trade winds blow from the east. Between about thirty and sixty degrees north and south, westerly winds prevail. Winds and currents in the Indian Ocean follow a different, but still regular and reliable, pattern. During the summer months monsoon winds blow from the southeast throughout the Indian Ocean basin, whereas during the winter they blow from the northwest. Once mariners understood these patterns, they were able to take advantage of prevailing winds and currents to sail to almost any part of the earth.

The volta do mar   Prevailing winds and currents often forced mariners to take indirect routes to their destinations. European vessels sailed easily from the Mediterranean to the Canary Islands, for example, since regular trade winds blew from the northeast. But those same trade winds complicated the return trip. By the mid-fifteenth century Portuguese mariners had developed a strategy called the *volta do mar* ("return through the sea") that enabled them to sail from the Canaries to Portugal. Instead of trying to force their way against the trade winds—a slow and perilous business—they sailed northwest into the open ocean until they found westerly winds and then turned east for the last leg of the homeward journey.

Although the *volta do mar* took mariners well out of their way, experience soon taught that sailing around contrary winds was much faster, safer, and more reliable than butting up against them. Portuguese and other European mariners began to rely on the principle of the *volta do mar* in sailing to destinations other than the Canary Islands. When Vasco da Gama departed for India, for example, he sailed south to the Cape Verde Islands and then allowed the trade winds to carry him southwest into the Atlantic Ocean until he approached the coast of Brazil. There da Gama caught the prevailing westerlies that enabled him to sail east, round the Cape of Good Hope, and enter the Indian Ocean. As they became familiar with the wind systems of the world's oceans, European mariners developed variations on the *volta do mar* that enabled them to travel reliably to coastlines throughout the world.

Voyages of Exploration: From the Mediterranean to the Atlantic

Exploratory voyaging began as early as the thirteenth century. In 1291 the Vivaldi brothers departed from Genoa in two ships with the intention of sailing around Africa to India. They did not succeed, but the idea of exploring the Atlantic and establishing a maritime trade route from the Mediterranean to India persisted. During the fourteenth century Genoese, Portuguese, and Spanish mariners sailed frequently into the Atlantic Ocean and rediscovered the Canary Islands. The Guanche people had settled the Canaries from their original home in Morocco, but there had been no contact between the Guanches and other peoples since the time of the Roman empire. Iberian mariners began to visit the Canaries regularly, and in the fifteenth century Castilian forces conquered the islands and made them an outpost for further exploration.

Dom Henrique   The pace of European exploration quickened after 1415 when Dom Henrique of Portugal (1394–1460) conquered the Moroccan port of Ceuta and sponsored a series of voyages down the west African coast. Portuguese merchants soon established fortified trading posts at São Jorge da Mina (in modern Ghana) and other strategic locations. There they exchanged European horses, leather, textiles, and metalwares for gold and slaves. Portuguese explorations continued after Henrique's death, and

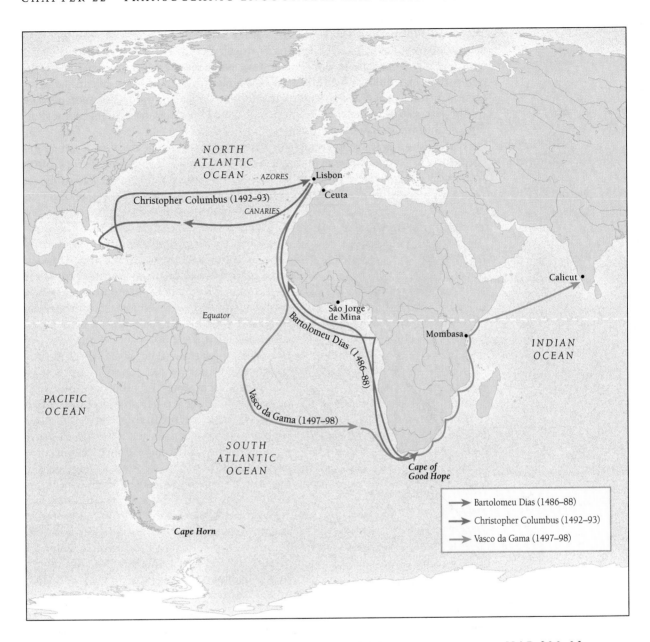

MAP [22.2]

European exploration in the Atlantic Ocean.

in 1488 Bartolomeu Dias rounded the Cape of Good Hope and entered the Indian Ocean. He did not proceed further because of storms and a restless crew, but the route to India, China, and the spice-bearing islands of southeast Asia lay open. The sea route to the Indian Ocean offered European merchants the opportunity to buy silk, spices, and pepper at the source, rather than through Muslim intermediaries, and to take part in the flourishing trade of Asia described by Marco Polo.

Portuguese mariners did not immediately follow up Dias's voyage, because domestic and foreign problems distracted royal attention from voyages to Asia. In 1497, however, Vasco da Gama departed Lisbon with a fleet of four armed merchant ships bound for India. His experience was not altogether pleasant. His fleet went more than three months without seeing land, and his cargoes excited little

Vasco da Gama

interest in Indian markets. His return voyage was especially difficult, and less than half of his crew made it safely back to Portugal. Yet his cargo of pepper and cinnamon was hugely profitable, and Portuguese merchants began immediately to organize further expeditions. By 1500 they had built a trading post at Calicut, and Portuguese mariners soon called at ports throughout India and the Indian Ocean basin. By the late sixteenth century, English and Dutch mariners had followed the Portuguese into the Indian Ocean basin.

Christopher Columbus

While Portuguese navigators plied the sea route to India, the Genoese mariner Cristoforo Colombo, known in English as Christopher Columbus (1451–1506), proposed sailing to the markets of Asia by a western route. On the basis of wide reading in geographical literature, Columbus believed that the Eurasian landmass covered 270 degrees of longtitude and that the earth was a relatively small sphere with a circumference of about 17,000 nautical miles. (In fact, the Eurasian landmass from Portugal to Korea covers only 140 degrees of longtitude, and the earth's circumference is almost 25,000 nautical miles.) By Columbus's calculations, Japan should be less than 2,500 nautical miles west of the Canary Islands. (The actual distance between the Canaries and Japan is more than 10,000 nautical miles.) This geography suggested that sailing west from Europe to Asian markets would be profitable, and Columbus sought royal sponsorship for a voyage to prove his ideas. The Portuguese court declined his proposal, partly out of scepticism about his geography and partly because Dias's voyage of 1488 already pointed the way toward India.

The earliest surviving world globe, produced in 1492 by the German cartographer Martin Behaim, depicts the eastern hemisphere quite accurately but shows almost no land west of Iberia except for east Asia • Germanisches Nationalmuseum Nürnberg

Eventually Fernando and Isabel of Spain agreed to underwrite Columbus's expedition, and in August 1492 his fleet of three ships departed Palos in southern Spain. He sailed south to the Canaries, picked up supplies, and then turned west with the trade winds. On the morning of 12 October 1492, he made landfall at an island in the Bahamas that the native Taino inhabitants called Guanahaní and that Columbus rechristened San Salvador (also known as Watling Island). Thinking that he had arrived in the spice islands known familiarly as the Indies, Columbus called the Tainos "Indians." In search of gold he sailed around the Caribbean for almost three months, and at the large island of Cuba he sent a delegation to seek the court of the emperor of China. When Columbus returned to Spain, he reported to his royal sponsors that he had reached islands just off the coast of Asia.

Hemispheric Links

Columbus never reached the riches of Asia, and despite three additional voyages across the Atlantic Ocean, he obtained very little gold in the Caribbean. Yet news of his voyage spread rapidly throughout Europe, and hundreds of Spanish, English, French, and Dutch mariners soon followed in his wake. Particularly in the early sixteenth century, many of them continued to seek the passage to Asian waters that

Columbus himself had pursued. Over a longer term, however, it became clear that the American continents and the Caribbean islands themselves held abundant opportunities for entrepreneurs. Thus Columbus's voyages to the western hemisphere had unintended but momentous consequences, since they established links between the eastern and western hemispheres and paved the way for the conquest, settlement, and exploitation of the Americas by European peoples.

Voyages of Exploration: From the Atlantic to the Pacific

While some Europeans sought opportunities in the Americas, others continued to seek a western route to Asian markets. The Spanish military commander Vasco Nuñez de Balboa sighted the Pacific Ocean in 1513 while searching for gold in Panama, but in the early sixteenth century no one knew how much ocean lay between the Americas and Asia. Indeed, no one even suspected the vast size of the Pacific Ocean, which covers one-third of the earth's surface.

The reconnaissance of the Pacific Ocean basin began with the Portuguese navigator Fernão de Magalhães (1480–1521), better known as Ferdinand Magellan. While sailing in the service of Portugal, Magellan had visited ports throughout the Indian Ocean basin and had traveled east as far as the spice islands of Maluku. He believed that the spice islands and Asian markets lay fairly close to the western coast

Ferdinand Magellan

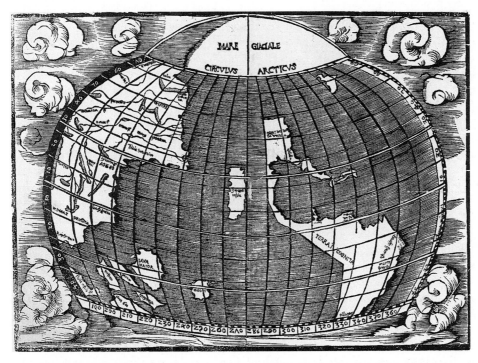

A map prepared about 1512 by the Polish cartographer Jan Stobnicza shows eloquently that it took a long time for geographers to realize the extent of the Americas and the Pacific Ocean. Here "Cipangu" (Japan) lies just west of Mexico, with the Asian mainland just beyond. ● Osterreichische National Bibliothek, Vienna. Photo: Bildarchiv, ONB Wien

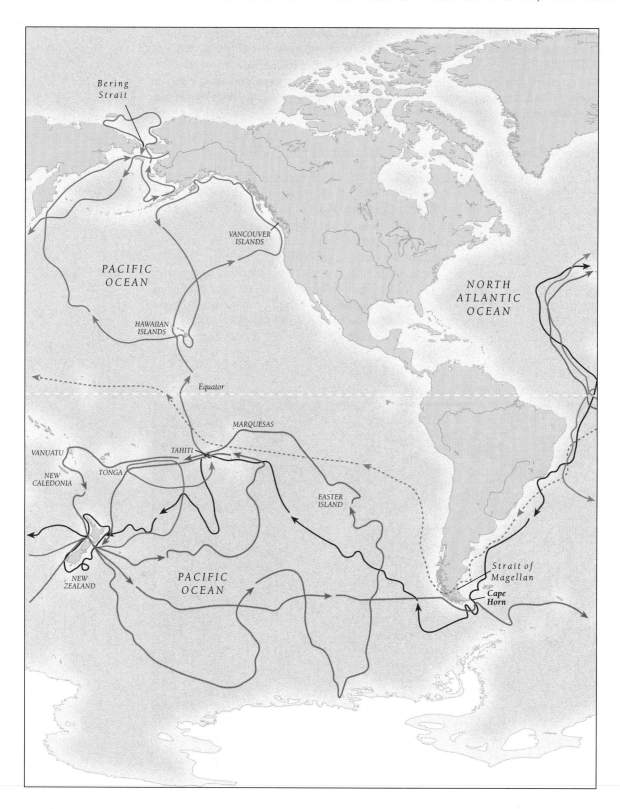

MAP [22.3]

European exploration in the Pacific Ocean.

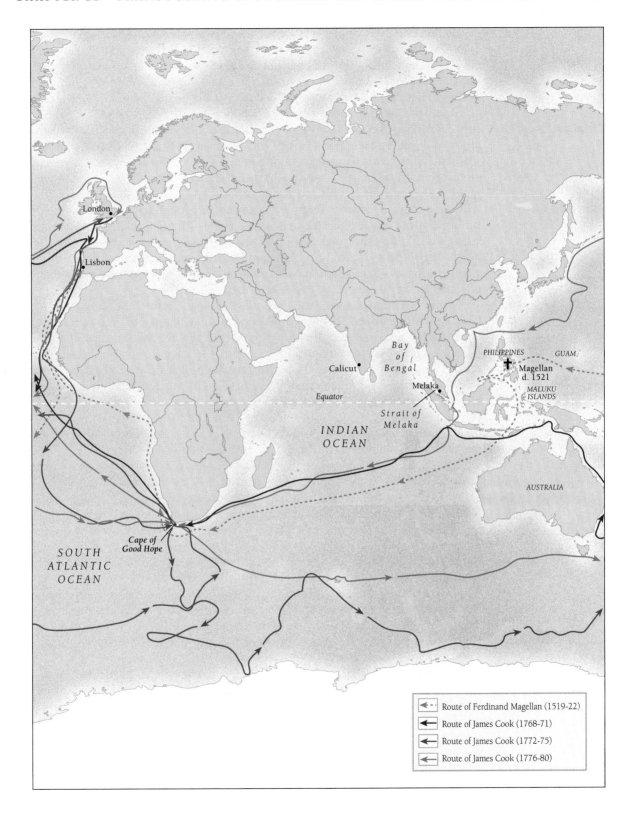

London

Lisbon

Calicut

Bay of Bengal

PHILIPPINES

GUAM

✝ Magellan d. 1521

Melaka

MALUKU ISLANDS

Equator

Strait of Melaka

INDIAN OCEAN

AUSTRALIA

Cape of Good Hope

SOUTH ATLANTIC OCEAN

Route of Ferdinand Magellan (1519-22)
Route of James Cook (1768-71)
Route of James Cook (1772-75)
Route of James Cook (1776-80)

of the Americas, and he decided to pursue Christopher Columbus's goal of establishing a western route to Asian waters. Because Portuguese mariners had already reached Asian markets through the Indian Ocean, they had little interest in Magellan's proposed western route. On his Pacific expedition and circumnavigation of the world (1519–1522), Magellan sailed in the service of Spain.

The Circumnavigation

Magellan's voyage was an exercise in endurance. He began by probing the eastern coast of South America in search of a strait leading to the Pacific. Eventually he found and sailed through the tricky and treacherous Strait of Magellan near the southern tip of South America. After exiting the strait, his fleet sailed almost four months before taking on fresh provisions at Guam. During that period crewmen survived on worm-ridden biscuits, leather that they had softened in the ocean, and water gone foul. Ship's rats that were unfortunate enough to fall into the hands of famished sailors quickly became the centerpiece of a meal. Lacking fresh fruits and vegetables in their diet, many of the crew fell victim to the dreaded disease of scurvy, which caused painful rotting of the gums, loss of teeth, abcesses, hemorrhaging, weakness, loss of spirit, and in most cases death. Scurvy killed twenty-nine members of Magellan's crew during the Pacific crossing.

Conditions improved after the fleet called at Guam, but its ordeal had not come to an end. From Guam, Magellan proceeded to the Philippine Islands, where he became involved in a local political dispute that took the lives of Magellan himself and 40 of his crew. The survivors continued on to the spice islands of Maluku, where they took on a cargo of cloves. Rather than brave the Pacific Ocean once again, they sailed home through the familiar waters of the Indian Ocean—and thus completed the first circumnavigation of the world—returning to Spain after a voyage of almost exactly three years. Of Magellan's five ships and 280 men, a single ship with 18 of the original crew returned. (Another 17 crewmen returned later by other routes so that 35 members of Magellan's original crew survived the expedition.)

Exploration of the Pacific

The Pacific Ocean is so vast that it took European explorers almost three centuries to chart its features. Spanish merchants built on information gleaned from Magellan's expedition and established a trade route between the Philippines and Mexico, but they did not continue to explore the ocean basin itself. English navigators, however, ventured into the Pacific in search of an elusive northwest passage from Europe to Asia. In fact, a northwest passage exists, but most of its route lies within the Arctic Circle. It is so far north that ice clogs its waters for much of the year, and it was only in the twentieth century that the Norwegian explorer Roald Amundsen traveled from the Atlantic to the Pacific by way of the northwest passage. Nevertheless, while searching for a passage, English mariners established many of the details of Pacific geography. In the sixteenth century, for example, Sir Francis Drake scouted the west coast of North America as far north as Vancouver Island.

Captain James Cook

Alongside Magellan, the most important of the Pacific explorers was Captain James Cook (1728–1779), who led three expeditions to the Pacific and died in a scuffle with the indigenous people of Hawai`i. Cook charted eastern Australia and New Zealand, and he added New Caledonia, Vanuatu, and Hawai`i to European maps of the Pacific. He probed the frigid waters of the Arctic Ocean and spent months at a time in the tropical islands of Tahiti, Tonga, and Hawai`i, where he showed deep interest in the manners, customs, and languages of Polynesian peoples. By the time Cook's voyages had come to an end, European geographers had compiled a reasonably accurate understanding of the world's ocean basins, their lands, and their peoples.

TRADE AND CONFLICT IN EARLY MODERN ASIA

The voyages of exploration taught European mariners how to sail to almost any coastline in the world. Once they arrived at their destinations, they sought commercial opportunities. In the eastern hemisphere they built a series of fortified trading posts that offered footholds in regions where established commercial networks had held sway for centuries. They even attempted to control the spice trade in the Indian Ocean but with limited success. They mostly did not have the human numbers or military power to impose their rule in the eastern hemisphere, although Spanish and Dutch forces established small island empires in the Philippines and Indonesia, respectively. Commercial and political competition in both the eastern and western hemispheres led to conflict between European peoples, and by the end of the Seven Years' War in 1763, English military and merchant forces had gained an initiative over their rivals that enabled them to dominate world trade and build the vast British empire of the nineteenth century.

Trading-Post Empires

Portuguese mariners built the earliest trading-post empire. Their goal was not to conquer territories, but to control trade routes by forcing merchant vessels to call at fortified trading sites and pay duties there. Vasco da Gama obtained permission from local authorities to establish a trading post at Calicut when he arrived there in 1498. By the mid-sixteenth century Portuguese merchants had built more than fifty trading posts between west Africa and east Asia. At São Jorge da Mina, they traded in west African slaves, and at Mozambique they attempted to control the south African gold trade. From Hormuz they controlled access to the Persian Gulf, and from Goa they organized trade in Indian pepper. At Melaka they oversaw shipping between the South China Sea and the Indian Ocean, and they channeled trade in cloves and nutmeg through Ternate in the spice islands of Maluku. Posts at Macau and Nagasaki offered access to the markets of China and Japan.

Portuguese Trading Posts

Equipped with heavy artillery, Portuguese vessels were able to overpower most other craft that they encountered, and they sometimes trained their cannon effectively onshore. The architect of their aggressive policy was Afonso d'Alboquerque, commander of Portuguese forces in the Indian Ocean during the early sixteenth century. Alboquerque's fleets seized Hormuz in 1508, Goa in 1510, and Melaka in 1511. From these strategic sites Alboquerque sought to control Indian Ocean trade by forcing all merchant ships to purchase safe-conduct passes and present them at Portuguese trading posts. Ships without passes were subject to confiscation, along with their cargoes. Alboquerque's forces punished violators of his policy by executing them or cutting off their hands. Alboquerque was confident of Portuguese naval superiority and its ability to control trade in the Indian Ocean. After taking Melaka, he boasted that the arrival of Portuguese ships sent other vessels scurrying and that even the birds left the skies and sought cover.

Afonso d'Alboquerque

Alboquerque's boast was an exaggeration. Although heavily armed, Portuguese forces did not have enough vessels to enforce the commander's orders. Arab, Indian, and Malay merchants continued to play prominent roles in Indian Ocean commerce, usually without taking the precaution of securing a safe-conduct pass. Portuguese ships transported perhaps half of the pepper and spices that Europeans consumed during the early and middle decades of the sixteenth century, but Arab

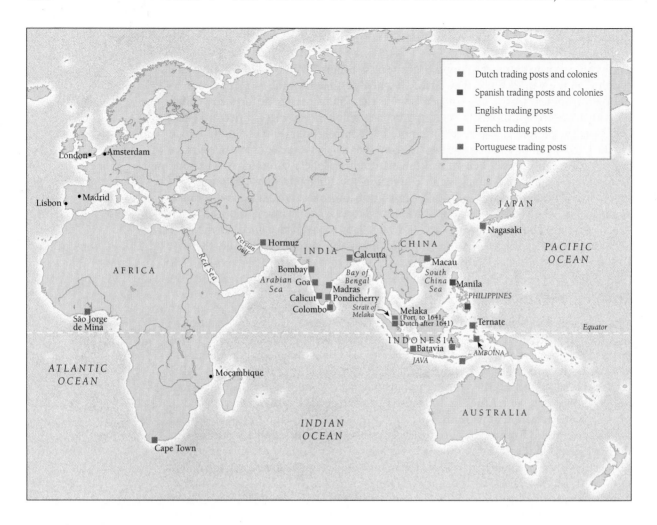

MAP [22.4]

European trading-post empires.

vessels delivered shipments through the Red Sea, which Portuguese forces never managed to control, to Cairo and Mediterranean trade routes.

By the late sixteenth century, Portuguese hegemony in the Indian Ocean was growing weak. Portugal was a small country with a small population—about one million in 1500—and was unable to sustain a large seaborne trading empire for very long. The crews of Portuguese ships often included Spanish, English, and Dutch sailors, who became familiar with Asian waters while in Portuguese service. By the late sixteenth century, investors in other lands began to organize their own expeditions to Asian markets. Most prominent of those who followed the Portuguese into the Indian Ocean were English and Dutch mariners.

English and Dutch Trading Posts   Like their predecessors, English and Dutch merchants built trading posts on Asian coasts and sought to channel trade through them, but they did not attempt to control shipping on the high seas. They occasionally seized Portuguese sites, most notably when a Dutch fleet conquered Melaka in 1641. Yet Portuguese authorities held many of their trading posts into the twentieth century: Goa remained the official capital of Portuguese colonies in Asia until Indian forces reclaimed it in 1961. Meanwhile, English and Dutch entrepreneurs established parallel networks. English merchants concentrated on India and built trading posts at Bombay, Madras, and

AFONSO D'ALBOQUERQUE SEIZES HORMUZ

• • •

Afonso d'Alboquerque the mariner had a son of the same name who in 1557 published a long set of historical Commentaries *on his father's deeds. His account of the battle for Hormuz vividly illustrates the effectiveness of Portuguese artillery, as well as the chaos and confusion of sea battles in early modern times.*

As some time had passed since the king [of Hormuz] had received information about the [Portuguese] fleet and the destruction that the great Afonso d'Alboquerque had wrought along the [Arabian] coast, he began to prepare himself to fight with him. For this end he gave orders to detain all the ships that came into the port of Hormuz and added a force of sixty great vessels into which he draughted off many soldiers and much artillery with everything that was required for the undertaking. And among these great vessels there was one belonging to the king of Cambay [in India] . . . and another of the prince of Cambay. . . . And besides these ships there were in the harbor about 200 galleys, which are long ships with many oars. . . . There were also many barks full of small guns and men wearing sword-proof dress and armed from head to foot, most of them being archers. All this fleet was rigged out with flags and standards and colored ensigns, and made a very beautiful appearance. . . .

When Afonso d'Alboquerque perceived the gleaming of the swords and waving of the bucklers and other doings of the Moors [Muslims] on shore, . . . he understood by these signs that the king was determined to give him battle. . . . When morning broke, . . . he ordered a broadside to be fired. The bombadiers took aim so that with the first two shots they fired they sent two large ships which were in front of them, with all their men, to the bottom—one being the prince of Cambay's ship. . . . Afonso Lopez da Costa, who was stationed on the land side, vanquished and sent to the bottom some portion of the galleys and guard boats that his artillery could reach. Manuel Telez, after having caused great slaughter upon some vessels, . . . ran into a large vessel that lay close to him and killed a part of the men in it, while the rest threw themselves into the sea, and those who were heavy-armed went down at once. João da Nova too with his artillery did great execution among the ships that lay along the piles, as did also Antonio do Campo and Francisco de Tavora among the galleys that had surrounded them, and all night long they kept on hooking their anchors together in order to catch the galleys in the middle of them. And although the Moors endeavored to avenge themselves with their artillery, our men were so well fortified with their defenses that they did them no harm, except on the upper deck, and with their arrows they wounded some people.

The fight was so confused on this side and on that, both with artillery and arrows, that it lasted some time without either party seeing each other by reason of the smoke. As soon as this cleared off, . . . and when Afonso saw the discomfiture of the king's fleet and the unexpected victory that Our Lord had sent him and the Moors throwing themselves into the sea from fear of our artillery, thinking that they could escape in that way by swimming, . . . [Afonso] called out to the captains to take to their boats and follow up the victory.

SOURCE: Afonso d'Alboquerque. *Commentaries of the Great Afonso Dalboquerque.* 4 vols. Trans. by Walter de Gray Birch. London: Hakluyt Society, 1875–84, 1:105, 112–14. (Translation slightly modified.)

Calcutta while the Dutch operated more broadly from Cape Town, Colombo, and Batavia (modern Jakarta on the island of Java).

English and Dutch merchants enjoyed two main advantages over their Portuguese predecessors. They sailed faster, cheaper, and more powerful ships, which offered both an economic and a military edge over their competitors. Furthermore, they conducted trade through an exceptionally efficient form of commercial organization—the joint-stock company—which enabled investors to realize handsome profits while limiting the risk to their investments.

The Trading Companies

English and Dutch merchants formed two especially powerful joint-stock companies: the English East India Company, founded in 1600, and its Dutch counterpart, the United East India Company, known from its initials as the VOC (Vereenigde Oost-Indische Compagnie), established in 1602. Private merchants advanced funds to launch these companies, outfit them with ships and crews, and provide them with commodities and money to trade. Although they enjoyed government support, the companies were privately owned enterprises. Unhampered by political oversight, company agents concentrated strictly on profitable trade. Their charters granted them the right to buy, sell, build trading posts, and even make war in the companies' interests.

The English and Dutch companies experienced immediate financial success. In 1601, for example, five English ships set sail from London with cargoes mostly of gold and silver coins valued at thirty thousand pounds sterling. When they returned in 1603, the spices that they carried were worth more than one million pounds sterling. The first Dutch expedition did not realize such fantastic profits, but it more than doubled the investments of its underwriters. Because of their advanced nautical technology, powerful military arsenal, efficient organization, and relentless pursuit of profit, the English East India Company and the VOC contributed to the early formation of a global network of trade.

European Conquests in Southeast Asia

Following voyages of exploration to the western hemisphere, Europeans conquered indigenous peoples, built territorial empires, and established colonies settled by European migrants. In the eastern hemisphere, however, they were mostly unable to force their will on large Asian populations and powerful centralized states. With the decline of the Portuguese effort to control shipping in the Indian Ocean, Europeans mostly traded peacefully in Asian waters alongside Arab, Indian, Malay, and Chinese merchants.

Yet in two island regions of southeast Asia—the Philippines and Indonesia—Europeans conquered existing authorities and imposed their rule. Though densely populated, neither the Philippines nor Indonesia had a powerful state when Europeans arrived there in the sixteenth century. Nor did imperial authorities in China or India lay claim to the island regions. Heavily armed ships enabled Europeans to bring massive force to bear and to establish imperial regimes that favored the interests of European merchants.

Conquest of the Philippines

Spanish forces approached the Philippines in 1565 under the command of Miguel López de Legazpi, who named the islands after King Philip II of Spain. Legazpi overcame local authorities in Cebu and Manila in almost bloodless contests. Because the Philippines had no central government, there was no organized resistance to the intrusion. Spanish forces faced a series of small, disunited chiefdoms, most of which soon fell before Spanish ships and guns. By 1575 Spanish forces controlled the coastal regions of the central and northern islands, and during the seventeenth century they extended their authority to most parts of the archipelago. The main region outside their control was the southern island of Mindanao, where a large Muslim community stoutly resisted Spanish expansion.

Manila

Spanish policy in the Philippines revolved around trade and Christianity. Manila was already a bustling, multicultural port city—an entrepot for trade particularly in silk—and it quickly became the hub of Spanish commercial activity in Asia. Chinese merchants were especially prominent in Manila. They occupied a specially designated commercial district of the city, and they accounted for about one-quarter of Manila's forty-two thousand residents in the mid-seventeenth century. They supplied the silk goods that Spanish traders shipped to Mexico in the so-called Manila galleons. Their commercial success brought suspicion on their community, and resentful Spanish and Filipino residents massacred Chinese merchants by the thousands in at least six major eruptions of violence in 1603, 1639, 1662, 1686, 1762, and 1819. Nevertheless, Spanish authorities continued to rely heavily on the wealth that Chinese merchants brought to Manila.

Apart from promoting trade, Spanish authorities in the Philippines also sought to spread Christianity throughout the archipelago. Spanish rulers and missionaries pressured prominent Filipinos to convert to Christianity in hopes of persuading others to follow their example. They opened schools to teach the fundamentals of Christian doctrine, along with basic literacy, in densely populated regions throughout the islands. The missionaries encountered stiff resistance in highland regions, where Spanish authority was not as strong as on the coasts, and resistance drew support from opponents of Spanish domination as well as from resentment of the newly arrived faith. Over the long term, however, Filipinos turned increasingly to Christianity, and by the nineteenth century the Philippines had become one of the most fervent Roman Catholic lands in the world.

Conquest of Java

Dutch mariners, who imposed their rule on the islands of Indonesia, did not worry about seeking converts to Christianity, but concentrated instead on the trade in spices, particularly cloves, nutmeg, and mace. The architect of Dutch policy was Jan Pieterszoon Coen, who in 1619 founded Batavia on the island of Java to serve as an entrepot for the VOC. Batavia occupied a strategic site near the Sunda Strait, and its market attracted both Chinese and Malay vessels. Coen's plan was to establish a VOC monopoly over spice production and trade, thus enabling Dutch merchants to reap enormous profits in European markets. Coen brought his naval power to bear on the small Indonesian islands and forced them to deliver spices only to VOC merchants. On larger islands like Java, he took advantage of tensions between local princes and authorities and extracted concessions from many in return for providing them with aid against the others. By the late seventeenth century, the VOC controlled all the ports of Java as well as most of the important spice-bearing islands throughout the Indonesian archipelago.

Dutch numbers were too few for them to rule directly over their whole southeast Asian empire. They made alliances with local authorities to maintain order in most regions, reserving for direct Dutch rule only Batavia and the most important spice-bearing islands such as clove-producing Amboina and the Banda Islands. They sought less to rule than to control the production of spices. The Dutch did not embark on campaigns of conquest for purposes of adding to their holdings, but they uprooted spice-bearing plants on islands they did not control and mercilessly attacked peoples who sold their spices to merchants not associated with the VOC. Monopoly profits from the spice trade not only enriched the VOC but also made the Netherlands the most prosperous land in Europe throughout most of the seventeenth century.

Commercial Rivalries and the Seven Years' War

The voyages of exploration led to conflicts not only between Europeans and Asians but also among Europeans themselves. Mariners competed vigorously for trade in Asia and the Americas, and their efforts to establish markets—and sometimes monopolies as well—led frequently to clashes with their counterparts from different lands.

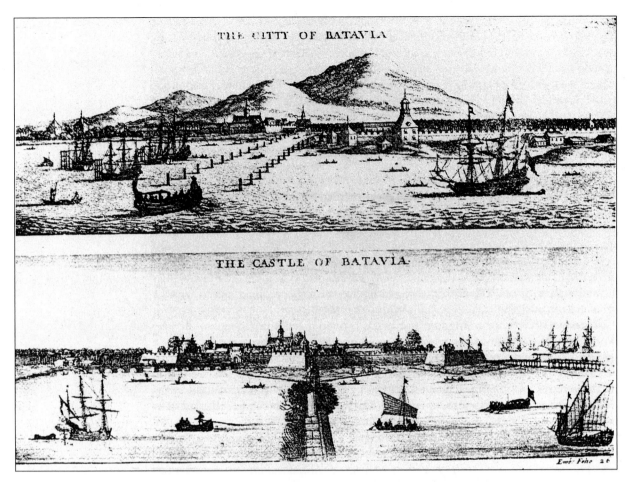

The city of Batavia as viewed from the sea in the mid-seventeenth century. The Dutch fortress stands at the center of the lower picture.
Warehouses and wharves lined the numerous canals that drained the low-lying land of the region.

Competition and Conflict   Indeed, throughout the seventeenth and early eighteenth centuries, commercial and political rivalries led to running wars between ships flying different flags. Dutch vessels were most numerous in the Indian Ocean, and they enabled the VOC to dominate the spice trade. Dutch forces expelled most Portuguese merchants from southeast Asia and prevented English mariners from establishing secure footholds there. By the early eighteenth century, trade in Indian cotton and tea from Ceylon had begun to overshadow the spice trade, and English and French merchants working from trading posts in India became the dominant carriers in the Indian Ocean. Fierce competition again generated violence: in 1746 French forces seized the English trading post at Madras, one of the three principal centers of British operations in India.

Commercial competition led to conflict also in the Caribbean and the Americas. English pirates and privateers preyed on Spanish shipping from Mexico, often seizing vessels carrying cargoes of silver. English and French forces constantly skirmished and fought over sugar islands in the Caribbean while also contesting territorial claims in North America. Almost all conflicts between European states in the eighteenth century spilled over into the Caribbean and the Americas.

Commercial rivalries combined with political differences and came to a head in the Seven Years' War (1756–1763). The Seven Years' War was a global conflict in that it took place in several distinct geographical theaters—Europe, India, the Caribbean, and North America—and involved Asian and indigenous American peoples as well as Europeans. Sometimes called "the great war for empire," the Seven Years' War had deep implications for global affairs, since it laid the foundation for 150 years of British imperial hegemony in the world.

The Seven Years' War

In Europe the war pitted Britain and Prussia against France, Austria, and Russia. In India, British and French forces each allied with local rulers and engaged in a contest for hegemony in the Indian Ocean. In the Caribbean, Spanish forces joined with the French in an effort to limit British expansion in the western hemisphere. In North America—where the Seven Years' War merged with a conflict already underway and sometimes goes by the name French and Indian War (1754–1763)—British and French armies made separate alliances with indigenous peoples in an effort to outmaneuver each other.

British forces fought little in Europe, where their Prussian allies held off massive armies seeking to surround and crush the expansive Prussian state. Elsewhere, however, British armies and navies handily overcame their enemies. They ousted French merchants from India and took control of French colonies in Canada, although they allowed French authorities to retain most of their Caribbean possessions. They allowed Spanish forces to retain Cuba but took Florida from the Spanish empire. Victory in the Seven Years' War placed Britain in a position to dominate world trade for the foreseeable future, and "the great war for empire" paved the way for the establishment of the British empire in the nineteenth century.

British Hegemony

GLOBAL EXCHANGES

European explorers and those who followed them established links between all lands and peoples of the world. Interaction between peoples in turn resulted in an unprecedented volume of exchange across the boundary lines of societies and cultural regions. Some of that exchange involved biological species: plants, food crops, animals, human populations, and disease pathogens all spread to regions they had not previously visited. These biological exchanges had differing and dramatic effects on human populations, destroying some of them through epidemic diseases and enlarging others through increased food supplies and richer diets. Commercial exchange also flourished in the wake of the voyages of exploration as European merchants traveled to ports throughout the world in search of trade. By the late sixteenth century, they had built fortified trading posts at strategic sites in the Indian, Atlantic, and Pacific Ocean basins. By the mid-eighteenth century they had established globe-girdling networks of trade and communication.

The Columbian Exchange

Processes of biological exchange were prominent features of world history well before modern times. The early expansion of Islam had facilitated the diffusion of plants and food crops throughout much of the eastern hemisphere during the period from about 700 to 1100 C.E., and transplanted species helped spark demographic and economic growth in all the lands where they took root. During the fourteenth century the spread of bubonic plague caused drastic demographic losses when epidemic disease struck Eurasian and north African lands.

Biological Exchanges

Yet the "Columbian exchange"—the global diffusion of plants, food crops, animals, human populations, and disease pathogens that took place after voyages of exploration by Christopher Columbus and other European mariners—had consequences much more profound than did earlier rounds of biological exchange. Unlike the earlier processes, the Columbian exchange involved lands with radically different flora, fauna, and diseases. For thousands of years the various species of the eastern hemisphere, the western hemisphere, and Oceania had evolved along separate lines. By creating links between these biological zones, the European voyages of exploration set off a round of biological exchange that permanently altered the world's human geography and natural environment.

Epidemic Diseases

Beginning in the early sixteenth century, infectious and contagious diseases brought sharp demographic losses to indigenous peoples of the Americas and the Pacific islands. The worst scourge was smallpox, but measles, diphtheria, whooping cough, and influenza also took heavy tolls. Before the voyages of exploration, none of these maladies had reached the western hemisphere or Oceania, and the peoples of those regions consequently had no inherited or acquired immunities to their pathogens. In the eastern hemisphere, these diseases had mostly become endemic: they claimed a certain number of victims from the ranks of infants and small children, but survivors gained immunity to the diseases through exposure at an early age. In some areas of Europe, for example, smallpox was responsible for 10 to 15 percent of deaths, but most victims were age ten or younger. Although its effects were tragic for individual families and communities, smallpox did not pose a threat to European society as a whole because it did not carry away adults, who were mostly responsible for economic production and social organization.

Population Losses

When infectious and contagious diseases traveled to previously unexposed populations, however, they touched off ferocious epidemics that sometimes destroyed entire societies. Beginning in 1519, epidemic smallpox ravaged the Aztec empire, often in combination with other diseases, and within a century the indigenous population of Mexico had declined by as much as 95 percent, from about twenty-one million to one million people. By that time Spanish conquerors had imposed their rule on Mexico, and the political, social, and cultural traditions of the indigenous peoples had either disappeared or fallen under Spanish domination.

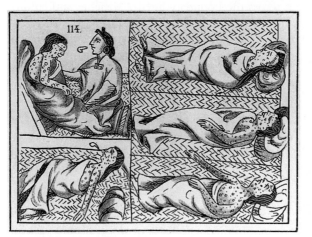

Smallpox victims in the Aztec empire. The disease killed most of those it infected and left disfiguring scars on survivors.   • Courtesy Dept. of Library Services, American Museum of Natural History. #4051(2)

Imported diseases took their worst tolls in densely populated areas like the Aztec and Inca empires, but they did not spare other regions. Smallpox and other diseases were so easily transmissible that they raced to remote areas of North and South America and sparked epidemics even before the first European explorers arrived in those regions. By the 1530s smallpox may have spread as far from Mexico as the Great Lakes in the north and the pampas of Argentina in the south.

When introduced to the Pacific islands, infectious and contagious diseases struck vulnerable populations with the same horrifying effects as in the Americas, albeit on a smaller scale. All told, disease epidemics sparked by the Columbian exchange probably caused the worst demographic calamity in all of world history. Between 1500 and 1800 upwards of one hundred million people may have died of diseases imported into the Americas and Pacific islands.

Over a longer term, however, the Columbian exchange increased rather than diminished human population because of the global spread of food crops and animals that it sponsored. Wheat, vines, horses, cattle, pigs, sheep, goats, and chickens went from Europe to the Americas where they sharply increased supplies of food and animal energy. Wheat grew well on the plains of North America and on the pampas of Argentina—regions either too dry or too cold for the cultivation of maize—and cattle transformed American grasses into meat and milk that humans could digest.

Food Crops and Animals

Food crops native to the Americas also played prominent roles in the Columbian exchange. American crops that took root in Africa, Asia, and Europe include maize, potatoes, beans, tomatoes, peppers, peanuts, manioc, papayas, guavas, avocados, pineapples, and cacao, to name only the most important. (A less nutritious transplant was tobacco.) Residents of the eastern hemisphere only gradually developed a taste for American crops, but by the eighteenth century maize and potatoes had contributed to a sharply increased number of calories in Eurasian diets. American bean varieties added protein, and tomatoes and peppers provided vitamins and zesty flavors in lands from western Europe to China. Peanuts and manioc flourished in tropical southeast Asian and west African soils that otherwise would not produce large yields or support large populations.

American Crops

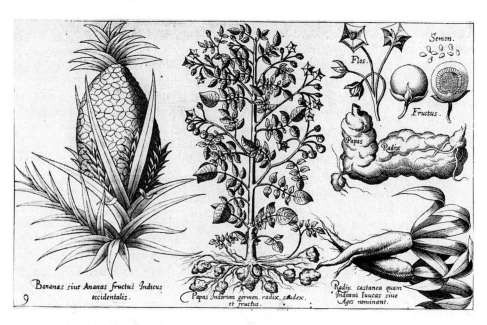

Illustrations in an early-seventeenth-century book depict pineapple, potatoes, and cassava—all plants native to the Americas and unknown to Europeans before the sixteenth century. • Courtesy of the James Ford Bell Library, University of Minnesota

Population Growth   The Columbian exchange of plants and animals caused a surge in world population. In 1500, as Eurasian peoples were recovering from epidemic bubonic plague, world population stood at about 425 million. By 1600 it had increased more than 25 percent to 545 million. Human numbers increased less rapidly during the next century, reaching 610 million in 1700. But thereafter they increased at a faster rate than ever before in world history. By 1750 human population stood at 720 million, and by 1800 it had surged to 900 million, having grown by almost 50 percent during the previous century. Much of the rise was due to the increased nutritional value of diets enriched by the global exchange of food crops and animals.

Migration   Alongside disease pathogens and plant and animal species, the Columbian exchange also involved the spread of human populations through transoceanic migration, whether voluntary or forced. During the period from 1500 to 1800, the largest contingent of migrants consisted of enslaved Africans transported involuntarily to South American, North American, and Caribbean destinations. A smaller but still sizable migration involved Europeans who traveled to the Americas and settled in lands depopulated by infectious and contagious diseases. During the nineteenth century European peoples traveled in massive numbers mostly to the western hemisphere but also to south Africa, Australia, and Pacific islands where diseases had diminished indigenous populations, and Asian peoples migrated to tropical and subtropical destinations throughout much of the world. In combination, these migrations have profoundly influenced modern world history.

The Origins of Global Trade

The trading-post empires established by Portuguese, Dutch, and English merchants linked Asian markets with European consumers and offered opportunities for European mariners to participate in the carrying trade within Asia. European vessels transported Persian carpets to India, Indian cottons to southeast Asia, southeast Asian spices to India and China, Chinese silks to Japan, and Japanese silver and copper to China and India. By the late sixteenth century, European merchants were as prominent as Arabs in the trading world of the Indian Ocean basin.

Transoceanic Trade   Besides stimulating commerce in the eastern hemisphere, the voyages of European merchant mariners also encouraged the emergence of a genuinely global trading system. As Europeans established colonies in the Caribbean and the Americas, for example, trade networks extended to all corners of the Atlantic Ocean basin. European manufactured goods traveled west across the Atlantic in exchange for silver from Mexican and Peruvian mines and agricultural products such as sugar and tobacco, both of which were in high demand among European consumers. Trade in human beings also figured in Atlantic commerce. European textiles, guns, and other manufactured goods went south to west Africa, where merchants exchanged them for African slaves, who then went to the tropical and subtropical regions of the western hemisphere to work on plantations.

The Manila Galleons   The experience of the Manila galleons illustrates the early workings of the global economy in the Pacific Ocean basin. For 250 years, from 1565 to 1815, Spanish galleons—sleek, fast, heavily armed ships capable of carrying large cargoes—regularly plied the waters of the Pacific Ocean between Manila in the Philippines and Acapulco on the west coast of Mexico. From Manila they took Asian luxury goods to Mexico and exchanged them for silver. Most of the precious metal made its way to China, where a thriving domestic economy demanded increasing quantities of silver, the basis of Chinese currency. In fact, the demand for silver was so high in China that European merchants exchanged it for Chinese gold, which they later traded

profitably for more silver as well as luxury goods in Japan. Meanwhile, some of the Asian luxury goods from Manila remained in Mexico or went to Peru, where they contributed to a comfortable way of life for Spanish ruling elites. Most, however, went overland across Mexico and then traveled by ship across the Atlantic to Spain and European markets.

By the late sixteenth century, European mariners had linked the ports of the world. During the next two centuries, the volume of global trade burgeoned, as English, Dutch, French, and other merchants contributed to the development of global markets. During the seventeenth century, for example, Dutch merchants imported, among other commodities, wheat from south Africa, cowry shells from India, and sugar from Brazil. The wheat fed domestic consumers, who increasingly worked as merchants, bankers, or manufacturers rather than as cultivators. English, Dutch, and other merchants eagerly purchased the cowry shells—which served as currency in much of sub-Saharan Africa—and exchanged them for slaves destined for plantations in the western hemisphere. The sugar went on the market at Amsterdam and found its way to consumers throughout Europe. During the eighteenth century world trade became even more intricate as mass markets emerged for commodities such as coffee, tea, sugar, and tobacco. By 1750 almost all parts of the world, with the exception of Australia, participated in global networks of commercial relations in which European merchant mariners played prominent roles.

Five Spanish galleons stand in the waters off the port of Acapulco on the Pacific coast of Mexico in this sixteenth-century engraving. Smaller craft ferry crewmen ashore, while dockworkers prepare to load cargo on the vessels.
● Rare Books Division. New York Public Library, Astor, Lenox and Tilden Foundations

Global commercial and biological exchanges arose from the efforts of European mariners to explore the world's waters and establish sea-lanes that would support long-distance trade. Their search for sea routes to Asia led them to the western hemisphere and the vast expanse of the Pacific Ocean. The geographical knowledge that they accumulated enabled them to link the world's regions into a finely articulated network of trade. But commercial exchange was not the only result of this global network. Food crops, animal stocks, disease pathogens, and human migrants also traveled the sea-lanes and dramatically influenced societies throughout the world. Transplanted crops and animal species led to improved nutrition and increasing populations throughout the eastern hemisphere. Epidemics sparked by unfamiliar disease pathogens ravaged indigenous populations in the Americas and the Pacific islands. Massive migrations of human communities transformed the social and cultural landscape of the Americas and encouraged increased mingling of the world's peoples. The European voyages of exploration, transoceanic trade networks, and the Columbian exchange pushed the world's regions toward interdependence and global integration.

CHRONOLOGY

1394–1460	Life of Dom Henrique of Portugal (Prince Henry the Navigator)
1488	Bartolomeu Dias's voyage around the Cape of Good Hope into the Indian Ocean
1492	Christopher Columbus's first voyage to the western hemisphere
1497–1499	Vasco da Gama's first voyage to India
1519–1522	Ferdinand Magellan's circumnavigation of the world
1565–1575	Spanish conquest of the Philippines
1756–1763	Seven Years' War
1768–1779	Captain James Cook's voyages in the Pacific Ocean

FOR FURTHER READING

K. N. Chaudhuri. *Trade and Civilisation in the Indian Ocean: An Economic History from the Rise of Islam to 1750.* Cambridge, 1985. A brilliant analysis that places the European presence in the Indian Ocean in its larger historical context.

———. *The Trading World of Asia and the English East India Company, 1660–1760.* Cambridge, 1978. The best study of the English East India Company and its role in world trade.

Carlo Cipolla. *Guns, Sails, and Empires: Technological Innovation and the Early Phases of European Expansion, 1400–1700.* New York, 1965. A well-written study of the naval and military technology available to European mariners.

Alfred W. Crosby. *The Columbian Exchange: Biological and Cultural Consequences of 1492.* Westport, Conn., 1972. Focuses on early exchanges of plants, animals, and diseases between Europe and America.

———. *Ecological Imperialism: The Biological Expansion of Europe, 900–1900.* Cambridge, 1986. An important study that examines the establishment of European biological species in the larger world.

Philip D. Curtin. *Cross-Cultural Trade in World History.* New York, 1984. Focuses on the roles of cross-cultural brokers in facilitating trade between different societies.

Stephen Frederic Dale. *Indian Merchants and Eurasian Trade, 1600–1750.* Cambridge, 1994. Scholarly analysis of Indian merchant communities trading in Russia, Persia, and central Asia in early modern times.

Andre Gunder Frank. *ReORIENT: Global Economy in the Asian Age.* Berkeley, 1998. Important and challenging analysis of global economic integration in the early modern world.

Jonathan L. Israel. *Dutch Primacy in World Trade, 1585–1740.* Oxford, 1989. A thorough examination of the Dutch seaborne empire at its height.

William H. McNeill. *Plagues and Peoples.* Garden City, N.Y., 1976. Examines the effects of infectious and contagious diseases in world history.

Anthony Pagden. *European Encounters with the New World: From Renaissance to Romanticism.* New Haven, 1993. Scholarly examination of early European responses to the peoples, societies, and environments they encountered in the Americas.

John H. Parry. *The Age of Reconnaissance.* Berkeley, 1982. Reliable and readable survey of European expansion.

M. N. Pearson. *The Portuguese in India.* Cambridge, 1987. A brief, lively, and up-to-date discussion of the early Portuguese empire in India.

William D. Phillips Jr. and Carla Rahn Phillips. *The Worlds of Christopher Columbus.* Cambridge, 1992. The best general study of Christopher Columbus.

Stuart B. Schwartz, ed. *Implicit Understandings: Observing, Reporting, and Reflecting on the Encounters between Europeans and Other Peoples in the Early Modern Era.* Cambridge, 1994. Fascinating collection of essays by specialists on cross-cultural perceptions in early modern times.

Sanjay Subrahmanyam. *The Career and Legend of Vasco da Gama.* Cambridge, 1997. The best critical study of the famous Portuguese mariner.

———. *The Portuguese Empire in Asia, 1500–1700: A Political and Economic History.* London, 1993. A sophisticated analysis of the Portuguese trading-post empire based on recent research.

James D. Tracy, ed. *The Political Economy of Merchant Empires: State Power and World Trade, 1350–1750.* Cambridge, 1991. Essays on the interconnections between political, military, and commercial relationships in early modern times.

———. *The Rise of Merchant Empires: Long-Distance Trade in the Early Modern World, 1350–1750.* Cambridge, 1990. Essays by specialists on global trade in early modern times.

Immanuel Wallerstein. *The Modern World-System.* 3 vols. to date. New York, 1974–. A controversial but influential interpretation of global political and economic development in modern times.

CHAPTER 23

THE TRANSFORMATION
OF EUROPE

• • •

In 1517 an obscure German monk posed a challenge to the Roman Catholic church. Martin Luther of Wittenberg denounced the church's sale of indulgences, a type of pardon that excused individuals from doing penance for their sins and thus facilitated their entry into heaven. Indulgences had been available since the eleventh century, but in order to raise funds for the reconstruction of St. Peter's basilica in Rome, church authorities began to market indulgences aggressively in the early sixteenth century. From their point of view, indulgences were splendid devices: they encouraged individuals to reflect piously on their behavior while also bringing large sums of money into the church's treasury.

To Martin Luther, however, indulgences were signs of greed, hypocrisy, and moral rot in the Roman Catholic church. Luther despised the pretentiousness of church authorities who arrogated to themselves powers that belonged properly to God alone: no human being had the power to absolve individuals of their sins and grant them admission to heaven, Luther believed, so the sale of indulgences constituted a massive fraud perpetrated on an unsuspecting public. In October 1517, following academic custom of the day, he offered to debate publicly with anyone who wished to dispute his views, and he denounced the sale of indulgences in a document called the *Ninety-Five Theses*.

Luther did not nail his work to the church door in Wittenberg, although a popular legend credited him with this heroic gesture, but news of the *Ninety-Five Theses* spread instantly: within a few weeks printed copies were available throughout Europe. Luther's challenge galvanized opinion among many who resented the power of the Roman church. It also drew severe criticism from religious and political authorities seeking to maintain the established order. Church officials subjected Luther's views to examination and judged them erroneous, and in 1520 Pope Leo X excommunicated the unrepentant monk. In 1521 the Holy Roman Emperor Charles V, a devout Roman Catholic, summoned Luther to an assembly of imperial authorities and demanded that he recant his views. Luther's response: "I cannot and will not recant anything, for it is neither safe nor right to act against one's conscience. Here I stand. I can do no other. God help me. Amen."

Martin Luther's challenge held enormous religious and political implications. Though expelled from the church, Luther still considered himself Christian—indeed, he considered his own faith true Christianity—and he held religious services

Martin Luther at age 42, depicted as a conscientious and determined man by the German painter Lucas Cranach in 1525. • Scala/Art Resource, NY for a community of devoted followers. Wittenberg became a center of religious dissent, which by the late 1520s had spread through much of Germany and Switzerland. During the 1530s dissidents known as Protestants—because of their protest against the established order—organized movements also in France, England, the Low Countries, and even Italy and Spain. By midcentury Luther's act of individual rebellion had mushroomed into the Protestant Reformation, which shattered the religious unity of western Christendom.

For all of its unsettling effects, the Protestant Reformation was only one of several powerful movements that transformed western European society during the early modern era. Another was the consolidation of strong centralized states, which took shape partly because of the Reformation. Between the sixteenth and eighteenth centuries, monarchs in western Europe took advantage of religious quarrels to tighten control over their societies. By curbing the power of the feudal nobility, expanding royal authority, and increasing control over their subjects, they built states much more powerful than the feudal monarchies of the middle ages. By the mid-eighteenth century some rulers had concentrated so much power in their own hands that historians refer to them as absolute monarchs.

Alongside religious conflict and the building of powerful states, capitalism and early modern science also profoundly influenced western European society in early modern times. Early capitalism pushed European merchants and manufacturers into unrelenting competition with each other and encouraged them to reorganize their businesses in search of maximum efficiency. Early modern science challenged traditional ways of understanding the world and the universe. Under the influence of scientific discoveries, European intellectuals sought an entirely rational understanding of human society as well as the natural world, and some sought to base European moral, ethical, and social thought on science and reason rather than Christianity.

Thus between 1500 and 1800, western Europe underwent a thorough transformation. Although the combination of religious, political, social, economic, intellectual, and cultural change was unsettling and often disruptive, it also strengthened European society. The states of early modern Europe competed vigorously and mobilized their human and natural resources in effective fashion. By 1800 several of them had become especially powerful, wealthy, and dynamic. They stood poised to play major roles in world affairs during the nineteenth and twentieth centuries.

THE FRAGMENTATION OF WESTERN CHRISTENDOM

In the third century C.E., Christian missionaries began to spread their faith from the Mediterranean basin throughout Europe, and by 1000 C.E. Christianity had established a foothold as far north as Scandinavia and Iceland. Although the peoples of western Europe spoke different languages, ate different foods, and observed different customs, the church of Rome provided them with a common religious and cultural heritage. During the sixteenth and seventeenth centuries, however, revolts against the Roman Catholic church shattered the religious unity of western Europe. Followers of Martin Luther and other Protestant reformers established a series of churches independent of Rome, and Roman Catholic leaders strengthened their own church against the challengers. Throughout early modern times, religious controversies fueled social tensions.

The Protestant Reformation

Martin Luther (1483–1546) attacked the sale of indulgences as an individual, but he soon attracted enthusiastic support from others who resented the policies of the Roman church. Luther was a prolific and talented writer, and he published scores of works condemning the Roman church. His cause benefitted enormously from the printing press, which had first appeared in Europe in the mid-fifteenth century. A sizable literate public inhabited European cities and towns, and readers eagerly consumed printed works on religious as well as secular themes. Printed editions of Luther's writings appeared throughout Europe and sparked spirited debates on indulgences and theological issues. His supporters and critics took their own works to the printers, and religious controversies kept the presses busy churning out pamphlets and treatises for a century and more.

Martin Luther

Luther soon moved beyond the issue of indulgences: he attacked the Roman church for a wide range of abuses and called for thorough reform of Christendom. He advocated the closure of monasteries, translation of the Bible from Latin into vernacular languages, and an end to priestly authority, including the authority of the pope himself. When opponents pointed out that his reform program ran counter to church policy, he rejected the authority of the church and its hierarchy and proclaimed that the Bible was the only source of Christian religious authority.

Luther's works drew an enthusiastic popular response, and in Germany they fueled a movement to reform the church along the lines of Luther's teachings. Lay Christians flocked to hear Luther preach in Wittenberg, and several princes of the Holy Roman Empire warmed to Luther's views—partly because of personal conviction but partly also because religious controversy offered opportunities for them to build their own power bases. During the 1520s and 1530s many of the most important German cities—Strasbourg, Nuremberg, and Augsburg, among others—passed laws prohibiting Roman Catholic observances and requiring all religious services to follow Protestant doctrine and procedures.

By the mid-sixteenth century about half the German population had adopted Lutheran Christianity, and reformers had launched Protestant movements and established alternative churches in other lands as well. By the late 1520s the prosperous cities of Switzerland—Zurich, Basel, and Geneva—had fledgling Protestant churches. The heavily urbanized Low Countries also responded enthusiastically to Protestant appeals. Protestants appeared even in Italy and Spain, although authorities in those lands handily suppressed their challenge to the Roman church.

Reform outside Germany

In England a Reformation took place for frankly political as well as religious reasons. Lutherans and other Protestants worked to build a following in England from the 1520s, but they faced stout government resistance until King Henry VIII (reigned 1509–1547) came into conflict with the pope. Henry wanted to divorce his wife, who had not borne a male heir, but the pope refused to allow him to do so. Henry's response was to sever relations with the Roman church and make himself Supreme Head of the Anglican church—an English pope, as it were. While Henry reigned, the theology of the English church changed little, but under pressure of reformers, his successors replaced Roman Catholic with Protestant doctrines and rituals. By 1560 England had permanently left the Roman Catholic community.

Meanwhile, an even more influential Reformation was taking shape in France and the French-speaking parts of Switzerland. The initiator was a French lawyer, John Calvin (1509–1564), who in the 1530s converted to Protestant Christianity. Because the French monarchy sought to suppress Protestants, Calvin slipped across

John Calvin

the border to French-speaking Geneva in Switzerland. There he organized a Protestant community and worked with local officials to impose a strict code of morality and discipline on the city. Calvin also composed an influential treatise, *Institutes of the Christian Religion* (first published in 1536 and frequently reprinted with revisions) that systematized Protestant teachings and presented them as a coherent and organized package.

Calvin's Geneva was not only a model Protestant community but also a missionary center. Calvinist missionaries were most active in France, where they attracted strong interest in the cities, but they ventured also to Germany, the Low Countries, England, Scotland, and even distant Hungary. They established churches in all these lands and worked for reform along Protestant lines. They were most successful in the Netherlands and Scotland. By the late sixteenth century, Lutherans, Anglicans, and Calvinists together had built communities large enough that a return to religious unity in western Christendom was inconceivable.

The Catholic Reformation

In response to the Protestant Reformation, Roman Catholic authorities undertook a massive reform effort within their own church. To some extent their efforts represented a reaction to Protestant success. Yet Roman Catholic authorities also sought to define points of doctrine so as to clarify differences between Roman and Protestant churches, to persuade Protestants to return to the Roman church, and to deepen the sense of spirituality and religious commitment in their own community. Taken together, their efforts constituted the Catholic Reformation.

Two institutions were especially important for defining the Catholic Reformation and advancing its goals—the Council of Trent and the Society of Jesus. The Council of Trent was an assembly of bishops, cardinals, and other high church officials who met intermittently between 1545 and 1563 to address matters of doctrine

The Council of Trent

Under inspiration of the Catholic Reformation, many devout individuals sought mystic union with God. One of the most famous of the mystics was St. Teresa of Avila (in Spain), who founded a strict order of nuns and often experienced religious visions. A famous sculpture by the Italian artist Gianlorenzo Bernini depicts St. Teresa in an ecstatic trance accompanied by an angel. • Scala/Art Resource, NY

and reform. Drawing heavily on the works of the thirteenth-century scholastic theologian St. Thomas Aquinas, the council defined the elements of Roman Catholic theology in detail. The council acknowledged that abuses had alienated many people from the Roman church, and it took steps to reform the church. The council demanded that church authorities observe strict standards of morality, and it required them to establish schools and seminaries in their districts to prepare priests properly for their roles.

While the Council of Trent dealt with doctrine and reform, the Society of Jesus went on the offensive and sought to extend the boundaries of the reformed Roman church. The society's founder was St. Ignatius Loyola (1491–1556), a Basque nobleman and soldier who in 1521 suffered a devastating leg wound that ended his military career. While recuperating he read spiritual works and popular accounts of saints' lives, and he resolved to put his energy into religious work. In 1540, together with a small band of disciples, he founded the Society of Jesus. *St. Ignatius Loyola*

Ignatius required that members of the society, known as Jesuits, complete a rigorous and advanced education. They received instruction not only in theology and philosophy but also in classical languages, literature, history, and science. As a result of this preparation—and their unswerving dedication to the Roman Catholic church—the Jesuits made extraordinarily effective missionaries. They were able to outargue most of their opponents and acquired a reputation for discipline and determination. They often served as counsellors to kings and rulers and used their influence to promote policies that benefited the Roman church. They also were the most prominent of the early Christian missionaries outside Europe: in the wake of the European reconnaissance of the world's oceans, Jesuits attracted converts in India, China, Japan, the Philippines, and the Americas, thus making Christianity a genuinely global religion. *The Society of Jesus*

Witch-Hunts and Religious Wars

Europeans took religion seriously in the sixteenth century, and religious divisions helped to fuel social and political conflict. Apart from wars, the most destructive violence that afflicted early modern Europe was the hunt for witches, which was especially prominent in regions like the Rhineland where tensions between Protestants and Roman Catholics ran high.

Like many other peoples, Europeans had long believed that certain individuals possessed unusual powers to influence human affairs or discover secret information such as the identity of a thief. During the late fifteenth century, theologians developed a theory that witches derived their powers from the devil. According to this theory, witches made agreements to worship the devil in exchange for supernatural powers, including the ability to fly through the night on brooms, pitchforks, or animals. Theorists believed that the witches regularly flew off to distant places to attend the "witches' sabbath," a gathering that featured devil worship, lewd behavior, and the concoction of secret potions, culminating in sexual relations with the devil himself.

Although the witches' sabbath was sheer fantasy, fears that individuals were making alliances with the devil sparked a massive hunt for witches. Witchcraft became a convenient explanation for any unpleasant turn of events—failure of a crop, outbreak of a fire, an unexpected death, or inability to conceive a child. About 110,000 individuals underwent trial as suspected witches during the sixteenth and seventeenth centuries, and about 60,000 of them died either by hanging or by burning at the stake. *Witch-Hunting*

Although men were among the victims, most convicted witches were women. Indeed, women may have accounted for 95 percent or more of the condemned. Many of the women were poor, old, single, or widowed—individuals who lived on the margins of their societies and were easy targets for accusers, since they had few protectors. Witch-hunting was mostly a European affair, but it also spread to European colonies in the Americas. The most intense witch-hunt in the Americas took place in seventeenth-century New England, where a population of about one hundred thousand colonists tried 234 individuals for witchcraft and executed 36 of them by hanging.

By 1700 the fear of witches had largely diminished. Accusations, trials, and executions occurred only sporadically thereafter. The last legal execution for witchcraft in Europe took place in Switzerland in 1782. For the better part of two centuries, however, the intermittent pursuit of witches revealed clearly the stresses and strains that afflicted European society during early modern times.

Religious Wars   Religious tensions even led to outright war between Protestant and Roman Catholic communities. Religious wars wracked France for thirty-six years (1562–1598), for example, and they also complicated relations between Protestant and Roman Catholic states. In 1588 King Philip II of Spain (reigned 1556–1598) attempted to force England to return to the Roman Catholic church by sending the Spanish Armada—a huge flotilla consisting of 130 ships and thirty thousand men—to dethrone the Protestant Queen Elizabeth. The effort collapsed, however, when English forces disrupted the Spanish fleet by sending blazing, unmanned ships into its midst. Then a ferocious gale scattered Spanish vessels throughout the North Sea.

Religious convictions also aggravated relations between The Netherlands and Spain by fueling the revolt of the Dutch provinces from their overlord, the king of Spain. In 1567 Philip sent an army to tighten his control over the provinces and to

A la fin ces Voleurs infames et perdus,
Comme fruits malheureux a cet arbre pendus
Monstrent bien que le crime (horrible et noire engeance)
Est luy mesme instrument de honte et de vengeance,
Et que c'est le Destin des hommes vicieux
D'esprouuer tost ou tard la iustice des Cieux.

The Thirty Years' War offered abundant opportunity for undisciplined mercenary soldiers to prey on civilian populations. Only rarely, as in the mass hanging depicted in this engraving of 1633, did soldiers receive punishment for their criminal acts. ● Anne S. K. Brown Military Collection, Brown University Library

suppress the Calvinist movement there. Resistance escalated into a full-scale rebellion. By 1610 the seven northern provinces (the modern Netherlands) had won their independence and formed a republic known as the United Provinces, leaving ten southern provinces (modern Belgium) under Spanish and later Austrian rule until the nineteenth century.

The religious wars culminated in a massive continental conflict known as the Thirty Years' War (1618–1648). The war opened when the Holy Roman emperor attempted to force his Bohemian subjects to return to the Roman Catholic church, and the main battleground was the emperor's territory in Germany. Other parties soon entered the fray, however, and by the time the war ended Spanish, French, Dutch, German, Swedish, Danish, Polish, Bohemian, and Russian forces had taken part in the conflict.

The Thirty Years' War

The motives that prompted these states to enter the war were sometimes political or economic, but religious differences complicated the other issues and made them more difficult to resolve. Regardless of the motives, the Thirty Years' War was the most destructive European conflict before World War I. Quite apart from violence and brutalities committed by undisciplined soldiers, the war damaged economies and societies throughout Europe and led to the deaths of about one-third of the German population.

THE CONSOLIDATION OF SOVEREIGN STATES

Although fundamentally a religious movement, the Reformation had strong political implications and centralizing monarchs readily made use of religious issues in their efforts to build strong states and enhance their authority. Ruling elites had their own religious preferences, and they often promoted a Protestant or Roman Catholic cause out of personal conviction. Religious controversies also offered splendid opportunities for ambitious subordinates who built power bases by appealing to particular religious communities. Over the long run, centralizing monarchs profited most from religious controversy generated by the Reformation. While the Holy Roman Empire fell into disarray because of political and religious quarrels, monarchs in England, France, and Spain augmented their revenues, enhanced their authority, and created powerful states that increasingly guided public affairs in western Europe.

The Attempted Revival of Empire

After the dissolution of the Carolingian empire in the ninth century C.E., there was no effective imperial government in western Europe. The so-called Holy Roman Empire emerged in the tenth century, but its authority extended only to Germany and northern Italy, and even there the emperors encountered stiff opposition from powerful princes and thriving cities. During the early sixteenth century, it seemed that Emperor Charles V (reigned 1519–1556) might establish the Holy Roman Empire as the preeminent political authority in Europe, but by midcentury it was clear that there would be no revival of empire. Thus unlike China, India, and Ottoman lands in southwest Asia and north Africa, early modern Europe developed as a region of independent states.

After 1273 all Holy Roman emperors came from the Habsburg family, whose ancestral homeland was in Austria. Through marriage alliances with princely and royal families, the Habsburgs accumulated rights and titles to lands throughout Europe

Charles V

MAP [23.1]

Sixteenth-century Europe.

and beyond. Charles V inherited authority over the Habsburgs' Austrian domains as well as the duchy of Burgundy (including the wealthy provinces of the Low Countries) and the kingdom of Spain (including its possessions in Italy and the Americas). When he became emperor in 1519, he acquired authority over Germany, Bohemia, Switzerland, and parts of northern Italy. His empire stretched from Vienna in Austria to Cuzco in Peru.

Imperial Fragmentation   In spite of his far-flung holdings, Charles did not extend his authority throughout Europe or even establish a lasting imperial legacy. Throughout his reign Charles had to devote much of his attention and energy to the Lutheran movement and to imperial princes who took advantage of religious controversy to assert their independence. Moreover, Charles did not build an administrative structure for his empire, but instead ruled each of his lands according to its own laws and customs. He was able to draw on the financial resources of wealthy lands like the Low Countries and Spain to maintain a powerful army. Yet Charles did not have the ambition to extend his authority by military force, but used his army mostly to put down rebellions.

Foreign Challenges

Foreign difficulties also prevented Charles from establishing his empire as the arbiter of Europe. The prospect of a powerful Holy Roman Empire struck fear in the kings of France, and it caused concern among the sultans of the Ottoman empire as well. Charles's holdings surrounded France, and the French kings suspected that the emperor wanted to absorb their realm and extend his authority throughout Europe. To forestall this possibility, the French kings created every obstacle they could for Charles. Even though they were staunch Roman Catholics, they aided German Lutherans and encouraged them to rebel. The French kings even allied with the Muslim Ottoman Turks against the emperor.

For their part the Ottoman sultans did not want to see a powerful Christian empire threaten their holdings in eastern Europe and their position in the Mediterranean basin. With the encouragement of the French king, Turkish forces conquered Hungary in 1526, and three years later they even laid siege briefly to Vienna. Moreover, during the early sixteenth century Ottoman forces imposed their rule beyond Egypt and embraced almost all of north Africa. By midcentury Turkish holdings posed a serious threat to Italian and Spanish shipping in the Mediterranean.

Thus numerous domestic and foreign problems prevented Charles V from establishing his vast empire as the supreme political authority in Europe. His inability to suppress the Lutherans was especially disappointing to Charles, and in 1556, after agreeing that imperial princes and cities could determine the religious faith observed in their jurisdictions, the emperor abdicated his throne and retired to a monastery in Spain. His empire did not survive intact. Charles bestowed his holdings in Spain, Italy, the Low Countries, and the Americas on his son, King Philip II of Spain, while his brother Ferdinand inherited the Habsburg family lands in Austria and the imperial throne.

The New Monarchs

In the absence of effective imperial power, guidance of public affairs fell to the various regional states that had emerged during the middle ages. The city-states of Italy were prominent because of their economic power: since the eleventh century they had been Europe's most important centers of trade, manufacturing, and finance. The most powerful European states, however, were the kingdoms of England, France, and Spain. During the late fifteenth and sixteenth centuries, rulers of these lands, known as the "new monarchs," marshaled their resources, curbed the feudal nobility, and built strong centralized regimes.

Finance

The new monarchs included Henry VIII of England, Louis XI and Francis I of France, and Fernando and Isabel of Spain. All the new monarchs sought to enhance their treasuries by developing new sources of finance. The French kings levied direct taxes on sales, households, and the salt trade. A new sales tax dramatically boosted Spanish royal income in the sixteenth century. For fear of provoking rebellion, the English kings did not introduce new taxes, but they increased revenues by raising fines and fees for royal services. Moreover, after Henry VIII severed ties between the

English and Roman churches, he dissolved the monasteries and confiscated church wealth in England. This financial windfall enabled Henry to enhance royal power by increasing the size of the state and adding to its responsibilities. After the English Reformation, for example, the state provided poor relief and support for orphans, which previously had been responsibilities of churches and monasteries.

State Power   With their increased income the new monarchs enlarged their administrative staffs, which enabled them to collect taxes and implement royal policies more reliably than before. The French and Spanish monarchs also maintained standing armies that vastly increased their power with respect to the nobility. Their armies with thousands of infantrymen were too large for individual nobles to match, and they equipped their forces with cannons that were too expensive for nobles to purchase. The English kings did not need a standing army to put down the occasional rebellion that flared in their island realm and so did not go to the expense of supporting one. Yet they too increased their power with respect to the nobles by subjecting them to royal justice and forcing them to comply with royal policy.

The debates and disputes launched by the Protestant Reformation helped monarchs increase their power. In lands that adopted Protestant faiths—including England, much of Germany, Denmark, and Sweden—rulers expropriated the monasteries and used church wealth to expand their powers. This option was not open to Roman Catholic kings, but Protestant movements provided them with a justification to mobilize resources, which they used against political as well as religious adversaries.

The Spanish Inquisition   The Spanish Inquisition was the most distinctive institution that relied on religious justifications to advance state ends. Fernando and Isabel founded the Spanish Inquisition in 1478, and they obtained papal license to operate the institution as a royal agency. Its original task was to ferret out those who secretly practiced Judaism or Islam, but Charles V charged it with responsibility also for detecting Protestant heresy in Spain. Throughout the late fifteenth and sixteenth century, however, the Spanish Inquisition served political as well as religious purposes.

Inquisitors had broad powers to investigate suspected cases of heresy. Popular legends have created an erroneous impression of the Spanish Inquisition as an institution running amok, framing innocent victims and routinely subjecting them to torture. In fact, inquisitors usually observed rules of evidence, and they released many suspects after investigations turned up no sign of heresy. Yet when they detected heresy, inquisitors could be ruthless. They sentenced hundreds of victims to hang from the gallows or burn at the stake and imprisoned many others in dank cells for extended periods of time. Fear of the inquisition intimidated many into silence, and a strict Roman Catholic orthodoxy prevailed in Spain. The inquisition deterred nobles from adopting Protestant views out of political ambition, and it used its influence on behalf of the Spanish monarchy. From 1559 to 1576, for example, inquisitors imprisoned the archbishop of Toledo—the highest Roman Catholic church official in all of Spain—because of his political independence.

Constitutional States and Absolute Monarchies

During the seventeenth and eighteenth centuries, as they sought to restore order after the Thirty Years' War, European states developed along two lines. Rulers in England and the Netherlands shared authority with representative institutions and created constitutional states, whereas monarchs in France, Spain, Austria, and Prus-

When the Spanish Inquisition detected traces of Protestant heresy, the punishment could be swift and brutal. In this engraving of about 1560, a large crowd observes the execution of heretics (top right) by burning at the stake. • Bibliothèque Nationale de France

sia concentrated power in their own hands and created a form of state known as absolute monarchy. In Russia (discussed in chapter 28) centralizing rulers also built a powerful state on the model of absolute monarchies to the west.

The island kingdom of England and the maritime Dutch republic did not have written constitutions specifying the powers of the state, but during the seventeenth century they evolved governments that claimed limited powers and recognized rights pertaining to individuals and representative institutions. In England constitutional government arose from a bitter dispute between kings and parliaments that culminated in civil war (1642–1649). Parliamentary forces executed King Charles I in 1649, deposed King James II in 1688, and established parliamentary supremacy in English politics. In the Netherlands constitutional government arose from representative assemblies that organized local affairs after the United Provinces gained their independence from Spain.

In both England and the Dutch republic, wealthy merchants were especially prominent in political affairs, and state policy in both lands favored maritime trade and the building of commercial empires overseas. The constitutional states allowed entrepreneurs to pursue their economic interests with minimal interference from public authorities, and during the late seventeenth and eighteenth centuries both experienced extraordinary prosperity as a result of these policies.

Constitutional States

Absolutism

Whereas constitutional states devised ways to share power and authority, absolutism stood on a theoretical foundation known as the divine right of kings. This theory held that kings derived their authority from God and served as "God's lieutenants upon earth." There was no role in divine-right theory for common subjects or even nobles in public affairs: the king made law and determined policy. Noncompliance or disobedience merited punishment, and rebellion was a despicable act tantamount to blasphemy. In fact, absolute monarchs always relied on support from nobles and other social groups as well, but the claims of divine-right theory clearly reflected efforts at royal centralization.

The most successful absolutist state was the French monarchy. The architect of French absolutism was a prominent church official, Cardinal Richelieu, who served as chief minister to King Louis XIII from 1624 to 1642. Richelieu worked systematically to undermine the power of the nobility and enhance the authority of the king. He destroyed nobles' castles and ruthlessly crushed aristocratic conspiracies. As a counterweight to the nobility, Richelieu built a large bureaucracy staffed by commoners loyal to the king. He also appointed officials to supervise the implementation of royal policy in the provinces. Finally, Richelieu attacked French Calvinists, who often allied with independent nobles, and destroyed their political and military power, although he allowed them to continue observing their faith. By midcentury France was under control of a tightly centralized absolute monarchy.

The Sun King

The ruler who best epitomized royal absolutism was King Louis XIV (reigned 1643–1715), who once reportedly declared that he was himself the state: "*l'état, c'est moi.*" Known as *le roi soleil*—"the sun king"—Louis surrounded himself with splendor befitting one who ruled by divine right. During the 1670s he built a magnificent residence at Versailles, a royal hunting lodge near Paris, and in the 1680s he moved his court there. Louis's palace at Versailles was the largest building in Europe, with 230 acres of formal gardens and 1,400 fountains. Because Louis did not want to wait years for saplings to grow, he ordered laborers to dig up twenty-five thousand fully grown trees and haul them to Versailles for transplanting.

The sun king was the center of attention at Versailles. Court officials hovered around him and tended to his every need. All prominent nobles established residences at Versailles for their families and entourages. Louis strongly encouraged them to live at court, where he and his staff could keep an eye on them, and ambitious nobles gravitated there anyway in hopes of winning influence with the king. Louis himself was the arbiter of taste and style at Versailles, where he lavishly patronized painters, sculptors, architects, and writers whose creations met with his approval.

While nobles living at Versailles mastered the intricacies of court ritual and attended banquets, concerts, operas, balls, and theatrical performances, Louis and his ministers ran the state. In effect, Louis provided the nobility with luxurious accommodations and endless entertainment in exchange for absolute rule. From Versailles Louis and his advisors promulgated laws and controlled a massive standing army that kept order throughout the land. They also promoted economic development by supporting the establishment of new industries, building roads and canals, abolishing internal tariffs, and encouraging exports. Finally, they waged a series of wars designed to enlarge French boundaries and establish France as the preeminent power in Europe.

Absolutism outside France

Louis XIV was not the only absolute monarch of early modern Europe. King Philip II had established an absolute monarchy in Spain during the sixteenth century, and his Habsburg heirs attempted to pursue absolutist policies throughout the seventeenth century. In Spain, however, expenses far exceeded revenues, and the royal

King Louis XIV and his entourage approach the main gate of Versailles (bottom right). Though only partially constructed at the time of this painting (1668), Versailles was already a spacious and luxurious retreat for Louis and his court.   • Giraudon/Art Resource, NY

treasury could not support the army and bureaucracy that absolute government required: between 1596 and 1680 the Spanish kings canceled their debts five times. Rulers in Austria, Prussia, and Russia looked upon absolutist France as a model for centralized government. All built magnificent palaces in imitation of Versailles, maintained splendid royal courts, and sought to increase royal control over political, military, and financial affairs. Prussian and Russian rulers also built powerful states that played major roles in European affairs from the eighteenth century forward.

The European States System

Whether they relied on absolutist or constitutional principles, European governments of early modern times built states much more powerful than those of their medieval predecessors. This round of state development led to difficulties within Europe, since conflicting interests fueled interstate competition and war. In the absence of an imperial authority capable of imposing and maintaining order in western Europe, sovereign states had to find ways to resolve conflicts by themselves.

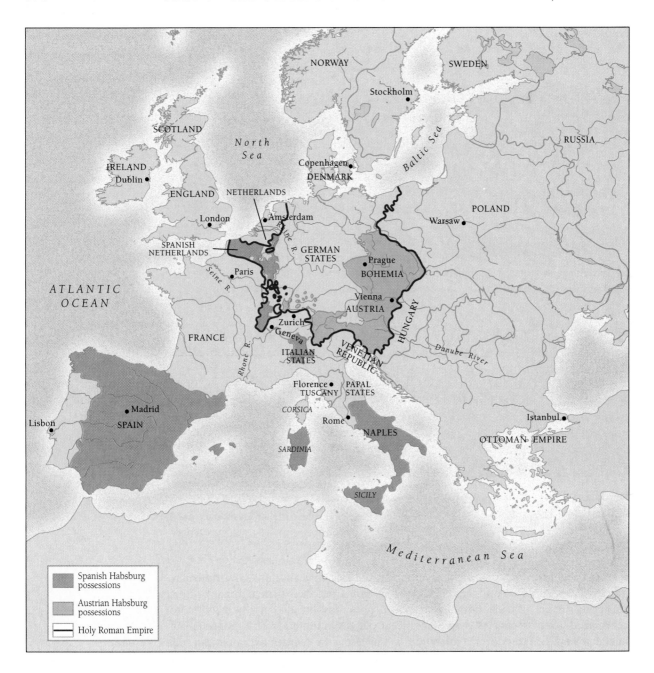

MAP [23.2]

Europe after the Peace
of Westphalia.

*The Peace
of Westphalia*

The Thirty Years' War demonstrated the chaos and devastation that conflict could bring. In an effort to avoid tearing their society apart, European states ended the Thirty Years' War with the Peace of Westphalia (1648), which laid the foundations for a system of independent, competing states. Almost all the European states participated in drafting the Peace of Westphalia, and by the treaty's terms they regarded each other as sovereign and equal. They also mutually recognized their rights to organize their own domestic affairs, including religious affairs. Rather than envisioning imperial or papal or some other sort of supreme authority, the Peace of Westphalia entrusted political and diplomatic affairs to states acting in their own interests. European religious unity had disappeared, and the era of the sovereign state had arrived.

The Peace of Westphalia did not bring an end to war. Indeed, war was almost constant in early modern Europe. Most conflicts were minor affairs inaugurated by monarchs seeking to extend their authority to new lands or to reclaim territories seized by others, but they nevertheless disrupted local economies and drained resources. A few wars, however, grew to sizable proportions. Most notable among them were the wars of Louis XIV and the Seven Years' War. Between 1668 and 1713, the sun king sought to expand his borders east into Germany and to absorb Spain and the Spanish Netherlands into his kingdom. This prospect prompted England, the United Provinces, and Austria to mount a coalition against Louis. Later the Seven Years' War (1756–1763) pitted France, Austria, and Russia against Britain and Prussia, and it merged with conflicts between France and Britain in India and North America to become a global war for imperial supremacy.

Coalition against Louis (handwritten margin note)

The Balance of Power

These shifting alliances illustrate the principal foundation of European diplomacy in early modern times—the balance of power. No ruler wanted to see another state dominate all the others. Thus when any particular state began to wax strong, others formed coalitions against it. Balance-of-power diplomacy was risky business: it was always possible that a coalition might repress one strong state only to open the door for another. Yet in playing balance-of-power politics, statesmen prevented the building of empire and ensured that Europe would be a land of independent, sovereign, competing states.

Military Development

Frequent wars and balance-of-power diplomacy drained the resources of individual states but strengthened European society as a whole. European states competed vigorously and sought to develop the most expert military leadership and the most effective weapons for their arsenals. States organized military academies where officers received advanced education in strategy and tactics and learned how to maintain disciplined forces. Demand for powerful weapons stimulated the development of a sophisticated armaments industry that turned out ever more lethal products. Gun foundries manufactured cannons of increasing size, range, power, and accuracy, as well as small arms that allowed infantry to unleash withering volleys against their enemies.

In China, India, and Islamic lands, imperial states had little or no incentive to encourage similar technological innovation in the armaments industry. These states possessed the forces and weapons they needed to maintain order within their boundaries, and they rarely encountered foreign threats backed up with superior armaments. In Europe, however, failure to keep up with the latest improvements in arms technology could lead to defeat on the battlefield and decline in state power. Thus Europeans continuously sought to improve their military arsenals, and as a result European armaments outperformed all others.

EARLY CAPITALIST SOCIETY

While the Protestant Reformation and the emergence of sovereign states brought religious and political change, a rapidly expanding population and economy encouraged the development of capitalism, which in turn led to a restructuring of European economy and society. Technologies of communication and transportation enabled businessmen to profit from distant markets, and merchants and manufacturers increasingly organized their affairs with the market rather than local communities in mind. Capitalism brought great wealth to European society but it also encouraged social change that sometimes caused painful adjustments.

The Old Stock Exchange of Amsterdam, depicted here in a painting of the mid-seventeenth century, attracted merchants, investors, entrepreneurs, and businessmen from all over Europe. There they bought and sold shares in joint-stock companies such as the VOC and dealt in all manner of commodities traded in Amsterdam. • Amsterdams Historisch Museum

Population Growth and Urbanization

American Food Crops   The foundation of European economic expansion in early modern times was a rapidly growing population, which reflected improved nutrition and decreasing mortality. The Columbian exchange enriched European diets by introducing new food crops to European fields and tables. Most notable of the introductions was the potato, which enjoyed the reputation of being an aphrodisiac during the sixteenth and seventeenth centuries. Although potatoes probably did not inspire much romantic ardor, they provided a welcome source of carbohydrates for peasants and laborers who were having trouble keeping up with the rising price of bread. From Ireland to Russia and from Scandinavia to the Mediterranean, cultivators planted potatoes and harvested crops that added calories to European diets. American maize also made its way to Europe. Maize, however, served mostly as feed for livestock rather than a food for human consumption, although peasants sometimes used cornmeal to make bread or porridges like polenta. Other American crops, such as tomatoes and peppers, added vitamins to European diets.

While recently introduced American crops improved European diets, old diseases lost some of their ferocity. Smallpox continued to carry off about 10 percent of Europe's infants, and dysentery, influenza, tuberculosis, and typhus also claimed victims among young and old, rich and poor alike. Yet better nourished populations were better able to resist these maladies. Bubonic plague, a massive epidemic killer during the fourteenth and fifteenth centuries, receded from European society. After its initial onslaught in the mid-fourteenth century, plague made periodic appearances throughout the early modern era. After the mid-seventeenth century, however, epidemics were rare and isolated events. The last major outbreaks of plague in Europe occurred in London in 1660 and Marseilles in 1720. By the mid-seventeenth century epidemic disease was almost negligible as an influence on European population.

Although European birth rates did not rise dramatically in early modern times, decreasing mortality resulted in rapid population growth. In 1500 the population of Europe, including Russia, was about 81 million. During the sixteenth century, as Europe recovered from epidemic plague, the population rose to 100 million. The Thirty Years' War—along with the famine and disease that the war touched off—led to population decline from about 1620 to 1650, but by 1700 European population had rallied and risen to 120 million. During the next century it grew by another 50 percent to 180 million.

Population Growth

Rapid population growth drove a process of equally rapid urbanization. Some cities grew because rulers chose them as sites of government. Madrid, for example, was a minor town with a few thousand inhabitants until 1561 when King Philip II decided to locate his capital there. By 1600 the population of Madrid had risen to 65,000, and by 1630 it had reached 170,000. Other cities were commercial and industrial as well as government centers, and their numbers expanded along with the European economy. In the mid-sixteenth century, for example, the population of Paris was about 130,000, and London had about 60,000 inhabitants. A century later the population of both cities had risen to half a million. Other European cities also experienced growth, even if it was not so dramatic as in the cases of Madrid, Paris, and London: Amsterdam, Berlin, Copenhagen, Dublin, Stockholm, Vienna, and others became prominent European cities during the early modern era.

Urbanization

Early Capitalism and Protoindustrialization

Population growth and rapid urbanization helped spur a round of remarkable economic development. This economic growth coincided with the emergence of capitalism—an economic system in which private parties make their goods and services available on a free market and seek to take advantage of market conditions to profit from their activities. Whether they are single individuals or large companies, private parties own the land, machinery, tools, equipment, buildings, workshops, and raw materials needed for production. Private parties pursuing their own economic interests hire workers and decide for themselves what to produce; economic decisions are the prerogative of capitalist businessmen, not governments or social superiors. The center of a capitalist system is the free market in which businessmen compete with each other and the forces of supply and demand determine the prices received for goods and services. If businessmen organize their affairs efficiently, they realize handsome profits when they place their goods and services on the market. Otherwise, they incur losses and perhaps even lose their businesses.

The Nature of Capitalism

The desire to accumulate wealth and realize profits was by no means new. Ever since the introduction of agriculture and the production of surplus crops, some individuals and groups had accumulated great wealth. Indeed, for several thousand years before the early modern era, merchants in China, southeast Asia, India, southwest Asia, the Mediterranean basin, and sub-Saharan Africa had pursued commercial ventures in hopes of realizing profits. Banks, investors, and insurance underwriters had supported privately organized commercial ventures throughout much of the eastern hemisphere since the postclassical era (500–1500 C.E.).

Supply and Demand

During early modern times, however, European merchants and entrepreneurs transformed their society in a way that none of their predecessors had done. The capitalist economic order developed as businessmen learned to take advantage of market conditions by building efficient networks of transportation and communication. Dutch merchants might purchase cheap grain from Baltic lands like Poland or Russia, for example, store it in Amsterdam until they learned about a famine in the Mediterranean and then transport it and sell it in southern France or Spain. Their enormous profits fueled suspicions that they took advantage of those in difficulty, but their activities also supplied hungry communities with the necessities of life, even if the price was high.

Private parties organized an array of institutions and services to support early capitalism. Banks, for example, appeared in all the major commercial cities of Europe: they held funds on account for safekeeping and granted loans to merchants or entrepreneurs launching new business ventures. Banks also published business newsletters—forerunners of the *Wall Street Journal* and *Fortune* magazine—that provided readers with reports on prices, information about demand for commodities in distant markets, and political news that could have an impact on business. Insurance companies mitigated financial losses from risky undertakings like transoceanic voyages. Stock exchanges arose in the major European cities and provided markets where investors could buy and sell shares in joint-stock companies and trade in other commodities as well.

Joint-Stock Companies

Joint-stock companies were especially important institutions in early capitalist society. Large trading companies like the English East India Company and its Dutch counterpart, the Vereenigde Oost-Indische Compagnie (VOC), spread the risks attached to expensive business enterprises and also took advantage of extensive communications and transportation networks. The trading companies organized commercial ventures on a larger scale than ever before in world history. They were the principal foundations of the global economy that emerged in early modern times, and they were the direct ancestors of contemporary multinational corporations.

Governments also played important roles in promoting capitalism. They recognized and protected individuals' rights to possess private property, enforced contracts, and settled disputes between parties to business transactions. Governments also chartered joint-stock companies and authorized some of them to explore, conquer, and colonize distant lands in search of commercial opportunities. Merchants were especially influential in the affairs of the English and Dutch states, and these lands adopted policies that were the most favorable to capitalist enterprises throughout the early modern era.

The development of capitalism encouraged European entrepreneurs to organize new ways to manufacture goods. For centuries craft guilds had monopolized the production of goods such as textiles and metalwares in European towns and cities. Guilds fixed prices and wages, and they regulated standards of quality. They did not seek to realize profits so much as to protect markets and preserve their members' places in society. As a result, they actively discouraged competition and sometimes resisted technological innovation.

Capitalist entrepreneurs seeking profits found the guilds cumbersome and inflexible, so they sidestepped them and moved production into the countryside. Instead of relying on urban artisans to produce cloth, for example, they organized a "putting-out system" by which they delivered unfinished materials like raw wool to rural households. Men and women in the countryside would then spin the wool into yarn, weave the yarn into cloth, cut the cloth according to patterns, and assemble the pieces into garments. The entrepreneur paid workers for their services, picked up the finished goods, and sold them on the market. During the seventeenth and eighteenth centuries, entrepreneurs moved the production of cloth, nails, pins, pots, and many other goods into the countryside through the putting-out system.

The Putting-out System

Because rural labor was usually plentiful, entrepreneurs spent relatively little on wages and realized handsome profits on their ventures. The putting-out system represented an early effort to organize efficient industrial production. Indeed, historians refer to the seventeenth and eighteenth centuries as an age of "protoindustrialization." The putting-out system remained a prominent feature of European society until the rise of industrial factories in the nineteenth century.

Social Change in Early Modern Europe

Capitalist economic development brought unsettling change to European lands. The putting-out system, for example, introduced considerable sums of money into the countryside. Increased wealth brought material benefits, but it also undermined long-established patterns of rural life. The material standards of rural life rose dramatically: peasant households acquired more cabinets, furnishings, and tableware, and rural residents wore better clothes, ate better food, and drank better wine. Individuals suddenly acquired incomes that enabled them to pursue their own economic interests and to become financially independent of their families and neighbors. When young adults and women began to earn their own incomes, however, many feared that they might slip out of the control of their families and abandon their kin who continued to work at agricultural tasks.

Capitalism also posed moral challenges. Medieval theologians had regarded profit-making activity as morally dangerous, since profiteers looked to their own advantage rather than the welfare of the larger community. Church officials even attempted to forbid the collection of interest on loans, since they considered interest an unearned and immoral profit. But profit was the lifeblood of capitalism, and bankers were not willing to risk large sums of money on business ventures without realizing handsome returns on their investments in the form of interest. Even as it transformed the European economy, capitalism found spokesmen who sought to explain its principles and portray it as a socially beneficial form of economic organization. Most important of the early apostles of capitalism was the Scottish philosopher Adam Smith (1723–1790), who held that society would prosper when individuals pursued their own economic interests.

Profits and Ethics

Nevertheless, the transition to capitalist society was long and painful. When individuals abandoned the practices of their ancestors and declined to help those who had fallen on hard times, their neighbors readily interpreted their actions as expressions of selfishness rather than economic prudence. Thus capitalist economic practices generated deep social strains, which often manifested themselves in violence. Bandits plagued the countryside of early modern Europe, and muggers turned whole sections of large cities into danger zones. Some historians believe that witch-hunting activities reflected social tensions generated by early capitalism and that accusations of witchcraft represented hostility toward women who were becoming economically independent of their husbands and families.

ADAM SMITH ON THE CAPITALIST MARKET

• • •

Adam Smith devoted special thought to the nature of early capitalist society and the principles that made it work. In 1776 he published a lengthy book entitled An Inquiry into the Nature and Causes of the Wealth of Nations, *a vastly influential work that championed free, unregulated markets and capitalist enterprise as the principal ingredients of prosperity. Smith's optimism about capitalism sprang from his conviction that society as a whole benefits when individuals pursue their own economic interests and trade on a free market.*

Every individual is continually exerting himself to find out the most advantageous employment for whatever capital he can command. It is his own advantage, indeed, and not that of the society, which he has in view. . . .

As every individual, therefore, endeavours as much as he can both to employ his capital in the support of domestic industry, and so to direct that industry that its produce may be of the greatest value, every individual necessarily labours to render the annual revenue of the society as great as he can. He generally, indeed, neither intends to promote the public interest, nor knows how much he is promoting it. By preferring the support of domestic to that of foreign industry, he intends only his own security; and by directing that industry in such a manner as its produce may be of the greatest value, he intends only his own gain, and he is in this, as in many other cases, led by an invisible hand to promote an end which was no part of his intention. Nor is it always the worse for the society that it was no part of it. By pursuing his own interest he frequently promotes that of the society more effectually than when he really intends to promote it. I have never known much good done by those who affected to trade for the public good. It is an affectation, indeed, not very common among merchants, and very few words need be employed in dissuading them from it.

What is the species of domestic industry which his capital can employ, and of which the produce is likely to be of the greatest value, every individual, it is evident, can, in his local situation, judge much better than any statesman or lawgiver can do for him. The statesman, who should attempt to direct private people in what manner they ought to employ their capitals, would not only load himself with a most unnecessary attention, but assume an authority which could safely be trusted, not only to no single person, but to no council or senate whatever, and which would nowhere be so dangerous as in the hands of a man who had folly and presumption enough to fancy himself fit to exercise it.

To give the monopoly of the home market to the produce of domestic industry, in any particular art or manufacture, is in some measure to direct private people in what manner they ought to employ their capitals, and must, in almost all cases, be either a useless or a hurtful regulation. If the produce of domestic can be brought there as cheap as that of foreign industry, the regulation is evidently useless. If it cannot, it must generally be hurtful. It is the maxim of every prudent master of a family, never to attempt to make at home what it will cost him more to make than to buy. The tailor does not attempt to make his own shoes, but buys them of the shoemaker. The shoemaker does not attempt to make his own clothes, but employs a tailor. The farmer attempts to make neither the one nor the other, but employs those different artificers. All of them find it for their interest to employ their whole industry in a way in which they have some advantage over their neighbours, and to purchase with a part of its produce, or, what is the same thing, with the price of a part of it, whatever else they have occasion for.

SOURCE: Adam Smith. *An Inquiry into the Nature and Causes of the Wealth of Nations.* Edinburgh: 1863, pp. 198–200.

In some ways capitalism favored the nuclear family as the principal unit of society. *The Nuclear Family*
For centuries European couples had mostly married late—in their mid-twenties—and
set up independent households. Early capitalism offered opportunities for these independent families to increase their wealth by cultivating agricultural crops or producing goods for sale on the market. As nuclear families became more important economically, they also became more socially and emotionally independent. Love
between a man and a woman became a more important consideration in the making
of marriages than the interests of the larger extended families, and affection between
parents and their children became a much more important ingredient of family life.
Capitalism did not necessarily cause these changes in family life, but it certainly encouraged developments that helped to define the nature and role of the family in
modern European society.

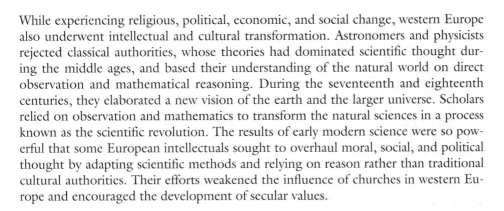

SCIENCE AND ENLIGHTENMENT

While experiencing religious, political, economic, and social change, western Europe
also underwent intellectual and cultural transformation. Astronomers and physicists
rejected classical authorities, whose theories had dominated scientific thought during the middle ages, and based their understanding of the natural world on direct
observation and mathematical reasoning. During the seventeenth and eighteenth
centuries, they elaborated a new vision of the earth and the larger universe. Scholars
relied on observation and mathematics to transform the natural sciences in a process
known as the scientific revolution. The results of early modern science were so powerful that some European intellectuals sought to overhaul moral, social, and political
thought by adapting scientific methods and relying on reason rather than traditional
cultural authorities. Their efforts weakened the influence of churches in western Europe and encouraged the development of secular values.

The Reconception of the Universe

Until the seventeenth century European astronomers based their understanding of *The Ptolemaic*
the universe on the work of the Greek scholar Claudius Ptolemy of Alexandria. *Universe*
About the middle of the second century C.E., Ptolemy composed a work known as
the *Almagest* that synthesized theories about the universe. Ptolemy envisioned a
motionless earth surrounded by a series of nine hollow, concentric spheres that revolved around it. Each of the first seven spheres had one of the observable heavenly
bodies—the sun, the moon, Mercury, Venus, Mars, Jupiter, and Saturn—embedded
in its shell. The eighth sphere held the stars, and an empty ninth sphere surrounded
the whole cosmos and provided the spin that kept all the others moving. Beyond the
spheres Christian astronomers located heaven, the realm of God.

Following Ptolemy, astronomers believed that the heavens consisted of matter
unlike any found on earth. Glowing like perfect jewels in the night skies, heavenly
bodies were composed of a pure substance that did not experience change or corruption, and they were not subject to the physical laws that governed the world
below the moon. They followed perfect circular paths in making their revolutions
around the earth.

Although theoretically attractive, this cosmology did not mesh readily with the *Planetary*
erratic movements of the planets—a term that comes from the Greek word *planetes*, *Movement*

A woodcut illustration depicts the Ptolemaic universe with the earth at the center surrounded by spheres holding the planets and stars. • Corbis-Bettmann

meaning "wanderer." From the vantage point of the earth, the planets often followed regular courses through the skies, but they sometimes slowed down, stopped, or even turned back on their courses—motions that would be difficult to explain if the planetary spheres revolved regularly around the earth. Astronomers went to great lengths to explain planetary behavior as the result of perfect circular movements. The result was an awkward series of adjustments known as epicycles—small circular revolutions that planets made around a point in their spheres, even while the spheres themselves revolved around the earth.

As astronomers accumulated data on planetary movements, most of them sought to reconcile their observations with Ptolemaic theory by adding increasing numbers of epicycles to

The Copernican Universe

their cosmic maps. In 1543, however, the Polish astronomer Nicolaus Copernicus published a treatise *On the Revolutions of the Heavenly Spheres* that broke with Ptolemaic theory and pointed European science in a new direction. Copernicus argued that the sun rather than the earth stood at the center of the universe and that the planets, including the earth, revolved around the sun.

Compared to Ptolemy's earth-centered universe, this new theory harmonized much better with observational data, but it did not receive a warm welcome. Copernicus's ideas not only challenged prevailing scientific theories but also threatened cherished religious beliefs. His theory implied that the earth was just another planet and that human beings did not occupy the central position in the universe. To some it also suggested the unsettling possibility that there might be other populated worlds in the universe—a notion that would be difficult to reconcile with Christian teachings, which held that the earth and humanity were unique creations of God.

The Scientific Revolution

Although it was unpopular in many quarters, Copernicus's theory inspired some astronomers to examine the heavens in fresh ways. As evidence accumulated, it became clear that the Ptolemaic universe simply did not correspond with reality. Astronomers based their theories on increasingly accurate observational data, and they relied on mathematical reasoning to organize the data. Gradually, they abandoned the Ptolemaic in favor of the Copernican model of the universe. Moreover, some of them began to apply their analytical methods to mechanics—the branch of science that deals with moving bodies—and by the mid-seventeenth century accurate observation and mathematical reasoning dominated both mechanics and astronomy. Indeed, reliance on observation and mathematics transformed the study of the natural world and brought about the scientific revolution.

The works of two mathematicians—Johannes Kepler of Germany and Galileo Galilei of Italy—rang the death knell for the Ptolemaic universe. Kepler (1571–1630) demonstrated that planetary orbits are elliptical, not circular as in Ptolemaic theory. Galileo (1564–1642) showed that the heavens were not the perfect, unblemished realm that Ptolemaic astronomers assumed, but rather a world of change, flux, and many previously unsuspected sights. Galileo took a recently invented instrument—the telescope—turned it skyward, and reported observations that astonished his contemporaries. With his telescope he could see spots on the sun and mountains on the moon—observations that discredited the notion that heavenly bodies were smooth, immaculate, unchanging, and perfectly spherical. He also noticed four of the moons that orbit the planet Jupiter—bodies that no human being had ever before observed—and he caught sight of previously unknown distant stars, which implied that the universe was much larger than anyone had previously suspected.

Galileo Galilei

In addition to his astronomical discoveries, Galileo also contributed to the understanding of terrestrial motion. He designed ingenious experiments to show that the velocity of falling bodies depends not on their weight, but rather on the height from which they fall. This claim brought him scorn from scientists who subscribed to scientific beliefs deriving from Aristotle, but it helped scientists to understand better how moving bodies behave under the influence of earth's gravitational pull. Galileo also anticipated the modern law of inertia, which holds that a moving body will continue to move in a straight line until some force intervenes to check or alter its motion.

The new approach to science culminated in the work of the English mathematician Isaac Newton (1642–1727), who depended on accurate observation and mathematical reasoning to construct a powerful synthesis of astronomy and mechanics. Newton outlined his views on the natural world in an epoch-making volume of 1687 entitled *Mathematical Principles of Natural Philosophy*. Newton's work united the heavens and the earth in a vast, cosmic system. He argued that a law of universal gravitation regulates the motions of bodies throughout the universe, and he offered precise mathematical explanations of the laws that govern movements of bodies on the earth. Newton's laws of universal gravitation and motion enabled him to synthesize the sciences of astronomy and mechanics. They also allowed him to explain a vast range of seemingly unrelated phenomena, such as the ebb and flow of the tides, which move according to the gravitational pull of the moon, and the eccentric orbits of planets and comets, which reflect the gravitational influence of the sun, the earth, and other heavenly bodies. Until the twentieth century Newton's universe served as the unquestioned framework for the physical sciences.

Isaac Newton

Newton's work symbolized the scientific revolution, but it by no means marked the end of the process by which observation and mathematical reasoning transformed European science. Inspired by the dramatic discoveries of astronomers and physicists, other scientists began to turn away from classical authorities and construct fresh approaches to the understanding of the natural world. During the seventeenth and eighteenth centuries, anatomy, physiology, microbiology, chemistry, and botany

An anonymous portrait of Isaac Newton depicts a serious scholar searching intently to discover the principles that govern the universe.

● Corbis-Bettmann

underwent a thorough overhaul, as scientists tested their theories against direct observation of natural phenomena and explained them in rigorous mathematical terms.

The Enlightenment

Newton's vision of the universe was so powerful and persuasive that its influence extended well beyond science. His work suggested that rational analysis of human behavior and institutions could lead to fresh insights about the human as well as the natural world. From Scotland to Sicily and from Philadelphia to Moscow, European and Euro-American thinkers launched an ambitious project to transform all human thought. Like the early modern scientists, they abandoned Aristotelian philosophy, Christian religion, and other traditionally recognized authorities, and they sought to subject the human world to purely rational analysis. The result of their work was a movement known as the Enlightenment.

Science and Society   Enlightenment thinkers sought to discover natural laws that governed human society in the same way that Newton's laws of universal gravitation and motion regulated the universe. Their search took different forms. The English philosopher John Locke (1632–1704) sought to identify the principles of psychology and argued that all human knowledge comes from sense perceptions. The Scottish philosopher Adam Smith turned his attention to economic affairs and held that laws of supply and demand determine what happens in the marketplace. The French nobleman Charles Louis de Secondat, better known as the Baron de Montesquieu (1689–1755), sought to establish a science of politics and discover principles that would foster political liberty in a prosperous and stable state.

The center of Enlightenment thought was France, where prominent intellectuals known collectively as *philosophes* ("philosophers") advanced the cause of reason. The philosophes were not philosophers in the traditional sense of the term so much as public intellectuals who popularized the ideas of others. They addressed their works more to the educated public than to scholars: instead of formal philosophical treatises, they mostly composed histories, novels, dramas, satires, and pamphlets on religious, moral, and political issues.

Voltaire   More than any other philosophe, François-Marie Arouet (1694–1778) epitomized the spirit of the Enlightenment. Writing under the pen name Voltaire, he published his first book at age seventeen. By the time of his death at age eighty-four, his published writings included some ten thousand letters and filled seventy volumes. With stinging wit and sometimes bitter irony, Voltaire championed individual freedom and attacked any institution sponsoring intolerant or oppressive policies. Targets of his caustic wit included the French monarchy and the Roman Catholic

Socially prominent women deeply influenced the development of Enlightenment thought by organizing and maintaining salons—gatherings where philosophes, scientists, and intellectuals discussed the leading ideas of the day. Though produced in 1814, this painting depicts the Parisian salon of Mme. Geoffrin (center left), a leading patron of the French philosophes, about 1775. In the background is a bust of Voltaire, who lived in Switzerland at the time. • Erich Lessing/Art Resource, NY

church. When the king of France sought to save money by reducing the number of horses kept in royal stables, for example, Voltaire suggested that it would be more effective to get rid of the asses who rode the horses. Voltaire also waged a long literary campaign against the Roman Catholic church, which he held responsible for fanaticism, intolerance, and incalculable human suffering. Voltaire's battle cry was *écrasez l'infame*—"crush the damned thing," meaning the church that he considered an agent of oppression.

Deism

Some philosophes were conventional Christians, and a few turned to atheism. Like Voltaire, however, most of them were deists who believed in the existence of a god but denied the supernatural teachings of Christianity, such as Jesus' virgin birth and his resurrection. To the deists the universe was an orderly realm. Deists held that a powerful god set the universe in motion and established natural laws that govern it, but did not take a personal interest in its development or intervene in its affairs. In a favorite simile of the deists, god was like a watchmaker who did not need to intefere constantly in his creation, since it operated by itself according to rational and natural laws.

The Theory of Progress

Most philosophes were optimistic about the future of the world and humanity. They expected knowledge of human affairs to advance as fast as modern science, and they believed that rational understanding of human and natural affairs would bring about a new era of constant progress. In fact, progress became almost an ideology of the philosophes, who believed that natural science would lead to greater human control over the world while rational sciences of human affairs would lead to individual freedom and the construction of a prosperous, just, and equitable society.

The philosophes' fond wishes for progress, prosperity, and social harmony did not come to pass. Yet the Enlightenment helped to bring about a thorough transformation of European society. It weakened the influence of organized religion, although it by no means destroyed institutional churches. Enlightenment thought encouraged the replacement of Christian values, which had guided European thought on religious and moral affairs for more than a millennium, with a new set of secular values arising from reason rather than revelation. Furthermore, the Enlightment encouraged political and cultural leaders to subject society to rational analysis and intervene actively in its affairs in the interests of promoting progress and prosperity. In many ways the Enlightenment legacy continues to influence European and Euro-American societies.

During the early modern era, European society experienced a series of profound and sometimes unsettling changes. The Protestant Reformation ended the religious unity of western Christendom, and intermittent religious conflict disrupted European society for a century and more. Centralizing monarchs strengthened their realms and built a society of sovereign, autonomous, and intensely competitive states. Capitalist entrepreneurs reorganized the production and distribution of manufactured goods, and although their methods led to increased wealth, their quest for efficiency and profits clashed with traditional values. Modern science based on direct observation and mathematical explanations emerged as a powerful tool for the investigation of the natural world, and its influence extended even to thought about human affairs. Some people rejected traditional religious beliefs altogether and worked toward the construction of a new moral thought based strictly on science and reason. At just the time that European merchants, colonists, and adventurers were seeking opportunities in the larger world, European society was becoming more powerful, more experimental, and more competitive than ever before.

CHRONOLOGY

1473–1543	Life of Nicolaus Copernicus
1478	Foundation of the Spanish Inquisition
1483–1546	Life of Martin Luther
1491–1556	Life of Ignatius Loyola
1509–1547	Reign of King Henry VIII
1509–1564	Life of John Calvin
1517	Publication of the *Ninety-Five Theses*
1519–1556	Reign of Emperor Charles V

1540	Foundation of the Society of Jesus
1545–1563	Council of Trent
1556–1598	Reign of King Philip II
1564–1642	Life of Galileo Galilei
1571–1630	Life of Johannes Kepler
1588	Spanish Armada
1618–1648	Thirty Years' War
1632–1704	Life of John Locke
1642–1727	Life of Isaac Newton
1643–1715	Reign of King Louis XIV
1648	Peace of Westphalia
1689–1755	Life of the Baron de Montesquieu
1694–1778	Life of Voltaire
1723–1790	Life of Adam Smith

FOR FURTHER READING

William J. Bouwsma. *John Calvin: A Sixteenth-Century Portrait*. New York, 1989. A penetrating examination of one of the principal Protestant reformers.

Fernand Braudel. *Civilization and Capitalism, 15th to 18th Century*. 3 vols. Trans. by S. Reynolds. New York, 1981–84. A rich analysis of early capitalist society by one of the greatest historians of the twentieth century.

Richard S. Dunn. *The Age of Religious Wars, 1559–1715*. 2nd ed. New York, 1979. Reliable survey of political, social, economic, and cultural history.

Robert S. Duplessis. *Transitions to Capitalism in Early Modern Europe*. Cambridge, 1997. A valuable synthesis of recent research on early capitalism and protoindustrialization.

Elizabeth L. Eisenstein. *The Printing Press as an Agent of Change*. 2 vols. Cambridge, 1979. An insightful study that examines the significance of printing for the Protestant Reformation and the scientific revolution.

G. R. Elton. *Reformation Europe, 1517–1559*. New York, 1963. An older but insightful analysis of Reformation Europe, with emphasis on religious and political developments.

Peter Gay. *The Enlightenment: An Interpretation*. 2 vols. New York, 1966–69. A classic study making the case for the Enlightenment as a turning point in European cultural history.

Margaret Jacob. *The Cultural Meaning of the Scientific Revolution*. New York, 1989. Explores the larger cultural and social implications of early modern science.

E. L. Jones. *The European Miracle: Environments, Economies, and Geopolitics in the History of Europe and Asia*. 2nd ed. Cambridge, 1987. Examines European politics and economic growth in comparative perspective.

———. *Growth Recurring: Economic Change in World History*. Oxford, 1988. Compares processes of economic growth in China, Europe, and Japan.

Leonard Krieger. *Kings and Philosophers, 1689–1789*. New York, 1970. A thoughtful analysis of European history during an age of absolutism and Enlightenment.

Thomas S. Kuhn. *The Structure of Scientific Revolutions*. 3rd ed. Chicago, 1997. An influential theoretical work that views scientific thought in larger social and cultural context.

Brian P. Levack. *The Witch-Hunt in Early Modern Europe*. New York, 1987. A compact but comprehensive survey of European witchcraft beliefs and pursuit of witches in the sixteenth and seventeenth centuries.

William H. McNeill. *The Pursuit of Power: Technology, Armed Force, and Society since A.D. 1000*. Chicago, 1982. Insightful analysis exploring the influence of sovereign states and early capitalism on military technology and organization.

Heiko A. Oberman. *Luther: Man between God and the Devil*. Trans. by E. Walliser-Schwartzbart. New Haven, 1989. A perceptive study of the first Protestant reformer by a foremost scholar.

Geoffrey Parker. *The Military Revolution: Military Innovation and the Rise of the West, 1500–1800.* Cambridge, 1988. A thoughtful essay on European military affairs in early modern times.

Eugene F. Rice Jr. and Anthony Grafton. *The Foundations of Early Modern Europe, 1460–1559.* 2nd ed. New York, 1994. Excellent introduction to political, social, economic, and cultural developments.

Simon Schama. *The Embarrassment of Riches: An Interpretation of Dutch Culture in the Seventeenth Century.* New York, 1987. A marvelous popular study of the wealthy Dutch republic at its height.

Keith Thomas. *Religion and the Decline of Magic.* New York, 1971. A riveting analysis of popular culture in early modern times, especially strong on the explanation of magic and witchcraft.

CHAPTER 24

NEW WORLDS: THE AMERICAS AND OCEANIA — *Islands*

· · ·

A young woman named Doña Marina played a remarkable role in the Spanish conquest of Mexico. Born about 1500 to a noble family in central Mexico, Doña Marina's mother tongue was Nahuatl, the principal language of the Aztec empire. When she was a girl, Doña Marina's family sent her to the Mexican coast as a slave, and her new family later passed her on to their neighbors in the Yucatan peninsula. During her travels she became fluent in Maya as well as her native Nahuatl language.

When Hernán Cortés arrived on the Mexican coast in 1519, his small army included a Spanish soldier who had learned the Maya language during a period of captivity in the Yucatan. But he had no way to communicate with the Nahuatl-speaking peoples of central Mexico until a Maya chieftain presented him with twelve young women, including Doña Marina, when he entered into an alliance with the foreigner. Doña Marina's linguistic talents enabled Cortés to communicate through an improbable chain of languages—from Spanish to Maya to Nahuatl and then back again—while making his way to the Aztec capital of Tenochtitlan. (Doña Marina soon learned Spanish and thus eliminated the Maya link in the linguistic chain.)

Doña Marina provided Cortés with intelligence and diplomatic as well as linguistic services. On several occasions she learned of plans by native peoples to overwhelm and destroy the tiny Spanish army, and she alerted Cortés to the danger in time for him to forestall an attack. Once she was able to report the precise details of a planned ambush because she played along with an effort to bring her into the scheme. She also helped Cortés negotiate with emissaries from Tenochtitlan and other major cities of central Mexico. Indeed, in the absence of Doña Marina's services, it is difficult to see how Cortés's small band could have survived to see the Aztec capital.

Apart from facilitating the Spanish conquest of the Aztec empire, Doña Marina also played a role in the formation of a new society in Mexico. In 1522, one year after the fall of Tenochtitlan, she gave birth to a son fathered by Cortés, and in 1526 she bore a daughter to a Spanish captain whom she had married. Her offspring were not the first children born in the western hemisphere of indigenous and Spanish parentage, but they symbolize the early emergence of a mestizo population in Mexico. Doña Marina died soon after the birth of her daughter, probably in 1527, but during her short life she contributed to the thorough transformation of Mexican society.

Doña Marina (center) translates for Hernán Cortés (seated at top) as he enters into an alliance with the ruler of Tlaxcala. • Benson Latin American Collection, General Libraries, University of Texas at Austin

Until 1492 the peoples of the eastern and western hemispheres had almost no dealings with each other. About 1000 C.E. Viking explorers established a short-lived colony in modern Newfoundland, and sporadic encounters between European fishermen and indigenous peoples of North America were likely before Christopher Columbus undertook his first voyage across the Atlantic Ocean. It is possible, too, that an occasional Asian or Austronesian mariner reached the Pacific coast of North or South America before 1492. Yet travel between the eastern hemisphere, the western hemisphere, and Oceania was too irregular and infrequent to generate interaction between peoples of different societies until the fifteenth century.

After 1492, however, the voyages of European mariners led to permanent and sustained contact between the peoples of the eastern hemisphere, the western hemisphere, and Oceania. The resulting encounters brought profound and often violent change to American and Pacific lands. European peoples possessed powerful military weapons, horses, and sailing ships that provided them with technological advantages over the peoples they encountered in the Americas and the Pacific islands. Moreover, most Europeans also enjoyed complete or partial immunity to diseases that caused demographic disasters when introduced to the western hemisphere and Oceania. Because of their technological advantages and the massive depopulation that followed from epidemic diseases, European peoples were able to establish a presence throughout the Americas and much of the Pacific basin.

The European presence did not lead to immediate change in Australia and the Pacific islands, although it laid a foundation for dramatic and often traumatic change in the nineteenth and twentieth centuries. In the western hemisphere, however, large numbers of European migrants helped to bring about a profound transformation of American societies in early modern times. In Mexico and Peru, Spanish conquerors established territorial empires ruled from Spain. In Brazil, Portuguese entrepreneurs founded sugar plantations and imported African slaves to perform the heavy labor required for their operation. In North America, French, English, and Dutch fur traders allied with indigenous peoples who provided them with animal skins, and their more sedentary compatriots founded settler societies concentrating on the production of cash crops for export. Throughout the western hemisphere, peoples of European, African, and American ancestry interacted to fashion a new world.

 ## COLLIDING WORLDS

When European peoples first sought to establish their presence in the Americas, they brought a range of technology unavailable to the peoples they encountered in the western hemisphere. Even more important than European technology, however, were divisions between indigenous peoples that Europeans were able to exploit and the effects of epidemic diseases that devastated native societies. Soon after their arrival in the western hemisphere, Spanish conquerors toppled the Aztec and Inca empires and imposed their own rule in Mexico and Peru. In later decades Portuguese planters built sugar plantations on the Brazilian coastline. French, English, and Dutch migrants displaced indigenous peoples in North America and established settler colonies under the rule of European peoples.

The Spanish Caribbean

The first site of interaction between European and American peoples was the Caribbean. When Spanish mariners arrived there, the Tainos (also known as Arawaks) were the most prominent people in the region. During the late centuries B.C.E., the ancestors of the Tainos had sailed in canoes from the Orinoco River valley in South America to the Caribbean islands, and by about 900 C.E. they had settled throughout the region. The Tainos cultivated manioc and other crops, and they lived in small villages under the authority of chiefs who allocated land to families and supervised community affairs. They showed interest in the glass, beads, and metal tools that Spanish mariners brought as trade goods and offered little resistance to the visitors.

Tainos

Christopher Columbus and his immediate followers made the island of Hispaniola (which embraces modern Haiti and the Dominican Republic) the base of Spanish operations in the Caribbean. There Spanish settlers established the fort of Santo Domingo, which became the capital of the Spanish Caribbean. Columbus's original plan was to build forts and trading posts where merchants could trade with local peoples for products desired by European consumers. Within a few years of Spanish arrival, however, it became clear that the Caribbean region offered no silks or spices for the European market. If Spanish settlers wanted to maintain their presence in the Caribbean, they would need to find some way to make a living.

Spanish Arrival

The settlers first attempted to support their society by mining gold. Deposits of gold were thin in the Caribbean, but they were sufficient to keep miners busy until about 1515. Spanish settlers were too few in number to mine gold—and in any case they were not inclined to perform heavy physical labor—so the miners came largely from the ranks of the Tainos. Recruitment of labor came through an institution known as the *encomienda*, which gave Spanish settlers (*encomenderos*) the right to compel Tainos to work in their mines or fields. In return for labor *encomenderos* assumed responsibility to look after their workers' health and welfare and to encourage their conversion to Christianity.

Conscription of Taino labor was a brutal business. *Encomenderos* worked their charges hard and punished them severely when they did not deliver the expected quantities of gold or work sufficiently hard in the fields. Tainos occasionally organized rebellions, but their bows, arrows, and slings had little effect against horse-mounted Spanish forces wielding steel swords and firearms. By about 1515 social disruption and physical abuse had brought decline to Taino populations on the large Caribbean islands—Hispaniola, Jamaica, Puerto Rico, and Cuba—favored by Spanish settlers.

Serious demographic decline set in only after 1518, however, when smallpox reached the Caribbean region and touched off devastating epidemics among the peoples of the western hemisphere. To replace laborers lost to disease, *encomenderos* launched raiding parties to kidnap and enslave Tainos and other peoples. This tactic exposed additional victims to introduced diseases and hastened the decline of indigenous populations.

Smallpox

Under pressure of epidemic disease, the native population of the Caribbean plummeted from about six million in 1492 to a few thousand in the 1540s. Native societies themselves also passed out of existence. Only a few Taino cultural elements survived the sixteenth century: canoe, hammock, hurricane, barbecue, maize, and tobacco all derive from Taino words, but the society that generated them had largely disappeared by the middle of the sixteenth century. In its place Spanish settlers built a European-style society. During the seventeenth century French, English, and Dutch settlers also flocked to the Caribbean, established sugar plantations, and imported African slaves to perform heavy labor. By the mid-seventeenth century Caribbean society consisted of a small class of European adminstrators and large masses of African slaves.

The Conquest of Mexico and Peru

Spanish interest soon shifted from the Caribbean to the American mainland, where settlers hoped to find more resources to exploit. During the early sixteenth century, Spanish *conquistadores* ("conquerors") pressed beyond the Caribbean islands, moving west into Mexico and south into Panama and Peru. Between 1519 and 1521 Hernán Cortés and a small band of men brought down the Aztec empire in Mexico, and between 1532 and 1533 Francisco Pizarro and his followers toppled the Inca empire in Peru. These conquests laid the foundations for colonial regimes that would transform the Americas.

FIRST IMPRESSIONS OF SPANISH FORCES

• • •

As the Spanish army made its way to Tenochtitlan, Motecuzoma dispatched a series of emissaries to communicate with Cortés and learn his intentions. The reports that came back were not reassuring. They brought disturbing news about Spanish weapons, armor, horses, and dogs that were much larger and more aggressive than the small, barkless animals that were native to Mexico.

And when [Motecuzoma] had heard what the messengers reported, he was terrified, he was astounded. . . .

Especially did it cause him to faint away when he heard how the gun, at [the Spaniards'] command, discharged [the shot]; how it resounded as if it thundered when it went off. It indeed bereft one of strength; it shut off one's ears. And when it discharged, something like a round pebble came forth from within. Fire went showering forth; sparks went blazing forth. And its smoke smelled very foul; it had a fetid odor which verily wounded the head. And when [the shot] struck a mountain, it was as if it were destroyed, dissolved. And a tree was pulverized; it was as if it vanished; it was as if someone blew it away.

All iron was their war array. In iron they clothed themselves. With iron they covered their heads. Iron were their swords. Iron were their crossbows. Iron were their shields. Iron were their lances.

And those which bore them upon their backs, their deer [that is, horses], were as tall as roof terraces.

And their bodies were everywhere covered; only their faces appeared. They were very white; they had chalky faces; they had yellow hair, though the hair of some was black. Long were their beards; they also were yellow. They were yellow-headed. [The black men's hair] was kinky, it was curly.

And their food was like fasting food—very large, white, not heavy like [tortillas]; like maize stalks, good-tasting as if of maize stalk flour; a little sweet, a little honeyed. It was honeyed to eat; it was sweet to eat.

And their dogs were very large. They had ears folded over; great dragging jowls. They had fiery eyes—blazing eyes; they had yellow eyes—fiery yellow eyes. They had thin flanks—flanks with ribs showing. They had gaunt stomachs. They were very tall. They were nervous; they went about panting, with tongues hanging out. They were spotted like ocelots; they were varicolored.

And when Motecuzoma heard all this, he was much terrified. It was as if he fainted away. His heart saddened; his heart failed him.

SOURCE: Bernardino de Sahagún, *Florentine Codex: General History of the Things of New Spain,*
13 vols. Trans. by Arthur J. O. Anderson and Charles E. Dibble. Salt Lake City:
University of Utah Press, 1950–82, 13:19–20. (Translation slightly modified.)

The conquest of Mexico began with an expedition to search for gold on the American mainland. In 1519 Cortés led about 450 men to Mexico and made his way from Veracruz on the Gulf coast to the island city of Tenochtitlan, the stunningly beautiful Aztec capital situated in Lake Texcoco. They seized the emperor Motecuzoma II, who died in 1520 during a skirmish between Spanish forces and residents of Tenochtitlan. Aztec forces soon drove the conquistadores from the capital, but Cortés built a small fleet of ships, placed Tenochtitlan under seige, and in 1521 starved the city into surrender.

Hernán Cortés

Steel swords, muskets, cannons, and horses offered Cortés and his men some advantage over the forces they met and help to account for the Spanish conquest of the Aztec empire. Yet weaponry alone clearly would not enable Cortés's tiny force to overcome a large, densely populated society of about twenty-one million. Quite apart from military technology, Cortés's expedition benefited from divisions among the indigenous peoples of Mexico. With the aid of Doña Marina, the conquistadores forged alliances with peoples who resented domination by the Mexica, the leaders of the Aztec empire, and who reinforced the small Spanish army with thousands of veteran warriors. Native allies also provided Spanish forces with logistical support and secure bases in friendly territory.

As in the Caribbean, epidemic disease also aided Spanish efforts. During the seige of Tenochtitlan, smallpox raged through the city, killing inhabitants by the tens of thousands and fatally sapping the strength of defensive forces. Smallpox rapidly spread beyond the capital, raced through Mexico, and carried off so many people that Aztec society was unable to function. Only in the context of this massive depopulation is it possible to understand the Spanish conquest of Mexico.

Epidemic Disease

Francisco Pizarro experienced similar results when he led a Spanish expedition from Central America to Peru. Pizarro set out in 1530 with 180 men, later joined by reinforcements to make a force of about 600. The conquistadores arrived in Peru just after a bitter dispute within the Inca ruling house, and it was a simple matter for them to exploit differences between the factions. Already by 1533 they had taken the Inca capital at Cuzco. Under pretext of holding a conference, they called the Inca ruling elites together, seized them, and killed most of them. They spared the Inca ruler Atahualpa until he had delivered a large quantity of gold to Pizarro. Then they strangled him and decapitated his body.

Francisco Pizarro

In this illustration from Felipe Guaman Poma de Ayala's letter of complaint to the Spanish king, conquistadores decapitate Atahualpa after executing him by strangulation in 1533.   • Det Kongelige Bibliotek, Copenhagen

Several considerations help to explain how Pizarro's tiny force was able to topple the Inca empire. Many subjects of the empire despised the Incas as overlords and tax collectors and put up little resistance to Pizarro's forces. Epidemic disease also discouraged resistance: smallpox had spread from Mexico and Central America to Peru in the 1520s, long before Pizarro's arrival, and had already taken a heavy toll among Andean populations. Pizarro and his army actually faced more threats from fresh Spanish interlopers than from native peoples. The conquest of Peru took longer than the conquest of Mexico, but by 1540 Spanish forces had established themselves securely as lords of the land.

Iberian Empires in the Americas

The conquests of Mexico and Peru were the results not of Spanish royal policy, but rather of individual efforts by freelance adventurers. During the early days after the conquests, Cortés and Pizarro allocated lands and labor rights to their troops under the *encomienda* system, which they transferred from the Caribbean to the American mainland. Gradually, however, the Spanish monarchy extended its control over the growing American empire, and by about 1570 the semiprivate regime of the conquistadores had given way to formal rule under the Spanish crown. Bureaucrats charged with the implementation of royal policy and the administration of royal justice replaced the soldiers of fortune who had conquered Mexico and Peru. The conquistadores did not welcome the arrival of the bureaucrats, but with the aid of Spanish lawyers, tax collectors, and military forces, royal officials had their way.

Spanish Colonial Administration
Spanish administrators established two centers of authority in the Americas—Mexico (which they called New Spain) and Peru (known as New Castile)—each governed by a viceroy who was responsible to the king of Spain. In Mexico they built a new capital, Mexico City, on top of Tenochtitlan. In Peru they originally hoped to rule from the Inca capital of Cuzco, but they considered the high altitude unpleasant and also found the Andean city too inaccessible for their purposes. In 1535 they founded Lima and transferred the government to the coast where it was accessible to Spanish shipping.

The viceroys were the king's representatives in the Americas, and they wielded considerable power. The kings of Spain attempted to ensure that their viceroys would not build personal power bases and become independent by subjecting them to the review of courts known as *audiencias* staffed by university-educated lawyers. The *audiencias* heard appeals against the viceroys' decisions and policies and had the right to address their concerns directly to the Spanish king. Furthermore, the *audiencias* conducted reviews of viceroys' performance at the end of their terms, and negative reviews could lead to severe punishment.

Nevertheless, the viceroys largely determined policy within their jurisdictions, partly because of the difficulty of communicating with the central government in Spain. It often took two years to receive a reply to a query from Mexico or Peru, and many replies simply asked for further information rather than providing firm directives. Even when viceroys received clear orders that they did not like, they found ways to procrastinate: they often responded to the king that "I obey, but I do not enforce," implying that with additional information the king would alter his decision.

New Cities
Spanish rule in the Americas led to the rapid establishment of cities throughout the viceroyalties. Like their compatriots in Spain, colonists preferred to live in cities even when they derived their income from the agricultural production of their landed estates. As the numbers of migrants increased, they expanded the territory under Spanish imperial authority and built a dense network of bureaucratic control based in recently founded cities. The jurisdiction of the viceroyalty of New Spain

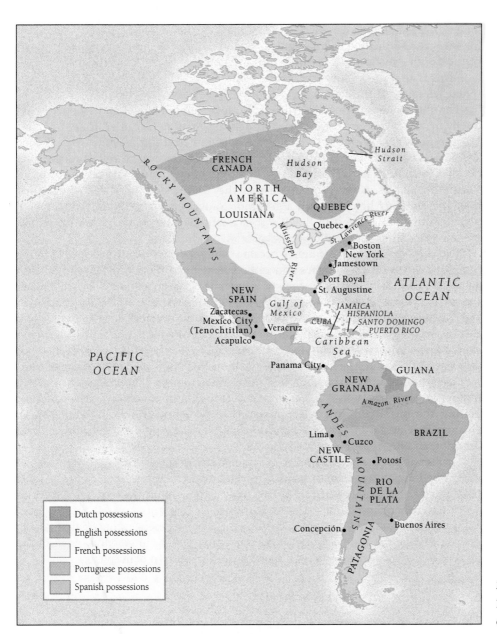

MAP [24.1]

European empires and colonies in the Americas.

reached from Mexico City as far as St. Augustine in Florida (founded in 1565). Administrators in Lima oversaw affairs from Panama (founded in 1519) to Concepción (founded in 1550) and Buenos Aires (founded in 1536).

Portuguese Brazil

While Spanish conquistadores and administrators built a territorial empire in Mexico and Peru, Portuguese forces established an imperial presence in Brazil. The Portuguese presence came about by an odd twist of diplomatic convention. In 1494 Spain and Portugal signed the Treaty of Tordesillas, which divided the world along an imaginary north-south line 370 leagues west of the Azores and Cape Verde Islands. According to this agreement, Spain could claim any land west of that line, so long as it was not already under Christian rule, and Portugal gained the same rights for lands east of the line. Thus Portugal gained territory along the northeastern part of the South American continent, a region known as Brazil from the many brazil-wood trees that grew along the coast, while the remainder of the western hemisphere fell under Spanish control.

The Portuguese mariner Pero Alvares Cabral sighted Brazil and stopped there briefly in 1500 while making a tack through the Atlantic Ocean en route to India. His compatriots did not display much immediate interest in the land. When French and Dutch mariners began to visit Brazilian shores, however, the Portuguese king decided to consolidate his claim to the land. He granted large coastal territories to Portuguese nobles in the expectation that they would develop and colonize their holdings, and later he dispatched a governor to oversee affairs and implement royal policy. Portuguese interest in Brazil rose dramatically after midcentury when entrepreneurs established profitable sugar plantations on the coast.

Colonial American Society

The cities of the Iberian empires became centers of European-style society in the Americas: the spires of churches and cathedrals defined their skylines, and Spanish and Portuguese were the languages of government, business, and society. Beyond the urban districts, however, indigenous ways of life persisted. In the Amazon basin and Paraguay, for example, native peoples produced little agricultural surplus, and there were no mineral deposits to attract European migrants. The few Spanish and Portuguese colonists who ventured to those regions learned to adapt to indigenous societies and customs: they ate bread made of manioc flour, made use of native hammocks and canoes, and communicated in the Guaraní and Tupi languages. Indeed, indigenous languages flourish even today throughout much of Latin America: among the more prominent are Nahautl in Mexico, Quiché in Mexico and Guatemala, Guaraní in Paraguay, and Quechua in the Andean highlands of Peru, Ecuador, and Bolivia.

Spanish and Portuguese peoples saw the western hemisphere more as a land to exploit and administer than as a place to settle and colonize. Nevertheless, sizable contingents of migrants settled permanently in the Americas. Between 1500 and 1800 upwards of five hundred thousand Spanish migrants crossed the Atlantic, alongside one hundred thousand Portuguese. Their presence contributed to the making of a new world—a world characterized by intense interaction between the peoples of Europe, Africa, and the Americas—in the western hemisphere.

Settler Colonies in North America

Throughout the sixteenth century Spanish explorers sought opportunities north of Mexico and the Caribbean. They established towns, forts, and missions from modern Florida as far north as Virginia on the east coast of North America, and they scouted shorelines off Maine and Newfoundland. On the west coast they ventured into modern Canada and established a fort on Vancouver Island. By midcentury, French, English, and Dutch mariners sailed the North Atlantic in search of fish and a northwest passage to Asia, and by the early seventeenth century they were dislodging Spanish colonists north of Florida. Their search for a northwest passage proved fruitless, but they harvested immense quantities of fish from the cod-filled banks off Labrador, Newfoundland, Nova Scotia, and New England.

Foundation of Colonies

More important, in the early seventeenth century they began to plant permanent colonies on the North American mainland. French settlers established colonies at Port Royal (Nova Scotia) in 1604 and Quebec in 1608, and English migrants founded Jamestown in 1607 and the Massachusetts Bay colony in 1630. Dutch entrepreneurs built a settlement at New Amsterdam in 1623, but the colony did not remain long in Dutch hands: an English fleet seized it in 1664, rechristened it New York, and absorbed it into English colonial holdings. During the seventeenth and eighteenth centuries, French migrants settled in eastern Canada, and French explorers and traders scouted the St. Lawrence, Ohio, and Mississippi Rivers, building forts all the way to the Gulf of Mexico. Meanwhile, English settlers established colonies along the east coast of the present-day United States of America.

Life in these early settlements was extremely difficult. Most of the settlers did not expect to cultivate food crops, but rather hoped to sustain their communities by producing valuable commodities such as fur, pitch, tar, or lumber, if not silver and gold. They relied heavily on provisions sent from Europe, and when supply ships did not arrive as expected, they sometimes avoided starvation only because indigenous peoples provided them with food. In Jamestown food shortages and disease became so severe that only sixty of the colony's five hundred inhabitants survived the winter of 1609–1610. Some settlers went so far as to disinter corpses and consume the flesh of their departed neighbors. One man even slaughtered and ate his wife.

Colonial Government

The French and English colonies in North America differed in several ways from Iberian territories to the south. Whereas Iberian explorations had royal backing, private investors played larger roles in French and English colonial efforts. Individuals put up the money to finance expeditions to America, and they retained much more control over their colonies' affairs than did their Iberian counterparts. Although English colonies were always subject to royal authority, for example, they also maintained their own assemblies and influenced the choice of royal governors: there were no viceroys or *audiencias* in the North American colonies. At the conclusion of the Seven Years' War (1763), the French colony in Canada fell under British control, and it too soon acquired institutions of self-government.

Relations with Indigenous Peoples

French and English colonies differed from Iberian territories also in their relationships with indigenous peoples. French and English migrants did not find large, centralized states like the Aztec and Inca empires. Nor did they encounter agricultural peoples living in densely settled societies. Although most of them spoke Algonquian, Iroquois, or Sioux languages, the peoples of eastern North America had formed dozens of distinct societies. Many of them practiced agriculture, but most also relied on hunting and consequently moved their villages frequently in pursuit of game. They did not claim ownership of precisely bounded territories, but they regularly migrated between well-defined regions.

When European settlers saw forested lands not bearing crops, they staked out farms and excluded the indigenous peoples who had frequently visited the lands during the course of their migrations. The availability of fertile farmland soon attracted large numbers of European migrants. Upwards of 150,000 English migrants moved to North America during the seventeenth century alone, and sizable French, German, Dutch, and Irish contingents joined them in the search for land.

European migrants took pains to justify their claims to American lands. English settlers in particular sought to provide legal cover for their expanding communities by negotiating treaties with the peoples whose lands they colonized. Quite apart from legal niceties, migrants also justified their occupation on the grounds that they made productive use of the land, whereas native peoples merely used it as a hunting park. In Europe hunting was a pastime that only aristocratic and privileged classes could enjoy. Settlers did not recognize that hunting was a way of life, not a sport or hobby, for the peoples of North America.

A painting of the English settlement at Jamestown in the early seventeenth century illustrates the precarious relations between European settlers and indigenous peoples. Note the heavy palisades and numerous cannons deployed within the fort, as well as the imposing figure of the native chief Powhatan depicted outside the settlement's walls. • Courtesy of Whitehall-Robins Company. Photograph by Don Eiler

Conflict   French and English settlers frequently clashed with native peoples who resented intrusions on their hunting grounds, but the conflicts differed from the campaigns of conquest carried out by the conquistadores in Mexico and Peru. English settlers negotiated rights to American lands by treaty, but native peoples did not appreciate the fine points of English law and frequently mounted raids on farms and villages. During an assault of 1622, for example, they massacred almost one-third of the English settlers in the Chesapeake region. Attacks on their communities brought reprisals from settlers, who ruthlessly destroyed the fields and villages of native peoples. Edward Waterhouse, who survived the raid of 1622, went so far as to advocate annihilation of the indigenous population: "Victorie may bee gained many waies: by force, by surprize, by [causing] famine [through] burning their Corne, by destroying and burning their Boats, Canoes, and Houses, by breaking their fishing Weares [nets], by assailing them in their huntings, whereby they get the greatest part of their sustenance in Winter, by pursuing and chasing them with our horses, and blood-Hounds to draw after them, and Mastives [mastiffs] to teare them."

Indeed, a combination of epidemic disease and violent conflict dramatically reduced the indigenous population of North America in early modern times. In 1492 the native population of the territory now embraced by the United States was greater than five million, perhaps as high as ten million. By the mid-sixteenth century, however, smallpox and other diseases had begun to spread north from Mexico and ravage native societies in the plains and eastern woodlands of North America. Between 1600 and 1800 about one million English, French, German, Dutch, Irish, and Scottish migrants crossed the Atlantic and sought to displace native peoples as they pursued economic opportunities in North America. By 1800 indigenous peoples in the territory of the present-day United States numbered only six hundred thousand, as against almost five million settlers of European ancestry and about one million slaves of African ancestry. Although the settler colonies of North America differed markedly from the Iberian territorial empires to the south, they too contributed greatly to the transformation of the western hemisphere.

COLONIAL SOCIETY IN THE AMERICAS

The European migrants who flooded into the western hemisphere interacted both with the native inhabitants and with African peoples whom they imported as enslaved laborers. Throughout the Americas relations between individuals of American, European, and African ancestry soon led to the emergence of mestizo populations. Yet European peoples and their Euro-American offspring increasingly dominated political and economic affairs in the Americas. They mined precious metals, cultivated cash crops like sugar and tobacco, and trapped fur-bearing animals to supply capitalist markets that met the voracious demands of European consumers. Over time they also established their Christian religion as the dominant faith of the western hemisphere.

The Formation of Multicultural Societies

Many parts of the Americas remained outside European control until the nineteenth century. Only rarely did Europeans venture into the interior regions of the American continents in the sixteenth century, and those who did, like the adventurer Alvar Nuñez Cabeza de Vaca, often found themselves at the mercy of the native inhabitants. Cabeza de Vaca was a Spanish nobleman who joined an expedition of some three hundred men who went from Hispaniola to explore Florida in 1527. Most members of the expedition soon perished because of inadequate supplies, the harsh environment, and clashes with indigenous forces. Cabeza de Vaca and a small group of survivors built small boats to make their way west across the Gulf of Mexico to New Spain. But disaster struck when the strong current of the Mississippi River pushed the flotilla into the gulf and a fierce storm destroyed the makeshift vessels. The shipwrecked adventurers washed up near modern Galveston, Texas, and soon fell captive to native inhabitants. For the next eight years, Cabeza de Vaca and three companions lived in several different societies, serving sometimes as slaves and sometimes as physicians, before finding their way to Mexico in 1536.

Cabeza de Vaca

Although their influence reached the American interior only gradually, European migrants radically transformed the social order in the regions where they established imperial states or settler colonies. All European territories became multicultural societies where peoples of varied ancestry lived together under European or Euro-American dominance. Spanish and Portuguese territories soon became not only multicultural but ethnically mixed as well, largely because of migration patterns. Migrants to the Iberian colonies were overwhelmingly men: about 85 percent of the Spanish migrants were men, and the Portuguese migration was even

Mestizo Societies

During the eighteenth century Euro-American artists often depicted families to illustrate the physical characteristics of individuals of different ancestry. The household scene here presents a mestizo father, a Spanish mother, and their daughter, referred to as a *castiza*.

• Museo Nacional de Historia, Mexico City

more male-dominated than the Spanish. Because of the small numbers of European women, Spanish and Portuguese migrants entered into relationships with native women, which soon gave rise to an increasingly mestizo (or mixed) society.

Most Spanish migrants went to Mexico, where there was soon a growing population of mestizos—individuals of Spanish and native parentage, like the children of Doña Marina. Women were more prominent among the migrants to Peru than to Mexico, and Spanish colonists there lived mostly in cities where they maintained a more distinct community than did their counterparts in Mexico. In the colonial cities Spanish migrants married among themselves and re-created a European-style society. In less settled regions, however, Spanish men associated with native women and gave rise to mestizo society.

With few European women available in Brazil, Portuguese men readily entered into relations both with native women and with African slave women. Brazil soon had large populations not only of mestizos, but also of mulattoes born of Portuguese and African parents, *zambos* born of indigenous and African parents, and other combinations arising from these groups themselves. Indeed, marriages between members of different racial and ethnic communities became very common in colonial Brazil and generated a society even more thoroughly mixed than that of mestizo Mexico.

In both the Spanish and the Portuguese colonies, migrants born in Europe known as *peninsulares* (those who came from the Iberian peninsula) stood at the top of the social hierarchy, followed by *criollos* or creoles, individuals born in the Americas of Iberian parents. In the early days of the colonies, mestizos lived on the fringes of society. As time went on, however, the numbers of mestizos grew, and they became essential contributors to their societies, especially in Mexico and Brazil. Meanwhile, mulattoes, zambos, and other individuals of mixed parentage became prominent groups in Brazilian society, although they were usually subordinate to European migrants, Euro-American creoles, and even mestizos. In all the Iberian colonies, imported slaves and conquered peoples stood at the bottom of the social hierarchy.

The Social Hierarchy

The social structure of the French and English colonies in North America differed markedly from that of the Iberian colonies. Women were more numerous among the French and especially the English migrants than in Spanish and Portuguese communities, and settlers mostly married within their own groups. French fur traders often associated with native women and generated *métis* (the French equivalent of mestizos) in regions around forts and trading posts. In French colonial cities like Port Royal and Quebec, however, liaisons between French and native peoples were less common.

North American Societies

Mingling between peoples of different ancestry was least common in the English colonies of North America. Colonists disdained the native peoples they encountered and regarded them as lazy heathens who did not recognize private property and did not exert themselves to cultivate the land. Later they also scorned imported African slaves as inferior beings. These attitudes fueled a virulent racism, as English settlers attempted to maintain sharp boundaries between themselves and peoples of American and African ancestry.

Yet even English settlers interacted with American and African peoples, and they readily borrowed useful cultural elements from other communities. They learned about American plants and animals, for example, and they used native terms to refer to unfamiliar animals such as racoons and opossums or trees such as hickory and pecan. They adapted mocassins and deerskin clothes, and they gave up European military customs of marching in massed ranks and announcing their presence with drums and flying colors. From their slaves they borrowed African food crops and techniques for the cultivation of rice. Yet unlike their Iberian neighbors to the south, the English settlers strongly discouraged relationships between individuals of different ancestry and mostly refused to accept or even acknowledge offspring of mixed parentage.

Mining and Agriculture in the Spanish Empire

From the Spanish perspective the greatest attractions of the Americas were precious metals, which drew thousands of migrants from all levels of Spanish society. The conquistadores thoroughly looted the easily accessible treasures of the Aztec and Inca empires. Ignoring the artistic or cultural value of artifacts, the conquerors simply melted down silver and gold treasures and fashioned them into ingots. Their followers opened mines to extract the mineral wealth of the Americas in more systematic fashion.

Gold was not the most abundant American treasure. Silver far outweighed gold in quantity and value, and much of Spain's American enterprise focused on its extraction. Silver production concentrated on two areas: the thinly populated Mexican north, particularly the region around Zacatecas, and the high, cold central Andes, particularly the stunningly rich mines of Potosí. Both sites employed large numbers of indigenous laborers. Many laborers went to Zacatecas as their home villages experienced the pressures of conquest and disease. Over time they became professional miners, spoke Spanish, and lost touch with the communities of their birth.

Silver Mining

Mining operations at Potosí gave rise to a large settlement that housed miners and others who supplied food, made charcoal, fashioned tools, and supported the enterprise. In this illustration from the mid-1580s, llamas laden with silver ore descend the mountain (background) while laborers work in the foreground to crush the ore and extract pure silver from it.   •   Courtesy of The Hispanic Society of America, New York

At Potosí Spanish administrators recruited laborers by adapting the Inca sytem of draft labor to their needs: they requisitioned laborers from local officials, who dispatched individuals from villages to work for several months in the mines. The rapid growth of the mines at Potosí created an explosive demand for labor. Spanish prospectors discovered a large vein of silver near Potosí in 1545, and by 1600 the boom town had a population of 150,000, including as many as fifty-eight thousand temporary laborers.

The Global Significance of Silver

The mining industries of Mexico and Peru powered the Spanish economy in the Americas and even stimulated the world economy of early modern times. Silver produced profits for private investors and revenues for the crown. The Spanish government reserved a fifth of the silver production for itself. This share, known as the *quinto*, represented the principal revenue that the crown derived from its American possessions. American silver helped Spanish kings finance a powerful army and bureaucracy, but much of it also went well beyond Spain to lubricate the larger world economy.

Most American silver made its way across the Atlantic to Spain and markets throughout Europe, and from there European merchants traded it for silk, spices, and porcelain in the markets of Asia. Some silver went from Acapulco on the west coast of Mexico across the Pacific in the Manila galleons, and from Manila it also made its way to Asian markets. No matter which direction it went or which oceans it crossed, American silver quickly traveled throughout the world and powerfully stimulated global trade.

Apart from mining, the principal occupations in Spanish America were farming, stock raising, and craft production. The organization of mining industries created opportunities for cultivators, herders, and artisans to provision mining towns with food, wine, textiles, tools, furniture, and craft items. By the seventeenth century the most prominent site of agricultural and craft production in Spanish America was the estate, or hacienda, which produced foodstuffs for its own use as well as for sale to local markets in nearby mining districts, towns, and cities. The products of the hacienda were mostly of European origin: wheat, grapes, and meat from pigs and cattle were the most prominent agricultural products. Bordering the large estates were smaller properties owned by Spanish migrants or creoles as well as sizable tracts of land held by indigenous peoples who practiced subsistence agriculture.

The Hacienda

The major sources of labor for the haciendas were native populations and small numbers of imported slaves. Most native peoples worked as temporary and seasonal laborers under the *encomienda* system, which Spanish conquerors transferred from the Caribbean to the American mainland. Because *encomenderos* often abused their laborers by overworking them and skimping on their maintenance, Spanish officials replaced *encomiendas* with the *repartimiento* system in the late sixteenth century. Like *encomiendas*, the *repartimiento* system compelled native communities to supply laborers for Spanish mines and farms, but it provided that laborers were subject to work only for limited periods of time and that Spanish employers had to compensate the laborers with fair wages.

Labor Systems

Compulsory labor drafts fostered callous treatment by employers and also promoted low worker productivity. Thus Spanish managers had an economic incentive to pay higher wages and provide better conditions for motivated workers. The *repartimiento* system did not disappear, but by the early seventeenth century forced labor had begun to give way to a market system in which laborers worked freely for wages. By the mid-seventeenth century *repartimiento* labor was on the wane in Mexico, although it survived longer in Peru.

The Spanish regimes in the Americas met considerable resistance from indigenous peoples. Resistance took various forms: rebellion, half-hearted work under the *encomienda* and *repartimiento* systems, and retreat into the mountains and forests where Spanish power did not reach. Indigenous peoples sometimes turned to Spanish law and administrators in search of aid against oppressive colonists. In 1615, for example, Felipe Guaman Poma de Ayala, a native of Peru, fired off a 1,200-page letter—accompanied by some four hundred hand-drawn illustrations—to King Philip III of Spain asking for protection for native peoples against rapacious colonists. Guaman Poma's letter went astray: the king never saw it. The missive somehow made its way to Denmark, where it remained unknown in a library until 1908.

Resistance to Spanish Rule

Guaman Poma's complaint serves as a record of grievances against Spanish overlords. The author wrote passionately of men ruined by overtaxation and women driven to prostitution, of Spanish colonists who grabbed the lands of native peoples and Spanish priests who seduced the wives of native men. Guaman Poma warned the king that the peoples of Peru were dying fast because of disease and abuse. If Philip wanted anything to remain of his Andean empire, he should intervene and protect the indigenous peoples of the land.

Felipe Guaman Poma de Ayala depicted himself several times in his letter of complaint. Here, kneeling, he presents a copy of his work to the king of Spain. In fact, Guaman Poma never traveled to Spain, and his letter probably never reached the king. Nevertheless, Guaman Poma's illustrations offer remarkable images of early colonial Peru. • Det Kongelige Bibliotek, Copenhagen

Sugar and Slavery in Portuguese Brazil

While the Spanish American empire concentrated on the extraction of silver, the Portuguese empire in Brazil depended on the production and export of sugar. The different economic and social foundations of the Spanish and Portuguese empires led to different patterns of labor recruitment. Spanish conquistadores subjugated sedentary peoples with effective administrative systems and compelled them to provide labor in the mines and estates of Mexico and Peru. Portuguese nobles and entrepreneurs established sugar plantations in regions without the administrative machinery to recruit workers and relied instead on imported African slaves as laborers. Indeed, Africans and their descendants became the majority of the population in Brazil, not simply an auxiliary labor force as in Spanish America.

The Engenho   Colonial Brazilian life revolved around the sugar mill, or *engenho*. Strictly speaking, the term *engenho* (related to the English word *engine*) referred only to the mill itself, but it came to represent a complex of land, labor, buildings, animals, capital, and technical skills related to the production of sugar. Unlike other crops, sugarcane required extensive processing to yield molasses or refined sugar as a profitable export. Thus *engenhos* always combined agricultural and industrial enterprises. They depended both on heavy labor for the planting and harvesting of cane and on the specialized skills of individuals who understood the intricacies of the sugar-making process. As a result, *engenhos* were among the most complex business enterprises in the Americas.

In a colonial economy where sugar figured as the most important export, the Portuguese planters and owners of sugar mills were a privileged class, exercising political, social, and economic power. As long as they contributed to the government's revenues, they could usually count on strong royal support. The planters acted like landed nobility, but the nature of their enterprises required them to pay attention to affairs like businessmen. They operated on very small profit margins. Their exalted social position often disguised difficult financial predicaments, and turnover in the business was always high.

Like their Spanish counterparts, Portuguese colonists first tried to enlist local populations as laborers. Unlike the inhabitants of Mexico and Peru, however, the peoples of Brazil were not sedentary cultivators. They resisted efforts to commandeer their labor, evaded Portuguese forces by retreating to interior lands, and took every opportunity to escape captors who managed to force them into servitude. From the Portuguese perspective, relying on native peoples as laborers had an additional drawback. As elsewhere in the Americas, epidemic diseases devastated indigenous populations. During the 1560s smallpox and measles ravaged the whole Brazilian coast, making it difficult for Portuguese settlers even to find potential laborers, let alone force them to work. *The Search for Labor*

Faced with these difficulties, the colonists turned to another labor source: the African slave. Portuguese plantation managers imported slaves as early as the 1530s, but they began to rely on African labor on a large scale only in the 1580s. The labor demands of cane cultivation and sugar production exacted a heavy toll from slave communities. Arduous working conditions, mistreatment, tropical heat, poor nutrition, and inadequate housing combined to produce high rates of disease and mortality: *engenhos* typically lost 5 to 10 percent of their slaves annually. In Brazil as in most other plantation societies, the number of deaths in the slave population usually exceeded the number of births, so there was a constant demand for more slaves. *Slavery*

The system had its critics, but government officials mostly left matters of labor management to slave owners. To them the balance sheet of sugar production dictated practices that paid scant heed to the preservation of slaves' lives, as long as the owners realized profits. Indeed, if a slave lived five to six years, the investment of the average owner doubled and permitted him to purchase a new and healthy slave without taking a monetary loss. Hence owners had little economic incentive to improve conditions for slaves or to increase their birthrates. Children required financial outlays for at least twelve years, which from the perspective of the owner represented a financial loss. All told, the business of producing Brazilian sugar was so brutal that every ton of the sweet substance cost one human life.

Fur Traders and Settlers in North America

European mariners first frequented North American shores in search of fish. Although fishing was a profitable enterprise, trade in furs became far more lucrative. The North American fur trade began when fishermen bartered for fur with local peoples. After explorers found a convenient entrance to rich fur-producing regions through the Hudson Strait and Hudson Bay, they began the systematic exploitation of the northern lands. Royal agents, adventurers, businessmen, and settlers began to connect large parts of the North American interior by a chain of forts and trading posts. Indigenous peoples trapped animals for Europeans and exchanged the pelts for manufactured goods such as wool blankets, iron pots, firearms, and distilled spirits. The hides went mostly to Europe, where capitalist markets experienced burgeoning demand for beaver skin hats and fur clothing. *The Fur Trade*

The fur trade generated tremendous conflict. American beaver populations, which were the chief targets of the trade, declined so rapidly that trappers constantly had to push further inland in search of untapped beaver grounds. When hunting grounds became depleted, native peoples poached or invaded others' territories, which frequently led to war. *Effects of the Fur Trade*

The fur trade also took place in the context of competition between European states. This competitive atmosphere contributed to further conflict, as indigenous peoples became embroiled in their patrons' rivalries. During the mid-seventeenth century, for example, Iroquois peoples who were allies of Dutch fur traders in New Amsterdam launched a war against Hurons living north of the Great Lakes. Equipped with firearms supplied by their Dutch allies, the Iroquois sought to exterminate the Hurons and extend their trapping to the northern lands. Hurons survived the war, although in greatly diminished numbers, but the Iroquois vastly increased their strength and destroyed Huron power.

Settler Society   European settler-cultivators posed an even more serious challenge to native ways of life than did the fur traders, since they displaced indigenous peoples from the land and turned hunting grounds into plantations. The earliest colonists experienced difficult times, since European crops like wheat did not grow well in their settlements. Indeed, many of the early colonies would have perished except for maize, game, and fish supplied by native peoples. Over time, however, French and especially English migrants stabilized their societies and distinguished them sharply from those of indigenous peoples.

Cash Crops

European moralists often denounced tobacco as a noxious weed, and they associated its use with vices like drunkenness, gambling, and prostitution. Nevertheless, its popularity surged in Europe, and later in Africa and Asia as well, after its introduction from the Americas. ● Arents Collections, New York Public Library. Astor, Lenox and Tilden Foundations

As colonists' numbers increased, they sought to integrate their American holdings into the larger capitalist economy of the Atlantic Ocean basin by producing cash crops that they could market in Europe. In the English colonies of Virginia and Carolina, settlers concentrated on the cultivation of tobacco. As early as 1616 Virginia colonists exported 2,300 pounds of tobacco. European demand for the addictive weed resulted in skyrocketing exports amounting to two hundred thousand pounds in 1624 and three million pounds in 1638. By the eighteenth century settlers in the southern colonies had established plantation complexes that produced rice and indigo as well as tobacco, and by the nineteenth century cotton also had become a prominent plantation crop.

Indentured Labor   The plantations created high demand for cheap labor. Colonists in North America displaced indigenous peoples but could not subjugate them or induce them to labor in their fields. Planters initially met the demand for cheap labor by recruiting indentured servants from Europe. People who had little future in Europe—the chronically unemployed, orphans, political prisoners, and criminals—were often willing to sell a portion of their working lives in exchange for passage across the Atlantic and a new start in life. Throughout the seventeenth and eighteenth centuries, indentured servants streamed into the American colonies in hopes that after they had satisfied their obligation to provide four to seven years of labor they might become independent artisans or planters themselves. (The indentured labor trade in the Americas continued on a smaller scale even into the early twentieth century.) Some indentured servants went on to become prominent figures in colonial society, but many died of disease or overwork before completing their terms of labor, while others found only marginal employment.

Most indentured servants eventually gained their freedom, but other suppliers of cheap labor remained in bondage all their lives. As in lands colonized by Iberian peoples, English settlers in North America found uses for slave labor from Africa. The first African slaves reached Virginia about 1610, but their numbers remained small until the late seventeenth century. Between 1670 and 1720, however, planters increasingly replaced European indentured servants with African slaves. By 1750 about 120,000 black slaves tilled Chesapeake tobacco, and another 180,000 cultivated Carolina rice.

Slavery in North America

Slave labor was not prominent in the northern colonies, principally because the land and climate were not suitable for the cultivation of labor-intensive cash crops. Nevertheless, the economies of these colonies profited handsomely from slavery. Many New England merchants traded in slaves destined for the West Indies: by the

An eighteenth-century engraving depicts work on a plantation: African slaves prepare flour and bread from manioc (left) while others hang tobacco leaves to dry in a shed (right). A male turkey—a fowl native to the Americas—ignores the bustle and displays his feathers (right foreground). ● Arents Collections, New York Public Library. Astor, Lenox and Tilden Foundations

mid-eighteenth century half the merchant fleet of Newport carried human cargo. The economies of New York and Philadelphia benefited from the building and out-fitting of slave vessels, and the seaports of New England became profitable centers for the distillation of rum. The chief ingredient of this rum was slave-produced sugar from the West Indies, and merchants traded much of the distilled spirits for slaves on the African coast. Thus, although the southern plantation societies became most directly identified with a system that exploited African labor, all the North American colonies participated in and profited from the slave trade.

Christianity and Native Religions in the Americas

Like Buddhists and Muslims in earlier centuries, European explorers, conquerors, merchants, and settlers took their religious traditions with them when they traveled overseas. The desire to spread Christianity was a prominent motive behind European ventures overseas, and missionaries soon made their way to the Americas as well as other lands where Europeans established a presence.

Spanish Missionaries   From the beginning of Spanish colonization in Mexico and Peru, priests served as representatives of the crown and reinforced civil administrators. Franciscan, Do-minican, and Jesuit missionaries campaigned to Christianize indigenous peoples. In Mexico, for example, a group of twelve Franciscan missionaries arrived in 1524. They founded a school in Tlatelolco, the bustling market district of the Aztec capital of Tenochtitlan, where they educated the sons of prominent noble families in Latin, Spanish, and Christian doctrine. The missionaries themselves learned native lan-guages and sought to explain Christianity in terms understandable to their audi-ences. They also compiled a vast amount of information about native societies in hopes of learning how best to communicate their message. The work of Franciscan Bernardino de Sahagún was especially important. Sahagún preserved volumes of in-formation about the language, customs, beliefs, literature, and history of Mexico be-fore the arrival of Spanish forces there. His work remained largely unstudied until the twentieth century, but in recent times it has shed enormous light both on Aztec society and on the methods of early missionaries in Mexico.

Survival of Native Religions   Christian missionaries encountered considerable resistance in the Americas. In both Mexico and Peru, indigenous peoples continued to observe their inherited faiths into the seventeenth century and beyond, even though Spanish authorities sponsored the Roman Catholic faith and tried to eliminate the worship of pagan deities. Native peoples honored idols in caves and inaccessible mountain sites, and they may have occasionally even continued to sacrifice human victims to their tradi-tional gods.

Yet Christianity won adherents in Spanish America. In the wake of conquest and epidemic disease, many native leaders in Mexico concluded that their gods had abandoned them and looked to the missionaries for spiritual guidance. When native peoples adopted Christianity, however, they blended their own interests and tradi-tions with the faith taught by Spanish missionaries. When they learned about Roman Catholic saints, for example, they revered saints with qualities like those of their in-herited gods or those whose feast days coincided with traditional celebrations.

The Virgin of Guadalupe   In Mexico Christianity became especially popular after the mid-seventeenth cen-tury, as an increasingly mestizo society took the Virgin of Guadalupe almost as a na-tional symbol. According to legends, the Virgin Mary appeared before a peasant near Mexico City in 1531. The site of the apparition soon became a popular local shrine visited mostly by Spanish settlers. By the 1640s the shrine attracted pilgrims from all parts of Mexico, and the Virgin of Guadalupe gained a reputation for working miracles on behalf of individuals who visited her shrine. The popularity of the Virgin of Guadalupe helped to ensure that Roman Catholic Christianity would dominate cultural and religious matters in Mexico.

French and English Missions

French and English missionaries did not attract nearly as many converts to Christianity in North America as their Spanish counterparts did in Mexico and Peru. Partly this was because French and English colonists did not rule over conquered populations of sedentary cultivators: it was much more difficult to conduct missions among peoples who frequently moved about the countryside than among those who lived permanently in villages, towns, or cities. In addition, English colonists displayed little interest in converting indigenous peoples to Christianity. The colonists did not discourage converts, but they made little effort to seek them, nor did they welcome native converts into their agricultural and commercial society. By contrast, French missionaries worked actively among native communities in the St. Lawrence, Mississippi, and Ohio River valleys and experienced modest success in spreading Christianity. Even though native peoples did not embrace Christianity, however, the burgeoning settlements of French and especially English colonists guaranteed that European religious traditions would figure prominently in North American society.

EUROPEANS IN THE PACIFIC

Though geographically distant from the Americas, Australia and the Pacific islands underwent experiences similar to those that transformed the western hemisphere in early modern times. Like their American counterparts, the peoples of Oceania had no inherited or acquired immunities to diseases that were common to peoples throughout the eastern hemisphere, and their numbers plunged when epidemic disease struck their populations. For the most part, however, Australia and the Pacific islands experienced epidemic disease and the arrival of European migrants later than did the Americas. European mariners thoroughly explored the Pacific basin between the sixteenth and eighteenth centuries, but only in Guam and the Mariana Islands did they establish permanent settlements before the late eighteenth century. Nevertheless, their scouting of the region laid a foundation for much more intense interactions between European, Euro-American, Asian, and Oceanic peoples during the nineteenth and twentieth centuries.

Australia and the Larger World

At least from the second century C.E., European geographers had speculated about *terra australis incognita*—"unknown southern land"—that they thought must exist in the world's southern hemisphere to balance the huge landmasses north of the equator. As European mariners reconnoitered the Atlantic and Pacific Oceans during early modern times, they watched expectantly for a southern continent. Yet their principal interest was trade, and they rarely abandoned the pursuit of profit to sail out of their way in search of an unknown land.

Dutch Exploration

When they visited the islands of southeast Asia in the quest for spices, however, they approached Australia from the west. Portuguese mariners most likely charted much of the western and northern coast of Australia as early as the 1520s, but Dutch sailors made the first recorded European sighting of the southern continent in 1606. The Dutch VOC authorized exploratory voyages, but mariners found little to encourage further efforts. In 1623, after surveying the dry landscapes of western Australia, the Dutch mariner Jan Carstenzs reported that his party had not seen "one fruit-bearing tree, nor anything that man could make use of: there are no mountains or even hills, so that it may be safely concluded that the land contains no metals, nor yields any precious woods," and he described the land as "the most arid and barren region that could be found anywhere on earth."

Nevertheless, Dutch mariners continued to visit Australia. By the mid-seventeenth century they had scouted the continent's northern, western, and southern coasts, and they had ascertained that New Guinea and Tasmania were islands separate from Australia itself. Dutch explorers were so active in the reconnaissance of Australia that Europeans referred to the southern continent as "New Holland" throughout the seventeenth century. Yet neither Dutch nor any other European seamen visited the eastern coast until James Cook approached Australia from the southeast and charted the region in 1770, barely escaping destruction on the Great Barrier Reef.

Although European mariners explored Australian coastlines in the seventeenth and eighteenth centuries, they made only brief landfalls and had only fleeting encounters with indigenous peoples. The aboriginal peoples of Australia had formed many distinct foraging and fishing societies, but European visitors did not linger long enough to become familiar with either the peoples or their societies. Because they were nomadic foragers rather than sedentary cultivators, Europeans mostly considered them wretched savages. In the absence of tempting opportunities to trade, European mariners made no effort to establish permanent settlements in Australia.

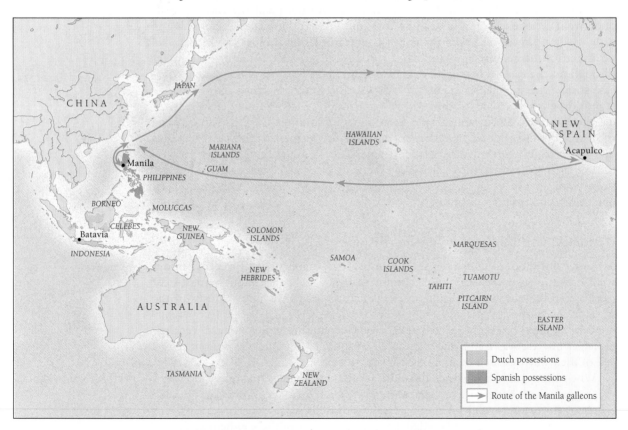

MAP [24.2]

European exploration and settlement in the Pacific.

Only after Cook's charting of the eastern coast in 1770 did European peoples *British Colonists* become seriously interested in Australia. Cook dropped anchor for a week at Botany Bay (near modern Sydney) and reported that the region was suitable for settlement. In 1788 a British fleet arrived at Sydney carrying about one thousand passengers, eight hundred of them convicts, who established the first European settlement in Australia as a penal colony. For half a century Europeans in Australia numbered only a few thousand, most of them convicts who herded sheep. Free settlers did not outnumber convicted criminal migrants until the 1830s. Thus exploratory voyages of the seventeenth and eighteenth centuries led to fleeting encounters between European and aboriginal Australian peoples, but only in the nineteenth and twentieth centuries did a continuing stream of European migrants and settlers link Australia more directly to the larger world.

The Pacific Islands and the Larger World

The entry of European mariners into the Pacific Ocean basin did not bring immediate change to most of the Pacific islands. As in the case of Australia, European merchants and settlers did not arrive in the Pacific islands in large numbers until the late eighteenth century. Guam and the Mariana Islands underwent dramatic change already in the sixteenth century, however, and the ventures of European merchants and explorers in the Pacific basin set the stage for profound upheavals in other island societies during the nineteenth and twentieth centuries.

Ferdinand Magellan and his crew became the first Europeans to cross the Pa- *Spanish Voyages* cific Ocean in 1521. Before reaching the Philippines, they encountered only one *in the Pacific* inhabited island group—the Marianas, dominated by Guam. In 1565 Spanish mariners inaugurated the Manila galleon trade between Manila and Acapulco. Since their primary goal was to link New Spain to Asian markets, they rarely went out of their way to explore the Pacific Ocean or to search for other islands. Spanish vessels visited the Marquesas, Tuamotu, Cook, Solomon, and New Hebrides islands in the sixteenth century, and it is likely that one or more stray ships fetched up in Hawai`i. Yet Spanish mariners found little to interest them in most of the Pacific islands and did not establish regular communications with island peoples. They usually sailed before the trade winds from Acapulco to Manila on a route that took them south of Hawai`i and north of other Polynesian islands. On the return trip they sailed before the westerlies on a route that took them well north of all the Pacific islands.

The only Pacific islands that attracted substantial Spanish interest in the sixteenth *Guam* century were Guam and the Marianas. Manila galleons called regularly at Guam, which lay directly on the route from Acapulco to Manila. For more than a century, they took on fresh provisions and engaged in mostly peaceful trade with the indigenous Chamorro people. During the 1670s and 1680s, Spanish authorities decided to consolidate their position in Guam and bring the Mariana Islands under the control of the viceroy of New Spain in Mexico. They dispatched military forces to the islands to impose Spanish rule and subject the Chamorro to the spiritual authority of the Roman Catholic church. The Chamorro stoutly opposed these efforts, but a smallpox epidemic of 1688 severely reduced their numbers and crippled their resistance. By 1695 the Chamorro population had declined from about fifty thousand at midcentury to five thousand, partly because of Spanish campaigns but mostly because of smallpox. By the end of the seventeenth century, Spanish forces had established garrisons throughout the Mariana Islands and relocated surviving Chamorro into communities supervised by Spanish authorities.

Visitors and Trade   Like the aboriginal peoples of Australia, the indigenous peoples of the Pacific islands had mostly fleeting encounters with European visitors during early modern times. By the late eighteenth century, however, growing European and Euro-American interest in the Pacific Ocean basin led to sharply increased interactions between islanders and mariners. English and French mariners explored the Pacific basin in search of commercial opportunities and the elusive northwest passage from Europe to Asia. They frequently visited Tahiti after 1767, and they soon began to trade with the islanders: European mariners received provisions and engaged in sexual relations with Tahitian women in exchange for nails, knives, iron tools, and textiles. Although trade was mostly peaceful, misunderstandings often led to minor skirmishes, and European captains occasionally trained their cannons on fleets of war canoes or villages in the Pacific islands. James Cook lost his life in 1779 when disputes over petty thefts escalated into a bitter conflict between his crew and the islanders of Hawai`i.

By the late eighteenth century, whalers had begun to venture into Pacific waters in large numbers, followed by missionaries, merchants, and planters. By the early nineteenth century, European and Euro-American peoples had become prominent figures in all the major Pacific islands groups. During the nineteenth and twentieth centuries, interactions between islanders, visitors, and migrants brought rapid change to Pacific islands societies.

Hawaiian canoes and James Cook's ships share Kealakekua Bay in Hawai`i in this sketch by a member of Cook's crew. Tensions between Hawaiians and Englishmen soon mounted, however, and led to the skirmish that claimed Cook's life. • *Public Record Office, London*

The Americas underwent thorough transformation in early modern times. Smallpox and other diseases sparked ferocious epidemics that devastated indigenous populations and undermined their societies. In the wake of severe depopulation, European peoples toppled imperial states, established mining and agricultural enterprises, imported enslaved African laborers, and founded colonies throughout much of the western hemisphere. Some indigenous peoples disappeared entirely as distinct groups. Others maintained their communities, identities, and cultural traditions but fell increasingly under the influence of European migrants and their Euro-American offspring. In Oceania only Guam and the Mariana Islands felt the full effects of epidemic disease and migration in the early modern era. By the late eighteenth century, however, European and Euro-American peoples with advanced technologies had thoroughly explored the Pacific Ocean basin, and epidemic diseases traveled with them to Australia and the Pacific islands. As a result, during the nineteenth and twentieth centuries, Oceania underwent a social transformation similar to the one experienced earlier by the Americas.

CHRONOLOGY

1492	First voyage of Christopher Columbus to the western hemisphere
1494	Treaty of Tordesillas
1518	Smallpox epidemic in the Caribbean
1519–1521	Spanish conquest of Mexico
1532–1540	Spanish conquest of Peru
1545	Spanish discovery of silver near Potosí
1604	Foundation of Port Royal (Nova Scotia)
1607	Foundation of Jamestown
1608	Foundation of Quebec
1623	Foundation of New Amsterdam
1630	Foundation of the Massachusetts Bay Colony
1688	Smallpox epidemic on Guam

FOR FURTHER READING

James Axtell. *The Invasion Within: The Contest of Cultures in Colonial North America*. New York, 1985. Insightful study of the interactions between French, English, and indigenous peoples in colonial North America.

Alvar Nuñez Cabeza de Vaca. *Castaways*. Trans. by F. M. López-Morillas. Berkeley, 1993. A new translation of Cabeza de Vaca's account of his shipwreck and travels through what is now the southwestern United States to Mexico.

Colin G. Callaway. *New Worlds for All: Indians, Europeans, and the Remaking of Early America*. Baltimore, 1997. Scholarly synthesis examining interactions and cultural exchanges between European and indigenous American peoples.

William Cronon. *Changes in the Land: Indians, Colonists, and the Ecology of New England*. New York, 1983. Brilliant study concentrating on the different ways English colonists and native peoples in colonial New England used the environment.

Bernal Díaz del Castillo. *The Conquest of New Spain*. Trans. by J. M. Cohen. Harmondsworth, 1963. A conveniently available translation of Bernal Díaz's account of the conquest of Mexico from the viewpoint of a soldier.

Nancy M. Farriss. *Maya Society under Colonial Rule: The Collective Enterprise of Survival*. Princeton, 1984. A richly detailed analysis of early interactions between Spanish colonists and the Maya of the Yucatan.

K. R. Howe. *Where the Waves Fall: A New South Sea Island History from First Settlement to Colonial Rule*. Honolulu, 1984. A thoughtful survey of Pacific islands history emphasizing interactions between islanders and visitors.

Jacques Lafaye. *Quetzlcóatl and Guadalupe: The Formation of Mexican National Consciousness, 1531–1813*. Trans. by B. Keen. Chicago, 1976. Examines the blending of indigenous with Spanish beliefs and the role of religion in the formation of a Mexican national consciousness.

Miguel León-Portilla. *The Broken Spears: The Aztec Account of the Conquest of Mexico*. Rev. ed. Boston, 1992. Offers translations of indigenous accounts of the Spanish conquest of the Aztec empire.

James Lockhart. *The Nahuas after the Conquest*. Stanford, 1992. A thorough, scholarly analysis of indigenous society in central Mexico from the sixteenth to the eighteenth century.

James Lockhart and Stuart B. Schwartz, *Early Latin America: A History of Colonial Spanish America and Brazil*. New York, 1982. The best survey of colonial Latin American history.

Sabine MacCormack. *Religion in the Andes: Vision and Imagination in Early Colonial Peru*. Princeton, 1991. Analyzes the encounter between native religious beliefs and Spanish Christianity in Peru.

Gary B. Nash. *Red, White, and Black: The Peoples of Early America*. 3rd ed. Englewood Cliffs, N.J., 1992. Outstanding survey of early American history focusing on the interactions between peoples of European, African, and American ancestry.

Stuart B. Schwartz. *Sugar Plantations and the Formation of Brazilian Society*. Cambridge, 1985. Examines the roles of sugar and slavery in early colonial Brazil.

Steve J. Stern. *Peru's Indian Peoples and the Challenge of Spanish Conquest*. 2nd ed. Madison, 1993. Scholarly analysis concentrating on the social history of indigenous peoples following the Spanish conquest of Peru.

David J. Weber. *The Spanish Frontier in North America*. New Haven, 1992. A comprehensive study of Spanish efforts to explore and colonize lands north of Mexico.

Richard White. *The Middle Ground: Indians, Empires, and Republics in the Great Lakes Region, 1650–1815*. Cambridge, 1991. Insightful study of relations between French, English, and indigenous peoples in the Great Lakes region.

CHAPTER 25

AFRICA AND THE ATLANTIC WORLD

. . .

Between 1760 and 1792, a west African man known to history as Thomas Peters crossed the Atlantic Ocean four times. In 1760 slave raiders captured Peters, whose original African name is unknown, marched him to the coast, and sold him to French slave merchants. He traveled in a slave ship to the French colony of Louisiana, where he probably worked on a sugar plantation. But Peters was not a docile servant. He attempted to escape at least three times, and his master punished him by beating him, branding him with a hot iron, and forcing him to wear shackles around his legs. During the 1760s his French master sold Peters to an English planter, and about 1770 a Scottish landowner in North Carolina bought him.

During the 1770s, as English colonists in North America prepared to rebel against the British government in the interests of "life, liberty, and the pursuit of happiness," slaves of African ancestry considered their own prospects and looked for ways to obtain personal freedom. Peters was among them. When war broke out, he made his way with his wife and daughter to British lines and joined the Black Pioneers, a company of escaped slaves who fought to maintain British rule in the colonies. When the colonists won the war, Peters escaped to Nova Scotia with his family and many other former slaves.

Blacks were legally free in Nova Scotia, but the white ruling elites forced them to till marginal lands and live in segregated villages. In hopes of improving their lot, some two hundred black families designated Peters as their spokesman and sent him to London to petition the government for better treatment or resettlement in a more favorable land. In 1790 Peters sailed to England, where he promoted the establishment of a colony for former slaves in Sierra Leone. His efforts succeeded, and the next year he returned to Nova Scotia to seek recruits for the colony. In 1792 he led 1,196 blacks aboard a convoy of fifteen ships and began his fourth crossing of the Atlantic Ocean. The colonists arrived safely at Freetown, and Peters served as a leader of the black community there. His time was short—he lived for less than four months after arriving in Sierra Leone—but through his own life and experiences Thomas Peters personified the links connecting the lands of the Atlantic Ocean basin.

Below decks on an illegal slave ship seized by a British antislavery patrol in 1846. • National Maritime Museum, London/Bridgeman Art Library, London and New York

For the most part the peoples of sub-Saharan Africa continued to follow established patterns of life in early modern times. They built states and organized societies based on kinship groups as their Bantu-speaking predecessors had done for centuries. In west Africa and coastal east Africa, they also traded regularly with Muslim merchants from north Africa and southwest Asia.

Yet the establishment of global trade networks brought deep change to sub-Saharan Africa. Commercial opportunities drew European vessels to the coasts of west Africa, and maritime trade soon turned west African attention to the Atlantic. Maritime commerce did not put an end to the trans-Saharan caravan trade that linked west Africa to the Mediterranean, but it helped promote the emergence of prosperous port cities and the establishment of powerful coastal kingdoms that traded through the ocean rather than the desert. In central Africa and south Africa, European merchants brought the first substantial opportunities for long-distance trade, since Muslim merchants had not ventured to those regions in large numbers.

Trade through the Atlantic profoundly affected African society because it involved human beings. African peoples had made a place for slavery in their own societies for centuries, and they had also supplied slaves to Muslim merchants who transported them to markets in the Mediterranean and the Indian Ocean basin. The Atlantic slave trade, however, was vastly larger than the African and Islamic slave trades, and it had more serious consequences for African society. Between the fifteenth and nineteenth centuries, it not only siphoned millions of people from their own societies but also provoked turmoil in much of sub-Saharan Africa, as peoples raided each others' communities in search of captives for sale to slave traders.

The vast majority of Africans sold into the Atlantic slave trade went to destinations in the Caribbean or the Americas. Most worked on plantations cultivating cash crops for export, although some worked as domestic servants, miners, or laborers. Together they made up the largest migration in history before the nineteenth century and gave rise to an African diaspora in the western hemisphere. Under the restrictive conditions of slavery, they did not reconstitute African societies, but they also did not join European or Euro-American society. Instead, they preserved some African traditions and blended them with European and American traditions to create hybrid African-American societies.

AFRICAN POLITICS AND SOCIETY IN EARLY MODERN TIMES

For perhaps three millennia (2000 B.C.E. to 1000 C.E.), Bantu-speaking peoples spread agriculture and iron metallurgy throughout sub-Saharan Africa. Many organized themselves into villages and clans governed by kinship groups rather than formal states. As their numbers grew, they devised political structures and built a series of chiefdoms and regional kingdoms. Muslim merchants, who ventured to sub-Saharan Africa after the eighth century, brought trade that encouraged the formation of large kingdoms and empires in west Africa and thriving city-states in east Africa.

African peoples continued to form states during the early modern era, but under the influence of maritime trade the patterns of state development changed. Regional kingdoms replaced the imperial states of west Africa as peoples organized their societies to take advantage of Atlantic as well as trans-Saharan commerce. The city-states of east Africa fell under the domination of Portuguese merchant-mariners seeking commercial opportunities in the Indian Ocean basin. The extension of trade networks also led to the formation of regional kingdoms in central Africa and south Africa. As the volume of long-distance trade grew, both Islam and Christianity became more prominent in sub-Saharan African societies.

The Islamic States of West Africa and East Africa

Between the eighth and sixteenth centuries, powerful kingdoms and imperial states ruled the savannas of west Africa. The earliest was the kingdom of Ghana, which originated perhaps as early as the fifth or sixth century and established its dominance in the region in the eighth century. By controlling and taxing the trans-Saharan trade in gold, the kings of Ghana gained the financial resources they needed to field a large army and influence affairs in much of west Africa. In the thirteenth century the Mali empire replaced Ghana as the preeminent power in west Africa, but the Mali rulers continued the Ghana policy of controlling trans-Saharan trade.

By the fifteenth century the Mali empire had begun to weaken, and the expansive state of Songhay emerged to take its place as the dominant power of the western grasslands. Based in the trading city of Gao, Songhay rulers built a flourishing city-state perhaps as early as the eighth century. In the early fifteenth century, they rejected Mali authority and mounted raids deep into Mali territory. In 1464 the Songhay ruler

The Songhay Empire

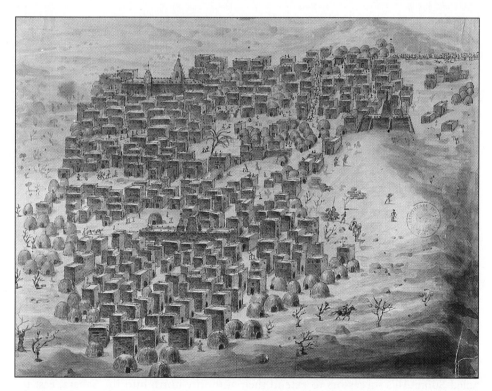

Timbuktu, the commercial and cultural center of the Mali and Songhay empires, as sketched by a French traveler in 1828. Though long in decline, the city's mosques, mud-brick dwellings, and crowds of people bespeak a prosperous community. ● Bibliothèque Nationale de France

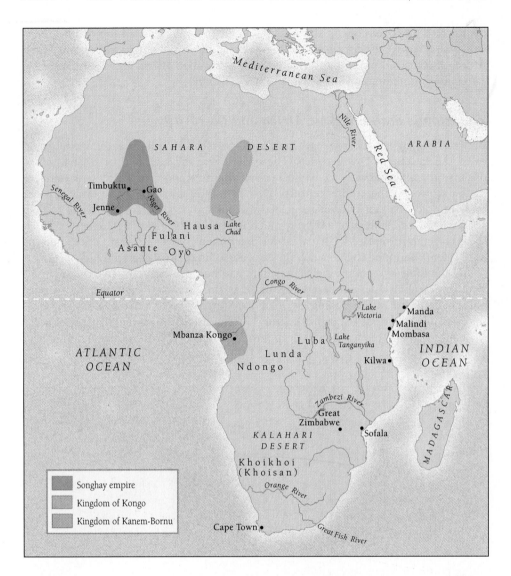

MAP [25.1]

African states in early
modern times.

Sunni Ali (reigned 1464–1493) embarked on a campaign to conquer his neighbors and consolidated the Songhay empire (1464–1591). He brought the important trading cities of Timbuktu and Jenne under his control and used their wealth to dominate the central Niger valley.

Sunni Ali's administrative apparatus was more elaborate than that of his predecessors in Ghana and Mali. He appointed governors to oversee provinces and instituted a hierarchy of command that turned his army into an effective military force. He also created an imperial navy to patrol the Niger River, which was an extremely important commercial highway in the Songhay empire. Songhay military might enabled Sunni Ali's successors to extend their authority north into the Sahara, east toward Lake Chad, and west toward the upper reaches of the Niger River.

The Songhay emperors presided over a prosperous land. The capital city of Gao had about seventy-five thousand residents, many of whom participated in the lucrative trans-Saharan trade that brought salt, textiles, and metal goods south in exchange for gold and slaves. The emperors were all Muslims: they supported mosques, built schools to teach the Quran, and maintained an Islamic university at Timbuktu. Like the rulers of Ghana and Mali, the Songhay emperors valued Islam as a cultural foundation for cooperation with Muslim merchants and Islamic states in north Africa. Nevertheless, the Songhay emperors did not abandon traditional religious practices: Sunni Ali often consulted pagan diviners and magicians.

The Songhay empire dominated west Africa for most of the sixteenth century, but it was the last of the great imperial states of the grasslands. In 1591 a musket-bearing Moroccan army trekked across the Sahara and opened fire on the previously invincible Songhay military machine. Songhay forces withered under the attack, and subject peoples took the opportunity to revolt against Songhay domination.

Fall of Songhay

As the Songhay empire crumbled, a series of small, regional kingdoms and city-states emerged in west Africa. The kingdom of Kanem-Bornu dominated the region around Lake Chad, and the Hausa people established thriving commercial city-states to the west. In the forests south of the grasslands, Oyo and Asante peoples built powerful regional kingdoms. On the coasts Diula, Mande, and other trading peoples established a series of states that entered into commercial relations with European merchant-mariners who called at west African ports after the fifteenth century. The increasing prominence of Atlantic trade in west African society worked against the interests of imperial states like Mali and Songhay, which had relied on control of trans-Saharan trade to finance their empires.

While regional states displaced the Songhay empire in west Africa, the Swahili city-states of east Africa fell on hard times. When the Portuguese mariner Vasco da Gama made his way up the east African coast en route to India in 1497 and 1498, he skirmished with local forces at Mozambique and Mombasa. On his second voyage to India in 1502, he forced the ruler of Kilwa to pay tribute, and his followers trained their cannons on Swahili ports all along the east African coast. In 1505 a massive Portuguese naval expedition subdued all the Swahili cities from Sofala to Mombasa. Portuguese forces built administrative centers at Mozambique and Malindi and constructed forts throughout the region in hopes of controlling trade in east Africa. They did not succeed in this effort, but they disrupted trade patterns enough to send the Swahili cities into a decline from which they never fully recovered.

Swahili Decline

The Kingdoms of Central Africa and South Africa

As trade networks multiplied and linked all regions of sub-Saharan Africa, an increasing volume of commerce encouraged state-building in central Africa and south Africa. In central Africa the principal states were the kingdoms of Kongo, Ndongo, Luba, and Lunda in the basin of the Congo River (also known as the Zaire River). Best known of them was the kingdom of Kongo, since abundant written records throw light on its experience in early modern times. The kingdom emerged in the fourteenth century. Its rulers built a centralized state with officials overseeing military, judicial, and financial affairs, and by the late fifteenth century Kongo embraced much of the modern-day Republic of Congo and Angola.

The Kingdom of Kongo

In 1482 a small Portuguese fleet reconnoitered the estuary of the Congo River and initiated commercial relations with the kingdom of Kongo. Within a few years, Portuguese merchants had established a close political and diplomatic relationship with the kings of Kongo. They supplied the kings with advisors, provided a military

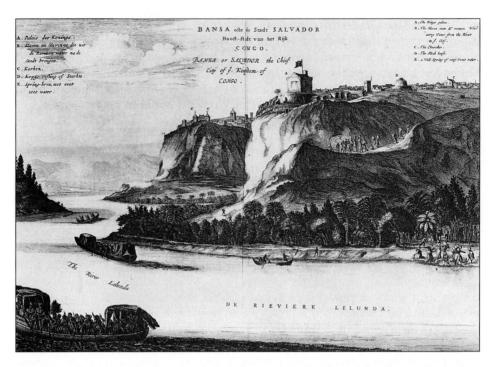

An engraving depicts São Salvador in Angola in the late seventeenth century. A flag flies over the royal palace while the Portuguese citadel (to the right of the palace) guards the city. Churches appear at the center and on the far right side of the engraving. • Rare Books Division, New York Public Library. Astor, Lenox and Tilden Foundations

garrison to support the kings and protect Portuguese interests, and brought tailors, shoemakers, masons, miners, and priests to Kongo.

The kings of Kongo converted to Christianity as a way to establish closer commercial relations with Portuguese merchants and diplomatic relations with the Portuguese monarchy. King Affonso I (reigned 1506–1543) became a devout Roman Catholic and sought to convert all his subjects to Christianity. Portuguese priests in Kongo reported that he attended religious services daily and studied the Bible so zealously that he sometimes neglected to eat. The Kongo capital of Mbanza— known to Europeans as São Salvador—had so many churches during the sixteenth century that contemporaries referred to it as "Kongo of the Bell."

Slave-Raiding in Kongo   Relations with Portugal brought wealth and foreign recognition to Kongo but also led eventually to the destruction of the kingdom and the establishment of a Portuguese colony in Angola. In exchange for the textiles, weapons, advisors, and craftsmen that they brought to Kongo, Portuguese merchants sought high-value merchandise such as gold, silver, ivory, and most of all slaves. They sometimes embarked on slaving expeditions themselves, but more often they made alliances with local authorities in interior regions and provided them with weapons in exchange for slaves. Some of their local allies were enemies of the kings of Kongo, while others were royal subordinates. In either case Portuguese tactics undermined the authority of the kings, who appealed repeatedly but unsuccessfully for the Portuguese to cease or at least to limit their trade in slaves.

By the late sixteenth century, Kongo was a land torn by strife. Invaders ravaged the kingdom and allied with Portuguese merchants, who appreciated the many war captives delivered to them as slaves. By 1665 relations between Portuguese merchants and the kings of Kongo had deteriorated to the point that the two sides went to war. Portuguese forces defeated the Kongolese army and decapitated the king. Soon thereafter, Portuguese merchants began to withdraw from Kongo in search of more profitable business in the kingdom of Ndongo to the south.

Portuguese explorers referred to Ndongo as Angola from the title of the king, *ngola*. During the sixteenth century Ndongo had grown from a small chiefdom to a powerful regional kingdom. It attracted the interest of Portuguese merchants who hoped to find gold or silver ores within its boundaries. Ndongo had no precious metals, but Portuguese adventurers found abundant supplies of slaves there. Portuguese forces began to campaign in Ndongo in the early seventeenth century, and by the end of the century they ruled the land as the Portuguese colony of Angola.

The Kingdom of Ndongo

The conquest of Angola did not come easily. For forty years Queen Nzinga (reigned 1623–1663) led spirited resistance against Portuguese forces. Nzinga came from a long line of warrior kings. She dressed as a male warrior when leading troops in battle and insisted that her subjects refer to her as king rather than queen. She sometimes went so far in playing male roles as to travel with a group of "concubines"—young men dressed as women companions of the "king." She mobilized central African peoples against her Portuguese adversaries, and she also allied with Dutch mariners, who traded frequently on the African coast during the mid-seventeenth century. Her aim was to drive the Portuguese from her land, then expel the Dutch, and finally create a vast central African empire embracing the entire lower Congo basin.

Queen Nzinga

Although she was a cunning strategist and effective military leader, Nzinga could not overcome Portuguese arms and the political divisions that plagued central African peoples. She stymied Portuguese efforts to control her realm, but she was unable to evict them from central Africa. When she died, Portuguese forces faced less capable resistance, and they soon consolidated their control over Angola, the first European colony in sub-Saharan Africa.

The Portuguese Colony of Angola

Historical records do not shed as much light on the political structures of south Africa as they do on Kongo and Angola, but it is clear that in the south, as in central Africa, regional kingdoms dominated political affairs. Kingdoms had begun to emerge as early as the eleventh century, largely under the influence of trade. Merchants from the Swahili city-states of coastal east Africa sought gold, ivory, and slaves from the interior regions of south Africa. By controlling local commerce chieftains increased their wealth, enhanced their power, and extended their authority. By 1300 rulers of one such kingdom had built a massive, stone-fortified city known as Great Zimbabwe, near the city of Nyanda in modern Zimbabwe, and they dominated the gold-bearing plain between the Zambesi and Limpopo Rivers until the late fifteenth century.

Regional Kingdoms in South Africa

After the fifteenth century a series of smaller kingdoms displaced the rulers of Great Zimbabwe, and Portuguese and Dutch mariners began to play a role in south African affairs. In search of commercial opportunities, Europeans struck alliances with local peoples and intervened in disputes with the aim of supporting their allies and advancing their own interests. They became especially active after Dutch mariners built a trading post at Cape Town in 1652. There they encountered the

European Arrival in South Africa

Queen Nzinga of Ndongo speaks with a Portuguese diplomat at his headquarters. The diplomat refused
to provide Nzinga with a chair, so she seated herself on the back of a servant while her "concubines"
looked on at the right. • Weidenfeld and Nicholson

hunting-and-gathering Khoikhoi people, whom they referred to pejoratively as Hot-
tentots. With the aid of firearms, they claimed lands for themselves and comman-
deered Khoikhoi labor with relative ease. By 1700 large numbers of Dutch colonists
had begun to arrive in south Africa, and by midcentury they had established settlements throughout the region bounded by the Orange and the Great Fish Rivers.
Their conquests laid the foundation for a series of Dutch and British colonies, which
eventually became the most prosperous European possessions in sub-Saharan Africa.

Islam and Christianity in Early Modern Africa

Indigenous religions remained influential throughout sub-Saharan Africa in early
modern times. Although most African peoples recognized a supreme, remote creator god, they devoted most of their attention to powerful spirits who were thought
to intervene directly in human affairs. African peoples associated many of these spirits with prominent geographical features such as mountains, waters, or forests. Others they thought of as the "living dead"—spirits of ancestors who roamed the world,
distributing rewards to descendants who led worthy lives and honored the memories
of departed kin and meting out punishments to those who did not.

Islam in Sub-   Although most Africans continued to observe their inherited religions, both
Saharan Africa Islam and Christianity attracted increasing interest in sub-Saharan Africa. Islam was
most popular in the commercial centers of west Africa and the Swahili city-states of

east Africa. In the sixteenth century the trading city of Timbuktu had an Islamic university and 180 schools that taught the Quran. Students flocked to Timbuktu by the thousands from all parts of west Africa.

Most African Muslims blended Islam with indigenous beliefs and customs. The result was a syncretic brand of Islam that not only made a place for African beliefs in spirits and magic but also permitted men and women to associate with each other on much more familiar terms than was common in north Africa, Arabia, and southwest Asia. Although it appealed to Africans, this syncretic Islam struck many devout Muslims as impure and offensive. Muslim merchants and travelers from north Africa and Arabia often commented on their shock at seeing women in tropical Africa who went out in public with bare breasts and socialized freely with men outside their own families.

Some Muslims in sub-Saharan Africa also shared these concerns about the purity of Islam. Most important of them were the Fulani, originally a pastoral people who for centuries kept herds of cattle in the savannas of west Africa. By the late seventeenth century, many Fulani had settled in cities, where they observed a strict form of Islam like that practiced in north Africa and Arabia. Beginning about 1680 and continuing through the nineteenth century, the Fulani led a series of military campaigns to establish Islamic states and impose their own brand of Islam in west Africa.

The Fulani and Islam

The Fulani did not by any means stamp out African religions, nor did they eliminate indigenous elements from the syncretic Islam practiced in west Africa. But they founded powerful states in what is now Guinea, Senegal, Mali, and northern Nigeria, and they promoted the spread of Islam beyond the cities to the countryside. They even established schools in remote towns and villages to teach the Quran and Islamic doctrine. Their campaigns strengthened Islam in sub-Saharan Africa and laid a foundation for new rounds of Islamic state-building and conversion efforts in the nineteenth and twentieth centuries.

Like Islam, Christianity made compromises with traditional beliefs and customs when it spread in sub-Saharan Africa. The Portuguese community in Kongo and Angola supported priests and missionaries who introduced Roman Catholic Christianity to central Africa. They found strong interest among rulers like King Affonso I of Kongo and his descendants, who eagerly adopted European-style Christianity as a foundation for commercial and political alliances with Portugal. Beyond the ruling courts, however, Christian teachings blended with African traditions to form syncretic cults. Africans regarded Christian missionaries as magicians and wore crosses and other Christian symbols as amulets to ward off danger from angry spirits.

Christianity in Sub-Saharan Africa

A particularly influential syncretic cult was the Antonian movement in Kongo, which flourished in the early eighteenth century, when the Kongolese monarchy faced challenges throughout the realm. The Antonian movement began in 1704 when an aristocratic woman called Dona Beatriz, formerly a priestess of an African religion, proclaimed that she had received communications from St. Anthony of Padua, a thirteenth-century Franciscan missionary and popular preacher. (Though buried in Padua, St. Anthony was a native of Portugal and was very popular among Portuguese missionaries, including those who worked in Kongo.) Dona Beatriz gained a reputation for working miracles and curing diseases, and she used her prominence to promote an African form of Christianity. She taught that Jesus Christ had been a black African man, that Kongo was the true holy land of Christianity, and that heaven was for Africans. She urged Kongolese to ignore European missionaries and heed her disciples instead, and she sought to harness the widespread popular interest in her teachings and use it to end the wars plaguing Kongo.

The Antonian Movement

The kings of Kongo retained their Christian faith even after their relations with Portuguese merchants and missionaries became strained in the seventeenth century. Here King Alvaro II—with European-style boots and a cross attached to his left sleeve—receives a Dutch embassy in 1642. ● Rare Books Division, New York Public Library. Astor, Lenox and Tilden Foundations

Dona Beatriz's movement was a serious challenge to Portuguese missionaries in Kongo. In 1706 they persuaded King Pedro IV of Kongo to arrest the charismatic prophetess on suspicion of heresy. Upon examining her, the missionaries satisfied themselves that Dona Beatriz was a false prophet and that she knowingly taught false doctrine. On their recommendation the royal government sentenced her to death and burned her at the stake. Yet the Antonian movement did not disappear: Dona Beatriz's disciples continued working to strengthen the monarchy and reconstruct Kongolese society. In 1708 an army of almost twenty thousand Antonians challenged King Pedro, whom they considered an unworthy ruler. Their efforts illustrate clearly the tendency of Kongolese Christians to fashion a faith that reflected their own needs and concerns as well as the interests of European missionaries.

Social Change in Early Modern Africa

Despite increased state-building activity and political turmoil, African society followed long-established patterns during the early modern era. Kinship groups, for example, the most important social units that emerged after the Bantu migrations, continued to serve as the basis of social organization and sometimes political organization as well. Within agricultural villages throughout sub-Saharan Africa, clans under the leadership of prominent men organized the affairs of their kinship groups and disciplined those who violated community standards. In regions where kingdoms and empires had not emerged, clan leaders consulted with each other and governed large regions. Indeed, even in lands ruled by formal states, clan leaders usually implemented state policy at the village level.

Yet interaction with European peoples brought change to African society in early modern times. Trade brought access to European textiles and metal goods. Africans had produced textiles and high-quality steel for centuries before the arrival of Portuguese mariners, but European products of different materials and styles became popular as complements to native African wares.

Trade also brought new food crops to sub-Saharan Africa. In the mid-sixteenth century American crops such as manioc, maize, and peanuts arrived in Africa aboard Portuguese ships. These crops supplemented bananas, yams, and millet, the principal staple foods that Bantu-speaking peoples had spread throughout sub-Saharan Africa. The most important American crop was manioc because of its high yield and because it thrived in tropical soils not well suited to cultivation of the other crops.

American Food Crops in Sub-Saharan Africa

By the eighteenth century bread made from manioc flour had become a staple food in much of west Africa and central Africa, where it helped to underwrite steady population growth. In 1500 C.E. the population of sub-Saharan Africa was about thirty-four million. By 1600 it had increased by almost one-third to forty-four million, and it continued climbing to fifty-two million in 1700 and sixty million in 1800. This strong demographic expansion is all the more remarkable because it took place precisely when millions of Africans underwent an involuntary, forced migration to destinations in the Caribbean and the Americas. Despite this migration, American food crops supported expanding populations in all regions of sub-Saharan Africa during early modern times.

Population Growth

THE ATLANTIC SLAVE TRADE

Of all the processes that linked Africa to the larger Atlantic world in early modern times, the most momentous was the Atlantic slave trade. From the fifteenth to the nineteenth century, European peoples looked to Africa as a source of labor for massive plantations that they established in the western hemisphere. In exchange for slaves African peoples received European manufactured products—most notably firearms, which they sometimes used to strengthen military forces that then sought further recruits for the slave trade. Only in the early nineteenth century did the Atlantic slave trade come to an end. During the course of the century, most states abolished the institution of slavery itself.

Foundations of the Slave Trade

The institution of slavery appeared in remote antiquity, and until the nineteenth century many all settled agricultural peoples made some place for slaves in their societies. Slavery was common throughout Africa after the Bantu migrations spread agriculture to all parts of the continent. As in other societies, most slaves came from the ranks of war captives, although criminals and individuals expelled from their clans also frequently fell into slavery. Once enslaved, an individual had no personal or civil rights. Owners could order slaves to perform any kind of work, punish them at will, and sell them as chattel. African slaves usually worked as cultivators in societies far from their homes, although some worked as administrators, soldiers, or even highly placed advisors. The Songhay emperors, for example, often employed slaves as administrators and soldiers, since the rulers distrusted free nobles, whom they considered excessively ambitious and undependable.

Slavery in Africa

Law and society made African slavery different from bondage in Europe, Asia, and other lands. African law did not recognize private property, but rather vested ownership of land in communities. Thus wealth and power in Africa came not from the possession of land, but rather from control over the human labor that made the land productive. Slaves were a form of private investment, a type of heritable property, and a means of measuring wealth. Those who controlled large numbers of individuals were able to harvest more crops and accumulate more wealth than others. Africans routinely purchased slaves to enlarge their families and enhance their power. Often they assimilated slaves into their kinship groups so that within a generation a slave might obtain both freedom and an honorable position in a new family or clan.

The Islamic Slave Trade   After the eighth century Muslim merchants from north Africa, Arabia, and Persia sought African slaves for sale and distribution to destinations in the Mediterranean basin, southwest Asia, India, and even southeast Asia and China. Muslim merchants obtained their human wares through established African networks that supplied slaves to continental consumers. Then the merchants transported their slaves across the Sahara desert by camel caravan for distribution in the Mediterranean basin or boarded them on ships at the Swahili port cities of east Africa for delivery to destinations across the Indian Ocean. During a millennium and more of the Islamic slave trade, which lasted into the twentieth century, as many as ten million Africans may have left their homeland in servitude.

By the time Europeans ventured to sub-Saharan Africa in the fifteenth and sixteenth centuries, traffic in slaves was a well-established feature of African society, and a system for capturing, selling, and distributing slaves had functioned effectively for more than five hundred years. When Europeans began to pursue commercial interests in Africa and the Americas, the slave trade expanded dramatically. After 1450 European peoples tapped existing networks and expanded commerce in African slaves from the Mediterranean and the Indian Ocean to the Atlantic Ocean basin. This Atlantic slave trade brought about an enormous involuntary migration that influenced the development of societies throughout the Atlantic Ocean basin.

Human Cargoes

The Atlantic slave trade began small, but it grew steadily and eventually reached massive proportions. The earliest European slave traders were Portuguese explorers who reconnoitered the west African coast in the mid-fifteenth century. In 1441 a raiding party seized twelve African men and took them to Portugal as slaves. Portuguese mariners soon learned that they could purchase slaves instead of capturing them, and by 1460 the mariners were delivering five hundred slaves per year to Portugal and Spain. In Europe African slaves usually worked as miners, porters, or domestic servants, since free peasants and serfs cultivated the land.

The Early Slave Trade   Slave traders also delivered their human cargoes to Portuguese island colonies in the Atlantic. There was no supply of labor to work plantations in the Azores, Madeiras, Cape Verde Islands, and São Tomé, all of which were uninhabited when explorers discovered them in the fifteenth century. The Portuguese population was too small to provide large numbers of colonists. Sugar planters on the island of São Tomé in particular called for slaves in increasing quantities. They relied on slave labor, and production soared along with the demand for sugar in Europe. By the 1520s some two thousand slaves per year went to São Tomé. Soon thereafter Portuguese entrepreneurs extended the use of slave labor to South America. During the 1530s Portuguese planters imported slaves directly from Kongo and Angola to Brazil, which eventually became the wealthiest of the sugar-producing lands of the western hemisphere.

Meanwhile, Spanish explorers and conquerors also sought laborers to work lands in the Caribbean and the Americas. As imported diseases ravaged indigenous populations in the western hemisphere, the conquerors found themselves in possession of vast stretches of land but few laborers to work it. The Spanish attempted to harness the labor of those who survived the diseases, but native peoples frequently revolted against their overlords or simply escaped into the hinterlands. Gradually Spanish settlers began to rely on imported African slaves as laborers. In 1518 the first shipment of slaves went directly from west Africa to the Caribbean, where they worked on recently established sugar plantations. During the 1520s Spanish authorities introduced slaves to Mexico, Peru, and Central America, where they worked as cultivators and miners. By the early seventeenth century, English colonists had introduced slaves also to the North American mainland.

The demand for labor in the western hemisphere stimulated a profitable commerce known as the **triangular trade**, since European ships often undertook voyages of three legs. On the first leg they carried European manufactured goods—mostly cloth and metal wares, especially firearms—that they exchanged in Africa for slaves. The second leg took enslaved Africans to Caribbean and American destinations. Upon arrival merchants sold their human cargoes to plantation owners for two to three times what they had cost on the African coast. Sometimes they exchanged slaves for cash, but in sugar-producing regions they often bartered slaves for sugar or molasses. Then they filled their vessels' hulls with American products before embarking on their voyage back to Europe.

A bronze plaque from Benin offers an early African view of Europeans: it depicts a Portuguese soldier armed with a musket and accompanied by a dog.

● © The British Museum

Triangular Trade

At every stage of the process, the slave trade was a brutal and inhumane business. The original capture of slaves in Africa was almost always a violent affair. As European demand for slaves grew, some African chieftains organized raiding parties to

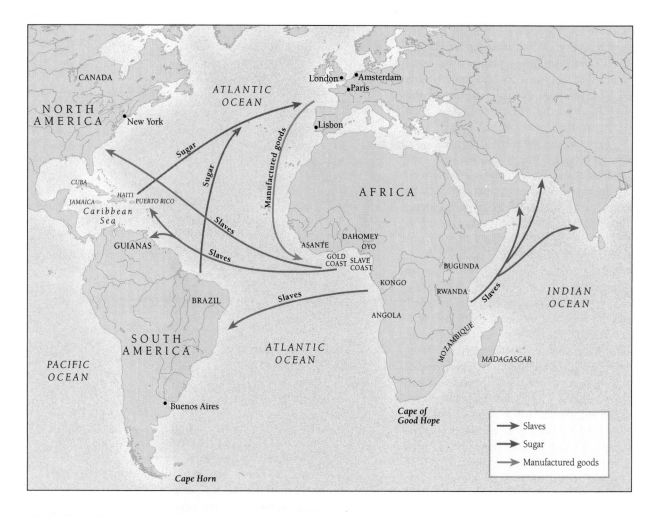

MAP [25.2]

The Atlantic slave trade.

seize individuals from neighboring societies. Others launched wars for the purpose of capturing victims for the slave trade. They often snatched individuals right out of their homes, fields, or villages: millions of lives changed instantly, as slave raiders grabbed their quarries and then immediately spirited them away in captivity. Bewilderment and anger was the lot not only of the captives but also of their family members, who would never again see their kin.

The Middle Passage   Following capture, enslaved individuals underwent a forced march to the coast where they lived in holding pens until a ship arrived to transport them to the western hemisphere. Then they embarked on the dreadful "middle passage," the trans-Atlantic journey aboard filthy and crowded slave ships. Enslaved passengers traveled below decks in hideously cramped quarters. Most ships provided slaves with enough room to sit upright, although not to stand, but some forced them to lie in chains on shelves with barely half a meter (twenty inches) of space between them. Conditions were so bad that many slaves attempted to starve themselves to death or mounted revolts. Ship crews attempted to preserve the lives of slaves, intending to sell them for a profit at the end of the voyage, but often treated the unwilling passengers with cruelty and contempt. Crew members used tools to pry open the mouths of those who refused to eat and pitched sick individuals into the ocean rather than have them infect others or waste limited supplies of food.

OLAUDAH EQUIANO ON THE MIDDLE PASSAGE

• • •

Olaudah Equiano (1745–1797) was a native of Benin in west Africa. When he was ten years old, slave raiders seized him and his sister at home while their parents were tending the fields. He spent the next twenty-one years as a slave. Then Equiano purchased his freedom and worked against the slave trade for the rest of his life. In his autobiography of 1789, Equiano described the horrors of the middle passage.

The first object which saluted my eyes when I arrived on the coast was the sea, and a slave ship which was then riding at anchor and waiting for its cargo. These filled me with astonishment, which was soon converted into terror when I was carried on board. I was immediately handled and tossed up to see if I were sound by some of the crew, and I was now persuaded that I had gotten into a world of bad spirits and that they were going to kill me. . . .

I was not long suffered to indulge my grief; I was soon put down under the decks, and there I received such a salutation in my nostrils as I had never experienced in my life: so that with the loathsomeness of the stench and crying together, I became so sick and low that I was not able to eat, nor had I the least desire to taste anything. I now wished for the last friend, death, to relieve me; but soon, to my grief, two of the white men offered me eatables, and on my refusing to eat, one of them held me fast by the hands and laid me across I think the windlass and tied my feet while the other flogged me severely. I had never experienced anything of this kind before, and although not being used to the water I naturally feared that element the first time I saw it, yet nevertheless if I could have gotten over the nettings I would have jumped over the side, but I could not; and besides, the crew used to watch very closely over those of us who were not chained down to the decks, lest we should leap into the water: and I have seen some of these poor African prisoners most severely cut for attempting to do so, and hourly whipped for not eating. This indeed was often the case with myself. . . .

One day when we had a smooth sea and moderate wind, two of my wearied countrymen who were chained together (I was near them at the time), preferring death to such a life of misery, somehow made through the nettings and jumped into the sea: immediately another quite dejected fellow, who on account of his illness was suffered to be out of irons, also followed their example; and I believe many more would very soon have done the same if they had not been prevented by the ship's crew, who were instantly alarmed. Those of us that were the most active were in a moment put down under the deck, and there was such a noise and confusion amongst the people of the ship as I never heard before, to stop her and get the boat to go after the slaves. However, two of the wretches were drowned, but they got the other and afterwards flogged him unmercifully for thus attempting to prefer death to slavery. In this manner we continued to undergo more hardships than I can now relate, hardships which are inseparable from this accursed trade.

SOURCE: Olaudah Equiano. *The Interesting Narrative of the Life of Olaudah Equiano, or Gustavus Vassa, the African, Written by Himself,* 2 vols. London, 1789. (Translation slightly modified.)

Barring difficulties, the journey to Caribbean and American destinations took four to six weeks, during which heat, cold, and disease levied a heavy toll on the human cargo. During the early days of the slave trade on particularly cramped ships, mortality sometimes exceeded 50 percent. As the volume of the trade grew, slavers built larger ships, carried more water, and provided better nourishment and facilities for their cargoes, and mortality eventually declined to about 5 percent per voyage. Over the course of the Atlantic slave trade, however, approximately one-quarter of individuals enslaved in Africa did not survive the middle passage.

The Impact of the Slave Trade in Africa

*Volume of the
Slave Trade*

Before 1600 the Atlantic slave trade operated on a modest scale. Annual export figures varied considerably, but on average about two thousand slaves left Africa for American destinations during the fifteenth and sixteenth centuries. During the seventeenth century slave exports rose dramatically to twenty thousand per year, as European peoples settled in the western hemisphere and called for African labor to cultivate their lands. The high point of the slave trade came in the eighteenth century, when the number of slaves exported to the Americas averaged fifty-five thousand per year. During the 1780s slave arrivals averaged eighty-eight thousand per year, and in some individual years they exceeded one hundred thousand. From beginning to end the Atlantic slave trade brought about the involuntary migration of about twelve million Africans to the western hemisphere. Another four million or more died resisting seizure or during captivity before arriving at their intended destination.

The impact of the slave trade varied over time and from one African society to another. The kingdoms of Rwanda and Bugunda on the great lakes and the herding societies of the Masai and Turkana of east Africa largely escaped the slave trade, partly because they resisted it and partly because their lands were distant from the major slave ports on the west African coast. Other societies flourished during early modern times and benefited economically from the slave trade. Those Africans who raided, took captives, and sold slaves to Europeans profited handsomely from the trade, as did the port cities and the states that coordinated trade with European merchants. Asante, Dahomey, and Oyo peoples, for example, took advantage of the slave trade to obtain firearms from European merchants and build powerful states in west Africa. In the nineteenth century, after the abolition of slavery, some African merchants complained bitterly about losing their livelihood and tried to undermine the efforts of the British navy to patrol Atlantic waters and put an end to slave trading.

*Social Effects
of the Slave Trade*

On the whole, however, Africa suffered serious losses from the slave trade. The Atlantic slave trade alone deprived African societies of about sixteen million individuals, in addition to another several million consumed by the continuing Islamic slave trade during the early modern era. Although total African population rose during the early modern era, partly because American food crops enriched diets, several individual societies experienced severe losses because of the slave trade. West African societies between Senegal and Angola were especially vulnerable to slave raiding because of their proximity to the most active slave ports.

While diverting labor from Africa to other lands, the slave trade also distorted African sex ratios, since approximately two-thirds of all exported slaves were males. Slavers preferred young men between fourteen and thirty-five years of age, since they had the best potential to repay their buyers' investments by providing heavy labor over an extended period of time. This preference for male slaves had social implications for lands that provided slaves. By the late eighteenth century, for example, women made up more than two-thirds of the adult population of Angola. This sexual imbalance encouraged Angolans to practice polygamy and forced women to take on duties, such as working in the fields, that formerly had fallen to men.

*Political Effects
of the Slave Trade*

Apart from its demographic and social effects, the slave trade also brought turmoil to African societies. During early modern times African peoples fought many wars for reasons that had little or nothing to do with the slave trade, but it encouraged them to participate also in conflicts that might never have occurred in the absence of the trade.

Violence escalated especially after the late seventeenth century, when African peoples increasingly exchanged slaves for European firearms. When the kingdom of Dahomey obtained effective firearms, for example, its armies were able to capture slaves from unarmed neighboring societies and exchange them for more weapons. During the eighteenth century Dahomey expanded rapidly and absorbed neighboring societies by increasing its arsenal of firearms and maintaining a constant flow of slaves to the coast. Indeed, the Dahomey army, which included a regiment of women soldiers, became largely a slave-raiding force. By no means did all African states take such advantage of the slave trade, but Dahomey's experience illustrates the potential of the slave trade to alter the normal patterns of African politics and society.

THE AFRICAN DIASPORA

Some slaves worked as urban laborers or domestic servants, and in Mexico and Peru many worked also as miners. The vast majority, however, provided agricultural labor on plantations in the Caribbean or the Americas. There they cultivated cash crops that made their way into commercial arteries linking lands throughout the Atlantic Ocean basin. Although deprived of their freedom, slaves often resisted their bondage, and they built hybrid cultural traditions compounded of African, European, and American elements. Most European and American states ended the slave trade and abolished slavery during the nineteenth century. By that time the African diaspora—the dispersal of African peoples and their descendants—had left a permanent mark throughout the western hemisphere.

Plantation Societies

Most African slaves went to plantations in the tropical and subtropical regions of the western hemisphere. When European peoples arrived in the Caribbean and the Americas, they found vast stretches of fertile land and almost immediately began to envision huge profits from plantations that would satisfy the growing European demand for sugar and other agricultural commodities. Spanish colonists established the first of these plantations in 1516 on the island of Hispaniola (which embraces modern Haiti and the Dominican Republic) and soon extended them to Mexico as well. Beginning in the 1530s Portuguese entrepreneurs organized plantations in Brazil, and by the early seventeenth century English, Dutch, and French plantations had also appeared in the Caribbean and the Americas.

Many of these plantations produced sugar, which was one of the most lucrative cash crops of early modern times. But plantations produced other crops as well. During the seventeenth century tobacco rivaled sugar as a profitable product. Rice also became a major plantation product, as did indigo. By the eighteenth century many plantations concentrated on the cultivation of cotton, and coffee had begun to emerge as a plantation specialty.

Cash Crops

Regardless of the crops they produced, Caribbean and American plantations had certain elements in common. All of them specialized in the production of some agricultural crop in high demand: plantations often maintained gardens that produced food for the local community, but their purpose was to profit from the production and export of commercial crops. In efforts to operate efficiently and profitably, plantations relied almost exclusively on slave labor: plantation communities often included a hundred or more slaves, whose uncompensated labor services helped keep

In an engraving of 1667, a European supervisor (lower right) directs slaves on a sugar plantation in Barbados as they haul cane, crush it to extract its juice, boil it to produce molasses, and distill the product into rum. • Arents Collection. Rare Books Division, New York Public Library. Astor, Lenox and Tilden Foundations

their agricultural products competitive. Plantations also featured a sharp, racial division of labor: small numbers of European or Euro-American supervisors governed plantation affairs, and large numbers of African or African-American slaves performed most of the community's physical labor.

In spite of their structural similarities, plantation societies differed considerably from one region to another. In the Caribbean and South America, slave populations usually were unable to sustain their numbers by natural means. Many slaves fell victim to tropical diseases like malaria and yellow fever. On the plantations they faced brutal working conditions and low standards of sanitation and nutrition. Moreover, slaves had low rates of reproduction because plantation owners mostly imported male slaves and allowed only a few to establish families. Thus in the Caribbean and South America, plantation owners imported continuing streams of slaves from Africa to maintain their work forces. Of all the slaves delivered from Africa to the western hemisphere, about half went to Caribbean destinations, and another third went to Brazil. Smaller numbers went to other destinations in South America and Central America.

Only about 5 percent of enslaved Africans went to North American destinations. Diseases there were less threatening than in the Caribbean and Brazil, and in some ways the conditions of slaves' lives were less harsh than in the more southerly regions. North American planters imported larger numbers of female slaves and encouraged their slaves to form families and bear children. Their support for slave families was especially strong in the eighteenth century, when the prices of fresh slaves from Africa rose dramatically.

Slaves were vulnerable to cruel treatment that often provoked them to run away from their plantations or even mount revolts. A French visitor to Brazil in the early nineteenth century depicted a Portuguese overseer administering a brutal whipping to a bound slave on a plantation near Rio de Janeiro. ● From Debret. *Voyages Pittoresque et Historiques au Bresil, 1816–1831,* New York Public Library. Astor, Lenox and Tilden Foundations

Resistance to Slavery

No matter where they lived, slaves did not meekly accept their servile status, but like Thomas Peters resisted it in numerous ways. Some forms of resistance were mild but costly to slave owners: slaves often worked slowly for their masters but diligently in their own gardens, for example. They occasionally sabotaged plantation equipment or work routines. A more serious form of resistance involved running away from the plantation community. Runaways known as maroons gathered in mountainous, forested, or swampy regions and built their own self-governing communities. Maroons often raided nearby plantations for arms, tools, provisions, and even slaves to increase their own numbers or to provide labor for their communities. Many maroons had gained military experience in Africa, and they organized escaped slaves into effective military forces. Maroon communities flourished throughout slave-holding regions of the western hemisphere, and some of them survived for centuries. In present-day Suriname, for example, the Saramaka people maintain an elaborate oral tradition that traces their descent from eighteenth-century maroons.

Slave Revolts

The most dramatic form of resistance to slavery was the slave revolt. Slaves far outnumbered others in most plantation societies, and they had the potential to organize and overwhelm their masters. Slave revolts brought stark fear to plantation owners and supervisors, and they often resulted in widespread death and destruction. Yet slave revolts almost never brought slavery itself to an end, because the European and Euro-American ruling elites had access to arms, horses, and military forces that extinguished most rebellions. Only in the French sugar colony of Saint-Domingue did a slave revolt abolish slavery as an institution (1793). Indeed, the slaves of Saint-Domingue declared independence from France, renamed the land Haiti, and established a self-governing republic (1804). The Haitian revolution terrified slave owners and inspired slaves throughout the western hemisphere, but no other slave rebellion matched its accomplishments.

The Making of African-American Cultural Traditions

Enslaved Africans did not enjoy the luxury of maintaining their inherited cultural traditions in the western hemisphere. They often preserved African traditions, including languages and religions, but had to adapt to societies compounded of various European and American as well as African elements. When packed in slave ships for the middle passage, they found themselves in the company of Africans from societies other than their own. When sold to masters in the Caribbean and the Americas, they joined societies shaped by European and American traditions. In adapting to new circumstances, slaves constructed distinctive African-American cultural traditions.

African and Creole Languages

European languages were the dominant tongues in the slave societies of the western hemisphere, but African languages also influenced communication. Occasionally African slaves from a particular region were numerous enough to speak among themselves in their native tongues. More often they spoke a creole tongue that drew on several African and European languages. In the low country of South Carolina and Georgia, for example, slaves made up about three-quarters of the population in the eighteenth century and regularly communicated in the creole languages Gullah and Geechee, respectively.

African-American Religions

Like their languages, slaves' religions also combined elements from different societies. Some slaves shipped out of Africa were Christians, and many others converted to Christianity after their arrival in the western hemisphere. Most Africans and African-Americans did not practice European Christianity, however, but rather a syncretic faith that made considerable room for African interests and traditions. Because they developed mostly in plantation societies under conditions of slavery, these syncretic religions usually did not create an institutional structure or establish a hierarchy of priests and other church officials. Yet in several cases—most notably Vodou in Haiti, Santeria in Cuba, and Candomblé in Brazil—they became exceedingly popular among slaves.

All the syncretic, African-American religions drew inspiration from Christianity: they met in parish churches, sought personal salvation, and made use of European Christian paraphernalia like holy water, candles, and statues. Yet they also preserved African traditions. They associated African deities with Christian saints and relied heavily on African rituals like drumming, dancing, and sacrificing animals. Indeed, the core of these syncretic faiths was often participation in rituals like those observed in Africa. They also preserved beliefs in spirits and supernatural powers: magic, sorcery, witchcraft, and spirit possession all played prominent roles in African-American religions.

African-American Cultural Traditions

African traditions also made their effects felt throughout much of the western hemisphere. Slaves introduced African foods to Caribbean and American societies and helped give rise to distinctive hybrid cuisines. They combined African okra, for example, with European-style sauteed vegetables and American shellfish to produce magnificent gumbos, which found their way to Euro-American as well as African-American tables. (*Okra* and *gumbo* are both African words.) Slaves introduced rice cultivation to tropical and subtropical regions, including South Carolina, Georgia, and Louisiana, and added variety to American diets. They also built houses, fashioned clay pots, and wove grass baskets in west African styles. In many ways the African diaspora influenced the ways all peoples lived in plantation societies.

The End of the Slave Trade and the Abolition of Slavery

Almost as old as the Atlantic slave trade itself were voices calling for its abolition. The American and French revolutions stimulated the abolitionist cause. The American call for "life, liberty, and the pursuit of happiness" and the French appeal for "liberty, equality, and fraternity" suggested that there was a universal human right to freedom and equality.

Olaudah Equiano

Africans also took up the struggle to abolish commerce in human beings. Frequent slave revolts in the eighteenth and nineteenth centuries made the institution of slavery an expensive and dangerous business. Some freed slaves contributed to the abolitionist cause by writing books that exposed the brutality of institutional slavery. Most notable of them was the west African Olaudah Equiano (1745–1797), who in 1789 published an autobiography detailing his experiences as a slave and free man. Captured at age ten in his native Benin (in modern Nigeria), Equiano worked as a slave in the West Indies, Virginia, and Pennsylvania. He accompanied one of his masters on several campaigns of the Seven Years' War before purchasing his freedom in 1766. Equiano's book became a best-seller, and the author traveled throughout the

Olaudah Equiano as depicted in the first edition of his autobiography (1789). • Manuscripts, Archives and Rare Books Division, Schomburg Center for Research in Black Culture, The New York Public Library. Astor, Lenox and Tilden Foundations

British isles giving speeches and denouncing slavery as an evil institution. He lobbied government officials and members of Parliament, and his efforts strengthened the antislavery movement in England.

Quite apart from moral and political arguments, economic forces also contributed to the end of slavery and the slave trade. Plantations, slavery, and the slave trade continued to flourish as long as they were profitable, notwithstanding the efforts of abolitionists. Yet it gradually became clear that slave labor did not come cheap. The possibility of rebellion forced slave societies to maintain expensive military forces. Even in peaceful times slaves often worked unenthusiastically, but owners had to care for them throughout their lives no matter how hard they

The Economic Costs of Slavery

worked. Furthermore, in the late eighteenth century a rapid expansion of Caribbean sugar production led to declining prices. About the same time, African slave traders and European merchants sharply increased the prices they charged for fresh slaves.

As the profitability of slavery declined, Europeans began to shift their investments from sugarcane and slaves to newly emerging manufacturing industries. Investors soon found that wage labor in factories was cheaper than slave labor on plantations. As an additional benefit, free workers spent much of their income on manufactured goods. Meanwhile, European investors realized that leaving Africans in Africa where they could secure raw materials and buy manufactured goods in exchange was good business. Thus European entrepreneurs began to look upon Africa as something other than a source of slave labor.

End of the Slave Trade

In 1803 Denmark abolished trade in slaves, and other lands followed the Danish example: Great Britain in 1807, the United States in 1808, France in 1814, the Netherlands in 1817, and Spain in 1845. The end of the legal commerce in slaves did not abolish the institution of slavery itself, however, and as long as plantation slavery continued, a clandestine trade shipped slaves across the Atlantic. British naval squadrons sought to prevent this trade by patrolling the west coast of Africa conducting search and seizure operations, and gradually the illegal slave trade ground to a halt. The last documented ship that carried slaves across the Atlantic arrived in Cuba in 1867.

The Abolition of Slavery

The abolition of the institution of slavery itself was a long and drawn-out process: emancipation of all slaves came in 1833 in British colonies, 1848 in French colonies, 1865 in the United States, 1886 in Cuba, and 1888 in Brazil. Saudi Arabia and Angola abolished slavery in the 1960s. Officially, slavery no longer exists, but millions of people live in various forms of servitude even today. According to the Anti-Slavery Society for the Protection of Human Rights, debt bondage, contract labor, sham adoptions, servile marriages, and other forms of servitude still oppress more than two hundred million people, mostly in Africa, south Asia, and Latin America. Meanwhile, the legacy of the Atlantic slave trade remains visible throughout much of the western hemisphere, where the African diaspora has given rise to distinctive African-American communities.

During the early modern era, the peoples of sub-Saharan Africa organized societies on the basis of kinship groups as they had since the early days of the Bantu migrations. They also built states and traded with Islamic societies as they had since the eighth century C.E. Yet African peoples also experienced dramatic changes as they participated in the formation of an integrated Atlantic Ocean basin. The principal agents of change were European merchant-mariners who sought commercial opportunities in sub-Saharan Africa. They brought European manufactured goods and introduced American food crops that fueled population growth throughout Africa. But they also encouraged vast expansion of existing slave-trading networks as they sought laborers for plantations in the western hemisphere. The Atlantic slave trade violently removed sixteen million or more individuals from their home societies, and it led to political turmoil and social disruption throughout much of sub-Saharan Africa. Enslaved Africans and their descendants were mostly unable to build states or organize societies in the western hemisphere. But they formed an African diaspora that maintained some African traditions and profoundly influenced the development of societies in all slave-holding regions of the Caribbean and the Americas. They also collaborated with others to bring about an end to the slave trade and the abolition of slavery itself.

CHRONOLOGY

1441	Beginning of the Portuguese slave trade
1464–1493	Reign of Sunni Ali
1464–1591	Songhay empire
1506–1543	Reign of King Affonso I
1623–1663	Reign of Queen Nzinga
1706	Execution of Dona Beatriz
1745–1797	Life of Olaudah Equiano
1793–1804	Haitian revolution
1807	End of the British slave trade
1865	Abolition of slavery in the United States

FOR FURTHER READING

Paul Bohannan and Philip D. Curtin. *Africa and Africans.* 3rd ed. Prospect Heights, Ill., 1988. General discussion of African society, religion, and history by an anthropologist and a historian.

Michael L. Conniff and Thomas J. Davis. *Africans in the Americas: A History of the Black Diaspora.* New York, 1994. A comprehensive survey of African-European relations, the slave trade, and the African diaspora.

Philip D. Curtin. *The Rise and Fall of the Plantation Complex: Essays in Atlantic History.* 2nd ed. Cambridge, 1998. Examines plantation societies and slavery as institutions linking lands throughout the Atlantic Ocean basin.

———, ed. *Africa Remembered: Narratives by West Africans from the Era of the Slave Trade.* Madison, 1967. Translations of works in which ten enslaved Africans recounted their memories of early modern Africa.

Basil Davidson. *The African Slave Trade.* Rev. ed. Boston, 1980. A popular history of the slave trade by a prominent student of African history.

David Brion Davis. *Slavery and Human Progress.* New York, 1984. A rich and thoughtful book that places African slavery in a larger historical context.

Olaudah Equiano. *Equiano's Travels.* Ed. by Paul Edwards. Oxford, 1967. An abridged and conveniently available edition of Equiano's autobiography.

Leland Ferguson. *Uncommon Ground: Archaeology and Early African America, 1650–1800.* Washington, 1992. Enriches the understanding of slave society in the southeastern United States on the basis of recent archaeological discoveries.

Joseph E. Harris, ed. *Global Dimensions of the African Diaspora.* 2nd ed. Washington, 1993. A collection of scholarly essays on Africans in the Americas and the larger world.

Anne Hilton. *The Kingdom of Kongo.* Oxford, 1985. A synthesis of recent scholarship.

Patrick Manning. *Slavery and African Life: Occidental, Oriental, and African Slave Trades.* Cambridge, 1990. Concentrates on the impact of the slave trade on Africa.

Sidney W. Mintz and Richard Price. *The Birth of African-American Culture: An Anthropological Perspective.* Boston, 1992. A provocative study analyzing the transformation of African cultural traditions under the influence of slavery.

Richard Price. *First-Time: The Historical Vision of an Afro-American People*. Baltimore, 1983. Fascinating reconstruction of the experiences and historical self-understanding of the Saramaka maroons of modern Suriname.

James Rawley. *The Transatlantic Slave Trade: A History*. New York, 1981. A reliable survey concentrating on the roles of European and Euro-American peoples in the slave trade.

Mechal Sobel. *The World They Made Together: Black and White Values in Eighteenth Century Virginia*. Princeton, 1987. Argues persuasively that African-American slaves deeply influenced the development of early American society.

Barbara L. Solow, ed. *Slavery and the Rise of the Atlantic System*. Cambridge, 1991. An important collection of scholarly essays on slavery and its implications for the history of the Atlantic Ocean basin.

John Thornton. *Africa and Africans in the Making of the Atlantic World, 1400–1800*. 2nd ed. New York, 1997. A rich analysis of African peoples and their roles in the Atlantic Ocean basin.

———. *The Kongolese Saint Anthony: Dona Beatriz Kimpa Vita and the Antonian Movement, 1684–1706*. Cambridge, 1998. Excellent scholarly study of Dona Beatriz and the Antonian movement in the kingdom of Kongo.

Jan Vansina. *Kingdoms of the Savanna*. Madison, 1966. The best history of central Africa in early modern times.

———. *Paths in the Rainforest: Toward a History of Political Tradition in Equatorial Africa*. Madison, 1990. A thoughtful analysis that considers both native traditions and external influences on African history.

CHAPTER 26

TRADITION AND CHANGE
IN EAST ASIA

• • •

In January 1601 a mechanical clock chimed the hours for the first time in the city of Beijing. In the early 1580s devices that Chinese called "self-ringing bells" had arrived at the port of Macau, where Portuguese merchants awed local authorities with their chiming clocks. Reports of them soon spread throughout southern China and beyond to Beijing. The Roman Catholic missionary Matteo Ricci conceived the idea of capturing the emperor's attention with mechanical clocks and then persuading him and his subjects to convert to Christianity. From his post at Macau, Ricci let imperial authorities know that he could supply the emperor with a chiming clock. When Emperor Wanli granted him permission to travel to Beijing and establish a mission there, Ricci took with him both a large mechanical clock intended for public display and a smaller self-ringing bell for the emperor's personal use.

Chiming mechanical clocks enchanted Wanli and his court and soon became the rage in elite society throughout China. Wealthy Chinese merchants did not hesitate to pay handsome sums for the devices, and Europeans often found that their business in China went better if they presented gifts of self-ringing bells to the government officials they dealt with. By the eighteenth century the imperial court maintained a workshop to manufacture and repair mechanical clocks and watches. Most Chinese could not afford to purchase mechanical clocks, but commoners also had opportunities to admire self-ringing bells. Outside their residence in Beijing, Matteo Ricci and his missionary colleagues installed a large mechanical clock that regularly attracted crowds of curious neighbors when it struck the hours.

Chiming clocks did not have the effect that Ricci desired. The emperor showed no interest in Christianity, and the missionaries attracted only small numbers of Chinese converts. Yet by opening the doors of the imperial court to the missionaries, the self-ringing bells symbolized the increasing engagement between Asian and European peoples.

By linking all the world's regions and peoples, the European voyages of exploration inaugurated a new era in world history. Yet transoceanic connections influenced different societies in very different ways. In contrast to sub-Saharan Africa, where the Atlantic slave trade bred instability and provoked turmoil, east Asian lands benefited greatly from long-distance trade, since it brought silver that stimulated their economies. East Asian societies benefited also from American plant crops that made their way across the seas as part of the Columbian exchange.

Dutch ships and Japanese vessels mingle in Nagasaki harbor. • Laurie Platt Winfrey, Inc.

Unlike the Americas, where Europeans profoundly influenced historical development from the time of their arrival, east Asian societies largely controlled their own affairs until the nineteenth century. Europeans were active on the coastlines, but they had little influence on internal affairs in the region. Because of its political and cultural preeminence, China remained the dominant power in east Asia. Long-standing political, social, and cultural traditions endowed Chinese society with a sense of stability and permanence. Beneath the surface, however, Chinese society experienced rapid and profound change, most notably economic and social transformations that affected virtually all aspects of society.

During the seventeenth and eighteenth centuries, Japan also underwent major transformations. The Tokugawa shoguns unified the Japanese islands for the first time and laid a foundation for long-term economic growth. While tightly restricting contacts and relations with the larger world, Tokugawa Japan generated a distinctive set of social and cultural traditions. These developments helped fashion a Japan that would play a decisive role in global affairs by the twentieth century.

THE QUEST FOR POLITICAL STABILITY

During the thirteenth and fourteenth centuries, China experienced the trauma of rule by the Yuan dynasty (1279–1368) of nomadic Mongol warriors. Mongol overlords ignored Chinese political and cultural traditions, and they displaced Chinese bureaucrats in favor of Turkish, Persian, and other foreign administrators. When the Yuan dynasty came to an end, the Ming emperors who succeeded it sought to erase all signs of Mongol influence and restore traditional ways to China. Rulers of the succeeding Qing dynasty were themselves Manchus of nomadic origin, but they too worked zealously to promote Chinese ways. The Ming and Qing emperors were intensely conservative, and they looked to the Tang and Song dynasties for precedents to guide their political and cultural policies. In an effort to maintain Chinese political and cultural traditions, the Ming and Qing emperors fashioned a state that governed China for more than half a millennium.

The Ming Dynasty

Ming Government   When the Yuan dynasty collapsed, the Ming dynasty (1368–1644) restored native rule to China. Emperor Hongwu (1368–1398), founder of the Ming ("brilliant") dynasty, drove the Mongols out of China and built a tightly centralized state. Hongwu made extensive use of mandarins, imperial officials who traveled throughout the land and oversaw implementation of government policies. He also placed great trust in eunuchs on the thinking that they could not generate families and hence would not build power bases that would challenge imperial authority. Emperor Yongle (1403–1424) launched a series of naval expeditions that sailed throughout the Indian Ocean basin and showed Chinese colors as far away as Malindi in east Africa. Yongle's successors discontinued the expensive maritime expeditions but maintained the tightly centralized state that Hongwu had established.

The Ming emperors were determined to prevent new invasions. In 1421 Yongle moved the capital from Nanjing in the south to Beijing so as to keep closer watch on the Mongols and other nomadic peoples in the north. The early Ming emperors commanded powerful armies that controlled the Mongols militarily, but by the mid-fifteenth century they had lost their effectiveness. Mongol forces massacred several Chinese armies in the 1440s, and in 1449 they captured the Ming emperor himself.

The later Ming emperors sought to protect their realm by building new fortifications, including the Great Wall of China, along the northern border. The Great Wall had precedents dating back to the fourth century B.C.E., and the first emperor of the Qin dynasty had ordered construction of a long defensive wall during the third century B.C.E. These early walls had all fallen into ruin, however, and the Great Wall was a Ming-dynasty project. Workers by the hundreds of thousands labored throughout the late fifteenth and sixteenth centuries to build a formidable stone and brick barrier that ran some 2,500 kilometers (1,550 miles). The Great Wall was ten to fifteen meters (thirty-three to forty-nine feet) high, and it featured watch towers, signal towers, and accommodations for troops deployed on the border.

The Great Wall

The Ming emperors also set out to eradicate Mongol and other foreign influences and to create a stable society in the image of the Chinese past. With Ming encouragement, for example, individuals abandoned the Mongol names and dress that many had adopted during the Yuan dynasty. Respect for Chinese traditions facilitated the restoration of institutions that the Mongols had ignored or suppressed. The government sponsored study of Chinese cultural traditions, especially Confucianism, and provided financial support for imperial academies and regional colleges. Most important, the Ming state restored the system of civil service examinations that Mongol rulers had neglected.

The vigor of early Ming rule did not survive beyond the mid-sixteenth century, when a series of problems weakened the dynasty. From the 1520s to the 1560s, pirates and smugglers operated almost at will along the east coast of China. (Although Ming officials referred to the pirates as Japanese, in fact most of them were Chinese.)

Ming Decline

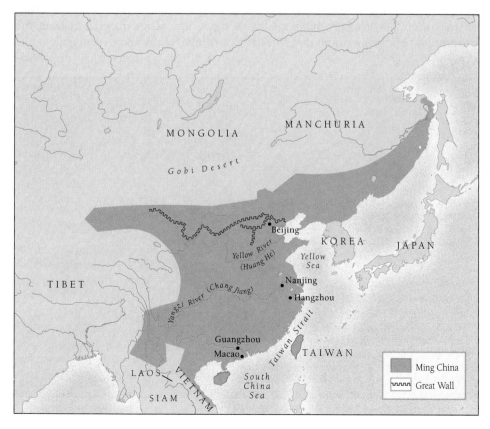

MAP [26.1]

Ming China.

Both the Ming navy and coastal defenses were ineffective, and conflicts with pirates often led to the disruption of coastal communities and sometimes even interior regions. In 1555, for example, a band of sixty-seven pirates went on a three-month rampage during which they looted a dozen cities in three provinces and killed more than four thousand people.

Suppression of pirates took more than forty years, partly because of an increasingly inept imperial government. The later Ming emperors lived extravagantly in the Forbidden City, a vast imperial enclave in Beijing, and received news about the outside world from eunuch servants and administrators. The emperors sometimes ignored government affairs for decades on end while satisfying their various appetites. Throughout his long reign, for example, Emperor Wanli (1572–1620) refused to meet with government officials. Instead, while indulging his taste for wine and opium, he conducted business through eunuch intermediaries. Powerful eunuchs won the favor of the later Ming emperors by procuring concubines for them and providing for their amusement. The eunuchs then used their power and position to enrich themselves and lead lives of luxury. As their influence increased, corruption and inefficiency spread throughout the government and weakened the Ming state.

Ming Collapse When a series of famines struck China during the early seventeenth century, the government was unable to organize effective relief efforts. Peasants in famine-struck regions ate grass roots and tree bark. During the 1630s peasants organized revolts throughout China, and they gathered momentum as one city after another withdrew its loyalty from the Ming dynasty. Manchu invaders from the north allied with the rebels and joined them in attacking the Ming dynasty. By the early 1640s the combined rebel and Manchu forces controlled most of China and turned toward the capital at Beijing. Sheltered from bad news by court eunuchs, the last Ming emperor reportedly did not even know the location of rebel forces until they began to clamber over the walls of the Forbidden City. As rebels looted the imperial quarter, the emperor and his family committed suicide. The Ming dynasty came to an end.

Emperor Yongle designed the Forbidden City as a vast, walled imperial retreat in central Beijing. Here a sculptured lion guards the Forbidden City's Gate of Supreme Harmony.

● © 1996 Harvey Lloyd/ The Stock Market

The Qing Dynasty

When the Ming dynasty fell, Manchus poured into China from their homeland of Manchuria north of the Great Wall. They overwhelmed the Chinese rebel forces, seized Beijing, and proceeded to occupy all of China. The victors proclaimed a new dynasty, the Qing ("pure"), which ruled China until the early twentieth century (1644–1911).

The Manchus mostly were pastoral nomads, although many had turned to agriculture and settled in the rich farmlands of southern Manchuria. Their ancestors had traded with China since the Qin dynasty, and they had frequently clashed with their neighbors over land and resources in northern China and southern Manchuria. During the late sixteenth and early seventeenth centuries, an ambitious chieftain named Nurhaci (reigned 1616–1626) unified Manchu tribes into a centralized state, promulgated a code of laws, and organized a powerful military force. During the 1620s and 1630s, the Manchu army expelled Ming garrisons in Manchuria, captured Korea and Mongolia, and launched small-scale invasions into China. After their seizure of Beijing in 1644, the Manchus moved to extend their authority throughout China. For almost forty years they waged campaigns against Ming loyalists and other rebels in southern China until by the early 1680s the Manchus had consolidated the Qing dynasty's hold throughout the land.

The Manchus

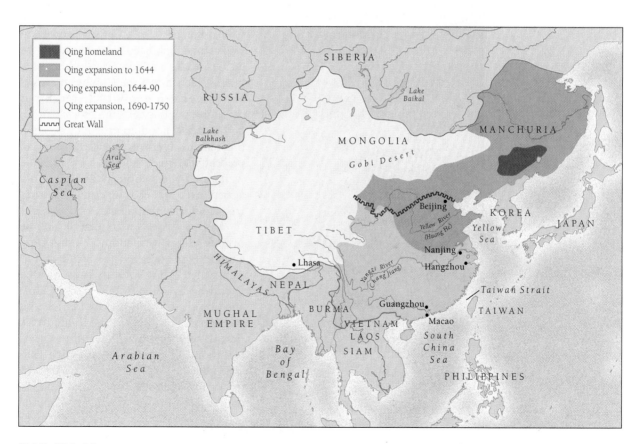

MAP [26.2]

The Qing empire.

The establishment of the Qing dynasty was due partly to Manchu military prowess and partly to Chinese support for the Manchus. During the 1630s and 1640s, many Chinese generals deserted the Ming dynasty because of its corruption and inefficiency. Confucian scholar-bureaucrats also worked against the Ming, since they despised the eunuchs who dominated the imperial court. The Manchu ruling elites were schooled in Chinese language and Confucian thought, and they often enjoyed more respect from the scholar-bureaucrats than did the emperor and high administrators of the Ming dynasty itself.

The Manchus were careful to preserve their own ethnic and cultural identity. They not only outlawed intermarriage between Manchus and Chinese but also forbade Chinese from traveling to Manchuria and from learning the Manchurian language. Qing authorities also forced Chinese men to shave the front of their heads and grow a Manchu-style queue as a sign of submission to the dynasty.

Kangxi and His Reign

Though painted in the nineteenth century, this portrait depicts Kangxi in his imperial regalia as he looked at about age 50. • Portrait of the Emperor K'ang Hsi, 19th century, Ch'ing Dynasty. The Metropolitan Museum of Art, Rogers Fund, 1942. (42.141.2) Photograph © 1980 The Metropolitan Museum.

Until the nineteenth century strong imperial leadership muted tensions between Manchu rulers and Chinese subjects. The long reigns of two particularly effective emperors, Kangxi (1661–1722) and Qianlong (1736–1795), helped the Manchus consolidate their hold on China. Kangxi was a Confucian scholar as well as an enlightened ruler. He was a voracious reader and occasionally composed poems. He studied the Confucian classics and sought to apply their teachings through his policies. Thus, for example, he organized flood-control and irrigation projects in observance of the Confucian precept that rulers should look after the welfare of their subjects and promote agriculture. He also generously patronized Confucian schools and academies.

Kangxi was also a conqueror, and he oversaw the construction of a vast Qing empire. He conquered the island of Taiwan, where Ming loyalists had retreated after their expulsion from southern China, and absorbed it into his empire. Like his predecessors of the Han and Tang dynasties, Kangxi sought to forestall problems with nomadic peoples by projecting Chinese influence into central Asia. His conquests in Mongolia and central Asia extended almost to the Caspian Sea, and he imposed a Chinese protectorate over Tibet. Kangxi's grandson Qianlong continued this expansion of Chinese influence by making Vietnam, Burma, and Nepal vassal states of the Qing dynasty.

Qianlong's reign marked the height of the Qing dynasty. Like Kangxi, Qianlong was a sophisticated and learned man. He reportedly composed more than one hundred thousand poems, and he was a discriminating connoisseur of painting and calligraphy. During his long, peaceful, and prosperous reign, the imperial treasury bulged so much that on four separate occasions Qianlong canceled tax collections. Toward the end of his reign, Qianlong paid less attention to imperial affairs and delegated many responsibilities to his favorite eunuchs. His successors continued this practice, devoting themselves to hunting and the harem, and by the nineteenth century the Qing dynasty faced serious difficulties. Throughout the reign of Qianlong, however, China remained a wealthy and well-organized land.

Qianlong and His Reign

The Son of Heaven and the Scholar-Bureaucrats

Although Qing rulers usually appointed Manchus to the highest political posts, they relied on the same governmental apparatus that the Ming emperors had established. Both the Ming and Qing dynasties presided over a tightly centralized state, which they administered through a bureaucracy staffed by Confucian scholars. For more than five hundred years, the autocratic state created by the Ming emperor Hongwu governed China's fortunes.

If the emperor of China during the Ming and Qing dynasties was not quite a god, he certainly was more than a mere mortal. Chinese tradition held that he was the "Son of Heaven," the human being designated by heavenly powers to maintain order on the earth. He led a privileged life within the walls of the Forbidden City. Hundreds of concubines resided in his harem, and thousands of eunuchs looked after his desires. His daily activities were carefully choreographed performances in the form of inspections, audiences, banquets, and other official duties. Everything about his person and the institution he represented conveyed a sense of awesome authority. The imperial wardrobe and personal effects bore designs forbidden to all others, for instance, and the written characters of the emperor's name were taboo throughout the realm. Individuals who had the rare privilege of a personal audience with the emperor had to perform the kowtow—three kneelings and nine head knockings. Those who gave even minor offense faced severe punishment. Even the highest official could have his bare buttocks flogged with bamboo canes, a punishment that sometimes brought victims to the point of death.

The Son of Heaven

Day-to-day governance of the empire fell to scholar-bureaucrats appointed by the emperor. With few exceptions these officials came from the class of well-educated and highly literate men known as the scholar-gentry. These men had earned academic degrees by passing rigorous civil service examinations, and they dominated China's political and social life.

The Scholar-Bureaucrats

Preparations for the examinations began at an early age. Sometimes they took place in local schools, which like the civil service examinations were open only to males. Wealthy families often engaged the services of tutors, who made formal education available also to girls. By the time boys were eleven or twelve years old, they had memorized several thousand characters that were necessary to deal with the Confucian curriculum, including the *Analects* of Confucius and other standard works. They followed these studies with instruction in calligraphy, poetry, and essay composition. Diligent students also acquainted themselves with a large corpus of commentaries, histories, and literary works in preparing for civil service examinations.

The examinations consisted of a battery of tests administered at the district, provincial, and metropolitan levels. Stiff official quotas restricted the number of

Civil-Service Examinations

successful candidates in each examination—only three hundred students could pass metropolitan examinations—and students frequently took the examinations several times before earning a degree.

Writing the examinations was a grueling ordeal. At the appointed hour candidates presented themselves at the examination compound. Each candidate brought a water pitcher, a chamber pot, bedding, food, an inkstone, ink, and brushes. After guards had verified their identities and searched them for hidden printed materials, the new arrivals proceeded along narrow lanes to a honeycomb of small, cell-like rooms barely large enough to accommodate one man and his possessions. Aside from a bench, a makeshift bed, and boards that served as a desk, the rooms were empty. For the next three days and two nights, the cramped rooms were home to the candidates, who spent all their time writing "eight-legged essays"—literary compositions with eight distinct sections—on questions posed by the examiners. There were no interruptions, nor was there any communication between candidates. If someone died during the examination period, officials wrapped his body in a straw mat and tossed it over the high walls that ringed the compound.

The Examination System and Chinese Society

The possibility of bureaucratic service—with prospects for rich social and financial rewards—assured that competition for degrees was ferocious at all levels. As a result, cheating candidates and corrupt examiners occasionally compromised the system. Yet a degree did not assure government service. During the Qing dynasty the empire's one million degree holders competed for twenty thousand official civil service positions. Those who passed only the district exams had few opportunities for bureaucratic employment and usually spent their careers "plowing with the writing brush" by teaching in local schools or serving as family tutors. Those who passed the metropolitan examinations, however, could look forward to powerful positions in the imperial bureaucracy.

The examination system was a pivotal institution. By opening the door to honor, power, and rewards, the examinations encouraged serious pursuit of a formal education. Furthermore, since the system did not erect social barriers before its recruits, it provided an avenue for upward social mobility. Years of education and travel to examination sites were expensive, so candidates from wealthy families enjoyed advantages over others, but the exams themselves were open to all males regardless of age or social class. Finally, in addition to selecting officials for government service, the education and examination system molded the personal values of those who managed day-to-day affairs in imperial China. By concentrating on Confucian classics and neo-Confucian commentaries, the examinations guaranteed that Confucianism would be at the heart of Chinese education and that Confucians would govern the state.

 ## ECONOMIC AND SOCIAL CHANGES

By modeling their governmental structure on the centralized imperial states of earlier Chinese dynasties, the Ming and Qing emperors succeeded in their goal of restoring and maintaining traditional ways in China. They also sought to preserve the traditional hierarchical and patriarchal social order. Yet while the emperors promoted conservative political and social policies, China experienced economic and social changes, partly as a result of influences from abroad. Agricultural production increased dramatically—especially after the introduction of new food crops from the Americas—and fueled rapid population growth. Meanwhile, global trade brought

China enormous wealth, which stimulated the domestic economy by encouraging increased trade, manufacturing, and urban growth. These developments deeply influenced Chinese society and partly undermined the stability that the Ming and Qing emperors sought to preserve.

The Patriarchal Family

Moralists portrayed the Chinese people as one large family, and they extended family values to the larger society. Filial piety, for example, not only implied duties of children toward their fathers but also loyalty of subjects toward the emperor. Like the imperial government, the Chinese family was hierarchical, patriarchal, and authoritarian. The father was head of the household, and he passed leadership of the family to his eldest son. The veneration of ancestors, which the state promoted as a matter of Confucian propriety, strengthened the authority of the patriarchs by honoring the male line of descent in formal family rituals. Filial piety was the cornerstone of family values. Children had the duty to look after their parents' happiness and well-being, and a crucial obligation was to support parents in their old age. Young children heard stories of sons who went so far as to cut off parts of their bodies to ensure that their parents had enough to eat!

Filial Piety

The social assumptions of the Chinese family extended into patrilineal descent groups such as the clan. Sometimes numbering into the thousands, clan members came from all social classes, though members of the gentry usually dominated a given clan. Clans assumed responsibilities that exceeded the capacities of the nuclear family, such as the maintenance of local order, organization of local economies, and provision for welfare. Clan-supported education gave poor but promising relatives the opportunity to succeed in the civil service examinations. The principal motives behind this charity were corporate self-interest as well as altruism. A government position brought prestige and prosperity to the entire clan, so educational support was a prudent investment. Finally, clans served as a means for the transmission of Confucian values from the gentry leaders to all social classes within the clan.

Within the family Confucian principles subjected women to the authority of men. The subordination of females began at an early age. Chinese parents preferred boys over girls. Whereas a boy might have the opportunity to take the official examinations, become a government official, and thereby bring honor and financial reward to the entire clan, parents regarded a girl as a social and financial liability. After years of expensive upbringing, most girls would marry and become members of other households. Under these circumstances it was not surprising that life was precarious for newborn girls, who were the primary victims of infanticide.

Gender Relations

During the Ming and Qing dynasties, patriarchal authority over females probably became tighter than ever before in China. Since ancient times, relatives had discouraged widows from remarriage, but social pressures increased during the Ming dynasty. Friends and relatives not only encouraged widows to honor the memory of their departed husbands but also heaped posthumous honors on those who committed suicide and followed their spouses to the grave.

Moreover, foot binding, a custom that probably originated in the Song dynasty, became exceptionally popular during the late Ming and Qing dynasties. Tightly constrained and even deformed by strips of linen, bound feet could not grow naturally and so would not support the weight of an adult woman. Bound feet were small and dainty, and they sometimes inspired erotic arousal among men. The practice of foot

Foot Binding

binding became most widespread among the wealthy classes, since it demonstrated an ability to support women who could not perform physical labor, but commoners sometimes bound the feet of especially pretty girls in hopes of arranging favorable marriages that would enhance the family's social standing.

Marriage itself was a contractual affair whose principal purpose was to continue the male line of descent. A bride became a member of the husband's family, and there was no ambiguity about her position in the household. On her wedding day, as soon as she arrived at her husband's home, the bride performed ritual acts demonstrating subservience to her husband and her new family. Women could not divorce their husbands, but men could put aside their wives in cases where there was no offspring or where the wife was guilty of adultery, theft, disobedience to her husband's family, or even being too talkative.

Thus custom and law combined to strengthen patriarchal authority in Chinese families during the Ming and Qing dynasties. Yet while family life continued to develop along traditional lines, the larger Chinese society underwent considerable change between the sixteenth and eighteenth centuries.

Population Growth and Economic Development

China was a predominantly agricultural society, a fact that meshed agreeably with the Confucian view that land was the source of everything praiseworthy. The emperor himself acknowledged the central importance of agriculture by plowing the first furrow of the season. Yet only a small fraction of China's land is suitable for planting: even today only about 11 percent is in cultivation. To feed the country's large population, China's farmers relied on an intensive, garden-style form of agriculture that was highly productive. On its strong agrarian foundation, China supported a large population and built the most highly commercialized economy of the preindustrial world.

American Food Crops

This engraving depicts a peasant couple in harness pulling a plow. Note that the man wears the braided queue that Manchus required their male Chinese subjects to wear. • General Research Division, New York Public Library. Astor, Lenox and Tilden Foundations

By intensively cultivating every available parcel of land, Chinese peasants increased their yields of traditional food crops—especially rice, wheat, and millet—until the seventeenth century. Beginning about the mid-seventeenth century, as peasants approached the upper limits of agricultural productivity, Spanish merchants coming by way of the Philippines introduced American food crops to China. American maize, sweet potatoes, and peanuts permitted Chinese farmers to take advantage of soils that previously had gone uncultivated. The introduction of new crops increased the food supply and supported further population growth.

In spite of recurring epidemic diseases such as plague, which claimed the lives of *Population Growth* millions, China's population rose rapidly from 100 million in 1500 to 160 million in 1600. Partly because of rebellion and war, it fell to 140 million in the mid-seventeenth century, but returned to 160 million by 1700 and then surged to 225 million by 1750, thus registering more than a 40 percent increase in half a century. This rapid demographic growth set the stage for economic and social problems, since agricultural production could not keep pace with population over a long term. Acute problems did not occur until the nineteenth century, but per capita income in China began to decline as early as the reign of Qianlong.

While an increasing population placed pressure on Chinese resources, the growing commercial market offered opportunities for entrepreneurs. Because of demographic expansion, entrepreneurs had access to a large labor force that was both occupationally and geographically mobile, so they were able to recruit workers readily at low cost. After the mid-sixteenth century the Chinese economy benefited also from the influx of Japanese and American silver, which stimulated trade and financed further commercial expansion.

Global trade brought tremendous prosperity to China, especially during the early *Foreign Trade* Qing dynasty. Chinese workers produced vast quantities of silk, porcelain, lacquerware, and tea for consumers in the Indian Ocean basin, central Asia, and Europe. The silk industry was especially well organized: weavers worked in workshops for regular wages producing fine satins and brocades for export. Chinese imports were relatively few: they included spices from Maluku, exotic products like birds and animal skins from tropical regions, and small quantities of woolen textiles from Europe. Compensation for exports came most importantly in the form of silver bullion, which supported the silver-based Chinese economy and fueled manufacturing.

Economic growth and commercial expansion took place mostly in an atmosphere of tight government regulation. During the early fifteenth century, the Ming emperor Yongle sought to establish a Chinese presence in the Indian Ocean basin,

Ming and Qing craftsmen produced high-quality porcelain coveted by connoisseurs and wealthy consumers throughout the world. This bowl produced about 1723 to 1735 depicts fish swimming in a pond with lotus plants. • Erich Lessing/Art Resource, NY

and he sponsored a series of seven massive maritime expeditions (1405–1433) led by the eunuch admiral Zheng He. The Chinese fleets included as many as 317 vessels and twenty-eight thousand men. Zheng He called at ports from Java to Malindi, suppressed pirates in southeast Asian waters, intervened in local conflicts in Sumatra and Ceylon, intimidated local authorities with shows of force in southern Arabia and Mogadishu, and made China's presence felt throughout the Indian Ocean basin.

After the reign of Yongle, however, the Ming government withdrew its support for expensive maritime expeditions and even tried to prevent Chinese subjects from dealing with foreign peoples. In its effort to pacify southern China during the later seventeenth century, the Qing government tried to end maritime activity altogether. An imperial edict of 1656 forbade "even a plank from drifting to the sea," and in 1661 the emperor Kangxi ordered evacuation of the southern coastal regions. These policies had only a limited effect—small Chinese vessels continued to trade actively in Japan and southeast Asian ports—and when Qing forces pacified southern China in the 1680s, government authorities rescinded the strictest measures. Nevertheless, foreign trade fell under the surveillance and tight control of imperial authorities. In western Europe capitalist merchants and manufacturers largely made their own economic decisions and trusted their fates to the free markets, but in China government policy played a much larger role in trade and economic organization.

Government and Technology China's economic expansion took place in the absence of technological innovation. During the Tang and Song dynasties, Chinese engineers had produced a veritable flood of inventions, and China was the world's leader in technology. Yet by early Ming times, technological innovation had slowed. Imperial armed forces adopted European cannons and advanced firearms for their own uses—thus borrowing forms of gunpowder technology that had originated in China and that Europeans had refined and improved—but little innovation in agricultural and industrial technologies occurred during the Ming and Qing dynasties.

Part of the explanation for the slowdown has to do with role of the government. During the Tang and Song dynasties, the imperial government had encouraged technological innovation as a foundation of military and economic strength. In contrast, the Ming and Qing regimes favored political and social stability over technological innovation, which they feared would lead to unsettling change. Alongside government policy, the abundance and ready availability of skilled workers also discouraged technological innovation. When employers wanted to increase production, they found that hiring additional workers was less costly than making large investments in new technologies. In the short run this tactic maintained relative prosperity in China while keeping most of the population gainfully employed. Over the longer term, however, it ensured that China lost technological ground to European peoples, who embarked on a round of stunning technological innovation beginning about the mid-eighteenth century.

Gentry, Commoners, Soldiers, and "Mean People"

Privileged Classes Leaving aside the emperor and his family, scholar-bureaucrats and gentry occupied the most exalted positions in Chinese society. Because of their official positions, the scholar-bureaucrats ranked slightly above gentry. Nevertheless, scholar-bureaucrats had much in common with the gentry: they came largely from gentry ranks, and after leaving government service they usually rejoined gentry society. The scholar-bureaucrats and gentry functioned as intermediaries between the imperial government and local society. By organizing water control projects and public security measures, they played a crucial role in the management of local society.

EMPEROR QIANLONG ON CHINESE TRADE WITH ENGLAND

· · ·

Qing administrators tightly restricted foreign trade. Foreign merchants had to deal with government-approved agents outside the city walls of Guangzhou and had to depart as soon as they had completed their business. In 1793 a British diplomat representing King George III of England bestowed gifts on Emperor Qianlong and petitioned for the right to trade at ports other than Guangzhou. In a letter to King George, Qianlong outlined his views on Chinese trade with England. His letter also bespeaks clearly the importance of government policy for commerce and economic affairs in China.

You, O king, from afar have yearned after the blessings of our civilization, and in your eagerness to come into touch with our influence have sent an embassy across the sea bearing a memorandum. I have already taken note of your respectful spirit of submission, have treated your mission with extreme favor and loaded it with gifts, besides issuing a mandate to you, O king, and honoring you with the bestowal of valuable presents. . . .

Yesterday your ambassador petitioned my ministers to memorialize me regarding your trade with China, but his proposal is not consistent with our dynastic usage and cannot be entertained. Hitherto, all European nations, including your own country's barbarian merchants, have carried on their trade with our Celestial Empire at Guangzhou. Such has been the procedure for many years, although our Celestial Empire possesses all things in prolific abundance and lacks no product within its own borders. There was therefore no need to import the manufactures of outside barbarians in exchange for our own produce. But as the tea, silk, and porcelain which the Celestial Empire produces are absolute necessities to European nations and to yourselves, we have permitted, as a signal mark of favor, that trading agents should be established at Guangzhou, so that your wants might be supplied and your country thus participate in our beneficence. But your ambassador has now put forward new requests which completely fail to recognize our throne's

principle to "treat strangers from afar with indulgence," and to exercise a pacifying control over barbarian tribes the world over. . . . Your England is not the only nation trading at Guangzhou. If other nations, following your bad example, wrongfully importune my ear with further impossible requests, how will it be possible for me to threat them with easy indulgence? Nevertheless, I do not forget the lonely remoteness of your island, cut off from the world by intervening wastes of sea, nor do I overlook your excusable ignorance of the usages of our Celestial Empire. I have consequently commanded my ministers to enlighten your ambassador on the subject, and have ordered the departure of the mission. . . .

If, after the receipt of this explicit decree, you lightly give ear to the representations of your subordinates and allow your barbarian merchants to proceed to Zhejiang and Tianjin, with the object of landing and trading there, the ordinances of my Celestial Empire are strict in the extreme, and the local officials, both civil and military, are bound reverently to obey the law of the land. Should your vessels touch the shore, your merchants will assuredly never be permitted to land or to reside there, but will be subject to instant expulsion. In that event your barbarian merchants will have had a long journey for nothing. Do not say that you were not warned in due time! Tremblingly obey and show no negligence! A special mandate!

SOURCE: J. O. P. Brand. *Annals and Memoirs of the Court of Peking*. Boston: Houghton Mifflin, 1914, pp. 325–31. (Translation slightly modified.)

Scholar-bureaucrats and gentry were easy to identify. They wore distinctive clothing—black gowns with blue borders adorned with various rank insignia—and commoners addressed them with honorific terms. They received favorable legal treatment that reflected their privileged status. As a rule, commoners could not call members of privileged classes to appear as witnesses in legal proceedings. They also enjoyed immunity from corporal punishment and exemption from labor service and taxes.

Most of the gentry owned land, which was their major source of income. As long as they did not have to perform physical labor, some gentry also supplemented their income by operating pawn and rice shops. Many of them were also silent business partners of merchants and entrepreneurs. Their principal source of income, however, came from the government service to which only they had access by virtue of their academic degrees. In contrast to landed elites elsewhere, who often lived on rural estates, China's gentry resided largely in cities and towns, where they tended to political, social, and financial affairs.

Working Classes   Confucian tradition ranked three broad classes of commoners below the gentry: peasants, artisans or workers, and merchants. By far the biggest class consisted of peasants, a designation that covered everyone from day laborers to tenant farmers to petty landlords. Confucian principles regarded peasants as the most honorable of the three classes, since they performed honest labor and provided the food that supported the entire population.

The category of artisans and workers encompassed a wide spectrum of occupations. Despite their lower status, craftsmen, tailors, barbers, physicians, and workers in manufacturing plants generally enjoyed higher income than peasants. Artisans and workers were usually employees of the state or of gentry and merchant families, but they also pursued their occupations as self-employed persons.

Merchants   Merchants, from street peddlers to men of enormous wealth and influence, ranked at the bottom level of the Confucian social hierarchy. Because moralists looked upon them as unscrupulous social parasites, merchants enjoyed little legal protection, and government policy was always critically important to their pursuits. Yet Chinese merchants often garnered official support for their enterprises, either through bribery of government bureaucrats or through profit-sharing arrangements with gentry families. Indeed, the participation of gentry families in commercial ventures such as warehousing, money lending, and pawnbroking blurred the distinction between gentry and merchants. In addition, merchants blurred the distinction further by providing their sons with an education that prepared them for government examinations, which in turn could result in promotion to gentry status and appointment to civil service positions.

The prominence of artisans and merchants pointed up the social and economic development of China since the time of Confucius. Although China was still a basically agricultural land, manufacturing and commerce had become much more economically important than in ancient times. As a result, those who could recognize and exploit opportunities had the potential to lead comfortable lives and even to climb into the ranks of the privileged gentry class.

Lower Classes   Beyond the Confucian social hierarchy were members of the military forces and the so-called mean people. Confucian moralists regarded armed forces as a wretched but necessary evil and attempted to avoid military dominance of society by placing civilian bureaucrats in the highest command positions, even at the expense of military effectiveness. The mean people included slaves, indentured servants, entertainers, prostitutes, and other marginal groups like the "beggars of Jiangsu" and the "boat people of Guangdong."

THE CONFUCIAN TRADITION AND NEW CULTURAL INFLUENCES

The Ming and Qing emperors looked to Chinese traditions for guidance in framing their cultural as well as their political and social policies. They provided generous support for Confucianism, particularly in the form of neo-Confucianism articulated by the twelfth-century scholar Zhu Xi, and they ensured that formal education in China revolved around Confucian thought and values. Yet the Confucian tradition was not the only cultural alternative in Ming and Qing China. Demographic and urban growth encouraged the emergence of a vibrant popular culture in Chinese cities, and European missionaries reintroduced Roman Catholic Christianity to China and acquainted Chinese intellectuals with European science and technology as well.

Neo-Confucianism and Pulp Fiction

Imperial sponsorship of Chinese cultural traditions meant primarily support for the Confucian tradition, especially as systematized by the Song dynasty scholar Zhu Xi, the most prominent architect of neo-Confucianism. Zhu Xi combined the moral, ethical, and political values of Confucius with the logical rigor and speculative power of Buddhist philosophy. He emphasized the values of self-discipline, filial piety, and obedience to established rulers, all of which appealed to Ming and Qing emperors seeking to maintain stability in their vast realm. Cultural policies of the Ming and Qing dynasties made the neo-Confucian tradition the reigning imperial ideology from the fourteenth to the early twentieth century.

In order to promote Confucian values, the Ming and Qing emperors supported educational programs at several levels. They funded the Hanlin Academy, a research institute for Confucian scholars in Beijing, and maintained provincial schools throughout China where promising students could study for the civil service examinations. The exams themselves encouraged the cultivation of Confucian values, since they focused largely on Confucian texts and neo-Confucian commentaries.

Confucian Education

Ming and Qing courts also provided generous funding for other projects emphasizing Chinese cultural traditions. The Ming emperor Yongle sponsored the compilation of the *Yongle Encyclopedia,* a vast collection of Chinese philosophical, literary, and historical texts that filled almost twenty-three thousand scrolls. During the Qing dynasty both Kangxi and Qianlong organized similar projects. Kangxi's *Collection of Books* was smaller than the *Yongle Encyclopedia,* but it was more influential because the emperor had it printed and distributed, whereas Yongle's compilation was available only in three manuscript copies. Qianlong's *Complete Library of the Four Treasuries* was too large to publish—it ran to 93,556 pamphlet-size volumes—but the emperor deposited manuscript copies in seven libraries throughout China.

While the imperial courts promoted Confucianism, a lively popular culture took shape in the cities of China. Most urban residents did not have an advanced education and knew little about Confucius, Zhu Xi, or other intellectual luminaries. Many of them were literate businessmen, however, and they preferred entertainment and diversion more intellectually engaging than that found in local teahouses and wine shops. Popular novels met their needs.

Popular Culture

Confucian scholars looked down on popular novels as crude fiction that had little to do with the realities of the world. Printing made it possible to produce books cheaply and in mass quantities, however, and urban residents eagerly consumed the

Popular Novels

fast-paced novels that flooded Chinese cities during the Ming and Qing eras. Many of the novels had little literary merit, but their tales of conflict, horror, wonder, excitement, and sometimes unconcealed pornography appealed to readers.

Yet many popular novels also offered thoughtful reflections on the world and human affairs. The historical novel *The Romance of the Three Kingdoms,* for example, explored the political intrigue that followed the collapse of the Han dynasty. *The Dream of the Red Chamber* told the story of cousins deeply in love who could not marry because of their families' wishes. Through the prism of a sentimental love story, the novel shed fascinating light on the dynamics of wealthy scholar-gentry families. In a different vein, *Journey to the West* dealt with the seventh-century journey to India of the famous Buddhist monk Xuanzang. In the popular novel Xuanzang's traveling companion was a monkey with magical powers who among other things could jump 10,000 kilometers (6,215 miles) in a single bound. While promoting Buddhist values, *Journey to the West* also made the trickster monkey a wildly popular and celebrated character in Chinese literature. As recently as 1987 Chinese-American novelist Maxine Hong Kingston adapted this character to modern times in her novel *Tripmaster Monkey.*

The Return of Christianity to China

Nestorian Christians had established churches and monasteries in China as early as the seventh century C.E., and Roman Catholic communities were prominent in Chinese commercial centers during the Yuan dynasty. After the outbreak of epidemic plague and the collapse of the Yuan dynasty in the fourteenth century, however, Christianity disappeared from China. When Roman Catholic missionaries returned in the sixteenth century, they had to start from scratch in their efforts to win converts and establish a Christian community.

Matteo Ricci   The most prominent of the missionaries were the Jesuits, who worked to strengthen Roman Catholic Christianity in Europe and also to spread their faith abroad. Founder of the mission to China was the Italian Jesuit Matteo Ricci (1552–1610), who had the ambitious goal of converting China to Christianity, beginning with the emperor Wanli. Ricci was a brilliant and learned man, as well as a polished diplomat, and he became a popular figure at the Ming court. Upon arrival at Macau in 1582, Ricci immersed himself in the study of the Chinese language and the Confucian classics. He had a talent for languages, and his phenomenal memory enabled him to master the thousands of characters used in literary Chinese writing. By the time he first traveled to Beijing and visited the imperial court in 1601, Ricci was able to write learned Chinese and converse fluently with Confucian scholars.

Ricci's mastery of Chinese language and literature opened doors for the Jesuits, who then dazzled their hosts with European science, technology, and mechanical gadgetry. Ricci and his colleagues had an advanced education in mathematics and astronomy, and they were able to correct Chinese calendars that consistently miscalculated solar eclipses. The Jesuits also prepared maps of the world—with China placed diplomatically at the center—on the basis of geographical knowledge that Europeans had gained during their voyages through the world's seas. The Jesuits even supervised the casting of high-quality bronze cannons for Ming and early Qing armies.

The Jesuits piqued Chinese curiosity also with mechanical devices. Finely ground glass prisms became popular because of their refraction of sunlight into its component parts. Harpsichords also drew attention, and Jesuits with musical talents often composed songs for their hosts. Most popular of all, however, were the devices that Chinese called "self-ringing bells"—spring-driven mechanical clocks that kept tolerably accurate time, chimed the hours, and sometimes even struck the quarter hours as well.

The Jesuits sought to capture Chinese interest with European science and technology, but their ultimate goal was always to win converts. They portrayed Christianity as a faith very similar to Chinese cultural traditions. Ricci, for example, wrote a treatise entitled *The True Meaning of the Lord of Heaven* in which he argued that the doctrines of Confucius and Jesus were very similar, if not identical. Over the years, according to Ricci, neo-Confucian scholars had altered Confucius's own teachings, so adoption of Christianity by Chinese would represent a return to a more pure and original Confucianism. The Jesuits also held religious services in the Chinese language and allowed converts to continue the time-honored practice of venerating their ancestors.

In spite of their tolerance, flexibility, and genuine respect for their hosts, the Jesuits attracted few converts in China. By the mid-eighteenth century Chinese

Confucianism and Christianity

Matteo Ricci (left) with Xu Quangqi, his most famous Chinese disciple. Both men wear the distinctive gowns of educated, refined scholar-gentry. A distinguished scholar who held an appointment at the Hanlin Academy, Xu helped Ricci translate Euclid's geometrical works into Chinese. • Rare Books Division, New York Public Library. Astor, Lenox and Tilden Foundations

Christians numbered about two hundred thousand—a tiny proportion of the Chinese population of 225 million. Chinese hesitated to adopt Christianity partly because of its exclusivity: for centuries, Chinese had honored Confucianism, Daoism, and Buddhism at the same time. Like Islam, though, Christianity claimed to be the only true religion, so conversion implied that Confucianism, Daoism, and Buddhism were inferior or even fallacious creeds—a proposition most Chinese were unwilling to accept.

Ultimately, the Roman Catholic mission in China came to an end because of squabbles between the Jesuits and members of the Franciscan and Dominican orders, who also sought converts in China. Jealous of the Jesuits' presence at the imperial court, the Franciscans and Dominicans complained to the pope about their rivals' tolerance of ancestor veneration and willingness to conduct Chinese-language services. The pope sided with the critics and in the early eighteenth century issued several proclamations ordering missionaries in China to suppress ancestor veneration and conduct services according to European standards. In response to this demand, the emperor Kangxi ordered an end to the preaching of Christianity in China. Although he did not strictly enforce the ban, the mission weakened, and by the mid-eighteenth century it had effectively come to an end.

End of the Jesuit Mission

The Roman Catholic mission to China did not attract large numbers of Chinese converts, but it nonetheless had important cultural effects. Besides making European science and technology known in China, the Jesuits also made China known in Europe. In letters, reports, and other writings distributed widely throughout Europe, the Jesuits described China as an orderly and rational society. The Confucian civil service system attracted the attention of European rulers, who began to design their own civil service bureaucracies in the eighteenth century. The rational morality of Confucianism also appealed to the Enlightenment philosophes, who sought alternatives to Christianity as the foundation for ethics and morality. For the first time since Marco Polo, the Jesuits made first-hand observations of China available to Europeans and stimulated strong European interest in east Asian societies.

THE UNIFICATION OF JAPAN

During the late sixteenth and early seventeenth centuries, the political unification of Japan ended an extended period of civil disorder. Like the Ming and Qing emperors in China, the Tokugawa shoguns sought to lay a foundation for long-term political and social stability, and they provided generous support for neo-Confucian studies in an effort to promote traditional values. Indeed, the Shoguns went even further than their Chinese counterparts by promoting conservative values and tightly restricting foreign influence in Japan. As in China, however, demographic expansion and economic growth fostered social and cultural change in Japan, and merchants introduced Chinese and European influences into Japan.

The Tokugawa Shogunate

From the twelfth through the sixteenth century, a *shogun* ("military governor") ruled Japan through feudal vassals who received political rights and large estates in exchange for military services. Theoretically, the shogun ruled as a temporary stand-in for the Japanese emperor, the ultimate source of political authority. In fact, however, the emperor was nothing more than a figurehead, and the shogun sought to monopolize power. After the fourteenth century the conflicting ambitions of shoguns and feudal vassals led to constant turmoil, and by the sixteenth century Japan was in a state of civil war. Japanese historians often refer to the sixteenth century as the era of *sengoku*—"the country at war."

Tokugawa Ieyasu   Toward the end of the sixteenth century, powerful states emerged in several regions of Japan, and a series of military leaders brought about the unification of the land. In 1600 the last of these chieftains, Tokugawa Ieyasu (reigned 1600–1616), established a military government known as the Tokugawa *bakufu* ("tent government," since it theoretically was only a temporary replacement for the emperor's rule). Ieyasu and his descendants ruled the bakufu as shoguns from 1600 until the end of the Tokugawa dynasty in 1867.

The principal aim of the Tokugawa shoguns was to stabilize their realm and prevent the return of civil war. Consequently, the shoguns needed to control the *daimyo* ("great names"), powerful territorial lords who ruled most of Japan from their vast, hereditary landholdings. The 260 or so daimyo functioned as near-absolute rulers within their domains. Each maintained a government staffed by warrior vassals, supported an independent judiciary, established schools, and circulated

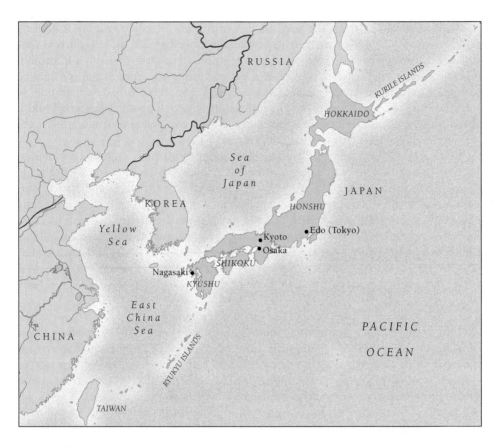

MAP [26.3]
Tokugawa Japan.

paper money. Moreover, after the mid-sixteenth century, many daimyo established relationships with European mariners, from whom they learned how to manufacture and use gunpowder weapons. During the last decades of the *sengoku* era, cannons and personal firearms had played prominent roles in Japanese conflicts.

From the castle town of Edo (modern Tokyo), the shogun governed his own personal domain and sought to extend his control to the daimyo. The shoguns instituted the policy of "alternate attendance," which required daimyo to maintain their families at Edo and spend every other year at the Tokugawa court. This policy enabled the shoguns to keep an eye on the daimyo, and as a side effect it encouraged daimyo to spend their money on lavish residences and comfortable lives in Edo rather than investing it in military forces that could challenge the bakufu. The shoguns also subjected marriage alliances between daimyo families to bakufu approval, discouraged the daimyo from visiting each other, and required daimyo to obtain permits for construction work on their castles. Even meetings between the daimyo and the emperor required the shogun's permission.

In an effort to prevent European influences from destabilizing the land, the Tokugawa shoguns closely controlled relations between Japan and the outside world. They knew that Spanish forces had conquered the Philippine Islands in the sixteenth century, and they feared that Europeans might jeopardize the security of the bakufu itself. Even if Europeans did not conquer Japan, they could cause serious problems by making alliances with daimyo and supplying them with weapons.

Control of the Daimyo

Control of Foreign Relations

Thus during the 1630s the shoguns issued a series of edicts sharply restricting Japanese relations with other lands that remained in effect for more than two centuries. The policy forbade Japanese from going abroad on pain of death and prohibited the construction of large ships. It expelled Europeans from Japan, prohibited foreign merchants from trading in Japanese ports, and even forbade the import of foreign books. The policy allowed carefully controlled trade with Asian lands, and it also permitted small numbers of Chinese and Dutch merchants to trade under tight restrictions at the southern port city of Nagasaki.

During the seventeenth century Japanese authorities strictly enforced this policy. In 1640 a Portuguese merchant ship arrived at Nagasaki in hopes of engaging in trade in spite of the ban. Officials beheaded sixty-one of the party and spared thirteen others so they could relate the experience to their compatriots. Yet authorities gradually loosened the restrictions, and the policy never led to the isolation of Japan from the outside world. Throughout the Tokugawa period Japan carried on a flourishing trade with China, Korea, Taiwan, and the Ryukyu Islands, and Dutch merchants regularly brought news of European and larger world affairs.

Economic and Social Change

By ending civil conflict and maintaining political stability, the Tokugawa shoguns set the stage for economic growth in Japan. Ironically, peace and a booming economy encouraged social change that undermined the order that the bakufu sought to preserve.

Economic growth had its roots in increased agricultural production. New crop strains, new methods of water control and irrigation, and the use of fertilizer brought increased yields of rice. Production of cotton, silk, indigo, and sake also increased dramatically. In many parts of Japan, villages moved away from subsistence farming in favor of production for the market. Between 1600 and 1700 agricultural production doubled.

Population Growth

Increased agricultural production brought about rapid demographic growth: during the seventeenth century the Japanese population rose by almost one-third from twenty-two million to twenty-nine million. Thereafter, however, Japan underwent a demographic transition, as many families practiced population control in order to maintain or raise their standard of living. Between 1700 and 1850 the Japanese population grew moderately from twenty-nine million to thirty-two million. Contraception, late marriage, and abortion all played roles in limiting population growth, but the principal control measure was infanticide, euphemistically referred to as "thinning out the rice shoots." Japanese families resorted to these measures primarily because Japan was land poor. During the seventeenth century populations in some areas strained resources, causing financial difficulties for local governments and distress for rural communities.

The Tokugawa era was an age of social as well as demographic change in Japan. Because of Chinese cultural influence, the Japanese social hierarchy followed Confucian precepts in ranking the ruling elites—including the shogun, daimyo, and samurai warriors—as the most prominent and privileged class of society. Beneath them were peasants and artisans. Merchants ranked at the bottom, as they did in China.

Social Change

The extended period of peace ushered in by Tokugawa rule undermined the social position of the ruling elites. Since the twelfth century the ruling elites had basically been warriors who lived by the code of *bushido* ("the way of the warrior"). Without wars to fight daimyo and samurai mostly became administrators and government functionaries. Some daimyo and samurai even turned to scholarship, a pursuit that their martial ancestors would have utterly despised. As they lost their accustomed place in society, many of the ruling elite also fell into financial difficulty. Their principal income came in the form of rice collected from peasant cultivators of their lands. They readily converted rice into money through brokers, but the price of rice did not keep pace with other costs. Moreover, daimyo and samurai lived in expensive and sometimes ostentatious style—particularly daimyo who sought to impress others with their wealth while residing at Edo in alternate years. Many of them became indebted to rice brokers and gradually declined into genteel poverty.

Meanwhile, as in China, merchants became increasingly wealthy and prominent. Japanese cities flourished throughout the Tokugawa era—the population of Edo approached one million by 1700—and merchants prospered handsomely in the vibrant urban environment. Rice dealers, pawnbrokers, and sake merchants soon controlled more wealth than the ruling elites. Those who became especially wealthy sometimes purchased elite ranks or contracted marriages with elite families in efforts to improve their social standing. Others did not go to such lengths but won respect anyway, in spite of occupations that ranked low in the ideal Confucian social order.

Neo-Confucianism and Floating Worlds

Japan had gone to school in China, and the influence of China continued throughout the Tokugawa era. Formal education began with study of Chinese language and literature. As late as the nineteenth century, many Japanese scholars wrote their philosophical, legal, and religious works in Chinese. The common people embraced Buddhism, which had come to Japan from China, and Confucianism was the most influential philosophical system.

Like the Ming and Qing emperors in China, the Tokugawa shoguns promoted the neo-Confucianism of Zhu Xi. With its emphasis on filial piety and loyalty to superiors, neo-Confucianism provided a respectable ideological underpinning for the bakufu. The shoguns patronized scholars who advocated neo-Confucian views, which figured prominently in the educational curriculum. All those who had a formal education—including the sons of merchants as well as offspring of government officials—received constant exposure to neo-Confucian values. By the early eighteenth century, neo-Confucianism had become the official ideology of the Tokugawa bakufu.

Neo-Confucianism in Japan

Yet even with Tokugawa sponsorship, neo-Confucianism did not dominate intellectual life in Japan. Although most scholars recognized Japan's debt to Chinese intellectual traditions, some sought to establish a sense of Japanese identity that did not depend on cultural kinship with China. Particularly during the eighteenth century, scholars of "native learning" scorned neo-Confucianism and even Buddhism as alien cultural imports and emphasized instead the importance of folk traditions and the indigenous Shinto religion for Japanese identity. Many scholars of native learning viewed Japanese people as superior to all others and xenophobically regarded foreign influence as perverse. They urged the study of Japanese classics and glorified the supposed purity of Japanese society before its adulteration by Chinese and other foreign influences.

Native Learning

While scholars of neo-Confucianism and native learning debated issues of philosophy and Japanese identity, the emergence of a prosperous merchant class encouraged the development of a vibrant popular culture. During the seventeenth and eighteenth centuries, an exuberant middle-class culture flourished in cities like Kyoto, the imperial capital; Edo, Japan's largest city and home to bureaucrats and daimyo; and Osaka, the commercial hub of the islands. In these and other cities, Japan's finest creative talents catered to middle-class appetites.

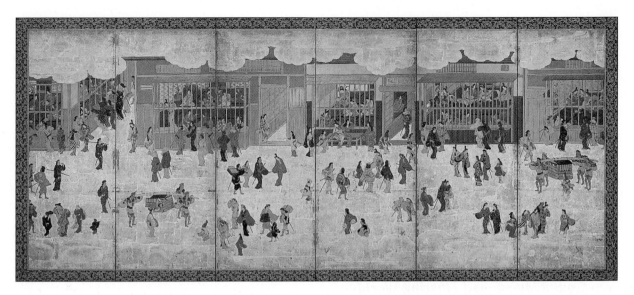

The cortesan district of Kyoto hummed with activity in the mid-seventeenth century. In this woodblock print courtesans await clients behind the wooden grill while urban residents fill the streets. • *Scenes from the Pleasure Quarters of Kyoto,* 17th century, Edo Period. One of a pair of 6-panel folding screens. Denman Waldo Ross Collection. Courtesy, Museum of Fine Arts, Boston

Floating Worlds   The centers of Tokugawa urban culture were the "floating worlds" (*ukiyo*), entertainment and pleasure quarters where teahouses, theaters, brothels, and public baths offered escape from social responsibilities and the rigid rules of conduct that governed public behavior in Tokugawa society. In contrast to the solemn, serious proceedings of the imperial court and the bakufu, the popular culture of urban residents was secular, satirical, and even scatological. The main expressions of this lively culture were prose fiction and new forms of theater.

Ihara Saikaku (1642–1693), one of Japan's most prolific poets, helped create a new genre of prose literature, the "books of the floating world." Much of his fiction revolved around the theme of love. In *The Life of a Man Who Lived for Love,* for example, Ihara chronicled the experiences of a townsman who devoted his life, beginning at the tender age of eight, to a quest for sexual pleasure. Ihara's treatment of love stressed the erotic rather than the aesthetic, and the brief, episodic stories that made up his work appealed to literate urban residents who were not inclined to pore over dense neo-Confucian treatises.

Beginning in the early seventeenth century, two new forms of drama became popular in Japanese cities. One was *kabuki* theater, which usually featured several acts consisting of lively and sometimes bawdy skits where stylized acting combined with lyric singing, dancing, and spectacular staging. A crucial component of kabuki was the actor's ability to improvise and embellish the dialogue, for the text of plays served only as guides for the dramatic performance. The other new dramatic form was *bunraku,* the puppet theater. In bunraku chanters accompanied by music told a story acted out by puppets. Manipulated by a team of three, each puppet could execute the subtlest and most intricate movements, such as brushing a tear from the eye with the sleeve of a kimono. Both kabuki and bunraku attracted enthusiastic audiences in search of entertainment and diversion.

A colored woodcut by Okumura Masanobu depicts the audience at a seventeenth-century kabuki theater. Enthusiastic actors often ran down wooden ramps and played their roles among the audience. • © The British Museum

Christianity and Dutch Learning

Alongside neo-Confucianism, native learning, and middle-class popular culture, Chris- *Christian Missions*
tian missionaries and European merchants contributed their own distinctive threads to
the cultural fabric of Tokugawa Japan. The Jesuit Francis Xavier traveled to Japan in
1549 and opened a mission to seek converts to Christianity. In the early decades of
their mission, Jesuits experienced remarkable success in Japan. Several powerful
daimyo adopted Christianity and ordered their subjects to do likewise. The principal
interest of the daimyo was to establish trade and military alliances with Europeans, but
many Japanese converts became enthusiastic Christians and worked to convert their
compatriots to the new faith. By the 1580s about 150,000 Japanese had converted to
Christianity, and by 1615 Japanese Christians may have numbered half a million.

Although Christians were only a tiny minority of the Japanese population, the
popularity of Christianity generated a backlash among government officials and
moralists seeking to preserve Japanese religious and cultural traditions. The Tokugawa shoguns restricted European access to Japan largely because of concerns that
Christianity might serve as a cultural bridge for alliances between daimyo and European adventurers, which in turn could lead to destabilization of Japanese society and

even threats to the bakufu. Meanwhile Buddhist and Confucian scholars resented the Christian conviction that their faith was the only true doctrine.

Anti-Christian Campaign

Between 1587 and 1639 shoguns promulgated several decrees ordering a halt to Christian missions and commanding Japanese Christians to renounce their faith. In 1612 the shoguns began rigorous enforcement of these decrees. They tortured and executed European missionaries who refused to leave the islands, as well as Japanese Christians who refused to abandon their faith. They often executed victims by crucifixion or burning at the stake, which Tokugawa authorities regarded as especially appropriate for Christians. By the late seventeenth century, the anti-Christian campaign had claimed tens of thousands of lives, and Christianity survived as a secret, underground religion observed only in rural regions of southern Japan.

Dutch Learning

Tokugawa policies ensured that Christianity would not soon reappear in Japan, but they did not entirely prevent contacts between Europeans and Japanese. After 1639 Dutch merchants trading at Nagasaki became Japan's principal source of information about Europe and the world beyond east Asia. A small number of Japanese scholars learned Dutch in order to communicate with the foreigners. Their studies, which they called "Dutch learning," brought considerable knowledge of the outside world to Japan. After 1720 Tokugawa authorities lifted the ban on foreign books, and Dutch learning began to play a significant role in Japanese intellectual life.

European art influenced Japanese scholars interested in anatomy and botany because of its accurate representations of objects. Scholars translated Dutch medical and scientific treatises into Japanese and learned to draw according to the principles of linear perspective, which enabled them to prepare textbooks that were more accurate than the Chinese works they had previously used. European astronomy was also popular in Japan, since it enabled scholars to improve calendars and issue accurate predictions of eclipses and other celestial events. By the mid-eighteenth century the Tokugawa shoguns themselves had become enthusiastic proponents of Dutch learning, and schools of European medicine and Dutch studies flourished in several Japanese cities.

Both China and Japan controlled their own affairs throughout the early modern era and avoided the turmoil that afflicted societies in the Americas and much of sub-Saharan Africa. After driving the Mongols to the steppelands of central Asia, rulers of the Ming dynasty built a powerful centralized state in China. They worked diligently to eradicate all vestiges of Mongol rule and restore traditional ways by reviving Chinese political institutions and providing state sponsorship for neo-Confucianism. In the interest of stability, authorities also restricted foreign merchants' access to China and limited the activities of Christian missionaries. The succeeding Qing dynasty pursued similar policies. The Ming and Qing dynasties both brought political stability, but China experienced considerable social and economic change in early modern times. American food crops helped increase agricultural production, which fueled rapid population growth, and global trade stimulated the Chinese economy, which improved the position of merchants and artisans in society. The experience of Tokugawa Japan was much like that of Ming and Qing China. The Tokugawa bakufu brought political order to the Japanese islands and closely controlled foreign relations, but a vibrant economy promoted social change that enhanced the status of merchants and artisans.

CHRONOLOGY

1368–1644	Ming dynasty (China)
1368–1398	Reign of Emperor Hongwu
1403–1424	Reign of Emperor Yongle
1552–1610	Life of Matteo Ricci
1572–1620	Reign of Emperor Wanli
1600–1867	Tokugawa shogunate (Japan)
1616–1626	Reign of Nurhaci
1642–1693	Life of Ihara Saikaku
1644–1911	Qing dynasty (China)
1661–1722	Reign of Kangxi
1736–1795	Reign of Qianlong

FOR FURTHER READING

George Elison. *Deus Destroyed: The Image of Christianity in Early Modern Japan.* Cambridge, Mass., 1973. Scholarly study of the Jesuit mission in Japan and its end during the early Tokugawa era.

Mark Elvin. *The Pattern of the Chinese Past: A Social and Economic Interpretation.* Stanford, 1973. A brilliant analysis of Chinese history concentrating on economic, social, and technological themes.

Jacques Gernet. *China and the Christian Impact.* Trans. by J. Lloyd. Cambridge, 1985. A careful study of the Jesuit mission in China, concentrating on the cultural differences between Chinese and Europeans.

Susan B. Hanley. *Economic and Demographic Change in Pre-Industrial Japan, 1600–1868.* Princeton, 1977. Argues that the Tokugawa period was crucial for the development of modern Japanese history.

Harry D. Harootunian. *Things Seen and Unseen: Discourse and Ideology in Tokugawa Nativism.* Chicago, 1988. A challenging scholarly analysis of the efforts by Tokugawa thinkers to construct a distinctive Japanese identity.

Ping-ti Ho. *Studies on the Population of China, 1368–1953.* Chicago, 1959. A venerable study that is the point of departure for modern studies in Chinese demography.

Ray Huang. *1587: A Year of No Significance.* New Haven, 1981. A very good history of the late Ming, with insights into daily life.

Donald Keene. *The Japanese Discovery of Europe, 1720–1830.* Rev. ed. Stanford, 1969. A highly readable account of Japanese encounters with Europe by way of Dutch merchants.

Ichisada Miyazaki. *China's Examination Hell: The Civil Service Examinations in Imperial China.* Trans. by Conrad Schirokauer. New Haven, 1981. Explores all aspects of the labyrinthine civil service examination system.

Susan Naquin and Evelyn S. Rawski. *Chinese Society in the Eighteenth Century.* New Haven, 1987. A lucid and well-organized discussion of Chinese social history.

Jonathan D. Spence. *The Death of Woman Wang.* New York, 1978. Engaging reconstruction of life in rural China during the early Qing dynasty.

———. *Emperor of China: Self-Portrait of K'ang-Hsi.* New York, 1974. Outstanding introduction to the reign of Kangxi based partly on recently discovered documents, some written by the emperor himself.

Ronald P. Toby. *State and Diplomacy in Early Modern Japan: Asia in the Development of the Tokugawa Bakufu.* Princeton, 1984. An important study dealing with Japanese trade and relations with other lands under Tokugawa rule.

Conrad Totman. *Early Modern Japan.* Berkeley, 1993. An outstanding survey of Tokugawa ecological, political, social, economic, and cultural history.

H. Paul Varley. *Japanese Culture.* 3rd ed. Honolulu, 1984. Places the cultural history of the Tokugawa era in its larger historical context.

Frederic Wakeman Jr. *The Great Enterprise: The Manchu Reconstruction of the Imperial Order in Seventeenth-Century China,* 2 vols. Berkeley, 1985. Important scholarly analysis of early Qing history.

Arthur Waldron. *The Great Wall of China: From History to Myth.* Cambridge, 1990. Fascinating work that places the Great Wall of Ming China in the context of earlier efforts to build defensive walls.

THE ISLAMIC EMPIRES

· · · ·

In 1635 Shah Jahan, the emperor of Mughal India, took his seat on the Peacock Throne. Seven years in the making, the Peacock Throne is probably the most spectacular seat on which any mortal human being has rested. Shah Jahan ordered the throne encrusted with ten-million rupees' worth of diamonds, rubies, emeralds, and pearls. Atop the throne itself stood a magnificent, golden-bodied peacock with a huge ruby and a fifty-carat, pear-shaped pearl on its breast and a brilliant elevated tail fashioned of blue sapphires and other colored gems.

Yet for all its splendor, the Peacock Throne ranks a distant second among Shah Jahan's artistic projects: pride of place goes to the incomparable Taj Mahal. Built over a period of eighteen years as a tomb for Shah Jahan's beloved wife Mumtaz Mahal, who died in childbirth in 1631, the Taj Mahal is a graceful and elegant monument both to the departed empress and to Shah Jahan's Islamic faith.

The emperor and his architects conceived the Taj Mahal as a vast allegory in stone symbolizing the day when Allah would cause the dead to rise and undergo judgment before his heavenly throne. Its gardens represented the gardens of paradise, and the four water channels running through them symbolized the four rivers of the heavenly kingdom. The domed marble tomb of Mumtaz Mahal represented the throne of Allah, and the four minarets surrounding the structure served as legs supporting the divine throne. Craftsmen carved verses from the Quran throughout the Taj Mahal. The main gateway to the structure features the entire text of the chapter promising that on the day of judgment, Allah will punish the wicked and gather the faithful into his celestial paradise.

The Peacock Throne and the Taj Mahal testify to the wealth of the Mughal empire, and the tomb of Mumtaz Mahal bespeaks also the fundamentally Islamic character of the ruling dynasty. But the Mughal realm was not the only well-organized Islamic empire of early modern times. The Ottoman dynasty ruled a powerful empire that expanded from its base in Anatolia to embrace much of eastern Europe, Egypt, and north Africa. The Safavid dynasty never expanded far beyond Persia, but its rulers challenged the Ottomans for dominance in southwest Asia, and the Safavid realm prospered from its role in trade networks linking China, India, Russia, southwest Asia, and the Mediterranean basin.

All three Islamic empires of early modern times had Turkish ruling dynasties. The Ottomans, Safavids, and Mughals came from nomadic, Turkish-speaking peoples of central Asia who conquered the settled agricultural lands of Anatolia, Persia, and India, respectively. All three dynasties retained political and cultural traditions

The Süleymaniyye mosque built for Sultan Süleyman the Magnificent by the Ottoman architect Sinan Pasha in 1556. • © Harvey Lloyd/The Stock Market

that their ancestors had adopted while leading nomadic lives on the steppes, but they also adapted readily to the city-based agricultural societies that they conquered. The Ottoman dynasty made especially effective use of the gunpowder weapons that transformed early modern warfare, and the Safavids and Mughals also incorporated gunpowder weapons into their arsenals. All three dynasties officially embraced Islam and drew cultural guidance from Islamic values.

During the sixteenth and early seventeenth centuries, the three Islamic empires presided over expansive and prosperous societies. About the mid-seventeenth century, however, they all began to weaken. Their waning fortunes reflected the fact that they had ceased to expand territorially and gain access to new sources of wealth. Instead, each empire waged long, costly wars that drained resources without bringing compensating benefits. Furthermore, the Islamic empires made little investment in economic and technological development. By the mid-eighteenth century the Safavid empire had collapsed, and the Ottoman and Mughal realms were rapidly falling under European domination.

 ## FORMATION OF THE ISLAMIC EMPIRES

The Islamic empires began as small warrior principalities in frontier areas. They expanded at varying rates and with varying degrees of success at the expense of neighboring states. As they grew, they devised elaborate administrative and military institutions. Under the guidance of talented and energetic rulers, each empire organized an effective governmental apparatus and presided over a prosperous society.

The Ottoman Empire

Osman   The Ottoman empire was an unusually successful frontier state. The term *Ottoman* derived from Osman Bey, founder of the dynasty that continued in unbroken succession from 1289 until the dissolution of the empire in 1923. Osman was chief (*bey*) of a band of seminomadic Turks who migrated to northwestern Anatolia in the thirteenth century. Osman and his followers sought above all to become *ghazi,* Muslim religious warriors. In his encomium of the Ottomans, the poet Ahmadi described their ethos: "The Ghazi is the instrument of the religion of Allah, a servant of God who purifies the earth from the filth of polytheism; the Ghazi is the sword of God, he is the protector and the refuge of the believers. If he becomes a martyr in the ways of God, do not believe that he has died—he lives in beatitude with Allah, he has eternal life."

Ottoman Expansion   The Ottomans' location on the borders of the Byzantine empire afforded them ample opportunity to wage holy war. Their first great success came in 1326 with the capture of the beautiful Anatolian city of Bursa, which became the capital of the Ottoman principality. Around 1352 they established a foothold in Europe when they seized the fortress of Gallipoli while aiding a claimant to the Byzantine throne. Numerous *ghazi,* many of them recent converts, soon flocked to join the Ottomans. The city of Edirne (Adrianople) became a second Ottoman capital and served as a base for further expansion into the Balkans. As warriors settled in frontier districts and pushed their boundaries forward, they took spoils and gathered revenues that enriched both the *ghazi* and the central government. Bursa developed into a major commercial and intellectual center with inns, shops, schools, libraries, and mosques.

The city of Bursa in western Anatolia was the first great Ottoman conquest, and it served as the empire's first capital and site of the royal cemetery. It was also an important cultural center and emporium for the silk trade and textile production. • Adam Woolfitt/Woodfin Camp & Associates

A formidable military machine drove Ottoman expansion. Ottoman military leaders initially organized *ghazi* recruits into two forces: a light cavalry and a volunteer infantry. As the Ottoman state became more firmly established, it added a professional cavalry force equipped with heavy armor and financed by land grants. After expanding into the Balkans, the Ottomans created a supremely important force composed of slave troops. Through an institution known as the *devshirme,* the Ottomans required the Christian population of the Balkans to contribute young boys to become slaves of the sultan. The boys received special training, learned Turkish, and converted to Islam. According to individual ability, they entered either the Ottoman civilian administration or the military. Those who became soldiers were known as Janissaries, from the Turkish *yeni cheri* ("new troops"). The Janissaries quickly gained a reputation for esprit de corps, loyalty to the sultan, and readiness to employ new military technology. Besides building powerful military forces, the Ottomans outfitted their forces with gunpowder weapons and used them effectively in battles and sieges.

The capture of Constantinople in 1453 by Mehmed II (reigned 1451–1481)— known as Mehmed the Conqueror—opened a new chapter in Ottoman expansion. With its superb location and illustrious heritage, Constantinople became the new Ottoman capital, subsequently known as Istanbul, and Mehmed worked energetically to stimulate its role as a commercial center. With the capture of the great city behind him, Mehmed presented himself not just as a warrior sultan but as a true emperor, ruler of the "two lands" (Europe and Asia) and the "two seas" (the Black Sea and the Mediterranean). He laid the foundations for a tightly centralized, absolute monarchy, and his army faced no serious rival. He completed the conquest of Serbia, moved into southern Greece and Albania, eliminated the last Byzantine outpost at Trebizond, captured Genoese ports in the Crimea, initiated a naval war with

Mehmed the Conqueror

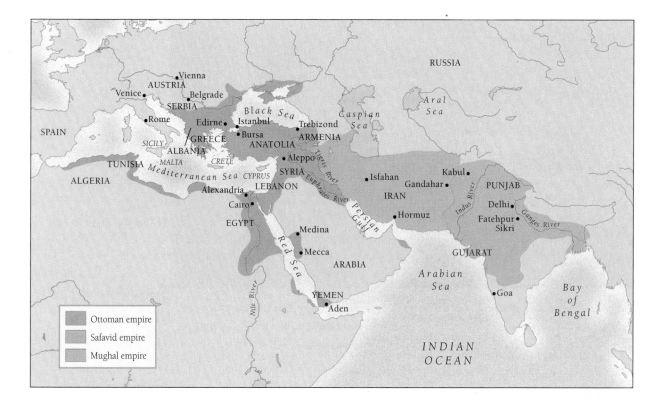

MAP [27.1]

The Ottoman, Safavid, and Mughal empires.

Süleyman the Magnificent

Venice in the Mediterranean, and reportedly hoped to cross the Straits of Otranto, march on Rome, and capture the pope himself. Toward the end of his life he launched an invasion of Italy and briefly occupied Otranto, but his successors abandoned Mehmed's plans for expansion in western Europe.

The Ottomans continued their expansion in the early sixteenth century when sultan Selim the Grim (reigned 1512–1520) occupied Syria and Egypt. Ottoman imperialism climaxed in the reign of Süleyman the Magnificent (reigned 1520–1566). Süleyman vigorously promoted Ottoman expansion both in southwest Asia and in Europe. In 1534 he conquered Baghdad and added the Tigris and Euphrates valleys to the Ottoman domain. In Europe he kept the rival Habsburg empire on the defensive throughout his reign. He captured Belgrade in 1521, defeated and killed the king of Hungary at the battle of Mohács in 1526, consolidated Ottoman power north of the Danube, and in 1529 subjected the Habsburgs' prized city of Vienna to a brief but nonetheless terrifying siege.

Under Süleyman the Ottomans also became a major naval power. In addition to their own Aegean and Black Sea fleets, the Ottomans inherited the navy of the Mamluk rulers of Egypt. A Turkish corsair, Khayr al-Din Barbarossa Pasha, who had challenged Spanish forces in Tunisia and Algeria, placed his pirate fleet under the Ottoman flag and became Süleyman's leading admiral. Thus Süleyman was able to challenge Christian vessels throughout the Mediterranean and Portuguese fleets in the Red Sea and Indian Ocean. The Ottomans seized the island of Rhodes from the Knights of St. John, besieged Malta, secured Yemen and Aden, and even dispatched a squadron to attack the Portuguese fleet at Diu in India.

The Safavid Empire

In 1499 a twelve-year-old boy named Ismail left the swamps of Gilan near the Caspian Sea, where he had hidden from the enemies of his family for five years, to seek his revenge. Two years later he entered Tabriz at the head of an army and laid claim to the ancient Persian imperial title of shah. The young Shah Ismail (reigned 1501–1524) also proclaimed that the official religion of his realm would be Twelver Shiism, and he proceeded to impose it, by force when necessary, on the formerly Sunni population. Over the next decade he seized control of the Iranian plateau and launched expeditions into the Caucasus, Anatolia, Mesopotamia, and central Asia.

The Safavids

For propaganda purposes Shah Ismail and his successors carefully controlled accounts of their rise to power—and expediently changed the story when circumstances warranted. They traced their ancestry back to Safi al-Din (1252–1334), leader of a Sufi religious order in northwestern Persia. The famous tomb and shrine of Safi al-Din at Ardabil became the home of his family (named "Safavids" after the holy man himself), the headquarters of his religious movement, and the center of a determined, deliberate conspiracy to win political power for his descendants. The Safavids changed their religious preferences several times in the hope of gaining popular support before settling on a form of Shiism that appealed to the nomadic Turkish tribes moving into the area in the post-Mongol era.

Twelver Shiism

Twelver Shiism held that there had been twelve infallible imams (or religious leaders) after Muhammad, beginning with the prophet's cousin and son-in-law Ali. The twelfth or "hidden" imam had gone into hiding around 874 to escape persecution, but the Twelver Shiites believed he was still alive and would one day return to take power and spread his true religion. Ismail's father had instructed his Turkish followers to wear a distinctive red hat with twelve pleats in memory of the twelve Shiite imams, and they subsequently became known as the *qizilbash* ("red heads"). Safavid propaganda also suggested that Ismail was himself the hidden imam, or even an incarnation of Allah. Although most Muslims, including most Shiites, would have regarded these pretensions as utterly blasphemous, the *qizilbash* enthusiastically accepted them, since they resembled traditional Turkish conceptions of leadership that associated military leaders with divinity. The *qizilbash* believed that Ismail would make them invincible in battle, and they became fanatically loyal to the Safavid cause.

Shah Ismail's curious blend of Shiism and Turkish militancy gave his regime a distinctive identity, but it also created some powerful enemies. Foremost among them were the staunchly Sunni Ottomans who detested the Shiite Safavids and feared the spread of Safavid propaganda among the nomadic Turks in their own territory. As soon as Selim the Grim became sultan, he launched a persecution of Shiites in the Ottoman empire and prepared for a full-scale invasion of Safavid territory.

Battle of Chaldiran

At the critical battle on the plain of Chaldiran (1514), the Ottomans deployed heavy artillery and thousands of Janissaries equipped with firearms behind a barrier of carts. Although the Safavids knew about gunpowder technology and had access to firearms, they declined to use devices that they saw as unreliable and unmanly. Trusting in the protective charisma of Shah Ismail, the *qizilbash* cavalry fearlessly attacked the Ottoman line and suffered devastating casualties. Ismail had to slip away, and the Ottomans temporarily occupied his capital at Tabriz. The Ottomans badly damaged the Safavid state but lacked the resources to destroy it completely, and the two empires remained locked in intermittent conflict for the next two centuries.

Shah Ismail and the *qizilbash.* Thia miniature painting from a Safavid manuscript depicts the shah and his *qizilbash* warriors wearing the distinctive red pleated cap that was their emblem of identity. ● © The British Library

Later Safavid rulers recovered from the disaster at Chaldiran. They relied more heavily than Ismail had on the Persian bureaucracy and its administrative talents. Ismail's successors abandoned the extreme Safavid ideology that associated the emperor with Allah in favor of more conventional Twelver Shiism, from which they still derived legitimacy as descendants and representatives of the imams. They also assigned land grants to the *qizilbash* officers to retain their loyalty and give them a stake in the survival of the regime.

Shah Abbas the Great (reigned 1588–1629) fully revitalized the Safavid empire. He moved the capital to the more central location of Isfahan, encouraged trade with other lands, and reformed the administrative and military institutions of the empire. He incorporated "slaves of the royal household" into the army, increased the use of gunpowder weapons, and sought European assistance against the Ottomans and the Portuguese in the Persian Gulf. With newly strengthened

Shah Abbas the Great military forces, Shah Abbas led the Safavids to numerous victories. He attacked and defeated the nomadic Uzbeks in central Asia, expelled the Portuguese from Hormuz, and harassed the Ottomans mercilessly in a series of wars from 1603 to the end of his reign. His campaigns brought most of northwestern Iran, the Caucasus, and Mesopotamia under Safavid rule.

The Mughal Empire

Babur In 1523 Zahir al-Din Muhammad, known as Babur ("the Tiger"), a Chagatai Turk who claimed descent from both Chinggis Khan and Tamerlane, suddenly appeared in northern India. Unlike the Ottomans, who sought to be renowned *ghazis,* or the

Safavids, who acted as champions of Shiism, Babur made little pretense to be anything more than an adventurer and soldier of fortune in the manner of his illustrious ancestors. His father had been the prince of Farghana, and Babur's great ambition was to transform his inheritance into a glorious central Asian empire. Yet envious relatives and Uzbek enemies frustrated his ambitions.

Never able to extend his authority much beyond Kabul and Qandahar and reduced at times to hardship and a handful of followers, Babur turned his attention to India. With the aid of gunpowder weapons, including both artillery and firearms, Babur mounted invasions in 1523 and 1525, and he took Delhi in 1526. Ironically, Babur cared little for the land he had conquered. Many in his entourage wanted to take their spoils of war and leave the hot and humid Indian climate, which ruined their finely crafted compound bows, but Babur elected to stay. He probably hoped to use the enormous wealth of

The Royal Mosque of Isfahan, centerpiece of the city as rebuilt by Shah Abbas at the end of the sixteenth century. With its combination of an open space flanked by markets, the palace, and religious structures, Isfahan stands as a unique example of urban planning in Islamic lands. • William Hubbell/Woodfin Camp & Associates

India to build a vast central Asian empire like that of Tamerlane—an elusive dream that his successors would nonetheless continue to cherish. By the time of his death in 1530, Babur had built a loosely knit empire that stretched from Kabul through the Punjab to the borders of Bengal. He founded a dynasty called the *Mughal* (a Persian term for "Mongol"), which expanded to embrace almost all the Indian subcontinent.

The real architect of the Mughal empire was Babur's grandson Akbar (reigned *Akbar* 1556–1605), a brilliant and charismatic ruler. Akbar gathered the reins of power in his own hands in 1561 following an argument with Adham Khan, a powerful figure at the imperial court and commander of the Mughal army. Akbar threw Adham Khan out a window, then dragged him back from the palace courtyard, and tossed him out again to make sure he was dead. Thereafter Akbar took personal control of the Mughal government and did not tolerate challenges to his rule. He created a

A CONQUEROR AND HIS CONQUESTS: BABUR ON INDIA

• • •

Babur was a talented writer as well as a successful warrior. His memoirs make fascinating reading and provide a unique perspective on early Mughal India. His writings include his reflections on the territories he conquered in India, which he compared unfavorably to his central Asian homeland, and on his decision to stay in India and found an empire.

Most of the inhabitants of India are infidels, called Hindus, believing mainly in the transmigration of souls; all artisans, wage-earners and officials are Hindus. In our countries the desert dwellers get tribal names; here people settled in the cultivated villages also get tribal names. Again, every artisan follows the trade handed down to him from his forefathers.

India is a country of few charms. The people lack good looks and good manners. They have no social life or exchange of visits. They have no genius or intelligence, no polite learning, no generosity of magnanimity, no harmony or proportion in their arts and crafts, no lead-wire or carpenter's square. They lack good horses and good dogs; grapes, melons, and any good fruit; ice and cold water; good food or good bread in the markets. They have no baths and no advanced educational institutions. . . . There are no running streams in their gardens or residences, no waters at all except the large rivers and the swamps in the ravines and hollows. Their residences have no pleasant and salubrious breezes, and in their construction [there is] no form or symmetry. . . .

Among the charms that India does possess is that it is a large country, with large quantities of gold and silver. Its air in the rainy season is very fine. Sometimes it rains ten or fifteen or even twenty times a day, and in such torrents that rivers flow where no water was previously. While it rains, and throughout the rainy season, the air is remarkably fine, not to be surpassed for mildness and pleasantness. Its only fault is its great humidity, which spoils bows. . . .

It was the hot season when we came to Agra. All the inhabitants had run away in terror. We could find neither grain for ourselves nor corn for our horses. The villages, out of hostility and hatred for us, had taken to thieving and highway-robbery, and it was impossible to travel on the roads. We had not yet the opportunity to distribute the treasure and to assign men in strength to each district. Moreover, the year was a very hot one, pestilential simooms [sandstorms] were striking people down in heaps, and masses were beginning to die off.

For all these reasons, most of the the best warriors were unwilling to stay in India; in fact, they determined to leave. . . .

When I discovered this unsteadiness among my people, I summoned all the leaders and took counsel. I said, "Without means and resources there is no empire and conquest, and without lands and followers there is no sovereignty and rule. By the effort of long years, through much tribulation and the crossing of distant lands, by flinging ourselves into battle and danger, we have through God's favor overcome so many enemies and conquered such vast lands. And now, what force compels us, what necessity has arisen, that we should, without cause, abandon a country taken at such risk of life? And if we returned to Kabul, we would again be left in poverty and weakness. Henceforth, let no well-wisher of mine speak of such things! But let not those turn back from going who cannot bear the hardship and have determined to leave." With such words I reasoned with them and made them, willy-nilly, quit their fears.

SOURCE: Babur. *The Babur-nama in English (Memoirs of Babur)*, Trans. by Annette Susannah Beveridge. London: Luzac, 1922. (Translation slightly modified.)

centralized administrative structure with ministries regulating the various provinces of the empire. His military campaigns consolidated Mughal power in Gujarat and Bengal. He destroyed the Hindu kingdom of Vijayanagar, thus laying the foundation for later Mughal expansion in southern India.

Although he was a no-nonsense ruler, Akbar was also a thoughtful, reflective man deeply interested in religion and philosophy. He pursued a policy of religious toleration that he hoped would reduce tensions between Hindu and Muslim communities in India. Although illiterate (probably due to dyslexia), he was extremely intelligent and had books read to him daily. Instead of imposing Islam on his subjects, he encouraged the elaboration of a syncretic religion called the "divine faith" that focused attention on the emperor as a ruler common to all the religious, ethnic, and social groups of India.

The Mughal empire reached its greatest extent under Aurangzeb (reigned 1659–1707). During his long reign Aurangzeb waged

This manuscript illumination from about 1590 depicts Akbar (at top, shaded by attendants) inspecting construction of a new imperial capital at Fatehpur Sikri. • Victoria & Albert Museum, London/Art Resource, NY

a relentless campaign to push Mughal authority deep into southern India. By the early eighteenth century, Mughals ruled the entire subcontinent except for a small region at the southern tip.

Aurangzeb

Although he greatly expanded Mughal boundaries, Aurangzeb presided over a troubled empire. He faced rebellions throughout his reign, and religious tensions generated conflicts between Hindus and Muslims. Aurangzeb was a devout Muslim, and he broke with Akbar's policy of religious toleration. He demolished several famous Hindu temples and replaced them with mosques. He also imposed a tax on Hindus in an effort to encourage conversion to Islam. His promotion of Islam appealed strongly to the Mughals themselves and other Indian Muslims as well, but it provoked deep hostility among Hindus and enabled local leaders to organize movements to resist or even rebel against Mughal authority.

IMPERIAL ISLAMIC SOCIETY

Despite many differences, there were striking similarities in the development of Ottoman, Safavid, and Mughal societies. All relied on bureaucracies that drew inspiration from the steppe traditions of Turkish and Mongol peoples as well as from the heritage of Islam. They adopted similar economic policies and sought ways to maintain harmony in societies that embraced many different religious and ethnic groups. Rulers of all the empires also sought to enhance the legitimacy of their regimes by providing for public welfare and associating themselves with literary and artistic talent.

The Dynastic State

The Ottoman, Safavid, and Mughal empires were all military creations, regarded by their rulers as their personal possessions by right of conquest. The rulers exercised personal command of the armies, appointed and dismissed officials at will, and adopted whatever policies they wished. In theory, the emperors owned all land and granted use of it to peasant families on a hereditary basis in return for the payment of fixed taxes. The emperors and their families derived revenues from crown lands, and revenues from other lands supported military and administrative officials.

The Emperors and Islam
In the Ottoman, Safavid, and Mughal empires, the prestige and authority of the dynasty derived from the personal piety and the military prowess of the ruler and his ancestors. The Safavids were prominent leaders of a Sufi religious order, and the Ottomans and Mughals associated closely with famous Sufis. Devotion to Islam encouraged rulers to extend their faith to new lands. The *ghazi* ideal of spreading Islam by fighting infidels or heretics resonated with the traditions of Turkish and Mongolian peoples: on the steppes fighting was routine, and successful warriors became charismatic leaders.

Steppe Traditions
The autocratic authority wielded by the rulers of the Islamic empires also reflected steppe traditions. The early emperors largely did as they pleased, irrespective of religious and social norms. The Ottoman sultans, for example, unilaterally issued numerous legal edicts. The greatest of these were the many *kanun* ("laws") issued by Süleyman—Europeans called him "Süleyman the Magnificent," but the Ottomans referred to him as Süleyman Kanuni, "the Lawgiver." Safavid and Mughal rulers went even further than the Ottomans in asserting their spiritual authority. Shah Ismail did not hesitate to force his Shiite religion on his subjects. Akbar issued a decree in 1579 claiming broad authority in religious matters, and he promoted his own eclectic religion, which glorified the emperor as much as Islam.

Steppe practices also brought succession problems. In the steppe empires the ruler's relatives often managed components of the states, and succession to the throne became a hot contest between competing members of the family. The Mughal empire in particular became tied up in family controversies: conflicts among Mughal princes and rebellions of sons against fathers were recurrent features throughout the history of the empire. The Safavids also engaged in murderous struggles for the throne. Shah Abbas himself lived in fear that another member of the family would challenge him. He kept his sons confined to the palace and killed or blinded relatives he suspected, almost wiping out his family in the process.

The early Ottomans assigned provinces for the sultan's sons to administer but kept the empire as a whole tightly unified. After the fifteenth century, however, the sultans moved to protect their position by eliminating family rivals. Mehmed the Conqueror decreed that a ruler could legally kill off his brothers after taking the throne. His successors observed this tradition in Turko-Mongol style—by strangling victims with a silk bow string so as not to shed royal blood—until 1595, when the new sultan executed nineteen brothers, many of them infants, as well as fifteen expectant mothers. After that episode sultans confined their sons in special quarters of the imperial harem and forbade them to go outside except to take the throne.

Women and Politics

Even though Muslim theorists universally agreed that women should have no role in public affairs and decried the involvement of women in politics as a sure sign of decadence, women played important roles in managing the Islamic empires. Many Ottoman, Safavid, and Mughal emperors followed the example of Chinggis Khan, who revered his mother and his first wife. In the Islamic empires the ruler's mother and his chief wife or favorite concubine enjoyed special privileges and authority. Ottoman courtiers often complained loudly about the "rule of women," thus offering eloquent testimony to the power that women could wield. Süleyman the Magnificent, for example, became infatuated with Hürrem Sultana (also known as Roxelana), a concubine of Ukrainian origin. Süleyman elevated her to the status of a legal wife, consulted her on state policies, and deferred to her judgment even to the point of executing his eldest son for treason when Hürrem wanted him eliminated to secure the succession of her own child. After Hürrem's death Süleyman constructed a mausoleum for her next to his own in the courtyard of the great mosque in Istanbul.

Women also played prominent political roles in the Safavid and Mughal empires. In Safavid Persia, Mahd-e Olya, the wife of one shah, was the de facto ruler. Her efforts to limit the power of the *qizilbash* so enraged them that they murdered her. The aunt of another shah scolded the ruler for neglecting his duties and used her own money to raise an army to put down a revolt. The Mughal emperor Jahangir was content to let his wife Nur Jahan run the government, and even the conscientious Muslim Aurangzeb listened to his daughter's political advice. Shah Jahan's devotion to his wife Mumtaz Mahal has become world famous because of the Taj Mahal.

The Taj Mahal, a sumptuous mosque and tomb built between 1632 and 1649 by Shah Jahan in memory of his wife Mumtaz Mahal, also known as Empress Nur Jahan. ● Gerard Champlong/The Image Bank

Agriculture and Trade

Food Crops   Productive agricultural economies were the foundations of all the Islamic empires. Each extracted surplus agricultural production and used it to finance armies and bureaucracies. Mostly the Islamic empires relied on crops of wheat and rice that had flourished for centuries in the lands they ruled. The Columbian exchange brought American crops to all the Islamic empires but without the same dramatic effects as in Europe, east Asia, and Africa. European merchants introduced maize, potatoes, tomatoes, and other crops to the Islamic empires, and the new arrivals soon found a place in regional cuisines. Potatoes appeared in the curries of southern India, and tomatoes enlivened dishes in the Ottoman empire as well as other Mediterranean lands. Maize did not appeal to human palates in the Islamic empires, but it became popular as feed for animal stocks, especially in the Ottoman empire.

The Columbian exchange strongly encouraged consumption of coffee and tobacco, especially in the Ottoman and Safavid empires. Although native to Ethiopia and cultivated in southern Arabia, coffee did not become popular in Islamic lands until the sixteenth century. Like sugar, it traveled to Europe and from there to the Americas, where plantations specialized in the production of tropical crops for the world market. By the eighteenth century American producers and European merchants supplied Muslim markets with both coffee and sugar.

Tobacco   According to the Ottoman historian Ibrahim Pechevi, English merchants introduced tobacco around 1600, claiming it was useful for medicinal purposes. Within a few decades it had spread throughout the Ottoman empire. The increasing popularity of coffee drinking and pipe smoking encouraged businessmen to establish coffeehouses where customers could indulge their appetites for caffeine and nicotine at the same time. The popularity of coffeehouses provoked protest from moralists who worried that these popular attractions were dens of iniquity that distracted men from their religious duties and attracted crowds of idlers and riffraff. Pechevi complained about the hideous odor of tobacco, the messy ashes, and the danger that smoking could cause fires, while religious leaders claimed that coffee was an illegal beverage and that it was worse to frequent a coffeehouse than a tavern. Sultan Murad IV went so far as to outlaw coffee and tobacco and to execute those who continued to partake. This, however, was a losing battle. Both pastimes eventually won widespread acceptance, and the coffeehouse became a prominent social institution in the Islamic empires.

Population Growth   American food crops had less demographic effect in the Islamic empires than in other parts of the world. The population of India surged during early modern times, growing from 105 million in 1500 to 135 million in 1600, 165 million in 1700, and 190 million in 1800. But population growth in India resulted more from intensive agriculture along traditional lines than from the influence of new crops. The Safavid population grew less rapidly, from 5 million in 1500 to 6 million in 1600, and to 8 million only in 1800. Ottoman numbers grew from 9 million in 1500 to 28 million in 1600, as the empire enlarged its boundaries to include populous regions in the Balkans, Egypt, and southwest Asia. After 1600, however, the Ottoman population declined to about 24 million, where it remained until the late nineteenth century. The decline reflected loss of territory more than a shrinking population, but even in the heartland of Anatolia, Ottoman numbers did not expand nearly as dramatically as those of other lands in early modern times. From 6 million in 1500, the population of Anatolia rose to 7.5 million in 1600, 8 million in 1700, and 9 million in 1800.

The Islamic empires ruled lands that had figured prominently in long-distance trade for centuries and participated actively in global trade networks in early modern times. In the Ottoman empire, for example, the early capital at Bursa was also the terminus of a caravan route that brought raw silk from Persia to supply the Italian market. The Ottomans also granted special trading concessions to merchants from England and France to cement alliances against common enemies in Spain and central Europe. Aleppo became an emporium for foreign merchants engaged primarily in the spice trade and served as local headquarters for the operations of the English Levant Company.

Trade

Shah Abbas promoted Isfahan as a commercial center, extending trading privileges to foreign merchants and even allowing Christian monastic orders to set up missions there to help create a favorable environment for trade. European merchants sought Safavid raw silk, carpets, ceramics, and high-quality craft items. The English East India Company, the French East India Company, and the Dutch VOC all traded actively with the Safavids. To curry favor with them, the English company sent military advisors to help introduce gunpowder weapons to Safavid armed forces and provided a navy to help them retake Hormuz in the Persian Gulf from the Portuguese.

A bustling bazaar in Mughal India. At the center of this painting, a soothsayer attracts a crowd as he consults a manual while telling fortunes. Sacks of coins at his side suggest that he has done good business. Elsewhere in the market consumers buy watermelons, cloth, and peanuts. ● Museum Rietberg-Zurich. Photo: Wettstein & Kauf

The Mughals did not pay as much attention to foreign trade as the Ottomans and Safavids did, partly because of the enormous size and productivity of the domestic Indian economy and partly because the Mughal rulers concentrated on their land empire and had little interest in maritime affairs. Nevertheless, the Mughal treasury derived significant income from foreign trade. The Mughals allowed the creation of trading stations and merchant colonies by Portuguese, English, French, and Dutch merchants. Indian merchants formed trading companies of their own, ventured overland as far as Russia, and sailed the waters of the Indian Ocean to port cities from Persia to Indonesia.

Religious Affairs in the Islamic Empires

All the Islamic empires had populations that were religiously and ethnically diverse, and imperial rulers had the daunting challenge of maintaining harmony between

Religious Diversity

different religious communities. The Ottoman empire included large numbers of Christians and Jews in the Balkans, Armenia, Lebanon, and Egypt. The Safavid empire embraced sizable Zoroastrian and Jewish communities, as well as many Christian subjects in the Caucasus. The Mughal empire was especially diverse. Most Mughal subjects were Hindus, but large numbers of Muslims lived alongside smaller communities of Jains, Zoroastrians, Christians, and devotees of syncretic faiths such as Sikhism.

Christian Mission in India

Portuguese Goa became the center of a Christian mission in India. Priests at Goa sought to attract converts to Christianity and established schools that provided religious instruction for Indian children. In 1580 several Portuguese Jesuits traveled to the Mughal court at Akbar's invitation. They had visions of converting the emperor to Christianity and then spreading their faith throughout India, but their hopes went unfulfilled. Akbar received the Jesuits cordially and welcomed their participation in religious and philosophical discussions at his court, but he declined to commit to an exclusive faith that he thought would alienate many of his subjects.

Indeed, Akbar was cool even to his own Islamic faith. In his efforts to find a religious synthesis that would serve as a cultural foundation for unity in his diverse empire, he supported the efforts of the early Sikhs, who combined elements of both Hinduism and Islam in a new syncretic faith. He also attempted to elaborate his own "divine faith" that would emphasize loyalty to the emperor and help bridge differences among the many religious and ethnic groups of his realm.

Status of Religious Minorities

The Islamic empires relied on a long-established model to deal with subjects who were not Muslims. They did not require conquered peoples to convert to Islam but extended to them the status of a protected people (*dhimmi*). In return for their loyalty and payment of a special tax known as *jizya, dhimmi* communities retained their personal freedom, kept their property, practiced their religion, and handled their own legal affairs. In the Ottoman empire, for example, autonomous religious communities known as *millet* retained their own civil laws, traditions, and languages. *Millet* communities usually also assumed social and administrative functions in matters concerning birth, marriage, death, health, and education.

The situation in the Mughal empire was different, since its large number of religious communities made a *millet* system impractical. Mughal rulers reserved the most powerful military and administrative positions for Muslims, but in the day-to-day management of affairs, Muslims and Hindus cooperated closely. Some Mughal emperors sought to forge links between religious communities. Akbar in particular worked to integrate Muslim and Hindu elites. In an effort to foster communication and understanding among the different religious communities of his realm, he abolished the *jizya;* tolerated all faiths; and sponsored discussions and debates between Muslims, Hindus, Jains, Zoroastrians, and Christians.

Promotion of Islam

Policies of religious tolerance were not popular with many Muslims, who worried that they would lose their religious identity and that toleration might lead to their absorption into Hindu society as another caste. They therefore insisted that Mughal rulers create and maintain an Islamic state based on Islamic law. When Aurangzeb reached the Mughal throne in 1659, this policy gained strength. Aurangzeb reinstated the *jizya* and promoted Islam as the official faith of Mughal India. His policy satisfied zealous Muslims but at the cost of deep bitterness among his Hindu subjects. Tension between Hindu and Muslim communities in India persisted throughout the Mughal dynasty and beyond.

Cultural Patronage of the Islamic Emperors

As the empires matured, the Islamic rulers sought to enhance their prestige through public works projects and patronage of scholars. They competed to attract outstanding religious scholars, poets, artists, and architects to their courts. They lavished resources on mosques, palaces, government buildings, bridges, fountains, schools, hospitals, and soup kitchens for the poor.

Capital cities and royal palaces were the most visible expressions of imperial majesty. The Ottomans beautified both Bursa and Edirne, but they took particular pride in Istanbul. Dilapidated and deserted after the conquest, it quickly revived and became a bustling, prosperous city of more than a million people. At its heart was the great Topkapi palace, which housed government offices, such as the mint, and meeting places for imperial councils. At its core was the sultan's residence with its harem, gardens, pleasure pavilions, and a repository for the most sacred possessions of the empire, including the mantle of the prophet Muhammad. Sultan Süleyman the Magnificent was fortunate to be able to draw on the talents of the architectural genius Sinan Pasha (1489–1588) to create the most celebrated of all the monuments of Istanbul. Sinan built a vast religious complex called the Süleymaniye, which blended Islamic and Byzantine architectural elements. It combined tall, slender minarets with large domed buildings supported by half domes in the style of the Byzantine church Hagia Sofia (which the Ottomans converted into the mosque of Aya Sofya).

Istanbul

In a seventeenth-century painting the emperor Akbar presides over discussions between representatives of various religious groups. Two Jesuits dressed in black robes kneel at the left.

● Reproduced by kind permission of the Trustees of the Chester Beatty Library, Dublin

Shah Abbas made his capital, Isfahan, into the queen of Persian cities and one *Isfahan* of the most precious jewels of urban architectural development anywhere in the world: its inhabitants still boast that "Isfahan is half the world." Abbas concentrated markets, the palace, and the royal mosque around a vast polo field and public square. Broad, shaded avenues and magnificent bridges linked the central city to its suburbs. Safavid architects made use of monumental entryways, vast arcades, spacious courtyards, and intricate, colorful decoration. Unlike the sprawling Ottoman and Mughal palaces, the Safavid palaces in Isfahan were relatively small and emphasized natural settings with gardens and pools. They were also much more open than Topkapi, with its series of inner courts and gates. Ali Qapu, the palace on the square in Isfahan, had a striking balcony, and most of the palaces had large, open verandas. The point was not only to enable the shah to observe outside activities but also to emphasize his visibility and accessibility, qualities long esteemed in the Persian tradition of kingship.

To some extent, in accordance with steppe traditions, the early Mughals regarded the capital as wherever the ruler happened to camp. Yet they too came to sponsor urban development. Their work skillfully blended central Asian traditions with elements of Hindu architecture, and they built on a scale that left no doubt about their wealth and resources. They constructed scores of mosques, fortresses, and palaces and sometimes created entire cities.

Fatehpur Sikri   The best example was Fatehpur Sikri, a city planned and constructed by Akbar that served as his capital from 1569 to 1585. It commemorated his conquest of the prosperous commercial province of Gujarat in a campaign that enabled Akbar to head off both Portuguese attacks and Ottoman intervention there. With its mint, records office, treasury, and audience hall, the new city demonstrated Akbar's strength and imperial ambitions. Fatehpur Sikri was also a private residence and retreat for the ruler, reproducing in stone a royal encampment with exquisite pleasure palaces where Akbar indulged his passions for music and conversation with scholars and poets. At yet another level, it was a dramatic display of Mughal piety and devotion, centered on the cathedral mosque and the mausoleum of Akbar's Sufi guru, Shaykh Salim Chisti. Despite their intensely Islamic character, many of the buildings

Fatehpur Sikri, built by Akbar in the 1570s, commemorated the emperor's military conquests and housed the tomb of his religious guide. It included a palace, an audience hall where Akbar attended religious and philosophical debates, and a great mosque. ● Byron Crader/Ric Ergenbright

consciously incorporated Indian elements such as verandas supported by columns and decorations of stone elephants. Even the tomb of Shaykh Chisti bore some resemblance to a Hindu shrine. Unfortunately, Akbar selected a poor site for the city and soon abandoned it because of its bad water supply.

The Taj Mahal

The most famous of the Mughal monuments—and one of the most prominent of all Islamic edifices—was the Taj Mahal. Shah Jahan had twenty thousand workers toil for eighteen years to erect the exquisite white marble mosque and tomb. He originally planned to build a similar mausoleum out of black marble for himself, but his son Aurangzeb deposed him before he could carry out the project. Shah Jahan spent his last years confined to a small cell with a tiny window, and only with the aid of a mirror was he able to catch the sight of his beloved wife's final resting place.

THE EMPIRES IN TRANSITION

The Islamic empires underwent radical change between the sixteenth and eighteenth centuries. The Safavid empire disappeared entirely. In 1722 a band of Afghan tribesmen marched all the way to Isfahan, blockaded the city until its starving inhabitants resorted to cannibalism, forced the shah to abdicate, and executed thousands of Safavid officials, as well as many members of the royal family. After the death of Aurangzeb in 1707, Mughal India experienced provincial rebellions and foreign invasions. By midcentury the subcontinent was falling under British imperial rule. By 1700 the Ottomans, too, were on the defensive: the sultans lost control over remote provinces such as Lebanon and Egypt, and throughout the eighteenth and nineteenth centuries European and Russian states placed political, military, and economic pressure on the shrinking Ottoman realm.

The Deterioration of Imperial Leadership

Strong and effective central authority was essential to the Islamic empires, and Muslim political theorists never tired of emphasizing the importance of rulers who were diligent, virtuous, and just. Weak, negligent, and corrupt rulers would allow institutions to become dysfunctional and social order to break down. The Ottomans were fortunate in having a series of talented sultans for three centuries, and the Safavids and Mughals produced their share of effective rulers as well.

Dynastic Decline

Eventually, however, all three dynasties had rulers who were incompetent or more interested in spending vast sums of money on personal pleasures than in tending to affairs of state. Moreover, all three dynasties faced difficulties because of suspicion and fighting among competing members of their ruling houses. The Ottomans sought to limit problems by confining princes in the palace, but this measure had several negative consequences. The princes had no opportunity to gain experience in government, but they were exposed to plots and intrigues of the various factions maneuvering to bring a favorable candidate to the throne. Notorious examples of problem rulers included Süleyman's successor Selim the Sot (reigned 1566–1574) and Ibrahim the Crazy (reigned 1640–1648), who taxed and spent to such excess that government officials deposed and murdered him. Several energetic rulers and talented ministers attempted to keep the government on track. Nonetheless, after the late seventeenth century, weak rule increasingly provoked mutinies in the army, provincial revolts, political corruption, economic oppression, and insecurity throughout the Ottoman realm.

Religious Tensions   Political troubles often arose from religious tensions. Conservative Muslim clerics strongly objected to policies and practices that they considered affronts to Islam. Muslim leaders had considerable influence in the Islamic empires because of their monopoly of education and their deep involvement in the everyday lives and legal affairs of ordinary subjects. The clerics mistrusted the emperors' interests in unconventional forms of Islam such as Sufism, complained bitterly when women or subjects who were not Muslims played influential political roles, and protested any exercise of royal authority that contradicted Islamic law.

In the Ottoman empire disaffected religious students often joined the Janissaries in revolt. A particularly serious threat came from the Wahhabi movement in Arabia, which denounced the Ottomans as dangerous religious innovators who were unfit to rule. Conservative Muslims fiercely protested the construction of an astronomical observatory in Istanbul and forced the sultan to demolish it in 1580. In 1742 they also forced the closure of the Ottoman printing press, which they regarded as an impious technology.

The Safavids, who began their reign by crushing Sunni religious authorities, fell under the domination of the very Shiites they had supported. Shiite leaders pressured the shahs to persecute Sunnis, non-Muslims, and even the Sufis who had helped establish the dynasty. Religious tensions also afflicted Mughal India. Already in the seventeenth century, the conservative Shaykh Ahmad Sirhindi (1564–1624) fearlessly rebuked Akbar for his policy of religious tolerance and his interest in other faiths. In the mid-eighteenth century, as he struggled to claim the Mughal throne, Aurangzeb drew on Sirhindi's ideas when he required non-Muslims to pay the poll tax and ordered the destruction of Hindu temples. These measures inflamed tensions between the various Sunni, Shiite, and Sufi branches of Islam and also fueled animosity among Hindus and other Mughal subjects who were not Muslims.

Economic and Military Decline

In the sixteenth century all the Islamic empires had strong domestic economies and played prominent roles in global trade networks. By the eighteenth century, however, domestic economies were under great stress, and foreign trade had declined dramatically or had fallen under the control of European powers. The Islamic empires were well on their way to becoming marginal lands that depended on goods produced elsewhere.

Economic Stagnation   The high cost of maintaining an expensive military and administrative apparatus helped to bring about economic decline in the Islamic empires. As long as the empires were expanding, they were able to finance their armies and bureaucracies with fresh resources extracted from newly conquered lands. When expansion slowed, ceased, or reversed, however, they faced the problem of supporting their institutions with limited resources. The long, costly, and unproductive wars fought by the Ottomans with the Habsburgs in central Europe, by the Safavids and Ottomans in Mesopotamia, and by Aurangzeb in southern India exhausted the treasuries of the Islamic empires without making fresh resources available to them. As early as 1589 the Ottomans tried to pay the Janissaries in debased coinage and immediately provoked a mutiny. The next 150 years witnessed at least six additional military revolts.

As expansion slowed and the empires lost control over remote provinces, officials reacted to the loss of revenue by raising taxes, selling public offices, accepting bribes, or resorting to simple extortion. All these measures were counterproductive. Although they might provide immediate cash, they did long-term economic damage.

To make matters worse, the governments viewed foreign trade as just another opportunity to bring in revenue. The Ottomans expanded the privileges enjoyed by foreign merchants, and the Mughals encouraged the establishment of Dutch and English trading outposts and welcomed the expansion of their business in India. Imperial authorities were content to have foreign traders come to them. None made serious efforts to establish commercial stations abroad, although Indian merchants organized their own private trading companies.

As they lost initiative to western European peoples in economic and commercial affairs, the Islamic empires also experienced military decline because they did not seek actively to improve their military technologies. As early as the fifteenth century, the Ottomans had relied heavily on European technology in gunnery; indeed, the cannon that Mehmed the Conqueror used in 1453 to breach the defensive wall of Constantinople was the product of a Hungarian gun-founder. During the sixteenth and early seventeenth centuries, the Islamic empires were able to purchase European weapons in large numbers and attract European expertise that kept their armies supplied with powerful gunpowder weapons. In 1605, for example, the cargo of an English ship bound for Anatolia included seven hundred barrels of gunpowder, one thousand musket barrels, five hundred fully assembled muskets, and two thousand sword blades, alongside wool textiles and bullion.

All the Islamic empires fought numerous wars, many of which exhausted resources without adding to the productive capacities of the empires. This illustration depicts Ottoman forces (right) clashing with heavily armored Austrian cavalry near Budapest in 1540. • Topkapi Palace Museum. Photograph: Ergun Catagy

Military Decline

By about the mid-seventeenth century, European military technology was advancing so rapidly that the Islamic empires could not keep pace. None of the empires had a large armaments industry, so they had to rely on foreign suppliers. They still were able to purchase European weapons and expertise, but their arsenals became increasingly dated, since they depended on technologies that European peoples had already replaced. By the late eighteenth century, the Ottoman navy, which had long influenced maritime affairs in the Mediterranean, Red Sea, Persian Gulf, and Arabian Sea, was closing its shipbuilding operations and ordering new military vessels from foreign shipyards.

Cultural Insularity

While experiencing economic and military decline, the Islamic empires also neglected cultural developments in the larger world. Europeans who visited the Islamic empires attempted to learn as much as possible about the language, religion, social customs, and history of the host countries. They published accounts of their travels that became extremely popular in their homelands, and they advocated serious study of Islamic lands. In the early seventeenth century, for example, the English scholar William Bedwell described Arabic as the only important language of trade, diplomacy, and religion from Morocco to the China seas.

Cultural Conservatism

There is little evidence of a flow of information in the other direction. Few Muslims traveled willingly to the infidel lands of "the Franks." Muslim rulers and their Muslim subjects were absolutely confident of their superiority and believed that they had nothing to learn from Europeans. As a result, most Muslims remained largely oblivious to cultural and technological developments. Not until 1703 was there an attempt to introduce European scientific instruments such as the telescope into astronomical observatories. Then conservative Muslim clerics soon forced the removal of the foreign implements, which they considered impious and unnecessary.

The Printing Press

The early experience of the printing press in the Islamic empires illustrates especially well the resistance of conservative religious leaders to cultural imports from western Europe. Jewish refugees from Spain introduced the first printing presses to Anatolia in the late fifteenth century. Ottoman authorities allowed them to operate presses in Istanbul and other major cities as long as they did not print books in the Turkish or Arabic language. Armenian and Greek printers soon established presses in the Ottoman realm and published books in their own languages. Not until 1729 did government authorities lift the ban on the printing of books in Turkish and Arabic languages. During the next thirteen years, a Turkish press published seventeen books dealing mostly with history, geography, and language before conservative Muslims forced its closure in 1742. Only in 1784 did a new Turkish press open, and printing spread throughout the Ottoman empire soon thereafter.

Printing also caught on slowly in Mughal India. Jesuit missionaries in Goa published books, including translations of the Bible into Indian and Arabic languages, as early as the 1550s. Yet Mughal rulers displayed little interest in the press, and printing did not become prominent in Indian society until the establishment of British colonial rule in Bengal in the eighteenth century.

Thus like imperial China and Tokugawa Japan, the Islamic empires resisted the introduction of cultural influences from western European societies. Rulers of the Islamic empires readily accepted gunpowder weapons as enhancements to their military and political power, but they and their subjects drew little inspiration from European religion, science, or ideas. Moreover, under the influence of conservative religious leaders, Islamic authorities actively discouraged the circulation of writings that might pose unsettling challenges to the social and cultural order of the Islamic empires. Like the Ming, Qing, and Tokugawa rulers, the Ottoman, Safavid, and Mughal emperors preferred political and social stability to the risks that foreign cultural innovations might bring.

Like China and Japan, the Islamic empires largely retained control of their own affairs throughout the early modern era. Ruling elites of the Ottoman, Safavid, and Mughal empires came from nomadic Turkish stock, and they all drew on steppe traditions in organizing their governments. But the rulers also adapted steppe traditions to the needs of settled agricultural societies and devised institutions that maintained order over a long term. During the sixteenth and seventeenth centuries, all the Islamic empires enjoyed productive economies that enabled merchants to participate actively in the global trade networks of early modern times. By the early eighteenth century, however, these same empires were experiencing economic difficulties that led to political and military decline. Like the Ming, Qing, and Tokugawa rulers in east Asia, the Islamic emperors mostly sought to limit foreign and especially European influences in their realms. The Islamic emperors ruled lands that were religiously and ethnically diverse, and most of them worried that the expansion of foreign religious and cultural traditions would threaten political and social stability. They allowed their subjects to practice faiths other than Islam, and the Mughal emperor Akbar even promoted a syncretic religion in hopes that it would defuse tensions between Hindus and Muslims. For the most part, however, rulers of the Islamic empires followed the advice of conservative Muslim clerics, who promoted Islamic values and fought the introduction of foreign cultural imports, such as the printing press and European science, that might undermine their authority. By the late eighteenth century, the Safavid empire had collapsed, and economic stagnation and cultural insularity had severely weakened the Ottoman and Mughal empires.

CHRONOLOGY

1451–1481	Reign of Mehmed the Conqueror
1453	Ottoman conquest of Constantinople
1501–1524	Reign of Shah Ismail
1514	Battle of Chaldiran
1520–1566	Reign of Süleyman the Magnificent
1556–1605	Reign of Akbar
1588–1629	Reign of Shah Abbas the Great
1659–1707	Reign of Aurangzeb
1722	Fall of the Safavid dynasty

FOR FURTHER READING

Esin Atil. *The Age of Sultan Süleyman the Magnificent*. Washington, 1987. Richly illustrated volume that emphasizes Süleyman's role as a patron of the arts.

Franz Babinger. *Mehmed the Conqueror and His Time*. Trans. by R. Manheim. Princeton, 1978. A magisterial biography of the sultan who conquered Constantinople.

Palmira Brummett. *Ottoman Seapower and Levantine Diplomacy in the Age of Discovery*. Albany, 1994. A scholarly study of Ottoman military strategy and diplomacy in the Mediterranean during the sixteenth century.

Stephen Frederic Dale. *Indian Merchants and Eurasian Trade, 1600–1750*. Cambridge, 1994. Examines the workings of an Indian trading community that conducted business in Persia, central Asia, and Russia.

Suraiya Faroghi. *Towns and Townsmen of Ottoman Anatolia*. Cambridge, 1989. A valuable contribution to understanding of the Ottoman domestic economy.

Naimur Rahman Farooqi. *Mughal-Ottoman Relations*. Delhi, 1989. Illustrates the tensions between the two empires and uses them to shed new light on the motivations behind Akbar's policies.

Irfan Habib. *The Agrarian System of Mughal India, 1556–1707*. Bombay, 1963. A penetrating and influential assessment of the role of agriculture in the Mughal economy and the development of the empire.

Halil Inalçik. *The Ottoman Empire: The Classical Age, 1300–1600*. New York, 1973. A reliable survey by the foremost historian of the early Ottoman empire.

Halil Inalçik and Donald Quataert, eds. *An Economic and Social History of the Ottoman Empire, 1300–1914*. Cambridge, 1994. An exhaustive survey of Ottoman economic history.

Norman Itzkowitz. *Ottoman Empire and Islamic Tradition*. Chicago, 1972. A brief but insightful survey of Ottoman history.

Çemal Kafadar. *Between Two Worlds: The Construction of the Ottoman State*. Berkeley, 1995. Studies the origins and early development of the Ottoman empire.

Bernard Lewis. *The Muslim Discovery of Europe*. New York, 1982. An important study that charts Muslim interest in European affairs.

Bruce Masters. *The Origins of Western Economic Dominance in the Middle East: Mercantilism and the Islamic Economy in Aleppo, 1600–1750*. New York, 1988. A stimulating case study of an important trading city caught between a central government in chaos and European mercantile pressure.

David Morgan. *Medieval Persia, 1040–1797*. London, 1988. A brief and insightful survey that examines Persian history through the Safavid dynasty.

Leslie Pierce. *The Imperial Harem: Women and Sovereignty in the Ottoman Empire*. Oxford, 1993. Challenges many stereotypes about the role of women in the imperial Ottoman elite.

John F. Richards. *The Mughal Empire*. Cambridge, 1993. A concise and reliable overview of Mughal history, concentrating on political affairs.

Roger Savory. *Iran under the Safavids*. Cambridge, 1980. A rich and authoritative survey of Safavid history, especially interesting for its views on Safavid origins, culture, and commercial relations.

Stanford J. Shaw. *History of the Ottoman Empire and Modern Turkey*. 2 vols. Cambridge, 1976–77. A comprehensive survey of Ottoman history.

Douglas E. Streusand. *The Formation of the Mughal Empire*. Delhi, 1989. A new interpretation of the establishment and development of Mughal rule.

Paul Wittek. *The Rise of the Ottoman Empire*. London, 1938. Still the most insightful and stimulating interpretation of the *ghazi* role in the making of the Ottoman empire.

Madeline Zilfi. *The Politics of Piety: The Ottoman Ulema in the Postclassical Age 1600–1800*. Minneapolis, 1988. Examines the influence and changing role of the Ottoman religious leadership.

THE RUSSIAN EMPIRE IN EUROPE AND ASIA

· · ·

In 1681 Tsar Fedor II ordered the holy man Avvakum burned at the stake. The fiery end of Avvakum's life marked a stunning reversal of fortune for a priest who had been an advisor on religious issues to Tsar Fedor's father. Once a spiritual leader charged with reforming Orthodoxy, the branch of Christianity that had come to Russia in the tenth century from the Byzantine empire, Avvakum had become deeply suspicious of efforts to reform the Russian Orthodox church with the aid of Greek biblical and liturgical texts. Eventually, he broke with his colleagues over matters of liturgy and ritual and even charged that his opponents represented the Antichrist come to Russia.

Exiled to Siberia, this charismatic priest attracted followers and met with members of other sects who also believed that the Russian Orthodox church had corrupted the true religion so much that it offered damnation rather than salvation. During the mid-seventeenth century approximately forty groups of these devout dissidents boarded boats and took their own lives in dramatic fashion—by setting their vessels ablaze as they sailed down Russia's rivers. Viewing the horrid spectacle, an English envoy reported that Russia resembled "the suburbs of hell." Although their numbers amounted to only 20 percent of the population, religious dissidents constituted a potent threat to the tsarist state because they represented the limits of its control.

Avvakum's life reflected the emergence of Russia as a power in both Europe and Asia during early modern times. His break with the Orthodox church represented a reaction against Russian interactions and cultural exchanges with western European peoples. He witnessed the transformation of the principality of Muscovy, which from its capital city of Moscow governed much of Russia, into a powerful absolutist state with extensive Asian territories. His Siberian exile was possible only because of the eastward expansion of this empire, and his death bespoke the costs of opposition to Russian state-building efforts.

Between the late fifteenth and the eighteenth centuries, Russia underwent a profound transformation. From a small territorial state centered on Moscow, it grew into a huge Eurasian empire. During the course of its expansion, Russia acquired a powerful, centralized, imperial government under the tsars, and the Romanov family established a dynasty that ruled Russia from 1610 to 1917.

Tsar Peter the Great with a pair of shears, about to remove the beard of a conservative subject.

· AKG London

The rapid expansion of the empire brought Russian peoples into interactions with a wide variety of neighbors, including Europeans, Ottoman Turks, central Asian Muslims, and the indigenous peoples of Siberia and northern Asia. In many cases Russian expansion led to conflict with other peoples, but it also stimulated commercial and cultural exchanges. It led most notably to the influence of western European political and cultural traditions in Russia. The tsars tried to control western influences, favoring only those that might benefit their state, while social and religious conservatives sought to reject them altogether. By the early eighteenth century, however, the Russian state and military forces had drawn deep inspiration from western European models.

By no means did Russia become completely transformed along western European lines. Until the mid-nineteenth century, for example, Russian society depended on the agricultural labor of unfree serfs. Despite increasing trade and manufacturing, agriculture dominated the Russian economy until the mid-twentieth century. Although French philosophes found favor at the tsarist court in the eighteenth century, Enlightenment thought became familiar only to a privileged intellectual elite and barely touched Russian society as a whole. Nevertheless, selective borrowing and adaptation of western European models greatly strengthened Russian society. By the eighteenth century Russia was playing a prominent and increasingly important role in Eurasian affairs.

FOUNDATIONS OF THE ABSOLUTIST STATE

Political leaders began to build states in Russia about the mid-ninth century. For almost five hundred years, the princes of Kiev (in modern Ukraine) dominated Russia. They built a wealthy, commercial society with extensive political, economic, and cultural connections to the Vikings of Scandinavia and the Greek population of Constantinople. In the late 1230s, however, nomadic Mongols conquered Kiev, and descendants of Chinggis Khan ruled Russia for more than 250 years. In the late fifteenth century, as Mongol states fell into disorder, the princes of Moscow worked to recover the territories of Kiev and subject them again to Russian rule.

The Gathering of the Russian Land

In 1480 Ivan III, the grand prince of Moscow (reigned 1462–1505), later known as Ivan the Great, stopped paying tribute to the Mongol khan. By refusing to acknowledge the khan's supremacy, Ivan in effect declared Russian independence from Mongol rule. Although Ivan's dramatic gesture symbolized a turning point in Russian history, by 1480 the process by which the princes of Moscow imposed their rule on Russia had in fact been underway for more than a century. The princes of Moscow began to expand their holdings as early as the mid-fourteenth century. From their base around the small commercial town of Moscow, they acquired new territories by war, marriage, and even outright purchase. By the mid-fifteenth century their state was the most powerful of several Russian principalities under Mongol rule.

Ivan III

Ivan III continued the policy of "gathering the Russian land" and fashioned Moscow into a large and powerful state. His territorial acquisitions were impressive: Muscovy, the principality ruled from Moscow, almost tripled in size as he brought Russian-speaking peoples under his rule. The most important addition to his territo-

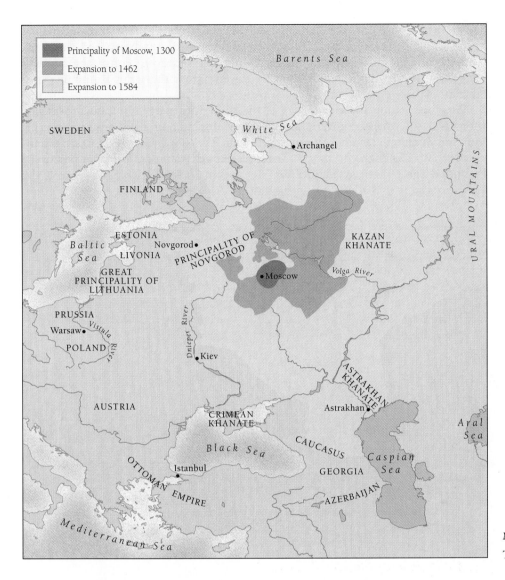

MAP [28.1]

The expansion of Muscovy.

ries came with the acquisition of the prosperous trading city of Novgorod in the 1470s. A hub of the lucrative fur trade and a member of the Hanseatic League of Baltic commercial cities, Novgorod was an autonomous city-state that governed its own affairs through a town council. The city's merchants had strong ties to Poland and Lithuania to the west, and Ivan wanted to make sure that the wealth of Novgorod did not strengthen neighboring states. Thus he demanded that the city acknowledge his authority in 1471. When Novgorod's merchants organized an uprising in 1478, Ivan put down the rebellion, ended the city's independence, and absorbed it into his state.

Ivan sought to consolidate his hold over his territorial acquisitions by recruiting peasants and offering them freedom to settle in recently conquered lands. Known as *cossacks* (from a Turkish word meaning "free men"), these peasants played a huge

Cossacks

role in the expansion of the Russian empire. Particularly in the steppelands to the south, the cossacks undertook their own campaigns of expansion and vastly extended the range of Russian influence. During the sixteenth century the cossacks conquered the Volga River valley and moved across the Ural Mountains into Siberia.

While expanding the boundaries of the Muscovite state, Ivan also provided it with a strong centralized government. He drew inspiration for this project especially from the Byzantine empire. Although Ottoman Turks had conquered Constantinople in 1453 and put an end to the Byzantine empire, Ivan sought to appropriate the Byzantine legacy for his own purposes. He married Sophia Palaeologus, niece of the

A seventeenth-century crowd prepares for Easter observances in the plaza now known as Red Square outside the Kremlin in Moscow. The churches reflect Russian architectural traditions, but the design of the walled Kremlin itself was the work of Italian and English architects. • The Fotomas Index

last Byzantine emperor, and called himself *tsar* (sometimes spelled *czar*)—a Russian-ized form of the term *caesar,* which Byzantine rulers had borrowed from the classical Roman empire to signify their imperial status. He made the Byzantine double-headed eagle the symbol of his authority, and he adopted the elaborate pomp and ceremony of the Byzantine court for use in Muscovy. He also sought to beautify and glorify his capital, and under influence of his wife Sophia he commissioned Italian architects to rebuild the Kremlin, the fortress that stood at the heart of Moscow.

Like the Byzantine emperors, Ivan III ruled not only as head of state but also as head of the church. Like absolutist rulers in western Europe, he claimed to derive his authority directly from God. Establishing that claim sometimes put the secular gov-ernment at odds with organized religion because it implied the authority of the ruler over the church. For the most part, however, the expanding Muscovite state cooper-ated harmoniously with the Russian Orthodox church, which expanded its own influ-ence as the Muscovite state grew. Orthodox clergy affirmed that God appointed the tsar to his position. By the early sixteenth century, Orthodox monks had begun to refer to Moscow as the "third Rome." They held that Germanic invaders had con-quered the first Rome and that the Ottoman Turks had toppled the second Rome, Constantinople. Only Moscow survived as the seat of true Christian faith, and its prominence was due largely to the expansionist and centralizing policies of Ivan III.

The Third Rome

The Time of Troubles

In spite of Ivan III's claims to divine-right rule, the tsarist court encountered oppo-sition to its centralizing and expansionist policies. Most prominent of the opponents were rulers of minor principalities facing absorption into the Muscovite state and es-pecially the powerful *boyars,* the elite military aristocracy comparable to feudal knights in western Europe and samurai in Japan. Resistance to the policy of central-ization climaxed during the reign of Ivan III's grandson, Ivan IV, who became known as Ivan the Terrible because of the severity and cruelty of his response.

Tsar Ivan IV (reigned 1533–1584) is one of the most curious and compelling fig-ures in Russian history. Only three years old when his father died, Ivan began to rule officially when he reached the age of sixteen, when he also married into the powerful and ambitious boyar clan of the Romanovs. Following in the footsteps of Ivan III, he embarked on a series of reforms intended to improve administration and root out corruption in both government and church. Distancing himself from boyar clan rival-ries, Ivan ruled with the help of his Chosen Council, an inner circle of advisors who owed their proximity to the tsar to their talents rather than their families. Ivan also inaugurated the practice of calling "assemblies of the land," meetings of representa-tives who informed him of local situations throughout Russia. Thus Ivan IV sought to create an administration that functioned independently of personal whims.

Ivan IV

Other facets of Ivan's personality, however, overwhelmed his constructive desire to build a more effective government. Long suspicious of the boyars who impeded his efforts at reshaping the Russian government, Ivan suspected them of murdering his beloved wife Anastasia (1560). In 1564 he abdicated the throne in highly sensa-tional fashion, claiming that obstructionist boyars prevented him from governing ef-fectively. When a large delegation of panic-stricken subjects appealed to him to re-turn, he agreed on the condition that he receive powers to deal with treacherous boyars, as well as complete control over a vast portion of Muscovite territory that he called the *oprichnina,* the "land apart." This new power allowed Ivan to confiscate large estates and redistribute them among his supporters.

Ivan's Reign of Terror

Ivan went further to create a new aristocracy, the *oprichniki,* settled on the redistributed lands. He fashioned this newly privileged class into a private army whose members dressed in black and wore insignia displaying a dog's head and a broom, symbolic of their determination to hunt down treason and sweep it out of Russia. Under Ivan's guidance the *oprichniki* laid waste to numerous civilian populations, including that of Novgorod. Observers wrote of giant frying pans set up in the center of Moscow to cook suspected traitors and of *oprichniki* skinning victims alive with taunts that the innocent among them would grow new skins.

It is difficult to account for Ivan's behavior. To some extent his policies reflected the fact that he faced dangerous enemies. Creation of the *oprichnina* had weakened Russia, leaving the state vulnerable to attacks from Poland in the west and the Mongols in the southeast. But Ivan also turned on faithful *oprichniki,* subjecting numerous servitors to the same grotesque punishments inflicted on his supposed enemies. It is possible too that medical problems help to explain Ivan's eccentric behavior. A twentieth-century autopsy showed that the tsar suffered from a debilitating spinal disorder, and historical records attest that he frequently turned to drugs and alcohol in an effort to relieve his severe pain. In any case Ivan's reign ended effective boyar opposition to Russian autocracy.

War and Famine

Count S. D. Sheremetev costumed as Field Marshal Boris Sheremetev for the imperial ball at the Winter Palace, February 1903. Count Sheremetev wears the traditional dress of boyars, including the distinctive bearskin cloak. • Courtesy of Priscilla Roosevelt. From *Life on the Russian Country Estate* (Yale University Press, 1995)

When Ivan died in 1584, after fifty-one years on the throne, he left no capable heir, having killed his oldest son himself. Russia soon fell into civil war, which helped to bring a devastating famine on the land, and neighboring Poland and Sweden took advantage of the chaos by invading Russian territories. This so-called time of troubles lasted fifteen furious years (1598–1613). Popular yearning for a legitimate head of state led to the brief reigns of two pretenders—both claiming to be Dmitrii, a deceased son of Ivan the Terrible miraculously restored to life—and an uprising led by a former slave confirmed that deep social problems plagued Russia.

In 1610, when Polish and Swedish armies seriously threatened the integrity of Muscovy, volunteer armies rallied to expel the invaders and then took it upon themselves to resolve their differences and elect a tsar. Representatives from around the country selected the boyar Mikhail Romanov, a young relative of Ivan IV's first wife Anastasia, as the new tsar. Romanov's dynasty endured until 1917, rarely facing challenges to its legitimacy despite the wide variety of tsars and tsarinas who occupied the imperial throne.

WESTERNIZATION AND EMPIRE

The establishment of the Romanov dynasty settled the dynastic question in Russia, but it did not bring political stability. Trade and military conflicts led to interactions between Russian and neighboring peoples, and the tsars became increasingly aware that western European technology outstripped their own. By the mid-seventeenth century the tsarist court was the site of a spirited debate about whether or not Russia should follow the example of western European societies. Tsar Peter I and Tsarina Catherine II resolved the issue by undertaking a massive program of westernization. Their policies greatly strengthened the tsarist state and helped consolidate a Russian empire with extensive holdings in eastern Europe, central Asia, and northern Asia. Territorial expansion made Russia a vast, multicultural empire that sprawled over one-sixth of the earth's land.

A Window on the West

Since the mid-seventeenth century, as a concession to the merchants of Moscow, the tsars had limited the trading rights of western European merchants in Russia. Among other things, they required foreign merchants to reside in a suburb of Moscow known as Germantown and conduct their business there. By 1676 approximately eighteen thousand western Europeans lived in Russia, the vast majority of them in Germantown. In Japan the Tokugawa shoguns restricted Dutch merchants to the port of Nagasaki because they wanted to guard against contaminating ideas from Europe. Compared to the shoguns, Russia's tsars were more open to outside influences, yet they too sought to control the introduction of ideas from western Europe.

Germantown became the playground for the future tsar Peter I (reigned 1682–1725), widely known as Peter the Great. Last in line to the throne, Peter spent much of his youth away from the imperial court. In Germantown he developed a fascination for technology, especially shipbuilding and navigation. More taken with inventions than with government, the young Peter gladly allowed his half sister Sophia to rule as regent for himself and his older but feeble and sickly half brother. As Peter grew older, however, he entered court politics and maneuvered Sophia out of position. By 1689 he had established himself as tsar.   *Peter I*

Soon after taking the imperial throne, Peter instituted a policy of forced and rapid modernization. He fully appreciated modern science, and he considered it urgent for Russia to match western European achievements. He worked to base political administration on pragmatic procedures and to establish Russian industries based on the most advanced science and technology available. He sent Russians abroad to study and embarked on his own tour of Germany, the Netherlands, and England in 1697–98 to learn about western European military and industrial technology. He traveled incognito in the hope that western Europeans would speak more frankly with a commoner than with an emperor. But the tsar, who stood two meters (six feet and seven inches) tall, fooled few in his simple sailor's uniform. His traveling companions often behaved crudely by western European standards: they consumed beer, wine, and brandy in quantities that astonished their hosts, and King William III sent Peter a bill for damage done by his entourage at the country home where they lodged in England. (Among other things, Peter had ruined the gardens by having his men march through them in military formation.) But Peter observed western European government and society at work, and he resolved to remodel Russia along more efficient lines.

*Peter's Program
of Westernization*

Upon returning to Moscow, Peter set Russia spinning. He did not imitate all the features of western European societies: he was too much of an autocrat to find any interest in the institutions of representative government that he encountered in England and the Netherlands. But unlike the rulers of China, Japan, and the Islamic empires, who sought to limit foreign influences in their lands, Peter instituted a policy of conscious westernization by selectively adopting western European models and using them to guide the reform of Russian government and society.

Military Reform

Peter's commitment to reform derived from his ambition to make Russia one of Europe's great military powers. He reformed the army by offering better pay and drafting peasants who served for life as professional soldiers. He provided his forces with extensive training and equipped them with modern weapons. He ordered aristocrats to study mathematics and geometry so they could calculate how to aim cannons accurately, and he refused permission for them to marry until they successfully completed their studies. By the time of his death, the Russian army was the largest in Europe with three hundred thousand troops, and it proved its effectiveness in a prolonged struggle known as the Great Northern War (1700–1722) that Peter waged against Sweden. Recognizing the importance of merchant and naval fleets to western European states, Peter also determined to create a Russian navy that would dominate the Baltic and the northern seas. Shipbuilding, sailing, and navigation had intrigued Peter since his boyhood in Germantown, and as tsar he began the construction of a navy even before he had any port facilities suitable for military vessels.

*Bureaucratic
Reform*

Peter also overhauled the government bureaucracy to facilitate tax collection and encourage industrial production. Because Russia had only a very small educated urban class, Peter relied on nobles to serve as government officials. He established the Table of Ranks, which permitted officials to move along fourteen stations according to merit. Old titles, such as boyar, disappeared along with the bearskin robes favored by the old nobility. Besides providing opportunities for social mobility based on merit, the Table of Ranks also underscored the subservience of individuals to the state. By emphasizing that the tsar himself was an energetic servant of the state rather than a privileged parasite, Peter made the abstract political concept a psychological reality.

Social Reform

In his effort to westernize Russia, Peter also brought change to sex and gender relations. He abolished the *terem*, the Russian equivalent of a harem, which kept upper-class women secluded from men outside their own families, and encouraged social mixing of the sexes, especially in towns and cities. His transformation of Russia even involved a cosmetic makeover, as he commanded his subjects to wear western clothing and ordered men to shave their traditional beards. These policies, which were extremely unpopular among conservative Russians, provoked spirited protest among those who resented the increasing influence of western European ways. Yet Peter considered westernization so important that he reportedly went into the streets himself and hacked the beards off recalcitrants' faces. In the face of stiff opposition, however, the tsar eventually compromised by allowing men to keep their beards if they paid extra taxes, an option that many chose well into the nineteenth century.

St. Petersburg

Perhaps the best symbol of Peter's policy of westernization was St. Petersburg, a "window on the west" that he opened in 1702 when he ordered the construction of a new capital city on the Baltic Sea. The city rose near the site of a Swedish fort captured during the Great Northern War, and the tsar named it after his patron saint. The construction of St. Petersburg cost an estimated ten thousand serfs' lives and hence bore the nickname "the city built on bones." Yet the new city provided a

PETER THE GREAT AND THE FOUNDING OF ST. PETERSBURG

• • •

Jakob Staehlin von Storcksburg was an aristocratic German scholar who traveled to Russia in 1735 and spent more than twenty years there, mostly in St. Petersburg. Von Storcksburg was a great admirer of Peter the Great and collected scores of stories and anecdotes about the tsar, his deeds, and his character. In one the traveler detailed the lengths that Peter went to in founding St. Petersburg.

Long before the Swedish war [the Great Northern War], Peter had conceived the project of obtaining a port on the Baltic, that he might there construct the ships necessary to the execution of his designs.

As soon as he was master of the country in which St. Petersburg is situated, he determined to build a city there and laid the foundations of it in 1703. He surrounded it with fortifications on one side of the Neva [River] and placed the admiralty on the other.

This spot of ground contained before only a single fisherman's hut by the side of the fort; and this very hut afforded the monarch a retreat at the commencement of his undertaking. It is now carefully preserved under a roof as a precious monument of the prodigious labors of the Russian hero. . . .

At length, in 1714, finding himself in peaceful possession of his conquests and at the eve of an advantageous peace, the tsar saw with much joy that he should soon be freed from all the obstacles that had opposed the execution of his designs, and particularly the desire he felt to turn all his attention to the civilization of his empire. He therefore published a ukase, or ordinance, to hasten the building of his new city.

He required all landholders, clergy as well as laymen, and monasteries as well as gentlemen, to build houses proportioned to their means . . . on the ground marked out in lots of twelve, twenty, thirty, and forty yards long, and to render them habitable in the space of two years, under pain of confiscation of their property.

To facilitate the execution of his orders, and that no one might have an impediment or excuse, he made an abundant provision of materials and established an architect's office under the direction of Tressins, an Italian, where plans, according to the extent of the ground, were given *gratis*. . . . Timber, piles, and lime were sent in such quantities from Ladoga and Novgorod that they were to be bought at a very moderate price.

Planks, laths, and beams were all furnished by a great number of sawing mills turned by wind or water. . . .

A great number of workmen were collected by the tsar's order from all parts of Russia to work at his new city and pave the streets. He had long before directed all vessels or carriages that might come loaded to St. Petersburg to bring a certain quantity of stones besides their usual load or cargo, and to deliver them at the entrance of the town to a commissary appointed for that purpose.

SOURCE: Jakob Staehlin von Storcksburg. *Original Anecdotes of Peter the Great.* London: J. Murray, 1788, pp. 190–98. (Translation slightly modified.)

haven for Russia's fledgling navy and offered access to western European lands through the Baltic Sea.

Peter worked zealously to establish St. Petersburg as a center of efficient government. He transferred many government offices to the new capital and ordered nobles to build houses there even before wrapping up his victory against Sweden. He invested vast sums in buildings and fountains, mostly designed by Italian architects, that recalled the cities of western Europe. After Peter, Russia claimed two capitals: the original capital of Moscow in the Russian heartland and the new administrative center and tsarist residence in St. Petersburg.

The Limits of Westernization

The most able of Peter the Great's successors was Catherine II (reigned 1762–1795), also known as Catherine the Great, who continued to pursue Peter's policy of westernization—or at least she did so until it seemed that western European influences might threaten the tsarist autocracy. Born into the ruling family of the minor Baltic principality of Anhalt-Zerbst, Catherine found herself in an arranged marriage to a grandson of Peter the Great. Her marriage was unhappy, however, and she allied with the leading nobles at the tsarist court to displace her feeble husband. Catherine's remarkable skill at fashioning herself into a Russian ruler supported by the nobility stands as a testament to her adaptability. Making the Russian language and Orthodox faith her own, she left behind a significantly more powerful empire than the one she had entered as a nervous bride.

Catherine II   Like Peter, Catherine attempted to increase the effectiveness of the tsarist bureaucracy by appointing officials with a modern, western European–style education, and she worked to rationalize the administration of her realm. She organized the Russian empire into fifty administrative provinces, each supervised by a governor-general. She spelled out the rights and obligations of the nobility and the urban classes in her Charter of the Nobility and the parallel Charter of the Towns. Catherine was an autocrat in the mold of the enlightened despots of eastern Europe, and even though she sought economic development of Russia's towns, she was not willing to grant them any substantial autonomy. She took care to keep the nobles happy, however, since she owed her rule to their support. She confirmed them in their privileges, and she extended their rights over the peasants on their lands.

Catherine the Great, depicted in 1762 in the style and dress of western European rulers. • Novosti/Sovfoto

Catherine had high respect for western European lands, especially France. She encouraged nobles to travel in western Europe, and by the late eighteenth century, educated aristocrats often communicated among themselves in French. Catherine herself became deeply infatuated with the philosophes of the Enlightenment, and she corresponded extensively with the philosophe Denis Diderot. She considered the philosophes' ideas for liberal social reform, but she was not willing to grant reforms that would weaken her hold on society. As she pointed out to Diderot, "You write on paper, but I have to write on human skin, which is far more ticklish."

Catherine thought of herself as an enlightened despot. Like Maria Theresa of Austria and Frederick II of Prussia, she sought to devise policies that would improve her subjects' lives without detracting from her own power and authority. She restricted the punishments that noble landowners could inflict on the serfs who worked their lands, for example, and she sought to eliminate common penalties such as torture, beating, and the mutilation of individuals by cutting off their noses, ears, or tongues.

Catherine's interest in reform cooled rapidly, however, when it resulted in challenges to her rule. She faced a particularly unsettling trial in 1773 when the cossack Emelian Pugachev mounted a serious rebellion in the steppelands north of the Caspian Sea. Pugachev's rebellious force was a motley collection of disgruntled cossacks, exiles, peasants, and serfs. They sought an end to taxes, government supervision, and the military draft, and they demanded the right to possess their own land and elect their own leaders. During a year of bitter violence, Pugachev's army killed thousands of noble landowners, government officials, and Orthodox priests. The imperial army crushed the uprising in late 1774, captured Pugachev, and took him to Moscow in chains. In spite of Catherine's interest in humane punishments, her government beheaded Pugachev, quartered his body, and displayed its parts throughout the city as a warning against rebellion.

Pugachev's Rebellion

Pugachev's rebellion alarmed the tsarina and led her to tighten her grip on Russian affairs, but the outbreak of the French Revolution in 1789 effectively ended Catherine's interest in reform inspired by western European societies. The storming of the Bastille by Parisian crowds soon led to a reign of terror against monarchy and nobility. During the last years of her reign, Catherine abandoned the program of westernization and adopted extremely conservative policies for fear that further reform might encourage revolutionary turmoil in Russia. After more than a century of westernization, the tsarist autocracy adopted policies like those of contemporary rulers in China, Japan, and the Islamic empires aimed at limiting foreign and especially western European influence.

The End of Reform

The Russian Empire in Europe

Political consolidation led to the development of a powerful state with considerable financial resources at its disposal and a technologically advanced military at its command. This situation helps to explain the remarkable transformation of the small principality of Muscovy into a vast empire that survived until 1991. Expansion begun under Ivan the Great continued incrementally, pushing westward into Europe, especially Poland, Lithuania, and the Ottoman-controlled Balkan peninsula. Then during the reign of Ivan the Terrible, Russia began its eastward movement into Siberia and the former Mongol territories. By the late eighteenth century the Russian empire was a vast, multicultural realm that embraced much of the Eurasian landmass from Poland to the Pacific Ocean, and Russian explorers had even ventured tentatively into North America and the Pacific islands.

During the early stages of Russian expansion, the tsars sought to recapture territories associated with the Kievan state and return Russia to dominance in eastern Europe. The biggest target of this expansive effort was Poland. The ebbing of Mongol power had led to the rise of Lithuania, which united with Poland into a kingdom that stretched from the Baltic Sea as far as the Black Sea. In 1569, when Ivan IV's reign of terror engulfed Russia, Poland-Lithuania organized into a dual republican state with

Poland-Lithuania

MAP [28.2]

Imperial Russia in the eighteenth century.

separate administrative and legal systems, but ruled in common by an elected king and parliament. Although the state dominated much of eastern Europe, the political structure of the Polish-Lithuanian republic eventually became too unstable to mediate conflicts effectively and ultimately left it vulnerable.

Despite their ethnic similarities, Russia and Poland had gone separate ways religiously: Poland was Roman Catholic, as was Lithuania. Several Orthodox Slavic territories, such as Belarus and Ukraine, fell within the borders of Poland-Lithuania and feared Roman Catholic influence, especially after Jesuit missionaries began to visit Ukraine in the sixteenth century. Because of the Orthodox faith that they shared with Russia—and because their peasants resented oppressive Polish landlords—these smaller Slavic communities gravitated toward the empire emerging around Moscow.

The Absorption of Ukraine

Animosity against Poland directly inspired the union of Ukraine with Russia. The Ukrainian adventurer Bogdan Khmelnitsky, seeking revenge against Poland for the murder of his son, united the peasants of Ukraine against their Polish rulers and sought union with Moscow on the basis of the Orthodox faith they held in common. Russian cooperation with Khmelnitsky led to war with Poland, and the fighting lasted thirteen years, with tremendous costs for all belligerents. It ended in 1667 with a partition of Ukraine, and Kiev returned to the empire that it had once served as capital city.

The Partition of Poland

Poland's political woes increased. The Polish parliament operated under a crippling handicap in that it required unanimous consent to make law: a single negative vote could prevent the passage of any legislation. This policy generated such acute instability that the Polish state could not defend itself at the end of the eighteenth century when its predatory neighbors—Russia, Austria, and Prussia—partitioned the Polish-Lithuanian republic and absorbed its regions into their own states. Polish resentment kept the historical memory alive, and the Poles rose against Russia in 1830 and 1863 before regaining their independence in 1918.

As Russia annexed territory from the disintegrating Polish state, it absorbed large numbers of Jews into its ethnic mix. Poland had institutionalized tolerance of Jews in 1265. Thereafter Poland became Europe's most important sanctuary for Jews until the Nazi conquest of Poland in World War II. Following the partitions, Catherine II prohibited Jews from moving out of the territory in which they lived unless they obtained official permission to do so. The restriction of Jews to this notorious Pale of Settlement provided a focus for anti-Semitism and motivated many Jews from this region to leave Russia and migrate to the United States at the end of the nineteenth century.

During the later decades of the eighteenth century, Russia expanded south into Ottoman territories in Europe. Tsarist forces pushed into Balkan regions that the Ottomans could no longer defend and made common cause with Greek Orthodox Christians who resented their Turkish overlords. Russia annexed the Crimea outright, and the army made plans to march on Istanbul. As the Russian military advanced, however, western European powers became alarmed at the prospect that Russia would gain control of the Black Sea, the Bosporus, and the Dardanelles and hence would enjoy free access to the Mediterranean. British and French diplomats overcame their own disagreements and cooperated to prevent further Russian expansion in the region. Nevertheless, the Slavic peoples of Russia and the Balkans forged a relationship that influenced the history of the Balkan peninsula through two world wars and many bitter civil conflicts in the twentieth century.

Southern Expansion

The Russian Empire in Asia

While building an empire in the settled, agricultural lands of eastern Europe, Russia also expanded into the more sparsely populated and less technologically developed regions of central Asia and northern Asia. The Mongol empires had broken into the separate khanates of Kazan, Astrakhan, and the Crimea by the sixteenth century. Ivan IV's army marched into Kazan in 1552 and annexed neighboring Astrakhan shortly thereafter. These conquests gave Russians control over the Volga River and offered opportunities for trade with Safavid Persia and the Ottoman empire through the Caspian Sea. Expansion into central Asia continued through the late nineteenth century and brought significant populations of Turkish and Mongol peoples under Russian rule.

In search of warm-water ports, tsarist forces continued to push south to the Caspian Sea and the Caucasus, a vibrant multiethnic region embracing the modern-day states of Georgia, Armenia, and Azerbaijan. Georgia, an ancient kingdom whose ruling dynasty traced its ancestry back to King David of Israel, was especially attractive to Russian imperialists. Although independent of both the Greek and the Russian churches, Georgians were Orthodox Christians who feared the Ottoman Turks and sought a Russian protectorate in 1783. Russia soon absorbed Georgia when the tsar declared the established kingdom extinct and coopted the native nobility by granting its members the same privileges enjoyed by Russian aristocrats. With its luxuriant scenery and mineral baths, Georgia became a favorite vacation spot for Russian aristocrats and remains a prime holiday destination today.

The Caucasus

Siberia

The dense forests and frozen tundras of Siberia offered a much less hospitable environment than the steppelands, but Russian explorers and merchants made their way into northern Asia as well as central Asia during the seventeenth and eighteenth centuries. The Russian conquest of Asia began in 1581 when the wealthy Stroganov merchant family hired a freebooting cossack adventurer named Ermak to capture the khanate of Sibir in the Ural Mountains. The Stroganovs wanted access to Siberian furs, a major source of wealth that lured the tsarist state eastward, just as North American furs attracted the interest of English, French, and Dutch merchants. Adapting an old Mongol practice of exacting tribute in furs, the Russian government established small fortified settlements throughout Siberia that coerced local peoples to supply pelts on a regular basis.

Native Peoples of Siberia

Siberia was home to some twenty-six distinct ethnic groups that lived by hunting, trapping, fishing, or herding reindeer. These indigenous peoples varied widely in language and religion, and they responded to the arrival of Russian adventurers in different ways. Some groups readily accepted iron tools, woven cloth, flour, tea, and liquor for the skins of fur-bearing animals such as otter, lynx, marten, Arctic fox, and especially the sleek black sable. Others resented the ever-increasing demands for fur tributes and resisted Russian encroachment on their lands. Russian forces then re-

A woodcut illustration depicts indigenous peoples of Siberia delivering fur tribute to Russian merchants in a walled, riverside fort. • Oregon Historical Society. OrHi 97421

sorted to punishing raids and hostage taking to induce Siberian peoples to deliver furs. The Yakut people of the Lena and Aldan River valleys of central Siberia mounted a revolt against Russian oppression in 1642 and experienced a brutal retribution that continued for forty years, forcing many Yakut out of their settlements and reducing their population by an estimated 70 percent. Quite apart from military violence, the peoples of Siberia also reeled under attack from contagious diseases such as smallpox that previously had not penetrated the forests and tundras. Epidemics of the mid-seventeenth century reduced the populations of many Siberian peoples by more than half.

As violence and disease sharply diminished the delivery of furs, the Russian government soon recognized that its interests were to protect the "small peoples," as state officials called the indigenous inhabitants of Siberia. Peter the Great sent missionaries in hopes of converting Siberian peoples to Orthodox Christianity and bringing them into Russian society. But few Siberians expressed an interest in Christianity, and those few came mostly from the ranks of criminals, abandoned hostages, slaves, and others who had little status in their native societies. Furthermore, once indigenous peoples converted to Christianity, they were no longer obligated to pay fur tributes to the state. The tsarist government therefore demonstrated less zeal in its religious mission than did the Spanish and Portuguese monarchs, who made the spread of Roman Catholic Christianity a prime goal of imperial expansion. Orthodox missionaries managed to attract a few Siberian converts but mostly served the needs of Russian merchants, adventurers, and explorers. The peoples of Siberia mostly continued to practice their inherited religions guided by native shamans.

The trappers and soldiers who extended Russian authority into Siberia included adventurous cossacks, social misfits, convicted criminals, and even prisoners-of-war. The harsh terrain discouraged a few, but it also limited Moscow's long reach. Serfdom did not extend east of the Ural Mountains, so disgruntled peasants had some motivation to flee to Siberia. By 1763 the 420,000 Russian migrants nearly doubled the native population of Siberia. The tsarist government used Siberia as an immense prison, a place to exile disagreeable individuals such as the priest Avvakum, and later as a site of forced labor camps.

Russian Population of Siberia

Russia's eastward expansion did not end in Siberia. Russian officials commissioned the Danish navigator Vitus Bering to undertake two maritime expeditions (1725–1730 and 1733–1742) in search of a northeast passage to Asian ports. Bering sailed through the icy Arctic Ocean and the Bering Strait that separates Siberia from Alaska and explored northern Asia as far as the Kamchatka Peninsula. Other Russian explorers pushed further into Alaska, which the tsarist government sold to the United States in 1867, and proceeded south through western Canada into northern California. By 1800 Russian mariners had also begun to explore the Pacific Ocean and had sailed as far south as the Hawaiian Islands. Indeed, they built a small fort on the island of Kauai and engaged in trade there early in the nineteenth century. Russians did not establish a permanent presence in North America or the Pacific islands, but their ventures into those regions bespoke a dynamic and expansive society.

American and Pacific Explorations

A SOCIETY IN TENSION

As the tsars gathered the Russian land and built a Eurasian empire, Russia became a vast but sparsely populated land. In 1700 Russia was thirty times the size of France, but with a population of about fifteen million it had fewer inhabitants. As Russian rulers stretched the boundaries of their realm, they faced the challenge of mobilizing a labor force to settle and cultivate the empire's land. They did so by restricting the mobility of Russian peasants and tying them to the land as serfs. Peter the Great sponsored the establishment of factories, but Russia remained a predominantly rural and agricultural society.

Muscovite Society before Westernization

Rural Life   In the absence of manufacturing industries and well-developed trade networks, agriculture dominated the Russian economy. Agricultural society revolved around the peasant village. There peasants often lived in extended families, and the male heads of their households gathered periodically to make decisions for the entire village. They allocated village lands according to the needs of individual families and negotiated with the owners of the land, who were mostly nobles, and with agents of the tsar, such as tax collectors and military recruiters. Peasant women tended to domestic chores and took primary responsibilty for arranging marriages—a role that offered them considerable social influence, since marriages created alliances between families in the village community. Unlike their counterparts in most of the world, Russian women retained control of their dowries after marriage, and as a result they enjoyed a degree of financial independence rarely known to women elsewhere.

Though photographed in the late nineteenth century, these woodchoppers look much like their ancestors of the sixteenth and seventeenth centuries. • Ria-Novosti/Sovfoto

Some peasants were free, especially in Siberia and other regions recently added to the Russian empire, since the tsars encouraged migration to newly conquered regions by offering generous terms to peasants who settled there. In European Russia, however, most peasants were serfs tied to lands owned by nobles, the crown, or monasteries that their ancestors had cultivated for generations. During the sixteenth and seventeenth centuries, as the Russian empire expanded, the conditions of serfdom became increasingly tight because of efforts by noble landowners and the tsarist state to ensure the availability of a rural labor force. Landowners constantly pressured the tsars to limit serfs' rights to marry or move off the land, since their holdings would be worthless without cultivators, and to enhance their own rights to recapture serfs who escaped. In 1649 the government promulgated a law code that placed serfs under strict control of their landlords. Serfs were not slaves, but during the late seventeenth and eighteenth centuries lords increasingly sold serfs as if they were private property.

Serfdom

The law code of 1649 also tightened state control over the Russian labor force by establishing a rigid, castelike social order that sharply restricted both occupational and geographical mobility. It required artisans and merchants to register their infant children into their fathers' occupations and to introduce them to the family trade. It also established a hierarchy of nobles, capped by fifty-two distinguished boyar families, who owed military and political services to the state. The law code of 1649 largely reflected the interests of this nobility, since it provided them with a legal foundation to mobilize a labor force and enabled them to derive an income from the agricultural production of serfs working their estates. Some nobles also owned small towns and derived further income from taxes levied on the craft production and trade carried on there.

During the reign of Catherine the Great, nobles gained a free hand over their estates and the serfs who worked them. Catherine sought noble support for her centralizing policies and her desire to hire educated experts of common birth for administrative and military positions. In exchange for their support, she granted them extensive rights in their own domains. Nobles gained rights to deploy laborers as they saw fit, levy taxes on serfs attached to their lands, and administer punishments through courts that they controlled. Catherine's bargain with the nobility greatly strengthened tsarist authority, but it did so by subjecting most Russians to the harsh and sometimes arbitrary rule of noble landlords.

Catherine and the Nobility

The Growth of Trade and Industry

Interactions with European and Asian peoples did not alter the fundamentally agricultural character of Russian society, but they stimulated trade and motivated Peter the Great to encourage the development of heavy industry. Direct trade with western European lands began in the mid-sixteenth century after an English expedition searching for a northeast passage to Asian markets made its way north around Scandinavia and into the White Sea. Tsar Ivan IV had the crew escorted to Moscow and offered the sailors concessions to trade in Russia. Dutch and other mariners followed English merchants to northern Russia. The port of Archangel (founded in 1584) soon became a flourishing trading city where merchants exchanged Russian furs, leather, and grain for western European armaments, textiles, paper, and silver.

European Trade

Meanwhile, Russian expansion to the south and east led to increased trade with Asian peoples. As the Russians acquired territory in the south, they found opportunities to engage in trade with merchants from Safavid Persia, the Ottoman empire, and even Mughal India. The Volga and other rivers flowing into the Caspian Sea offered access to the flourishing economies of the Islamic empires, and Astrakhan on the Volga delta became a bustling trade city mirroring Archangel in the north. During the seventeenth and eighteenth centuries, Astrakhan was home to a community of about two hundred foreign merchants from as far away as northern India, and one hundred or more additional Indian merchants made annual commercial trips to the Caspian. Some Indian merchants made their way up the Volga River and traded in Moscow and elsewhere in the Russian interior, whereas others devised plans (which they never realized) to extend their activities to the Baltic Sea and take their business to western Europe.

Asian Trade

The increasing prominence of foreign merchants in the imperial economy sparked deep resentment among Russian merchants, who were few in number and poorly organized in comparison with their western European and Asian competitors.

Russian merchants lodged protests with the tsarist government and demanded restrictions on the activities of foreign merchants. The tsars responded by requiring foreign merchants to reside and conduct their business in officially approved districts, such as the Germantown suburb of Moscow or border cities like Archangel and Astrakhan, and by forbidding them to trade in particularly lucrative commodities such as tobacco and alcohol. Yet these measures did little to diminish the influence of foreign commerce in Russia. Some foreign merchants simply ignored the restrictions or bribed their way around them, while others joined forces with Russian merchants and conducted business with local partners. In any case foreign trade and merchandise deeply influenced the Russian economy.

Industrial Development

Peter the Great's policy of westernization increased the prominence of foreigners in Russia. On his tour of western Europe in 1697–98, Peter avidly sought out technical experts willing to work abroad, and he lured about one thousand engineers, shipbuilders, military officers, teachers, and industrial specialists to Russia. He offered loans, subsidies, tax breaks, and tariff protection to those who would establish factories in Russia, and his efforts resulted in the opening of about two hundred new industrial plants. Most of the new factories produced iron, armaments, or textiles, and others turned out glass, paper, and leather goods.

This early effort at industrialization was all the more remarkable because of Russia's lack of cities and chronic shortage of labor. Moscow had a population of about 150,000 when Peter took the throne, but all other Russian cities combined had only another 300,000. In the absence of an urban working class, Peter drafted factory laborers from the ranks of serfs—an imperial decree of 1721 permitted factory owners to purchase serfs from landowners—as well as soldiers, beggars, prostitutes, criminals, and orphans.

During Peter the Great's reign, St. Petersburg took shape as a splendid capital. The Winter Palace illustrates Peter's interest in western European architectural styles.   •   Tom Owen Edmunds/The Image Bank

Peter's economic policies did not put Russia on a par with England or the Netherlands as an industrial power, but they laid a foundation for the development and diversification of a fundamentally agricultural society. During the eighteenth century, for example, Russia's population more than doubled, from fifteen million to thirty-seven million. Some of the increase reflected territorial gains by the expanding Russian empire, but much of it came about because of improved economic conditions. A growing population led to increased urbanization. By 1800 St. Petersburg had become the largest city in Russia with a population exceeding two hundred thousand, even though it was not yet a century old. Other cities throughout the Russian empire also experienced rapid growth.

Population Growth

CULTURAL CLASHES

European influences touched Russian cultural and religious life as well as political and economic matters. During the seventeenth century the Russian Orthodox church experienced a bitter dispute between reformers who sought to adapt ritual and liturgy from eastern European and Greek Orthodox churches for use in Russia. With the aid of the tsars, the reformers ultimately had their way, but the Russian church lost its autonomy and fell under the control of the tsarist autocracy. During the later seventeenth and eighteenth centuries, Peter the Great and Catherine the Great sponsored the introduction of western European thought and educational curricula into Russia. Cultural exchanges enlivened Russian intellectual life, but the outbreak of the French Revolution prompted Catherine to curtail her support for western European ideas.

Crisis in the Church

The spirit of reform and regulation that inspired official Russia also influenced church leaders, some of whom had long wanted to revise liturgy and rituals. They too looked west for inspiration—not to western Europe, however, but to Orthodox Greece and eastern Europe. Ceremony plays

Church Reform

St. Basil's Cathedral, located just outside the Kremlin in Moscow, was the most prominent seat of authority in the Russian Orthodox church. • Harald Sund/the Image Bank

a crucial role in Orthodox Christianity because community members receive divine grace not as individuals, but by meeting and performing rituals together. The reformers were particularly anxious to standardize ritual practices, and they sought to reform Russian Orthodox ritual according to the most accurate religious texts and the most authentic practices of Orthdox Christians in Greece and eastern Europe.

Patriarch Nikon

During the mid-seventeenth century the leader of the reform party was a strong-willed monk named Nikon who served as patriarch of Moscow, the spiritual head of the Russian Orthodox church. Nikon and the reformers established schools and academies that offered instruction in Latin and Greek as well as Church Slavonic, the ritual language of the Russian Orthodox church, and they built churches in the Byzantine style.

One of their innovations became the cause of a deep schism in the Russian church—their requirement that like Orthodox priests in other lands, Russian priests make the sign of the cross with three fingers rather than two. Although the issue might seem minor, many conservatives took it as a symbol of a church leadership that had turned its back on true and traditional ways. Even though he had the backing of the tsar, Nikon faced tremendous resistance to his reforms. With the aid of ninety cannons, for example, the conservative monks at the fortified Solovestskii monastery, located within the Arctic Circle on an island in the White Sea, held out for more than seven years (1668–1676) against a tsarist force promoting church reform.

Avvakum and Old Belief

Led by the priest Avvakum, religious conservatives refused to accept Nikon's reforms and campaigned to restore traditional practices. Avvakum and his followers feared that reformed rituals would compromise the community's eligibility to receive the grace of God and thus would threaten their eternal salvation. They blamed serfdom on outsiders. They regarded state tax collectors as agents of the Antichrist, the cosmic foe of God who appears in the apocalyptic book of Revelation in the New Testament. They went further and associated all this evil with the tsar, who supported Nikon and the reformers.

The tsarist government outlawed Avvakum's sectarianism, known as Old Belief, exiled many of its adherents (including Avvakum) to Siberia, and subjected others to torture and execution. In 1681 the tsar condemned Avvakum to execution at the stake, and the next year he declared all Old Belief treasonous and punishable by death. This policy proved divisive, so the government reached an uneasy and unofficial truce with the Old Believers, allowing them to practice their faith if they did so quietly or in out-of-the-way places like Siberia. Old Belief itself split into different sects and never established a coherent theology. Yet it endured and proved especially attractive to conservative Russian merchants who faced challenges from western European entrepreneurs. In the early twentieth century, many of Russia's most prominent politicians, industrialists, and patrons of the arts came from Old Believer families.

Tsarist Control over the Church

Like the religious wars in western Europe, the schism weakened the Russian Orthodox church and detracted from the authority of religious leaders. It also strengthened the tsarist state by offering it opportunities to extend its own authority over the church. Indeed, between the sixteenth and eighteenth centuries, the tsars progressively increased their control over the church until Peter the Great made it essentially a department of religious affairs in his government.

As the Russian empire expanded, church and political leaders cooperated in many ways, but wealth and economic power also brought the church into conflict with centralizing rulers. Large monasteries rivaled many cities in the resources at their disposal. They formed centers of learning, and the church hierarchy wielded considerable political influence. The tsars had good reason to want to secularize their landholdings because the monasteries, the largest of which even boasted military fortifications, could serve as bases of operations against them. During periods of civil stress, some citadels of faith, such as the Solovestskii monastery, became military fortresses. Thus beginning with Ivan III, centralizing tsars sought to appropriate church property whenever possible and to increase tsarist authority over the church.

This policy culminated in the reign of Peter the Great, who displaced the patriarch of Moscow and established a state council that supervised church affairs. The tsar himself named members to the council and appointed a military officer to oversee the council's work. The tsar also selected bishops for the Russian church and required parish clergy to support the government by reporting criminal, rebellious, treasonous, or otherwise suspicious behavior to state authorities. By the early eighteenth century, the tsarist autocracy had effectively turned the Russian church into a department of the state government.

Westernization and the Enlightenment in Russia

The westernizing tsars, Peter and Catherine, added new wrinkles to Russian cultural life by sponsoring the introduction of western European art, literature, and ideas. Impressed by its grace and athleticism, for example, Peter brought in the ballet, which had originated in France but soon took on a vibrant Russian identity that continues to the present day.

His program of westernization also had an educational dimension. Before Peter formal education had been almost a monopoly of the Russian Orthodox church, and apart from monastic schools geared to the preparation of clergy, Russia had no advanced educational institutions. In an effort to establish an alternative tradition of secular education, in 1714 Peter created a system of elementary schools that taught

Education

In 1756 Catherine the Great began construction of the Hermitage, shown here, to house her art collection. The Hermitage itself reflects the influence of western European architectural styles, and many of the items conserved there were works of French, Italian, and Dutch artists.   •   © Tom Tracy/The Stock Market

reading, writing, and basic science in Russia's provincial capitals. Ten years later he founded an academy of sciences that offered advanced instruction along western European lines in mathematics, natural sciences, geography, languages, philosophy, history, economics, and law.

Catherine continued Peter's interest in secular education and in some ways carried it further. She sought to expand Peter's elementary schools into a vast network of primary education that would educate all children except for serfs, and she opened the first Russian schools for girls. (She initially wanted girls' schools to offer the same curricula that boys studied, but she later decided that the girls, who made up about 7 percent of Russia's twenty-two thousand schoolchildren, should learn homemaking skills.) Her ambitious educational plans had limited results—partly because there were not enough teachers to staff the schools and partly because of aristocratic resistance to the extension of formal education to the lower classes. Nevertheless, she laid a foundation for widespread primary education.

Enlightenment Influences

Catherine also sponsored the introduction of Enlightenment values in Russia. Where Peter had looked to western Europe for technology, Catherine looked for philosophy. She generously subsidized the publications of the French philosophes, and like enlightened despots in Prussia and Austria, she sought to harness the cultural forces of the Enlightenment for the benefit of her realm. In a melodramatic gesture intended to demonstrate the benefits of science to an ill-educated populace, she had herself inoculated against smallpox in 1768. By 1800 some two million Russians had followed her example.

With Catherine's encouragement Russian literature flourished. Poets and playwrights turned a wooden language used in church liturgy and bureaucratic documents into a creative instrument for self-expression. Although at first they simply imitated western European styles and genres, Russian writers soon developed a literature that captured the experiences of their own society. Like the Enlightenment philosophes whom she admired, Catherine appreciated satire and diversity of opinion, even when she was the target—although to be sure her critics remained more guarded than forthright. The empress herself contributed to Russian literary expression by translating a bit of Shakespeare and writing several plays.

The Intelligentsia

Catherine's encouragement of cultural experimentation facilitated the emergence of an intellectual class known as the *intelligentsia*. Although the writers and critics who composed the intelligentsia had no legal status, they enjoyed recognition as an unofficial social estate and worked strenuously to influence public opinion and state policy. Their principal means of communication were "thick journals," monthly compendia with news on the latest developments in science, philosophy, and the arts, which became the principal platforms for political and cultural debate in the late eighteenth century. Government censors kept a close eye on their contents, but writers found ways to express provocative views in thick journals by addressing sensitive issues indirectly. Many government officials were themselves educated men who found thick journals intriguing. Even censors, who had to possess university degrees, often found the journals engaging.

The End of Experimentation

The outbreak of the French Revolution brought a speedy end to intellectual and cultural experimentation in Russia. Catherine feared that further efforts at reform might inspire rebellion, and during her last years she cut her ties with western European intellectuals. The policy of westernization lost imperial sponsorship, but questions of relations between Russian and western European societies continued to spark intense debate throughout the nineteenth and twentieth centuries.

Russia grew from a small regional state to a vast continental empire during early modern times. After throwing off Mongol rule, the princes of Moscow founded an absolutist state and greatly expanded their realm. Between the late fifteenth and late eighteenth centuries, the Russian tsars absorbed extensive territories in eastern Europe, central Asia, and northern Asia. While bringing additional resources to the state, this expansion also led to problems in Russian society. It strained labor resources because the Russian population was not large enough to settle and work all the newly acquired territories, especially in the vast tundras of Siberia. Tsars and nobles sought to ensure a reliable labor supply by tightening the conditions of serfdom, which caused deep discontent among the peasantry. Expansion set the stage for further conflict by encouraging interaction between Russian and western European societies. When reforming tsars sought to strengthen Russia by remodeling it along western European lines, they provoked opposition from nobles, merchants, church officials, and others who preferred traditional ways. The tsars actively promoted reform from the late seventeenth to the late eighteenth century and, unlike the rulers of China, Japan, and the Islamic empires, encouraged selective imitation of western European examples. After the outbreak of the French Revolution, however, the tsars feared that further change would spark rebellion. As a result, they sharply limited western European influence in Russia and largely abandoned the program of reform.

CHRONOLOGY

1462–1505	Reign of Ivan III (Ivan the Great)
1533–1584	Reign of Ivan IV (Ivan the Terrible)
1598–1613	The "time of troubles"
1610–1917	Romanov dynasty
1681	Execution of Avvakum
1682–1725	Reign of Peter I (Peter the Great)
1700–1722	Great Northern War
1702	Founding of St. Petersburg
1725–1742	Maritime expeditions of Vitus Bering
1762–1795	Reign of Catherine II (Catherine the Great)
1773–1774	Pugachev's rebellion

FOR FURTHER READING

Paul Avrich. *Russian Rebels, 1600–1800*. New York, 1972. A fascinating and spirited account of major peasant rebellions preceding the revolutionary upheaval of 1917.

James H. Billington. *The Icon and the Axe: An Interpretive History of Russian Culture*. New York, 1966. A rich, imaginative, and evocative analysis of Russian cultural history in its political context.

Robert Crummey. *The Formation of Muscovy, 1304–1613*. London, 1987. An erudite and measured study, among the most informative about Russia's transition from feudalism to absolutism.

———. *Aristocrats and Servitors: The Boyar Elite in Russia, 1613–1689*. Princeton, 1983. A companion volume to *The Formation of Muscovy* that examines the construction of a centralized tsarist state before the reign of Peter the Great.

Stephen Frederic Dale. *Indian Merchants and Eurasian Trade, 1600–1750*. Cambridge, 1994. Examines the workings of an Indian trading community that conducted business in Persia, central Asia, and Russia.

Isabel de Madariaga. *Russia in the Age of Catherine the Great*. New Haven, 1981. In addition to the biographical insights offered into Catherine's life, this book highlights the larger social, cultural, and political transformations that Russia underwent during her reign.

Paul Dukes. *The Making of Russian Absolutism, 1613–1801*. 2nd ed. London, 1990. A succinct study of two disparate centuries, the seventeenth and eighteenth, and two influential tsars, Peter and Catherine.

Richard Hellie. *Enserfment and Military Change in Muscovy*. Chicago, 1971. The most thorough study of the origins and evolution of serfdom, this book also offers a social history of the military during the pivotal seventeenth century.

Daniel Kaiser and Gary Marker. *Reinterpreting Russian History: Readings, 860s–1860s*. New York, 1994. This collection blends primary sources with secondary works, offering insights into political, social, economic, and cultural history.

Robert J. Kaiser. *The Geography of Nationalism in Russia and the USSR*. Princeton, 1994. Establishes a historical framework for analyzing the many nationalities that made up Russia and the USSR.

Michael Khodarkovsky. *Where Two Worlds Meet: The Russian State and the Kalmyk Nomads, 1600–1771*. Ithaca, 1992. One of the first major studies to look at Russian imperial expansion through the eyes of colonized peoples.

Nicholas Riasanovsky. *The Image of Peter the Great in Russian History and Thought*. Oxford, 1985. Examines the significance of Peter's reputation for relations between Russia and western European societies.

Yuri Slezkine. *Arctic Mirrors: Russia and the Small Peoples of the North*. Ithaca, 1994. Thoughtful analysis of Russian relations with the hunting, fishing, and herding peoples of Siberia.

Ronald Suny. *The Making of the Georgian Nation*. Bloomington, 1988. Studies Russian absorption of the Caucasus from the perspective of the native Georgians.

David Turnock. *The Making of Eastern Europe: From Earliest Times to 1815*. New York, 1988. An especially useful survey that examines broader movements that affected eastern Europe as a geographical region.

AN AGE OF REVOLUTION, INDUSTRY, AND EMPIRE, 1750–1914

．．．

During the early modern era, from 1500 to 1800, peoples from all parts of the world entered into sustained interactions with each other for the first time in history. Commercial, biological, and cultural exchanges influenced the development of societies in all the world's regions. European peoples in particular benefited from increased global interactions because they established the principal maritime links between the world's regions. As a result, they realized enormous profits from interregional trade, and they were also able to establish large empires and flourishing settler colonies in the Americas.

During the period from about 1750 to 1914, European peoples parlayed their advantageous position into global hegemony: by the late nineteenth century, European powers controlled affairs in most of Asia and almost all of Africa, while their Euro-American cousins dominated the Americas. Even tiny Pacific islands fell under the rule of European and Euro-American peoples. Three historical developments—revolution, industrialization, and imperialism—help to explain how European and Euro-American peoples came to dominate so much of the world.

Revolution transformed European and American societies in the late eighteenth and early nineteenth centuries. Revolution broke out first in North America, where thirteen British colonies rebelled and won their independence. These colonies joined together to form a new republic, the United States of America, which drew heavily on the Enlightenment values of freedom, equality, and popular sovereignty in justifying its existence as an independent land. The success of the American revolution inspired the people of France to undertake a thorough transformation of their own society: after abolishing the monarchy and the aristocracy, they established a republic based on freedom, equality, and popular sovereignty. Although turmoil soon brought down the French republic, Enlightenment values continued to influence public affairs in France after the revolution. From France revolution moved back to the western hemisphere, where the French colony of Saint-Domingue (modern Haiti) and Iberian colonies in Mexico and South America won their independence.

Revolutions had a profound effect on the organization of societies in the Atlantic Ocean basin. First in Europe and later in the

Americas as well, revolutions and the conflicts that followed from them encouraged the formation of national identities. States seeking to pursue the interests of national communities were able to mobilize popular support on a scale never before achieved and often enjoyed success in conflicts with neighboring peoples who had not been able to organize effective national states. The idea of organizing states around national communities eventually influenced political development throughout the world.

While organizing themselves into national states, western European and North American peoples also embarked on processes of industrialization. By harnessing inanimate sources of energy and organizing production in factories, industrialists were able to produce high-quality goods at low cost. Because industrialization encouraged continuous innovation, industrial societies were also able to improve constantly on their economic performance. Industrialization caused a great deal of discomfort and dislocation, as workers adjusted from the rhythms of agricultural society to the demands of factories, machines, and managers seeking efficiencies in production. Over time, however, industrial societies became economically much stronger than agricultural societies, and industrial production brought about general improvement in material standards of living. After originating in Britain in the late eighteenth century, industrialization spread rapidly to western Europe and North America, and by the late nineteenth century to Russia and Japan as well. Even the lands that did not undergo processes of industrialization until the twentieth century immediately felt the effects of industrialization, as demand rose for agricultural products and natural resources needed by industrial societies.

Alongside increased material standards of living, industrialization also brought political, military, and economic strength. Particularly in western Europe and the United States, where it occurred alongside the formation of national communities, industrial-ization helped underwrite processes of imperialism and colonialism. Industrial lands developed powerful transportation, communication, and military technologies that agricultural societies could not match. Railroads, steamships, telegraphs, and lethal weapons enabled western European peoples to impose their rule in most of Asia and Africa in the nineteenth century, just as Euro-American settlers relied on industrial technologies to drive the indigenous peoples of North America and South America onto marginal lands. Toward the end of the nineteenth century, the United States and Japan used their own industrial technologies to increase their presence in the larger world and thus joined western European lands as global imperial and colonial powers.

Revolution, industrialization, and imperialism had effects felt around the world. Western European and North American lands vastly strengthened their position in the world by exercising political or economic influence over other societies. In some lands, particularly the Ottoman empire, Russia, China, and Japan, reformers worked to restructure their societies and increase their influence in global affairs by building national states that harnessed the energies of their populations. In doing so they studied the experience of western European lands and sought to adapt the principles of European political and social organization to their own societies. In the absence of a revolution that toppled ruling elites, however, critics found it very difficult to bring about meaningful reform, since privileged classes resisted change that threatened their position in their own societies. Colonized peoples had even less opportunity to bring about political and social reform, but they frequently resisted imperial powers by mounting rebellions and organizing anti-colonial movements. Revolution, industry, and empire fueled conflict throughout the world in the nineteenth century, and in combination they forced the world's peoples to deal with each other more systematically than ever before in history.

ASIA	AFRICA	EUROPE	AMERICAS AND OCEANIA
1760	**1760**	**1760**	**1760**
Chinese emperor Qianlong (r. 1736–1796) Ottoman sultan Selim III (1789–1807)		Voltaire (1694–1778) and Jean-Jacques Rousseau (1712–1778) Seven Years' War (1756–1763) James Watt invents the steam engine (1765) French revolution begins (1789) *Declaration of the Rights of Man and the Citizen* (1789) Olympe de Gouge's *Declaration of the Rights of Woman and the Female Citizen* (1791) Mary Wollstonecraft's *A Vindication of the Rights of Women* (1792)	American revolution (1775–1783) *Declaration of Independence* (1776) United States president George Washington (1732–1799) British surrender at Yorktown (1781) Peace of Paris (1783) and American independence Slave revolt in Saint-Domingue (1791) Toussaint Louverture (1744–1803)
1800	**1800**	**1800**	**1800**
Ram Mohan Roy (1772–1833) Ottoman sultan Mahmud II (1808–1839)	Slave trade ends Great Britain (1807), United States (1808), France (1814), Netherlands (1817)	Napoleon's final defeat at Waterloo (1815) Congress of Vienna (1814–1815) Austrian minister Klemens von Metternich (1773–1959) George Stephenson invents the steam locomotive (1815)	Independence of Haiti (1804) Louisiana Purchase (1803) War of 1812 (1812–1815)
1820	**1820**	**1820**	**1820**
Chinese cholera epidemic (1822–1824) Thomas Raffles founds Singapore (1824)	Slavery abolished Great Britain (1833), France (1848), United States (1865), Cuba (1886)	Russo-Turkish war (1828–1829) Origins of utopian socialism	Independence of Brazil Brazilian emperor Pedro I (1822–1834) Monroe Doctrine (1823) Central American Federation (1824–1838) splits into Guatemala, El Salvador, Honduras, Nicaragua, and Costa Rica Simón Bolívar (1783–1830), José de San Martín (1778–1850), and Bernardo O'Higgins (1778–1842)
1840	**1840**	**1840**	**1840**
Tanzimat era (1839–1876) Reforms of Mizuno Tadakuni (1841–1843) Opium War (1839–1842) Treaty of Nanjing (1843) Taiping rebellion (1850–1864) Hong Xiuquan captures Nanjing (1853) Commodore Perry arrives in Japan (1853) Indian sepoy uprising (1857)		Rebellions of 1848 Karl Marx's *Manifesto of the Communist Party* (1848) Crimean war (1853–1856) Charles Darwin's *The Origin of Species* (1859)	Treaty of Waitangi (1840) Mexican-American War (1845–1848) Seneca Falls Convention (1848) United States president Abraham Lincoln (1809–1865)

ASIA	AFRICA	EUROPE	AMERICAS AND OCEANIA
1860	**1860**	**1860**	**1860**
Meiji restoration (1868)	Construction of Suez Canal	Russian tsar Alexander II	U.S. Civil War (1861–1865)
Ito Hirobumi (1841–1909)	(1859–1869)	(1855–1881)	First Canadian prime minister
Japan sends warships to Korea	King Leopold II establishes	Italian unification (1866)	John A. McDonald
(1876)	Congo Free State	Count Camillo di Cavour	(1815–1891)
Promulgation of the Ottoman	Exploration under Stanley,	(1810–1861)	Annexation of Tahiti (France),
constitution (1876)	Livingston, Speke,	Giuseppe Garibaldi	Fiji (Britain), and Marshall
Vietnam, Cambodia, and Laos	and Burton	(1807–1882)	Islands (Germany)
fall to France (1859–1893)	Discovery of diamonds	German unification (1871)	Battle of Little Big Horn
	in South Africa (1866)	Otto von Bismarck	(1876)
		(1815–1898)	
1880	**1880**	**1880**	**1880**
Ottoman sultan Abd	British occupation of Egypt	Cecil Rhodes (1835–1902)	Northwest Rebellion (1885)
al-Hamid II (r. 1876–1908)	(1882)	Queen Victoria (1837–1901)	Massacre at Wounded Knee
Indian National Congress	Berlin Conference		(1890)
founded (1885)	(1884–1885)		Spanish-American War (1898)
Burma falls to Britain (1886)	Discovery of gold in South		
Promulgation of the Meiji	Africa (1886)		
constitution (1889)	Scramble for Africa		
Sino-Japanese War	(1875–1900)		
(1894–1895)	Battle of Omdurman (1898)		
Empress Dowager Cixi			
(1835–1908)			
Kang Youwei (1852–1927)			
Liang Qichao (1873–1929)			
Hundred Days Reforms			
(1898)			
Boxer Rebellion (1899–1900)			
1900	**1900**	**1900**	**1900**
Russo-Japanese War	Belgium takes control of		Construction of Panama
(1904–1905)	Belgian Congo (1908)		Canal (1904–1914)
Young Turks revolt (1908)			Mexican revolution
Mustapha Kemal (1881–1938)			(1911–1920)
Emperor Puyi abdicates throne			Porfirio Díaz (1830–1915),
(1912)			Emiliano Zapata
			(1897–1919), and
			Francisco Villa (1878–1923)

REVOLUTIONS
AND NATIONAL STATES
IN THE ATLANTIC WORLD

· · ·

Marie Gouze was a French butcher's daughter who educated herself by reading books, moved to Paris, and married a junior army officer. Under the name Olympe de Gouges she won some fame as a journalist, actress, and playwright. Gouges was as flamboyant as she was talented, and news of her well-publicized love affairs scandalized Parisian society.

Gouges was also a revolutionary and a strong advocate of women's rights. She responded enthusiastically when the French revolution broke out in July 1789, and she applauded in August when revolutionary leaders proclaimed freedom and equality for all citizens in the Declaration of the Rights of Man and the Citizen. It soon became clear, however, that in the view of revolutionary leaders, freedom and equality pertained only to male citizens. They welcomed women's contributions to the revolution but withheld the right to vote and left women under the patriarchal authority of their fathers and husbands.

Gouges campaigned fervently to raise the standing of women in French society. She called for more education and demanded that women share equal rights in family property. She challenged patriarchal authority and appealed to Queen Marie Antoinette to use her influence to advance women's rights. In 1791 Gouges published a "Declaration of the Rights of Woman and the Female Citizen," which claimed the same rights for women that revolutionary leaders had granted to men in August 1789. She asserted that freedom and equality were inalienable rights of women as well as men, and she insisted on the rights of women to vote, speak their minds freely, participate in the making of law, and hold public office.

Gouges's declaration attracted a great deal of attention but little support. Revolutionary leaders dismissed her appeal as a publicity stunt and refused to put women's rights on their political agenda. In 1793 they executed her because of her affection for Marie Antoinette and her persistent crusade for women's rights. Yet Gouges's campaign illustrated the power of the Enlightenment ideals of freedom and equality. Revolutionary leaders stilled her voice, but once they had proclaimed freedom and equality as universal human rights, they were unable to suppress demands to extend them to new constituencies.

Liberty, personified as a woman, leads the French people in a famous painting by Eugène Delacroix.
· Giraudon/Art Resource, NY

Violence rocked lands throughout much of the Atlantic Ocean basin in the late eighteenth and early nineteenth centuries, as a series of revolutions brought dramatic political and social change in the European and Euro-American world. Revolution broke out first in the British colonies of North America, where colonists asserted their independence and founded a new republic. A few years later revolutionaries abolished the French monarchy and thoroughly reorganized French society. Revolutionary ideas soon spread to other lands. They inspired popular movements throughout Europe and prompted Latin American peoples to seek independence from Spanish and Portuguese colonial rule. In Saint-Domingue revolution led to the abolition of slavery as well as independence from French rule. By the 1830s peoples had reorganized political and social structures throughout western Europe and the Americas.

Apart from affecting individual lands, the revolutions of the late eighteenth and early nineteenth centuries had two results of deep global significance. First, they helped to spread a cluster of Enlightenment ideas concerning freedom, equality, and popular sovereignty. Revolutionary leaders argued that political authority arose from the people and worked to establish states in the interests of the people rather than the rulers. Usually they instituted republican forms of government, in which constituents selected delegates to represent their interests. In fact, early revolutionaries extended political rights to a privileged group of white men, but they justified their actions in general terms that invited new consituencies to seek enfranchisement. Ideas about freedom, equality, and popular sovereignty spread globally after the American and French revolutions as social reformers and revolutionaries struggled throughout the nineteenth and twentieth centuries to make freedom and equality a reality for oppressed groups and subject peoples throughout the world. By the mid-twentieth century nearly every state in the world formally recognized the freedom and equality of all its citizens—even if they did not always honor their official positions—and claimed authority to rule on the basis of popular sovereignty.

While promoting Enlightenment values, revolutions also encouraged the consolidation of national states as the principal form of political organization. As peoples defended their states from enemies and sometimes mounted attacks on foreign lands, they developed a powerful sense of identity with their compatriots, and nationalist convictions inspired them to work toward the foundation of states that would advance the interests of the national community. During the nineteenth century strong national identities and movements to build national states profoundly influenced the political experiences of European states. Strong nationalist sentiments created problems for multicultural states like the Austrian empire, which embraced several distinct linguistic and ethnic communities, but also fueled movements to unify lands like Italy and Germany, which previously had no national state. During the late nineteenth and twentieth centuries, efforts to harness nationalist sentiments and form states based on national identity became one of the most powerful and dynamic movements in world history.

POPULAR SOVEREIGNTY AND POLITICAL UPHEAVAL

Drawing on Enlightenment ideals, revolutionaries of the eighteenth and nineteenth centuries sought to fashion a fair and equitable society by instituting governments that were responsive to the needs and interests of the peoples they governed. In justifying their policies, revolutionaries attacked monarchical and aristocratic regimes and argued for popular sovereignty—the notion that legitimate political authority resides not in kings but rather in the people who made up a society. In North America colonists declared independence from British rule and instituted a new government founded on the principle of popular sovereignty. Soon thereafter, French revolutionaries abolished the monarchy and revamped the social order. Yet revolutionaries in France were unable to devise a stable alternative to the monarchy, and French society experienced turmoil for more than twenty years. In the early nineteenth century, Napoleon Bonaparte imposed military rule on France and helped spread revolutionary ideas to much of western Europe.

Enlightened and Revolutionary Ideas

Throughout history kings or emperors ruled almost all settled agricultural societies. Small societies occasionally instituted democratic governments, in which all citizens participated in political affairs, or republican governments, in which delegates represented the interests of various constituencies. Some societies, especially those with weak central leadership, also relied on aristocratic governments, in which privileged elites supervised public affairs. But hierarchical rule flowing from a king or emperor was by far the most common form of government in settled agricultural societies.

In justifying their rule, kings and emperors throughout the world often identified themselves with deities or claimed divine sanction for their authority. Some rulers were priests, and most others cooperated closely with religious authorities. On the basis of their association with divine powers, kings and emperors claimed sovereignty—political supremacy and the authority to rule. In imperial China, for example, dynastic houses claimed to rule in accordance with the "mandate of heaven," while in early modern Europe centralizing monarchs often asserted a "divine right of kings" to rule as absolute monarchs.

During the seventeenth and eighteenth centuries, *philosophes* and other advocates of Enlightenment ideas (discussed in chapter 23) began to question long-standing notions of sovereignty. The philosophes rarely challenged monarchical rule, but sought instead to make kings responsible to the people they governed. They commonly regarded government as the result of a contract between rulers and ruled. The English philosopher John Locke (1632–1704) formulated one of the most influential theories of contractual government. In his *Second Treatise of Civil Government,* published in 1690, Locke held that government arose in the remote past when people decided to work together, form civil society, and appoint rulers to protect and promote their common interests. Individuals granted political rights to their rulers but retained personal rights to life, liberty, and property. Any ruler who violated these rights was subject to deposition. Furthermore, according to Locke, because individuals voluntarily formed society and established government, rulers derived their authority from the consent of those whom they governed. If subjects withdrew their consent, they had the right to replace their rulers. In effect, Locke's political thought relocated sovereignty, removing it from rulers as divine agents and vesting it in the people of a society.

Enlightenment thinkers addressed issues of freedom and equality as well as sovereignty. Philosophes like Voltaire (1694–1778) resented the persecution of religious minorities and the censorship of royal officials, who had the power to prevent printers from publishing works that did not meet the approval of political and religious authorities. They called for religious toleration and freedom to express their views openly. When censors prohibited the publication of their writings in France,

Popular Sovereignty

Individual Freedom

they often worked with French-speaking printers in Switzerland or the Netherlands who published their books and smuggled them across the border into France.

Political and Legal Equality

Many Enlightenment thinkers also called for equality. They condemned the legal and social privileges enjoyed by aristocrats, who in the philosophes' view made no more contribution to the larger society than a peasant, artisan, or craftsman. They recommended the creation of a society in which all individuals would be equal before the law. The most prominent advocate of political equality was the French-Swiss thinker Jean-Jacques Rousseau (1712–1778), who identified with simple working people and deeply resented the privileges enjoyed by elite classes. In his influential book *The Social Contract* (1762), Rousseau argued that members of a society were collectively the sovereign. In an ideal society all individuals would participate directly in the formulation of policy and the creation of laws. In the absence of royalty, aristocrats, or other privileged elites, the general will of the people would carry the day.

Enlightenment thought on freedom, equality, and popular sovereignty reflected the interests of educated and talented men who sought to increase their influence and enhance their status in society. Most Enlightenment thinkers were of common birth but comfortable means. While seeking to limit the prerogatives of ruling and aristocratic classes, they did not envision a society in which they would share political rights with women, children, peasants, laborers, slaves, or people of color.

Global Influence of Enlightenment Values

Nevertheless, Enlightenment thought constituted a serious challenge to long-established notions of political and social order. Revolutionary leaders in Europe and the Americas readily adopted Enlightenment ideas when justifying their efforts to overhaul the political and social structures they inherited. Over the longer term Enlightenment political thought influenced the organization of states and societies throughout the world. Enlightenment ideals did not spread naturally or inevitably. Rather, they spread when social reformers and revolutionaries claimed and fought for rights previously denied to them by ruling authorities and elite classes. Arguments for freedom, equality, and popular sovereignty originally served the interests of relatively privileged European and Euro-American men, but many other groups made effective use of them in seeking the extension of political rights.

The American Revolution

In the mid-eighteenth century there was no sign that North America might become a center of revolution. Residents of the thirteen British colonies there regarded themselves as British subjects: they recognized British law, read English-language books, and often braved the stormy waters of the North Atlantic Ocean to visit friends and family in England. They benefited handsomely from British rule. Trade brought prosperity to the colonies, and British military forces protected colonists' interests. From 1754 to 1763, for example, British forces waged an extremely expensive conflict in North America known as the French and Indian War. This conflict merged with a larger contest for imperial supremacy, the Seven Years' War (1756–1763), in which British and French forces battled each other in Europe and India as well as North America. Victory in the Seven Years' War ensured that Britain would dominate global trade and that British possessions, including the North American colonies, would prosper.

tax

Tightened British Control of the Colonies

After the mid-1760s, however, North American colonists became increasingly disenchanted with British imperial rule. Faced with staggering financial difficulties arising from the Seven Years' War, the British Parliament passed legislation to levy new taxes and bring order to a far-flung trading empire. Parliament expected that the North American colonies would bear a fair share of the empire's tax burden and respect imperial trade policies. But parliamentary legislation proved extremely unpopular in North America. Colonists especially resented the imposition of taxes on molasses by the Sugar Act (1764), on publications and legal documents by the Stamp Act (1765), on a wide variety of imported items by the Townshend Act (1767), and on tea by the Tea Act (1773). They objected to strict enforcement of navigation laws—some of them a century old, but widely disregarded—that required cargoes to travel in British ships and clear British customs. Colonists also took offense at the Quartering Act (1765), which required them to provide housing and accommodations for British troops.

In responding to British policies, colonists argued that they should govern their own affairs rather than follow instructions from London. They responded to new parliamentary levies with the slogan "no taxation without representation." They boycotted British products, physically attacked British officials, and mounted protests such as the Boston Tea Party (1773), in which colonists dumped a cargo of tea into Boston harbor rather than pay duties under the Tea Act. They also organized the Continental Congress (1774), which coordinated the colonies' resistance to British policies. By 1775 tensions were so high that British troops and a colonial militia skirmished at the village of Lexington, near Boston. The war of American independence had begun.

On 4 July 1776 the Continental Congress adopted a document entitled "The unanimous Declaration of the thirteen united States of America." This Declaration of Independence drew deep inspiration from Enlightenment political thought in justifying the colonies' quest for independence. The document asserted "that all men are created equal, that they are endowed by their Creator with certain unalienable Rights, that among these are Life, Liberty, and the pursuit of Happiness." It echoed John Locke's contractual theory of government in arguing that individuals established governments to secure these rights and in holding that governments derive their power and authority from "the consent of the governed." When any government infringes upon individuals' rights, the document continued, "it is the Right of the People to alter or abolish it, and to institute new Government." The Declaration of Independence presented a long list of specific abuses charged to the British crown and concluded by proclaiming the colonies "Free and Independent States" with "full Power to levy War, conclude Peace, contract Alliances, establish Commerce, and to do all other Acts and Things which Independent States may of right do."

The Declaration of Independence

It was one thing to declare independence, but a different matter altogether to make independence a reality. At the beginning of the war for independence, Britain enjoyed many advantages over the rebels: a strong government with clear lines of authority, the most powerful navy in the world, a competent army, and a sizable population of loyalists in the colonies. But to wage war in a distant land full of opponents, Britain had to ship supplies and reinforcements across a stormy ocean. Meanwhile, the rebels benefited from the military and economic support of European states that were eager to chip away at British hegemony in the Atlantic Ocean basin: France, Spain, the Netherlands, and several German principalities contributed to the American quest for independence. Moreover, George Washington (1732–1799) provided strong and imaginative military leadership for the colonial army while local militias employed guerrilla tactics effectively against British forces.

In this painting by American artist John Trumbull, authors of the Declaration of Independence, including John Adams, Thomas Jefferson, and Benjamin Franklin, stand before a desk at the Continental Congress in Philadelphia. • Yale University Art Gallery

By 1780 all combatants were weary of the conflict. Rather than risk the possibility that France might establish a close alliance with the North American colonies, British forces surrendered to George Washington at Yorktown, Virginia, in October 1781. In September 1783 diplomats concluded the Peace of Paris, by which the British government formally recognized American independence.

Building an Independent State   The leaders of the fledgling land organized a state that reflected Enlightenment principles. They created a federal republic in which the thirteen former colonies retained a great deal of autonomy over local affairs. They based the federal government on popular sovereignty, and they agreed to follow a written constitution that guaranteed freedom of speech and religion. They did not grant political and legal equality to all inhabitants of the newly independent land. They accorded full rights only to men of property, withholding them from landless men, women, slaves, and indigenous peoples. Over time, however, disenfranchised groups claimed and struggled for political and legal rights. Their campaigns involved considerable personal sacrifice and sometimes led to violence, since those in possession of rights did not always share them readily with others. With the extension of civil rights, American society broadened the implications of the Enlightenment values of freedom and equality as well as popular sovereignty.

MAP [29.1]

The American Revolution.

The French Revolution

French revolutionaries also drew inspiration from Enlightenment political thought, but the French revolution was a more radical affair than its American counterpart. American revolutionary leaders sought independence from British imperial rule, but they were content to retain British law and much of their British social and cultural heritage. By contrast, French revolutionary leaders repudiated existing society, often referred to as the *ancien régime* ("the old order"), and sought to replace it with new political, social, and cultural structures.

Serious fiscal problems put France on the road to revolution. In the 1780s approximately half of the French royal government's revenue went to pay off war debts—some of them arising from French support for colonists in the war of American independence—and another quarter went to French armed forces. King Louis XVI (reigned 1774–1793) was unable to raise more revenue from the overburdened

The Estates General

peasantry, so he sought to increase taxes on the French nobility, which had long been exempt from many levies. Aristocrats protested this effort and forced Louis to summon the Estates General, an assembly that represented the entire French population through groups known as estates. In the *ancien régime* there were three estates, or political classes. The first estate consisted of about one hundred thousand Roman Catholic clergy, and the second included some four hundred thousand nobles. The third estate embraced the rest of the population—about twenty-four million serfs, free peasants, and urban residents ranging from laborers, artisans, and shopkeepers to physicians, bankers, and attorneys. Though founded in 1303, the Estates General had not met since 1614.

In May 1789 King Louis called the Estates General into session at the royal palace of Versailles in hopes that it would authorize new taxes. Louis never controlled the assembly. Representatives of the third estate arrived at Versailles demanding sweeping political and social reform. Although some members of the lower clergy and a few prominent nobles supported reform, the first and second estates stymied efforts to push measures through the Estates General.

The National Assembly

On 17 June 1789, after six weeks of fruitless debate, representatives of the third estate took the dramatic step of seceding from the Estates General. Meeting at an indoor tennis court, they declared themselves the National Assembly, the true representative of the French people. They swore further that they would not disband until they had provided France with a written constitution. This assertion of popular sovereignty caused great excitement in nearby Paris. On 14 July 1789 a Parisian crowd stormed the Bastille, a royal arsenal and jail, in search of weapons and ammunition. The military garrison protecting the Bastille surrendered to the crowd but only after killing many of the attackers. To vent their rage, members of the crowd hacked the defenders to death. One assailant used his pocketknife to sever the garrison commander's head, which the victorious crowd mounted on a pike and paraded around the streets of Paris. News of the event soon spread, sparking insurrections in cities throughout France.

A contemporary print depicts the storming of the Bastille in 1789. The deeds of common people working in crowds became a favorite theme of artists after the outbreak of the French revolution. ● Bulloz/ Musée Carnavalet

THE DECLARATION OF THE RIGHTS OF MAN AND THE CITIZEN

• • •

While developing their program of reform, members of the National Assembly consulted closely with Thomas Jefferson, the principle author of the American Declaration of Independence, who was the U.S. ambassador to France in 1789. Thus it is not surprising that the Declaration of the Rights of Man and the Citizen reflects the influence of American revolutionary ideas.

First Article. Men are born and remain free and equal in rights. Social distinctions may be based only on common utility.

Article 2. The goal of every political association is the preservation of the natural and inalienable rights of man. These rights are liberty, property, security, and resistance to oppression.

Article 3. The principle of all sovereignty resides essentially in the nation. No body and no individual can exercise authority that does not flow directly from the nation.

Article 4. Liberty consists in the freedom to do anything that does not harm another. The exercise of natural rights of each man thus has no limits except those that assure other members of society their enjoyment of the same rights. These limits may be determined only by law. . . .

Article 6. Law is the expression of the general will. All citizens have the right to participate either personally or through their representatives in the making of law. The law must be the same for all, whether it protects or punishes. Being equal in the eyes of the law, all citizens are equally eligible for all public honors, offices, and occupations, according to their abilities, without any distinction other than that of their virtues and talents. . . .

Article 11. The free communication of thoughts and opinions is one of the most precious rights of man: every citizen may thus speak, write, and publish freely, but will be responsible for abuse of this freedom in cases decided by the law. . . .

Article 13. For the maintenance of public military force and for the expenses of administration, common taxation is necessary: it must be equally divided among all citizens according to their means. . . .

Article 15. Society has the right to require from every public official an accounting of his administration.

Article 16. Any society in which guarantees of rights are not assured and separation of powers is not defined has no constitution at all.

Article 17. Property is an inviolable and sacred right. No one may be deprived of property except when public necessity, legally determined, clearly requires it, and on condition of just and prearranged compensation.

SOURCE: Déclaration des droits de l'homme et du citoyen. Translated by Jerry H. Bentley.

Emboldened by popular support, the National Assembly undertook a broad program of political and social reform. The Declaration of the Rights of Man and the Citizen, which the National Assembly promulgated in August 1789, articulated the guiding principles of the program. Reflecting the influence of American revolutionary ideas, the Declaration of the Rights of Man and the Citizen proclaimed the equality of all men, declared that sovereignty resided in the people, and asserted individual rights to liberty, property, and security.

Between 1789 and 1791 the National Assembly reconfigured French society. Taking "liberty, equality, and fraternity" as its goals, the Assembly abolished the feudal system along with the many fees and labor services that peasants owed to their landlords. It dramatically altered the role of the church in French society by seizing church lands, abolishing the first estate, defining clergy as civilians, and requiring clergy to take an oath of loyalty to the state. It also promulgated a constitution that

Liberty, Equality, and Fraternity

made the king the chief executive official but deprived him of legislative authority. France became a constitutional monarchy in which men of property—about half the adult male population—had the right to vote in elections to choose legislators. Thus far, the French revolution represented an effort to put Enlightenment political thought into practice.

The Convention   The revolution soon took a radical turn. Alarmed by the disintegration of monarchical authority, rulers of Austria and Prussia invaded France to support the king and restore the *ancien régime*. Revolutionary leaders responded by establishing the Convention, a new legislative body elected by universal male suffrage, which abolished the monarchy and proclaimed France a republic. The Convention rallied the French population by instituting the *levée en masse*, a "mass levy" or universal conscription that drafted people and resources for use in the war against invading forces. The Convention also rooted out enemies at home. It made frequent use of the guillotine, a recently invented machine that brought about supposedly humane executions by quickly severing a victim's head—whereas beheading with a sword or ax often led to needless suffering because executioners frequently needed several whacks to get the job done. In 1793 King Louis XVI and his wife Queen Marie Antoinette themselves went to the guillotine when the Convention found them guilty of treason.

Revolutionary chaos reached its peak in 1793 and 1794 when Maximilien Robespierre (1758–1794) and the radical Jacobin party dominated the Convention. The Jacobins believed passionately that France needed complete restructuring, and they unleashed a campaign of terror to promote their revolutionary agenda. They sought to eliminate the influence of Christianity in French society by closing churches and forcing priests to take wives. They promoted a new "cult of reason" as a secular alternative to Christianity. They reorganized the calendar, keeping months of thirty days but replacing seven-day weeks with ten-day units that recognized no day of religious observance. The Jacobins also proclaimed the inauguration of a new historical era with the Year I, which began with the establishment of the French republic (1792 in the Christian calendar). They encouraged citizens to display their revolutionary zeal by wearing working-class clothes. They granted increased rights to women by permitting them to inherit property and divorce their husbands, although they did not allow women to vote or participate in political affairs. The Jacobins also made frequent use of the guillotine: between the summer of 1793 and the summer of 1794, they executed about forty thousand people and imprisoned another three hundred thousand suspected enemies of the revolution. The feminist Olympe de Gouges (1748–1793) was herself a victim of the Jacobins, who did not appreciate her efforts to extend the rights of freedom and equality to women.

The guillotine was an efficient killing machine. In this contemporary print the executioner displays the just-severed head of King Louis XVI to the crowd assembled to witness his execution.

• Bibliothèque Nationale de France

Many victims of this reign of terror were fellow radicals who fell out of favor with Robespierre and the Jacobins. The instability of revolutionary leadership eventually undermined confidence in the regime itself. In July 1794 the Convention arrested Robespierre and his allies, convicted them of tyranny, and sent them to the guillotine. A group of conservative men of property then seized power and ruled France under a new institution known as the Directory (1795–1799). Though more pragmatic than previous revolutionary leaders, members of the Directory were unable to resolve the economic and military problems that plagued revolutionary France. In seeking a middle way between the *ancien régime* and radical revolution, they lurched from one policy to another, and the Directory faced constant challenges to its authority. It came to an end in November 1799 when a young general named Napoleon Bonaparte staged a coup d'état and seized power.

The Directory

The Reign of Napoleon

Born to a minor noble family of Corsica, a Mediterranean island annexed by France in 1768, Napoleon Bonaparte (1769–1821) studied at French military schools and became an officer in the army of King Louis XVI. A brilliant military leader, he became a general at age 24. He was a fervent supporter of the revolution and defended the Directory against a popular uprising in 1795. In a campaign of 1796–97, he drove the Austrian army from northern Italy and established French rule there. In 1798 he mounted an invasion of Egypt to gain access to the Red Sea and threaten British control of the sea route to India, but the campaign ended in a complete British victory. Politically ambitious, Napoleon returned to France and joined the Directory. When Austria, Russia, and Britain formed a coalition to attack France and end the revolution, he overthrew the Directory, imposed a new constitution, and named himself first consul with almost unchecked power to rule the French republic for ten years. In 1802 he became consul for life, and two years later he crowned himself emperor.

Napoleon brought political stability to a land torn by revolution and war. He made peace with the Roman Catholic church and in 1801 concluded an agreement with the pope. The pact, known as the Concordat, provided that the French state would retain church lands seized during the revolution, but the state agreed to pay clerics' salaries, recognize Roman Catholic Christianity as the preferred faith of France, and extend freedom of religion to Protestant Christians and Jews. This measure won Napoleon a great deal of support from people who supported the political and social goals of the revolution but balked at radicals' efforts to replace Christianity with a cult of reason.

Napoleonic France

In 1804 Napoleon promulgated the Civil Code, a revised body of civil law, which also helped stabilize French society. The Civil Code affirmed the political and legal equality of all adult men and established a merit-based society in which individuals qualified for education and employment because of talent rather than birth or social standing. The code protected private property, and Napoleon allowed aristocratic opponents of the revolution to return to France and reclaim some of their lost property. The Civil Code confirmed many of the moderate revolutionary policies of the National Assembly but retracted measures passed by the more radical Convention. The code restored patriarchal authority in the family, for example, by making women and children subservient to male heads of households.

Although he approved the Enlightenment ideal of equality, Napoleon was no champion of intellectual freedom or representative government. He limited free speech and routinely censored newspapers and other publications. He established a secret police force that relied heavily on spies and detained suspected political opponents by the thousands. He made systematic use of propaganda to manipulate public opinion. He ignored elective bodies and surrounded himself with loyal military officers who ensured that representative assemblies did not restrict his authority. When he crowned himself emperor, he founded a dynasty that set his family above and apart from the people in whose name they ruled.

Napoleon's Empire   While working to stabilize France, Napoleon also sought to extend his authority throughout Europe. He was an imaginative tactician and strategist, the greatest general of his time. Full of revolutionary zeal and inspired by his leadership, Napoleon's armies conquered the Iberian and Italian peninsulas, occupied the Netherlands, and

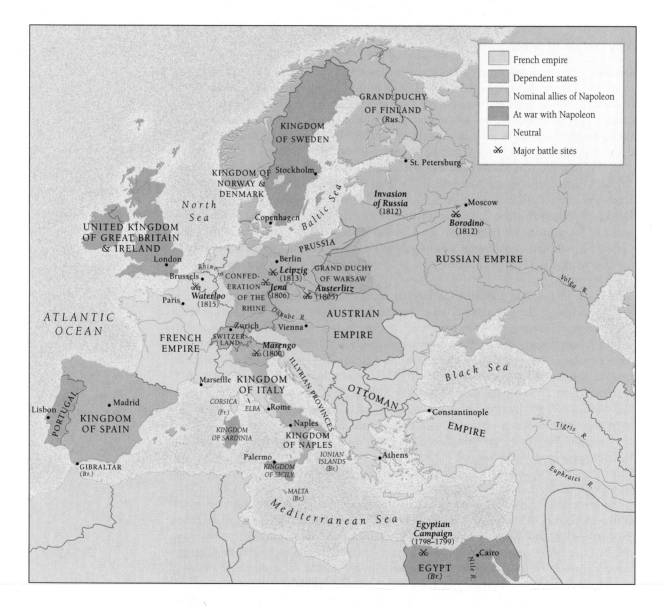

MAP [29.2]

Napoleon's empire.

inflicted humiliating defeats on Austrian and Prussian forces. Napoleon sent his brothers and other relatives to rule the conquered and occupied lands, and he forced Austria, Prussia, and Russia to ally with him and respect French hegemony in Europe.

Napoleon's empire began to unravel in 1812, when he decided to invade Russia. Convinced that the tsar was conspiring with his British enemies, Napoleon led a "Grand Army" of six hundred thousand men to Moscow. He captured the city, but the tsar withdrew and refused to surrender. Russian patriots set Moscow ablaze, leaving Napoleon's massive army without adequate shelter or supplies. Napoleon ordered a retreat, but the bitter Russian winter destroyed his army. Napoleon had defied the combined forces of Britain, Austria, and Prussia, but he was no match for "General Winter." The Grand Army disintegrated, and a battered remnant of only thirty thousand men limped back to France.

Napoleon's disastrous Russian campaign emboldened his enemies. A coalition of British, Austrian, Prussian, and Russian armies converged on France and forced Napoleon to abdicate his throne in April 1814. The victors restored the French monarchy and exiled Napoleon to the tiny Mediterranean island of Elba, near Corsica. But Napoleon's adventure had not yet come to an end. In March 1815 he escaped from Elba, returned to France, and reconstituted his army. For a hundred days he ruled France again before a British army defeated him at Waterloo in Belgium. Unwilling to take further chances with the wily general, European powers banished Napoleon to the remote and isolated island of St. Helena in the South Atlantic Ocean, where he died of natural causes in 1821.

The Fall of Napoleon

THE INFLUENCE OF REVOLUTION

The Enlightenment ideals promoted by the American and French revolutions—freedom, equality, and popular sovereignty—appealed to peoples throughout Europe and the Americas. In the Caribbean and South America, they inspired revolutionary movements: slaves in the French colony of Saint-Domingue rose against their overlords and established the independent republic of Haiti, and Euro-American leaders mounted independence movements in Central America and South America. The ideals of the American and French revolutions also encouraged social reformers to organize broader programs of liberation. Whereas the American and French revolutions guaranteed political and legal rights to white men, social reformers sought to extend these rights to women and slaves of African ancestry. During the nineteenth century all European and Euro-American states abolished slavery, but former slaves and their descendants remained an underprivileged and often oppressed class in most of the Atlantic world. The quest for women's rights also proceeded slowly during the nineteenth century.

The Haitian Revolution

The only successful slave revolt in history took place on the Caribbean island of Hispaniola in the aftermath of the French revolution. By the eighteenth century Hispaniola was a major center of sugar production with hundreds of prosperous plantations. The Spanish colony of Santo Domingo occupied the eastern part of the island (modern Dominican Republic), and the French colony of Saint-Domingue occupied the western part (modern Haiti). Saint-Domingue was one of the richest of all European colonies in the Caribbean: sugar, coffee, and cotton produced there accounted for almost one-third of France's foreign trade.

Saint-Domingue Society

In 1790 the population of Saint-Domingue included about forty thousand white French settlers, thirty thousand *gens de couleur* (free people of color, including mulattoes as well as freed slaves), and some five hundred thousand black slaves, most of whom were born in Africa. Led by wealthy planters, white residents stood at the top of society. *Gens de couleur* farmed small plots of land, sometimes with the aid of a few slaves, or worked as artisans in the island's towns. Most of the colony's slaves toiled in the fields under brutal conditions. Planters worked their slaves so hard and provided them with so little care that mortality was very high. Many slaves ran away into the mountains. By the late eighteenth century, Saint-Domingue had many large communities of maroons (escaped slaves), who maintained their own societies and sometimes attacked plantations in search of food, weapons, tools, and additional recruits. As planters lost laborers, they imported new slaves from Africa and other Caribbean islands. This pattern continued throughout the eighteenth century, when prices of new slaves from Africa rose dramatically.

The American and French revolutions prepared the way for a violent political and social revolution in Saint-Domingue. Because French policy supported North American colonists against British rule, colonial governors in Saint-Domingue sent about eight hundred *gens de couleur* to fight in the American war of independence. In North America the *gens de couleur* became familiar with ideas of freedom and equality and returned to Saint-Domingue with the intention of reforming society there. When the French revolution broke out in 1789, white settlers in Saint-Domingue sought the right to govern themselves, but they opposed proposals to grant political and legal equality to the *gens de couleur*. By May 1791 civil war had broken out between white settlers and *gens de couleur*.

Slave Revolt

The conflict expanded dramatically when a charismatic Vodou priest named Boukman organized a slave revolt. In August 1791 some twelve thousand slaves began killing white settlers, burning their homes, and destroying their plantations. Within a few weeks the rebels attracted almost one hundred thousand slaves into their ranks. Saint-Domingue quickly descended into chaos as white, *gens de couleur,* and slave factions battled each other. Many slaves were battle-tested veterans of wars in Africa, and they drew on their military experience to organize large armies. Slave leaders also found recruits and reinforcements in Saint-Domingue's maroon communities. Foreign armies soon complicated the situation: French troops arrived in 1792 to restore order, and British and Spanish forces intervened in 1793 in hopes of benefiting from France's difficulties.

Boukman died while fighting shortly after launching the revolt, but slave forces eventually overcame white settlers, *gens de couleur,* and foreign armies. Their successes were due largely to the leadership of François-Dominique Toussaint

The slave rebellion in Saint-Domingue struck fear in the hearts of European and Euro-American peoples. This French print depicts outnumbered white settlers under attack on a plantation.

• The Granger Collection, New York

Toussaint Louverture

(1744–1803), who after 1791 called himself Louverture—from the French *l'ouverture,* meaning "the opening," or the one who created an opening in enemy ranks. The son of slaves, Toussaint learned to read and write from a Roman Catholic priest. Because of his education and intelligence, he worked as a domestic servant rather than a field hand. He rose to the position of livestock overseer on the plantation, and he became an astute judge of human character. When the slave revolt broke out in 1791, Toussaint helped his masters escape to a safe place, then left the plantation and joined the rebels.

Toussaint was a skilled organizer, and by 1793 he had built a strong, disciplined army. He shrewdly played French, British, and Spanish forces against one another while also jockeying for power with other black and mulatto generals. By 1797 he led an army of twenty thousand that controlled most of Saint-Domingue. In 1801 he promulgated a constitution that granted equality and citizenship to all residents of Saint-Domingue. He stopped short of declaring independence from France, however, because he did not want to provoke Napoleon into attacking the island.

Nevertheless, in 1802 Napoleon dispatched twenty thousand troops to restore French authority in Saint-Domingue. Toussaint attempted to negotiate a peaceful settlement, but the French commander arrested him and sent him to France, where he died in jail of maltreatment in 1803. By the time he died, however, yellow fever had ravaged the French army in Saint-Domingue, and the black generals who succeeded Toussaint had defeated the remaining troops and driven them out of the colony. Late in 1803 they declared independence, and on 1 January 1804 they proclaimed the establishment of Haiti, named after a prominent mountain, which became the second independent republic in the western hemisphere.

The Republic of Haiti

Wars of Independence in Latin America

Revolutionary ideals traveled beyond Saint-Domingue to the Spanish and Portuguese colonies in the Americas. Though governed by *peninsulares* (colonial officials from Spain or Portugal), the Iberian colonies all had a large, wealthy, and powerful class of Euro-American *criollos* or creoles, individuals born in the Americas of Spanish or Portuguese ancestry. In 1800 the *peninsulares* numbered about 30,000, and the creole population was 3.5 million. The Iberian colonies also had a large population—about 10 million in all—of less privileged classes. Black slaves formed a majority in Brazil, but elsewhere indigenous peoples and individuals of mixed ancestry such as mestizos and mulattoes were most numerous.

Latin American Society

Creoles benefited greatly during the eighteenth century, as they established plantations and ranches in the colonies and participated in rapidly expanding trade with Spain and Portugal. Yet the creoles also had grievances. Like British colonists in North America, the creoles resented administrative control and economic regulations imposed by the Iberian powers. They drew inspiration from Enlightenment political thought and occasionally took part in tax revolts and popular uprisings. The creoles desired neither social reform like that promoted by Robespierre nor the establishment of an egalitarian society like Haiti. Basically they sought to displace the *peninsulares* but retain their privileged position in society: political independence on the model of the United States in North America struck them as an attractive alternative to colonial status. Between 1810 and 1825 creoles led movements that brought independence to most Iberian colonies in the Americas and established Euro-American elites as the dominant powers in their societies.

Mexican Independence

The struggle for independence began in the wake of Napoleon's invasion of Spain and Portugal (1807), which weakened royal authority in the Iberian colonies. By 1810 revolts against Spanish rule had broken out in Argentina, Venezuela, and Mexico. The most serious was a peasant rebellion in Mexico led by a parish priest, Miguel de Hidalgo (1753–1811), who rallied indigenous peoples and mestizos against colonial rule. Hidalgo called for a new government, redistribution of wealth, equality for peasants, and the return of land to indigenous peoples. Conservative creoles soon captured Hidalgo and executed him, but his rebellion continued to flare for three years after his death.

Colonial rule came to an end in 1821, when the creole general Augustín de Iturbide (1783–1824) seized the capital, named himself emperor of Mexico, and declared independence from Spain. Neither Iturbide nor his empire survived for long. Though an able general, Iturbide was an incompetent administrator, and in 1822 creole elites deposed him and established a republic. Two years later the southern regions of the Mexican empire declared their own independence. They formed a Central American Federation until 1838, then split into the independent states of Guatemala, El Salvador, Honduras, Nicaragua, and Costa Rica.

Simón Bolívar

In South America creole elites like Simón Bolívar (1783–1830) led the movement for independence. Born in Caracas (in modern Venezuela), Bolívar was a fervent republican steeped in Enlightenment ideas about popular sovereignty. Inspired by the example of George Washington, he took up arms against Spanish rule in 1811. In the early days of his struggle, Bolívar experienced many reversals and twice went into exile. In 1819, however, he assembled an army that surprised and crushed the Spanish army in Colombia. Later he campaigned in Venezuela, Ecuador, and Peru, coordinating his efforts with other creole leaders like José de San Martín (1778–1850) in Argentina and Bernardo O'Higgins (1778–1842) in Chile. By 1824 creole forces had overcome Spanish armies and deposed Spanish rulers throughout South America.

Simón Bolívar, creole leader of the independence movement in Latin America, was a favorite subject of painters in the nineteenth century. This portrait depicts him as a determined and farsighted leader. • Van Bucher/Photo Researchers

Bolívar's goal was to weld the former Spanish colonies of South America into a great confederation like the United States in North America. During the 1820s independent Venezuela, Colombia, and Ecuador formed a republic called Gran Colombia, and Bolívar attempted to bring Peru and Bolivia (named for Bolívar himself) into the confederation. By 1830, however, strong political and regional differences had undermined Gran Colombia. As the confederation disintegrated, a bitterly disappointed Bolívar pronounced South America "ungovernable" and lamented that "those who have served the revolution have plowed the sea." Shortly

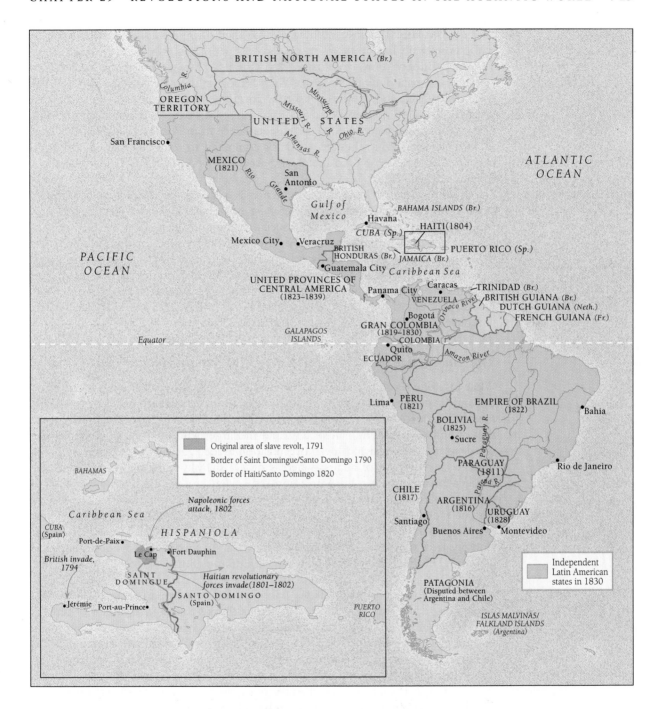

MAP [29.3]

Latin America in 1830.

after the breakup of Gran Colombia, Bolívar died of tuberculosis while en route to self-imposed exile in Europe.

Brazilian Independence   Independence came to Portuguese Brazil at the same time as to Spanish colonies, but by a different process. When Napoleon invaded Portugal in 1807, the royal court fled Lisbon and established a government in exile in Rio de Janeiro. In 1821 the king returned to Portugal, leaving his son Pedro in Brazil as regent. The next year Brazilian creoles called for independence from Portugal, and Pedro agreed to their demands. He refused his father's command to return to Lisbon, led resistance to Portuguese forces in Brazil, and accepted appointment as Emperor Pedro I (reigned 1822–1834).

Creole Dominance   Although Brazil achieved independence as a monarchy rather than a republic, creole elites dominated Brazilian society just as they did in former Spanish colonies. Indeed, independence brought little social change in Latin America. The *peninsulares* returned to Europe, but Latin American society remained as rigidly stratified as it had been in 1800. The newly independent states granted military authority to local strongmen, known as *caudillos,* allied with creole elites. The new states also permitted the continuation of slavery, confirmed the wealth and authority of the Roman Catholic church, and repressed the lower orders. The principal beneficiaries of independence in Latin America were the creole elites.

The Emergence of Ideologies: Conservatism and Liberalism

While inspiring revolutions and independence movements in other lands, the American and French revolutions also prompted political and social theorists to crystallize the modern ideologies of conservatism and liberalism. An *ideology* is a coherent vision of human nature, human society, and the larger world that proposes some particular form of political and social organization as ideal. Some ideologies seek to justify the current state of affairs, whereas others sharply criticize the status quo in arguing for movement toward an improved society. In all cases ideologists seek to design a political and social order appropriate for their communities.

Conservatism   The modern ideology of conservatism arose as political and social theorists responded to the challenges of the American and especially the French revolution. Conservatives viewed society as an organism that changed very slowly over the generations. The English political philosopher Edmund Burke (1729–1797) held, for example, that society was a compact between a people's ancestors, the present generation, and their descendants as yet unborn. While admitting the need for gradual change that came about by general consensus, Burke condemned radical or revolutionary change, which in his view could only lead to anarchy. Thus Burke approved of the American revolution, which he took as an example of natural change in keeping with the historical development of North American society, but he denounced the French revolution as a chaotic and irresponsible assault on society.

Liberalism   In contrast to conservatives, liberals took change as normal and welcomed it as the agent of progress. They viewed conservatism as an effort to justify the status quo, maintain the privileges enjoyed by favored classes, and avoid dealing with injustice and inequality in society. For liberals the task of political and social theory was not to stifle change but to manage it in the best interests of society. Liberals championed the Enlightenment values of freedom and equality, which they believed would lead to higher standards of morality and increased prosperity for the whole society. They usually favored republican forms of government in which citizens elected representatives to legislative bodies, and they called for written constitutions that guaranteed freedom and equality for all citizens and that precisely defined the political structure and institutions of their societies.

The most prominent exponent of early liberalism was John Stuart Mill (1806–1873), an English philosopher, economist, and social reformer. Mill tirelessly promoted the freedom of individuals to pursue their own economic and intellectual interests. He tried to ensure that powerful minorities, such as wealthy businessmen, would not curb the freedoms of the poorly organized majority, but he also argued that it was improper for the majority to impose its will on minorities with different interests and values. He advocated universal suffrage as the most effective way to advance individual freedom, and he called for taxation of business profits and high personal incomes to forestall the organization of wealthy classes into groups that threatened individual liberties. Mill went further than most liberals in seeking to extend the rights of freedom and equality to women and working people as well as men of property.

Testing the Limits of Revolutionary Ideals: Slavery

The Enlightenment ideals of freedom and equality were watchwords of revolution in the Atlantic Ocean basin. Yet different revolutionaries understood the implications of freedom and equality in very different ways. In North America revolution led to political independence, a broad array of individual freedoms, and the legal equality of adult white men. In France it destroyed the hierarchical social order of the *ancien régime* and temporarily extended political and legal rights to all citizens, although Napoleon and later rulers effectively curbed some of those rights. In Haiti revolution brought independence from French rule and the end of slavery as well as freedom and equality for all citizens. In South America it led to independence from Iberian rule and societies dominated by creole elites. In the wake of the Atlantic revolutions, social activists in Europe and the Americas considered the possibility that the ideals of freedom and equality might have further implications as yet unexplored. They turned their attention especially to the issues of slavery and women's rights.

The campaign to end the slave trade and abolish slavery began in the eighteenth century. Freed slaves like Olaudah Equiano (1745–1797) were among the earliest critics of slavery. Beginning in the 1780s European Christian moralists also voiced opposition to slavery.

Movements to End the Slave Trade

Only after the American, French, and Haitian revolutions, however, did the antislavery movement gain momentum. The leading spokesman of the movement was William Wilberforce (1759–1833), a prominent English philanthropist elected in 1780 to a seat in Parliament. There he tirelessly attacked slavery on moral and religious grounds. After the Haitian revolution he attracted supporters who feared that continued reliance on slave labor would result in more and larger slave revolts, and in 1807 Parliament passed Wilberforce's bill to end the slave trade. Under British pressure, other states also banned commerce in slaves: the United States in 1808, France in 1814, the Netherlands in 1817, and Spain in 1845. The British navy, which dominated the North Atlantic Ocean, patrolled the west coast of Africa to ensure compliance with the law. But the slave trade died slowly, as illegal trade in African slaves continued on a small scale: the last documented ship to carry slaves across the Atlantic Ocean arrived in Cuba in 1867.

Movements
to Abolish Slavery

The abolition of slavery itself was a much bigger challenge than ending the slave trade because owners had property rights in their slaves. Planters and merchant elites strongly resisted efforts to alter the system that provided them with abundant supplies of inexpensive labor. Nevertheless, the end of the slave trade doomed the institution of slavery in the Americas. In Haiti the end of slavery came with the revolution. In much of South America, slavery ended with independence from Spanish rule, as Simón Bolívar freed slaves who joined his forces and provided constitutional guarantees of free status for all residents of Gran Colombia.

Meanwhile, as they worked to ban traffic in human labor, Wilberforce and other moralists also launched a campaign to free slaves and abolish the institution of slavery itself. In 1833, one month after Wilberforce's death, Parliament provided twenty million pounds sterling as compensation to slave owners and abolished slavery throughout the British empire. Other states followed the British example: France abolished slavery in 1848, the United States in 1865, Cuba in 1886, and Brazil in 1888.

Freedom without
Equality

Abolition brought legal freedom for African and African-American slaves, but it did not bring political equality. In most lands other than Haiti, African-American peoples had little influence in society. Property requirements, literacy tests, poll taxes, and campaigns of intimidation effectively prevented them from voting. Nor did emancipation bring social and economic improvements for former slaves and their descendants. White creole elites owned most property in the Americas, and they kept blacks in subordination by forcing them to accept low-paying work. A few African-Americans owned small plots of land, but they could not challenge the economic and political power of creole elites.

Testing the Limits of Revolutionary Ideals: Women's Rights

Women participated alongside men in the movement to abolish slavery, and their experience inspired feminist social reformers to seek equality with men. They pointed out that women suffered many of the same legal disabilities as slaves: they had little access to education, they could not enter professional occupations that required advanced education, and they were legally deprived of the right to vote. They drew on Enlightenment thought in making a case for women's rights, but in spite of support from prominent liberals like John Stuart Mill, they had little success before the twentieth century.

Enlightenment
Ideals and Women

Enlightenment thought called for the restructuring of government and society, but the philosophes mostly held conservative views on women and their roles in family and society. Rousseau, for example, advised that girls' education should prepare them to become devoted wives and mothers. Yet social reformers found Enlightenment thought extremely useful in arguing for women's rights. Drawing on the political thought of John Locke, for example, the English writer Mary Astell (1666–1731) suggested that absolute sovereignty was no more appropriate in a family than in a state. Astell also reflected Englightenment influence in asking why, if all men were born free, all women were born slaves?

During the eighteenth century advocates of women's rights were particularly active in Britain, France, and North America. Among the most prominent was the British writer Mary Wollstonecraft (1759–1797). Although she had little schooling, Wollstonecraft avidly read books at home and gained an informal self-education. In 1792 she published an influential essay entitled *A Vindication of the Rights of Women*. Like Astell, Wollstonecraft argued that women possessed all the rights that Locke had granted to men. She insisted on the right of women to education: it

Parisian women were the leaders of the crowd that marched to Versailles, protested high food prices, and forced the king and queen to return to Paris in October 1789. • Bulloz/Musée Carnavalet

would make them better mothers and wives, she said, and would enable them to contribute to society by preparing them for professional occupations and participation in political life.

Women and Revolution

Women played crucial roles in the revolutions of the late eighteenth and early nineteenth centuries. Some women supported the efforts of men by sewing uniforms, rolling bandages, or managing farms, shops, and businesses. Others actively participated in revolutionary activities. In October 1789, for example, about six thousand Parisian women marched to Versailles to protest the high price of bread. Some of them forced their way into the royal apartments and demanded that the king and queen return with them to Paris—along with the palace's supply of flour. In the early 1790s pistol-wielding members of the Republican Revolutionary Women patrolled the streets of Paris. The fate of Olympe de Gouges made it clear, however, that revolutionary women had little prospect of holding official positions or playing a formal role in public affairs.

Under the National Assembly and the Convention, the French revolution brought increased rights for women. The republican government provided free public education for girls as well as boys, granted wives a share of family property, and legalized divorce. Yet the revolution did not bring women the right to vote or to play major roles in public affairs. Under the Directory and Napoleon's rule, women lost even the rights that they had won in the early days of the revolution. In other lands women never gained as much as they did in revolutionary France. In the United States and the independent states of Latin America, revolution brought legal equality and political rights only for adult white men, who retained patriarchal authority over their wives and families.

Women's Rights Movements

Nevertheless, throughout the nineteenth century social reformers pressed for women's rights as well as the abolition of slavery. The American feminist Elizabeth Cady Stanton (1815–1902) was an especially prominent figure in this movement. In 1840 Stanton went to London to attend an antislavery conference but found that the organizers barred women from participation. Infuriated, Stanton returned to the United States and began to build a movement for women's rights. She organized a conference of feminists who met at Seneca Falls, New York, in 1848. The conference passed twelve resolutions demanding that lawmakers grant women rights equivalent to those enjoyed by men. The resolutions called specifically for women's rights to vote, attend public schools, enter professional occupations, and participate in public affairs.

The women's rights movement experienced limited success in the nineteenth century. More women received formal education than before the American and French revolutions, and women in Europe and North America participated in academic, literary, and civic organizations. Rarely did they enter the professions, however, and nowhere did they enjoy the right to vote. Yet by seeking to extend the promises of Enlightenment political thought to blacks and women as well as white men, social reformers of the nineteenth century laid a foundation that would lead to large-scale social change in the twentieth century.

THE CONSOLIDATION OF NATIONAL STATES IN EUROPE

The Enlightenment ideals of freedom, equality, and popular sovereignty inspired political revolutions in much of the Atlantic Ocean basin, and the revolutions in turn helped spread Enlightenment values. The wars of the French revolution and the Napoleonic era also inspired the development of a particular type of community identity that had little to do with Enlightenment values—nationalism. Revolutionary wars involved millions of French citizens in the defense of their country against foreign armies and the extension of French influence to neighboring states. Wartime experiences encouraged peoples throughout Europe to think of themselves as members of distinctive national communities. Throughout the nineteenth century European nationalist leaders worked to fashion states based on national identities and mobilized citizens to work in the interests of their own national communities, sometimes by fostering jealousy and suspicion of other national groups. By the late nineteenth century, national identities were so strong that peoples throughout Europe responded enthusiastically to ideologies of nationalism, which promised glory and prosperity to those who worked in the interests of their national communities.

Nations and Nationalism

One of the most influential concepts of modern political thought is the idea of the nation. The word *nation* refers to a type of community that became especially prominent in the nineteenth century. At various times and places in history, individuals have associated themselves primarily with families, clans, cities, regions, and religious faiths. During the nineteenth century European peoples came to identify strongly with communities they called nations. Members of a nation considered themselves a distinctive people born into a unique community that spoke a common language, observed common customs, inherited common cultural traditions, held common values, and shared common historical experiences. Often they also honored common religious beliefs, although they sometimes overlooked differences of faith and construed the nation as a political, social, and cultural rather than religious unit.

Intense feelings of national identity fueled ideologies of nationalism. Advocates of nationalism insisted that the nation must be the focus of political loyalty. Zealous nationalist leaders maintained that members of their national communities had a common destiny that they could best advance by organizing independent national states and resolutely pursuing their national interests. Ideally, in their view, the boundaries of the national state embraced the territory occupied by the national community, and its government promoted the interests of the national group, sometimes through conflict with other peoples.

Early nationalist thought often sought to deepen appreciation for the historical experiences of the national community and foster pride in its cultural accomplishments. During the late eighteenth century, for example, Johann Gottfried von Herder (1744–1803) sang the praises of the German *Volk* ("people") and their powerful and expressive language. In reaction to Enlightenment thinkers and their quest for a scientific, universally valid understanding of the world, early cultural nationalists like Herder focused their attention on individual communities and relished their uniqueness. They emphasized historical scholarship, which they believed would illuminate the distinctive characteristics of their societies. They also valued the study of literature, which they considered the best guide to the *Volksgeist,* the popular soul or spirit or essence of their community. For this reason the German brothers Jakob and Wilhelm Grimm collected popular poetry, stories, songs, and tales as expressions of the German *Volk.*

Cultural Nationalism

During the nineteenth century nationalist thought became much more strident than the cultural nationalism of Herder or the brothers Grimm. Advocates of nationalism demanded loyalty and solidarity from members of the national group. In lands where they were minorities or where they lived under foreign rule, they sought to establish independent states to protect and advance the interests of the national community.

Political Nationalism

In Italy, for example, the nationalist activist Giuseppe Mazzini (1805–1872) formed a group called Young Italy that promoted independence from Austrian and Spanish rule and the establishment of an Italian national state. Mazzini likened the nation to a family and the nation's territory to the family home. Austrian and Spanish authorities forced Mazzini to lead much of his life in exile, but he used the opportunity to encourage the organization of nationalist movements in new lands. By the mid-nineteenth century Young Italy had inspired the development of nationalist movements in Ireland, Switzerland, and Hungary.

While it encouraged political leaders to work toward the establishment of national states for their communities, nationalism also had strong potential to stir up conflict between different groups of people. The more nationalists identified with their own national communities, the more they distinguished themselves both from peoples in other lands and from minority groups within their own societies.

This divisive potential of nationalism helps to explain the emergence of Zionism, a movement founded in the late nineteenth century to establish a Jewish state in Palestine. Unlike Mazzini's Italian compatriots, Jews did not inhabit a well-defined territory, but rather lived in states throughout Europe. As national communities tightened their bonds, nationalist leaders often became distrustful of minority populations. Suspicion of Jews fueled anti-Semitic persecution in much of Europe. In Russia and Poland, anti-Semitic violence was especially acute, as cossacks and army units led pogroms against Jewish communities. During the late nineteenth and twentieth centuries, millions of Jews migrated to other European lands or to North

Nationalism and Anti-Semitism

A portrait of the Italian nationalist leader Giuseppe Mazzini as a disappointed but determined idealist.

• The Granger Collection, New York

America to escape this violence. Anti-Semitism was not as severe in France as in Russia and Poland, but it reached a fever pitch there after a military court convicted Alfred Dreyfus, a Jewish army officer, of spying for Germany in 1894. Although he was innocent of the charges and eventually had the verdict reversed on appeal, Dreyfus was the focus of bitter debates about the trustworthiness of Jews in French society.

Among the reporters at Dreyfus's trial was a Jewish journalist from Vienna, Theodor Herzl (1860–1904). Shocked at the anti-Semitism he witnessed, Herzl became convinced that Jews would never be able to live securely in Europe. In 1897 he launched the Zionist movement to establish a Jewish state in Palestine, the land that the Hebrew kings David and Solomon had ruled in the tenth century B.C.E. During the next half

Zionism century, Jewish migrants trickled into Palestine, and in 1948 they won recognition for the Jewish state of Israel. Although it arose in response to exclusive nationalism in Europe, however, Zionism provoked a resentful nationalism among Palestinians displaced by Jewish settlers. Conflict between Jews and Palestinians continues to the present day.

The Emergence of National Communities

The French revolution and the wars that followed it heightened feelings of national identity throughout Europe. In France the establishment of a republic based on liberty, equality, and fraternity inspired patriotism and encouraged citizens to rally to the defense of the revolution when foreign armies threatened it. Revolutionary leaders took the tricolored flag as a symbol of the French nation, and they adopted a rousing marching tune, the "Marseillaise," as an anthem that inspired pride and identity with the national community. In Spain, the Netherlands, Austria, Prussia, and Russia, national consciousness surged in reaction to the arrival of revolutionary and Napoleonic armies. Opposition to Napoleon and his imperial designs also inspired national feeling in Britain.

The Congress After the fall of Napoleon, conservative political leaders feared that heightened
of Vienna national consciousness and ideas of popular sovereignty would encourage further experimentation with revolution and undermine European stability. Meeting as the Congress of Vienna (1814–1815), representatives of the "great powers" that defeated Napoleon—Britian, Austria, Prussia, and Russia—attempted to restore the pre-revolutionary order. Under the guidance of the influential foreign minister of Austria, Prince Klemens von Metternich (1773–1859), the Congress dismantled Napoleon's empire, returned sovereignty to Europe's royal families, restored them to the thrones they had lost during the Napoleonic era, and created a diplomatic order based on a

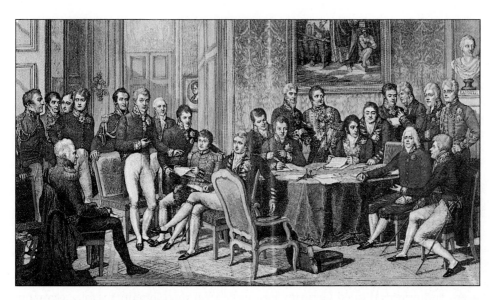

The charming and polished courtier Prince Klemens von Metternich (standing at left center) dominated the Congress of Vienna. Here delegates to the congress are gathered at the Habsburg palace in Vienna.

• By Jean-Baptiste Isabey, AKG Photo London

balance of power that prevented any one state from dominating the others. A central goal of Metternich himself was to suppress national consciousness, which he viewed as a serious threat to the multicultural Austrian empire that included Germans, Italians, Magyars, Czechs, Slovaks, Poles, Serbs, and Croats among its subjects.

The efforts of Metternich and the Congress of Vienna to restore the *ancien régime* had limited success. The European balance of power established at Vienna survived for almost a century, until the outbreak of a general continental and global war in 1914. Metternich and the conservative rulers installed by the Congress of Vienna took measures to forestall further revolution: they censored publications to prevent communication of seditious ideas and relied on spies to identify nationalist and republican activists. By 1815, however, it was impossible to suppress national consciousness and ideas of popular sovereignty.

From the 1820s through the 1840s, a wave of rebellions inspired by nationalist sentiments swept through Europe. The first uprising occurred in 1821 in the Balkan peninsula, where the Greek people sought independence from the Ottoman Turks, who had ruled the region since the fifteenth century. Many western Europeans sympathized with the Greek cause. The English poet Lord Byron even joined the rebel army and in 1824 died (of a fever) while serving in Greece. With the aid of Britain, France, and Russia, the rebels overcame the Ottoman forces in the Balkans by 1827 and won formal recognition of Greek independence in 1830.

Nationalist Rebellions

In 1830 rebellion showed its face throughout Europe. In France, Spain, Portugal, and some of the German principalities, revolutionaries inspired by liberalism called for constitutional government based on popular sovereignty. In Belgium, Italy, and Poland, they demanded independence and the formation of national states as well as popular sovereignty. By the mid-1830s authorities had put down the uprisings, but in 1848 a new round of rebellions shook European states. The uprisings of 1848 brought down the French monarchy and seriously threatened the Austrian empire, where subject peoples clamored for constitutions and independence. Prince Metternich resigned his office as Austrian foreign minister and unceremoniously fled Vienna as rebels took control of the city. Uprisings also rocked cities in Italy, Prussia, and German states in the Rhineland.

By the summer of 1849, the veteran armies of conservative rulers had put down the last of the rebellions. Metternich returned to Vienna and resumed oversight of the European balance of power. Advocates of national independence and popular sovereignty remained active, however, and the potential of their ideals to mobilize popular support soon became dramatically apparent.

The Unification of Italy and Germany

The most striking demonstration of the power that national sentiments could unleash involved the unification of Italy and Germany. Since the fall of the Roman empire, Italy and Germany had been disunited lands. A variety of regional kingdoms, city-states, and ecclesiastical states ruled the Italian peninsula for more than a thousand years, and princes divided Germany into more than three hundred semiautonomous jurisdictions. The Holy Roman Empire claimed authority over Germany and much of Italy, but the emperors were rarely strong enough to enforce their claims.

As they dismantled Napoleon's empire and sought to restore the *ancien régime,* delegates at the Congress of Vienna placed much of northern Italy under Austrian rule. Most of southern Italy was already subject to Spanish authority. As national sentiment surged throughout nineteenth-century Europe, Italian political leaders worked to win independence from foreign rule and establish an Italian national state. Mazzini's Young Italy movement attracted discontented idealists throughout the peninsula. In 1820, 1830, and 1848, they mounted major uprisings that threatened but did not dislodge foreign rule in Italy.

Cavour and Garibaldi   The unification of Italy came about when practical political leaders like Count Camillo di Cavour (1810–1861), prime minister to King Vittore Emmanuele II of Piedmont and Sardinia, combined forces with nationalist advocates of independence. Cavour was a cunning diplomat, and the kingdom of Piedmont and Sardinia was the most powerful of the Italian states. In alliance with France, Cavour expelled Austrian authorities from most of northern Italy in 1859. Then he turned his attention to southern Italy, where Giuseppe Garibaldi (1807–1882), a dashing soldier of fortune and a passionate nationalist, led the unification movement. With an army of about one thousand men outfitted in distinctive red shirts, Garibaldi swept through Sicily and southern Italy, outmaneuvering government forces and attracting enthusiastic recruits. In 1860 Garibaldi met King Vittore Emmanuele near Naples. Not ambitious to rule, Garibaldi delivered southern Italy into Vittore Emmanuele's hands, and the kingdom of Piedmont and Sardinia became the kingdom of Italy. During the next decade the new monarchy absorbed several additional territories, including Venice, Rome, and their surrounding regions.

In Germany as in Italy, unification came about when political leaders harnessed nationalist aspirations. The Congress of Vienna created a German Confederation composed of 39 states dominated by Austria and Prussia. Metternich and other conservative German rulers stifled nationalist movements, and the suppression of the rebellions of 1848 left German nationalists frustrated at their inability to found a national state.

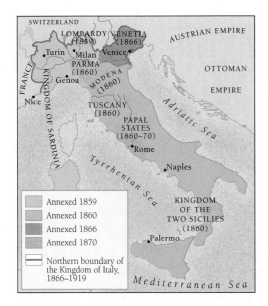

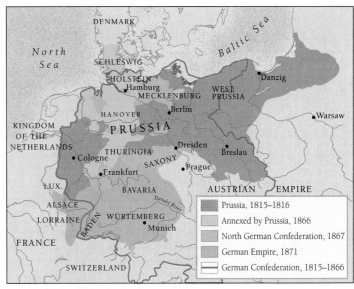

MAP [29.4]

The unification of Italy and Germany.

Otto von Bismarck

In 1862 King Wilhelm I of Prussia appointed a wealthy landowner, Otto von Bismarck (1815–1898), as his prime minister. Bismarck was a master of *Realpolitik* ("the politics of reality"). He succinctly expressed his realistic approach in his first speech as prime minister: "The great questions of the day will not be settled by speeches or majority votes—that was the great mistake of 1848 and 1849—but by blood and iron."

It was indeed blood and iron that brought about the unification of Germany. As prime minister, Bismarck reformed and expanded the Prussian army. Between 1864 and 1870 he intentionally provoked three wars—with Denmark, Austria, and France—and whipped up German sentiment against the enemies. In all three conflicts Prussian forces quickly shattered their opponents, swelling German pride. In 1871 the Prussian king proclaimed himself emperor of the Second Reich—meaning the Second German Empire, following the Holy Roman Empire—which embraced almost all German-speaking peoples outside Austria and Switzerland in a powerful and dynamic national state.

The unification of Italy and Germany made it clear that when coupled with strong political, diplomatic, and military leadership, nationalism had enormous potential to mobilize people who felt a sense of national kinship. Italy, Germany, and other national states went to great lengths to foster a sense of national community. They adopted national flags to serve as symbols of unity, national anthems to inspire patriotism, and national holidays to focus public attention on individuals and events of special importance for the national community. They established bureaucracies that took censuses of national populations and tracked vital national statistics involving birth, marriage, and death. They built schools that instilled patriotic values in students, and they recruited young men into armies that defended national interests and sometimes went on the offensive to enhance national prestige. By the end of the nineteenth century, the national state had proven to be a powerful model of political organization in Europe. By the mid-twentieth century it had become well-nigh universal, as political leaders adopted the national state as the principal form of political organization throughout the world.

Wearing a white jacket, Otto von Bismarck (center) witnesses the crowning of King Wilhelm I of Prussia as German emperor. The coronation followed the victory of Prussia over France in 1871, and it took place in the royal palace at Versailles. • Schloss Friedrichsruhe/Bridgeman Art Library International, Ltd., London and NY

The Enlightenment ideals of freedom, equality, and popular sovereignty inspired revolutionary movements throughout much of the Atlantic Ocean basin in the late eighteenth and early nineteenth centuries. In North America colonists threw off British rule and founded an independent federal republic. In France revolutionaries abolished the monarchy, established a republic, and refashioned the social order. In Saint-Domingue rebellious slaves threw off French rule, established an independent Haitian republic, and granted freedom and equality to all citizens. In Latin America creole elites led movements to expel Spanish and Portuguese colonial authorities and found independent republics. During the nineteenth century adult white men were the main beneficiaries of movements based on Enlightenment ideals, but social reformers launched campaigns to extend freedom and equality to Africans, African-Americans, and women.

Meanwhile, as they fought each other in wars sparked by the French revolution, European peoples developed strong feelings of national identity and worked to establish states that advanced the interests of national communities. Nationalist thought was often divisive: it pitted national groups against one another and fueled tensions especially in large multicultural states. But nationalism also had strong potential to contribute to state-building movements, and nationalist appeals played prominent roles in the unification of Italy and Germany. During the nineteenth and twentieth centuries, peoples throughout the world drew inspiration from Enlightenment ideals and national identities when seeking to build or restructure their societies.

CHRONOLOGY

1632–1704	Life of John Locke
1694–1778	Life of Voltaire
1712–1778	Life of Jean-Jacques Rousseau
1744–1803	Life of Toussaint Louverture
1748–1793	Life of Olympe de Gouges
1768–1821	Life of Napoleon Bonaparte
1773–1859	Life of Klemens von Metternich
1774–1793	Reign of King Louis XVI
1775–1781	American revolution
1783–1830	Life of Simón Bolívar
1789–1799	French revolution
1791–1803	Haitian revolution
1799–1814	Reign of Napoleon
1805–1872	Life of Giuseppe Mazzini
1807–1882	Life of Giuseppe Garibaldi
1810–1830	Wars of independence in Latin America
1810–1861	Life of Camillo di Cavour
1814–1815	Congress of Vienna
1815–1898	Life of Otto von Bismarck
1821–1827	War of Greek independence
1859–1870	Unification of Italy
1864–1871	Unification of Germany

FOR FURTHER READING

Benedict Anderson. *Imagined Communities: Reflections on the Origin and Spread of Nationalism.* Rev. ed. London, 1991. A pioneering work that analyzes the means and the processes by which peoples came to view themselves as members of national communities.

Bernard Bailyn. *The Ideological Origins of the American Revolution.* 2nd ed. Cambridge, Mass., 1992. A fundamental study of pamphlets and other publications that criticized British colonial policy in North America.

Reinhard Bendix. *Kings or People: Power and the Mandate to Rule.* Berkeley, 1978. A challenging but important comparative study of popular sovereignty and its displacement of monarchical authority.

Linda Colley. *Britons: Forging the Nation, 1707–1837.* New Haven, 1992. A detailed analysis of the emergence of British national identity.

Geoffrey Ellis. *Napoleon.* New York, 1997. An excellent biography of a pivotal figure in modern European history.

Carolyn Fick. *The Making of Haiti: The Saint Domingue Revolution from Below.* Knoxville, 1990. A valuable study focusing on the role of slaves in the Haitian revolution.

François Furet. *Revolutionary France, 1770–1880*. Trans. by A. Nevill. Oxford, 1992. An influential interpretation emphasizing the ideological dimension of the French revolution.

Eric Hobsbawm. *Nations and Nationalism Since 1780: Programme, Myth, and Reality*. 2nd ed. Cambridge, 1992. A brief interpretation of nationalism in Europe and the larger world.

_____ and Terence Ranger, eds. *The Invention of Tradition*. Cambridge, 1983. A fascinating collection of essays examining the rituals and other traditions that modern states have relied on to enhance their authority.

Lester D. Langley. *The Americas in the Age of Revolution, 1750–1850*. New Haven, 1997. A comparative study of revolutions and wars of independence in the western hemisphere.

Mary Beth Norton. *Liberty's Daughters: The Revolutionary Experience of American Women, 1750–1800*. Boston, 1980. Focuses on the role of women in the American revolution and the early republic.

Robert Palmer. *The Age of the Democratic Revolution: A Political History of Europe and America, 1760–1800*. 2 vols. Princeton, 1959–64. A classic study of the American and French revolutions and their influence in Europe and the Americas.

Simon Schama. *Citizens: A Chronicle of the French Revolution*. New York, 1989. Detailed narrative of the French revolution focusing on the experiences and decisions made by individual actors.

Gordon S. Wood. *The Radicalism of the American Revolution*. New York, 1991. A comprehensive synthesis emphasizing the role of republican and democratic ideas in the overthrow of monarchical institutions.

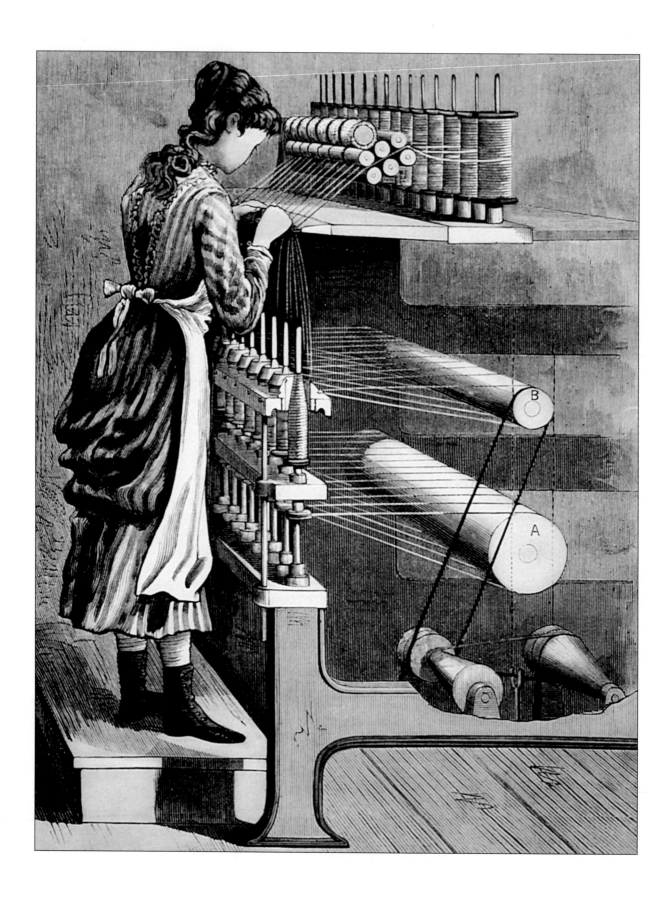

CHAPTER 30

THE MAKING
OF INDUSTRIAL SOCIETY

. . .

*I*n 1827, shortly after marrying at the age of twenty-three, Betty Harris took a job as a drawer in a coal pit near Manchester, England. A drawer's job involved crawling down narrow mine shafts and hauling loads of coal from the bottom of the pit, where miners chipped it from the earth, to the surface. From there the coal went to fuel the steam engines that powered the factories and mills of early industrial society. Drawers performed unskilled labor for low wages, but their work was essential for the emergence of industrial production.

While working, Harris wore a heavy belt around her waist. Hitched to the belt was a chain that passed between her legs and attached to the coal cart that she pulled through the mine shafts, often while creeping along on hands and knees. The belt strained against her body, and the mine shafts were steep and slippery. Yet every work day, even when she was pregnant, Harris strapped on her belt and chain at 6:00 A.M., removing her bindings only at the end of the shift twelve hours later.

Work conditions for Betty Harris were less than ideal. She labored in the coal pit with six other women and six boys and girls. All members of the crew experienced hardships and exploitation. Harris reported that drawing coal was "very hard work for a woman," and she did not exaggerate. She and her companions often had to crawl through water that collected in the mine shafts during rain storms, and the men who mined coal in the pits showed scant respect for the lowly, ill-paid drawers. The belts and chains worn by drawers often chafed their skin raw, and miners contributed to their physical discomfort by beating them for slow or clumsy work. The miners, many of whom shed their clothes and worked naked in the hot, oppressive coal pits, also took sexual liberties with the women and girl drawers: Harris personally knew several illegitimate children conceived during forced sexual encounters in the coal pits.

Betty Harris faced her own sexual problems once she arrived home. Exhausted from twelve hours of work, with only a one-hour break for a midday meal consisting of bread and butter, she often tried to discourage her husband's advances. Her husband had little patience, however, and Harris remarked that "my feller has beaten me many a time for not being ready." Harris's work schedule made comfortable family life impossible. A cousin had to care for her two children during the day, and Harris tended to them and her husband at night. The grinding demands of the coal pit took a toll: at age thirty-seven, after fourteen years in the mines, Harris admitted that "I am not so strong as I was, and cannot stand my work so well as I used to."

Young woman at work in a mechanized textile mill in the 1830s. • Corbis-Bettmann

Not all industrial workers suffered the indignities that coal drawers endured, but Betty Harris's experience nonetheless illustrates some of the deep changes that industrialization wrought in patterns of work and family life. Beginning in the late eighteenth century, workers and their families had to adjust to the sometimes harsh demands of the machine age. First in Britain, then in western Europe, North America, Russia, and Japan, machines and factories transformed agricultural societies into industrial societies. At the heart of this transformation were technological changes based on newly developed, inanimate sources of power that led to the extensive use of machinery in manufacturing. Machine production raised worker productivity, encouraged economic specialization, and promoted the growth of large-scale enterprise. Industrial machinery transformed economic production by turning out high-quality products quickly, cheaply, and efficiently. The process of industrialization encouraged rapid technological innovation and over the long term raised material standards of living in much of the world.

But the impact of industrialization went beyond economics, generating widespread and often unsettling social change as well. Early industrialists created a new work environment, the factory, which concentrated large numbers of workers under one roof to operate complicated machinery. The concentration of workers made it possible to rely on inanimate motive power such as water wheels or steam engines. Factories also enabled managers to impose work discipline and closely supervise the quality of production at their plants. By moving work outside the home, however, factories drew fathers, mothers, and children in different directions, altered traditional patterns of domestic life, and strained family relations in the industrial era.

Industrialization encouraged rapid urbanization and migration. New cities mushroomed to house workers who left the countryside for jobs in factories. Millions of migrants traveled even further, crossing the seas in search of opportunities in new lands. Often, however, early industrial workers found themselves living in squalor and laboring under dangerous conditions.

Social critics and reformers worked to alleviate the problems of early industrial society. Most scathing and influential of the critics were the German theorists Karl Marx and Friedrich Engels, who called for the destruction of capitalism and the establishment of a more just and equitable socialist society. Despite their appeals, industrialization flourished and spread rapidly from Britain to continental Europe, North America, and Asia. Although industrialization spread unevenly around the globe, it profoundly influenced social and economic conditions throughout the world, since industrial societies created a new international division of labor that made most African, Asian, and American lands dependent on the export of raw materials.

 ## PATTERNS OF INDUSTRIALIZATION

Industrialization refers to the process that transformed agricultural societies into industrial societies. The principal features of this process were technological and organizational changes that transformed manufacturing and led to increased productivity. Critical to industrialization were technological innovations that made it possible to produce goods by machines rather than by hand and that harnessed inanimate sources of energy such as coal and petroleum. Organizational changes accompanied technological innovations. By the end of the nineteenth century, the factory had become the predominant site of industrial production in Europe, the United States, and Japan. Factory production strongly encouraged the emergence of new divisions of labor, as interchangeable parts and belt-driven assembly lines made the mass production of goods a hallmark of industrialized societies. The need to invest in increasingly expensive equipment encouraged the formation of large businesses: by the mid-nineteenth century many giant corporations had joined together to control trade through trusts and cartels.

Technological Innovation

Industrialization came first to Britain. Several conditions favored a move there toward industrial production. Agricultural productivity was high, so many individuals were able to work at tasks other than cultivation. Skilled craftsmen were numerous, and they readily turned their talents to the invention and refinement of new machinery. Deposits of coal and iron ore were abundant, so entrepreneurs enjoyed access to raw materials crucial to industrialization. Navigable rivers and networks of canals reached most parts of the land and facilitated trade and transportation. London was home to sophisticated banking and financial institutions that supported fledgling businesses. Finally, liberal governments looked favorably on individual initiative and protected the interests of early industrialists.

Industrialization built on the economic development of early capitalist society, which raised material standards of living and increased demand for consumer items in early modern Europe (see chapter 23). Strong consumer demand encouraged manufacturers to seek greater efficiencies and increase their production. Beginning about the mid-eighteenth century, consumer demand encouraged a transformation of the British cotton industry.

During the seventeenth century English consumers had became fond of calicoes—inexpensive, brightly printed textiles imported from India. Cotton cloth came into demand because it was lighter, easier to wash, and quicker to dry than wool, which was the principal fabric of European clothes before the nineteenth century. Threatened by the popularity of cotton products, British wool producers persuaded Parliament to pass a series of laws to protect the domestic wool industry. The Calico Acts of 1701 and 1721 prohibited imports of printed cotton cloth and restricted the sale of calicoes at home. Parliament even passed a law requiring corpses to be buried in woolen shrouds, but legislation did not dampen consumers' enthusiasm for cotton. Consumer demand for cotton products drove the development of a British cotton textile industry.

Demand for cotton was so strong that producers had to speed up spinning and weaving to supply growing domestic and foreign markets. To increase production they turned to inventions that rapidly mechanized the cotton textile industry. In the early 1730s craftsmen began to invent labor-saving devices for spinning and weaving cotton, thereby moving away from hand-based techniques derived from the wool and linen industries. The first important technological breakthrough came in 1733 when the Manchester mechanic John Kay invented the flying shuttle. This device speeded up the weaving process and stimulated demand for thread. Within a few years competitions among inventors resulted in the invention of several mechanical spinning devices. The most important was Samuel Crompton's "mule," invented in 1779. Adapted for steam power by 1790, the mule became the device of choice for spinning cotton. The mule turned out strong, fine thread of much higher quality than any human worker could produce on a spinning wheel, and it worked fast as well. A worker using a steam-driven mule could produce a hundred times more thread than a preindustrial worker using a manual spinning wheel.

Mechanization of the Cotton Industry

The new spinning machines created an imbalance in manufacturing, since weavers could not keep up with the production of thread, so inventors turned their attention next to weaving. In 1785 Edmund Cartwright, a clergyman without training or experience in either mechanics or textiles, invented a power loom that inaugrated an era of mechanical weaving. Within two decades steam moved the power loom, and by the 1820s it had largely supplanted hand weavers in the cotton industry. A young boy working on two power looms could produce fifteen times more cloth than the fastest hand weaver. By 1830 half a million people worked in the cotton business, Britain's leading industry, which accounted for 40 percent of exports.

Steam Power   The most crucial technological innovation of the early industrial era was the invention of a general-purpose steam engine in 1765 by James Watt, an instrument maker at the University of Glasgow in Scotland. Steam engines burned coal to boil water and create steam, which drove mechanical devices that performed work. Even before Watt's time primitive steam engines had powered pumps that drew water out of coal mines, but those devices consumed too much fuel to be useful for other purposes. Watt's invention relied on steam to force a piston to turn a wheel, whose rotary motion converted a simple pump into an engine that had multiple uses. Watt's contemporaries used the term *horsepower* to measure the energy generated by his steam engine, which did the work of numerous animals. By 1800 more than a thousand of Watt's steam engines were in use in the British isles. They were especially prominent in the textile industry, where their application resulted in greater productivity for manufacturers and cheaper prices for consumers.

Iron and Steel   Innovation did not stop with cotton production and steam engines. The iron and steel industries also benefited from technological refinement, and the availability of inexpensive, high-quality iron and steel reinforced the move toward mechanization. After 1709 British smelters began to use coke (a purified form of coal) rather than more expensive charcoal as a fuel to produce iron. Besides being cheaper than charcoal, coke made it possible for producers to build bigger blast furnaces and turn out larger lots of iron. As a result, British iron production skyrocketed during the eighteenth century, while prices to consumers fell. Inexpensive iron fittings and parts made industrial machinery stronger, and iron soon became common in bridges, buildings, and ships.

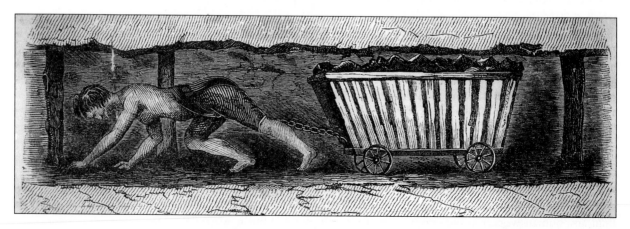

A girl working as a drawer in a British coal mine drags her coal cart with the aid of a belt and chain. Manually produced coal fueled the machines of early industrial society. • Corbis-Bettmann

The nineteenth century was an age of steel rather than iron. Steel is much harder, stronger, and more resilient than iron, but until the nineteenth century it was very expensive to produce. Between 1740 and 1850 a series of improvements simplified the process. In 1856 Henry Bessemer built a refined blast furnace known as the Bessemer converter that made it possible to produce steel cheaply and in large quantities. Steel production rose sharply, and steel quickly began to replace iron in tools, machines, and structures that required high strength.

Transportation

Steam engineering and metallurgical innovations both contributed to improvements in transportation technology. James Watt's steam engine did not adapt well to transportation uses because it consumed too much coal. After his patent expired, however, inventors devised high-pressure engines that required less fuel. In 1815 George Stephenson, a self-educated Englishman, invented the first steam-powered locomotive. In 1829 his Rocket won a contest by reaching a speed of 45 kilometers per hour (28 mph). Although they were more efficient than Watt's invention, Stephenson's engines still burned too much coal for use at sea. Sailing ships remained the most effective means of transport over the seas until the middle of the nineteenth century, when refined engines of high efficiency began to drive steamships.

Because they had the capacity to carry huge cargoes, railroads and steamships dramatically lowered transportation costs. They also contributed to the creation of dense transportation networks that linked remote interior regions and distant shores more closely than ever before in history. Between 1830 and 1870 British entrepreneurs laid about twenty thousand kilometers (thirteen thousand miles) of railroads, which linked industrial centers, coal fields, iron deposits, and port cities throughout the land—and also carried some 322 million passengers as well as cargoes of raw materials and manufactured goods. Steamships proved their own versatility by advancing up rivers to points that sailboats could not reach because of inconvenient twists, turns, or winds. Railroads and steamships benefited from the innovations that drove the industrialization process and in turn encouraged continuing industrialization by providing rapid and inexpensive transport.

The Factory System

In the emerging capitalist society of early modern Europe (discussed in chapter 23), most manufacturing took place under the putting-out system. To avoid guild restrictions on prices and wages, entrepreneurs in early modern Europe paid individuals to work on materials in their households. This proto-industrial system of production centered on the household and usually involved fewer than ten people. A few proto-industrial factories collected more

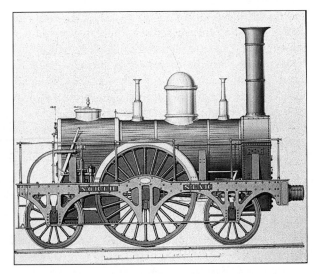

George Stephenson's North Star engine of 1837. • Science Museum, London/Bridgeman Art Library International, Ltd., London and NY

people under one roof to perform specialized tasks, but the largest preindustrial work forces consisted of unskilled laborers in mines and slaves on plantations.

The Factory   The factory system replaced the putting-out system and became the characteristic method of production in industrial economies. It began to emerge in the late eighteenth century, when technological innovations transformed the British textile industry, and by the mid-nineteenth century most cotton production took place in factories. Many of the newly invented machines were too large and expensive for home use, and it became necessary to move work to locations where entrepreneurs and engineers built complicated machinery for large-scale production. This centralization of production brought together more workers doing specialized tasks than ever before.

The factory system differed from earlier forms of industrial organization in that it made possible a high degree of coordination in the production process. The new environment enabled managers to make sure that work flowed through a series of steps on schedule. Factories also enabled managers to impose strict work discipline and closely supervise employees. Thus Josiah Wedgwood (1730–1795), an Englishman with a wooden leg who owned a porcelain factory, held his employees to high standards in an effort to produce the highest quality chinaware. When he spotted inferior work, he frequently dumped it on the factory floor and crushed it with his peg leg saying, "This will not do for Josiah Wedgwood!"

Working Conditions   The factory system allowed managers to improve worker productivity and realize spectacular increases in the output of manufactured goods. But the new environment also had unsettling effects on the nature of work. The factory system led to the emergence of an owner class whose capital financed equipment and machinery that were too expensive for workers to acquire. Industrial workers themselves became mere wage earners who had only their labor services to offer and who depended on their employers for their livelihood. In addition, any skills that they may have possessed as artisans soon became obsolete.

Equally disturbing was the new work discipline and the pace of work. Those accustomed to rural labor soon learned that the seasons, the rising and setting of the sun, and fluctuations in the weather no longer dictated work routines. Instead, clocks, machines, and shop rules established new rhythms of work. The factory whistle sounded the beginning and the end of the working day, and throughout the day workers had to keep pace with the monotonous movements of machines. At the same time they faced strict and immediate supervision, which made little allowance for a quick nap or socializing with friends. Floor managers pressured men, women, and children to speed up production and punished them when they did not meet expectations. Since neither the machines nor the methods of work took safety into account, early industrial workers constantly faced the possibility of maiming or fatal accidents.

Industrial Protest   In some instances machine-centered factories sparked violent protest. Between 1811 and 1816 organized bands of English hand craftsmen known as Luddites went on a rampage and destroyed textile machines that they blamed for their low wages and unemployment. They called their leader King Lud, after a legendary boy named Ludlam who broke a knitting frame to spite his father. The movement broke out in the hosiery and lace industries around Nottingham and then spread to the wool and cotton mills of Lancashire. The Luddites usually wore masks and operated at night. Because they avoided violence against people, they enjoyed considerable popular support. Nevertheless, by hanging fourteen Luddites in 1813, the government served notice that it was unwilling to tolerate violence even against machines, and the movement gradually died out.

Workers tend to a massive steam hammer under very dangerous conditions.   • Science Museum
Library, London

The Early Spread of Industrialization

Industrialization and the technological, organizational, and social transformations
that accompanied it might have originated in many parts of the world where abundant craft skills, agricultural production, and investment capital could support the
industrialization process. For half a century, however, industrialization took place
only in Great Britain. Aware of their head start, British entrepreneurs and government officials forbade the export of machinery, manufacturing techniques, and
skilled workers.

Yet Britain's monopoly on industrialization did not last forever, since enterprising businessmen recognized profitable opportunities in foreign lands and circumvented government regulations to sell machinery and technical know-how abroad.
Moreover, European and North American businessmen did their best to become acquainted with British industrial techniques and lure British experts to their own
lands. European and North American entrepreneurs did not hesitate to bribe or
even kidnap British engineers, and they also smuggled advanced machinery out of
the British isles. Sometimes they got poor value for their investments: they found
that it was difficult to attract the best British experts to foreign lands and had to
make do with drunkards or second-rate specialists who demanded high pay but
made little contribution to industrialization.

Nevertheless, by the mid-nineteenth century industrialization had spread to
France, Germany, Belgium, and the United States. The French revolution and the

*Industrialization
in Western Europe*

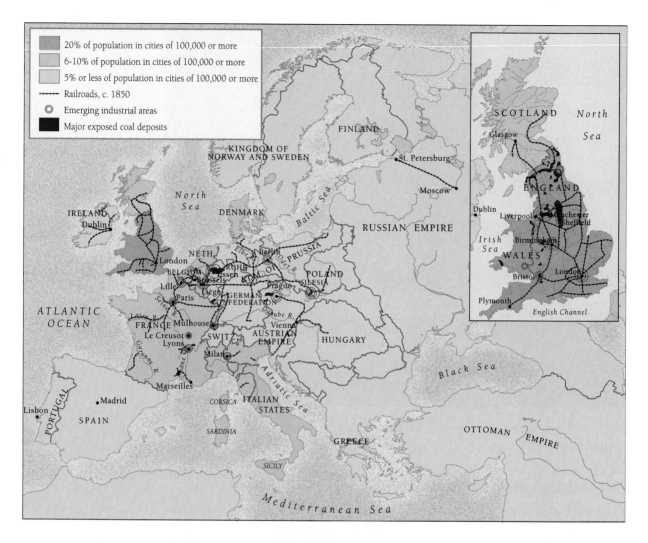

MAP [30.1]

Industrial Europe.

Napoleonic wars helped set the stage for industrialization in western Europe by abolishing internal trade barriers and dismantling guilds that discouraged technological innovation and restricted the movement of laborers. The earliest continental center of industrial production was Belgium, where coal, iron, textile, glass, and armaments production flourished in the early nineteenth century. About the same time France also moved toward industrialization. By 1830 French firms employed about fifteen thousand skilled British workers who helped establish mechanized textile and metallurgical industries in France. By the mid-nineteenth century French engineers and inventors were devising refinements and innovations that led to greater efficiencies especially in metallurgical industries. Later in the century a boom in railroad construction stimulated economic development while also leading to decreased transportation costs.

German industrialization proceeded more slowly than Belgian and French, partly because of political instability resulting from competition between the many German states. After the 1840s, however, German coal and iron production soared, and by the 1850s an extensive railroad network was under construction. After unification in 1871 Bismarck's government sponsored rapid industrialization in Germany. In the interests of strengthening military capacity, Bismarck encouraged the development of heavy industry, and the formation of huge businesses became a hallmark of German industrialization. The giant Krupp firm, for example, dominated mining, metallurgy, armaments production, and shipbuilding.

Industrialization transformed North America as well as western Europe in the nineteenth century. In 1800 the United States possessed abundant land and natural resources but few laborers and little money to invest in business enterprises. Both labor and investment capital came largely from Europe: migrants crossed the Atlantic in large numbers throughout the nineteenth century, and European bankers and businessmen eagerly sought opportunities to invest in businesses that made use of American natural resources. American industrialization began in the 1820s when entrepreneurs lured British craftsmen to New England and built a cotton textile industry. By midcentury well over a thousand mills were producing fabrics from raw cotton grown in the southern states, and New England had emerged as a site for the industrial production also of shoes, tools, and handguns. In the 1870s heavy iron and steel industries emerged in areas like western Pennsylvania and central Alabama where there were abundant supplies of iron ore and coal. By 1900 the United States had become an economic powerhouse, and industrialization had begun to spill over into southern Canada.

Industrialization in North America

The vast size of the United States was advantageous to industrialists because it made abundant natural resources available to them, but it also hindered travel and communication between the regions. To facilitate transportation and distribution, state governments built canals, and private investors established steamship lines and railroad networks. By 1860 rails linked the industrial northeast with the agricultural south and the midwestern cities of St. Louis and Chicago, where brokers funneled wheat and beef from the plains to the more densely populated eastern states. As in other lands, railroad construction spurred industrialization by providing cheap transportation and stimulating coal, iron, and steel industries.

Industrial Capitalism

Cotton textiles were the major factory-made products during the early phase of industrialization, but new machinery and techniques soon made it possible to extend the factory system to other industries. Furthermore, with refined manufacturing processes, factories could mass-produce standardized articles. An important contribution to the evolving factory system came from the American inventor Eli Whitney (1765–1825). Though best remembered as the inventor of the cotton gin, Whitney also developed the technique of using interchangeable parts in the making of firearms. In contrast to conventional methods, whereby a skilled worker made a complete musket, forming and fitting each unique part, Whitney designed machine tools with which unskilled workers made only a particular part that fit every musket of the same model. Before long, entrepreneurs applied Whitney's method to the manufacture of everything from watches and sewing machines to uniforms and shoes. By the middle of the nineteenth century, mass production of standardized articles was becoming the hallmark of industrial societies.

Mass Production

In 1913 Henry Ford improved manufacturing techniques further when he introduced the assembly line to automobile production. Instead of organizing production around a series of stations where teams of workers assembled each individual car using standardized parts, Ford designed a conveyor system that carried components past workers at the proper height and speed. Each worker performed a specialized task at a fixed point on the assembly line, which churned out a complete chassis every 93 minutes—a task that previously took 728 minutes. The subdivision of labor and the coordination of operations resulted in enormous productivity gains, enabling Ford Motor Company to produce half of the world's automobiles in the early twentieth century. With gains in productivity, car prices plummetted, allowing millions of ordinary people to purchase automobiles. The age of the motor car had arrived.

Big Business

As the factory evolved, so too did the organization of business. Industrial machinery and factories were expensive investments, and they encouraged businesses to organize on a large scale. Thus industrialization spurred the continuing development of capitalist business organization. Entrepreneurs in early modern Europe formed private businesses in the hopes of profiting from market-oriented production and trade. Some businesses, such as the English East India Company and other commercial concerns, organized joint-stock companies in the interests of spreading risk, achieving efficiency, and maximizing profits. With industrialization, manufacturers followed the lead of merchants by organizing on a large scale.

The Corporation

During the 1850s and 1860s, government authorities in Britain and France laid the legal foundations for the modern corporation, which quickly became the most common form of business organization in industrial societies. A corporation was a private business owned by hundreds, thousands, or even millions of individual and institutional investors who financed the business through the purchase of stocks representing shares in the company. When a corporation flourished, investors received dividends in proportion to their stake in the company. But if a corporation went bankrupt, laws protected shareholders from any liability or financial loss beyond the extent of their investments. Thus corporate organization was extremely attractive to investors. By the late nineteenth century, corporations controlled most businesses requiring large investments in land, labor, or machinery, including railroads, shipping lines, and industrial concerns that produced iron, steel, and armaments. Meanwhile, an array of investment banks, brokerage firms, and other financial businesses arose to serve the needs of industrial capitalists organized in corporations.

Monopolies, Trusts, and Cartels

To protect their investments, some big businesses of the late nineteenth century sought not only to outperform their competitors in the capitalist marketplace but also to eliminate competition altogether. Business firms formed associations to restrict markets or establish monopolies in their industries. Some monopolists sought to control industries through vertical organization, by which they would dominate all facets of a single industry. The industrial empire of the American petroleum producer John D. Rockefeller, for example, which he ruled through Standard Oil Company and Trust, controlled almost all oil drilling, processing, refining, marketing, and distribution in the United States. Control over all aspects of the petroleum industry enabled Standard Oil to operate efficiently, cut costs, and undersell its competitors. Vertical organization of this kind offered large corporations great advantages over smaller companies.

Other monopolists tried to eliminate competition by means of horizontal organization, which involved the consolidation or cooperation of independent companies in the same business. Thus cartels sought to ensure the prosperity of their members by absorbing competitors, fixing prices, regulating production, or dividing up markets. The German firm IG Farben, the world's largest chemical concern until the middle of the twentieth century, grew out of a complex merger of chemical and pharmaceutical manufacturers that controlled as much as 90 percent of production in chemical industries. By the end of the nineteenth century, some governments outlawed these combinations and broke them up. Yet when governments proved unwilling to confront large businesses, or when the public remained ignorant or indifferent, monopolistic practices continued well into the twentieth century.

INDUSTRIAL SOCIETY

Industrialization brought material benefits in its train: inexpensive manufactured products, rising standards of living, and population growth. Yet industrialization also unleashed dramatic and often unsettling social change. Massive internal and external migrations took place, as millions of people moved from the countryside to work in new industrial cities, and European migrants crossed the Atlantic by the tens of millions to seek opportunities in the less densely populated lands of the western hemisphere. Industrialization encouraged the emergence of new social classes—especially the middle class and the working class—and forced men, women, and children to adjust to distinctly new patterns of family and work life. Reformers sought to alleviate the social and economic problems that accompanied industrialization. The most influential critics were the socialists, who did not object to industrialization per se but worked toward the building of a more equitable and just society.

The Fruits of Industry

Industrialization brought efficiencies in production that flooded markets with affordable manufactured goods. In 1851 the bounty of industry went on display in London at the Crystal Palace, a magnificent structure made of iron and glass that enclosed trees, gardens, fountains, and manufactured products from around the world. Viewers flocked to the exhibition to see industrial products like British textiles, iron goods, and machine tools. Colt revolvers and sewing machines from the United States also attracted attention as representatives of the "American system of manufacture," which used interchangeable parts in producing large quantities of standardized goods at low prices. Observers marveled at the Crystal Palace exhibits and congratulated themselves on the achievements of industrial society.

In many ways industrialization raised material standards of living. Industrial production led to dramatic reductions in the cost of clothing, for example, so individuals were able to add variety to their wardrobes. By the early nineteenth century, all but the desperately poor could afford several changes of clothes, and light, washable underwear came into widespread use with the availability of inexpensive manufactured cotton. Industrial factories turned out tools that facilitated agricultural work, while steam-powered locomotives delivered produce quickly and cheaply to distant markets, so industrialization contributed as well to a decline in the price of food. Consumers in early industrial Europe also filled their homes with more furniture, cabinets, porcelain, and decorative objects than any but the most wealthy of their ancestors.

The populations of European and Euro-American peoples rose sharply during the eighteenth and nineteenth centuries, and they reflected the rising prosperity and standards of living that came with industrialization. Between 1700 and 1800 the population of Europe increased from 105 to 180 million, and during the nineteenth century it more than doubled to 390 million. Demographic growth in the western hemisphere—fueled by migration from Europe—was even more remarkable. Between 1700 and 1800 the population of North America and South America rose from 13 million to 24 million and then surged to 145 million by 1900. Demographic growth was most spectacular in the temperate regions of the western hemisphere. In Argentina, for example, population expanded from 300,000 in 1800 to 4.75 million in 1900—a 1,583 percent increase. In temperate North America—what is now the United States—population rose from 6 million to 76 million (1,266 percent) during the nineteenth century.

Population Growth

Exhibitors from around the world displayed fine handicrafts and manufactured goods at the Crystal Palace exhibition of 1851 in London. Industrial products from Britain and the United States particularly attracted the attention of visitors to the enchanting and futuristic exhibition hall. • Guild Hall Library, Corporation of London/Bridgeman Art Library International, Ltd., London and NY

To some extent this demographic expansion arose from increasingly intensive agricultural techniques and the diffusion of food crops. But the European and Euro-American population increase was due to changing patterns of birth and death rates as well as to growing supplies of food. In most preindustrial societies fertility was high, but famines and epidemics resulted in high mortality, especially child mortality, which prevented explosive population growth. High birth rates were common also in early industrializing societies, but death rates fell markedly because better diets and improved disease control reduced child mortality. Because more infants survived to adulthood, the population of early industrializing societies grew rapidly. By the late nineteenth century, better diets and improved sanitation led to declining levels of adult as well as child mortality, so populations of industrial societies expanded even faster. Britain and Germany, the most active sites of early industrialization, experienced especially fast population growth. Between 1800 and 1900 the British population increased from 10.5 million to 37.5 million while German numbers rose from 18 million to 43 million.

The Demographic Transition   Beginning in the nineteenth century, industrializing lands experienced a social change known as the *demographic transition,* which refers to shifting patterns of fertility and mortality. As industrialization transformed societies, fertility began a marked decline. In the short run mortality fell even faster than fertility, so the populations of industrial societies continued to increase. Over time, however, declining birth rates led to lower population growth and relative demographic stability. The principal reason for declining fertility in industrial lands was voluntary birth control through contraception. Married couples might have chosen to have fewer offspring because raising them cost more in industrial than in agricultural societies or because declining child mortality meant that any children born were more likely to survive to adulthood. In any case the demographic transition accompanied industrialization in western Europe, the United States, Japan, and other industrializing lands as well.

Urbanization and Migration

Industrialization and population growth strongly encouraged migration and urbanization. Within industrial societies migrants flocked from the countryside to urban centers in search of work. Industrial Britain led the world in urbanization. In 1800 about one-fifth of the British population lived in towns and cities of 10,000 or more inhabitants. During the following century a largely rural society became predominantly urban, with three-quarters of the population working and living in cities. This pattern repeated itself in continental Europe, the United States, Japan, and the rest of the world. By 1900 at least 50 percent of the population in industrialized lands lived in towns with populations of 2,000 or more. The increasing size of cities reflected this internal migration. In 1800 there were barely twenty cities in Europe with populations as high as 100,000, and there were none in the western hemisphere. By 1900 there were more than 150 large cities in Europe and North America combined. With a population of 6.5 million, London was the largest city in the world, followed by New York with 4.2 million, Paris with 3.3 million, and Berlin with 2.7 million.

City Life

While financiers and the captains of industry lived in elegant mansions and townhouses, workers and their families often occupied shoddy housing with no comforts or amenities. Coal-burning fires and industrial pollution so fouled the air that people flocked to parks and public gardens on weekends, and the well-to-do escaped to homes in the suburbs. Inadequate water supplies and unsanitary living conditions led to periodic epidemics of typhus and cholera, and dysentery and tuberculosis were also common maladies.

By the later nineteenth century, though, government authorities were tending to the problems of the early industrial cities. They improved municipal water supplies, expanded sewage systems, and introduced building codes that outlawed the construction of rickety tenements to accommodate poorly paid workers. These measures made city life safer and brought improved sanitation that helped to eliminate epidemic disease. City authorities also built parks and recreational facilities to make cities more livable.

Transcontinental Migration

While workers moved from the countryside to urban centers, rapid population growth in Europe encouraged massive migration to the Americas, especially to the United States. During the nineteenth and early twentieth centuries, about fifty million Europeans migrated to the western hemisphere, and this flow of humanity accounts for much of the stunning demographic growth of the Americas. Many of the migrants intended to stay for only a few years and fully expected to return to their homelands with a modest fortune made in the Americas. Indeed, some did return to Europe: about one-third of Italian migrants to the Americas made the trip back across the Atlantic. The vast majority, however, remained in the western hemisphere. They and their descendants transformed the Americas into Euro-American lands.

This landscape of cramped working-class housing was one of the original illustrations for Friedrich Engels's exposé, *The Condition of the Working Class in England.*

Most of the migrants came from the British isles in the early nineteenth century, from Germany, Ireland, and Scandinavia in the middle decades, and from eastern and southern Europe in the late nineteenth century. Migration reflected difficult political, social, and economic circumstances in Europe: British migrants often sought to escape dangerous factories and the squalor of early industrial cities, while most Irish migrants departed during the potato famines of the 1840s, and millions of Jews left the Russian empire in the 1890s because of the tsar's anti-Semitic policies. Many of these migrants entered the work force of the United States, where they settled in new industrial centers like New York, Pittsburgh, and Cleveland. Indeed, labor from abroad made it possible for the United States to undergo rapid industrialization in the late nineteenth century.

Industry and Society

As millions of people moved from the countryside to industrial centers, society underwent a dramatic transformation. Before industrialization, the vast majority of the world's peoples worked in rural areas as cultivators or herders. Rulers, aristocrats, priests, and a few others enjoyed privileged status, and small numbers of people worked in cities as artisans, craftsmen, bureaucrats, or professionals. Many societies also made use of slave labor, occasionally on a large scale.

Industrialization radically altered traditional social structures. It encouraged the disappearance of slavery in lands undergoing industrialization, partly because the economics of industrial society did not favor slave labor. Slaves were generally poor, so they did not consume the products of industrial manufacturers in large quantities. Industrialists preferred free wage laborers who spent their money on products that kept their factories busy.

Industrialization also helped bring new social classes into being. Captains of industry and enterprising businessmen became fabulously wealthy and powerful enough to overshadow the military aristocracy and other traditionally privileged classes. Less powerful than this new elite was the middle class, consisting of small business owners, factory managers, engineers, accountants, skilled employees of large corporations, and professionals such as teachers, physicians, and attorneys. Industrial production generated great wealth, and a large portion of it flowed to the middle class, which was a principal beneficiary of industrialization. Meanwhile, masses of laborers who toiled in factories and mines constituted a new working class. Less skilled than the artisans and craftsmen of earlier times, the new workers tended to machines or provided heavy labor for low wages. Concentrated in mining and industrial centers, the working class began to influence political affairs by the mid-nineteenth century.

New Social Classes

The most basic unit of social organization—the family—also underwent fundamental change during the industrial age. In preindustrial societies the family was the basic productive unit. Whether engaged in agriculture, domestic manufacturing, or commerce, family members worked together and contributed to the welfare of the larger group. Industrialization challenged the family economy and reshaped family life by moving economic production outside the home and introducing a sharp distinction between work and family life. During the early years of industrialization, family economies persisted as fathers, mothers, and children pooled their wages and sometimes even worked together in factories. Over time, however, it became less common for family members to work in groups. Workers left their homes each day to labor an average of fourteen hours in factories, and family members led increasingly separate lives.

Industrial Families

Men gained increased stature and responsibility in the industrial age as work dominated public life. When production moved outside the home, some men became owners or managers of factories while the majority served as wage workers. Industrial work seemed to be far more important than the domestic chores traditionally carried out by women, or even the agricultural and light industrial work performed by women and children. Men's wages also constituted the bulk of their families' income. Upper-class and middle-class men especially enjoyed increased prestige at home, since they usually were the sole providers who made their families' comfortable existence possible.

Men at Work and Play

Internalizing the work ethic of the industrial age, professional men dedicated themselves to self-improvement even in their leisure hours. They avidly read books and attended lectures on business or cultural themes. They also strove to instill their own values in the industrial workforce and impose work discipline on the laborers under their supervision. Threats of fines, beatings, and dismissal coerced workers into accepting factory rules against absenteeism, tardiness, and swearing. Through their support for churches and Sunday schools, factory owners sought to persuade workers to adopt middle-class norms of respectability and morality.

For their own part, industrial workers often resisted the work discipline and moral pressures they encountered at the factory. They frequently observed "Holy

Monday" and stayed home to lengthen their weekly break from work on Sundays. In their leisure time they flocked to sporting events: European soccer and American baseball both became popular sports during the early industrial era. They also gambled, socialized at bars and pubs, and staged fights between dogs or chickens. The middle and upper classes tried to suppress these activities and established urban police forces to control workers' public behavior. But efforts at regulation had limited success, and workers persistently pursued their own interests.

Women at Home and Work

Like men, women had worked long hours in preindustrial times. Agriculture and domestic manufacturing could easily accommodate women's dual role as mothers and workers, since the workplace was either at home or nearby. Industrialization dramatically changed the terms of work for women. When industry moved production from the home to the factory, married women were unable to work unless they left their homes and children in someone else's care.

Middle-class women generally did not work outside the home. For them, industrialization brought stringent confinement to the domestic sphere and pressure to conform to new models of behavior revolving around their roles as mothers and wives. In a book entitled *Woman in Her Social and Domestic Character* (1833), Mrs. John Sandford—who referred to herself by her husband's name rather than her own—described the ideal British woman. "Domestic life is the chief source of her influence," Sandford proclaimed, adding that "there is, indeed, something unfeminine in independence." (By *independence* Sandford meant taking a job or "acting the Amazon.") The model woman "knows that she is the weaker vessel" and takes pride in her ability to make the home a happy place for her husband and children.

Industrialization increased the demand for domestic servants as the middle class grew in both numbers and wealth. In the nineteenth century working women preferred domestic service over work in mines or even factories. One of every three European women became a domestic servant at some point in her life. Rural women sometimes had to move long distances to take positions in middle-class homes in cities, where they experienced adventure and independence from family control. Their employers replaced their parents as guardians, but high demand for servants ensured that women could switch jobs readily in search of more attractive positions. Young women servants often sent some of their earnings home, but many also saved wages for personal goals: amassing a dowry, for example, or building funds to start their own careers as clerks or secretaries.

Child Labor

Industrialization profoundly influenced the childhood experience. Like their elders, children in preindustrial societies had always worked in and around the family home. Industrial work, which took children away from home and parents for long hours with few breaks, made child labor seem especially pitiable and exploitative. Early reports from British textile mills described sensational abuses by overseers who forced children to work from dawn until dark and beat them to keep them awake. Yet many families needed their children's wages to survive, so they continued to send their offspring to the factories and mines. By the 1840s the British Parliament began to pass laws regulating child labor and ultimately restricted or removed children from the industrial workforce.

The Socialist Challenge

Among the most vocal and influential critics of early industrial society were the socialists, who worked to alleviate the social and economic problems generated by capitalism and industrialization. Socialists deplored economic inequalities, as represented by the vast difference in wealth between a captain of industry and a factory laborer, and

Once held almost exclusively by men, clerical jobs increasingly went to women as industrial society matured. Men assumed positions as managers who supervised their female employees.   •   Museum of the City of New York

Boys covered in thick, black dust work the coal mines of Pennsylvania. The harsh conditions of their work eventually led to the regulation of child labor.   •   Courtesy George Eastman House

Unlike working-class children, offspring of middle-class and upper-class families enjoyed leisure and luxury. Here the children of U.S. railroad executive George Jay Gould ride in miniature cars in Paris.
  •   Culver Pictures

they condemned the system that permitted the exploitation of laborers, especially women and children. Early socialists sought to expand the Enlightenment understanding of equality: they understood equality to have an economic as well as a political, legal, and social dimension, and they looked to the future establishment of a just and equitable society. While most socialists shared this general vision, they held very different views on the best way to establish and maintain an ideal socialist society.

Utopian Socialists   The term *socialism* first appeared around 1830, when it referred to the thought of social critics like Charles Fourier (1772–1837) and Robert Owen (1771–1858). Often called utopian socialists, Fourier, Owen, and their followers worked to establish ideal communities that would point the way to an equitable society. Fourier spent most of his life as a salesman, but he loathed the competition of the market system and called for social transformations that would better serve the needs of humankind. He painstakingly planned model communities held together by love rather than coercion in which everyone performed work in accordance with personal temperament and inclination. Owen, a successful businessman, transformed a squalid Scottish cotton mill town called New Lanark into a model industrial community. At New Lanark, Owen raised wages, reduced the workday from seventeen to ten hours, built spacious housing, and opened a store that sold goods at fair prices. Despite the costs of these reforms, the mills of New Lanark generated profits. Out of the two thousand residents of the community, five hundred were young children from the poorhouses of Glasgow and Edinburgh, and Owen devoted special attention to their education. He kept young children out of the factories and sent them to a school that he opened in 1816. Owen's indictment of competitive capitalism, his stress on cooperative control of industry, and his advocacy of improved educational standards for children left a lasting imprint on the socialist tradition.

The ideas of the utopian socialists resonated widely in the nineteenth century, and their disciples established experimental communities from the United States to Romania. Despite the enthusiasm of the founders, most of the communities soon encountered economic difficulties and political problems that forced them to fold. By the mid-nineteenth century most socialists looked not to utopian communities but to large-scale organization of working people as the best means to bring about a just and equitable society.

Marx and Engels   Most prominent of the nineteenth-century socialists were the German theorists Karl Marx (1818–1883) and Friedrich Engels (1820–1895). They scorned the utopian socialists as unrealistic dabblers whose ideal communities had no hope of resolving the problems of the early industrial era. Marx and Engels believed that social problems of the nineteenth century were inevitable results of a capitalist economy. They held that capitalism divided people into two main classes, each with its own economic interests and social status: the capitalists, who owned industrial machinery and factories (which Marx and Engels called the means of production), and the proletariat, consisting of wage workers who had only their labor to sell. Intense competition between capitalists trying to realize a profit resulted in ruthless exploitation of the working class. To make matters worse, Marx and Engels viewed the state and its coercive institutions, such as police forces and courts of law, as agencies of the capitalist ruling class. Their function was to maintain capitalists in power and enable them to continue their exploitation of the proletariat. Even music, art, literature, and religion served the purposes of capitalists, according to Marx and Engels, since they amused the working classes and diverted attention from their misery. Marx once referred to religion as "the opiate of the masses" because it encouraged workers to focus on a hypothetical realm of existence beyond this world rather than trying to improve their lot in society.

Marx developed these views fully in a long, theoretical work called *Capital.* Together with Engels, Marx also wrote a short, spirited tract entitled *Manifesto of the Communist Party* (1848). In the *Manifesto* Marx and Engels aligned themselves with the communists, who worked toward the abolition of private property and the institution of a radically egalitarian society. The *Manifesto* asserted that all human history has been the history of struggle between social classes. It argued that the future lay with the working class because the laws of history dictated that capitalism would inexorably grind to a halt. Crises of overproduction, underconsumption, and diminishing profits would shake the foundations of the capitalist order. Meanwhile, members of the constantly growing and thoroughly exploited proletariat would come to view the forcible overthrow of the existing system as the only alternative available to them. Marx and Engels believed that a socialist revolution would result in a "dictatorship of the proletariat," which would abolish private property and destroy the capitalist order. After the revolution was secure, the state would wither away. Coercive institutions would also disappear, since there would no longer be an exploiting class. Thus socialism would lead to a fair, just, and egalitarian society infinitely more humane than the capitalist order.

The Communist Manifesto

The doctrines of Marx and Engels came to dominate European and international socialism, and socialist parties grew rapidly throughout the nineteenth century. Political parties, trade unions, newspapers, and educational associations all worked to advance the socialist cause. Yet socialists disagreed strongly on the best means to reform society. Revolutionary socialists like Marx, Engles, and other communists urged workers to seize control of the state, confiscate the means of production, and distribute wealth equitably throughout society. Doubting that a revolution could succeed, evolutionary socialists placed their hopes in representative governments and called for the election of legislators who supported socialist reforms.

Although socialists did not win control of any government until the Russian revolution of 1917, their critiques persuaded government authorities to attack the abuses of early industrialization and provide security for the working classes. The British government began regulating hours and conditions of work, especially for women and children, in the Factory Act of 1833. In the Mines Act of 1842, Parliament prohibited underground employment for women, like the drawer Betty Harris, as well as for boys under the age of ten. In the 1880s, under the leadership of Otto von Bismarck, Germany introduced medical insurance, unemployment compensation, and retirement pensions to provide social security for working people in industrial society.

Social Reform

Trade unions also sought to advance the quest for a just and equitable society. As governments regulated businesses and enhanced social security, trade unions struggled to eliminate abuses of early industrial society and improve workers' lives by seeking higher wages and better working conditions for their members. Through most of the nineteenth century, both employers and governments considered trade unions illegal associations whose purpose was to restrain trade. Tensions ran high when union members went on strike, especially when employers sought to keep their businesses going by hiring replacement workers. In those cases violence frequently broke out, prompting government authorities to send in police or military forces to maintain order. Over the longer run, though, trade unions gradually improved the lives of working people and reduced the likelihood that a disgruntled proletariat would mount a revolution to overthrow industrial capitalist society. Indeed, trade unions became an integral part of industrial society because they did not seek to destroy capitalism but rather to make employers more responsive to their employees' needs and interests.

Trade Unions

MARX AND ENGELS ON BOURGEOISIE AND PROLETARIANS

. . .

Karl Marx and Friedrich Engels were the most scathing critics of early industrial society. Indeed, their critique extended to industrial capitalism in general. In their view, contemporary society pitted capitalists (whom they called the bourgeoisie in their Manifesto of the Communist Party*) against proletarians. Marx and Engels argued that in the short term capitalists would exploit the proletarians, but that over the longer run proletarians would become aware of their misery, rise up, and destroy capitalist society.*

The history of all hitherto existing society is the history of class struggles.

Freeman and slave, patrician and plebeian, lord and serf, guild-master and journeyman, in a word, oppressor and oppressed, stood in constant opposition to one another, carried on an uninterrupted, now hidden, now open fight, a fight that each time ended, either in a revolutionary reconstitution of society at large, or in the common ruin of the contending classes. . . .

The modern bourgeois society that has sprouted from the ruins of feudal society has not done away with class antagonisms. It has but established new classes, new conditions of oppression, new forms of struggle in place of the old ones.

Our epoch, the epoch of the bourgeoisie, possesses, however, this distinctive feature: it has simplified the class antagonisms. Society as a whole is more and more splitting up into two great hostile camps, into two great classes directly facing each other: Bourgeoisie and Proletariat. . . .

The bourgeoisie has stripped of its halo every occupation hitherto honoured and looked up to with reverent awe. It has converted the physician, the lawyer, the priest, the poet, the man of science, into its paid wage-labourers.

The bourgeoisie has torn away from the family its sentimental veil, and has reduced the family relation to a mere money relation. . . .

The need for a constantly expanding market for its products chases the bourgeoisie over the whole surface of the globe. It must nestle everywhere, settle everywhere, establish connexions everywhere. . . .

The weapons with which the bourgeoisie felled feudalism to the ground are now turned against the bourgeoisie itself.

But not only has the bourgeoisie forged the weapons that bring death to itself; it has also called into existence the men who are to wield those weapons—the modern working class—the proletarians.

In proportion as the bourgeoisie, i.e., capital, is developed, in the same proportion is the proletariat, the modern working class, developed—a class of labourers, who live only so long as they find work, and who find work only so long as their labour increases capital. These labourers, who must sell themselves piecemeal, are a commodity, like every other article of commerce, and are consequently exposed to all the vicissitudes of competition, to all the fluctuations of the market. . . .

The advance of industry, whose involuntary promoter is the bourgeoisie, replaces the isolation of the labourers, due to competition, by their revolutionary combination, due to association. The development of Modern Industry, therefore, cuts from under its feet the very foundation on which the bourgeoisie produces and appropriates products. What the bourgeoisie, therefore, produces, above all, is its own grave-diggers. Its fall and the victory of the proletariat are equally inevitable.

SOURCE: Karl Marx and Friedrich Engels, *Manifesto of the Communist Party.*
Trans. by Samuel Moore. London: W. Reeves, 1888.

Robert Koehler's painting *The Strike* depicts a situation verging toward violence, as workers mill about in a confrontation with factory owners, and one angry laborer crouches to pick up a stone.   •   Deutsches Historisches Museum, Berlin

GLOBAL EFFECTS OF INDUSTRIALIZATION

Early industrialization was a British, western European, and North American affair. By the late nineteenth century, Russia and Japan were beginning to industrialize. Quite apart from its spread beyond western Europe, industrialization had deep global implications because industrial powers used their tools, technologies, business organization, financial influence, and transportation networks to obtain raw materials from preindustrial societies around the world. Many lands that possessed natural resources became increasingly oriented to exporting raw materials but maintained little control over them, since representatives of industrial countries dominated the commercial and financial institutions associated with the trade. Some societies saw their home markets flooded with inexpensive manufactured products from industrial lands, which devastated traditional industries and damaged local economies.

The Continuing Spread of Industrialization

By the mid-nineteenth century industrialization processes were well underway in western Europe and North America as well as Britain. Industry brought economic and military power, and leaders in other lands began to seek their own paths to industrialization. After 1870 Russia and Japan embarked on campaigns of rapid industrialization. Government authorities took the lead in sponsoring industrialization in both lands, largely to strengthen their societies and enable them to resist military and economic pressures from western Europe and the United States.

Industrialization in Russia

In Russia the tsarist government promoted industrialization by encouraging the construction of railroads to link the distant regions of the massive empire. In 1860 Russia had less than 1,100 kilometers (700 miles) of railroads, but by 1900 there were more than 58,000 kilometers (36,000 miles). Most impressive of the Russian railroads was the trans-Siberian line, constructed between 1891 and 1904, which stretched more than 9,000 kilometers (5,600 miles) and linked Moscow with the port of Vladivostock on the Pacific Ocean. Apart from drawing the regions of the Russian empire together, railroads stimulated the development of coal, iron, and steel industries and enabled Russia to serve as a commercial link between western Europe and east Asia.

Russian industry experienced explosive growth when Count Sergei Witte served as finance minister (1892–1903). Witte oversaw construction of the trans-Siberian railroad, and he worked to push Russian industrialization by reforming commercial law, protecting infant industries, supporting steamship companies, and promoting nautical and engineering schools. He invited foreign investors to bring their capital and expertise to Russia, and he encouraged the establishment of savings banks to raise additional investment funds at home. By 1900 Russia produced half the world's oil, and Russian steel production ranked fourth in the world, behind the United States, Germany, and Britain. As a result of Witte's efforts, Russia also had enormous coal and iron industries, and government demand for weapons supported also a massive armaments industry.

Industrialization in Japan

In Japan, too, imperial authorities pushed industrialization. Because private sources of finance were limited, the government hired thousands of foreign experts to instruct Japanese workers and managers in the techniques of modern industry. The government also took the initiative by modernizing iron foundries and dockyards established during the Tokugawa shogunate, founding new businesses, and opening schools and universities specializing in scientific and technical fields. Government support was responsible for the construction of railroads, the opening of mines, the organization of a banking system, and the establishment of mechanized industries producing ships, armaments, silk, cotton, chemicals, and glass.

When businesses were able to operate on their own, the government sold them

The Tomioka silk factory, established in the 1870s, was one of the earliest mechanized textile factories in Japan. As in many textile mills in Europe and North America, male managers oversaw female factory workers. • Laurie Platt Winfrey, Inc.

to private entrepreneurs, who often built huge industrial empires known as *zaibatsu* ("wealthy cliques"). *Zaibatsu* were similar to the trusts and cartels that emerged in nineteenth-century Europe and the United States but most commonly organized around a single family. *Zaibatsu* usually operated and controlled companies in several industries. The Mitsui combine, for example, owned or had large investments in a multitude of enterprises engaged in banking, trade, mining, food processing, and textile manufacturing. By 1900, as a result of active government encouragement and the organization of large-scale enterprises that operated efficiently, Japan was the most industrialized land in Asia, and it was poised for dramatic economic and industrial expansion in the twentieth century.

The International Division of Labor

Industrialization brought great economic and military strength to societies that reconfigured themselves and relied on mechanized production. Their power encouraged other societies to work towards industrialization. Before the mid-twentieth century, however, these efforts had limited results outside Europe, North America, and Japan. In India, for example, entrepreneurs established a thriving industry in the production of jute—a natural, hemplike fiber used for making carpets, upholstery, and burlap bags—as well as a small domestic steel industry. But fledgling Indian industries lacked government support, and private investment capital was insufficient to bankroll industrialization on a large scale.

Nevertheless, industrialization had deep global ramifications. The industrialization process influenced the economic and social development of many societies because it promoted a new international division of labor. Industrial societies needed minerals, agricultural products, and other raw materials from sometimes distant regions of the world. Representatives of industrial societies searched the globe for raw materials to supply their factories.

Demand for Raw Materials

Large-scale global trade in agricultural products was nothing new. From the sixteenth through the eighteenth centuries, European countries had imported sugar, spices, tobacco, tea, coffee, cotton, and other products grown mostly on plantations. In the nineteenth century demand for these products increased sharply because of population growth. But industrial society fueled the demand for additional products as British, European, and U.S. industrialists sought the natural resources and agricultural products of Africa, the Americas, Asia, Australia, and eastern Europe. The mechanization of the textile industry, for example, produced a demand for large quantities of raw cotton, which came mostly from India, Egypt, and the southern rim of the United States. Similarly, new industrial technologies increased demand for products like rubber, the principal ingredient of belts and tires that were essential to industrial machinery, which came from Brazil, Malaya, and the Congo River basin.

In some lands specialization in the production and export of primary goods paved the way for economic development and eventual industrialization. This pattern was especially noticeable in lands settled by European colonists, including Canada, Argentina, Uruguay, South Africa, Australia, and New Zealand, each of which experienced economic growth through the export of primary products and the infusion of foreign capital and labor. The same societies had an additional advantage in that they were high-wage economies. High incomes fostered economic development in two ways: they created flourishing markets, and they encouraged entrepreneurs to counteract high wages and labor scarcity by inventing new labor-saving technologies.

Economic Development

Economic
Dependency

In most of Latin America, sub-Saharan Africa, south Asia, and southeast Asia, however, dependence on exporting primary products resulted in little or no industrialization. Export-oriented agriculture dominated many of these societies, where the major cash crops were sugar, cotton, and rubber. Foreign investors owned and controlled the plantations that produced these crops, and most of the profits generated went abroad, depriving domestic economies of investment funds that might have contributed to the building of markets and industries. The low wages of plantation workers made the situation worse by dampening demand for manufactured goods. The result was the concentration of wealth in the hands of a small group of people, whether local or foreign, who contributed little to the creation of a domestic market through consumption or investment. To compound the problem, both native and foreign financial interests adopted a free-trade policy that permitted unrestricted entry of foreign manufactures, further limiting opportunities for indigenous industrialization.

The new geographic division of labor, in which some of the world's peoples provided raw materials while others processed and consumed them, increased the volume of world trade and led to increased transportation on both sea and land. Bigger ships, larger docking facilities, and canals facilitated trade and transport. Although its benefits and rewards flowed primarily to Europe, North America, and Japan, the process of industrialization increasingly linked all the world's peoples and profoundly influenced the development of their societies.

An Eastern Steamboat, a watercolor by John Lewis Krimmel, depicted Robert Fulton's steamboat the *Paragon*. Steamboats transported passengers and cargo and helped spread industrialization around the world. • Metropolitan Museum of Art, Rogers Fund, 1942 (42.95.7). Photograph © 1995 The Metropolitan Museum of Art

The process of industrialization involved the harnessing of inanimate sources of energy, the replacement of handicraft production with machine-based manufacturing, and the generation of new forms of business and labor organization. Along with industrialization came demographic growth, large-scale migration, and rapid urbanization, which increased the demand for manufactured goods by the masses of working people. Societies that underwent industrialization enjoyed sharp increases in economic productivity: they produced large quantities of high-quality goods at low prices, and this increased productivity translated into higher material standards of living. Yet industrialization brought costs, in the form of unsettling social problems, as well as benefits. Family life changed dramatically in the industrial age as men, women, and children increasingly left their homes to work in factories and mines, often under appalling conditions. Socialist critics sought to bring about a more just and equitable society, and government authorities curtailed the worst abuses of the early industrial era. Governments and labor unions both worked to raise living standards and provide security for working people. Meanwhile, industrialization increasingly touched the lives of peoples around the world. Western European, North American, and Japanese societies followed Britain's lead into industrialization, while many African, Asian, and Latin American lands became dependent on the export of raw materials to industrial societies.

CHRONOLOGY

1730–1795	Life of Josiah Wedgwood
1733	John Kay invents the flying shuttle
1765	James Watt invents the steam engine
1765–1825	Life of Eli Whitney
1779	Samuel Crompton invents the spinning mule
1785	Edmund Cartwright invents the power loom
1797	Eli Whitney introduces interchangeable parts to the manufacturing process
1829	George Stephenson's locomotive, the Rocket, attains a speed of 45 kilometers per hour (28 mph)
1833	Factory Act restricts employment of women and children in textile factories
1842	Mines Act restricts employment of women and children in mines
1848	Karl Marx and Friedrich Engels publish the *Manifesto of the Communist Party*
1849–1915	Life of Sergei Witte
1851	Crystal Palace exhibition in London
1856	Bessemer converter invented
1913	Henry Ford introduces the assembly line to the manufacture of automobiles

FOR FURTHER READING

T. S. Ashton. *The Industrial Revolution, 1760–1830*. New York, 1968. A brief and readable survey of early industrialization in the British isles.

Rondo Cameron. *A Concise Economic History of the World from Paleolithic Times to the Present*. 3rd ed. New York, 1997. A comprehensive and useful work on economic development, concentrating on industrial Europe.

Daniel R. Headrick. *The Tentacles of Progress: Technology Transfer in the Age of Imperialism, 1850–1940*. New York, 1988. Concentrates on the political and cultural obstacles that hindered transfer of European technologies to colonial lands.

Tom Kemp. *Historical Patterns of Industrialization*. 2nd ed. London, 1993. Focuses on relationship between industrialization and the peasantry, banking institutions, and the state.

A. G. Kenwood and A. L. Lougheed. *Technological Diffusion and Industrialisation before 1914*. London, 1982. A balanced interpretation drawing on different theoretical perspectives raised by industrialization worldwide.

David S. Landes. *The Unbound Prometheus: Technological Change and Industrial Development in Western Europe from 1750 to the Present*. Cambridge, 1969. A comprehensive study of industrialization concentrating on the role of technological innovation.

——. *The Wealth and Poverty of Nations: Why Some Are So Rich and Some So Poor*. New York, 1998. A wide-ranging analysis arguing that social and cultural attitudes serve as the foundation of economic development.

Karl Marx and Friedrich Engels. *The Communist Manifesto*. Trans. by Samuel Moore. Harmondsworth, 1967. English translation of the most important tract of nineteenth-century socialism, with an excellent introduction by historian A. J. P. Taylor.

Joel Mokyr. *The Lever of Riches: Technological Creativity and Economic Progress*. New York, 1990. Examines European technological development in comparative context.

Peter N. Stearns. *The Industrial Revolution in World History*. Boulder, 1993. An excellent overview of industrialization, its European origins, its spread, and its effects in the larger world.

—— and Herrick Chapman. *European Society in Upheaval: Social History since 1750*. 3rd ed. New York, 1992. Important synthetic study examining the social effects of industrialization in Europe.

Mikulas Teich and Roy Porter, eds. *The Industrial Revolution in National Context: Europe and the USA*. Cambridge, 1996. A collection of essays by leading scholars who reappraise industrialization and explore the new approaches that have recently emerged.

E. P. Thompson. *The Making of the English Working Class*. New York, 1966. A classic work that analyzes the formation of working-class consciousness in England from 1790s to the 1830s.

Louise A. Tilly. *Industrialization and Gender Inequality*. Washington, D.C., 1993. A brief historiographical survey of debates on gender and industrialization in England, France, Germany, the United States, Japan, and China.

THE AMERICAS IN THE AGE OF INDEPENDENCE

· · ·

A village fish peddler, Fatt Hing Chin often roamed the coast of southern China in search of fish to sell at market. One day at the wharves, he heard a tale of mysterious but enticing mountains of gold beckoning young Chinese to cross the ocean. At nineteen years of age, Chin felt restlessness, and he longed for the glittering mountains. He learned that he could purchase passage on a foreign ship, but he also needed to be cautious. He did not want to alarm his parents, nor did he want to draw the attention of the authorities, who were reportedly arresting individuals seeking to leave China. Eventually he reconciled his parents to his plans, and in 1849 he boarded a Spanish ship to sail to California and join the gold rush.

Chin felt some uncertainty once at sea. Surprised at the large number of young Chinese men crammed in with him in the ship's hold, he shared their dismay as they remained confined for weeks to the vomit-laden cargo areas of the ship. Ninety-five days and nights passed before the hills of San Francisco came into view. Upon arrival the travelers met Chinese veterans of life in the United States who explained the need to stick together if they were to survive and prosper.

Chin hired out as a gold miner and headed for the mountains of gold. After digging and sifting for two years, he had accumulated his own little pile of gold. He wrote to his brothers and cousins, urging them to join him, and thus helped fuel the large-scale overseas migration of workers. Having made his fortune, though, Chin decided to return to China. Wealthy, he traveled more comfortably this time around, with a bunk and other amenities—and temptations. He participated in the gambling that took place at sea and lost half of his gold by the time the ship docked in Guangzhou. What remained still amounted to a small fortune. California gold provided him with the means to take a wife, build a house, and buy some land.

Although settled and prosperous, Chin remained restless and longed for the excitement of California. Leaving his pregnant wife, he sailed for California again after only a year in China. He returned to mining with his brother, but the gold was more difficult to find. Inspired by the luck of another migrant, Tong Ling, who managed to get one dollar for each meal he sold, Chin's cousins in San Francisco decided to open a restaurant. As one of them said, "If the foreign devils will eat his food, they will eat ours." Chin found the city much more comfortable than the mountains. "Let the others go after the gold in the hills," he said. "I'll wait for the gold to come to the city."

Nineteenth-century cowboys drive a herd of cattle north from Texas. • The Roland P. Murdock Collection, Wichita Art Museum, Wichita, Kansas

Fatt Hing Chin was one of the earliest Chinese migrants to settle in the Americas. His career path—from a miner in search of quick riches to an urban resident committed to a new homeland and hoping to profit from the service industry—was quite typical of Chinese migrants to the United States. Some went from mining to railroad construction or agricultural labor, but all contributed to the transformation of the Americas. Along with millions of others from Europe and Asia, Chinese migrants increased the ethnic diversity of American populations and stimulated political, social, and economic development in the western hemisphere.

During the late eighteenth and early nineteenth centuries, almost all the lands of the western hemisphere won their independence from European colonial powers. American peoples then struggled throughout the nineteenth century to build states and societies that realized their potential in an age of independence. The United States built the most powerful state in the western hemisphere and embarked on a westward push that brought almost all the temperate regions of North America under U.S. control. Canada built a federal state under British Canadian leadership. The varied lands of Latin America built smaller states that often fell under the sway of local military leaders. One issue that most American peoples wrestled with, regardless of their region, was the legacy of the Enlightenment. The effort to build societies based on freedom, equality, and constitutional government was a monumental challenge only partially realized in lands characterized by enormous social, economic, and cultural diversity.

The age of independence for the United States, Canada, and Latin America was a contentious era characterized by continuous mass migration and explosive economic growth, occasionally followed by deep economic stagnation, and punctuated with civil war, ethnic violence, class conflict, and battles for racial and sexual equality. Independence did not solve all the political and social problems of the western hemisphere, but rather created a new context in which American peoples struggled to build effective states, enjoy economic prosperity, and attain cultural cohesion. These goals were elusive throughout the nineteenth century, and in many ways remain so even in the present day. Nevertheless, the histories of these first lands to win independence from colonial powers inspired other peoples who later sought freedom from imperial rule, but they also served as portents of the difficulties faced by newly free states.

 ## THE BUILDING OF AMERICAN STATES

After winning independence from Britain, the United States fashioned a government and began to expand rapidly to the west. By midcentury the new republic had absorbed almost all the temperate lands of North America. Yet the United States was an unstable society composed of varied regions with diverse economic and social structures. Differences over slavery and the rights of individual states as opposed to the federal government sparked a massive civil war in the 1860s. This conflict resulted in the abolition of slavery and the strengthening of the federal state. The experience of Canada was very different from that of the United States. Canada gained independence from Britain without fighting a war, and even though Canada also was a land of great diversity, it avoided falling into a civil war. Although intermittently nervous about the possibility that the United States might begin to expand to the north, Canada established a relatively weak federal government, which presided over provinces that had considerable power over local affairs. Latin American lands were even more diverse than their counterparts to the north, and there was never any real possibility that they could join together in a confederation. Throughout the nineteenth century Latin America was a politically fragmented region, and many individual states faced serious problems and divisions within their own societies.

The United States: Westward Expansion and Civil War

After gaining independence the United States faced the need to construct a machinery of government. During the 1780s leaders from the rebellious colonies drafted a constitution that entrusted responsibility for general issues to a federal government, reserved authority for local issues for individual states, and provided for the admission of new states and territories to the confederation. Although the Declaration of Independence had declared that "all men are created equal," most individual states limited the vote to men of property. But the Enlightenment ideal of equality encouraged political leaders to extend the franchise: by the late 1820s most property qualifications had disappeared, and by midcentury almost all adult white men were eligible to participate in the political affairs of the republic.

While working to settle constitutional issues, Americans also began to expand rapidly to the west. After the American revolution, Britain ceded to the new republic all lands between the Appalachian Mountains and the Mississippi River, and the United States doubled in size. In 1803 Napoleon Bonaparte needed funds immediately to protect revolutionary France from its enemies, and he allowed the United States to purchase France's Louisiana Territory, which extended from the Mississippi River to the Rocky Mountains. Overnight the United States doubled in size again. Between 1804 and 1806 a geographical expedition led by Meriwether Lewis and William Clark mapped the territory and surveyed its resources. Settlers soon began to flock west in search of cheap land to cultivate. By the 1840s westward expansion was well underway, and many Americans spoke of a "manifest destiny" to occupy all of North America from the Atlantic to the Pacific Ocean.

Westward Expansion and "Manifest Destiny"

Westward expansion brought settlers and government forces in conflict with the indigenous peoples of North America, who resisted efforts to push them from their ancestral lands and hunting grounds. Native peoples forged alliances among themselves and also sought the backing of British colonial officials in Canada, but the U.S. army supported Euro-American settlers and gradually forced the continent open to their expansion. By 1840 U.S. forces had gained effective control of all territory east of the Mississippi River. They pushed some indigenous peoples into marginal lands, such as the swampy lowlands of southern Florida, and forced others to move to arid regions in the west. The most important of these relocations was the forced removal of Cherokees from the eastern woodlands to Oklahoma on the "Trail of Tears" (1837–1838).

Conflict with Indigenous Peoples

After 1840 the site of conflict between Euro-American and indigenous peoples shifted to the plains region west of the Mississippi River. There settlers and ranchers encountered peoples like the Sioux, Comanche, Pawnee, and Apache, who possessed firearms and outstanding equestrian skills. They offered fierce resistance to encroachment by Euro-American intruders on their lands, and they sometimes registered stunning victories over U.S. forces. In 1876, for example, a Sioux force annihilated an army under the command of Colonel George Armstrong Custer in the battle of Little Big Horn (in southern Montana). By the 1870s, however, U.S. forces

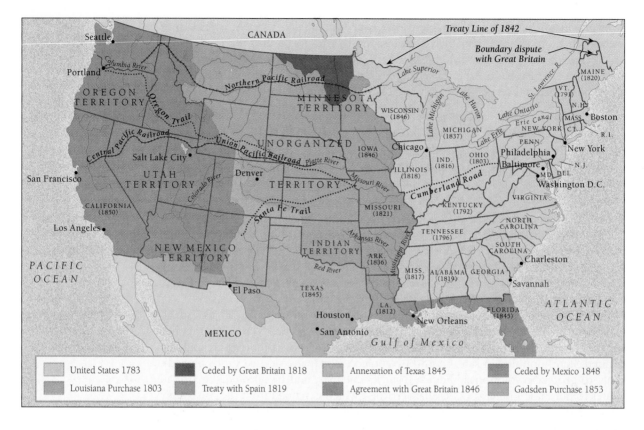

MAP [31.1]

Westward expansion of the United States.

were using cannons and deadly, rapid-fire Gatling guns, and with these weapons they broke the resistance of indigenous peoples, disarmed them, and opened the western plains to Euro-American expansion. The last large conflict came in 1890 at Wounded Knee (in southern South Dakota), where a U.S. force armed with machine guns massacred more than two hundred Sioux men, women, and children while seeking to prevent an uprising.

The Mexican-American War   Westward expansion also generated tension between the United States and Mexico, whose territories included Texas, California, and New Mexico (the territory that is now the American southwest). Texas declared independence from Mexico in 1836, largely because the many American migrants who had settled there wanted to run their own affairs. In 1845 the United States accepted Texas as a new state—against vigorous Mexican protest—and moved to consolidate its hold on the territory. These moves led to conflicts that rapidly escalated into the Mexican-American War (1845–1848). American forces inflicted a punishing defeat on the Mexican army, and by the Treaty of Guadalupe Hidalgo (1848), the United States paid Mexico fifteen million dollars for Texas north of the Rio Grande, California, and New Mexico.

While satisfying desires for the United States to realize its manifest destiny, westward expansion also created problems within the republic by aggravating tensions between regions. The most serious and divisive issue had to do with slavery, which had vexed American politics since independence. The Enlightenment ideal of equality clearly suggested that the appropriate policy was to abolish slavery, but the leaders of the American revolution and framers of the Constitution recognized the sanctity of private property, including slaves. American independence initially promoted

This photograph of a Sioux camp in South Dakota offers an idealized, pastoral, peaceful image of indigenous society in the United States in the 1890s. • Library of Congress

a surge of antislavery sentiment, as states from Delaware north abolished slavery within their jurisdictions. Abolition did not bring full equality for free blacks in northern states, but it hardened divisions between slave and free states. Westward expansion aggravated tensions further by raising the question of whether settlers could extend slavery to newly acquired territories.

Sectional Conflict

Opponents of slavery had dreamed that the institution would die a natural death with the decline of tobacco cultivation. Their hopes faded, however, with the invigoration of the slave system by the rise of cotton as a cash crop in the early nineteenth century, followed by westward expansion. The U.S. slave population rose sharply from five hundred thousand in 1770 to almost two million in 1820. As the numbers of slaves grew, antislavery forces fought to limit the spread of slavery to new territories. Beginning with the Missouri Compromise of 1820, a series of political compacts attempted to maintain a balance between slave and free states as the American republic admitted new states carved out of western territories. These compromises ultimately proved too brittle to endure, as proslavery and antislavery forces became more strident. Abraham Lincoln (1809–1865) predicted in 1858 that "a house divided against itself cannot stand," and he made the connection to slavery explicit: "I believe this government cannot endure permanently half *slave* and half *free*. . . . It will become *all* one thing, or *all* the other."

The election of Abraham Lincoln to the presidency in 1860 was the spark that ignited war between the states (1861–1865). Lincoln was an explicitly sectional candidate, convinced that slavery was immoral and committed to free soil—territories without slavery. Although slavery stood at the center of the conflict, the Civil War also revolved around issues central to the United States as a society: the nature of the Union, states' rights as opposed to the federal government's authority, and the imperatives of a budding industrial-capitalist system against those of an export-oriented plantation economy.

The U.S. Civil War

Abraham Lincoln as president. Lincoln opposed the spread of slavery, which he considered immoral. His election to the presidency sparked the outbreak of the Civil War. • The Lincoln Museum, Fort Wayne, Indiana

Eleven southern states withdrew from the Union in 1860 and 1861, affirming their right to dissolve the Union and their support for states' rights. Slavery and the cultivation of cotton as a cash crop had isolated the southern states from economic developments in the rest of the United States. By the mid-nineteenth century, the southern states were the world's major source of cotton, and the bulk of the crop went to the British isles. Manufactured goods consumed in the southern states came mostly from Britain, and almost all food came from the region's farms. Southerners considered themselves self-sufficient and believed that they did not need the rest of the United States. Northerners saw the situation differently. They viewed secession as illegal insurrection and an act of betrayal. They fought not only against slavery, but also against the concept of a state subject to blackmail by its constituent parts. They also fought for a way of life—their emerging industrial society—and an expansive western agricultural system based on free labor.

The first two years of the war ended in stalemate. The war changed character on 1 January 1863, however, when Abraham Lincoln signed the Emancipation Proclamation, making the abolition of slavery an explicit goal of the war. The Emancipation Proclamation struck at the heart of the southern war effort, since slaves constituted a sizable portion of the region's labor force. In practical terms the Emancipation Proclamation had little immediate effect on slaves' status, but its promise of abolition foreshadowed radical changes to come in southern life.

Ultimately, the northern states prevailed. They brought considerable resources to the war effort—some 90 percent of the country's industrial capacity and approximately two-thirds of its railroad lines—but still they fought four bitter years against a formidable enemy. The victory of the northern states ended slavery in the United States. Moreover, it ensured that the United States would remain politically united, and it enhanced the authority of the federal government in the American republic. Thus as European lands were building powerful states on the foundations of revolutionary ideals, liberalism, and nationalism, the United States also forged a strong central government to supervise westward expansion and deal with the political and social issues that divided the American republic.

The grotesquely twisted bodies of dead northern soldiers lay near a fence outside Antietam, Maryland, in 1862. The Civil War was the most costly in U.S. history in terms of lives lost.   •   Library of Congress

The Canadian Dominion: Independence without War

Canada did not fight a war for independence, and in spite of deep regional divisions, it did not experience bloody internal conflict. Instead, Canadian independence came gradually as Canadians and the British government agreed on general principles of autonomy. The distinctiveness of the two dominant ethnic groups, the British Canadians and the French Canadians, ensured that the process of building an independent society would not be smooth, but intermittent fears of U.S. expansion and concerns about the possibility of an invasion from the south helped submerge ethnic differences. By the late nineteenth century, Canada was a land in control of its own destiny, despite continuing ties to Britain and the looming presence of the United States to the south.

Autonomy and Division

Originally colonized by trappers and settlers from both Britain and France, the colony of New France passed into the British empire after the British victory in the Seven Years' War (1756–1763). Until the late eighteenth century, however, French Canadians outnumbered British Canadians, so imperial officials made large concessions to their subjects of French descent in order to forestall unnecessary strife. Officials recognized the Roman Catholic church and permitted continued observance of French civil law in Quebec and other areas of French Canadian settlement, which they governed through appointed councils staffed by local elites. British Canadians, by contrast, were Protestants who lived mostly in Ontario, followed British law, and governed themselves through elected representatives. After 1781 large numbers of British loyalists fled the newly formed United States to the south and sought refuge in Canada, thus greatly enlarging the size of the English-speaking community there.

Ethnic divisions and political differences could easily have splintered Canada, but the War of 1812 stimulated a sense of unity against an external threat. The United States declared war on Britain in retaliation for encroachments on U.S. rights during

The War of 1812

the Napoleonic wars, and the British colony of Canada formed one of the front lines of the conflict. U.S. military leaders assumed that they could easily invade and conquer Canada to pressure their foes. Despite the greater resources of the United States, however, Canadian forces repelled U.S. incursions. Their victories promoted a sense of Canadian pride, and anti-U.S. sentiments became a means for covering over differences among French Canadians and British Canadians.

After the War of 1812, Canada experienced an era of rapid growth. Expanded business opportunities drew English-speaking migrants, who swelled the population. This influx threatened the identity of Quebec, and discontent in Canada reached a critical point in the 1830s. The British imperial governors of Canada did not want a repeat of the American revolution, so between 1840 and 1867 they defused tensions by expanding home rule in Canada and permitting the provinces to govern their own internal affairs.

Dominion   Westward expansion of the United States and the American Civil War pushed Canada toward political autonomy. Fear of U.S. expansion helped stifle internal conflicts among Canadians and prompted Britain to grant independence to Canada. The British North America Act of 1867 joined Quebec, Ontario, Nova Scotia, and New Brunswick and recognized them as the Dominion of Canada. Other provinces joined the Dominion later. Each province had its own seat of government, provincial legislature, and lieutenant governor representing the British crown. The act created a federal government headed by a governor-general who acted as the British representative. An elected House of Commons and appointed Senate rounded out the framework of governance. Provincial legislatures reserved certain political matters for themselves, whereas others fell within the purview of the federal government. Without waging war, the Dominion of Canada had won control over all Canadian internal affairs, and Britain retained jurisdiction over foreign affairs until 1931.

John A. Macdonald (1815–1891) became the first prime minister of Canada, and he moved to incorporate all of British North America into the Dominion. He negotiated the purchase of the huge Northwest Territories from the Hudson's Bay Company in 1869, and he persuaded Manitoba, British Columbia, and Prince Edward Island to join the Dominion. Macdonald believed, however, that Canada's Dominion would remain symbolic—a mere "geographic expression," as he put it—until the government took concrete action to make Canadian unity and independence a reality. To strengthen the union he oversaw construction of a transcontinental railroad, completed in 1885. The railroad facilitated transportation and communications throughout Canada and eventually helped bring new provinces into the Dominion: Alberta and Saskatchewan in 1905 and Newfoundland in 1949. Although internal conflicts never disappeared, Dominion provided a foundation for Canadian independence and unity. Although maintaining ties to Britain and struggling to forge an identity distinct from its powerful neighbor to the south, Canada developed as a culturally diverse yet politically unified society.

Latin America: Fragmentation and Political Experimentation

Political unity was shortlived in Latin America. Simón Bolívar (1783–1830), hailed as the region's liberator, worked for the establishment of a large confederation that would provide Latin America with the political, military, and economic strength to

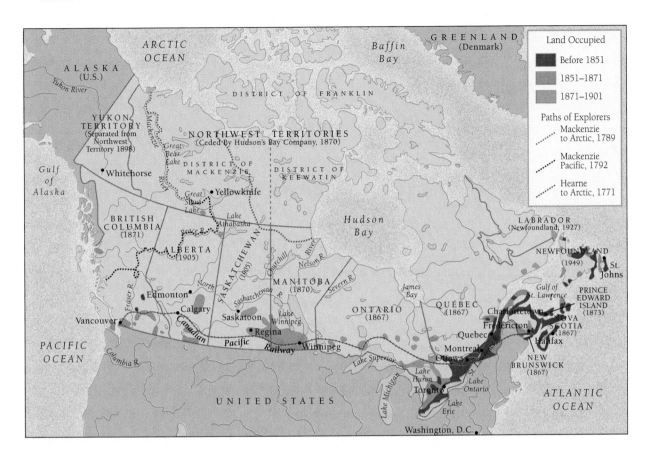

MAP [31.2]

The Dominion of Canada in the nineteenth century.

resist encroachment by foreign powers. The wars of independence that he led encouraged a sense of solidarity in Latin America. But Bolívar once admitted that "I fear peace more than war," and after the defeat of the common colonial enemy, solidarity was impossible to sustain. Bolívar's Gran Colombia broke into its three constituent parts—Venezuela, Colombia, and Ecuador—and the rest of Latin America fragmented into numerous independent states.

Following the example of the United States, creole elites usually established republics with written constitutions for the newly independent states of Latin America. Yet constitutions were much more difficult to frame in Latin America than in the United States. Before gaining independence, Latin American leaders had little experience with self-government, since Spanish and Portuguese colonial regimes were far more autocratic than the British imperial government in North America. Creole elites responded enthusiastically to Enlightenment values and republican ideals, but they had no experience putting their principles into practice. As a result, several Latin American lands lurched from one constitution to another as leaders struggled to create a machinery of government that would lead to political and social stability.

Creole elites also dominated the newly independent states and effectively prevented mass participation in public affairs. Less than 5 percent of the male population was active in Latin American politics in the nineteenth century, and millions of indigenous peoples lived entirely outside the political system. Without institutionalized means of expressing discontent or opposition, those disillusioned with the system had

Creole Elites and Political Instability

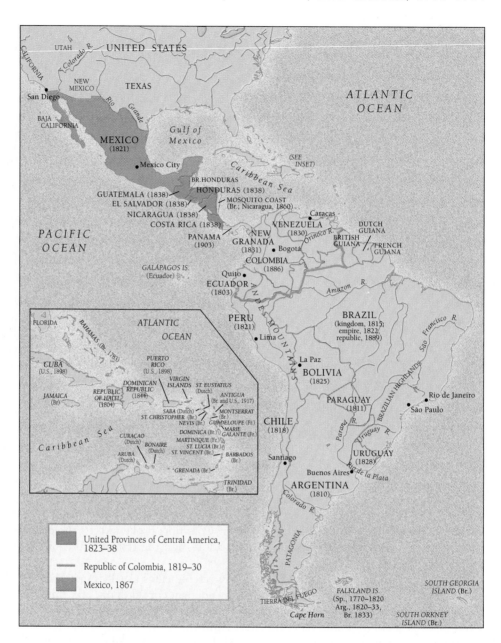

MAP [31.3]

Latin America in the
nineteenth century.

little choice beyond rebellion. Aggravating political instability were differences among elites. Whether they were urban merchants or rural landowners, Latin American elites divided into different camps as liberals or conservatives, centralists or federalists, secularists or Roman Catholics.

Conflicts with Indigenous Peoples

One thing elites agreed on was the policy of claiming American land for agriculture and ranching. This meant pushing aside indigenous peoples and establishing Euro-American hegemony in Latin America. Conflict was most intense in Argentina and Chile, where cultivators and ranchers longed to take over the South American plains. During the mid-nineteenth century, as the United States was crushing native

SIMÓN BOLÍVAR ON GOVERNMENT IN VENEZUELA

• • •

Often considered the liberator of South America because of his leadership during the drive for independence, Simón Bolívar devoted a great deal of thought to matters of statecraft. In this speech of 1819 to a congress considering the political destiny of Venezuela, Bolívar expressed his views on the problems and promises of Latin America. Later the same year he became president of Gran Colombia, which included modern Venezuela, Colombia, and Ecuador.

We are not Europeans; we are not Indians; we are but a mixed species of aborigines and Spaniards. Americans by birth and Europeans by law, we find ourselves engaged in a dual conflict: we are disputing with the natives for titles of ownership, and at the same time we are struggling to maintain ourselves in the country that gave us birth against the opposition of the invaders. Thus our position is most extraordinary and complicated. . . .

America . . . received everything from Spain, who, in effect, deprived her of the experience that she would have gained from the exercise of an active tyranny by not allowing her to take part in her own domestic affairs and administration. This exclusion made it impossible for us to acquaint ourselves with the management of public affairs. . . . In brief, Gentlemen, we were deliberately kept in ignorance and cut off from the world in all matters relating to the science of government. . . .

Despite these bitter reflections, I experience a surge of joy when I witness the great advances that our Republic has made since it began its noble career. Loving what is most useful, animated by what is most just, and aspiring to what is most perfect, Venezuela, on breaking away from Spain, has recovered her independence, her freedom, her equality, and her national sovereignty. By establishing a democratic republic, she has proscribed monarchy, distinctions, nobility, prerogatives, and privileges. She has declared for the rights of man and freedom of action, thought, speech, and press. These eminently liberal acts, because of the sincerity that has inspired them, will never cease to be admired. . . .

Permit me to call the attention of the Congress to a matter that may be of vital importance. We must keep in mind that our people are neither European nor North American; rather, they are a mixture of Africans and the Americans who originated in Europe. . . . It is impossible to determine with any degree of accuracy where we belong in the human family. The greater portion of the native Indians has been annihilated; Spaniards have mixed with Americans and Africans, and Africans with Indians and Spaniards. While we have all been born of the same mother, our fathers, different in origin and in blood, are foreigners, and all differ visibly as to the color of their skin: a dissimilarity which places upon us an obligation of the greatest importance.

Under the Constitution, which interprets the laws of Nature, all citizens of Venezuela enjoy complete political equality. Although equality may not have been the political dogma of Athens, France, or North America, we must consecrate it here in order to correct the disparity that apparently exists. My opinion, Legislators, is that the fundamental basis of our political system hinges directly and exclusively upon the establishment and practice of equality in Venezuela. . . .

Venezuela had, has, and should have a republican government. Its principles should be the sovereignty of the people, division of powers, civil liberty, proscription of slavery, and the abolition of monarchy and privileges. We need equality to recast, so to speak, into a unified nation, the classes of men, political opinions, and public customs.

SOURCE: Simón Bolívar, *Selected Works of Bolívar,* compiled by Vicente Lecuna, edited by Harold A. Bierck Jr., translated by Lewis Bertrand (New York: Colonial Press, 1951), 1:175–176, 181–183.

resistance to western expansion in North America, Argentine and Chilean forces brought modern weapons to bear in their campaign to conquer the indigenous peoples of South America. By the 1870s colonists had pacified the most productive lands and forced indigenous peoples either to assimilate to Euro-American society or to retreat to marginal lands that were unattractive to cultivators and ranchers.

Caudillos   Although creole elites agreed on the policy of conquering native peoples, division and discord in the newly independent states helped *caudillos,* or regional military leaders, come to power in much of Latin America. The wars of independence had lasted well over a decade, and they provided Latin America with military rather than civilian heroes. After independence, military leaders took to the political stage, appealing to populist sentiments and exploiting the discontent of the masses. One of the most notable caudillos was Juan Manuel de Rosas, who from 1835 to 1852 ruled an Argentina badly divided between the cattle-herding society of the pampas (the interior grasslands) and the urban elite of Buenos Aires. Rosas himself emerged from the *gaucho* ("cowboy") world of horsemanship and cattle ranching, and he used his skills to subdue other caudillos and establish control in Buenos Aires. Rosas called for regional autonomy in an attempt to reconcile competing interests, but he worked to centralize the government he usurped. He quelled rebellions, but he did so in bloody fashion. Critics often likened Rosas to historically infamous figures, calling him "the Machiavelli of the pampas" and "the Argentine Nero," and they accused him of launching a reign of terror in order to stifle opposition. One writer exiled by the caudillo compiled a chart that counted the number of Rosas's victims and the violent ways they met their ends:

Poisoned	4
Shot	1,393
Hanged	3,765
Assassinated	722
Killed in armed clashes	16,520
Total	22,404

Rosas did what caudillos did best: he restored order. In doing so, however, he made terror a tool of the government, and he ruled as a despot through his own personal army. While caudillo rule limited freedom and undermined republican ideals, it sometimes gave rise also to an opposition that aimed to overthrow the caudillos and work for liberal reforms that would promote more democratic forms of government.

Mexico: War   Independent Mexico experienced a succession of governments, from monarchy
and Reform   to republic to caudillo rule, but it also generated a liberal reform movement. The Mexican-American War caused political turmoil in Mexico and helped the caudillo General Antonio López Santa Ana consolidate his rule. After the defeat and disillusion of the war, however, a liberal reform movement attempted to reshape Mexican society. Led by President Benito Juárez (1806–1872), a Mexican of indigenous ancestry, *La Reforma* of the 1850s aimed to limit the power of the military and the Roman Catholic church in Mexican society. Juárez and his followers called for *tierra y libertad*—"land and liberty"—which would endow Mexicans with the means to make a living and enable them to participate in political affairs. The Constitution of 1857 set forth the ideals of *La Reforma*. It curtailed the prerogatives of priests and military elites, and it allowed the confiscation of church properties, which accounted for almost half of all the productive land in Mexico. The intent

behind land redistribution was to broaden the base of land ownership, especially among indigenous peoples, and thus improve conditions for the masses. In fact, however, speculators and large landowners, not indigenous peoples, bought most of the land.

La Reforma challenged the fundamental conservatism of Mexican elites, who led spirited opposition to political, social, and economic reform. By the early twentieth century, Mexico was a divided land moving toward civil war. The Mexican revolution (1911–1920), a bitter and bloody conflict, broke out when middle-class Mexicans joined with peasants and workers to over-

Samuel Chamberlain's lithograph *Street Fighting in the Calle de Iturbide* boldly illuminates the messy battles that took place during the Mexican-American War. • West Point Museum. Photo: Paulus Leeser

throw the powerful dictator Porfirio Díaz. The lower classes then took up weapons and followed the revolutionary leaders Emiliano Zapata and Francisco (Pancho) Villa, charismatic agrarian rebels who organized massive armies fighting for *tierra y libertad,* the goals of *La Reforma* in the 1850s. Although the poorly armed forces of Zapata and Villa enjoyed tremendous popular support, they were unable to capture Mexico's major cities, and they could not match the firepower of government armies. The Mexican revolution came to an end shortly after Zapata died in battle (1919) and government forces regained control of a battered land. Nevertheless, the Mexican Constitution of 1917 addressed the concerns of the revolutionaries by providing for land redistribution, universal suffrage, state-supported education, minimum wages and maximum hours for workers, and restrictions on foreign ownership of Mexican property and mineral resources.

Mexico: Revolution

In the form of division, rebellion, caudillo rule, and civil war, instability and conflict plagued Latin America throughout the nineteenth century. Many Latin American peoples lacked education, profitable employment, and political representation. Simón Bolívar himself once said that "independence is the only blessing we have gained at the expense of all the rest."

AMERICAN ECONOMIC DEVELOPMENT

During the nineteenth and early twentieth centuries, two principal influences—mass migration and British investment—shaped economic development throughout the Americas. But American states reacted in different ways to migration and foreign investment. The United States and Canada absorbed waves of migrants, exploited British capital, built industrial societies, and established economic independence.

The fragmented states of Latin America were unable to follow suit, however, as they struggled with the legacies of colonialism, slavery, and economic dependence on single export crops. Migrants to Latin America mostly worked not in factories, but on plantations owned or controlled by foreign investors.

Migration to the Americas

Underpinning the economic development of the Americas was the mass migration of European and Asian peoples to the United States, Canada, and Latin America. Gold discoveries drew prospectors hoping to make a quick fortune: the California gold rush of 1849 drew the largest crowd, but Canadian gold also lured migrants by the tens of thousands. Outnumbering gold prospectors were millions of European and Asian migrants who made their way to the factories, railroad construction sites, and plantations of the Americas. Following them were others who offered the support services that made life for migrant workers more comfortable and at the same time transformed the ethnic and cultural landscape of the Americas. Fatt Hing Chin's restaurant in San Francisco's Chinatown fed Chinese migrants, but it also helped introduce Chinese cuisine to American society. Migrants from all over the world found similar comforts as their foods, religious beliefs, and cultural traditions migrated with them to the Americas.

Industrial Migrants   After the mid-nineteenth century European migrants flocked to North America, where they filled the factories of the burgeoning industrial economy of the United States. Their lack of skills made them attractive to industrialists seeking workers to operate machinery or perform heavy labor at low wages. By keeping labor costs down, migrants helped increase the profitability and fuel the expansion of U.S. industry.

In the 1850s European migrants to the United States numbered 2.3 million—almost as many as had crossed the Atlantic during the half-century from 1800 to 1850—and the volume of migration surged until the early twentieth century. Increasing rents and indebtedness drove cultivators from Ireland, Scotland, Germany, and Scandinavia to seek opportunities in North America. Some of them moved to the Ohio and Mississippi River valleys in search of cheap and abundant land, but many stayed in the eastern cities and contributed to the early industrialization of the United States. By the late nineteenth century, most European migrants were coming from southern and eastern Europe. Poles, Russian Jews, Slavs, Italians, Greeks, and Portuguese were most prominent among the later migrants, and they settled largely in the industrial cities of the eastern states. They dominated the textile industries of the northeast, and without their labor, the remarkable industrial expansion that the United States experienced in the late nineteenth century would have been inconceivable.

Asian migrants further swelled the U.S. labor force and contributed to the construction of an American transportation infrastructure. Chinese migration grew rapidly after the 1840s, when British gunboats opened China to foreign influences. Officials of the Qing government permitted foreigners to seek indentured laborers in China and approved their migration to distant lands. Between 1852 and 1875 some two hundred thousand Chinese migrated to California. Some, like Fatt Hing Chin, negotiated their own passage and sought to make their fortune in the gold rush, but most traveled on indentured labor contracts that required them to cultivate crops or work on the Central Pacific Railroad. Another five thousand Chinese entered Canada to search for gold in British Columbia or work on the Canadian Pacific Railroad.

Prospectors searching for California gold in 1850. Notice that the white and Chinese prospectors work different sides of the sluice.

● Courtesy of the California History Room, California State Library, Sacramento

Plantation Migrants

While migrants to the United States contributed to the development of an industrial society, those who went to Latin American lands mostly worked on agricultural plantations. Some Europeans figured among these migrants. About four million Italians sought opportunities in Argentina in the 1880s and 1890s, for example, and the Brazilian government paid Italian migrants to cross the Atlantic and work for coffee growers who experienced a severe labor shortage after the abolition of slavery there (1888). Many Italian workers settled permanently in Latin America, especially Argentina, but some, popularly known as *golondrinas* ("swallows") because of their regular migrations, traveled back and forth annually between Europe and South America to take advantage of different growing seasons in the northern and southern hemispheres.

Other migrants who worked on plantations in the western hemisphere came from Asian lands. More than fifteen thousand indentured laborers from China worked in the sugarcane fields of Cuba during the nineteenth century, while Indian migrants traveled to Jamaica, Trinidad, Tobago, and Guyana. Laborers from both China and Japan migrated to Peru where they worked on cotton plantations in coastal regions, mined guano deposits for fertilizer, and helped build railroad lines. After the middle of the nineteenth century, expanding U.S. influence in the Pacific islands also led to Chinese, Japanese, Filipino, and Korean migrations to Hawai`i, where planters sought indentured laborers to tend sugarcane. About twenty-five thousand Chinese went to Hawai`i during the 1850s and 1860s, and later 180,000 Japanese also made their way to island plantations.

Economic Expansion in the United States

British Capital   British investment capital in the United States proved crucial to the early stages of industrial development by helping businessmen establish a textile industry. In the late nineteenth century, it also helped spur a vast expansion of U.S. industry by funding entrepreneurs who opened coal and iron ore mines, built iron and steel factories, and constructed railroad lines. The flow of investment monies was a consequence of Britain's own industrialization, which generated enormous wealth and created a need for investors to find profitable outlets for their funds. Stable, white-governed states and colonies were especially fertile grounds for British investment, which often provided the impetus for industrial expansion and economic independence in those regions. In the case of the United States, it helped create a rival industrial power that would eventually outperform Britain's own economy.

After the 1860s U.S. businesses made effective use of foreign investment capital as the reunited land recovered from the Civil War. The war determined that the United States would depend on wage labor rather than slavery, and entrepreneurs set about tapping American resources and building a continental economy.

Railroads   Perhaps the most important economic development of the later nineteenth century was the construction of railroad lines that linked all U.S. regions and helped create an integrated national economy. Because of its enormous size and environmental diversity, the United States offered an abundance of natural resources for industrial exploitation. But vast distances made it difficult to maintain close economic ties between regions until a boom in railroad construction created a dense transportation, communication, and distribution network. Before the Civil War the United States had about 50,000 kilometers (31,000 miles) of railroad lines, most of them short routes east of the Mississippi River. By 1900 there were more than 320,000 kilometers (200,000 miles) of track, and the American rail network stretched from coast to coast. Most prominent of the new lines was a transcontinental route, completed in 1869, running from Omaha, where connections provided access to eastern states, to San Francisco.

Railroads decisively influenced American economic development. They provided cheap transportation for agricultural commodities, manufactured goods, and individual travelers as well. Railroads hauled grain, beef, and hogs from the plains states, cotton and tobacco from the south, lumber from the northwest, iron and steel from the mills of Pittsburgh, and finished products from the eastern industrial cities. Quite apart from the transportation services they provided, railroads spurred the development of other industries: they required huge amounts of coal, wood, glass, and rubber, and by the 1880s some 75 percent of U.S. steel went to the railroad industry. Railroads also required the development of new managerial skills to operate large, complicated businesses. In 1850 few if any American businesses had more than a thousand employees. By the early 1880s, however, the Pennsylvania Railroad alone employed almost fifty thousand people, and the size of the business called for organization and coordination on an unprecedented scale. Railroads were the testing grounds where American managers developed the techniques they needed to run big businesses.

"Railroad Time"   Railroads even shaped the American sense of time. Until rapid and regular rail transportation became available, communities set their clocks by the sun. As a result, New York time was eleven minutes and forty-five seconds behind Boston time. When the

clock showed 12 noon in Chicago, it was 11:50 A.M. in St. Louis and 12:18 P.M. in Detroit. These differences in local sun times created scheduling nightmares for railroad managers, who by the 1880s had to keep track of more than fifty time standards. Observance of local time also created hazards because a small miscalculation in scheduling could bring two massive trains hurtling unexpectedly toward each other on the same track. To simplify matters, in 1883 railroad companies divided the North American continent into four zones in which all railroad clocks read precisely the same time. The general public quickly adopted "railroad time" in place of local sun time, and in 1918 the U.S. government legally established the four time zones as the nation's official framework of time.

Using wheelbarrows, picks, shovels, and baskets as their principal tools, Chinese laborers build a trestle in the Sierra Nevada mountains to serve the transcontinental railroad. • The Bancroft Library, University of California, Berkeley

Led by railroads, the U.S. economy expanded at a blistering pace between 1870 and 1900. Inventors designed new products and brought them to market: *Economic Growth* electric lights, telephones, typewriters, phonographs, film photography, motion picture cameras, and electric motors all made their appearance during this era. Strong consumer demand for these and other products fueled rapid industrial expansion and suggested to some that the United States had found the road to continuous progress and prosperity.

Yet the march of American industrialization did not go entirely unopposed: large-scale labor unions emerged alongside big business in the period from 1870 to 1900, and confrontations between businessmen seeking profits and workers seeking higher wages or job security sometimes grew ugly. A massive, coordinated strike of rail workers in 1877 shut down two-thirds of the nation's railroads. Violence stemming from the strike took the lives of one hundred people and resulted in ten million dollars' worth of property damage. Nevertheless, big business prevailed in its disputes with workers during the nineteenth century, often with support from federal or state governments, and by the early twentieth century the United States had emerged as one of the world's major industrial powers.

Canadian Prosperity

British investment deeply influenced the development of the Canadian as well as the U.S. economy in the nineteenth and early twentieth centuries. As in the United States, Canadian leaders took advantage of British capital to industrialize without allowing their economy to fall under British control. During the early nineteenth century, Britain paid relatively high prices for Canadian agricultural products and minerals, partly to keep the colony stable and discourage the formation of separatist movements. As a result, white Canadians enjoyed a high standard of living even before industrialization.

The National Policy   After the establishment of the Dominion, politicians started a program of economic development known as the National Policy. The idea was to attract migrants, protect nascent industries through tariffs, and build national transportation systems. The centerpiece of the transportation network was the transcontinental Canadian Pacific Railroad, built largely with British investment capital and completed in 1885. The Canadian Pacific railroad opened the western prairie lands to commerce, stimulated the development of other industries, and promoted the emergence of a Canadian national economy. The National Policy created some violent altercations with indigenous peoples who resisted encroachment on their lands and with trappers who resented disruption of their way of life, but it also promoted economic growth and independence. In Canada as in the United States, the ability to control and direct economic affairs was crucial to limiting the state's dependence on British capital.

As a result of the National Policy, Canada experienced booming agricultural, mineral, and industrial production in the late nineteenth and early twentieth centuries. Canadian population surged as a result of both migration and natural increase. Migrants flocked to Canada's shores from Asia and especially from Europe: between 1903 and 1914 some 2.7 million eastern European migrants settled in Canada. Fueled in part by this population growth, Canadian economic expansion took place on the foundation of rapidly increasing wheat production and the extraction of rich mineral resources, including gold, silver, copper, nickel, and asbestos. Industrialists also tapped Canadian rivers to produce the hydroelectric power necessary for manufacturing.

U.S. Investment   Canada remained wary of its powerful neighbor to the south, but did not keep U.S. economic influence entirely at bay. British investment dwarfed American investment throughout the nineteenth century: in 1914 British investment in Canada totaled $2.5 billion, compared to $700 million from the United States. Nevertheless, the U.S. presence in the Canadian economy grew. By 1918, Americans owned 30 percent of all Canadian industry, and thereafter the U.S. and Canadian economies became increasingly interdependent. Canada began to undergo rapid industrialization after the early twentieth century, as the province of Ontario benefitted from the spillover of U.S. industry in the northeastern states.

Latin American Dependence

Latin American states did not undergo industrialization or enjoy economic development like that of the United States and Canada. Colonial legacies help explain the lack of economic development in Latin American lands. Even when Spain and Portugal controlled the trade and investment policies of their American colonies, their home economies were unable to supply sufficient quantities of the manufactured goods that colonial markets demanded. As a result, they opened the colonies to European trade, which snuffed out local industries that could not compete with British, French, and German producers of inexpensive manufactured goods. Moreover, both in colonial times and after independence, Latin American elites—urban merchants and large landholders—retained control over local economies. Elites profited handsomely from European trade and investment and thus had little incentive to seek different economic policies or work toward economic diversification. Thus foreign investment and trade had more damaging effects in Latin American than in the United States or Canada.

British Investment

The relatively small size of Latin American markets limited foreign influence, which generally took the form of investment. British merchants had little desire to transform Latin American states into dependent trading partners for the simple reason that they offered no substantial market for British goods. Nevertheless, British investors took advantage of opportunities that brought them handsome profits and considerable control over Latin American economic affairs. In Argentina, for example, British investors encouraged the development of cattle and sheep ranching. After the 1860s and the invention of refrigerated cargo ships, meat became Argentina's largest export. British investors controlled the industry and reaped the profits, however, as Argentina became Britain's principal supplier of meat. Between 1880 and 1914 European migrants labored in the new export industries and contributed to the explosive growth of urban areas like Buenos Aires: by 1914 the city's population exceeded 3.5 million. Although migrant laborers rarely shared in the profits controlled by elites, the domination of urban labor by European migrants represented yet another form of foreign influence in Latin American economic affairs.

Attempted Industrialization

In a few lands, ruling elites made attempts to encourage industrialization, but with only limited success. The most notable of these efforts came when the dictatorial General Porfirio Díaz ruled Mexico (1876–1911). Díaz represented the interests of large landowners, wealthy merchants, and foreign investors. Under his rule railroad tracks and telegraph lines connected all parts of Mexico, and the production of mineral resources surged. A small steel industry produced railroad track and construction materials, and entrepreneurs also established glass, chemical, and textile industries. The capital, Mexico City, underwent a transformation during the Díaz years: it acquired paved streets, streetcar lines, and electric street lights. But the profits from Mexican enterprises did not support continuing industrial development. Instead they went into the pockets of the Mexican oligarchy and foreign investors who supported Díaz while a growing and discontented urban working class seethed with resentment at low wages, long hours, and foreign managers. Even as agriculture, railroad construction, and mining were booming, the standard of living for average Mexicans was declining in the late nineteenth century. Frustration with this state of affairs helps explain the sudden outbreak of violent revolution in 1911.

Despite a large proportion of foreign and especially British control, Latin American economies expanded rapidly in the late nineteenth century. Exports drove this growth: copper and silver from Mexico, bananas from Central America, rubber and coffee from Brazil, beef and wheat from Argentina, copper from Chile, tobacco and sugar from Cuba. As in the United States and Canada, foreign investment provided capital for development, but unlike the situation in the northern lands, control over industries and exports remained in foreign hands. Latin American economies were thus subject to decisions made in the interests of foreign investors, and unstable governments could do little in the face of strong foreign intervention. Controlled by the very elites who profited from foreign intervention at the expense of their citizens, Latin American governments helped promote the region's economic dependence, despite growth in industrial and export economies.

British and U.S. investors underwrote economic and industrial development in Latin America during the late nineteenth century, but most of the profits flowed outside the region. This copper mine in northwestern Mexico was built with U.S. investment. ● Courtesy of the Arizona Historical Society/Tucson. #97329

 ## AMERICAN CULTURAL AND SOCIAL DIVERSITY

In his "Song of Myself" (1855), U.S. poet Walt Whitman asked:

> Do I contradict myself?
> Very well then I contradict myself,
> (I am large, I contain multitudes.)

Much of the allure of the Americas derived from their vast spaces and diverse populations. The Americas were indeed large, and they contained multitudes. While diversity distinguished the Americas, it also provided abundant fuel for conflicts between ethnic groups, social classes, and those segregated into rigid castes based on race and gender. The social and cultural diversity of American societies challenged their ability to achieve cultural cohesion as well as political unity and democratically inclusive states. The lingering legacies of European conquest, slavery, migration, and patriarchy highlighted contradictions between the Enlightenment ideals of freedom and equality and the realities of life for native and African-American peoples, as well as recent migrants and women. American societies experienced ample strife in the age of independence. In efforts to maintain their own position and preserve social stability, the dominant political forces in the Americas often repressed demands for recognition by dispossessed groups.

Multicultural Society in the United States

By the late nineteenth century, the United States had become a boisterous multicultural society—the most culturally diverse land of the western hemisphere—whose population included indigenous peoples, Euro-American settlers, African-American laborers, and growing numbers of migrants from Europe and Asia. Walt Whitman described the United States as "not merely a nation but a teeming nation of nations." Yet political and economic power rested almost exclusively with white male elites of British and European ancestry. The United States experienced tension and occasional conflict as members of various constituencies worked for dignity, prosperity, and a voice in society. During the nineteenth century cultural and social tension swirled especially around indigenous peoples, African-American slaves and their descendants, women, and migrants.

Native Peoples

As they expanded to the west, Euro-American settlers and ranchers pushed indigenous peoples onto reservations. While promising to respect these lands, the U.S. government permitted settlers and railroads to encroach on the reservations and force native peoples into increasingly cramped and marginal territories. Meanwhile, the government tried to persuade indigenous peoples to join the larger society as farmers and small landowners. This policy was a complete failure, however, since most native peoples of the west came from seminomadic societies. They had little experience with settled agriculture or irrigation, nor did they have promising lands to cultivate in any case. Native peoples on the reservations lived in poverty and depended on the government to provide rudimentary education and health care. Those who left the reservations faced hostility as they sought to make a living in a society dominated by Euro-American peoples. With little education and limited understanding of Euro-American society, native peoples mostly found employment at low wages in mines or factories, and they often lived in poverty and under the suspicion of government authorities in the cities of North America.

Freed Slaves

The Civil War ended slavery, but it did not bring about instant equality for freed slaves and their African-American descendants. In an effort to establish a place for freed slaves in American society, northern forces sent armies of occupation to the southern states and forced them to undergo a program of social and political Reconstruction (1867–1877). They extended civil rights to freed slaves and provided black men with voting rights. Black and white citizens in southern states elected biracial governments for the first time in U.S. history, and freed slaves participated actively in the political affairs of the republic.

After Reconstruction, however, the armies of occupation went back north, and a violent backlash soon dismantled the reforms of Reconstruction. Freed slaves had not received land grants or any other means of economic support, so many had to work as sharecroppers for former slaveowners. Under these circumstances it was relatively easy for white southerners to take away the political and civil liberties that former slaves had gained under Reconstruction. By the turn of the century, U.S. blacks faced

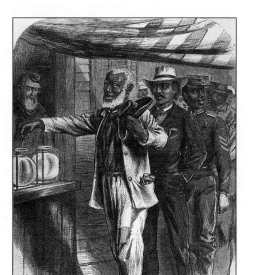

A lithograph from *Harper's Weekly* after the Civil War. An artisan, a middle-class African-American, and a black Union soldier are in the process of voting, perhaps for the first time in their lives.

• Corbis-Bettmann

THE MEANING OF FREEDOM FOR AN EX-SLAVE

• • •

Even before the conclusion of the Civil War brought slavery to an end in the United States, Jourdan Anderson had taken the opportunity to run away and claim his freedom. After the war his former master, Colonel P. H. Anderson, wrote a letter asking him to return to work on his Tennessee plantation. In responding from his new home in Dayton, Ohio, Anderson respectfully referred to the colonel as "my old master" and addressed him as "sir." Yet Anderson's letter makes it clear that his family's freedom and welfare were his principal concerns.

I want to know particularly what the good chance is you propose to give me. I am doing tolerably well here; I get $25 a month, with victuals and clothing; have a comfortable home for Mandy (the folks here call her Mrs. Anderson), and the children, Milly, Jane and Grundy, go to school and are learning well; the teacher says Grundy has a head for a preacher. They go to Sunday-School, and Mandy and me attend church regularly. We are kindly treated; sometimes we overhear others saying, "Them colored people were slaves" down in Tennessee. The children feel hurt when they hear such remarks, but I tell them it was no disgrace in Tennessee to belong to Col. Anderson. Many darkies would have been proud, as I used to was, to call you master. Now, if you will write and say what wages you will give me, I will be better able to decide whether it would be to my advantage to move back again.

As to my freedom, which you say I can have, there is nothing to be gained on that score, as I got my free-papers in 1864 from the Provost-Marshal-General of the Department at Nashville. Mandy says she would be afraid to go back without some proof that you are sincerely disposed to treat us justly and kindly—and we have concluded to test your sincerity by asking you to send us our wages for the time we served you. This will make us forget and forgive old scores, and rely on your justice and friendship in the future. I served you faithfully for thirty-two years and Mandy twenty years. At $25 a month for me, and $2 a week for Mandy, our earnings would amount to $11,680. Add to this the interest for the time our wages has been kept back and deduct what you paid for our clothing and three doctor's visits to me, and pulling a tooth for Mandy, and the balance will show what we are in justice entitled to. Please send the money by Adams Express, in care of V. Winters, esq, Dayton, Ohio. If you fail to pay us for faithful labors in the past we can have little faith in your promises in the future. We trust the good Maker has opened your eyes to the wrongs which you and your fathers have done to me and my fathers, in making us toil for you for generations without recompense. Here I draw my wages every Saturday night, but in Tennessee there was never any pay day for the negroes any more than for the horses and cows. Surely there will be a day of reckoning for those who defraud the laborer of his hire.

In answering this letter please state if there would be any safety for my Milly and Jane, who are now grown up and both good-looking girls. You know how it was with poor Matilda and Catherine. I would rather stay here and starve and die if it comes to that than have my girls brought to shame by the violence and wickedness of their young masters. You will also please state if there has been any schools opened for the colored children in your neighborhood, the great desire of my life now is to give my children an education, and have them form virtuous habits.

SOURCE: Leon F. Litwack, *Been in the Storm So Long: The Aftermath of Slavery* (New York: Knopf, 1979), pp. 334–335.

violence and intimidation when they tried to vote. Southern states fashioned a rigidly segregated society that deprived the African-American population of educational, economic, and political opportunities. Although freedom was better than slavery, it was far different from the hopeful visions of the slaves who had won their emancipation.

Even before the Civil War, a small but growing women's movement had emerged in the United States. At the Seneca Falls Convention in 1848, feminists issued a "declaration of sentiments" modeled on the Declaration of Independence— "We hold these truths to be self-evident: that all men and women are created equal"—and they demanded equal political and economic rights for U.S. women:

Women

> Now, in view of this entire disenfranchisement of one-half the people of this country, their social and religious degradation—in view of the unjust laws above mentioned, and because women do feel themselves aggrieved, oppressed, and fraudulently deprived of their most sacred rights, we insist that they have immediate admission to all the rights and privileges which belong to them as citizens of the United States.

Women fought for equal rights throughout the nineteenth century, and new opportunities for education and employment offered alternatives to marriage and domesticity. Women's colleges, reform activism, and professional industrial jobs allowed some women to pursue careers over marriage. Yet meaningful economic and political opportunities for women awaited the twentieth century.

Between 1840 and 1914 some twenty-five million European migrants landed on American shores, and in the late nineteenth century most of them hailed from southern and eastern European countries. Migrants introduced new foods, music, dances, holidays, sports, and languages to U.S. society and contributed to the cultural diversity of the western hemisphere. Yet white, native-born citizens of the United States began to feel swamped by the arrival of so many migrants. Distaste for foreigners often

Migrants

This photograph from the late nineteenth century captures the busy street life in San Francisco's Chinatown. Migrants flocked to urban centers and created ethnic enclaves like Chinatown for comfort and protection, transforming the urban landscapes of the Americas in the process. • California Historical Society, San Francisco. FIN-23115

resulted in hostility to the migrants who flooded into the expanding industrial cities. Migrants and their families tended to concentrate in certain districts such as Little Italy and Chinatown—partly out of choice, since they preferred neighbors with familiar cultural traditions, but partly also because native-born citizens discouraged the migrants from moving into other neighborhoods. Concerns about growing numbers of migrants with different cultural and social traditions eventually led to the exclusion of new arrivals from Asian lands: the U.S. government ordered a complete halt to migration from China in 1882 and Japan in 1908.

Canadian Cultural Contrasts

Ethnic Diversity   British and French settlers each viewed themselves as Canada's founding people. This cleavage, which profoundly influenced Canadian political development, masked much greater cultural and ethnic diversity in Canada. French and British settlers displaced the indigenous peoples, who remain a significant minority of Canada's population today. Slavery likewise left a mark on Canada. Slavery was legal in the British empire until 1833, and many early settlers brought their slaves to Canada. After the 1830s escaped slaves from the United States also reached Canada by way of the Underground Railroad. Blacks in Canada were free but not equal, segregated and isolated from the political and cultural mainstream. Chinese migrants also came to Canada: lured by gold rushes like the Fraser River rush of 1858 and by opportunities to work on the Canadian Pacific Railway in the 1880s, Chinese migrants lived mostly in segregated Chinatowns in the cities of British Columbia, and like blacks they had little voice in public affairs. In the late nineteenth and early twentieth centuries, waves of migrants brought even greater ethnic diversity to Canada. Between 1896 and 1914 three million migrants from Britain, the United States, and eastern Europe arrived in Canada.

Despite the heterogeneity of Canada's population, communities descended from British and French settlers dominated Canadian society, and conflict between the two communities was the most prominent source of ethnic tension throughout the nineteenth and twentieth centuries. After 1867, as British Canadians led the effort to settle the Northwest Territories and incorporate them into the Dominion, frictions between the two groups intensified. Westward expansion brought British Canadian settlers and cultivators in conflict with French Canadian fur traders and lumberjacks. The fur traders in particular often lived on the margins between European and indigenous societies. They frequently married or consorted with native women, giving rise to the *métis*, individuals of mixed European and indigenous ancestry.

The Métis *and Louis Riel*   A major outbreak of civil strife took place in the 1870s and 1880s. Native peoples and métis had moved west throughout the nineteenth century to preserve their land and trading rights, but the drive of British Canadians to the west threatened them. Louis Riel (1844–1885) emerged as the leader of the métis and indigenous peoples of western Canada. A métis himself, Riel abandoned his studies for the priesthood in Montreal and returned to his home in the Red River Settlement (in the southern part of modern Manitoba). Sensitive to his community's concern that the Canadian government threatened local land rights, Riel assumed the presidency of a provisional government in 1870. He led his troops in capturing Fort Garry (modern Winnipeg) and negotiated the incorporation of the province of Manitoba into the Canadian Dominion. Canadian government officials and troops soon outlawed his government and forced Riel into years of exile, during which he wandered through the United States and Quebec, even suffering confinement in asylums.

Work on the Canadian Pacific Railroad in the 1880s renewed the threat of white settlement to indigenous and métis society. The métis asked Riel to lead resistance to the railroad and British Canadian settlement. In 1885 he organized a military force of métis and native peoples in Saskatchewan and led an insurrection known as the Northwest Rebellion. The Royal Northwest Mounted Police quickly subdued the makeshift army, and government authorities executed Riel for treason.

Although the Northwest Rebellion never had a chance of success, the execution of Riel nonetheless reverberated throughout Canadian history. French Canadians took it as an indication of the state's readiness to subdue individuals who were culturally distinct and politically opposed to the drive for a nation dominated by British Canadian elites. In the very year when completion of the transcontinental railroad signified for some the beginnings of Canadian national unity, Riel's execution foreshadowed a long term of cultural conflict between Canadians of British, French, and indigenous ancestry.

Ethnicity, Identity, and Gender in Latin America

The heritage of Spanish and Portuguese colonialism and the legacy of slavery inclined Latin American societies toward the establishment of hierarchical distinctions based on ethnicity and color. At the top of society stood the creoles, individuals of European ancestry born in the Americas, while indigenous peoples, freed slaves, and their black descendants occupied the lowest rungs of the social ladder. In between were various groups of mixed ancestry, such as mestizos, mulattoes, zambos, and castizos. Although most Latin American states ended the legal recognition of these groups, the distinctions themselves persisted after independence and limited the opportunities available to peoples of indigenous, African, or mixed ancestry.

Migration and Cultural Diversity

Large-scale migration brought cultural diversity to Latin America in the nineteenth century. Indentured laborers who went from Asian lands to Peru, Brazil, Cuba, and other Caribbean destinations carried a great deal of cultural baggage. When their numbers were relatively small, as in the case of Chinese migrants to Cuba, they mostly intermarried and assimilated into the working classes without leaving much foreign influence on the societies they joined. When they were relatively more numerous, however, as in the case of Indian migrants to Trinadad and Tobago, they formed distinctive communities in which they spoke their native languages, prepared foods from their homelands, and observed their inherited cultural and social traditions. Migration of European workers to Argentina brought a lively diversity to the capital of Buenos Aires, which was perhaps the most cosmopolitan city of nineteenth-century Latin America. With its broad avenues, smart boutiques, and handsome buildings graced with wrought iron, Buenos Aires enjoyed a reputation as "the Paris of the Americas."

Latin American intellectuals seeking cultural identity usually saw themselves either as heirs of Europe or as products of the American environment. An eloquent spokesman who identified with Europe was the Argentine president Domingo Faustino Sarmiento (1811–1888). Sarmiento despised the rule of caudillos that had emerged after independence and worked for the development of a liberal and progressive society based on European values. In his widely read book *Facundo: Civilization and Barbarism* (1845), Sarmiento argued that it was necessary for Buenos Aires to bring discipline to the disorderly Argentine countryside. Deeply influenced by the Enlightenment, he characterized books, ideas, law, education, and art as products of cities, and he argued that only when cities dominated the countryside would social stability and genuine liberty be possible.

Gauchos

Sarmiento admired the bravery and independence of Argentina's *gauchos* (cowboys), but he considered it imperative that urban residents rather than ranchers make society's crucial decisions. Others took gauchos almost as a symbol of Latin American identity. Most gauchos were mestizos or castizos, but there were also white and black gauchos. For all intents and purposes, anyone who adopted gaucho ways became a gaucho, and gaucho society acquired an ethnic egalitarianism rarely found elsewhere in Latin America. Gauchos were most prominent in the Argentine pampas, but their cultural practices linked them to the cowboys, or *vaqueros,* found throughout the Americas. As pastoralists herding cattle and horses on the pampas, gauchos stood apart from both the indigenous peoples and the growing urban and agricultural elites who gradually displaced them with large land holdings and cattle ranches that spread to the pampas.

The gauchos led independent and self-sufficient lives that appealed broadly in hierarchical Latin American society. Gauchos lived off their own skills and needed only their horses to survive. They dressed distinctively, with sashed trousers, ponchos, and boots. Countless songs and poems lauded their courage, skills, and love-making bravado. Yet independence and caudillo rule disrupted gaucho life as the cowboys increasingly entered armies, either voluntarily or under compulsion, and as settled agriculture and ranches surrounded by barbed wire enclosed the pampas. The gauchos did not leave the pampas without resistance. The poet José Hernandez offered a romanticized vision of the gaucho life and protested its decline in his epic poem *The Gaucho Martín Fierro* (1873). Hernandez conveyed the pride of gauchos, particularly those who resisted assimilation to Euro-American society, by having Martín Fierro proclaim his independence and assert his intention to stay that way:

> I owe nothin' to nobody;
> I don't ask for shelter, or give it;
> and from now on, nobody
> better try to lead me around by a rope.

Nevertheless, by the late nineteenth century, gauchos were more symbols of Latin American identity than makers of a viable society.

Male Domination

Even more than in the United States and Canada, male domination was a central characteristic of Latin American society in the nineteenth century. Women could not vote or hold office, nor could they work or manage estates without permission from their male guardians. In rural areas women were liable to rough treatment and assault by gauchos and other men steeped in the values of *machismo*—a social ethic that honored male strength, courage, aggressiveness, assertiveness, and cunning. A few women voiced their discontent with male domination and machismo. In her poem "To Be Born a Man" (1887), for example, the Bolivian poet Adela Zamudio lamented bitterly that talented women could not vote, but ignorant men could, just by learning how to sign their names. Although Latin American lands did not generate a strong women's movement, they did begin to expand educational opportunities for girls and young women after the mid-nineteenth century. In large cities most girls received some formal schooling, and women usually filled teaching positions in the public schools that proliferated throughout Latin America in the late nineteenth century.

After gaining independence from European colonial powers, the states of the western hemisphere worked to build stable and prosperous societies. The independent American states faced difficult challenges—including vast territories, diverse populations, social tensions, and cultural differences—as they sought to construct viable societies on the Enlightenment principles of freedom, equality, and constitutional government. The United States and Canada built large federal societies in North America, whereas a series of smaller states governed affairs in Latin America. The United States in particular was an expansive society that absorbed Texas, California, and the northern territories of Mexico while extending its authority from the Atlantic to the Pacific Ocean. Throughout the hemisphere descendants of European settlers subdued indigenous American peoples and built societies dominated by Euro-American peoples. They established agricultural economies, exploited natural resources, and in some lands launched processes of industrialization. They accepted streams of European and Asian migrants, who contributed to American cultural diversity. All American lands experienced tensions arising from social, economic, cultural, and ethnic differences, which led occasionally to violent civil conflict and often to smoldering resentments and grievances. The making of independent American societies was not a smooth process, but it reflected the increasing interdependence of all the world's peoples.

CHRONOLOGY

1803	Louisiana Purchase
1804–1806	Lewis and Clark expedition
1812–1814	War of 1812
1835–1852	Rule of Juan Manuel de Rosas in Argentina
1837–1838	Trail of Tears
1845–1848	Mexican-American War
1848	Seneca Falls Convention
1849	California gold rush
1850s	*La Reforma* in Mexico
1861–1865	U.S. Civil War
1867	Establishment of the Dominion of Canada
1867–1877	Reconstruction in the United States
1869	Completion of the transcontinental railroad line in the United States
1876	Battle of Little Big Horn
1876–1911	Rule of Porfirio Díaz in Mexico
1885	Completion of the Canadian Pacific Railroad
1885	Northwest Rebellion
1890	Massacre at Wounded Knee
1911–1920	Mexican revolution

FOR FURTHER READING

Fernando Henrique Cardoso and Enzo Faletto. *Dependency and Development in Latin America*. Berkeley, 1979. A sophisticated treatment of economic development in Latin America.

William Cronon. *Nature's Metropolis: Chicago and the Great West*. New York, 1991. A valuable study exploring the role of Chicago in the economic development of the American west.

Tulio Halperín Donghi. *The Contemporary History of Latin America*. Trans. by J. C. Chasteen. Durham, 1993. An influential general history of Latin America from a Latin American point of view.

Ellen C. DuBois. *Feminism and Suffrage: The Emergence of an Independent Women's Movement in America, 1848–1869*. Ithaca, 1984. Traces the rise and character of the U.S. women's movement in the nineteenth century.

Stephen F. Haber. *Industry and Underdevelopment: The Industrialization of Mexico, 1890–1940*. Stanford, 1989. Using Mexico as a test case, the author argues that export-oriented economies did not preclude significant industrialization in Latin America.

Alan Knight. *The Mexican Revolution*. Cambridge, 1986. An excellent analysis of the Mexican Revolution.

Patricia Nelson Limerick. *The Legacy of Conquest: The Unbroken Past of the American West*. New York, 1987. A provocative work exploring the influences of race, class, and gender in the conquest of the American west.

Leon F. Litwack. *Been in the Storm So Long: The Aftermath of Slavery*. New York, 1979. The best study of the promises and perils of life for freed slaves after the U.S. Civil War.

James M. McPherson. *Battle Cry of Freedom: The Civil War Era*. New York, 1988. A balanced account of the Civil War by a renowned scholar.

J. R. Miller. *Skyscrapers Hide the Heavens: A History of Indian-White Relations in Canada*. Toronto, 1989. An important study of Canadian policies toward indigenous peoples.

Walter Nugent. *Crossings: The Great Transatlantic Migrations, 1870–1914*. Bloomington, 1992. Provides an overview and analysis of the mass migrations to North America in the nineteenth and twentieth centuries.

Ronald Takaki. *A Different Mirror: A History of Multicultural America*. Boston, 1993. A spirited account of the contributions made by peoples of European, African, Asian, and native American ancestry to the modern American society.

——. *Strangers from a Different Shore: A History of Asian Americans*. Boston, 1989. Fascinating survey of the experiences of Asian migrants who came to North America across the Pacific Ocean.

Richard White. *"It's Your Misfortune and None of My Own": A History of the American West*. Norman, Okla., 1991. Surveys the conquest, exploitation, and transformation of the American west.

Donald Worster. *Rivers of Empire: Water, Aridity, and the Growth of the American West*. New York, 1985. Focuses on the role of irrigation in the establishment of a Euro-American agricultural society in the arid west.

SOCIETIES AT CROSSROADS

. . .

Hong Xiuquan, the third son of a poor family, grew up in a farming village in southern China about fifty kilometers (thirty-one miles) from Guangzhou. Although he was arrogant and irritable, he showed intellectual promise. His neighbors made him village teacher so he could study and prepare for the civil service examinations, the principal avenue to government employment, since a position in the Qing bureaucracy would bring honor and wealth to both his family and his village. Between 1828 and 1837 Hong took the exams three times but failed to obtain even the lowest degree. This outcome was not surprising, since thousands of candidates competed for a degree, which only a few obtained. Yet the disappointment was too much for Hong. He suffered an emotional collapse, lapsed into a delirium that lasted about forty days, and experienced visions.

Upon recovering from his breakdown, Hong resumed his position as village teacher. After failing the civil service examinations a fourth time in 1843, he began studying the works of a Chinese missionary who explained the basic elements of Christianity. As he pondered the religious tracts, Hong came to believe that during his illness he had visited heaven and learned from God that he was the younger brother of Jesus Christ. He believed further that God had revealed to him that his destiny was to reform China and pave the way for the heavenly kingdom. Inspired by these convictions, Hong baptized himself and worked to build a community of disciples.

Hong's personal religious vision soon evolved into a political program: Hong believed that God had charged him with the establishment of a new order, one that necessitated the destruction of the Qing dynasty that had ruled China since 1644. In 1847 he joined the Society of God Worshipers, a religious group recently founded by disgruntled peasants and miners. Hong soon emerged as the group's guiding force, and in the summer of 1850 he led about ten thousand followers in rebellion against the Qing dynasty. On his thirty-seventh birthday, 11 January 1851, he assumed the title of "Heavenly King" and proclaimed his own dynasty, the *Taiping tianguo* ("Heavenly Kingdom of Great Peace"). Hong's followers, known as the Taipings, quickly grew from a ragtag band to a disciplined and zealous army of over one million men and women who pushed the Qing dynasty to the brink of extinction.

China was not the only land that faced serious difficulties in the nineteenth century: the Ottoman empire, the Russian empire, and Tokugawa Japan experienced problems similar to those of China during the late Qing dynasty. One problem

Japanese women wearing European-style clothes learn to play European musical instruments in the Meiji era. • Laurie Platt Winfrey, Inc.

common to the four societies was military weakness that left them vulnerable to foreign threats. The Ottoman, Russian, Qing, and Tokugawa armies all fought wars or engaged in military confrontations with the industrial lands of western Europe and the United States, and all discovered suddenly and unexpectedly that they were militarily much weaker than the industrial powers. European lands occasionally seized territories outright and either absorbed them into their own possessions or ruled them as colonies. More often, however, European and U.S. forces used their power to force concessions out of militarily weak societies. They won rights for European and U.S. businesses to seek opportunities on favorable terms and enabled industrial capitalists to realize huge profits from trade and investment in militarily weak societies.

Another problem common to the four societies was internal weakness due to population pressure, declining agricultural productivity, famine, falling government revenue, and corruption at all levels of government. Ottoman, Russian, Chinese, and Japanese societies all experienced serious domestic turmoil especially during the second half of the nineteenth century, as peasants mounted rebellions, dissidents struggled for reform, and political factions fought among themselves or conspired to organize coups. Military weakness often left leaders of the four societies unable to respond effectively to domestic strife, which sometimes provided western European powers and the United States with an excuse to intervene in order to protect their business interests.

Thus by the late nineteenth century, the Ottoman empire, the Russian empire, Qing China, and Tokugawa Japan were societies at crossroads. Unless they undertook a program of thoroughgoing political, social, and economic reform, they would continue to experience domestic difficulties and would grow progressively weaker in relation to industrial lands. Reformers in all four societies promoted plans to introduce written constitutions, limit the authority of rulers, make governments responsive to the needs and desires of the people, guarantee equality before the law, restructure educational systems, and begin processes of industrialization. Many reformers had traveled in Europe and the United States, where they experienced constitutional government and industrial society at first hand, and they sought to remodel their own societies along the lines of the industrial lands.

Vigorous reform movements emerged in all four lands, but they had very different results. In the Ottoman empire, the Russian empire, and Qing China, ruling elites and wealthy classes viewed reform warily and opposed any changes that might threaten their status. Reform in these three lands was halting, tentative, and sometimes abortive, and by the early twentieth century, the Ottoman, Romanov, and Qing dynasties were on the verge of collapse. In Japan, however, the Tokugawa dynasty fell and so was unable to resist change. Reform there was much more thorough than in the other lands, and by the early twentieth century, Japan was an emerging industrial power poised to expand its influence in the larger world.

THE OTTOMAN EMPIRE IN DECLINE

During the eighteenth century the Ottoman empire experienced military reverses and challenges to its rule. By the early nineteenth century, the Ottoman state could no longer ward off European economic penetration or prevent territorial dismemberment. As Ottoman officials launched reforms to regenerate imperial vigor, Egypt and other north African provinces declared their independence, and European states seized territories in the northern and western parts of the Ottoman empire. At the same time pressure from ethnic, religious, and nationalist groups threatened to fragment the polyglot empire. The once powerful realm slipped into decline, its sovereignty maintained largely by the same European powers who exploited its economy.

The Nature of Decline

By the late seventeenth century, the Ottoman empire had reached the limits of its expansion. Ottoman armies suffered humiliating defeats on the battlefield, especially at the hands of Austrian and Russian foes. Ottoman forces lagged behind European armies in strategy, tactics, weaponry, and training. Equally serious was a breakdown in the discipline of the elite Janissary corps, which had served as the backbone of the imperial armed forces since the fifteenth century. The Janissaries neglected their military training and turned a blind eye to advances in weapons technology. As its military capacity declined, the Ottoman realm became vulnerable to its more powerful neighbors.

Military Decline

Loss of military power translated into declining effectiveness of the central government, which was losing power in the provinces to its own officials. By the early nineteenth century, semi-independent governors and local notables formed private armies of mercenaries and slaves to support the sultan in Istanbul in return for recognition of autonomy. Increasingly these independent rulers also turned fiscal and administrative institutions to their own interests, collecting taxes for themselves and sending only nominal payments to the imperial treasury, thus depriving the central state of revenue.

The Ottoman government managed to maintain its authority in Anatolia and Iraq, the heart of the empire, but it suffered serious territorial losses elsewhere. Russian forces took over poorly defended territories in the Caucasus and central Asia, and the Austrian empire nibbled away at the western frontiers. Nationalist uprisings forced Ottoman rulers to recognize the independence of Balkan provinces, notably Greece (1830) and Serbia (1867).

Territorial Losses

Most significant, however, was the loss of Egypt. In 1798 the ambitious French general Napoleon invaded Egypt in hopes of using it as a springboard for an attack on the British empire in India. His campaign was a miserable failure: Napoleon had to abandon his army and sneak back to France, where he worked to consolidate the French revolution. But the invasion sparked turmoil in Egypt, as local elites battled to seize power after Napoleon's departure. The ultimate victor was the energetic general Muhammad Ali, who built a powerful army modeled on European forces and ruled Egypt from 1805 to 1848. He drafted peasants to serve as infantrymen, and he hired French and Italian officers to train his troops. He also launched a program of industrialization, concentrating on cotton textiles and armaments. Although he remained nominally subordinate to the Ottoman sultan, by 1820 he had established himself as the effective ruler of Egypt, which was the most powerful land in the Muslim world. He even invaded Syria and Anatolia, threatening to capture Istanbul and topple the Ottoman state. Indeed, the Ottoman dynasty survived only because British forces intervened out of fear that Ottoman collapse would result in a sudden and dangerous expansion of Russian influence. Nevertheless, Muhammad Ali made Egypt an essentially autonomous region within the Ottoman empire.

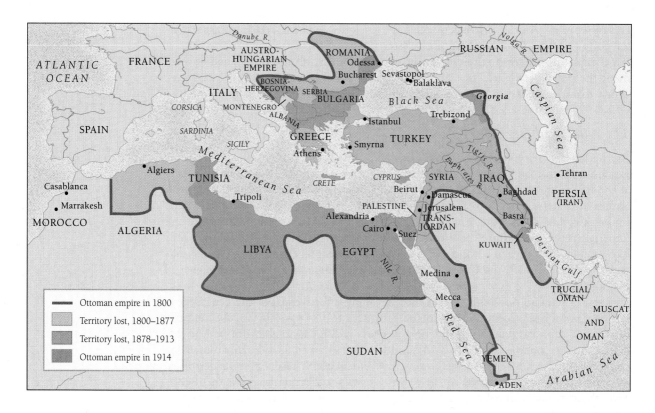

MAP [32.1]

Decline of the
Ottoman empire.

*Economic
Difficulties*

Economic ills aggravated the military and political problems of the Ottoman state. The volume of trade passing through the Ottoman empire declined throughout the later seventeenth and eighteenth centuries, as European merchants increasingly circumvented Ottoman middlemen and traded directly with their counterparts in India and China. By the eighteenth century the focus of European trade had shifted to the Atlantic Ocean basin, where the Ottomans had no presence at all.

Meanwhile, as European producers became more efficient in the eighteenth and nineteenth centuries, their textiles and manufactured goods began to flow into the Ottoman empire. Since they were inexpensive and high-quality products, they placed considerable pressure on Ottoman artisans and craftsmen, who frequently led urban riots to protest foreign imports. Ottoman exports consisted largely of raw materials such as grain, raw cotton, hemp, indigo, and opium, but they did not offset the value of imported European manufactures. Gradually, the Ottoman empire moved toward fiscal insolvency and financial dependency. After the middle of the nineteenth century, economic development in the Ottoman empire depended heavily on foreign loans, as European capital financed the construction of railroads, utilities, and mining enterprises. Interest payments grew to the point that they consumed more than half of the empire's revenues. In 1882 the Ottoman state was unable to pay interest on its loans and had no choice but to accept foreign administration of its debts.

The Capitulations

Nothing symbolized foreign influence more than the capitulations, agreements that exempted European visitors from Ottoman law and provided European powers with extraterritoriality—the right to exercise jurisdiction over their own citizens according to their own laws. The practice dated back to the sixteenth century, when Ottoman sultans signed capitulation treaties to avoid the burden of administering justice for communities of foreign merchants. By the nineteenth century, however,

Ottoman officials regarded the capitulations as humiliating intrusions on their sovereignty. Capitulations also served as instruments of economic penetration by European businessmen who established tax-exempt banks and commercial enterprises in the Ottoman empire, and they permitted foreign governments to levy duties on goods sold in Ottoman ports.

By the early twentieth century, the Ottoman state lacked the resources to maintain its costly bureaucracy. Expenditures exceeded revenues, and the state experienced growing difficulty paying the salaries of its employees in the palace household, the military, and the religious hierarchy. Declining incomes led to reduced morale, recruitment difficulties, and a rise in corruption. Increased taxation designed to offset revenue losses only led to increased exploitation of the peasantry and a decline in agricultural production. The Ottoman empire was ailing, and it needed a major restructuring to survive.

Reform and Reorganization

In response to recurring and deepening crises, Ottoman leaders launched a series of reforms designed to strengthen and preserve the state. Reform efforts began as early as the seventeenth century, when sultans sought to limit taxation, increase agricultural production, and end official corruption. Reform continued in the eighteenth century, as Sultan Selim III (reigned 1789–1807) embarked on a program to remodel his army along the lines of European forces. But the establishment of a new crack fighting force, trained by European instructors and equipped with modern weapons, threatened the elite Janissary corps, which reacted violently by rising in revolt, killing the new troops, and locking up the sultan. When Selim's successor tried to revive the new military force, rampaging Janissaries killed all male members of the dynasty save one, Selim's cousin Mahmud II, who became sultan (reigned 1808–1839).

The encroachment of European powers and the separatist ambitions of local rulers convinced Mahmud to launch his own reform program. Politically savvy, Mahmud ensured that his reforms were perceived not as dangerous infidel innovations, but rather as a restoration of the traditional Ottoman military. Nevertheless, his proposal for a new European-style army in 1826 brought him into conflict with the Janissaries. When the Janissaries mutinied in protest, Mahmud had them massacred by troops loyal to the sultan. This incident cleared the way for a series of reforms that unfolded during the last thirteen years of Mahmud's reign.

The Reforms of Mahmud II

Mahmud's program remodeled Ottoman institutions along western European lines. Highest priority went to the creation of a more effective army. European drill masters dressed Ottoman soldiers in European-style uniforms and instructed them in European weapons and tactics. Before long Ottoman recruits studied at military and engineering schools that taught European curricula. Mahmud's reforms went beyond military affairs. His government created a system of secondary education for boys to facilitate the transition from mosque schools, which provided most primary education, to newly established scientific, technical, and military academies. Mahmud also tried to transfer power from traditional elites to the sultan and his cabinet by taxing rural landlords, abolishing the system of military land grants, and undermining the *ulama,* the Islamic leadership. To make his authority more effective, the sultan established European-style ministries, constructed new roads, built telegraph lines, and inaugurated a postal service. By the time of Mahmud's death in 1839, the Ottoman empire had shrunk in size, but it was also more consolidated and powerful than it had been since the early seventeenth century.

Legal and Educational Reform

Continuing defeats on the battlefield and the rise of separatist movements among subject peoples prompted the ruling classes to undertake more radical restructuring of the Ottoman state. The tempo of reform increased rapidly during the *Tanzimat* ("reorganization") era (1839–1876). Once again, the army was a principal target of reform efforts, but legal and educational reforms also had wide-ranging implications for Ottoman society. In designing their program, Tanzimat reformers drew considerable inspiration from Enlightenment thought and the constitutional foundations of western European states.

Tanzimat reformers attacked Ottoman law with the aim of making it acceptable to Europeans so they could have the capitulations lifted and recover Ottoman sovereignty. Using the French legal system as a guide, reformers promulgated a commercial code (1850), a penal code (1858), a maritime code (1863), and a new civil code (1870–76). Tanzimat reformers also issued decrees designed to safeguard the rights of subjects. Key among them were measures that guaranteed public trials, rights of privacy, and equality before the law for all Ottoman subjects, whether Muslim or not. Matters pertaining to marriage and divorce still fell under religious law. But because state courts administered the new laws, legal reform undermined the *ulama* and enhanced the authority of the Ottoman state. Educational reforms also undermined the *ulama,* who controlled religious education for Muslims. A comprehensive plan for educational reform, introduced in 1846, provided for a complete system of primary and secondary schools leading to university-level instruction, all under the supervision of the state ministry of education. A still more ambitious plan, inaugurated in 1869, provided for free and compulsory primary education.

Opposition to the Tanzimat

Although reform and reorganization strengthened Ottoman society, the Tanzimat provoked spirited opposition from several distinct quarters. Harsh criticism came from religious conservatives, who argued that reformers posed a threat to the empire's Islamic foundation. Many devout Muslims viewed the extension of legal equality to Jews and Christians as an act contrary to the basic principles of Islamic law. Even some minority leaders opposed legal equality, fearing that it would diminish their own position as intermediaries between their communities and the Ottoman state. Criticism arose also from a group known collectively as the Young Ottomans. Although they did not share a common political or religious program—their views ranged from secular revolution to Islamic fundamentalism—Young Ottomans agitated for individual freedom, local autonomy, and political decentralization. Many Young Ottomans desired the establishment of a constitutional government along the lines of the British system. A fourth and perhaps the most dangerous critique of Tanzimat emerged from within the Ottoman bureaucracy itself. In part because of their exclusion from power, high-level bureaucrats were determined to impose checks on the sultan's power by forcing him to accept a constitution and if necessary even to depose the ruler.

The Young Turk Era

Reform and Repression

In 1876 a group of radical dissidents from the Ottoman bureaucracy seized power in a coup, formed a cabinet that included partisans of reform, and installed Abd al-Hamid II as sultan (reigned 1876–1909). Convinced of the need to check the sultan's power, reformers persuaded Abd al-Hamid to accept a constitution that limited his authority and established a representative government. Within a year, however, the sultan suspended the constitution, dissolved parliament, exiled many liberals, and executed others. For thirty years he ruled autocratically in an effort to rescue the empire from dismemberment by European powers. He continued to develop the army and administration according to Tanzimat principles, and he oversaw the formation of a police force, educational reforms, economic development, and the construction of railroads.

Sultan Abd al-Hamid II ruled the Ottoman empire from 1876 to 1909, when the Young Turks deposed him and sent him into exile. • Hulton Getty/Liaison Agency

Abd al-Hamid's despotic rule generated many liberal opposition groups. While intended to strengthen the state, reform and reorganization actually undermined the position of the sultan. As Ottoman bureaucrats and army officers received an education in European curricula, they not only learned modern science and technology but also became acquainted with European political, social, and cultural traditions. Many of them fell out of favor with Abd al-Hamid and spent years in exile, where they experienced European society firsthand. Educated subjects came to believe that the biggest problem of the Ottoman empire was the political structure that vested unchecked power in the sultan. For these dissidents Ottoman society was in dire need of political reform and especially of a written constitution that defined and limited the sultan's power.

The most active dissident organization was the Ottoman Society for Union and Progress, better known as the Young Turk Party, although many of its members were neither young nor Turkish. Founded in 1889 by exiled Ottoman subjects living in Paris, the Young Turk Party vigorously promoted reform, and its members made effective use of recently established newspapers to spread their message. Young Turks called for universal suffrage, equality before the law, freedom of religion, free public education, secularization of the state, and the emancipation of women. In 1908 the Young Turks inspired an army coup that forced Abd al-Hamid to restore parliament and the constitution of 1876. In 1909 they dethroned him and established Mehmed V Rashid (reigned 1909–1918) as a puppet sultan. Throughout the Young Turk era (1908–1918), Ottoman sultans reigned but no longer ruled.

The Young Turks

PROCLAMATION OF THE YOUNG TURKS

• • •

Beginning in the 1890s the Ottoman Society for Union and Progress, better known as the Young Turk Party, started agitating for the resignation of the Ottoman sultan Abd al-Hamid and the restoration of the constitution of 1876. After years of underground activity, the Young Turks forced the sultan to reestablish a parliamentary government and reinstate the constitution in 1908. Shortly thereafter the Young Turks outlined their plans for a new Turkish state.

1. The basis for the Constitution will be respect for the predominance of the national will. One of the consequences of this principle will be to require without delay the responsibility of the minister before the Chamber, and, consequently, to consider the minister as having resigned, when he does not have a majority of the votes of the Chamber.

2. Provided that the number of senators does not exceed one third the number of deputies, the Senate will be named (which is not provided for in article 62 of the Constitution) as follows: one third by the Sultan and two thirds by the nation, and the term of senators will be of limited duration.

3. It will be demanded that all Ottoman subjects having completed their twentieth year, regardless of whether they possess property or fortune, shall have the right to vote. Those who have lost their civil rights will naturally be deprived of this right.

4. It will be demanded that the right freely to constitute political groups be inserted in a precise fashion in the constitutional charter, in order that article 1 of the Constitution of 1293 (1876) be respected. . . .

7. The Turkish tongue will remain the official state language. Official correspondence and discussion will take place in Turk. . . .

9. Every citizen will enjoy complete liberty and equality, regardless of nationality or religion, and be submitted to the same obligations. All Ottomans, being equal before the law as regards rights and duties relative to the State, are eligible for government posts, according to their individual capacity and their education. Non-Muslims will be equally liable to the military law.

10. The free exercise of the religious privileges which have been accorded to different nationalities will remain intact. . . .

14. Provided that the property rights of landholders are not infringed upon (for such rights must be respected and must remain intact, according to the law), it will be proposed that peasants be permitted to acquire land, and they will be accorded means to borrow money at a moderate rate. . . .

16. Education will be free. Every Ottoman citizen, within the limits of the prescriptions of the Constitution, may operate a private school in accordance with the special laws.

17. All schools will operate under the surveillance of the state. In order to obtain for Ottoman citizens an education of a homogeneous and uniform character, the official schools will be open, their instruction will be free, and all nationalities will be admitted. Instruction in Turk will be obligatory in public schools. In official schools, public instruction will be free.

   Secondary and higher education will be given in the public and official schools indicated above; it will use the Turkish tongue as a basis. . . . Schools of commerce, agriculture and industry will be opened with the goal of developing the resources of the country.

SOURCE: Rondo Cameron, ed. *Civilization Since Waterloo: A Book of Source Readings* (Itasca, Ill.: F. E. Peacock, 1971), pp. 245–246.

While pursuing reform within Ottoman society, the Young Turks sought to maintain Turkish hegemony in the larger empire. They worked to make Turkish the official language of the empire, even though many subjects spoke Arabic or a Slavic language as their native tongue. Thus Young Turk policies aggravated tensions between Turkish rulers and subject peoples outside the Anatolian heartland of the Ottoman empire. Syria and Iraq were especially active regions of Arab resistance to Ottoman rule. In spite of their efforts to shore up the ailing empire, reformers could not turn the tide of decline: Ottoman armies continued to lose wars, and subject peoples continued to seek autonomy or independence. By the early twentieth century, the Ottoman empire survived principally because European diplomats could not agree on how to dispose of the empire without upsetting the European balance of power.

Young Turks celebrate the success of their coup, which forced the sultan to establish a constitutional government in 1908.

● Culver Pictures

THE RUSSIAN EMPIRE UNDER PRESSURE

Like the Ottoman empire, the Russian empire experienced battlefield reverses that laid bare the economic and technological disparity between Russia and western European powers. Determined to preserve Russia's status as a great land power, the tsarist government embarked on a program of reform. The keystone of these efforts was the emancipation of the serfs. Social reform paved the way for government-sponsored industrialization, which began to transform Russian society during the last decades of the nineteenth century. Political liberalization did not accompany social and economic reform, as the tsars refused to yield their autocratic powers. The oppressive political environment sparked opposition movements that turned increasingly radical in the late nineteenth century. In the early twentieth century, domestic discontent reached crisis proportions and exploded in revolution.

Military Defeat and Social Reform

The nineteenth-century tsars ruled a multiethnic, multilingual, multicultural empire that stretched from Poland to the Pacific Ocean. Only about half the population spoke the Russian language or observed the Russian Orthodox faith. The Romanov tsars ruled their diverse and sprawling realm through an autocratic regime in which all initiative came from the central administration. The tsars enjoyed the support of the Russian Orthodox church and a powerful class of nobles who owned most of the land and were exempt from taxes and military duty. Peasants made up the vast majority of the population, and most of them were serfs bound to the lands that they cultivated. Serfdom was little more than slavery, but most landowners, including the state, considered it as a guarantee of social stability.

The Crimean War   A respected and feared military power, Russia maintained its tradition of conquest and expansion. During the nineteenth century the Russian empire expanded in three directions: east into Manchuria, south into the Caucasus and central Asia, and southwest toward the Mediterranean. This last thrust led to interference in the Balkan provinces of the Ottoman empire. After defeating Turkish forces in a war of 1828 to 1829, Russia tried to establish a unilateral protectorate over the weakening Ottoman empire. This expansive effort threatened to upset the balance of power in Europe, which led to military conflict between Russia and a coalition including Britain, France, the Kingdom of Sardinia, and the Ottoman empire. The Crimean War (1853–1856) clearly revealed the weakness of the Russian empire, which could hold its own against Ottoman and Qing forces, but not against the industrial powers of western Europe. Unable to mobilize, equip, and transport troops to defeat European forces that operated under a mediocre command, Russian armies suffered devastating defeat. Russia's economy could not support the tsars' expansionist ambitions, and the Crimean War clearly demonstrated the weakness of an agrarian economy based on unfree labor. Military defeat compelled the tsarist autocracy to reevaluate the Russian social order and undertake an extensive restructuring program.

MAP [32.2]

The Russian empire in the nineteenth century.

The key to social reform in Russia was emancipation of the serfs. Opposition to serfdom had grown steadily since the eighteenth century, not only among radicals but also among high officials. While some objected to serfdom on moral grounds, most believed that it had become an obstacle to economic development and a viable state. Besides being economically inefficient, serfdom also was a source of rural instability and peasant revolt: hundreds of insurrections broke out during the first four decades of the nineteenth century. As Tsar Alexander II (reigned 1855–1881) succinctly suggested to the nobility of Moscow, "it is better to abolish serfdom from above than to wait until the serfs begin to liberate themselves from below." Accordingly, in 1861 the tsar abolished the institution of serfdom.

Tsar Alexander II of Russia. After signing the Treaty of Paris in 1856, ending the Crimean War, Alexander abolished serfdom in the Russian empire. • Library of Congress

Emancipation of the Serfs

The government sought to balance the interests of lords and serfs, but on balance the terms of emancipation were unfavorable to most peasants. The government compensated landowners for the loss of their land and the serfs who had worked it. Serfs won their freedom, had their labor obligations gradually canceled, and gained opportunities to become landowners. But the peasants won few political rights, and they had to pay a redemption tax for most of the lands they received. Many disappointed peasants believed that their rulers forced them to pay for land that was theirs by right. A few peasants prospered and improved their position as the result of emancipation, but most remained desperately poor. Emancipation resulted in little if any increase in agricultural production.

Other important reforms came in the wake of the serfs' emancipation. To deal with local issues of health, education, and welfare, the government created elected district assemblies, or *zemstvos,* in 1864. Although all classes, including peasants, elected representatives to these assemblies, the *zemstvos* remained subordinate to the tsarist autocracy, which retained exclusive authority over national issues, and the landowning nobility, which possessed a disproportionately large share of both votes and seats. Legal reform was more fruitful than experimentation with representative government. The revision of the judiciary system in 1864 created a system of law courts based on western European models, replete with independent judges and a system of appellate courts. Legal reforms also instituted trial by jury for criminal offenses and elected justices of the peace who dealt with minor offenses. These reforms encouraged the emergence of attorneys and other legal experts, whose professional standards contributed to a decline in judicial corruption.

Political and Legal Reform

Industrialization

Social and political reform coincided with industrialization in nineteenth-century Russia. Tsar Alexander II emancipated the serfs partly with the intention of creating a mobile labor force for emerging industries, and the tsarist government encouraged industrialization as a way of strengthening the Russian empire. Thus although Russian industrialization took place within a framework of capitalism, it differed from western European industrialization in that the motivation for development was political and military and the driving force was government policy rather than entrepreneurial initiative. Industrialization proceeded slowly at first, but it surged during the last two decades of the nineteenth century.

The Witte System   The prime mover behind Russian industrialization was Count Sergei Witte, minister of finance from 1892 to 1903. His first budget, submitted to the government in 1893, outlined his aims as "removing the unfavorable conditions which hamper the economic development of the country" and "kindling a healthy spirit of enterprise." Availing himself of the full power of the state, Witte implemented policies designed to stimulate economic development. The centerpiece of his industrial policy was a massive program of railway construction, which linked the far-flung regions of the Russian empire and also stimulated the development of other industries. Most important of the new lines was the trans-Siberian railway, which opened Siberia to large-scale settlement, exploitation, and industrialization. To raise domestic capital for industry, Witte remodeled the state bank and encouraged the establishment of savings banks. Witte supported infant industries with high protective tariffs while also securing large foreign loans from western Europe to finance industrialization. His plan worked. French and Belgian capital played a key role in developing the steel and coal industries, and British funds supported the booming petroleum industry in the Caucasus.

Russian merchants in nineteenth-century Novgorod wear both western European and traditional Russian dress while taking tea. • Hulton Getty/Liaison Agency

For a decade the Witte system played a crucial role in the industrialization of Russia, but peasant rebellions and strikes by industrial workers indicated that large segments of the population were unwilling to tolerate the low standard of living that Witte's policy entailed. Recently freed serfs often did not appreciate factory work, which forced them to follow new routines and adapt to the rhythms of industrial machinery. Industrial growth began to generate an urban working class, which endured conditions similar to those experienced by workers in other societies during the early stages of industrialization. Employers kept wages of overworked and poorly housed workers at the barest minimum. The industrial sections of St. Petersburg and Moscow became notorious for the miserable working and living conditions of factory laborers. In 1897 the government limited the maximum working day to 11.5 hours, but this measure did little to alleviate the plight of workers. The government prohibited the formation of trade unions and outlawed strikes, which continued to occur in spite of the restrictions. Economic exploitation and the lack of political freedom made workers increasingly receptive to revolutionary propaganda, and underground movements soon developed among them.

Industrial Discontent

Not everyone was dissatisfied with the results of intensified industrialization. Besides foreign investors, a growing Russian business class benefited from government policy that protected domestic industries and its profits. Russian entrepreneurs reaped rich rewards for their roles in economic development, and they had little complaint with the political system. In contrast to western European capitalists who had both material and ideological reasons to challenge the power of absolute monarchs and the nobility, Russian businessmen generally did not challenge the tsarist autocracy.

Repression and Revolution

During the last three decades of the nineteenth century, antigovernment protest and revolutionary activity increased. Hopes aroused by government reforms gave impetus to reform movements, and social tensions arising from industrialization fueled protest by groups whose aims became increasingly radical. Peasants seethed with discontent because they had little or no land, and increasingly mobile dissidents spread rebellious ideas between industrial cities. At the center of opposition were university students and a class of intellectuals collectively known as *intelligentsia*. Their goals and methods varied, but they generally sought substantial political reform and thorough social change. Most dissidents drew inspiration from western European socialism, but they despised the individualism, materialism, and unbridled capitalism of western Europe and thus worked toward a socialist system more in keeping with Russian cultural traditions. Many revolutionaries were anarchists, who refused to work on behalf of any formal government but simply sought to destroy existing institutions that they considered oppressive. Insofar as they had a positive political program, the anarchists wanted to vest all authority in local governing councils elected by universal suffrage.

Protest

Some activists saw the main potential for revolutionary action in the countryside, and between 1873 and 1876 hundreds of anarchists and other radicals traveled to rural areas to enlighten and rouse the peasantry. The peasants did not understand their impassioned speeches, but the police did and soon arrested the idealists. Tsarist authorities sentenced some to prison and banished others to the remote provinces of Siberia. Frightened by manifestations of radicalism, tsarist authorities resorted to repression:

Repression

they censored publications and sent secret police to infiltrate and break up dissident organizations. Repression, however, only radicalized revolutionaries further and encouraged them to conspiratorial activities.

In the Baltic provinces, Poland, the Ukraine, Georgia, and central Asia, dissidents opposed the tsarist autocracy on ethnic as well as political and social grounds. In those lands subject peoples speaking their own languages often used schools and political groups as foundations for separatist movements as they sought autonomy or independence from the Russian empire. Tsarist officials responded with a heavy-handed program of Russification to repress the use of languages other than Russian and to restrict educational opportunities to those loyal to the tsarist state. Throughout the Russian empire, Jews also were targets of suspicion, and tsarist authorities tolerated frequent pogroms (anti-Jewish riots) by subjects jealous of their Jewish neighbors' success in business affairs. To escape this violence, Jews migrated by the hundreds of thousands to western Europe and the United States in the late nineteenth century.

Terrorism   In 1876 a recently formed group called the Land and Freedom Party began to promote the assassination of prominent officials as a means to pressure the government into political reform. In 1879 a terrorist faction of the party resolved to assassinate Alexander II, who had emancipated the serfs and launched a program of political and social reform. After several unsuccessful attempts, an assassin exploded a bomb under Alexander's carriage in 1881. The first blast did little damage, but as Alexander inspected his carriage, a second and more powerful explosion killed the reforming tsar. The attack brought the era of reform to an end and prompted the tsarist autocracy to adopt an uncomprising policy of repression.

In 1894 Nicholas II (reigned 1894–1917) ascended the throne. A well-intentioned but weak ruler, Nicholas championed oppression and police control. To deflect attention from domestic issues and neutralize revolutionary movements, the tsar's government embarked on expansionist ventures in east Asia. Russian designs on Korea and Manchuria clashed with similar Japanese intentions, leading to a rivalry that ended in war. The Russo-Japanese war began with a Japanese surprise attack on the Russian naval squadron at Port Arthur in February 1904 and ended in May 1905 with the destruction of the Russian navy.

Damaged Russian naval vessel in Port Arthur, a casualty of the Japanese attack on the Russian fleet in 1904. • UPI/Corbis-Bettmann

Russian military defeats brought to a head simmering political and social discontent and triggered widespread disturbances. In January 1905 a group of workers marched on the tsar's Winter Palace in St. Petersburg to petition Nicholas for a popularly elected assembly and other political concessions. Government troops met the petitioners with rifle fire, killing 130. The news of this Bloody Sunday massacre caused an angry uproar throughout the empire that culminated in labor unrest, peasant insurrections, student demonstrations, and mutinies in both the army and navy. Organizing themselves at the village level, peasants discussed seizing the property of their landlords. Urban workers created new councils known as *soviets* to organize strikes and negotiate with employers and government authorities. Elected delegates from factories and workshops served as members of these soviets.

The Revolution of 1905

Revolutionary turmoil paralyzed Russian cities and forced the government to make concessions. Sergei Witte, whom Nicholas had appointed to conduct peace negotiations with Japan, urged the tsar to create an elected legislative assembly. The tsar reluctantly consented and permitted the establishment of the Duma, Russia's first parliamentary institution. Although the Duma lacked the power to create or bring down governments, from the Romanov perspective this act was a major concession. Still, the creation of the Duma did not end unrest. Between 1905 and 1907 disorder continued, and violence flared especially in the Baltic provinces, Poland, the Ukraine, Georgia, and central Asia, where ethnic tensions added to revolutionary sentiments. Through bloody reprisals the government eventually restored order, but the hour was late for the Romanov dynasty.

THE CHINESE EMPIRE UNDER SIEGE

The Chinese empire and the Qing dynasty experienced even more difficulties than did the Ottoman and Russian empires during the nineteenth century. European powers inflicted military defeats on Qing forces and compelled China's leaders to accepted a series of humiliating treaties. The provisions of these treaties undermined Chinese sovereignty, carved China into spheres of influences that set the stage for economic exploitation, and handicapped the Qing dynasty's ability to deal with domestic disorder. As the government tried to cope with foreign challenges, it also faced dangerous internal upheavals, the most important of which was the Taiping rebellion. Caught between aggressive foreigners and insurgent rebels, China's ruling elites developed reform programs to maintain social order, strengthen the state, and preserve the Qing dynasty. The reforms had limited effect, however, and by the early twentieth century, China was in seriously weakened condition.

The Opium War and the Unequal Treaties

In 1759 the emperor Qianlong restricted the European commercial presence in China to the waterfront at Guangzhou, where European merchants could establish warehouses. There Chinese authorities not only controlled European merchants but also the terms of trade. Foreign merchants could deal only with specially licensed Chinese firms known as *cohongs,* which bought and sold goods at set prices and operated under strict regulations established by the government. Besides the expense and inconvenience of the *cohong* system, European merchants had to cope with a market that had little demand for European products. As a result, European merchants paid for Chinese silk, porcelain, lacquerware, and tea largely with silver bullion.

The Opium Trade   Seeking increased profits in the late eighteenth century, officials of the British East India Company sought alternatives to bullion to exchange for Chinese goods. They gradually turned to trade in a product that was as profitable as it was criminal—opium. Using Turkish and Persian expertise, the East India Company grew opium in India and shipped it to China, where company officials exchanged it for Chinese silver coin. The silver then flowed back to British-controlled Calcutta and London, where company merchants used it to buy Chinese products in Guangzhou. The opium trade expanded rapidly: annual imports of opium in the early nineteenth century amounted to about 4,500 chests, each weighing 60 kilograms (133 pounds), but by 1839 some 40,000 chests of opium entered China annually to satisfy the habits of drug addicts. With the help of this new commodity, the East India Company easily paid for luxury Chinese products.

Trade in opium was illegal, but it continued unabated for decades because Chinese authorities made little effort to enforce the law. Indeed, corrupt officials often benefited personally by allowing the illegal trade to go on. By the late 1830s, however, government officials had become aware that China had a trade problem and a drug problem as well. The opium trade not only drained large quantities of silver bullion from China but also created serious social problems in southern China. When government authorities took steps in 1838 to halt the illicit trade, British merchants started losing money. In 1839 the Chinese government stepped up its campaign by charging the incorruptible Lin Zexu with the task of destroying the opium trade. Commissioner

Chinese opium smokers. Chinese efforts to stop opium imports led to humiliating defeat in the Opium War.   •   Historical Picture Archive/Corbis

Lin acted quickly, confiscating and destroying some twenty thousand chests of opium. His uncompromising policy ignited a war that ended with humiliating defeat for China.

The Opium War   Outraged by the Chinese action against opium, British commercial agents pressed their government into a military retaliation designed to reopen the opium trade. The ensuing conflict, known as the Opium War (1839–1842), made plain the military power differential between Europe and China. In the initial stages of the conflict, British naval vessels easily demonstrated their superiority on the seas. Meanwhile, equipped only with swords, knives, spears, and occasionally muskets, the defenders of Chinese coastal towns were no match for the controlled firing power of well-drilled British infantry armed with rifles. But neither the destruction of Chinese war fleets nor the capture of coastal forts and towns persuaded the Chinese to sue for peace.

LETTER OF LIN ZEXU TO QUEEN VICTORIA

• • •

In 1838 Qing Emperor Daoguang sent Lin Zexu to Guangzhou to put an end to imports of opium into China. A leading Confucian scholar, Lin worked to persuade Chinese and foreigners alike that opium was a harmful and evil drug. In 1839 he composed a letter to Great Britain's Queen Victoria seeking her support in halting the flow of opium. Although never delivered, the letter illustrates Lin's efforts to stem the flow of opium by reason and negotiation before he resorted to sterner measures.

You have traded in China for almost 200 years, and as a result, your country has become wealthy and prosperous.

As this trade has lasted for a long time, there are bound to be unscrupulous as well as honest traders. Among the unscrupulous are those who bring opium to China to harm the Chinese; they succeed so well that this poison has spread far and wide in all the provinces. You, I hope, will certainly agree that people who pursue material gains to the great detriment of the welfare of others can be neither tolerated by Heaven nor endured by men. . . .

I have heard that the areas under your direct jurisdiction such as London, Scotland, and Ireland do not produce opium; it is produced instead in your Indian possessions such as Bengal, Madras, Bombay, Patna, and Malwa. In these possessions the English people not only plant opium poppies that stretch from one mountain to another but also open factories to manufacture this terrible drug. As months accumulate and years pass by, the poison they have produced increases in its wicked intensity, and its repugnant odor reaches as high as the sky. Heaven is furious with anger, and all the gods are moaning with pain! It is hereby suggested that you destroy and plow under all of these opium plants and grow food crops instead, while issuing an order to punish severely anyone who dares to plant opium poppies again. If you adopt this policy of love so as to produce good and exterminate evil, Heaven will protect you, and gods will bring you good fortune. Moreover, you will enjoy a long life and be rewarded with a multitude of children and grandchildren! . . .

The present law calls for the imposition of the death sentence on any Chinese who has peddled or smoked opium. Since a Chinese could not peddle or smoke opium if foreigners had not brought it to China, it is clear that the true culprits of a Chinese's death as a result of an opium conviction are the opium traders from foreign countries. Being the cause of other people's death, why should they themselves be spared from capital punishment? A murderer of one person is subject to the death sentence; just imagine how many people opium has killed! This is the rationale behind the new law which says that any foreigner who brings opium to China will be sentenced to death by hanging or beheading. Our purpose is to eliminate this poison once and for all and to the benefit of all mankind. . . .

Our Celestial Empire towers over all other countries in virtue and possesses a power great and awesome enough to carry out its wishes. But we will not prosecute a person without warning him in advance; that is why we have made our law explicit and clear. If the merchants of your honorable country wish to enjoy trade with us on a permanent basis, they must fearfully observe our law by cutting off, once and for all, the supply of opium. Under no circumstance should they test our intention to enforce the law by deliberately violating it.

SOURCE: Dun J. Li, *China in Transition* (New York: Van Nostrand, 1969), pp. 64–67.

British forces broke the military stalemate when they decided to strike at China's jugular vein—the Grand Canal, which linked the Yangzi and Yellow River valleys—with the aid of steam-powered gunboats. Armed, shallow-draft steamers could travel speedily up and down rivers, projecting the military advantage that European ships enjoyed on the high seas deep into interior regions. In May 1842 a British armada of seventy ships—led by the gunboat *Nemesis*—advanced up the Yangzi River. The British fleet encountered little resistance, and by the time it reached the intersection of the river and the Grand Canal, the Chinese government sued for peace. China experienced similar military setbacks throughout the second half of the nineteenth century in conflicts with Britain and France (1856–1858), France (1884–1885), and Japan (1894–1895).

Unequal Treaties   In the wake of these confrontations came a series of pacts collectively known as the *unequal treaties.* Beginning with the Treaty of Nanjing, which Britain forced China to accept at the conclusion of the Opium War in 1842, these agreements guided Chinese relations with foreign states until 1943. The Treaty of Nanjing released Korea, Vietnam, and Burma (now known as Myanmar) from Chinese authority and thereby dismantled the Chinese system of tributary states. Other provisions placed Hong Kong under British authority, opened Chinese ports to commerce, legalized the opium trade, permitted the establishment of Christian missions throughout China, compelled the Qing government to extend most-favored-nation status to Britain, and granted extraterritoriality to British visitors in China. To facilitate sales of foreign goods, the treaty also prevented the Qing government from levying tariffs on imports. The Treaty of Nanjing governed relations only between Britain and China, but France, Germany, Denmark, the Netherlands, Spain, Belgium, Austria-Hungary, the United States, and Japan later concluded similar unequal treaties with China. By 1900 ninety Chinese ports were under the effective control of foreign powers, foreign merchants controlled much of the Chinese economy, Christian missionaries sought converts throughout China, and foreign gunboats patrolled Chinese waters.

The Taiping Rebellion

The debilitation of the Chinese empire at the end of the nineteenth century was as much a result of internal turmoil as it was a consequence of foreign intrusion. Large-scale rebellions in the later nineteenth century reflected the increasing poverty and discontent of the Chinese peasantry. Between 1800 and 1900 China's population rose by more that 50 percent from 330 million to 475 million. The amount of land under cultivation increased only slowly during the same period, so population growth strained Chinese resources. The concentration of land in the hands of wealthy elites aggravated peasant discontent, as did widespread corruption of government officials and increasing drug addiction. After 1850 rebellions erupted throughout China: the Nian rebellion (1851–1868) in the northeast, the Muslim rebellion (1855–1873) in the southwest, and the Tungan rebellion (1862–1878) in the northwest. Most dangerous of all was the Taiping rebellion (1850–1864), which raged throughout most of China and brought the Qing dynasty to the brink of collapse.

The Taiping Program   The village schoolteacher Hong Xiuquan provided both inspiration and leadership for the Taiping rebellion. His call for the destruction of the Qing dynasty and his program for the radical transformation of Chinese society appealed to millions of men and women. The Qing dynasty had ruled China since 1644, and Qing elites had adapted to Chinese ways, but many native Chinese subjects despised the

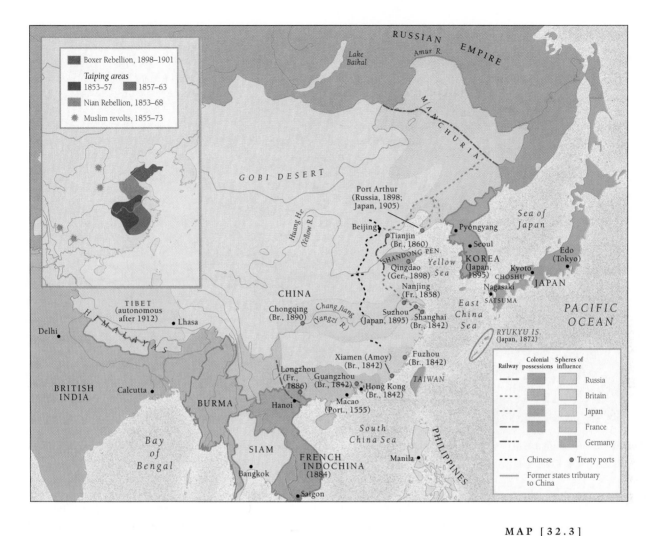

MAP [32.3]

East Asia in the nineteenth century.

Manchu ruling class as foreigners. The Taiping reform program contained many radical features that appealed to discontented subjects, including the abolition of private property, the creation of communal wealth to be shared according to needs, the prohibition of footbinding and concubinage, free public education, simplification of the written language, and literacy for the masses. Some Taiping leaders also called for the establishment of democratic political institutions and the building of an industrial society. Although they divided their army into separate divisions of men and women soldiers, the Taipings decreed the equality of men and women. Taiping regulations prohibited sexual intercourse among their followers, including married couples, but Hong and other high leaders maintained large harems.

After sweeping through southeastern China, Hong and his followers in the Society of God Worshipers took Nanjing in 1853 and made it the capital of their Taiping ("Great Peace") kingdom. From Nanjing they campaigned throughout China, and as the rebels passed through the countryside whole towns and villages joined them—often voluntarily, but sometimes under coercion. By 1855 a million Taipings were poised to attack Beijing. Qing forces repelled them, but five years later, firmly entrenched in the Yangzi River valley, the Taipings threatened Shanghai.

The final assault on the Taipings at Nanjing by Qing forces in 1864, an operation that caught common people and their livestock in crossfire. • © Collection Viollet

Taiping Defeat   The radical nature of the Taiping program ensured that the Chinese gentry would side with the Qing government to support a regime dedicated to the preservation of the established order. After imperial forces consisting of Manchu soldiers failed to defeat the Taipings, the Qing government created regional armies staffed by Chinese instead of Manchu soldiers and commanded by members of the scholar-gentry class. With the aid of European advisors and weapons, these regional armies gradually overcame the Taipings. By 1862 Hong Xiuquan had largely withdrawn from public affairs, as he sought solace in religious reflection and diversion in his harem. After a lingering illness, he committed suicide in June 1864. In the following months Nanjing fell, and government forces slaughtered some one hundred thousand Taipings. By the end of the year, the rebellion was over. But the Taiping rebellion had taken a costly toll. It claimed twenty million to thirty million lives, and it caused such massive declines in agricultural production that populations in war-torn regions frequently resorted to eating grass, leather, hemp, and even human flesh.

Reform Frustrated

The Taiping rebellion altered the course of Chinese history. Contending with aggressive foreign powers and lands ravaged by domestic rebellion, Qing rulers recognized that changes were necessary for the empire to survive. From 1860 to 1895

Qing authorities tried to fashion an efficient and benevolent Confucian government to solve social and economic problems while also adopting foreign technology to strengthen state power.

Most imaginative of the reform programs was the Self-Strengthening Movement (1860–1895), which flourished especially in the 1860s and 1870s. Empowered with imperial grants of authority that permitted them to raise troops, levy taxes, and run bureaucracies, several local leaders promoted military and economic reform. Adopting the slogan "Chinese learning at the base, Western learning for use," leaders of the Self-Strengthening Movement sought to blend Chinese cultural traditions with European industrial technology. While holding to Confucian values and seeking to reestablish a stable agrarian society, movement leaders built modern shipyards, constructed railroads, established weapons industries, opened steel foundries with blast furnaces, and founded academies to develop scientific expertise.

The Self-Strengthening Movement

Empress Dowager Cixi diverted government funds intended for the construction of modern warships to the building of a huge marble vessel to decorate a lake in the gardens of the Summer Palace near Beijing. • MacQuitty International Collection

Although it laid a foundation for industrialization, the Self-Strengthening Movement brought only superficial change to Chinese economy and society. It did not introduce enough industry to bring real military and economic strength to China. It also encountered obstacles in the imperial government: the empress dowager Cixi (1835–1908)—a former imperial concubine who established herself as effective ruler of China during the last fifty years of the Qing dynasty—diverted funds intended for the navy to build a magnificent marble boat to grace a lake in the imperial gardens. Furthermore, the movement foundered on a contradiction: industrialization would bring fundamental social change to an agrarian land, and education in European curricula would undermine the commitment to Confucian values.

In any case the Self-Strengthening Movement also did not prevent continuing foreign intrusion into Chinese affairs. During the latter part of the nineteenth century, foreign powers began to dismantle the Chinese system of tributary states. In 1885 France incorporated Vietnam into its colonial empire, and in 1886 Great Britain detached Burma from Chinese control. In 1895 Japan forced China to recognize the independence of Korea and cede the island of Taiwan and the Liaodong Peninsula in southern Manchuria. By 1898 foreign powers had carved China itself into spheres of economic influence. Powerless to resist foreign demands, the Qing government granted exclusive rights for railway and mineral development to Germany in Shandong Province, to France in the southern border provinces, to Great Britain in the Yangzi River valley, to Japan in the southeastern coastal provinces, and to Russia in Manchuria. Only distrust among the foreign powers prevented the total dismemberment of the Middle Kingdom.

Spheres of Influence

The Hundred Days
Reforms

These setbacks sparked the ambitious but abortive Hundred Days reforms of 1898. The leading figures of the reform movement were the scholars Kang Youwei (1858–1927) and Liang Qichao (1873–1929), who published a series of treatises reinterpreting Confucian thought in a way that justified radical changes in the imperial system. Kang and Liang did not seek to preserve an agrarian society and its cultural traditions so much as to remake China and turn it into a powerful modern industrial society. Impressed by their ideas, the young and open-minded Emperor Guangxu launched a sweeping program to transform China into a constitutional monarchy, guarantee civil liberties, root out corruption, remodel the educational system, encourage foreign influence in China, modernize military forces, and stimulate economic development. The broad range of reform edicts produced a violent reaction from members of the imperial household, their allies in the gentry, and the young emperor's aunt, the ruthless and powerful Empress Dowager Cixi. After a period of 103 days, Cixi nullified the reform decrees, imprisoned the emperor in the Forbidden City, and executed six leading reformers. Kang and Liang, the spiritual guides of the reform movement, escaped to Japan.

The Boxer Rebellion

Believing that foreign powers were pushing for her retirement, Cixi threw her support behind an antiforeign uprising known as the Boxer rebellion, a violent movement spearheaded by militia units calling themselves the Society of Righteous and Harmonious Fists. The foreign press referred to the rebels as Boxers. In 1899 the Boxers organized to rid China of "foreign devils" and their influences. With the empress dowager's encouragement, the Boxers went on a rampage in northern China, killing foreigners and Chinese Christians as well as Chinese who had ties to foreigners. Confident that foreign weapons could not harm them, some 140,000 Boxers besieged foreign embassies in Beijing in the summer of 1900. A heavily armed force of British, French, Russian, U.S., German, and Japanese troops quickly crushed the Boxer movement in bloody retaliation for the assault. The Chinese government had to pay a punitive indemnity and allow foreign powers to station troops in Beijing at their embassies and along the route to the sea.

Because Cixi had instigated the Boxers' attacks on foreigners, many Chinese regarded the Qing dynasty as bankrupt. Revolutionary uprisings gained widespread public support throughout the country, even among conservative Chinese gentry. Cixi died in November 1908, one day after the sudden, unexpected, and mysterious death of the emperor himself. In her last act of state, the empress dowager appointed the two-year-old boy Puyi to the imperial throne. But Puyi never had a chance to rule: revolution broke out in the autumn of 1911, and by early 1912 the last emperor of the Qing dynasty had abdicated his throne.

 ## THE TRANSFORMATION OF JAPAN

In 1853 a fleet of U.S. warships steamed into Tokyo Bay and demanded permission to establish trade and diplomatic relations with Japan. Representatives of European lands soon joined U.S. agents in Japan. Heavily armed foreign powers intimidated the Tokugawa shogun and his government, the *bakufu,* into signing unequal treaties providing political and economic privileges similar to those obtained earlier from the Qing dynasty in China. Opposition forces in Japan used the humiliating intrusion of foreigners as an excuse to overthrow the discredited shogun and the Tokugawa bakufu. After restoring the emperor to power in 1868, Japan's new rulers worked for the transformation of Japanese society to achieve political and economic equality with foreign powers. The changes initiated during the Meiji period turned Japan into the political, military, and economic powerhouse of east Asia.

From Tokugawa to Meiji

By the early nineteenth century, Japanese society was in turmoil. Declining agricultural productivity, periodic crop failures and famines, and harsh taxation contributed to economic hardship and sometimes even led to starvation among the rural population. A few cultivators prospered during this period, but many had to sell their land and become tenant farmers. Economic conditions in towns and cities, where many peasants migrated in search of a better life, were hardly better than those in the countryside. As the price of rice and other commodities rose, the urban poor experienced destitution and hunger. Even samurai and daimyo faced hardship because they fell in debt to a growing merchant class. Under these conditions Japan experienced increasing peasant protest and rebellion during the late eighteenth and early nineteenth centuries.

Crisis and Reform

The Tokugawa bakufu responded with conservative reforms. Between 1841 and 1843 the shogun's chief advisor, Mizuno Tadakuni, initiated measures to stem growing social and economic decline and to shore up the Tokugawa government. Mizuno canceled debts that samurai and daimyo owed to merchants, abolished several merchant guilds, and compelled peasants residing in cities to return to the land and cultivate rice. Most of his reforms were ineffective, and they provoked strong opposition that ultimately drove him from office.

Another problem facing the Tokugawa bakufu was the insistence on the establishment of diplomatic and commercial relations by foreign lands. Beginning in 1844, British, French, and U.S. ships visited Japan seeking to establish relations. The United States in particular sought ports where its Pacific merchant and whaling fleets could stop for fuel and provisions. Tokugawa officials refused all these requests and stuck to the policy of excluding all European and Euro-American visitors to Japan except for a small number of Dutch merchants, who carried on a carefully controlled trade in Nagasaki. In the later 1840s the bakufu began to make military preparations to resist potential attacks.

Foreign Pressure

The arrival of a U.S. naval squadron in Tokyo Bay in 1853 abruptly changed the situation. The American commander, Commodore Matthew C. Perry, trained his guns on the bakufu capital of Edo (modern Tokyo) and demanded that the shogun open Japan to diplomatic and commercial relations and sign a treaty of friendship. The shogun had no good alternative and so quickly acquiesced to Perry's demands. Representatives of Britain, the Netherlands, and Russia soon won similar rights. Like Qing diplomats a few years earlier, Tokugawa officials agreed to a series of unequal treaties that opened Japanese ports to foreign commerce, deprived the government of control over tariffs, and granted foreigners extraterritorial rights.

The sudden intrusion of foreign powers precipitated a domestic crisis in Japan that resulted in the collapse of the Tokugawa bakufu and the restoration of imperial rule. When the shogun complied with the demands of U.S. and European representatives, he aroused the opposition of conservative daimyo and the emperor, who resented the humiliating terms of the unequal treaties and questioned the shogun's right to rule Japan as "subduer of barbarians." Opposition to Tokugawa authority spread rapidly, and the southern domains of Choshu and Satsuma became centers of discontented samurai. By 1858 the imperial court in Kyoto—long excluded from playing an active role in politics—had become the focal point for opposition. Dissidents there rallied around the slogan: "Revere the emperor, expel the barbarians."

The End of Tokugawa Rule

A Japanese view of an audience of the first U.S. Consul, Townsend Harris, with the Tokugawa shogun and his officials in 1859. • Laurie Platt Winfrey, Inc.

The Meiji
Restoration

Tokugawa officials did not yield power quietly. Instead, they vigorously responded to their opponents by forcibly retiring dissident daimyo and executing or imprisoning samurai critics. In a brief civil war, however, bakufu armies suffered repeated defeats by dissident militia units trained by foreign experts and armed with imported weapons. With the Tokugawa cause doomed, the shogun resigned his office. On 3 January 1868 the boy emperor Mutsuhito—subsequently known by his regnal name Meiji ("Enlightened Rule")—took the reins of power. Emperor Meiji (1852–1912) reigned during a most eventful period in Japan's history.

Meiji Reforms

The Meiji restoration returned authority to the Japanese emperor and brought an end to the series of military governments that had dominated Japan since 1185. It also marked the birth of a new Japan. Determined to gain parity with foreign powers, a conservative coalition of daimyo, imperial princes, court nobles, and samurai formed a new government dedicated to the twin goals of prosperity and strength: "rich country, strong army." The Meiji government looked to the industrial lands of Europe and the United States to obtain the knowledge and expertise to strengthen Japan and win revisions of the unequal treaties. The Meiji government sent many students and officials abroad to study everything from technology to constitutions, and it also hired foreign experts to facilitate economic development and the creation of indigenous expertise.

Foreign Influences

Among the most prominent of the Meiji-era travelers were Fukuzawa Yukichi (1835–1901) and Ito Hirobumi (1841–1909). Fukuzawa began to study English soon after Perry's arrival in Japan, and in 1860 he was a member of the first Japanese mission to the United States. Later he traveled also in Europe, and he reported his observations of foreign lands in a series of popular publications. He lauded the constitutional government and modern educational systems that he found in the United States and western Europe, and he argued strongly for equality before the law in Japan. Hirobumi ventured abroad on four occasions. His most important journey came in 1882 and 1883, when he traveled to Europe to study foreign constitutions and administrative systems, as Meiji leaders prepared to fashion a new government. He was especially impressed with recently united Germany, and he drew inspiration from the German constitution in drafting a governing document for Japan.

The first goal of the Meiji leaders was to centralize political power, a ticklish task that required destruction of the old feudal order. After convincing daimyo to yield their lands to the throne in exchange for patents of nobility, reformers replaced the old domains with prefectures and metropolitan districts controlled by the central government. Reformers then appointed new prefectural governors to prevent the revival of old domain loyalties. As a result, most daimyo found themselves effectively removed from power. The government also abolished the samurai class and the stipends that supported it. Gone as well were the rights of daimyo and samurai to carry swords and wear their hair in the distinctive topknot that signified their military status. When Meiji leaders raised a conscript army, they deprived the samurai of the military monopoly they had held for centuries. Many samurai felt betrayed by these actions, and Meiji officials sought to ease their discontent by awarding them government bonds. As the bonds diminished in value because of inflation, former warriors had to seek employment or else suffer impoverishment. Frustrated by these new circumstances, some samurai rose in rebellion, but the recently created national army crushed all opposition. By 1878 the national government no longer feared military challenges to its rule.

Abolition of the Feudal Order

Japan's new leaders next put the regime on secure financial footing by revamping the tax system. Peasants traditionally paid taxes in grain, but because the value of grain fluctuated with the price of rice, so did government revenue. In 1873 the Meiji government converted the grain tax into a fixed-money tax, which provided the government with predictable revenues and left peasants to deal with market fluctuations in grain prices. The state also began to assess taxes on the potential productivity of arable land, no matter how much a cultivator actually produced. This measure virtually guaranteed that only those who maximized production could afford to hold on to their land. Others had to sell their land to more efficient producers.

Revamping the Tax System

The reconstruction of Japanese society continued in the 1880s under mounting domestic pressure for a constitution and representative government. These demands coincided with the rulers' belief that constitutions gave foreign powers their strength and unity. Accordingly, in 1889 the emperor promulgated the Meiji constitution as "a voluntary gift" to his people. Drafted under the guidance of Ito Hirobumi, this document established a constitutional monarchy with a legislature, known as the Diet, composed of a house of nobles and an elected lower house. The constitution limited the authority of the Diet and reserved considerable power to the executive branch of government. The "sacred and inviolable" emperor commanded the armed forces, named the prime minister, and appointed the cabinet. Both the prime minister and the cabinet were responsible to the emperor rather than the lower house, as in European parliamentary systems. The emperor also had the right to dissolve parliament, and whenever the Diet was not in session he had the prerogative of issuing ordinances. Effective power thus lay with the emperor, whom the parliament could

Constitutional Government

The opening of the Japanese parliament in 1891 by the Meiji emperor, seated at the right. The assembly's main chamber, shown here, followed the design of European parliament buildings.

● Hulton Getty/Liaison Agency

advise but never control. The Meiji constitution recognized individual rights, but it provided that laws could limit those rights in the interests of the state, and it established property restrictions on the franchise ensuring that delegates elected to the lower house represented the most prosperous social classes. In the elections of 1890 less than 5 percent of the adult male population was eligible to cast ballots. Despite its conservative features, the Meiji constitution provided greater opportunity for debate and dissent than ever before in Japanese society.

Remodeling the Economy   Economic initiatives matched efforts at political reconstruction. Convinced that a powerful economy was the foundation of national strength, the Meiji government created a modern transportation, communications, and educational infrastructure. The establishment of telegraph, railroad, and steamship lines tied local and regional markets into a national economic network. The government also removed barriers to commerce and trade by abolishing guild restrictions and internal tariffs. Aiming to improve literacy rates—40 percent for males and 15 percent for females in the nineteenth century—the government introduced a system of universal primary and secondary education. Universities provided advanced instruction for the best students, especially in scientific and technical fields. This infrastructure supported rapid industrialization and economic growth. While most economic enterprises were privately owned, the government controlled military industries and established pilot programs to stimulate industrial development. During the 1880s the government sold most of its enterprises to private investors who had close ties to governmental officials. The result was a concentration of enormous economic power in the hands of a small group of men, collectively known as *zaibatsu*, or financial cliques. By the early twentieth century, Japan had joined the ranks of the major industrial powers.

CHAPTER 32 SOCIETIES AT CROSSROADS 843

Economic development came at a price, as the Japanese people bore the social and political costs of rapid industrialization. Japanese peasants, for example, supplied much of the domestic capital that supported the Meiji program of industrialization. The land tax of 1873, which cost peasants 40 to 50 percent of their crop yields, produced almost 90 percent of government revenue during the early years of Meiji development. Foreign exchange to purchase industrial equipment came chiefly from the export of textiles produced in a labor-intensive industry staffed by poorly paid workers.

Costs of Economic Development

The difficult lot of peasants came to the fore in 1883 and 1884 with a series of peasant uprisings aimed at money lenders and government offices holding records of loans. The Meiji government deployed military police and army units to put down these uprisings, and authorities imprisoned or executed many leaders of the rebellions. Thereafter, the government did virtually nothing to alleviate the suffering of the rural population. Hundreds of thousands of families lived in destitution, haunted by malnutrition, starvation, and infanticide. Those who escaped rural society to take up work in the burgeoning industries learned that the state did not tolerate labor organizations that promoted the welfare of workers: Meiji law treated the formation of unions and the organization of strikes as criminal activities, and the government crushed a growing labor movement in 1901.

Nevertheless, in a single generation Meiji leaders transformed Japan into a powerful industrial society poised to play a major role in world affairs. Achieving political and economic equality with western European lands and the United States was the prime goal of Meiji leaders who sought an end to humiliating treaty provisions. Serving as symbols of Japan's remarkable development were the ending of extraterritoriality in 1899, the conclusion of an alliance with Britain as an equal power in 1902, and convincing displays of military prowess in victories over the Chinese empire (1894–1895) and the Russian empire (1904–1905).

During the nineteenth century Ottoman, Russian, Chinese, and Japanese societies faced severe challenges on both foreign and domestic fronts. Confrontations with western European and U.S. forces showed that the agrarian societies were militarily much weaker than industrializing lands. Ottoman, Russian, Chinese, and Japanese societies suffered also from domestic weaknesses brought on by growing populations, the slowing of agricultural productivity, official corruption, and declining imperial revenues. All these societies embarked on ambitious reform programs that drew inspiration from western European and U.S. models to solve the crises caused by domestic discontent and foreign intrusions on their sovereignty. But reform programs had very different results in different lands. In the Ottoman, Russian, and Chinese empires, conservative ruling elites were able to limit the scope of reform: while they generally supported industrialization and military reform, they stifled political and social reforms that might threaten their positions in society. In Japan, however, dissent led to the collapse of the Tokugawa bakufu, and reformers had the opportunity to undertake a much more thorough program of reform than did their counterparts in Ottoman, Russian, and Chinese societies. By the early twentieth century, on the basis of reforms implemented by Meiji leaders, Japan was becoming a political, military, and economic powerhouse.

CHRONOLOGY

1805–1848	Reign of Muhammad Ali in Egypt
1808–1839	Reign of Sultan Mahmud II
1814–1864	Life of Taiping leader Hong Xiuquan
1839–1842	Opium War
1839–1876	Tanzimat era
1850–1864	Taiping rebellion
1853	Arrival of Commodore Perry in Japan
1853–1856	Crimean War
1855–1881	Reign of Tsar Alexander II
1860–1895	Self-Strengthening Movement
1861	Emancipation of the Russian serfs
1868	Meiji restoration
1876	Promulgation of the Ottoman constitution
1889	Promulgation of the Meiji constitution
1894–1917	Reign of Tsar Nicholas II
1898	Hundred Days reforms
1905	Revolution of 1905 in Russia
1908–1918	Young Turk era

FOR FURTHER READING

William L. Blackwell. *The Industrialization of Russia: An Historical Perspective*. New York, 1982. A useful overview.

Carter V. Findley. *Bureaucratic Reform in the Ottoman Empire: The Sublime Porte, 1789–1922*. Princeton, 1980. An important scholarly work on bureaucratic reform and the development of the Ottoman civil service.

Fukuzawa Yukichi. *The Autobiography of Yukichi Fukuzawa*. Trans. by E. Kiyooka. New York, 1966. Fascinating autobiography of the former samurai who introduced Japan to the larger world on the basis of his travels in Europe and the United States.

Marius B. Jansen and Gilbert Rozman, eds. *Japan in Transition: From Tokugawa to Meiji*. Princeton, 1986. Important collection of essays exploring economic and social change during the era of the Meiji restoration.

Patrick Balfour Kinross. *The Ottoman Centuries: The Rise and Fall of the Turkish Empire*. New York, 1977. A general history of the Ottoman state.

Peter Kolchin. *Unfree Labor: American Slavery and Russian Serfdom*. Cambridge, Mass., 1987. A remarkable and stimulating comparative study of American slavery and Russian serfdom.

Tetsuo Najita and J. Victor Koschmann, eds. *Conflict in Modern Japanese History: The Neglected Tradition*. Princeton, 1982. Explores the role of conflict rather than consensus in Japanese society.

Sevket Pamuk. *The Ottoman Empire and European Capitalism, 1820–1913: Trade, Investment, and Production*. Cambridge, 1987. Closely examines complex economic entanglements.

James M. Polachek. *The Inner Opium War*. Cambridge, Mass., 1992. A recent scholarly treatment of the Opium War and its effects in China.

Hans Rogger. *Russia in the Age of Modernisation and Revolution, 1881–1917*. New York, 1983. An important study of Russian social and economic development.

Jonathan D. Spence. *God's Chinese Son: The Taiping Heavenly Kingdom of Hong Xiuquan*. New York, 1996. A recent and readable work on the Taiping rebellion.

Conrad D. Totman. *The Collapse of the Tokugawa Bakufu, 1862–1868.* Honolulu, 1980. A detailed political history of the bakufu's decline and fall.

Arthur Waley. *The Opium War through Chinese Eyes.* Stanford, 1968. Fascinating perspective on the Opium War drawing on eyewitness accounts by Chinese participants and observers.

Francis William Wcislo. *Reforming Rural Russia: State, Local Society, and National Politics, 1855–1914.* Princeton, 1990. Beginning with emancipation of the serfs, this work traces agrarian and political problems in Russian society.

Richard Wortman. *Scenarios of Power: Myth and Ceremony in the Russian Monarchy.* Princeton, 1995. An innovative study exploring the means by which Romanov rulers held on to their autocratic prerogatives despite fundamental changes in Russian society.

Avrahm Yarmolinsky. *Road to Revolution: A Century of Russian Radicalism.* New York, 1959. The most comprehensive introduction to Russian revolutionary movements in the nineteenth century.

THE BUILDING
OF GLOBAL EMPIRES

In the mid-nineteenth century south Africa was a land of limited appeal to European peoples. A small European population resided at the British port of Cape Town, a way station on the sea route from Europe to India, and a few cultivators of Dutch and British ancestry clashed bitterly with the more numerous Xhosa, Zulu, and other peoples who had long inhabited the region. The discovery of diamonds (1866) and rich gold deposits (1886) brought dramatic changes to the region as European prospectors flocked to south Africa to seek their fortune.

Among the arrivals was Cecil John Rhodes, an eighteen-year-old student at Oxford University, who in 1871 went to south Africa in search of a climate that would relieve his tuberculosis. Rhodes was persistent, systematic, and ambitious. He carefully supervised African laborers who worked his claims in the diamond fields, and he bought the rights to others' claims when they looked promising. By 1889, at age thirty-five, he had almost completely monopolized diamond mining in south Africa, and he controlled 90 percent of the world's diamond production. With ample financial backing, Rhodes built up a healthy stake in the gold-mining business, although he did not seek to monopolize gold the way he did diamonds. He also entered politics, serving as prime minister (1890–1896) of the British Cape Colony.

Yet Rhodes's ambitions went far beyond business and local politics. In his vision the Cape Colony would serve as a base of operations for the extension of British control to all of Africa, from Cape to Cairo. Rhodes led the movement to enlarge the colony by absorbing territories to the north settled by Dutch farmers. Under Rhodes's guidance, the colony annexed Bechuanaland (modern Botswana) in 1885, and in 1895 it added Rhodesia (modern Zambia and Zimbabwe) to its holdings. But Rhodes's plan did not stop with Africa: he urged the expansion of the British empire until it embraced all the world, and he even hoped to bring the United States of America back into the British fold. Rhodes considered British society the most noble, moral, and honorable in the world, and he regarded imperial expansion as a duty to humankind: "We are the finest race in the world," he said in 1877, "and the more of the world we inhabit, the better it is for the human race." In his sense of superiority to other peoples as well as his restless energy, his compulsion to expand, and his craving to extract mineral wealth from distant parts of the world, Rhodes represented well the views of European imperialists who carved the world into colonies during the nineteenth century.

The battle of Omdurman on the Nile River, 2 September 1898.   •   E-T Archive/Kobal

Throughout history strong societies have often sought to dominate their weaker neighbors by subjecting them to imperial rule. They have built empires for various reasons: to gain control over natural resources, to subdue potential enemies, to seize wealth, to acquire territory for expansion, and to win glory. From the days of ancient Mesopotamia and Egypt to the present, imperialism has been a prominent theme of world history.

During the second half of the nineteenth century, as the Ottoman and Qing empires weakened, a handful of western European states wrote a new chapter in the history of imperialism. Strong nationalist sentiments enabled them to mobilize their populations for purposes of overseas expansion. Industrialization equipped them with the most effective tools and the most lethal weapons available anywhere in the world. Three centuries of experience with maritime trade in Asia, Africa, the Americas, and Oceania provided them with unparalleled knowledge of the world and its peoples. With these advantages western European peoples conquered foreign armies, overpowered local rulers, and imposed their hegemony throughout the world. Toward the end of the century, the United States and Japan joined European states as new imperial powers.

The establishment of global empires had far-reaching effects. In many ways imperialism tightened links between the world's societies. Imperial powers encouraged trade between dominant states and their overseas colonies, for example, and they organized mass migrations of laborers to work in agricultural and industrial ventures. Yet imperialism also fostered divisions between the world's peoples. Powerful tools, deadly weapons, and global hegemony tempted European peoples to consider themselves superior to their subjects throughout the world: modern racism is one of the legacies of imperialism. Another effect of imperialism was the development of nationalism in subject lands. Just as the incursion of Napoleonic armies stimulated the development of nationalism in Europe, so the imposition of foreign rule provoked nationalist responses in colonized lands. Although formal empires almost entirely dissolved in the twentieth century, the influence of global imperialism continues to shape the contemporary world.

FOUNDATIONS OF EMPIRE

Even under the best of circumstances, campaigns to conquer foreign lands have always been dangerous and expensive ventures. They have arisen from a sense that foreign conquest is essential, and they have entailed the mobilization of political, military, and economic resources. In nineteenth-century Europe proponents of empire advanced a variety of political, economic, and cultural arguments to justify the conquest and control of foreign lands. The imperialist ventures that they promoted enjoyed dramatic success partly because of the increasingly sophisticated technologies developed by European industry.

Motives of Imperialism

Modern Imperialism   The building of empires is an old story in world history. By the nineteenth century, however, European observers recognized that empires of their day were different from those of earlier times. Accordingly, about midcentury they began to speak of *imperialism,* and by the 1880s the recently coined term had made its way into popular speech and writing throughout western Europe. In contemporary usage imperialism refers to the domination of European powers—and later the United States and Japan as well—over subject lands in the larger world. Sometimes this domination came in the old-fashioned way, by force of arms, but often it arose from trade, investment, and business activities that enabled imperial powers to profit from subject societies and influence their affairs without going to the trouble of exercising direct political control.

Like the building of empires, the establishment of colonies in foreign lands is a practice dating from ancient times. In modern parlance, however, colonialism refers not just to the sending of colonists to settle new lands but also to the political, social, economic, and cultural structures that enabled imperial powers to dominate subject lands. In some lands, such as North America, Chile, Argentina, Australia, New Zealand, and South Africa, European powers established settler colonies populated largely by migrants from the home societies. Yet contemporary scholars also speak of European colonies in India, southeast Asia, and sub-Saharan Africa, even though European migrants did not settle there in large numbers. European agents, officials, and businessmen effectively turned those lands into colonies and profoundly influenced their historical development by controlling their domestic and foreign policies, integrating local economies into the network of global capitalism, introducing European business techniques, transforming educational systems according to European standards, and promoting European cultural preferences.

Modern Colonialism

During the second half of the nineteenth century, many Europeans came to believe that imperial expansion and colonial domination were crucial for the survival of their states and societies—and sometimes for the health of their personal fortunes as well. European merchants and entrepreneurs sometimes became fabulously wealthy from business ventures in Asia or Africa, and they argued for their home states to pursue imperialist policies partly to secure and enhance their own enterprises. After making his fortune mining diamonds and gold, for example, Cecil Rhodes (1853–1902) worked tirelessly on behalf of British imperial expansion.

Cecil Rhodes resting in the gold fields of south Africa, about 1897. • Baldwin H. Ward/Corbis-Bettmann

Economic Motives of Imperialism

It is not difficult to understand why entrepreneurs like Rhodes would promote overseas expansion, but their interests alone could not have driven the massive imperialist ventures of the late nineteenth century. In fact, a wide range of motives encouraged European peoples to launch campaigns of conquest and control. Some advocates argued that imperialism was in the economic interests of European societies as well as individuals. They pointed out that overseas colonies could serve as reliable sources of raw materials not available in Europe that came into demand because of industrialization: rubber, tin, and copper were vital products, for example, and by the late nineteenth century petroleum also became a crucial resource for industrialized lands. Rubber trees were indigenous to the Amazon River basin, but imperialists established colonial rubber plantations in the Congo River basin and Malaya. Abundant supplies of tin were available from colonies in southeast Asia and copper in central Africa. The United States and Russia supplied most of the world's petroleum in the nineteenth century, but the oil fields of southwest Asia attracted the attention of European industrialists and imperialists alike.

Proponents of imperialism also held that colonies would consume manufactured products and provide a haven for migrants in an age of rapidly increasing European population. In fact, manufactured goods did not flow to most colonies in large quantities, and European migrants went overwhelmingly to independent states in the Americas rather than to overseas colonies. Nevertheless, arguments arising from national economic interest generated considerable support for imperialism.

Political Motives of Imperialism

As European states extended their influence overseas, a geopolitical argument for imperialism gained prominence. Even if colonies were not economically beneficial, imperialists held that it was crucial for political and military reasons to maintain them. Some overseas colonies occupied strategic sites on the world's sea-lanes, and others offered harbors or supply stations for commercial and naval ships. Advocates of imperialism sought to gain these advantages for their own states and—equally important—to deny them to rivals.

Imperialism had its uses also for domestic politics. In an age when socialists and communists directly confronted industrialists, European statesmen and national leaders sought to defuse social tension and inspire patriotism by focusing public attention on foreign imperialist ventures. Cecil Rhodes himself once observed that imperialism was an attractive alternative to civil war, and the German chancellor Otto von Bismarck worked to persuade both industrialists and workers that overseas expansion would benefit them all. By the end of the nineteenth century, European leaders frequently organized colonial exhibitions where subject peoples displayed their dress, music, and customs for tourists and the general public in imperial lands, all in an effort to win popular support for imperialist policies.

Cultural Justifications of Imperialism

Even spiritual motives fostered imperialism. Like the Jesuits in the early modern era, missionaries flocked to African and Asian lands in search of converts to Christianity. Missionaries often opposed imperialist ventures and defended the interests of their converts against European businessmen and colonial officials. Nevertheless, their spiritual campaigns provided a powerful religious justification for imperialism. Furthermore, missionaries often facilitated communications between imperialists and subject peoples, and they sometimes provided European officials with information they needed to maintain control of overseas colonies. Their settlements also served as convenient meeting places for Europeans overseas and as distribution centers for European manufactured goods.

RUDYARD KIPLING ON THE WHITE MAN'S BURDEN

· · ·

Rudyard Kipling lived in northern India for the first six years of his life. He grew up speaking Hindi, and he mixed easily with Indian subjects of the British empire. After attending a boarding school in England, he returned to India in 1882 and became a journalist and writer. Many of his works express his deep enchantment with India, but he also believed strongly in imperial rule. Indeed, he wrote his famous poem, entitled "The White Man's Burden," to encourage the United States to impose colonial rule in the Philippines. While recognizing the unpopularity of foreign rule, Kipling considered it a duty to bring order to colonial lands and to serve subject peoples.

Take up the White Man's Burden—
    Send forth the best ye breed—
Go bind your sons to exile
    To serve your captives' need;
To wait in heavy harness,
    On fluttered folk and wild—
Your new-caught, sullen peoples,
    Half-devil and half-child.

Take up the White Man's burden—
    In patience to abide,
To veil the threat of terror
    And check the show of pride;
By open speech and simple,
    An hundred times made plain,
To seek another's profit,
    And work for another's gain.

Take up the White Man's burden—
    The savage wars of peace—
Fill full the mouth of Famine
    And bid the sickness cease;
And when your goal is nearest
    The end for others sought,
Watch Sloth and heathen Folly
    Bring all your hope to nought.

Take up the White Man's burden—
    No tawdry rule of kings,
But toil of serf and sweeper—
    The tale of common things.

The ports ye shall not enter,
    The roads ye shall not tread,
Go make them with your living,
    And mark them with your dead.

Take up the White Man's burden—
    And reap his old reward:
The blame of those ye better,
    The hate of those ye guard—
The cry of hosts ye humor
    (Ah, slowly!) toward the light;—
"Why brought ye us from bondage,
    "Our loved Egyptian night?"

Take up the White Man's burden—
    Ye dare not stoop to less—
Nor call too loud on Freedom
    To cloak your weariness;
By all ye cry or whisper,
    By all ye leave or do,
The silent, sullen peoples
    Shall weigh your Gods and you.

Take up the White Man's burden—
    Have done with childish days—
The lightly proffered laurel,
    The easy, ungrudged praise.
Comes now, to search your manhood
    Through all the thankless years,
Cold, edged with dear-bought wisdom,
    The judgment of your peers!

SOURCE: Rudyard Kipling. "The White Man's Burden." *McClure's Magazine* 12:4 (1899): 290–291.

While missionaries sought to introduce Christianity to subject peoples, others worked to bring them "civilization" in the form of political order and social stability. French imperialists routinely invoked the *mission civilisatrice* ("civilizing mission") as justification for their expansion into Africa and Asia, and the English writer and poet Rudyard Kipling (1864–1936) defined the "white man's burden" as the duty of European and Euro-American peoples to bring order and enlightenment to distant lands.

Tools of Empire

Even the strongest motives would not have enabled imperialists to impose their rule throughout the world without the powerful technological advantages that industrialization conferred upon them. Ever since the introduction of gunpowder in the thirteenth century, European states had competed vigorously to develop increasingly powerful military technologies. Industrialization enhanced these efforts by making it possible to produce massive quantities of advanced weapons and tools. During the nineteenth century industrialists devised effective technologies of transportation, communication, and war that enabled European imperialists to have their way in the larger world.

Transportation Technologies   The most important innovations in transportation involved steamships and railroads. Small steamboats plied the waters of the United States and western Europe from the early nineteenth century. During the 1830s British naval engineers adapted steam power to military uses and built large, ironclad ships equipped with powerful guns. These steamships traveled much faster than any sailing vessel, and as an additional advantage they could ignore the winds and travel in any direction. Because they could travel much further upriver than sailboats, which depended on convenient winds, steamships enabled imperialists to project power deep into the interior regions of foreign lands. Thus in 1842 the British gunboat *Nemesis* led an expedition up the Yangzi River that brought the Opium War to a conclusion. Steam-powered gunboats later introduced European power to inland sites throughout Africa and Asia.

The construction of new canals enhanced the effectiveness of steamships. Both the Suez Canal (constructed 1859–1869) and the Panama Canal (constructed 1904–1914) facilitated the building and maintenance of empires by enabling naval vessels to travel rapidly between the world's seas and oceans. They also lowered the costs of trade between imperial powers and subject lands.

Once imperialists had gained control of overseas lands, railroads helped them to maintain their hegemony and organize local economies to their own advantage. Rail transportation enabled colonial officials and armies to travel quickly through the colonies. It also facilitated trade in raw materials and the distribution of European manufactured goods in the colonies.

Military Technologies   European industrialists also churned out massive quantities of increasingly powerful weapons. The most advanced firearms of the early nineteenth century were smooth-bore, muzzle-loading muskets. When large numbers of infantrymen fired their muskets at once, the resulting volley could cause havoc among opponents. Yet it took a skilled musketeer about one minute to reload his weapon, and because of its smooth bore, the musket was not a very accurate firearm. By midcentury European armies were using breech-loading firearms with rifled bores that were far more accurate and reliable than muskets. By the 1870s Europeans were experimenting with rifled machine guns, and in the 1880s they adopted the Maxim gun, a light and powerful weapon that fired eleven bullets per second.

Thousands of spectators gathered on the banks of the Suez Canal in 1869 to watch a parade of ships that opened the canal by proceeding from the Mediterranean to the Red Sea. • Mary Evans Picture Library

These firearms provided European armies with an arsenal vastly stronger than any other in the world. Accurate rifles and machine guns devastated opposing overseas forces, enabling European armies to impose colonial rule almost at will. In 1898, for example, a British army with twenty machine guns and six gunboats encountered a Sudanese force at Omdurman, near Khartoum on the Nile River. During five hours of fighting, the British force lost 368 men while machine guns and explosive charges fired from gunboats killed some eleven thousand Sudanese. The battle of Omdurman opened the door for British colonial rule in Sudan.

Communications Technologies

Communications also benefited from industrialization. Oceangoing steamships reduced the time required to deliver messages from imperial capitals to colonial lands. In the 1830s it took as long as two years for a British correspondent to receive a reply to a letter sent to India by sailing ship. By the 1850s, however, after the introduction of steamships, correspondence could make the round-trip between London and Bombay in four months. After the opening of the Suez Canal in 1869, steamships traveled from Britain to India in less than two weeks.

The invention of the telegraph made it possible to exchange messages even faster. Telegraph wires carried communications over land from the 1830s, but only in the 1850s did engineers devise reliable submarine cables for the transmission of messages through the oceans. By 1870 submarine cables carried messages between Britain and India in about five hours. By 1902 cables linked all parts of the British empire throughout the world, and other European states maintained cables to support communications with their own colonies. Their monopoly on telegraphic communications provided imperial powers with distinct advantages over their subject lands. Imperial officials could rapidly mobilize forces to deal with troubles, and merchants could respond quickly to developments of economic and commercial significance. Rapid communications was an integral structural element of empire.

EUROPEAN IMPERIALISM

Aided by powerful technologies, European states launched an unprecedented round of empire building in the second half of the nineteenth century. Imperial expansion began with the British conquest of India. Competition between imperial powers led to European intrusion into central Asia and the establishment of colonies in southeast Asia. Fearful that rivals might gain control over some region that remained free of imperial control, European states embarked on a campaign of frenzied expansion in the 1880s that brought almost all of Africa and Pacific Ocean territories into their empires.

The British Empire in India

The British empire in south Asia and southeast Asia grew out of the mercantile activities of the English East India Company, which enjoyed a monopoly on English trade with India. The East India Company obtained permission from the Mughal emperors of India to build fortified posts on the coastlines. There company agents traded for goods and stored commodities in warehouses until company ships arrived to transport them to Europe. In the seventeenth century company merchants traded mostly for Indian pepper and cotton, Chinese silk and porcelain, and fine spices from southeast Asia. During the eighteenth century tea and coffee became the most prominent trade items, and European consumers acquired a taste for both beverages that they have never lost.

Company Rule   After the death of the emperor Aurangzeb in 1707, the Mughal state entered a period of decline, and many local authorities asserted their independence of Mughal rule. The East India Company took advantage of Mughal weakness to strengthen and expand its trading posts. In the 1750s company merchants began campaigns of outright conquest in India, largely to protect their commercial interests from increasing disorder in the subcontinent. From their forts at Calcutta, Madras, and Bombay, the merchants extended their authority inland and won official rights to rule from the Mughal emperors and local authorities. They enforced their rule with a small British army and a large number of Indian troops known as *sepoys*.

A revolt by the sepoys led to the establishment of direct British imperial rule in India. In 1857 sepoy regiments received new Enfield rifles that fired bullets from cartridges. To protect them from moisture, the cartridges came in paper waxed with animal fat, and British officers instructed the sepoys to tear the paper off with their teeth. Hindu sepoys refused to comply out of concern that the protective fat came from cows, which they held sacred, and their Muslim counterparts refused on grounds that the fat might have come from pigs, which they considered foul. Even though British officials soon changed the procedures for packing and opening cartridges, in May 1857 Hindu sepoys staged a mutiny, killed their British officers, and proclaimed restoration of Mughal authority. Peasants and disgruntled elites joined the fray and transformed a minor mutiny into a large-scale rebellion that seriously threatened British rule in India. But the rebels had different interests and could not agree on a common program; in contrast, British forces benefited from powerful weapons and telegraphic communications, which enabled them to rush troops to trouble spots. The conflict produced some horrifying episodes of violence. At Cawnpore, near Lucknow, sepoys quickly overcame the British garrison and its population of 60 soldiers, 180 civilian men, and some 375 women and children. The rebels killed all the men—many of them as they surrendered—and two weeks later massa-

A contemporary British print depicted the atrocities at Cawnpore. At left, sepoys kill British troops and men from the garrison, while women and children fall in the foreground. At the right, rebels stuff their victims' corpses in a well.   •   National Army Museum, London

cred the women and children. When a fresh British force arrived, it exacted revenge by subjecting rebels and suspects to summary execution by hanging. Elsewhere British forces punished mutineers by blowing them to bits with a cannon. By May 1858 the British had crushed the rebellion and restored their authority in India.

British Imperial Rule

To stabilize affairs and forestall future problems, the British government preempted the East India Company and imposed direct imperial rule in India. In 1858 Queen Victoria (reigned 1837–1901) assigned responsibility for Indian policy to the newly established office of secretary of state for India. A viceroy represented British royal authority in India and administered the colony through an elite Indian civil service staffed almost exclusively by Englishmen. Indians served in low-level bureaucratic positions, but British officials formulated all domestic and foreign policy in India.

Under both the East India Company and direct colonial administration, British rule transformed India. As they extended their authority to all parts of India and Ceylon (modern Sri Lanka), British officials cleared forests, restructured land holdings, and encouraged the cultivation of crops like tea, coffee, and opium that were especially valuable trade items. They built extensive railroad and telegraph networks that tightened links between India and the larger global economy. They also constructed new canals, harbors, and irrigation systems to support commerce and agriculture.

British colonial authorities made little effort to promote Christianity, but they established English-style schools for the children of Indian elites, whom they sought as supporters of their rule. They also suppressed Indian customs that conflicted with European law or values. Most prominent of these customs was *sati*, the practice of burning widows on their husbands' funeral pyres. Although not universally observed, sati was not an uncommon practice among upper-class Hindus, who believed that women should serve their husbands loyally and follow them even in death. Under pressure from the East India Company, Indian law banned sati as early as 1829, but effective suppression of the practice came only after a long campaign by colonial authorities.

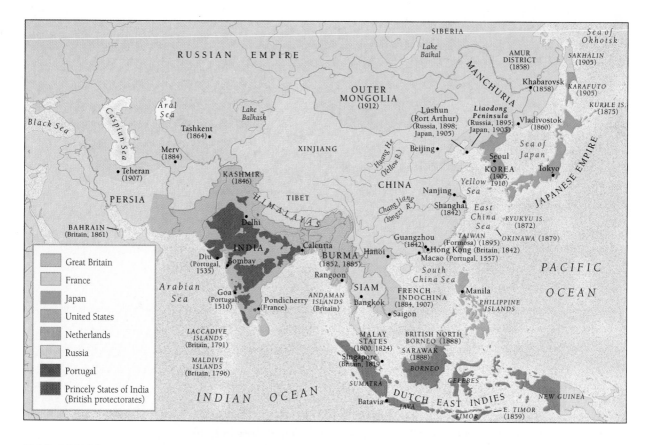

MAP [33.1]

Imperialism in Asia.

Imperialism in Central Asia and Southeast Asia

As the East India Company and British colonial agents tightened their grip on India, competition among European states kindled further empire-building efforts. Beginning in the early nineteenth century, French and Russian strategists sought ways to break British power and establish their own colonial presence in India. The French bid stalled after the fall of Napoleon, but Russian interest in India fueled a prolonged contest for power in central Asia.

The Great Game   Russian forces had probed central Asia as early as the sixteenth century, but only in the nineteenth century did they undertake a systematic effort to extend Russian authority south of the Caucasus. The weakening of the Ottoman and Qing empires turned central Asia into a political vacuum and invited Russian expansion into the region. By the 1860s cossacks had overcome Tashkent, Bokhara, and Samarkand, the great caravan cities of the silk roads, and approached the ill-defined northern frontier of British India. For the next half century, military officers and imperialist adventurers engaged in a risky pursuit of influence and intelligence that British agents referred to as the "Great Game."

Russian and British explorers ventured into parts of central Asia never before visited by Europeans. They mapped terrain, scouted mountain passes, and sought alliances with local rulers from Afghanistan to the Aral Sea—all in an effort to prepare for the anticipated war for India. In fact, the outbreak of global war in 1914 and the collapse of the tsarist state in 1917 ensured that the contest for India never took

Warships provide covering fire as British troops prepare to storm the Burmese port of Rangoon in 1824.

• © The British Library

place. Nevertheless, imperial expansion brought much of central Asia into the Russian empire and subjected the region to Russian hegemony that persisted until the disintegration of the Soviet Union in 1991.

Competition among European powers led also to further imperialism in southeast Asia. The Philippines had come under Spanish colonial rule in the sixteenth century, and many southeast Asian islands fell under Dutch rule in the seventeenth century. As imperial rivalries escalated in the nineteenth century, Dutch officials tightened their control and extended their authority throughout the Dutch East Indies, the archipelago that makes up the modern state of Indonesia. Along with cash crops of sugar, tea, coffee, and tobacco, exports of rubber and tin made the Dutch East Indies a valuable and productive colony.

In the interests of increasing trade between India, southeast Asia, and China, British imperialists moved in the nineteenth century to establish a presence in southeast Asia. As early as the 1820s, colonial officials in India conflicted with the kings of Burma (modern Myanmar) while seeking to extend their influence to the Irrawaddy River delta. By the 1880s they had established colonial authority in Burma, which became a source of teak, ivory, rubies, and jade. In 1824 Thomas Stamford Raffles founded the port of Singapore, which soon became the busiest center of trade in the Strait of Melaka. Administered by the colonial regime in India, Singapore served as the base for the British conquest of Malaya (modern Malaysia) in the 1870s and 1880s. Besides offering outstanding ports that enabled the British navy to control sea-lanes linking the Indian Ocean with the South China Sea, Malaya provided abundant supplies of tin and rubber.

British Colonies in Southeast Asia

Although foiled in their efforts to establish themselves in India, French imperialists built the large southeast Asian colony of French Indochina, consisting of the modern states of Vietnam, Cambodia, and Laos, between 1859 and 1893. Like their British counterparts in India, French colonial officials introduced European-style schools and sought to establish close connections with native elites. Unlike

French Indochina

their rivals, French officials also encouraged conversion to Christianity, and as a result the Roman Catholic church became prominent throughout French Indochina, especially Vietnam. By century's end all of southeast Asia had come under European imperial rule except for the kingdom of Siam (modern Thailand), which preserved its independence largely because colonial officials regarded it as a convenient buffer state between British-dominated Burma and French Indochina.

The Scramble for Africa

The most striking outburst of imperialism took place in Africa. As late as 1875 European peoples maintained a limited presence in Africa. They held several small coastal colonies and fortified trading posts, but their only sizable possessions were the Portuguese colonies of Angola and Mozambique, the French settler colony in northern Algeria, and a cluster of settler colonies populated by British and Dutch migrants in South Africa. After the end of the slave trade, a lively commerce developed around the exchange of African gold, ivory, and palm oil for European textiles, guns, and manufactured goods. This trade brought considerable prosperity and economic opportunity especially to west African lands.

Between 1875 and 1900, however, the relationship between Africa and Europe dramatically changed. Within a quarter century European imperial powers partitioned and colonized almost the entire African continent. Prospects of exploiting African resources and nationalist rivalries between European powers help to explain this frenzied quest for empire, often referred to as the "scramble for Africa."

European Explorers in Africa

European imperialists built on the information compiled by a series of adventurers and explorers who charted interior regions of Africa that Europeans had never before visited. Some went to Africa as missionaries. Best known of them was Dr. David Livingstone, a Scottish minister, who traveled through much of central and southern Africa in the mid-nineteenth century in search of suitable locations for mission posts. Other travelers were adventurers like the American journalist Henry Morton Stanley who undertook a well-publicized expedition to find Livingstone and report on his activities. Meanwhile, two English geographical enthusiasts, Richard Burton and John Speke, ventured into east Africa seeking the source of the Nile River. The geographical information compiled by these travelers held great interest for merchants eager to exploit business opportunities in Africa.

Especially exciting was reliable information about the great African rivers—the Nile, Niger, Congo, and Zambesi—and the access they provided to inland regions. In the 1870s King Leopold II of Belgium (reigned 1865–1909) employed Henry Morton Stanley to help develop commercial ventures and establish a colony called the Congo Free State (modern-day Republic of Congo) in the basin of the Congo River. To forestall competition from Belgium's much larger and more powerful European neighbors, Leopold announced that the Congo region would be a free-trade zone accessible to merchants and businessmen from all European lands. In fact, however, he carved out a personal colony and filled it with lucrative rubber plantations run by forced labor. Working conditions in the Congo Free State were so brutal, taxes so high, and abuses so many that humanitarians protested Leopold's colonial regime. In 1908 the Belgian government took control of the colony, known thereafter as Belgian Congo.

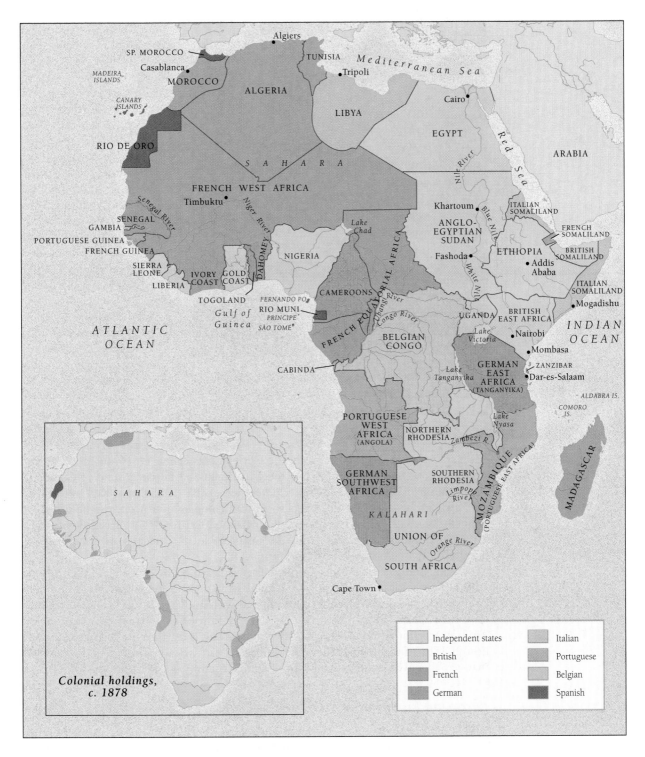

MAP [33.2]

Imperialism in Africa.

Henry Morton Stanley spent a great deal of time in the jungle, but here he appears, along with his gunbearer Kalulu, in front of a painted backdrop in a photographer's studio. • Hulton Getty/Liaison

As Leopold colonized central Africa, Britain established an imperial presence in Egypt. As Muhammad Ali and other Egyptian rulers sought to build up their army, strengthen the economy, and distance themselves from Ottoman authority, they borrowed heavily from European lenders. By the 1870s crushing debt forced Egyptian officials to impose high taxes, which provoked popular unrest and a military rebellion. In 1882 a British army occupied Egypt to protect British financial interests and ensure the safety of the Suez Canal, which was crucial to British communications with India.

The establishment of Belgian and British colonies in Africa alarmed European statesmen and heightened nationalist rivalries. In an

The Berlin Conference   effort to bring order to imperialism, the German chancellor, Otto von Bismarck, invited delegates of fourteen states to meet in Berlin and devise ground rules for the colonization of Africa. The Berlin Conference (1884–1885) produced agreement that any European state could establish African colonies after notifying the others of its intentions and occupying previously unclaimed territory. The Berlin Conference provided European diplomats with the justification they needed to draw lines on maps and carve a continent into colonies.

During the 1890s European imperialists sent armies to consolidate their claims and impose colonial rule in Africa. Armed with cannons and machine guns, they rarely failed to defeat African forces equipped with outdated muskets and sometimes only with spears. By the turn of the century, European colonies embraced all of Africa except for Ethiopia, where native forces fought off Italian efforts at colonization in 1896, and Liberia, a small republic in west Africa populated by freed slaves that was effectively a dependency of the United States.

European Imperialism in the Pacific

While scrambling for Africa, European imperial powers did not overlook opportunities to establish their presence in the Pacific Ocean basin. Imperialism in the Pacific took two main forms. In Australia and New Zealand, European powers established settler colonies and dominant political institutions. In most of the Pacific islands, however, they sought commercial opportunities and reliable bases for their operations, but did not wish to go to the trouble or expense of outright colonization. Only in the late nineteenth century did they begin to impose direct colonial rule on the islands.

European mariners reconnoitered Australia and made occasional landfalls from the early sixteenth century, but only after the Pacific voyages of Captain James Cook did Europeans travel to the southern continent in large numbers. In 1770 Cook anchored his fleet for a week at Botany Bay, near modern Sydney, and reported that the region would be suitable for settlement. In 1788 a British fleet with about one thousand settlers, most of them convicted criminals, arrived at Sydney harbor and established the colony of New South Wales. The migrants supported themselves mostly by herding sheep. Lured by opportunity, voluntary migrants outnumbered convicts by the 1830s, and the discovery of gold in 1851 brought a surge in migration to Australia. European settlers established communities also in New Zealand. Europeans first visited New Zealand while hunting whales and seals, but the islands' fertile soils and abundant stands of timber soon attracted their attention and drew large numbers of migrants.

Settler Colonies in the Pacific

European migration rocked the societies of Australia and New Zealand. Diseases like smallpox and measles devastated indigenous peoples at the same time that European migrants flooded into their lands. The aboriginal population of Australia fell from about 650,000 in 1800 to 90,000 in 1900, whereas the European population rose from a few thousand to 3.75 million during the same period. Similarly, the population of indigenous Maori in New Zealand fell from about 200,000 in 1800 to 45,000 a century later while European numbers climbed to 750,000.

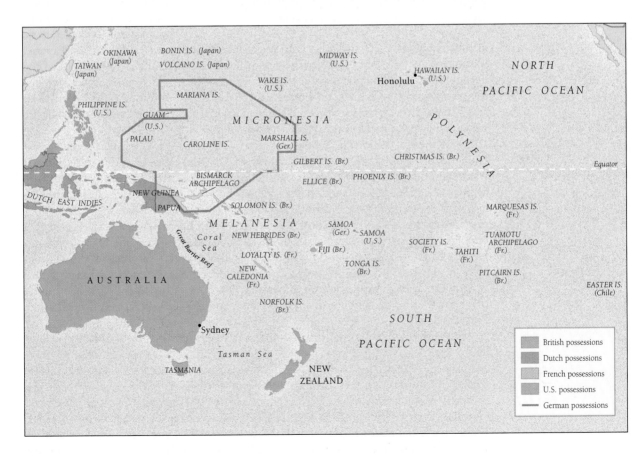

MAP [33.3]

Imperialism in Oceania.

An anonymous contemporary painting depicts the signing of the Treaty of Waitangi on 6 February 1840. British military and colonial officials look on as about fifty Maori chiefs put their names to the document. • Mary Evans Picture Library

Increasing migration also fueled conflict between European settlers and native populations. Large settler societies pushed indigenous peoples from their lands, often following violent confrontations. Because the nomadic foraging peoples of Australia did not occupy lands permanently, British settlers considered the continent *terra nullius*—"land belonging to no one"—that they could seize and put to their own uses. They undertook brutal military campaigns to evict aboriginal peoples from lands suitable for agriculture or herding, and by 1900 they had largely restricted native peoples to reservations located mostly in desert regions. A similar process took place in New Zealand. In 1840 settlers and missionaries persuaded Maori leaders to sign the Treaty of Waitangi, which placed the declining Maori population and the land of New Zealand under British protection. Settlers soon purchased titles to the best lands, provoking Maori resistance. Between 1860 and 1864 settlers and Maori fought a series of land wars that ended with victory for the settlers and confinement of the Maori to reservations.

Imperialists in Paradise

Even though imported diseases ravaged indigenous populations, the Pacific islands mostly escaped the fate of Australia and New Zealand, where settlers overwhelmed and overpowered native populations. During the nineteenth century the principal European visitors to Pacific islands were whalers, merchants, and missionaries. Whalers frequented ports where they could relax, refit their ships, and drink rum. Merchants sought fragrant sandalwood and succulent sea slugs, both of which fetched high prices in China. Missionaries established both Roman Catholic and Protestant churches throughout the Pacific Ocean basin. Naval vessels sometimes made a show of force or intervened in disputes between islanders and Europeans—or between competing groups of Europeans. Through most of the nineteenth century, however, imperialist powers had no desire to establish direct colonial rule over Pacific islands.

This situation changed in the late nineteenth century. Just as nationalist rivalries drove the scramble for Africa, so they encouraged imperialist powers to stake their claims in the Pacific. In an era of global imperialism, European states sought reliable coaling stations for their steamships and ports for their navies. France established a protectorate in Tahiti, the Society Islands, and the Marquesas as early as 1841 and imposed direct colonial rule in 1880. France also annexed New Caledonia in 1853. Britain made Fiji a crown colony in 1874, and Germany annexed several of the Marshall Islands in 1876 and 1878. At the Berlin Conference, European diplomats agreed on a partition of Oceania as well as Africa, and Britain, France, Germany, and the United States proceeded to claim almost all of the Pacific islands. By 1900 only the kingdom of Tonga remained independent, and even Tonga accepted British protection against the possibility of encroachments by other imperial powers.

Quite apart from their value as ports and coaling stations, the Pacific islands offered economic benefits to imperial powers. Hawai`i and Fiji were the sites of immensely productive sugarcane plantations. Samoa, French Polynesia, and many Melanesian and Micronesian islands were sources of copra—dried coconut, which produced high-quality vegetable oil for the manufacture of soap, candles, and lubricants. New Caledonia had rich veins of nickel, and many small Pacific islands had abundant deposits of guano—bird droppings that made excellent fertilizer.

THE EMERGENCE OF NEW IMPERIAL POWERS

Nineteenth-century imperialism was mostly a European affair. Toward the end of the century, however, two new imperial powers appeared on the world stage: the United States and Japan. Both lands experienced rapid industrialization in the late nineteenth century, and both built powerful armed forces. As European imperial powers planted their flags throughout the world, leaders of the United States and Japan decided that they too needed to establish a global imperial presence.

U.S. Imperialism in Latin America and the Pacific

The very existence of the United States was due to European imperialism. After the new republic had won its independence, U.S. leaders pursued their manifest destiny and brought almost all the temperate regions of North America under their authority. Like British migrants in Australia and New Zealand, Euro-American cultivators pushed indigenous peoples onto marginal lands and reservations. This domination of the North American continent represents a part of the larger story of European and Euro-American imperialism.

The fledgling United States also wielded power outside North America. In 1823 President James Monroe (in office 1817–1825) issued a proclamation that warned European states against imperialist designs in the western hemisphere. In essence Monroe claimed the Americas as a U.S. protectorate, and his proclamation, known as the Monroe Doctrine, served as a justification for U.S. intervention in hemispheric affairs. Until the late nineteenth century, the United States mostly exercised informal influence in the Americas and sought to guarantee free trade in the region. This policy benefited U.S. entrepreneurs and their European counterparts who worked to bring the natural resources and agricultural products of the Americas to the world market.

The Monroe Doctrine

As the United States consolidated its continental holdings, U.S. leaders became interested in acquiring territories beyond the temperate regions of North America. In 1867 the United States purchased Alaska from Russia and in 1875 claimed a protectorate over the islands of Hawai`i, where U.S. businessmen had established highly productive sugarcane plantations. The Hawaiian kingdom survived until 1893, when a group of planters and businessmen overthrew the last monarch, Queen Lili`uokalani, and invited the United States to annex the islands. U.S. president Grover Cleveland (in office 1885–1889 and 1893–1897) opposed annexation, but his successor, William McKinley (in office 1897–1901), was more open to American expansion and agreed to acquire the islands as U.S. possessions in 1898.

The Spanish-American War

Queen Liliʻuokalani, last monarch of Hawaiʻi, before her deposition in 1893. Wearing a European dress, the queen sits on a throne covered with a traditional royal cape made of bird feathers. • Brown Brothers

The United States emerged as a major imperial and colonial power after the brief Spanish-American War (1898–1899). War broke out as anticolonial tensions mounted in Cuba and Puerto Rico—the last remnants of Spain's American empire—where U.S. business interests had made large investments. In 1898 the U.S. battleship *Maine* exploded and sank in Havana harbor. U.S. leaders suspected sabotage and declared war on Spain. The United States easily defeated Spain and took possession of Cuba and Puerto Rico. After the U.S. navy destroyed the Spanish fleet at Manila in a single day, the United States also took possession of Guam and the Philippines, Spain's last colonies in the Pacific, to prevent them from falling under German or Japanese control.

The United States quickly established colonial governments in most of its new possessions. Instability and disorder prompted the new imperial power to intervene also in the affairs of Caribbean and Central American lands, even those that were not U.S. possessions, to prevent rebellion and protect American business interests. U.S. military forces occupied Cuba, the Dominican Republic, Nicaragua, Honduras, and Haiti in the early twentieth century.

The consolidation of U.S. authority in the Philippines was an especially difficult affair. The Spanish-American War coincided with a Filipino revolt against Spanish rule, and U.S. forces promised to support independence of the Philippines in exchange for an alliance against Spain. After the victory over Spain, however, President William McKinley decided to bring the Philippines under American control. The United States paid Spain twenty million dollars for rights to the colony, which was important to American businessmen and military leaders because of its strategic position in the South China Sea. Led by Emilio Aguinaldo—known to his followers as the George Washington of his country—Filipino rebels turned their arms against the new intruders. The result was a bitter insurrection that raged until 1902 and flared sporadically until 1906. The conflict claimed the lives of 4,200 American soldiers, fifteen thousand rebel troops, and some two hundred thousand Filipino civilians.

To facilitate communication and transportation between the Atlantic and Pacific Oceans, the United States sought to build a canal across some narrow stretch of land in Central America. Engineers identified the isthmus of Panama in northern Colombia as the best site for a canal, but Colombia was unwilling to cede land for the project. Under President Theodore Roosevelt (in office 1901–1909), an enthusiastic champion of imperial expansion, the United States supported a rebellion against Colombia in 1903 and helped rebels establish the breakaway state of Panama. In exchange for this support, the United States won the right to build a canal across Panama and to control the adjacent territory known as the Panama Canal Zone. When it opened in 1914, the Panama Canal strengthened both the military and the economic power of the United States.

The Panama Canal

Imperial Japan

Strengthened by rapid industrialization during the Meiji era, Japan joined the ranks of imperial powers in the late nineteenth century. Japanese leaders deeply resented the unequal treaties that the United States and European powers forced them to accept in the 1860s. They resolved to eliminate the diplomatic handicaps imposed by the treaties and to raise Japan's profile in the world. While founding representative political institutions to demonstrate their trustworthiness to American and European statesmen, Japanese leaders also made a bid to stand alongside the world's great powers by launching a campaign of imperial expansion.

The Japanese drive to empire began in the east Asian islands. During the 1870s Japanese leaders consolidated their hold on Hokkaido and the Kurile Islands to the north, and they encouraged Japanese migrants to populate the islands to forestall Russian expansion there. By 1879 they had also established their hegemony over Okinawa and the Ryukyu Islands to the south.

Early Japanese Expansion

In 1876 Japan purchased modern warships from Britain, and the newly strengthened Japanese navy immediately began to flex its muscles in Korea. After a confrontation between the Korean navy and a Japanese surveying vessel, Meiji officials dispatched a gunboat expedition and forced Korean leaders to submit to the same kind of unequal treaty that the United States and European states had imposed on Japan. As European and U.S. imperialists divided up the world in the 1880s and 1890s, Meiji political and military leaders made plans to project Japanese power abroad. They developed contingency plans for a conflict with China, staged maneuvers in anticipation of a continental war, and built a navy with the capacity to fight on the high seas.

Conflict erupted in 1894 over the status of Korea. Taking advantage of the unequal treaty of 1876, Japanese businesses had substantial interests in Korea. When an antiforeign rebellion broke out in Korea in 1893, Meiji leaders feared that the land might fall into anarchy and become an inviting target of European and U.S. imperialism. Qing rulers sent an army to restore order and reassert Chinese authority in Korea, but Meiji leaders were unwilling to recognize Chinese control over a land so important to Japanese business interests. Thus in August 1894 they declared war on China. The Japanese navy quickly gained control of the Yellow Sea and demolished the Chinese fleet in a battle lasting a mere five hours. The Japanese army then pushed Qing forces out of the Korean peninsula. Within a few months the conflict was over. When the combatants made peace in April 1895, Qing authorities recognized the independence of Korea, thus making it essentially a dependency of Japan.

The Sino-Japanese War

They also ceded Taiwan, the Pescadores Islands, and the Liaodong peninsula, which strengthened Japanese control over east Asian waters. Alongside territorial acquisitions, Japan also gained unequal treaty rights in China like those enjoyed by European and American powers.

The unexpected Japanese victory startled European imperial powers, especially Russia. Tensions between Japan and Russia soon mounted, as both imperial powers had territorial ambitions in the Liaodong peninsula, Korea, and Manchuria. During the late 1890s Japanese military leaders vastly strengthened both their navy and their army with an eye toward a future conflict with Russia.

The Russo-Japanese War   War broke out in 1904, and Japanese forces overran Russian installations before reinforcements could arrive from Europe. The enhanced Japanese navy destroyed the Russian Baltic fleet, which had sailed halfway around the world to support the war effort. By 1905 the war was over, and Japan won international recognition of its colonial authority over Korea and the Liaodong peninsula. Furthermore, Russia ceded the southern half of Sakhalin island to Japan, along with a railroad and economic interests in southern Manchuria. Victory in the Russo-Japanese War transformed Japan into a major imperial power.

 ## LEGACIES OF IMPERIALISM

Imperialism and colonialism profoundly influenced the development of world history. In some ways they tightened links between the world's peoples: trade and migration increased dramatically as imperial powers exploited the resources of subject lands and recruited labor forces to work in colonies throughout the world. Yet imperialism and colonialism also brought peoples into conflict and heightened senses of difference between peoples. European, Euro-American, and Japanese imperialists all came to think of themselves as superior to the peoples they overcame. Meanwhile, foreign intrusion stimulated the development of national identities in colonized lands, and over time these national identities served as a foundation for anticolonial independence movements.

Empire and Economy

One of the principal motives of imperialism was the desire to gain access to natural resources and agricultural products. As imperial powers consolidated their hold on foreign lands, colonial administrators reorganized subject societies so they would become efficient suppliers of timber, rubber, petroleum, gold, silver, diamonds, cotton, tea, coffee, cacao, and other products as well. As a result, global trade in these commodities surged during the nineteenth and early twentieth centuries. The advantages of this trade went mostly to the colonial powers, whose policies encouraged their subject lands to provide raw materials for processing in the industrialized societies of Europe, North America, and Japan.

Economic and Social Changes   Sometimes colonial rule transformed the production of crops and commodities that had long been prominent in subject societies. In India, for example, the cultivation of cotton began probably before 5000 B.C.E. For most of history cultivators spun thread and wove their own cotton textiles or else supplied local craftsmen with raw materials. In the nineteenth century, however, colonial administrators reoriented the cultivation of cotton to serve the needs of the emerging British textile industry. They encouraged cultivators to produce cotton for export rather than for

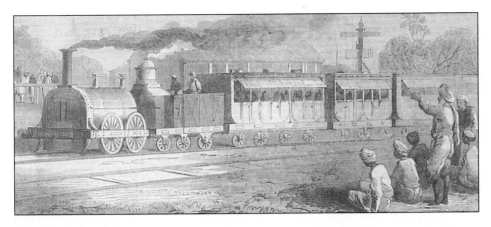

An engraving depicts the East India Railway about 1863. Though originally built to transport goods, railroads quickly became a popular means of passenger travel in India. • Mary Evans Picture Library

local consumption, and they built railroads deep into the subcontinent to transport raw cotton to the coast quickly, before rain and dust could spoil the product. They shipped raw cotton to England, where mechanized factories rapidly turned out large volumes of high-quality textiles. They also allowed the import of inexpensive British textiles, which undermined the Indian cotton industry. The value of raw cotton exported from India went from 10 million rupees in 1849 to 60 million rupees in 1860 and 410 million rupees in 1913, whereas the value of finished cotton products imported into India rose from 50,000 rupees in 1814 to 5.2 million rupees in 1829 and 30 million rupees in 1890. Thus colonial policies transformed India from the world's principal center of cotton manufacture to a supplier of raw cotton and a consumer of textiles produced in the British isles.

In some cases colonial rule led to the introduction of new crops that transformed both the landscape and the social order of subject lands. In the early nineteenth century, for example, British colonial officials introduced tea bushes from China to Ceylon and India. The effect on Ceylon was profound. British planters felled trees in much of the island, converted rain forests into tea plantations, and recruited Ceylonese women by the thousands to carry out the labor-intensive work of harvesting mature tea leaves. Consumption of tea in India and Ceylon was almost negligible, so increased supplies met the burgeoning demand for tea in Europe, where the beverage became accessible to individuals of all social classes. The value of south Asian tea exports rose from about 309,000 pounds sterling in 1866 to 4.4 million pounds sterling in 1888 and 6.1 million pounds sterling in 1900. Malaya and Sumatra underwent a similar social transformation after British colonial agents planted rubber trees there in the 1870s and established plantations to meet the growing global demand for rubber products.

Labor Migrations

Efforts to exploit the natural resources and agricultural products of subject lands led imperial and colonial powers to encourage mass migrations of workers during the nineteenth and early twentieth centuries. Two patterns of labor migration were especially prominent during the imperial and colonial era. European migrants went

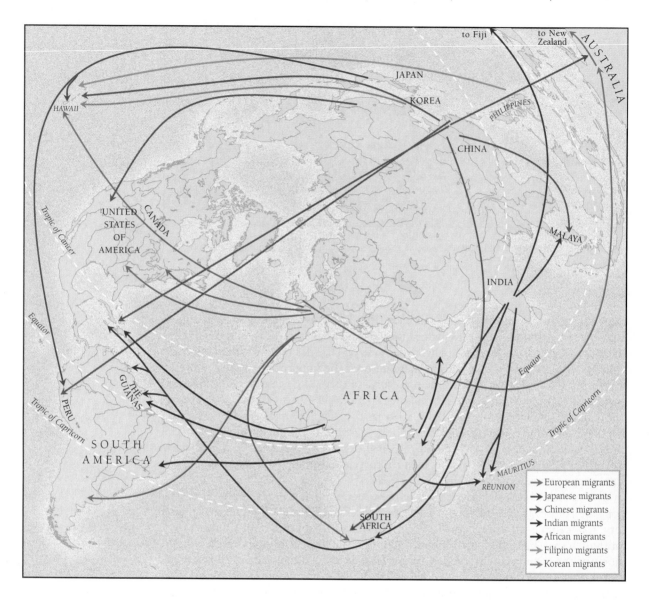

MAP [33.4]

Imperialism and migration.

mostly to temperate lands, where they worked as free cultivators or industrial laborers. By contrast, migrants from Asia, Africa, and the Pacific islands moved largely to tropical and subtropical lands, where they worked as indentured laborers on plantations or manual laborers for mining enterprises or large-scale construction projects. Between them, these two streams of labor migration profoundly influenced the development of societies especially in the Americas and the Pacific basin.

European Migration   Between 1800 and 1914 some fifty million European migrants left their homes and sought opportunities overseas. Most of these migrants left the relatively poor agricultural societies of southern and eastern Europe, especially Italy, Russia, and Poland, although sizable numbers came also from Britain, Ireland, Germany, and Scandinavia. A majority of the migrants—about thirty-two million—went to the United States. Many of the early arrivals went west in search of cheap land to cultivate. Later migrants settled heavily in the northeast, where they provided the labor that drove U.S. industrialization after the 1860s. Settler colonies in Canada, Argentina, Australia, New Zealand, and South Africa also drew large numbers of European migrants who mostly became free cultivators or herders but sometimes found employment as skilled laborers in mines or fledgling industries. Most European migrants traveled as free agents, but some went as indentured laborers. All of them were able to find opportunities in temperate regions of the world because of European and Euro-American imperialism in the Americas, south Africa, and Oceania.

In contrast to their European counterparts, migrants from Asia, Africa, and the Pacific islands generally traveled as indentured laborers. As the institution of slavery went into decline, planters sought large numbers of laborers to replace slaves who left the plantations. The planters relied primarily on contract laborers recruited from relatively poor and densely populated lands. Between 1820 and 1914 about 2.5 million indentured laborers left their homes to work in distant parts of the world. Labor recruiters generally offered workers free passage to their destinations and provided them with food, shelter, clothing, and modest compensation for their services in exchange for a commitment to work for five to seven years. Sometimes recruiters also offered free return passage to workers who completed a second term of service.

*Indentured Labor
Migration*

The majority of the indentured laborers came from India, but sizable numbers came also from China, Japan, Java, Africa, and the Pacific islands. Indentured laborers went mostly to tropical and subtropical lands in the Americas, the Caribbean, Africa, and Oceania. The indentured labor trade began in the 1820s when French and British colonial officials sent Indian migrants to work on sugar plantations in the Indian Ocean islands of Réunion and Mauritius. The arrangement worked well, and large numbers of Indian laborers later went to work on rubber plantations in Malaya and sugar plantations in south Africa, the Pacific island of Fiji, the Guianas, and the Caribbean islands of Trinidad, Tobago, and Jamaica. After the Opium War recruiters began to seek workers in China. Large numbers of Chinese laborers went to sugar plantations in Cuba and Hawai`i, guano mines in Peru, tin mines in Malaya, gold mines in south Africa and Australia, and railroad construction sites in the United States, Canada, and Peru. After the Meiji restoration in Japan, a large contingent of Japanese laborers migrated to Hawai`i to work on sugar plantations while a smaller group went to work in guano mines in Peru. Indentured laborers from Africa went mostly to sugar plantations in Réunion, the Guianas, and Caribbean islands. Those from Pacific islands went mostly to plantations in other Pacific islands and Australia.

All these large-scale migrations of the nineteenth century reflected the global influence of imperial powers. European migrations were possible only because European and Euro-American peoples had established settler societies in temperate regions around the world. Movements of indentured laborers were possible because colonial officials were able to recruit workers and dispatch them to distant lands where their compatriots had already established plantations or opened mines. In combination the nineteenth-century migrations profoundly influenced societies around the world by depositing large communities of people with distinctive ethnic identities in lands far from their original homes.

*Empire
and Migration*

Empire and Society

The policies adopted by imperial powers and colonial officials forced peoples of different societies to deal with one another on a regular and systematic basis. Their interactions often led to violent conflicts between colonizers and subject peoples. The sepoy rebellion was the most prominent effort to resist British colonial authority in

Colonial Conflict

India, but it was only one among thousands of insurrections organized by discontented Indian subjects between the mid-nineteenth and the mid-twentieth century. Colonized lands in southeast Asia and Africa also became hotbeds of resistance, as subject peoples revolted against foreign rule, tyrannical behavior of colonial officials, the introduction of European schools and curricula, high taxation, and requirements that subject peoples cultivate certain crops or provide compulsory labor for colonists' enterprises.

Many rebellions drew strength from traditional religious beliefs, and priests or prophets often led resistance to colonial rule. In Tanganyika, for example, a local prophet organized the massive Maji Maji rebellion (1905–1906) to expel German colonial authorities from east Africa. Rebels sprinkled themselves with "magic water" (*maji-maji*), which they believed would protect them from German weapons. The magic water was ineffective, and as many as seventy-five thousand insurgents died in the conflict. Nevertheless, rebellion was a constant threat to colonial rule. Even when subject peoples dared not revolt, since they could not match European weaponry, they resisted colonial rule by boycotting European goods, organizing political parties and pressure groups, publishing anticolonial newspapers and magazines, and pursuing anticolonial policies through churches and religious groups.

Colonial policies also led to conflicts among peoples brought together artificially into multicultural societies. When indentured laborers from different societies congregated on plantations, for example, tensions quickly developed between workers and their supervisors and among different groups of workers themselves. In Hawai`i, one of the most diverse multicultural societies created by the labor migrations of the nineteenth century, workers on sugar plantations came primarily from China, Japan, and Portugal, but there were also sizable contingents from the Philippines, Korea, and other Pacific islands. Workers and their families normally lived in villages dominated by their own ethnic groups, but there were plentiful opportunities for individuals and groups to conflict with each other at work, at play, or in the larger society. While the various ethnic communities readily adopted their neighbors' foods and sometimes took spouses from other groups, linguistic, religious, and cultural differences provided a foundation for strong ethnic identities throughout the plantation era and beyond.

Scientific Racism   Social and cultural differences were the foundation of an academic pursuit known as scientific racism, which became prominent especially after the 1840s. Theorists like the French nobleman Count Joseph Arthur de Gobineau (1816–1882) took race as the most important index of human potential. In fact, there is no such thing as a biologically pure race, but nineteenth-century theorists assumed that the human species consisted of several distinct racial groups. In his dense, four-volume *Essay on the Inequality of the Human Races* (1853–1855), Gobineau divided humanity into four main racial groups, each of which had its own peculiar traits. Gobineau characterized Africans as unintelligent and lazy; Asians as smart but docile; the native peoples of the Americas as dull and arrogant; and Europeans as intelligent, noble, and morally superior to others. Throughout the later nineteenth and early twentieth centuries, racist thinkers sought to identify racial groups on the basis of skin color, bone structure, nose shape, cranial capacity, and other physical characteristics. Agreeing uniformly that Europeans were superior to other peoples, race theorists clearly reflected the dominance of European imperial powers in the larger world.

After the 1860s scientific racists drew heavily from the writings of Charles Darwin (1809–1882), an English biologist whose book *The Origin of Species* (1859) argued that all living species had evolved over thousands of years in a ferocious contest for survival. Species that adapted well to their environment survived, reproduced, and flourished, according to Darwin, while others declined and went into extinction. The slogan "survival of the fittest" soon became a byword for Darwin's theory of evolution. Theorists known as Social Darwinists seized upon these ideas, which Darwin had applied exclusively to biological matters, and adapted them to explain the development of human societies. The English philosopher Herbert Spencer (1820–1903) relied on theories of evolution to explain differences between the strong and the weak: successful individuals and races had competed better in the natural world and consequently evolved to higher states than did other less fit peoples. On the basis of this reasoning, Spencer and others justified the domination of European imperialists over subject peoples as the inevitable result of natural scientific principles.

On a more popular level, there was no need for elaborate scientific theories to justify racist prejudices. Representatives of imperial and colonial powers routinely adopted racist views on the basis of personal experience, which seemed to teach their superiority to subject peoples. In 1896, for example, the British military officer Colonel Francis Younghusband reflected on differences between peoples that he noticed during his travels throughout China, central Asia, and India. He granted that Asian peoples were physically and intellectually equal to Europeans, but he held that

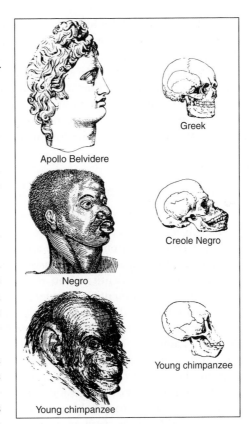

Popular Racism

Scientific racists often argued that Europeans had reached a higher stage of evolution than other peoples. An illustration from a popular book by Josiah Clark Nott and G. R. Glidden, *Indigenous Races of the Earth*, deliberately distorted facial and skull features to suggest a close relationship between African peoples and chimpanzees.
• General Research Collection, New York Public Library, Astor, Lenox and Tilden Foundations

No European can mix with non-Christian races without feeling his moral superiority over them. He feels, from the first contact with them, that whatever may be their relative positions from an intellectual point of view, he is stronger morally than they are. And facts show that this feeling is a true one. It is not because we are any cleverer than the natives of India, because we have more brains or bigger heads than they have, that we rule India; but because we are stronger morally than they are. Our superiority over them is not due to mere sharpness of intellect, but to that higher moral nature to which we have attained in the development of the human race.

Racist views were by no means a monopoly of European imperialists: U.S. and Japanese empire builders also developed a sense of superiority over the peoples they conquered and ruled. U.S. forces in the Philippines disparaged the rebels they fought there as "gooks," and they did not hesitate to torture enemies in a conflict justified by President McKinley as an effort to "civilize and Christianize" the Filipinos. In the 1890s Japanese newspapers portrayed Chinese and Korean peoples as dirty, backward, stupid, and cowardly. Some scholars concocted speculative theories that the Japanese people were more akin to the "Aryans," who supposedly had conquered much of the Eurasian landmass in ancient times, than to the "Mongolians" who populated China and Korea. After their victory in the Russo-Japanese War, political and military leaders came to believe that Japan had an obligation to oversee the affairs of their backward neighbors and help civilize their little Asian brothers.

Nationalism and Anticolonial Movements

While imperialists convinced themselves of their racial superiority, colonial rule provoked subject peoples to develop a sense of their own identities. Just as Napoleon's invasions aroused national feelings and led to the emergence of nationalist movements in Europe, so imperial expansion and colonial domination prompted the formation of national identities and the organization of anticolonial movements in subject lands. The potential of imperialism and colonialism to push subject peoples toward nationalism was most evident in India.

Ram Mohan Roy

During the nineteenth century educated Indian elites helped forge a sense of Indian identity. Among the most influential of them was Ram Mohan Roy (1772–1833), a prominent Bengali intellectual sometimes called the "father of modern India." Roy argued for the construction of a society based on both modern European science and the Indian tradition of devotional Hinduism. He supported some British colonial policies, such as the campaign to end the practice of sati, and he worked with Christian social reformers to improve the status of women by providing them with education and property rights. Yet Roy saw himself as a Hindu reformer who drew inspiration from the Vedas and Upanishads and who sought to bring Hindu spirituality to bear on the problems and conditions of his own time. During the last two decades of his life, Roy tirelessly published newspapers and founded societies to mobilize educated Hindus and advance the cause of social reform in colonial India.

Reform societies flourished in nineteenth-century India. Most of them appealed to upper-caste Hindus, but some were Muslim organizations, and a few represented the interests of peasants, landlords, or lower castes. After midcentury reformers increasingly called for self-government or at least greater Indian participation in government. Their leaders often had an advanced education in British universities, and they drew inspiration from European Enlightenment values, such as equality, freedom, and popular sovereignty. But they invoked those values to criticize the British colonial regime in India and to call for political and social reform.

The Indian National Congress

The most important of the reform groups was the Indian National Congress, founded in 1885 with British approval, as a forum for educated Indians to communicate their views on public affairs to colonial officials. Representatives from all parts of the subcontinent aired grievances about Indian poverty, the transfer of wealth from India to Britain, trade and tariff policies that harmed Indian businesses, the inability of colonial officials to provide effective relief for regions stricken by drought or famine, and British racism toward Indians. By the end of the nineteenth century, the Congress openly sought Indian self-rule within a larger imperial framework. In 1906 the congress joined forces with the All-India Muslim League, the most prominent organization working to advance the political and social interests of Muslims, who made up about 25 percent of the Indian population.

Much of western India experienced severe famine in 1896–97, and epidemics of bubonic plague broke out among weakened populations. British relief efforts were often heavy-handed and insensitive, and they did little to alleviate the problems.   •   © Royal Geographical Society

Faced with increasing demands for Indian participation in government, in 1909 colonial authorities granted a limited franchise that allowed wealthy Indians to elect representatives to local legislative councils. By that time, however, the drive for political reform had become a mass movement. Indian nationalists called for immediate independence, mounted demonstrations to build support for their cause, and organized boycotts of British goods. A few zealous nationalists turned to violence and sought to undermine British rule by bombing government buildings and assassinating colonial officials. Going into the twentieth century, Indian nationalism was a powerful movement that would bring independence from colonial rule in 1947.

Although local experiences varied considerably, Indian nationalism and independence movements served as models for anticolonial campaigns in other lands. In almost all cases the leaders of these movements were European-educated elites who absorbed Enlightenment values in European universities and then turned those values into an attack on European colonial rule in foreign lands.

The construction of global empires in the nineteenth century noticeably increased the tempo of world history. Armed with powerful transportation, communication, and military technologies, European peoples imposed their rule on much of Asia and almost all of Africa. They wielded enormous influence throughout the world, even where they did not establish imperial control, because of their wealth and economic power. Toward the end of the nineteenth century, the United States and Japan joined European states as global imperialists. All the imperial powers profoundly influenced the development of the societies they ruled. They shaped the economies and societies of their colonies by pushing them to supply natural resources and agricultural commodities in exchange for manufactured products. They created multicultural societies around the world by facilitating the movement of workers to lands where there was high demand for labor on plantations or in mines. They unintentionally encouraged the emergence of independence movements by provoking subject peoples to develop a sense of national identity. From the early twentieth century forward, much of world history has revolved around issues stemming from the world order of imperialism and colonialism.

CHRONOLOGY

1772–1833	Life of Ram Mohan Roy
1809–1882	Life of Charles Darwin
1816–1882	Life of Count Joseph Arthur de Gobineau
1824	Founding of Singapore by Thomas Stamford Raffles
1840	Treaty of Waitangi
1853–1902	Life of Cecil Rhodes
1857	Sepoy rebellion
1859–1869	Construction of the Suez Canal
1860–1864	Land wars in New Zealand
1865–1909	Reign of King Leopold II of Belgium
1884–1885	Berlin Conference
1885	Founding of the Indian National Congress
1894–1895	Sino-Japanese War
1897–1901	Term of office of U.S. president William McKinley
1898–1899	Spanish-American War
1901–1909	Term of office of U.S. president Theodore Roosevelt
1904–1905	Russo-Japanese War
1904–1914	Construction of the Panama Canal
1905–1906	Maji Maji rebellion

FOR FURTHER READING

Michael Adas. *Machines as the Measure of Men: Science, Technology, and Ideologies of Western Dominance.* Ithaca, 1988. Argues that European imperialists judged other peoples on the basis of their technological expertise.

———. *Prophets of Rebellion: Millenarian Protest Movements against the European Colonial Order.* Cambridge, 1987. Fascinating study focusing on five rebellions against European colonial rule led by religious leaders.

Benedict Anderson. *Imagined Communities: Reflections on the Origin and Spread of Nationalism.* Rev. ed. London, 1991. Examines the emergence of nationalism in Europe and its spread to other parts of the world during the era of imperialism.

W. G. Beasley. *Japanese Imperialism, 1894–1945.* Oxford, 1987. The best study of the topic, emphasizing the relationship between Japanese industrialization and imperialism.

A. Adu Boahen. *African Perspectives on Colonialism.* Baltimore, 1987. A valuable synthetic work that examines African responses to imperial intrusions and colonial regimes.

Nupur Chaudhuri and Margaret Strobel, eds. *Western Women and Imperialism: Complicity and Resistance.* Bloomington, 1992. A collection of essays examining the roles of women in the imperial era.

Bernard S. Cohn. *Colonialism and Its Forms of Knowledge: The British in India.* Princeton, 1996. Insightful essays on the cultural and intellectual manifestations of imperialism.

D. K. Fieldhouse. *The Colonial Empires: A Comparative Survey from the Eighteenth Century.* London, 1966. Concentrates on the political history of European empires.

John Gallagher. *The Decline, Revival and Fall of the British Empire.* Ed. by Anil Seal. Cambridge, 1982. A collection of essays that have deeply influenced scholarship on the British empire.

Ranajit Guha and Gayatri Chakravorty Spivak, eds. *Selected Subaltern Studies.* New York, 1988. A collection of essays dealing with the experiences of women, minorities, peasants, workers, rebels, and subordinate groups in colonial India.

Daniel R. Headrick. *The Tentacles of Progress: Technology Transfer in the Age of Imperialism, 1850–1940.* New York, 1988. Argues that imperial powers reserved the benefits of technological innovation for themselves by limiting the expertise that they shared with subject peoples.

——. *The Tools of Empire: Technology and European Imperialism in the Nineteenth Century.* New York, 1981. Surveys the role of transportation, communication, military, and medical technologies in the making of global empires.

Peter Hopkirk. *The Great Game: The Struggle for Empire in Central Asia.* New York, 1992. Exciting account of the contest for power known as the Great Game.

Victor G. Kiernan. *The Lords of Human Kind: European Attitudes to the Outside World in the Imperial Age.* Rev. ed. Harmondsworth, 1972. Influential study of European paternalism and condescension toward colonial subjects.

David Northrup. *Indentured Labor in the Age of Imperialism, 1834–1922.* Cambridge, 1995. Careful study of indentured labor migrations and working conditions.

Thomas Pakenham. *The Scramble for Africa, 1876–1912.* New York, 1991. Detailed popular history of empire building in sub-Saharan Africa.

Robert I. Rotberg. *The Founder: Cecil Rhodes and the Pursuit of Power.* New York, 1988. An insightful psychohistorical biography of Cecil Rhodes.

PART VII

THE TWENTIETH CENTURY

· · ·

By the end of the nineteenth century, Europeans and their descendants in North America dominated global affairs to an unprecedented extent, exercising political and economic control over peoples and their lands in most of Asia, nearly all of Africa, the Americas, and the Pacific islands. This global dominance was the outcome of three interconnected historical developments that took place between 1750 and 1914. Political revolutions in the Atlantic Ocean basin had encouraged the formation of national states, which could mobilize large-scale popular support. Extensive economic transformations paralleled the political reorganization of national communities, as peoples in western Europe and North America initiated processes of industrialization. Industrializing societies wielded enormous political and economic power. Their efficient transportation systems, fast communications networks, and powerful military technology supported imperial and colonial expansion. The ensuing cross-cultural encounters resulted in a high degree of interaction among the world's peoples.

During the twentieth century global interaction continued at an accelerating rate. Two world wars and an intervening economic depression testify to this development. In 1914 a Europe torn by national rivalries, colonial disputes, and nationalist aspirations plunged into war. A system of entangling alliances quickly transformed a local war between the kingdom of Serbia and the Austro-Hungarian empire into a European-wide conflict, which contemporaries simply called the Great War. As the imperial powers of Europe began to draw on the human and material resources of their colonies and dependencies and as lands such as the Ottoman empire, Japan, and the United States became belligerents, the Great War turned increasingly global in scope. By the time the war ended in 1918, the major European powers, including the victorious ones, had exhausted much of their economic wealth and political power. The war of 1914–1918 signaled the beginning of the end of Europe's global primacy.

As societies tried to come to terms with the political and economic devastation wrought by the Great War, an unprecedented economic contraction gripped the globe. Global interdependence ensured that after 1929 most of the world had to cope with the effects of the Great Depression. Spawning political turmoil and social misery, the Great Depression helped pave the way to fascist dictatorships in Italy and Germany and authoritarian regimes elsewhere. While the industrial world reeled under the impact of the Great Depression, the communist leadership of the Soviet Union, a state born out of revolution in 1917, embarked on a state-sponsored program of rapid industrialization. Despite great human suffering, a series of five-year plans transformed the Soviet Union into a major international power and the first socialist state. Meanwhile, the continued economic and political weakening of the European colonial powers encouraged political ferment in Asia, where nationalist movements tried to forge new identities free from imperial domination.

The depression years witnessed yet another global war. World War II began in China in 1931, when Japanese forces began to establish a colonial empire in Chinese territory. Independently of these developments, the conflict spread to Europe in the late 1930s where the Nazi regime had embarked on a policy of territorial expansion. By 1941 all the world's major powers had been sucked into a maelstrom of violence and suffering that engulfed most European societies, almost all of Asia and the Pacific, and parts of Africa. World War II proved to be more destructive than any previous war and counted among its victims more civilians than soldiers. With the United States and the Soviet Union playing the lead roles, the Allied forces brought the conflict to a victorious end in 1945.

World War II completed the economic and political weakening of European societies, and colonial powers found themselves unable to retain their grip on their global possessions. In the first three decades after World War II, an irresistible wave of independence movements swept away colonies and empires and led to the establishment of new nations in Africa and Asia. The end of empire was one of the most important outcomes of World War II, but the initial euphoria that accompanied freedom from imperial control was tempered by problems such as rapid population growth, lack of economic development, and regional and ethnic conflicts among the former colonial lands. The arrival of the cold war further complicated the task of building new societies in a postcolonial world.

Like the process of decolonization, the cold war contributed significantly to global political transformations after World War II. It was a strategic struggle that developed between the United States and its allies on the one hand and the Soviet Union and its allied countries on the other. Differences between political and economic systems and conflicting postwar national interests had transformed the wartime alliance between the two superpowers into a confrontation between the forces of capitalism and communism. The conflict produced a new set of global relationships, shaping the foreign policies, economic systems, and political institutions of nations throughout the world. While the two superpowers always avoided a direct clash of arms, the cold war spawned the formation of military and political alliances, the creation of client states, and a nuclear arms race of unprecedented scope. It also engendered diplomatic crises, interference in developing nations, and at times brought the world to the brink of nuclear annihilation. The cold war ended suddenly in the late 1980s as the Soviet-dominated regimes of central and eastern Europe dissolved under the impact of mostly peaceful revolutions. In 1991 the Soviet Union collapsed under the weight of economic mismanagement, political dissent, and ethnic discord.

Together, the cold war and decolonization have reshaped the world in the late twentieth century, but other transforming forces have also been at work. Key among them is globalization, a process that has widened the extent and form of cross-cultural interaction among the world's peoples. Technological advances that are dissolving old political, social, and economic barriers partly drive globalization. Improvements in information, communication, and transportation technologies, for instance, have encouraged the movement of peoples, diseases, and cultural preferences across political and geographic borders. In this highly interdependent world, the task of dealing with problems of a global magnitude—such as human rights, epidemic diseases, gender equity, and environmental pollution—increasingly require international cooperation. Governmental and nongovernmental international organizations have started to address global concerns, though most national states have been hesitant to surrender their sovereignty to international organizations such as the United Nations. Greater global integration has encouraged similar economic and political preferences and fostered common cultural values. But forces promoting distinct cultural traditions and political identities have also arisen to challenge the universalizing effects of globalization.

ASIA	AFRICA	EUROPE	AMERICAS AND OCEANIA
1910	**1910**	**1910**	**1910**
Chinese revolution and establishment of Republic (1911) Japan issues Twenty-one Demands to China (1915) Battle of Gallipoli (1915) Balfour Declaration (1917) May Fourth Movement (1919)	South Africa gains self-rule (1910) African National Congress created (1912)	World War I (1914–1918) Battles of Verdun and the Somme (1916) Treaty of Versailles (1919) Russian revolution (1917) Vladimir Ilych Lenin (1870–1924)	United States enters World War I (1917) Mexican Constitution of 1917
1920	**1920**	**1920**	**1920**
Mohandas Gandhi (1869–1948) Dr. Sun Yatsen (1866–1925) Jiang Jieshi unifies China (1927)		Lenin's New Economic Policy (1921) Benito Mussolini becomes leader of Italy (1922) First Soviet Five-Year Plan (1929) Joseph Stalin (1879–1953)	U.S. stock market collapses (1929) Great Depression begins
1930	**1930**	**1930**	**1930**
Mao Zedong (1893–1975) Long March (1934) Japanese invasions of Manchuria (1931) and China (1937)		Adolf Hitler becomes chancellor of Germany (1933) Nuremberg Laws (1935) and Kristallnacht (1938) Spanish Civil War (1936–1939) Munich Conference (1939) Nazi-Soviet Pact (1939) German invasion of Poland (1939)	Smoot-Hawley Tariff (1930) Mexican president Lázaro Cárdenas (1934–1940) Program of land distribution
1940	**1940**	**1940**	**1940**
Japanese bomb Pearl Harbor (1941) Battles of Midway (1942) and Okinawa (1945) Atomic bombs dropped on Hiroshima and Nagasaki (1945) India and Pakistan gain independence (1947) Muhammad Ali Jinnah (1876–1948) Israel gains independence (1948)	South Africa gains independence (1948) Afrikan National Party comes to power (1948) Establishment of apartheid	World War II (1939–1945) British Prime Minister Winston Churchill (1874–1965) Holocaust (1941–1945) Battle of Stalingrad (1942–1943) D-day invasion (1944) Split of East and West Germany (1949)	United States enters World War II (1941) United States president Franklin Delano Roosevelt (1882–1945) United States president Harry Truman (1884–1972) Yalta and Potsdam Conferences (1945) United Nations Conference (1945) Marshall Plan (1948) North Atlantic Treaty Organization formed (1949) Philippines gain independence (1946) Cold War (1947–1990)

ASIA	AFRICA	EUROPE	AMERICAS AND OCEANIA
1950	**1950**	**1950**	**1950**

Korean War (1950–1953)
Vietnamese capture
  of Dienbienphu (1954)
Bandung Conference (1955)
  and Nonaligned Movement
Indian Prime Minister
  Jawaharlal Nehru
  (1880–1964)
Great Leap Forward
  (1958–1961)
	Algerian War of Liberation
	  (1954–1962)
	African National Congress
	  issues its Freedom
	  Charter (1955)
	Morocco and Tunisia gain
	  independence (1956)
	Egyptian leader Gamel Abdel
	  Nasser (1918–1970)
	Suez Canal crisis (1956)
	Ghana gains independence
	  (1957)
	Kwame Nkrumah
	  (1909–1972)
		Nikita Khrushchev and
		  de-Stalinization
		  (1953–1964)
		Soviet Union sends troops
		  into Hungary (1956)
		European Economic
		  Community established
		  (1957)
			Argentine president Juan
			  Perón (1895–1974)
			Evita Perón (1919–1952)
			Fidel Castro seizes control
			  of Cuba (1959)

1960	**1960**	**1960**	**1960**

Vietnamese leader Ho Chi
  Minh (1890–1969)
Palestinian Liberation
  Organization formed (1964)
Yasser Arafat (b. 1929)
Great Proletarian Cultural
  Revolution (1966–1976)
	"Year of Africa" (1960)
	Sharpeville massacre (1960)
	Organization of African Unity
	  founded (1963)
	Kenya gains independence
	  (1963)
	Jomo Kenyatta (1895–1978)
	Mobutu Sese Seko seizes
	  control of Zaire in a
	  coup (1965)
	Kwame Nkrumah overthrown
	  in a coup (1966)
		Construction of Berlin
		  Wall (1961)
		Soviet Union sends troops
		  into Czechoslovakia (1968)
		Soviet leader Leonid Brezhnev
		  (1906–1982)
			Bay of Pigs invasion (1961)
			Cuban missile crisis (1962)
			Assassination of United States
			  president John F. Kennedy
			  (1963)
			United States president
			  Lyndon Johnson
			  (1908–1973)

1970	**1970**	**1970**	**1970**

Vietnam unified by North
  Vietnam (1976)
Iranian revolution (1979)
Ayatollah Ruhollah Khomeini
  (1900–1989)
	Angola gains independence
	  (1975)
		Soviet Union and United
		  States agree to SALT treaty
		  (1972)
			United States and Vietnam
			  sign Paris Peace Accords
			  (1973)

1980	**1980**	**1980**	**1980**

Assassination of Indira
  Gandhi (1984)
Iran-Iraq War (1980–1988)
Saddam Hussein (b. 1937)
Tiananmen Square (1989)
Deng Xiaoping (1904–1997)
	Zimbabwe gains
	  independence (1980)
	Egyptian leader Anwar Sadat
	  assassinated (1981)
		Polish leader Lech Walesa
		  and Solidarity
		Soviet Union withdraws
		  from Afghanistan (1989)	

1990	**1990**	**1990**	**1990**

Gulf War (1991)
Peace treaties between Arafat
  and Israeli prime minister
  Yitzhak Rabin (1993, 1995)
Afghan capital Kabul falls
  to Islamic Taliban (1996)
	F.W. de Klerk begins to
	  dismantle apartheid
	  system (1990)
	Nelson Mandela becomes
	  president of South Africa
	  (1994)
	Hutu genocidal slaughter
	  of Tutsis in Rwanda (1994)
	Laurent Kabila overthrows
	  Mobutu Sese Seko (1997)
	Zaire becomes Democratic
	  Republic of the Congo
		Collapse of Soviet Union
		  (1991)
		Mikhail Gorbachev's glasnost
		  and perestroika
		Boris N. Yeltsin becomes
		  Soviet leader
		Poland, Bulgaria, Hungary,
		  Czechoslovakia, Rumania,
		  and East Germany gain
		  independence	

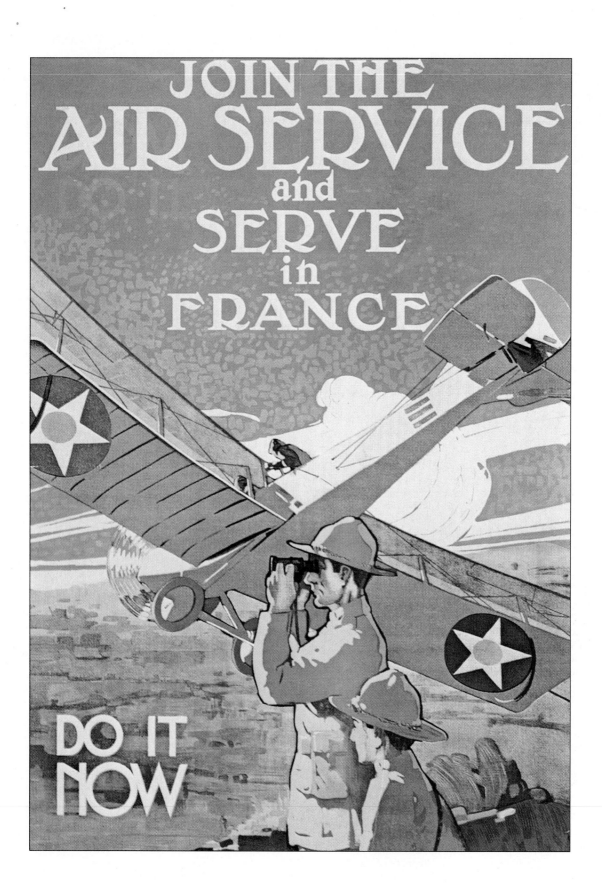

THE GREAT WAR: THE WORLD IN UPHEAVAL

. . .

Archduke Francis Ferdinand (1863–1914) was aware that his first official visit to Sarajevo was fraught with danger. This ancient city was the capital of Bosnia-Herzegovina, twin provinces that had been under Ottoman rule since the fifteenth century, but then were occupied and finally annexed by Austria-Hungary in 1908. These provinces had become the hotbed of pan-Serbian nationalism. Ferdinand was on record as favoring greater autonomy for the provinces, but his words carried little weight with most Serbian nationalists, who hated the dynasty and the empire the heir to the throne of Austria-Hungary represented.

It was a warm and radiant Sunday morning when Ferdinand's motorcade made its way through the narrow streets of Sarajevo. Waiting for him along the designated route were seven assassins armed with bombs and revolvers. The first would-be assassin did nothing, but the next man in line had more resolve and threw a bomb into the open car. Glancing off Ferdinand's arm, the bomb exploded near another vehicle and injured dozens of spectators. Trying to kill himself, the bomb-thrower swallowed cyanide and jumped into a nearby river. The old poison only made him vomit, and the water was too shallow for drowning.

Undeterred, Ferdinand went on to a reception at city hall; after the reception he instructed his driver to take him to the hospital where those wounded in the earlier attack were being treated. While Ferdinand was on his way to the hospital, a young Bosnian-Serb named Gavrilo Princip (1894–1918) lunged at the archduke's car and fired a revolver. The first bullet blew a gaping hole in the side of Ferdinand's neck. A second bullet intended for the governor of Bosnia went wild and entered the stomach of the expectant Duchess Sophie, the wife of the archduke. Turning to his wife, the archduke pleaded: "Sophie dear! Don't die! Stay alive for our children!" By the time medical aid arrived, however, both the duke and the duchess were dead.

In the meantime, Princip swallowed poison, which also only made him sick. When he tried to turn the gun on himself, a crowd intervened. After rescuing Princip from the mob, the police inflicted their own torture on the assassin: they kicked him, beat him, and scraped the skin from his neck with the edges of their swords. Three months later a court found Princip guilty of treason and murder, but because he committed his crime before his twentieth birthday, he could not be executed. Sentenced to twenty years in prison, Princip died in April 1918 from tuberculosis.

British recruiting poster. • Imperial War Museum, London

The assassination on 28 June, 1914 brought to a head the tensions between the Austro-Hungarian empire and the neighboring kingdom of Serbia. As other European powers took sides, the stakes far outgrew Austro-Serbian conflicts. Nationalist aspirations, international rivalries, and an inflexible alliance system transformed that conflict into a general European war and ultimately into a global struggle involving thirty-two nations. Twenty-eight of those nations, collectively known as the Allies and the Associated Powers, fought the coalition known as the Central Powers, which consisted of Germany, Austria-Hungary, the Ottoman empire, and Bulgaria. The shell-shocked generation that survived the carnage called this clash of arms simply the Great War. Sadly, though, a subsequent generation of survivors had occasion to rename the conflict World War I, for it was only the first of two wars that engulfed the world in the first half of the twentieth century.

The Great War lasted from August 1914 to November 1918 and ushered in history's most violent century. In geographic extent the conflict surpassed all previous wars, compelling men, women, and children on five continents to participate directly or indirectly in a struggle that many did not understand. The Great War also had the distinction of being the first total war in human history, as governments mobilized every available human and material resource for the conduct of war. This scope contrasts with past wars which, though frequently waged with ruthlessness and savage efficiency, tended to be less destructive, for they rarely engaged the passions of entire nations. Moreover, total war depended on industrial nations' capacity to fight with virtually unlimited means and to conduct combat on a vast scale. The industrial nature of the conflict meant that it was the bloodiest yet in the annals of organized violence. This clash of arms took the lives of millions of combatants and civilians alike, physically maimed untold multitudes, and emotionally scarred an entire generation. The number of military casualties alone passed a threshold beyond previous experience: roughly nine million soldiers died, and another twenty-one million combatants suffered injuries.

The war of 1914–1918 did more than destroy individual lives. It seriously damaged national economies. The most visible signs of this damage were huge public debts and soaring rates of inflation. The international economy witnessed a shift in power away from western Europe. By the end of the conflict, the United States loomed as an economic world power that, despite its self-imposed isolation during the 1920s and 1930s, would play a key role in global affairs in the coming decades. Politically, the war led to the redrawing of European boundaries, for it caused the demise of four dynasties and their empires—the Ottoman empire, the Russian empire, the Austro-Hungarian empire, and the German empire. The Great War also gave birth to nine new nations: Yugoslavia, Austria, Hungary, Czechoslovakia, Poland, Lithuania, Latvia, Estonia, and Finland. The war in part helped unleash the Bolshevik Revolution of 1917, which set the stage for an ideological conflict between capitalism and communism that endured to the end of the twentieth century. Finally, the Great War was responsible for an international realignment of power. It undermined the preeminence and prestige of European society, signaling an end to Europe's global primacy.

THE DRIFT TOWARD WAR

The catalyst for war was the assassination of Archduke Francis Ferdinand, heir to the throne of the Austro-Hungarian empire, by a Serbian nationalist. Yet without deeper underlying developments, the assassin's bullets would have had limited effect. The underlying causes for the war of 1914–1918 were many, including intense nationalism, frustrated national ambitions and ethnic resentments, the pursuit of exclusive economic interests, abrasive colonial rivalries, and a general struggle over the balance of power, both in Europe and the world at large. Between 1871 and 1914 European governments adopted foreign policies that steadily increased the danger of war. In order not to find themselves alone in a hostile world, national leaders sought alignments with other powers. Yet the establishment and maintenance in Europe of two hostile alliances—the Allies and the Central Powers—helped spread the war from the Balkans.

Nationalist Aspirations

The French Revolution and subsequent Napoleonic conquests spread nationalism throughout most of Europe (see chapter 29). Inherent in nationalism was the idea that peoples with the same ethnic origins, language, and political ideals had the right to form sovereign states; this concept is termed *self-determination*. But the dynastic and reactionary powers that dominated European affairs during the early nineteenth century either ignored or opposed the principle of self-determination, thereby denying national autonomy to Germans, Italians, and Belgians, among others. Before long, however, a combination of powerful nationalistic movements, revolutions, and wars allowed Belgians to gain independence from the Netherlands in 1830, promoted the unification of Italy in 1861, and secured the unification of Germany in 1871. Yet at the end of the nineteenth century, the issue of nationalism remained unresolved in other areas of Europe, most notably in eastern Europe and the Balkans. There the nationalist aspirations of subject minorities threatened to tear apart the multinational empires of the Ottoman, Habsburg, and Russian dynasties and with them the regional balance of power. In all these instances opposition to foreign rule played a large role in the construction of national identities and demands for self-determination.

The Ottoman empire had controlled the Balkan peninsula since the fifteenth century, but after 1829 the Turkish empire began to shrivel. European powers, especially Austria and Russia, were partly responsible for the shrinking of Ottoman territories in Europe, but the slicing away of Turkish territory resulted mostly from nationalist revolts by the sultan's subjects. Greece was the first to gain independence (in 1830), but within a few decades Serbia, Romania, and Bulgaria followed suit.

As the Ottoman territories succumbed to the forces of nationalism, the dual monarchy of Austria-Hungary confronted the nationalist aspirations of Slavic peoples—Poles, Czechs, Slovaks, Serbs, Croats, and Slovenes. Most menacing and militant were the Serbs, who pressed for unification with the independent kingdom of Serbia. Russia added fuel to this already volatile situation by promoting Pan-Slavism, a nineteenth-century movement that stressed the ethnic and cultural kinship of the various Slav peoples of eastern and east central Europe and sought to unite those peoples politically. Pan-Slavism, as advocated by Russian tsars, supported Slav nationalism in lands occupied by Austria-Hungary. The purpose behind this policy was to promote secession by Slav areas, thereby weakening Austrian rule and perhaps preparing territories for future Russian annexation. Russia's support of Serbia, which supported Slav nationalism, and Germany's backing of Austria-Hungary, which desperately tried to counter the threat of national independence, helped set the stage for international conflict.

National Rivalries

Aggressive nationalism was also manifest in economic competition and colonial conflicts, fueling dangerous rivalries among the major European powers. All the industrialized nations of Europe competed for foreign markets and engaged in tariff wars, but the most unsettling economic rivalry involved Great Britain and Germany. By the twentieth century Germany's rapid industrialization threatened British economic predominance. Whereas in 1870 the first industrial nation produced almost 32 percent of the world's total industrial output, compared to Germany's share of 13 percent, by 1914 Britain's share had dropped to 14 percent, roughly equivalent to that of Germany. British reluctance to accept the relative decline of British industry vis-à-vis German industry strained relations between the two economic powers.

The Naval Race   An expensive naval race further exacerbated tensions between the two nations. Both Germans and Britons convinced themselves that naval power was imperative to secure trade routes and protect merchant shipping. Moreover, military leaders and politicians saw powerful navies as a means of controlling the seas in times of war, a control that they viewed as decisive in determining the outcome of any war. Thus when Germany's political and military leaders announced their program to build a fleet with many large battleships, they threatened British naval supremacy. The British government moved to meet the German threat through the construction of super battleships known as *dreadnoughts*. But rather than discouraging the Germans from their naval buildup, the British determination to retain naval superiority stimulated the Germans to build their own flotilla of dreadnoughts. This expensive naval race contributed further to international tensions and outright hostilities between nations.

Colonial Disputes   Economic rivalries fomented colonial competition. During the late nineteenth and early twentieth centuries, European nations aggressively searched for new colonies or dependencies in an effort to bolster economic performance. But in their haste to conquer and colonize, the imperial powers stumbled over each other, repeatedly clashing in one corner of the globe or another: Britain and Russia faced off in Persia (modern-day Iran) and Afghanistan; Britain and France in Siam (modern-day Thailand) and the Nile valley; Britain and Germany in east and southwest Africa; Germany and France in Morocco and west Africa.

Virtually all the major powers engaged in the scramble for empire, but the competition between Britain and Germany and that between France and Germany were the most intense and dangerous. Germany, a unified nation only since 1871, embarked on the colonial race belatedly but aggressively, insisting that it too must have its "place in the sun." German imperial efforts were frustrated, however, by the simple fact that British and French imperialists had already carved up most of the world. German-French antagonisms and German-British rivalries went far toward shaping the international alliances that contributed to the spread of war after 1914.

Between 1905 and 1914 a series of international crises and two local wars not only raised tensions but almost precipitated a general European war. The first crisis resulted from a French-German confrontation over Morocco in 1905. Trying to isolate the French diplomatically, the German government announced its support of Moroccan independence, which French encroachment endangered. The French responded to German intervention by threatening war. An international conference in Algeciras, Spain, in the following year prevented a clash of arms, but similar crises threatened the peace in subsequent years. Contributing to the growing tensions in European affairs were the Balkan wars. Between 1912 and 1913, the states of the Balkan peninsula—including Bulgaria, Greece, Montenegro, Serbia, and Romania—

fought two consecutive wars for possession of European territories held by the Ottoman empire. The Balkan wars strained European diplomatic relations and helped shape the tense circumstances that led to the outbreak of the Great War.

Public pressure also contributed to national rivalries. Characteristic of many European societies was a high degree of political participation on the part of citizens who strongly identified with the state. These citizens wanted their nation to outshine others, particularly in the international arena. New means of communication nourished the public's desire to see their country "come in first," whether in the competition for colonies or in the race to the South Pole. The content of cheap, mass-produced newspapers, pamphlets, and books fueled feelings of national arrogance and aggressive patriotism. However, public pressure calling for national greatness placed policy makers and diplomats in an awkward situation. Compelled to achieve headline-grabbing foreign policy successes, these leaders ran the risk of paying for short-lived triumphs with long-lasting hostility from other countries.

Public Opinion

Entangling Alliances

In addition to a basic desire for security, escalating national rivalries and nationalist aspirations of subject minorities spawned a system of entangling alliances. While national interests guided the search for allies, each nation viewed its fulfillment of treaty obligations as crucial to self-preservation. Moreover, the complexity of those obligations could not hide the common characteristic underlying all the alliances: they outlined the circumstances under which countries would go to war to support each other. Intended to preserve the peace, rival alliance systems created a framework where even a small international crisis could set off a chain reaction leading to global war. Thus by 1914 Europe's major powers had transformed themselves into two hostile camps—the Triple Alliance and the Triple Entente.

The Triple Alliance, also known as the Central Powers, grew out of the close relationship that had developed between the leaders of Germany and Austria-Hungary during the last three decades of the nineteenth century. In 1879 the governments of the two empires formed the Dual Alliance, a defensive pact that assured reciprocal protection from a Russian attack and neutrality in case of an attack from any other power. Fear of a hostile France motivated Germans to enter into this pact, whereas Austrians viewed it as giving them a free hand in pursuing their Balkan politics without fear of Russian intervention. Italy, fearful of France, joined the Dual Alliance in 1882, thereby transforming it into the Triple Alliance. From the outset, however, the Italian policy of aggrandizement at the expense of Russia and Austria threatened to wreck the alliance. Thus the Italian declaration of war on the Ottoman empire in 1911 and the subsequent drive to annex the Tripoli region of northern Africa strained the Triple Alliance because the German government tried to cultivate friendly relations with the Turks.

The Central Powers

The Central Powers sought to protect the political status quo in Europe, but the leaders of other nations viewed this new constellation of power with suspicion. This response was especially true of French leaders, who neither forgot nor forgave Frances's humiliating defeat during the Franco-Prussian War of 1870–1871. The French government was therefore determined to curb the growing might of Germany at all costs.

The Allies

The tsarist regime of Russia was equally disturbed by the new alignment of powers, especially by Germany's support of Austria, while British leaders were traditionally suspicious of any nation that seemed to threaten the balance of power on the

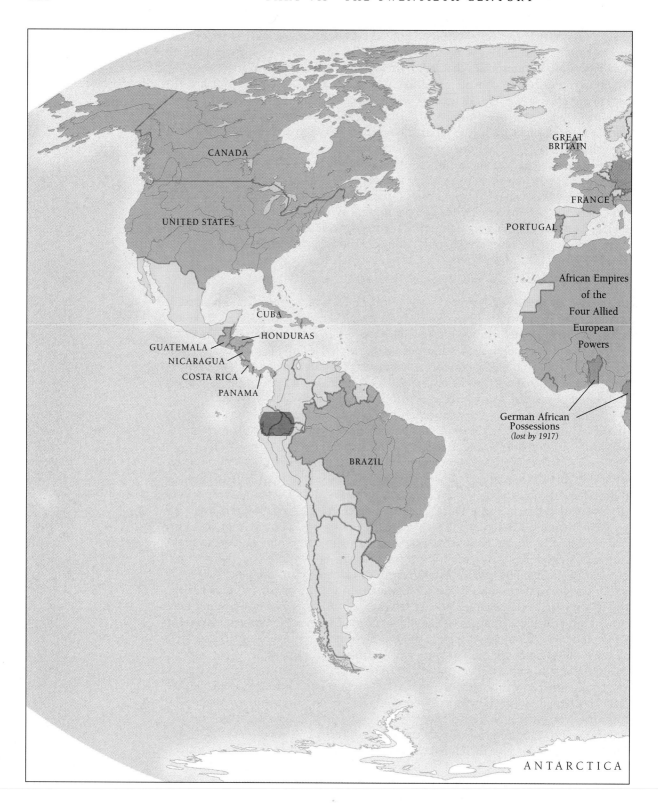

MAP [34.1]

The alliance systems of the Great War.

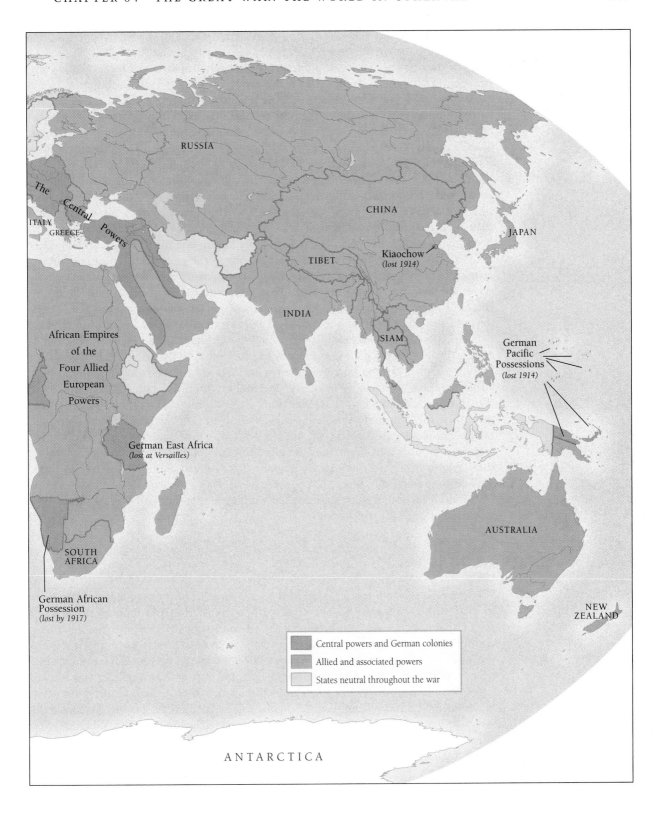

continent. The result was that the most unlikely bedfellows formed the Triple Entente, a combination of nations commonly referred to as the Allies. The Triple Entente originated in a series of agreements between Britain and France (1904) and between Britain and Russia (1907) that aimed to resolve colonial disputes. Between 1907 and 1914 cooperation between the leaders of Britain, France, and Russia led to the signing of a military pact in the summer of 1914. Reciprocal treaty obligations, which governments felt compelled to honor lest they face the risk of being alone in a hostile world, made it difficult for diplomats to contain what otherwise might be relatively small international crises.

War Plans   The preservation of peace was especially difficult because the military staffs of each nation had devised inflexible military plans and timetables that would be carried out in the event of war. For example, French military strategy revolved around Plan XVII, which amounted to a veritable celebration of offensive maneuvers. Indeed, the French master plan could be summed up in one word, attack, to be undertaken always and everywhere. This strategy viewed the enemy's intentions as inconsequential and gave no thought to the massive casualties that would invariably result. German war plans in particular played a crucial role in the events leading to the Great War. Germany's fear of encirclement encouraged its military planners to devise a strategy that would avoid a war on two fronts. It was based on a strategy developed in 1905 by General Count Alfred von Schlieffen (1833–1913). The Schlieffen plan called for a swift knockout of France, followed by defensive action against Russia. German planners predicated their strategy on the knowledge that the Russians could not mobilize their soldiers and military supplies as quickly as the French, thus giving German forces a few precious weeks during which they could concentrate their full power on France. However brilliantly conceived, the Schlieffen plan raised serious logistical problems, not the least of which was moving 180,000 men and their supplies into France and Belgium on five hundred trains, with fifty wagons each. More important, Germany's military strategy was a serious obstacle to those seeking to preserve the peace. In the event of Russian mobilization, Germany's leaders would feel compelled to stick to their war plans, thereby setting in motion a military conflict of major proportions.

 ## GLOBAL WAR

War came to Europe during harvest time, and most ordinary people heard the news as they worked in the fields. They reacted not with enthusiasm, but with shock and fear. Other people, especially intellectuals and young city dwellers, met the news with euphoria. Many of them had long expected war and saw it as a liberating release of pressure that would resolve the various political, social, and economic crises that had been building for years. The philosopher Bertrand Russell observed that the average Englishman positively wanted war, and the French writer Alain-Fournier noted that "this war is fine and just and great." In the capitals of Europe, people danced in the streets when their governments announced formal declarations of war. When the first contingents of soldiers left for the front, jubilant crowds threw flowers at the feet of departing men, who expected to return victorious after a short time.

Reality crushed any expectations of a short and triumphant war. On most fronts the conflict quickly bogged down and became a war of attrition in which the firepower of modern weapons slaughtered men by the millions. For the first time in history, belligerent nations engaged in total war. Even in democratic societies governments assumed dictatorial control to marshal the human and material resources required for continuous war. One result was increased participation of women in the labor force. Total war had repercussions that went beyond the borders of Europe. Imperial ties drew millions of Asians, Africans, and residents of the British dominions into the war to serve as soldiers and laborers. Struggles over far-flung colonies further underlined the global dimension of this war. Last, the war gained a global flavor through the entry of Japan, the United States, and the Ottoman empire, nations whose leaders professed little direct interest in European affairs.

The Guns of August

The shots fired from Gavrilo Princip's revolver on that fateful day of 28 June 1914 were heard around the world, for they triggered the greatest war in human history up to that point. By July, Austrian investigators had linked the assassins to a terrorist group known as the Black Hand. Centered in neighboring Serbia, this organization was dedicated to the unification of all south Slavs, or Yugoslavs, to form a greater Serbia. As far as Serbian nationalists were concerned, the principal obstacle to Slavic unity was the Austro-Hungarian empire, which explains why the heir to the Habsburg throne was a symbolic victim. This viewpoint also explains Austria's unyielding and violent response to the murder.

The assassination set in motion a flurry of diplomatic activity that quickly esca-   *Declarations of War*
lated into total war. Austrian leaders in Vienna were determined to teach the unruly Serbs a lesson, and on 23 July the Austrians issued a nearly unacceptable ultimatum to the government of Serbia. The Serbian government accepted all the terms of the ultimatum but one, which infringed on its sovereignty. The ultimatum demanded that Austrian officials take part in any Serbian investigation of persons found on Serbian territory connected to the assassination of Francis Ferdinand. On July 28, after declaring the Serbian reply to be unsatisfactory, Austria-Hungary declared war on Serbia. The drift toward war had begun, and statesmen and generals discovered that it could not be easily arrested. The subsequent sequence of events was largely determined by two factors: complex mobilization plans and the grinding logic of the alliance system. Mobilization called for the activation of military forces for imminent battle and the redirection of economic and social activities to support military efforts. Thus military planners were convinced that the timing of mobilization orders as well as adherence to precise timetables were crucial to the successful conduct of war.

On 29 July the Russian government mobilized its troops to defend its Serbian ally and itself from Austria. The tsar of Russia then ordered mobilization against Germany. Nicholas II (1868–1918) took this decisive step reluctantly and only after his military experts had convinced him that a partial mobilization against the Austrians would upset complex military plans and timetables. Delayed mobilization might invite defeat, they advised, should the Germans enter the war. This action precipitated a German ultimatum to Russia on 31 July, demanding that the Russian army ceases its mobilization immediately. Another ultimatum addressed to France demanded to know what France's intentions were in case Germany and Russia went to war. The Russians replied with a blunt "impossible," and the French never answered at all. Thus on 1 August the German government declared war on Russia, and France started to mobilize.

A German dispatch rider wearing a gas mask.   •   Imperial War
Museum, London

After waiting two more days, the Germans finally declared war on France on 3 August. On the same day, German troops invaded Belgium in accordance with the Schlieffen plan. Key to this plan was an attack on the weak left flank of the French army by massive German force through Belgium. The Belgian government, which had refused to permit the passage of German troops, called upon the signatories of the treaty of 1839, which had guaranteed Belgium's neutrality. On 4 August the British government, one of the signatories, sent an ultimatum to Germany demanding that Belgian neutrality be respected. When Germany's wartime leaders refused, the British immediately declared war. A local conflict had become a general European war.

Mutual Butchery

In the first weeks of August 1914, some twenty million young men donned uniform, took up rifles, and left for the front. Many of them looked forward to heroic charges, rapid promotions, and a quick homecoming. Some dreamed of glory and honor, and they believed that God was on their side. The inscription on the belt buckle of German recruits read *Gott mit uns* ("God is with us"), a sentiment echoed by Russian troops, who fought for "God and Tsar," and British soldiers, who went into battle "For God, King, and Country." Several years later Americans felt called upon to "make the world safe for democracy." Similar attitudes prevailed among the political and military leaders of the belligerent nations. The war strategies devised by the finest military thinkers of the time paid no attention to matters of defense. Instead, they were preoccupied by visions of sweeping assaults, envelopments, and, above all, swift triumphs.

The Western Front   The German thrust toward Paris in August 1914 came to a grinding halt along the river Marne, and both sides then undertook flanking maneuvers, a "race to the sea" that took them to the Atlantic coast. For the next three years, the battle lines remained virtually stationary, as both sides dug in and slugged it out in a war of attrition that lasted until the late autumn of 1918. Each belligerent tried to wear down the enemy by inflicting continuous damage and casualties, only to have their own forces suffer heavy losses in return. Trenches on the western front ran from the English Channel all the way to Switzerland. Farther south, Italy entered the war on the side of the Allies in 1915, but Allied hopes that the Italians would pierce Aus-

DULCE ET DECORUM EST

• • •

The Great War produced a wealth of poetry. The poetic response to war covered a range of moods from early romanticism and patriotism to cynicism, resignation, and the angry depiction of horror. Perhaps the greatest of all war poets was Wilfred Owen (1893–1918), whose poems are among the most poignant of the war. Owen, who enlisted for service on the western front in 1915, was injured in March 1917 and sent home. Declared fit for duty in August 1918, he returned to the front. German machine-gun fire killed him on 7 November, four days before the armistice, when he tried to cross the Sambre Canal.

Bent double, like old beggars under sacks,
Knock-kneed, coughing like hags, we cursed through sludge,
Till on the haunting flares we turned our backs
And towards our distant rest began to trudge.
Men marched asleep. Many had lost their boots
But limped on, blood-shod. All went lame; all blind;
Drunk with fatigue; deaf even to the hoots
Of gas-shells dropping softly behind.

Gas! GAS! Quick, boys!— An ecstasy of fumbling,
Fitting the clumsy helmets just in time;
But someone still was yelling out and stumbling
And floundering like a man in fire or lime.—
Dim, through the misty panes and thick green light
As under a green sea, I saw him drowning.

In all my dreams, before my helpless sight,
He plunges at me, guttering, choking, drowning.

If in some smothering dreams you too could pace
Behind the wagon that we flung him in,
And watch the white eyes writhing in his face,
His hanging face, like a devil's sick of sin;
If you could hear, at every jolt, the blood
Come gargling from the froth-corrupted lungs,
Obscene as cancer, bitter as the cud
Of vile, incurable sores on innocent tongues,—
My friend, you would not tell with such high zest
To children ardent for some desperate glory,
The old Lie: Dulce et decorum est
Pro patria mori.*

*Author's note: "Sweet and fitting is it to die for one's country" comes from a line by the Roman poet Horace (65–8 B.C.E.)

SOURCE: Edmund Blunden, ed. *The Poems of Wilfred Owen.* London: Chattus & Windus, 1933, p. 66.

---

trian defenses quickly faded. After the disastrous defeat at Caporetto in 1917, Italian forces maintained a defensive line only with the help of the French and British.

Stalemate

The stalemate on the western and southern fronts reflected technological developments that favored defensive tactics. Barbed wire, which had confined cattle on America's Great Plains, proved highly effective in frustrating the advance of men across "no man's land," the deadly territory between opposing trenches. Previously, imperialists had employed machine guns in Asia and Africa. During the Great War, European soldiers turned the same weapons on each other. A more unconventional weapon was poisonous gas, first used by German troops in the spring of 1915. Especially hated and much feared by troops in the trenches was mustard gas, a liquid agent that when exposed to air turned into a noxious yellow gas—hence its name. The effects of mustard gas did not appear for some twelve hours following exposure, but then it rotted the body from both within and without. After blistering the skin and damaging the eyes, the gas attacked the bronchial tubes, stripping off the mucous membrane. Death could take four to five weeks. In the meantime, victims endured excruciating pain and had to be strapped to their beds. Although gas claimed the lives of some eighty thousand men, it was ineffective from a tactical standpoint.

No-man's land on the western front. • Imperial War
Museum, London

Mutilated bodies on the western front. • AKG, London

No-Man's Land

The most courageous infantry charges, even when preceded by pulverizing artillery barrages and clouds of poisonous gas, were no match for determined defenders. Shielded by the dirt of their trenches, along with barbed wire and gas masks,
they simply unleashed a torrent of lethal metal with their machine guns and repeat-
ing rifles. In every sector of the front, those who fought rarely found the glory they
sought. Instead, they encountered death. No man's land was strewn with shell
craters, cadavers, and body parts. The grim realities of trench warfare—the wet,
cold, thigh-high mud, voracious lice, and corpse-fattened rats—contrasted sharply
with the ringing phrases of politicians and generals justifying the unrelenting slaughter. War had ceased to be a noble and sporting affair, if it ever was.

The Eastern Front

In eastern Europe and the Balkans, the battle lines were more fluid. After a
staunch defense, a combination of Austrian and German forces overran Serbia, Albania, and Romania. Farther north Russia took the offensive early by invading Prussia in
1914. The Central Powers recovered quickly, however, and by the summer of 1915
combined German-Austrian forces drove the Russian armies first out of East Prussia
and then out of Poland and established a defensive line extending from Riga to Cher-
novtsky. Russian counterattacks in 1916 and 1917 collapsed in a sea of casualties.
These Russian defeats undermined the popularity of the tsar and his government and
played a significant role in fostering revolutionary ferment within Russian society.

Bloodletting

There were many battles, but some were so horrific, so devastating, and so futile
that their names are synonymous with human slaughter. The casualties figures attested
to this. In 1916 the Germans tried to break the deadlock with a huge assault on the
fortress of Verdun. The French rallying cry was "They shall not pass," and they did
not—but at a tremendous cost: while the victorious French counted 315,000 dead,
the defeated Germans suffered a loss of 280,000. Survivors recovered fewer than
160,000 identifiable bodies. The rest were unrecognizable or had been blown to bits
by high explosives and sucked into the mud. To relieve the pressure on Verdun,
British forces counterattacked at the Somme, and by November they had gained a few
thousand yards at the cost of 420,000 casualties. The Germans suffered similar losses,
although in the end neither side gained any strategic advantage.

Dying and suffering were not limited solely to combatants: the Great War established rules of engagement that made civilians targets of warfare. Since they were crucial to the war effort, millions of people out of uniform became targets of enemy military operations. On 30 August 1914, Parisians looked up at the sky and saw a new weapon of war, a huge but silent German zeppelin (a hydrogen-filled dirigible) whose underbelly rained bombs, eventually killing one person. This event heralded a new kind of warfare—air war against civilians. A less novel but more

New Rules of Engagement

An Indian gun crew in the Somme area, 1916.

● National Archives

effective means of targeting civilian populations was the naval blockade. Military leaders on both sides used blockades to deny food to whole populations, hoping that starving masses would force their governments to capitulate.

Total War: The Home Front

Helmuth Karl von Moltke (1800–1891), former chief of the Prussian General Staff, showed an uncanny prescience long before 1914 when he predicted that future wars would not end with a single battle, because the defeat of a nation would not be acknowledged until the whole strength of its people was broken. He was right. As the Great War ground on, it became a conflict of attrition in which the organization of material and human resources was of paramount importance. War became total, fought between entire societies, not just between armies; and total victory was the only acceptable outcome that might justify the terrible sacrifices made by all sides. The nature of total war created a military front and a home front. The very term *home front* expressed the important reality that the outcome of the war hinged on how effectively each nation mobilized its economy and activated its noncombatant citizens to support the war effort.

Because patriotism and courage alone could not guarantee victory, the governments of belligerent nations assumed control of the home front. Initially ministers and generals shrank from compulsive measures, even conscription of recruits, but quickly changed their minds. Each belligerent government eventually militarized civilian war production, subordinating private enterprises to governmental control and imposing severe discipline on the labor process.

The Home Front

Economic measures were foremost in the minds of government leaders because the war created unprecedented demands for raw materials and manufactured goods. These material requirements compelled governments to abandon long-cherished ideals of a laissez-faire capitalist market economy and to institute tight controls over economic life. Planning boards reorganized entire industries, set production quotas and priorities, and determined what would be produced and consumed. Governmental authorities also established wage and price controls, extended work hours, and in some instances even restricted the movement of workers. Because bloody battlefields caused an insatiable appetite for soldiers, nations responded by extending military service. In Germany, for example, men between the ages sixteen and sixty were eligible to serve at the front. Yet by constantly tapping into the available male population, the war created an increasing demand for workers at home. Unemployment—a persistent feature of all prewar economies—vanished virtually overnight.

Women at War

As conscription took men out of the labor force, wartime leaders exhorted women to fill the gaps in the workforce. Thus as men marched out to war, women marched off to work. A combination of patriotism and high wages drew women into formerly "male" jobs. The lives of women changed as they bobbed their hair and left home or domestic service for the workplace. Some took over the management of farms and businesses left by their husbands who went off to fight. Others found jobs as postal workers and police officers. Behind the battle lines, women were most visible as nurses, doctors, and communications clerks.

Perhaps the most crucial work performed by women during the war was the making of shells. Several million women, and sometimes children, put in long, hard hours in munitions factories. This work exposed them to severe dangers. The first came simply from explosions, as keeping sparks away from highly volatile materials was impossible. Many women died in these incidents, although government censorship during the war made it difficult to know how many women perished in this fashion. The other, more insidious danger came from working with TNT explosives. Although the authorities claimed that this work was not dangerous, exposure to TNT caused severe poisoning, depending on the length of exposure. Even before serious illnesses manifested themselves, TNT poisoning marked its victims by turning their skin yellow and their hair orange. The accepted though ineffectual remedy for TNT poisoning was rest, good food, and plenty of fresh milk.

Women at work in an English munitions factory. ● Imperial War Museum, London

Middle- and upper-class women often reported that the war was a liberating experience, freeing them from older attitudes that had limited both their work and their personal life. At the very least, the employment of upper-class women spawned a degree of deliverance from parental control and gave women a sense of mission. They knew that they were important to the war effort. The impact of the Great War on the lives of working-class women, by contrast, was relatively minor. Many working-class women in cities had long been accustomed to earning wages, and for them war work proved less than liberating. Most of the belligerent governments promised equal pay for equal work, but in most instances this promise remained unfulfilled. Although women's industrial wages rose during the war, measurable gaps always remained between the incomes of men and women. In the end massive female employment was a transitory phenomenon. With few exceptions the Great War only briefly suspended traditional patterns of work outside the home. Nevertheless, the extension of voting rights to women shortly after the war, at least in Britain (1918, for women thirty years and older), Germany (1919), and Austria (1919), was in part due to the role women assumed during the Great War. Later in the century, war and revolution continued to serve as at least temporary liberating forces for women, as in Russia (1917) and China (1949) where new communist governments discouraged the patriarchal family system and supported sexual equality, including birth control.

To maintain the spirit of the home front and counter threats to national unity, governments everywhere resorted to the restriction of civil liberties, censorship of bad news, and vilification of the enemy through propaganda campaigns. While some government officials busily censored war news, people who had the temerity to criticize their nation's war effort were prosecuted as traitors. In France, for example, former prime minister Joseph Caillaux spent two years in prison awaiting trial because he had publicly suggested that the best interest of France would be to reach a compromise peace with Germany.

The propaganda offices of the belligerent nations tried to convince the public that military defeat would mean the destruction of everything worth living for, and to that end they did their utmost to discredit and dehumanize the enemy. Posters, pamphlets, and "scientific" studies depicted the enemy as subhuman savages who engaged in vile atrocities. While German propaganda depicted Russians as semi-Asiatic barbarians,

Propaganda

"The Heros of Belgium 1914." French propaganda poster expresses outrage at the German invasion of Belgium.
• National Archives

French authorities chronicled the atrocities committed by the German "Hun" in Belgium. In 1917 the *Times* of London published a story claiming that Germans converted human corpses into fertilizer and even food. With much less fanfare a later news story admitted that this information resulted from a sloppy translation: The German word for *horse* had been mistakenly translated as "human." German propaganda stooped equally low. One widely distributed poster invoked images of bestial black Allied soldiers raping German women, even pregnant women, to suggest the horrors that would follow if the nation's war effort failed. Most such atrocity stories originated in the fertile imagination of propaganda officers, and their falsehood eventually engendered public skepticism and cynicism. Ironically, public disbelief of wartime propaganda led to an inability to believe in the very real abominations perpetrated during subsequent wars.

Conflict in East Asia and the Pacific

To many Asian and African peoples, the Great War was a murderous European civil war that quickly turned into a global conflict. There were three reasons for the war's expansion. First, European governments carried their animosities into their colonies, embroiling them—especially African societies—in their war. Second, because Europe's human reserves were not enough to satisfy the appetite of war, the British and the French augmented their ranks by recruiting men from their colonies. Millions of Africans and Asians were drawn into the war. Behind their trenches the French employed laborers from Algeria, China, and French Indochina, and the British did not hesitate to draft Indian and African troops for combat. The British in particular relied on troops furnished by the dominion lands, including Australia, New Zealand, Canada, Newfoundland, and South Africa. Third, the Great War assumed global significance because the desires and objectives of some principal actors that entered the conflict—Japan, the United States, and the Ottoman empire—had little to do with the murder in Sarajevo or the other issues that drove the Europeans to battle. Japan's actions demonstrate this last point.

Japan's Entry into the War   On 15 August 1914 the Japanese government, claiming that it desired "to secure firm and enduring peace in Eastern Asia," sent an ultimatum to Germany demanding the handover of the German-leased territory of Jiaozhou (northeastern China) to Japanese authorities without compensation. The same note also demanded that the German navy unconditionally withdraw its warships from Japanese and Chinese waters. When the Germans refused to comply, the Japanese entered the war on the side of the Allies on 23 August 1914. Japanese forces took the fortress of Qingdao, a German-held port in China's Shandong Province, in November 1914, and between August and November of that year they took possession of the German-held Marshall Islands, the Mariana Islands, Palau, and the Carolines. Forces from New Zealand and Australia joined in the Japanese quest for German-held lands in the Pacific, capturing German-held portions of Samoa in August 1914 and German-occupied possessions in the Bismarck Archipelago and New Guinea.

The Twenty-one Demands   After seizing German bases in Shandong peninsula and on Pacific islands, Japan shrewdly exploited Allied support and European preoccupation to advance its own imperial interests in China. On 18 January 1915 the Japanese presented the Chinese government with twenty-one secret demands. The terms of this ultimatum, if accepted, would have reduced China to a protectorate of Japan. The most important demands were that the Chinese confirm the Japanese seizure of Shandong from Germany, grant Japanese industrial monopolies in central China, place Japanese

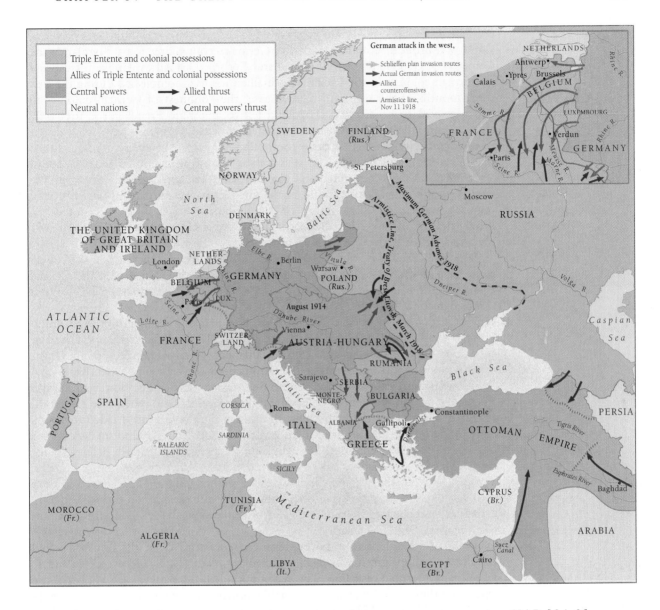

MAP [34.2]

The Great War in Europe and southwest Asia.

overseers in key government positions, give Japan joint control of Chinese police forces, restrict their arms purchases to Japanese manufacturers, and make those purchases only with the approval of the Tokyo government. China submitted to most of the demands but rejected others. Chinese diplomats leaked the note to the British authorities, who spoke up for China, thus preventing total capitulation. The Twenty-one Demands reflected Japan's determination to dominate east Asia, and they served as the basis for future Japanese pressure on China. Yet they had nothing to do with the Great War in Europe.

Battles in Africa and Southwest Asia

The geographic extent of the conflict also broadened beyond Europe when the Allies targeted German colonies in Africa for takeover. When the war of 1914–1918 erupted in Europe, all of sub-Saharan Africa (except Ethiopia and Liberia) consisted of European colonies, with the Germans controlling four: Togoland, the Cameroons, German Southwest Africa, and German East Africa. Unlike the capture of German colonies in the Pacific, which allied forces accomplished during the first three months of the war with relative ease, the conquest of German colonies in Africa proved to be difficult. Togoland fell to an Anglo-French force after only three weeks of fighting, but it took extended campaigns ranging over vast distances to subdue the remaining German footholds in Africa. The Allied force included British, French, and Belgian troops as well as large contingents of Indians, Arabs, and African soldiers. Fighting took place on land and sea; on lakes and rivers; in deserts, jungles, and swamps; and in the air. Germs were frequently more deadly than Germans; tens of thousands of Allied soldiers and workers succumbed to deadly tropical diseases. The German flag did not disappear from Africa until after the armistice took effect on 11 November 1918.

Gallipoli

The most extensive military operations outside Europe took place in the southwest Asian territories of the Ottoman empire, which was aligned with the Central Powers at the end of 1914. Seeking a way to break the stalemate on the western front, Winston Churchill (1874–1965), first lord of the Admiralty (British navy), suggested that an Allied strike against the Ottomans—a weak ally of the Central Powers—would hurt the Germans. Thus early in 1915 the British navy conducted an expedition to seize the approach to the Dardanelles in an attempt to open a warm-water supply line to Russia through the Ottoman-controlled straits. When British and French warships steamed to the Aegean Sea to open the straits, however, Turkish troops deployed at the strait at Gallipoli imposed heavy losses on the Allied navies.

After withdrawing the battleships, the British high command decided to land a combined force of English, Canadian, Australian, and New Zealand soldiers on the beaches of Gallipoli peninsula. The campaign was a disaster. Turkish defenders, ensconced in the cliffs above, quickly pinned down the Allied troops on the beaches. Trapped between the sea and the hills, Allied soldiers dug in and engaged in their own version of trench warfare. The resulting stalemate produced a total of 250,000 casualties on each side. Despite the losses, Allied leaders took nine months to admit that their campaign had failed.

Gallipoli was a debacle with long-term consequences. While the British directed the ill-fated campaign, it was mostly Canadians, Australians, and New Zealanders who suffered terrible casualties. This recognition led to a weakening of imperial ties and paved the way for emerging national identities. In Australia the date of the fateful landing, 25 April 1915, became enshrined as Anzac Day (an acronym for Australian and New Zealand Army Corps) and remains the country's most significant day of public homage. On the other side, the battle for the strait helped launch the political career of the commander of the Turkish division that defended Gallipoli. Mustapha Kemal (1881–1938) went on to play a crucial role in the formation of the modern Turkish state.

The Ottoman Empire

After successfully fending off Allied forces on the beaches of Gallipoli in 1915 and in Mesopotamia in 1916, Ottoman armies retreated slowly on all fronts. After yielding to the Russians in the Caucasus, Turkish troops were unable to defend the empire against invading British armies that drew heavily upon recruits from Egypt, India, Australia, and New Zealand. As the armies smashed the Ottoman state—one entering Mesopotamia and the other advancing from the Suez Canal toward Palestine—they received significant support from an Arab revolt against the Turks. In 1916, abetted by the British, the nomadic bedouin of Arabia under the leadership of Ibn Ali Hussain (sherif of Mecca and king of the Hejaz [1856–1931]) and others, rose up against Turkish rule. The success of the revolt gave birth to the legend of the romantic T. E. Lawrence of Arabia (1888–1935), a British adventurer, soldier, and author. Educated at Oxford University and trained as an archaeologist, Lawrence had learned Arabic during his visits to Syria and Palestine. In 1914 he began working for British intelligence services as a military advisor among the Arabs in revolt against Turkish rule, coordinating Arab attacks during the British advance toward Damascus.

Australian recruiting poster. • Fair Street Pictures

THE END OF THE WAR

The war produced strains within all the belligerent nations, but most of them managed, often ruthlessly, to cope with food riots, strikes, and mutinies. But in the Russian empire, the war amplified existing stresses to such an extent that the Romanov dynasty had to abdicate power in favor of a provisional government in the spring of 1917. Only a few months later, the provisional government yielded power to Bolshevik revolutionaries, who took Russia out of the war early in 1918. This blow to the Allies was more than offset by the entry of the United States into the conflict in 1917, which helped turn the tide of war in 1918. The resources of the United States finally compelled the exhausted Central Powers to sue for peace in November 1918.

In 1919 the victorious Allies gathered in Paris to hammer out a peace settlement that turned out to be a compromise that pleased few of the parties involved. The most significant consequence of the war was Europe's diminished role in the world. The war of 1914–1918 undermined Europe's power and simultaneously promoted nationalist aspirations among colonized peoples who began to clamor for self-determination and national independence. For the time being the major imperialist powers kept their grip on their overseas holdings, but the days of European preeminence were coming to an end.

Revolution in Russia

The February Revolution

The Great War had undermined the Russian state. In the spring of 1917, disintegrating armies, mutinies, and food shortages provoked a series of street demonstrations and strikes in Petrograd (St. Petersburg). The inability of police forces to suppress the uprisings, and the subsequent mutiny of troops garrisoned in the capital, convinced the well-meaning but incompetent tsar, Nicholas II (reigned 1894–1917), to abdicate the throne. Thus Russia ceased to be a monarchy, and the Romanov dynasty disappeared after three hundred years of uninterrupted rule. The February Revolution—the first of two revolutions in 1917—was an unplanned and incomplete affair.

The Struggle for Power

After its success in Petrograd, the revolution spread throughout the country, and political power in Russia shifted to two new agencies: the provisional government and the Petrograd soviet of Workers' and Soldiers' Deputies. *Soviets,* which were revolutionary councils organized by socialists, appeared for the first time during the Russian revolution of 1905 (see chapter 32). In 1917 soviets of Workers' and Soldiers' Deputies surfaced all over Russia, wielding considerable power through their control of factories and segments of the military. The period between February and October witnessed a political struggle between the provisional government and the powerful Petrograd soviet. At first the new government enjoyed considerable public support as it disbanded the tsarist police; repealed all limitations on freedom of speech, press, and association; and abolished laws that discriminated against ethnic or religious groups. But it failed to satisfy popular demands for an end to war and for land reforms. It claimed that, being provisional, it could not make fundamental changes such as confiscating land and distributing it among peasants. Any such change had to be postponed for decision by a future constituent assembly. The government also pledged itself to "unswervingly carry out the agreements made with the Allies" and promised to continue the war to a victorious conclusion. The Petrograd soviet, in contrast, called for an immediate peace.

V. I. Lenin

Into this tense political situation stepped Vladimir Ilyich Lenin (1870–1924), a revolutionary Marxist who had been living in exile in Switzerland. Born into a warm and loving family, Lenin grew up in the confines of a moderately prosperous family living in the provincial Russian town of Simbirsk. In 1887, shortly after his father's death, the police arrested and hanged his older brother for plotting to assassinate the tsar, an event that seared Lenin's youth. Following a brief career as a lawyer, Lenin spent many years abroad, devoting himself to studying Marxist thought and writing political pamphlets. In contrast to Marx, Lenin viewed the industrial working class as incapable of developing the proper revolutionary consciousness that would lead to effective political action. To Lenin the industrial proletariat required the leadership of a well-organized and highly disciplined party, a workers' vanguard that served as the catalyst for revolution and for the realization of a socialist society.

In a moment of high drama, the German High Command transported Lenin in 1917 to Russia in a sealed train, hoping that this committed antiwar activist would stir up trouble and bring about Russia's withdrawal from the war. Lenin headed the Bolsheviks, the radical wing of the Russian Social Democratic Party. In April he began calling for the transfer of legal authority to the soviets and advocated uncompromising opposition to the war. Initially, his own party opposed his radicalism, but he soon succeeded in converting his fellow Bolsheviks to his proposals.

STATE AND REVOLUTION

• • •

V. I. Lenin believed that the Great War would result in a revolutionary crisis that would lead to proletarian revolution. While hiding in Finland in the fall of 1917, Lenin composed the authoritative statement on Bolshevik political theory, published under the title State and Revolution *(1918). Lenin argued that the capitalist state had to be completely destroyed by a dictatorship of the proletariat before communism can be realized.* State and Revolution *was published after the Bolshevik seizure of power, prompting Lenin to write in a postscript: "It is more pleasant and useful to go through 'the experience of the revolution' than to write about it."*

In capitalist society, providing it develops under the most favorable conditions, we have a more or less complete democracy in the democratic republic. But this democracy is always hemmed in by the narrow limits set by capitalist exploitation, and consequently always remains, in reality, a democracy for the minority, only for the propertied classes, only for the rich. Freedom in capitalist society always remains about the same as it was in the ancient Greek republics: freedom for the slave-owners. Owing to the conditions of capitalist exploitation the modern wage slaves are so crushed by want and poverty that "they cannot be bothered with democracy," "they cannot be bothered with politics"; in the ordinary peaceful course of events the majority of the population is debarred from participation in public and political life.

But from this capitalist democracy—that is inevitably narrow, and stealthily pushes aside the poor, and is therefore hypocritical and false to the core—forward development does not proceed simply, directly and smoothly towards "greater and greater democracy," as the liberal professors and petty-bourgeois opportunists would have us believe. No, forward development, i.e., toward Communism, proceeds through the dictatorship of the proletariat; and cannot do otherwise, for the *resistance* of the capitalist exploiters cannot be *broken* by anyone else or in any other way.

. . . the dictatorship of the proletariat imposes a series of restrictions on the freedom of the oppressors, the exploiters, the capitalists. We must suppress them in order to free humanity from wage slavery, their resistance must be crushed by force; . . .

Only in Communist society, when the resistance of the capitalists has been completely crushed, when the capitalists have disappeared, when there are no classes (i.e., when there is no difference between the members of society as regards their relation to the social means of production), *only* then "the state . . . ceases to exist," and it *"becomes possible to speak of freedom."* Only then will there become possible and be realized a truly complete democracy, a democracy without any exceptions whatever.

SOURCE: V. I. Lenin. *The State and Revolution.* Peking: Foreign Languages Press, 1973, pp. 105–106.

The Bolsheviks, who were a small minority among revolutionary working-class parties, eventually gained control of the Petrograd soviet. Crucial to this development was the government's insistence on continuing the war, its inability to feed the population, and its refusal to undertake land reform. The tsarist regime's policies led to a growing conviction among workers and peasants that their problems could be solved only by the soviets. The Bolsheviks capitalized on this mood with effective slogans such as "All Power to the Soviets" and, most famous, "Peace, Land, and Bread." In September Lenin persuaded the Central Committee of the Bolshevik party to organize an armed insurrection and seize power in the name of the All-Russian National

The October Revolution

Congress of Soviets, which was then convening in Petrograd. During the night of 24 October and the following day, armed workers, soldiers, and sailors stormed the Winter Palace, the home of the provisional government. By the afternoon of 25 October, the virtually bloodless insurrection had run its course, and power had passed from the provisional government into the hands of Lenin and the Bolshevik Party. The U.S. journalist John Reed (1887–1920), who witnessed the Bolshevik seizure of power, understood the significance of the events when he referred to them as "ten days that shook the world." Lenin and his followers were poised to destroy the traditional patterns and values of Russian society and challenge the institutions of liberal society everywhere.

The Bolshevik rulers ended Russia's involvement in the Great War by signing the Treaty of Brest-Litovsk with Germany on 3 March 1918. The treaty gave the Germans possession or control of one-third of Russia's territory (the Baltic states, the Caucasus, Finland, Poland, and the Ukraine) and one-quarter of its population. The terms of the treaty were harsh and humiliating, but by taking Russia out of the war, it gave the new government an opportunity to deal with internal problems. Russia's departure from the war meant that Germany could concentrate all of its resources on the western front. There was small consolation in the fact that Russian autocracy no longer tainted the ideological purity of the Allied cause to "make the world safe for democracy."

U.S. Intervention and Collapse of the Central Powers

The year 1917 was crucial for yet another reason: it marked the entry of the United States into the war on the side of the Allies. In 1914 the American public firmly opposed intervention in a European war. Indeed, Woodrow Wilson (1856–1924) was elected president in 1916 because he campaigned on a nonintervention platform. This sentiment soon changed. Because U.S. companies sold huge amounts of supplies to the Allies, insistence on neutrality seemed hypocritical at best. With the war grinding on, the Allies began to take out large loans with American banks, which persuaded some Americans that an Allied victory made good financial sense. Allied propaganda also helped sway public opinion.

Submarine Warfare   The key factor in the U.S. decision to enter the war was Germany's resumption of unrestricted submarine warfare in February 1917. At the outset of the war, the government had asserted the traditional doctrine of neutral rights for its ships because it wanted to continue trading with belligerents, most notably the British and French. With its surface fleet bottled up in the Baltic, Germany's wartime leadership grew desperately dependent on its submarine fleet to strangle Britain economically and break the British blockade of the Central Powers. German military experts had calculated that submarine attacks against the ships of Great Britain and all the ships headed to Great Britain would bring about the defeat of Great Britain in six months. German subs often sank neutral merchant ships without first giving a warning as required by international law. On 7 May 1915 a German submarine sank the British passenger liner *Lusitania* off the Irish coast with a loss of 1,198 lives, including 128 U.S. citizens. Technically, the ship was a legitimate target, for it was carrying some 4,200 cases of ammunition and traveled through a declared war zone. Nevertheless, U.S. public opinion viewed the action as mass murder. During the next two years, the country's mood turned against Germany, and on 6 April 1917 the U.S. government broke off diplomatic relations with Germany and declared war.

Collapse

The corrosive effects of years of bloodletting began to show. For the first two years of the conflict, most people supported their governments' war efforts, but the continuing ravages of war took their toll everywhere. In April 1916 Irish nationalists mounted the Great Easter Rebellion, which attempted unsuccessfully to overthrow British rule in Ireland. The Central Powers suffered from food shortages as the result of the British blockade, and increasing numbers of people took to the streets to demonstrate against declining food rations. Food riots were complemented by strikes as prewar social conflicts reemerged. Governments reacted harshly to these challenges, pouncing on strikers, suppressing demonstrators, and jailing dissidents. Equally dangerous was the breakdown of military discipline. At the German naval base in Kiel, sailors revolted in the summer of 1917 and again, much more seriously, in the fall of 1918. In the wake of yet another failed offensive during the spring of 1917, which had resulted in ghastly casualties, French soldiers lost confidence in their leadership. When ordered to attack once again, they refused. The extent of the mutiny was enormous: fifty thousand soldiers were involved, resulting in 23,385 court martials and 432 death sentences. So tight was French censorship that the Germans, who could have taken advantage of this situation, did not learn about the mutiny until the war was over.

Against the background of civilian disillusionment and deteriorating economic conditions, Germany took the risk of throwing its remaining might at the western front in the spring of 1918. The gamble failed, and as the offensive petered out, the Allies broke through the front and started pushing the Germans back. Meanwhile, Bulgaria capitulated to the invading Allies on 30 September, the Ottomans concluded an armistice on 30 October, and Austria-Hungary surrendered on 4 November. Finally, the Germans accepted an armistice, which took effect on the eleventh hour of the eleventh day of the eleventh month of 1918. At last the guns went silent.

The Paris Peace Conference

The immediate effects of the Great War were all too obvious. Aside from the physical destruction, which was most visible in northern France and Belgium, the war had killed, disabled, orphaned, or rendered homeless millions of people. Conservative estimates suggest

German prisoners taken in France in the fall of 1918. • Imperial War Museum, London

Political leaders signing the Treaty of Versailles. ● National Portrait Gallery, Smithsonian Institution/Art Resource, NY

that the war killed fifteen million people, two-thirds of whom were soldiers, and wounded twenty million others. In the immediate postwar years, millions more succumbed to the effects of starvation, malnutrition, and epidemic diseases.

Before the costs of the war were fully assessed, world attention shifted to Paris. There, in 1919, the victorious powers convened to arrange a postwar settlement and set terms for the defeated nations. At the outset people on both sides of the war had high hopes for the settlement, but in the end it left a bitter legacy.

The Paris Settlement

Because the twenty-seven nations represented at Paris had different and often conflicting aims, many sessions of the conference deteriorated into pandemonium. Ultimately, the leaders of France, Britain, and the United States dominated the deliberations. The Allies did not permit representatives of the Central Powers to participate. In addition, the allies threatened to renew the war if the terms they laid down were not accepted. Significantly, the Soviet Union was not invited to the conference. Throughout this time the British blockade of Germany remained in effect, adding a sense of urgency to the proceedings. This situation later gave rise to the charge of a dictated peace, especially because no foreign troops had ever set foot on German soil.

The Peace Treaties

The final form of the treaties represented a series of compromises among the victors. The hardest terms originated with the French, who desired the destruction or the permanent weakening of German power. Thus in addition to requiring Germany to accept sole responsibility and guilt for causing the war, the victors demanded a reduction in the military potential of the former Central Powers. For example, the Treaty of Versailles denied the Germans a navy and air force and limited the size of the German army to one hundred thousand troops. In addition, the Allies prohibited Germany and Austria from entering into any sort of political union. Both the French and the British agreed that the defeated Central Powers must pay for the cost of the war and required the payment of reparations either in money or in kind. Although the German government as well as the public decried the Treaty of Versailles as being excessively harsh, it was no more severe in its terms than the Treaty of Brest-Litovsk that the Germans had imposed on Russia in 1918. The treaties also recognized successor states in eastern Europe that had sprung up at the end of the war at the expense of collapsing empires. In the final analysis the peace settlement was strategically weak because too few participants had a stake in maintaining it and too many had an interest in revising it. Judged by its long-terms result—particularly the outbreak of a second world war in a matter of decades—the peace settlement was a failure.

MAP [34.3]

Territorial changes in
Europe after the Great War.

*The League
of Nations*

   In an effort to avoid future destructive conflicts, the diplomats in Paris created
the League of Nations. The league was the first permanent international security organization whose principal mission was to maintain world peace. At the urging of
U.S. president Woodrow Wilson, the Covenant of the League of Nations was made
an integral part of the peace treaties, and every signatory to a peace treaty had to accept this new world organization. Initially, the league seemed to be the sign of a
new era: twenty-six of its forty-two original members were countries outside of Europe, suggesting that it transcended European interests.
   The treaty had two major flaws that rendered it ineffective. First, though designed
to solve international disputes through arbitration, it had no power to enforce its

decisions. Second, it relied on collective security as a tool for the preservation of peace. However, the basic conditions for collective security never materialized, because at any given time one or more of the major powers did not belong to the league. The United States never joined the league because the U.S. Senate rejected the idea. Germany, which viewed the league as a coterie of Allied victors, and Japan, which saw it as instrument of imperialism, both left the league in 1933, as did some smaller powers. Italy, chastised by the league for imperial adventures in Ethiopia, withdrew from it in 1937. The Soviet Union, which viewed the league as a tool of global capitalism, joined the organization in 1934, only to face expulsion in 1940. Although its failure to stop aggression in the 1930s led to its demise in 1940, the league established the pattern for a permanent international organization and served as a model for its successor, the United Nations.

Self-determination   One of the principal themes of the peace-making process was the concept of self-determination, which was promoted most intensely by Woodrow Wilson. Wilson believed that self-determination was the key to international peace and cooperation. With respect to Europe this principle sometimes translated into reality. For example, Poland and Czechoslovakia already existed as sovereign states, and by the end of the conference the principle of self-determination had triumphed in many areas that were previously under the control of the Austro-Hungarian and Russian empires. Yet in other instances peacemakers pushed the principle aside for strategic and security reasons. This was the case for Austria and Germany, whose peoples were denied the right to form one nation. At other times diplomats violated the notion of self-determination simply because they found it impossible to redraw national boundaries in accordance with nationalist aspirations without creating large minorities on one side or the other of a boundary line. Poland was one case in point; one-third of the population did not even speak Polish. An even more complicated situation existed in Czechoslovakia. The peoples who gave the republic its name—the Czechs and Slovaks—totaled only 67 percent of the population, with the remaining population consisting of Germans (22 percent), Ruthenes (6 percent), and Hungarians (5 percent).

The Mandate   However imperfect the results, the peacemakers at Paris tried to apply the princi-
System   ple of self-determination and nationality throughout Europe. Elsewhere, however, they did not do so. The unwillingness to apply the principle of self-determination became most obvious when the victors confronted the issue of what to do with Germany's former colonies and the Arab territories of the Ottoman empire. Because the United States rejected the establishment of old-fashioned colonies, the European powers came up with the enterprising idea of trusteeship. Article 22 of the Covenant of the League of Nations referred to the colonies and territories of the former Central Powers as areas "inhabited by peoples not yet able to stand by themselves under the strenuous conditions of the modern world." As a result, "the tutelage of such peoples should be entrusted to the advanced nations who . . . can best undertake this responsibility." The League divided the mandates into three classes based on the presumed development of their populations in the direction of fitness for self-government. The actual administration of the mandates fell to the victorious powers of the Great War.

The Germans interpreted the mandate system as a division of colonial booty by the victors, who had conveniently forgotten to apply the tutelage provision to their own colonies. German cynicism was more than matched by Arab outrage. The establishment of mandates in the former territories of the Ottoman empire violated promises (made to Arabs) by both French and British leaders during the war. They had promised Arab nationalists independence from the Ottoman empire even as they promised Jewish nationalists in Europe a homeland in Palestine. Where the

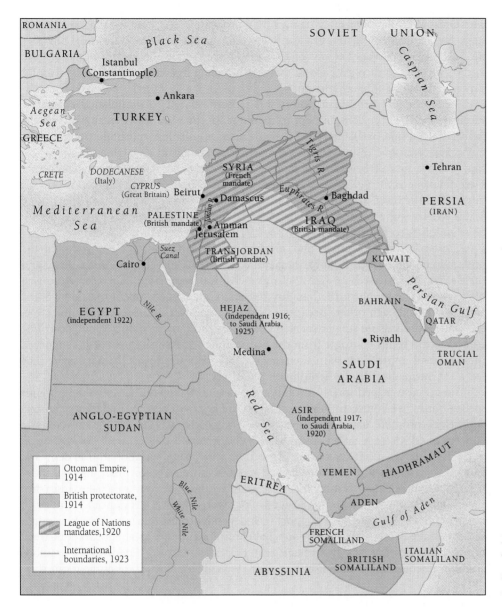

MAP [34.4]

Territorial changes in southwest Asia after the Great War.

Arabs hoped to form independent states, the French (in Lebanon and Syria) and the British (in Iraq and Palestine) established mandates. The Allies viewed the mandate system as a reasonable compromise between the reality of imperialism and the ideal of self-determination. To the peoples who were directly affected, the mandate system smacked of continued imperial rule draped in a cloak of respectability.

Challenges to European Preeminence

The Great War changed Europe forever, but to most Europeans the larger world and the continent's role in it remained essentially unchanged. With the imperial powers still ruling over their old colonies and new protectorates, it appeared that European global hegemony was even more secure. Yet this picture did not correspond to reality.

The Great War did irreparable damage to European power and prestige and set the stage for a process of decolonization that would gather momentum during and after the Second World War. The war of 1914–1918 accelerated the growth of nationalism in the European-controlled parts of the world, fueling desires for nothing less than independence and self-determination.

Weakened Europe   The decline in European power was closely related to diminished economic stature, a result of the commitment to total war. In time Europe overcame many war-induced economic problems, such as high rates of inflation and huge public debts, but other economic dislocations were both permanent and damaging. Most significant was the loss of overseas investments and foreign markets, which had brought huge financial returns. Nothing is more indicative of Europe's reduced economic might than the reversal of the economic relationship between Europe and the United States. Whereas the United States had been a debtor nation before 1914, owing billions of dollars to European investors, by 1919 it had become a major creditor.

A loss of prestige overseas and a weakening grip on colonies also reflected the undermining of Europe's global hegemony. Colonial subjects in Africa, Asia, and the Pacific often viewed the Great War as a civil war among the European nations, a bloody spectacle in which the haughty bearers of an alleged superior society vilified and slaughtered each other. Because Europe seemed weak, divided, and vulnerable, the white overlords no longer seemed destined to rule over colonized subjects. The colonials who returned home from the war in Europe and southwest Asia reinforced these general impressions with their own firsthand observations. In particular, they were less inclined to be obedient imperial subjects.

Revolutionary Ideas   The war also helped spread revolutionary ideas to the colonies. The U.S. war aims spelled out in the Fourteen Points had raised the hopes of peoples under imperial rule and helped promote nationalist aspirations. The peacemakers repeatedly invoked the concept of self-determination, and Wilson publicly proposed that in all colonial questions "the interests of the native populations be given equal weight with the desires of European governments." Wilson seemed to call for nothing less than national independence and self-rule. Nationalists struggling to organize anti-imperialist resistance also sought inspiration from the Soviet Union, whose leaders denounced all forms of imperialism and pledged their support to independence movements. Taken together, these messages were subversive to imperial control and had a great appeal for colonial peoples. The postwar disappointments and temporary setbacks experienced by nationalist movements did not diminish their desire for self-rule and self-determination.

The assassination of the Austrian archduke Francis Ferdinand had a galvanizing effect on a Europe torn by national rivalries, colonial disputes, and demands for self-determination. In the summer of 1914, inflexible war plans and a tangled alliance system had transformed a local war between Austria-Hungary and Serbia into a European-wide clash of arms. With the entry of the Ottoman empire, Japan, and the United States, the war of 1914–1918 became a global conflict. Although many belligerents organized their societies for total war and drew upon the resources of their overseas empires, the war remained at a bloody stalemate until the United States entered the conflict in 1917. The tide turned, and the combatants signed an armistice in November 1918. The Great War, a brutal encounter between societies and peoples, inflicted ghastly human casualties, severely damaged national economies, and discredited established political and cultural traditions. The war also altered the political landscape of many lands, destroying four dynasties and their empires and fostering the creation of several new European nations. In Russia the war served as a backdrop for the world's first successful socialist revolution. In the end the Great War sapped the strength of European colonial powers while it promoted nationalist aspirations among colonized peoples.

CHRONOLOGY

28 June 1914	Assassination of Archduke Francis Ferdinand
28 July 1914	Austrian declaration of war on Serbia
1 August 1914	German declaration of war on Russia
3 August 1914	German declaration of war on France
4 August 1914	British declaration of war on Germany
23 August 1914	Japan declaration of war on Germany
6 April 1917	United States declaration of war on Germany
1917	German resumption of unrestricted submarine warfare
1917	Bolshevik Revolution
11 November 1918	Armistice
1919–1920	Paris Peace Conference
1920	First meeting of the League of Nations

FOR FURTHER READING

Modris Eckstein. *Rites of Spring: The Great War and the Birth of the Modern Age*. Boston, 1989. An imaginative cultural study that ranges widely.

Gerald D. Feldman. *Army, Industry, and Labor in Germany, 1914–1918*. Princeton, 1966. A pioneering work on the impact of total war on the home front.

Paul Fussell. *The Great War and Modern Memory*. Oxford, 1975. An original and deeply moving piece of cultural history.

Felix Gilbert. *The End of the European Era, 1890 to the Present*. New York, 1979. An information-laden study that argues that the Great War destroyed Europe's centrality in the world.

Gerd Hardach. *The First World War, 1914–1918*. Berkeley, 1977. A brief and excellent introduction to the economic aspects of the conflict.

Margaret Randolph Higonnet et al. *Behind the Lines*. New Haven, 1990. Women's work and the war industry take center stage.

James Joll. *The Origins of the First World War*. 2nd ed. London, 1991. The most lucid and balanced introduction to a complex and controversial subject.

John Maynard Keynes. *The Economic Consequences of the Peace*. New York, 1920. A classic and devastating critique of the Versailles treaty.

Richard Pipes. *The Russian Revolution 1899–1919*. 2nd ed. London, 1992. An up-to-date and well-argued interpretation.

Erich Remarque. *All Quiet on the Western Front*. New York, 1958. A fictional account of trench warfare.

Barbara Tuchman. *The Guns of August*. New York, 1962. Spellbinding narrative of the coming of the war.

Robert Wohl. *The Generation of 1914*. Cambridge, 1979. Elegantly captures the ideas and attitudes of the generations that experienced the Great War.

NU DESCENDANT UN ESCALIER   MARCEL DUCHAMP

THE AGE OF ANXIETY, 1919–1939

. . .

Shanfei lived in interesting times. The daughter of a wealthy landowning man of the Chinese gentry, she grew up with luxuries and opportunities unknown to most other girls. Her father allowed her to attend school, and her mother clothed her in beautiful silk dresses. Shanfei, however, matured into a woman who rejected the rich trappings of her youth. Her formative years were marked by political ferment and the unsettling cultural changes that engulfed the globe in the wake of the Great War. The rise of nationalism and communism in China after the Revolution of 1911 and the Russian Revolution in 1917 guided the transformation of Shanfei—from a girl ruled by tradition and privilege she became an active revolutionary dedicated to the cause of women and communism.

With the exception of Shanfei's father, the members of her family in Hunan province took in the new spirit of the first decades of the twentieth century. Her brothers returned from school with strange and compelling ideas, including some that challenged the subordinate position of women in China. Shanfei's mother, to all appearances a woman who accepted her subservience to her husband, proved instrumental to Shanfei's departure from the common destiny of Chinese girls. She listened quietly to her sons as they discussed new views, and then she applied them to her daughter. She used every means at her disposal to convince her husband to educate their daughter—she wept, she begged, she cajoled. He relented, but still insisted not only that Shanfei receive an old-fashioned education but also that she submit to foot binding and childhood betrothal.

When Shanfei was eleven years old, her father suddenly died, and his death emboldened her mother. She ripped the bandages off Shanfei's feet and sent her to a modern school far from home. In the lively atmosphere of her school, Shanfei bloomed into an activist. At sixteen she incited a student strike against the administration of her school, transferred to an even more modern school, and became famous as a leader in the student movement. She went to school with men and broke tradition in her personal as well as political life. In 1926 Shanfei abandoned her studies to join the Communist Youth, and she also gave up her fiancé for a free marriage to the man she loved: a peasant who was also a leader of peasants in the communist movement.

Marcel Duchamp. *Nude Descending a Staircase, No. 2.* (1912). Exhibited in 1913 in New York, the painting attracted the scorn and ridicule of critics. The work immediately became a star attraction.

● Philadelphia Museum of Art: The Louise and Walter Arensberg Collection/© 2000 Artists Rights Society (ARS), New York/ADAGP, Paris/Estate of Marcel Duchamp

The amazing twists of fate that altered the destiny of Shanfei had parallels throughout the world after the Great War. Disillusion and radical upheaval marked areas as distinct as Europe, the lands of the former Russian empire, India, and China. European society, badly shaken by the effects of years of war, had experienced a shock to its system of values, beliefs, and traditions. Profound scientific and cultural transformations that came to the fore in the postwar decades also contributed to a sense of loss and anxiety. As peoples around the world struggled to come to terms with the aftermath of war, an unprecedented economic contraction gripped the international economy. Against the background of the Great Depression, dictators in Russia and Germany tried to translate blueprints for utopias into reality. While Joseph Stalin and his fellow communists recast the former tsarist empire into a dictatorship of the proletariat, Adolf Hitler and the Nazi party forged a new national community based on a racial state.

Elsewhere, European empires still appeared to dominate global relations. Beneath the surface, however, a deep nationalist ferment brewed. Nationalist movements had gathered strength, and in the postwar years resistance to foreign rule and desire for national unity were stronger than ever. This situation was especially true in India and China, where various visions of national identity competed with each other. The roots of all these developments lay in the global storm of a world war that had shaken the foundations of established traditions—and those foundations crumbled in Shanfei's home in Hunan as much as in the political capitals of Europe and the banks and industries that were collapsing under the pressure of the Great Depression.

 ## PROBING CULTURAL FRONTIERS

The Great War had discredited established social and political institutions and long-held beliefs about the superiority of European society. Writers, poets, theologians, and other intellectuals lamented the decline and imminent death of their society. While some wrote obituaries, however, others embarked on bold new cultural paths that established the main tendencies of modern thought and taste. Most of these cultural innovators had begun their work before the war, but it was in the two decades following the conflict that a revolution in science, psychology, art, and architecture attained its fullest development and potency.

The discoveries of physicists undermined the Newtonian universe—in which a set of inexorable natural laws governed events—with a new and disturbing cosmos. Uncertainty governed this strange universe, which lacked any objective reality. Equally discomforting were the insights of psychoanalysis, which suggested that human behavior was fundamentally irrational. Disquieting trends in the arts and architecture paralleled the developments in science and psychology. Especially in painting, an aversion to realism and a pronounced preference for abstraction heralded the arrival of new aesthetic standards.

Postwar Pessimism

"You are all a lost generation," noted Gertrude Stein (1874–1946) to her fellow American writer Ernest Hemingway (1899–1961). Stein had given a label to the group of American intellectuals and literati who congregated in Paris in the postwar years. This "lost generation" expressed in poetry and fiction the malaise and disillusion that characterized U.S. and European thought after the Great War. The vast majority of European intellectuals had rallied enthusiastically to the war in 1914, viewing it as a splendid adventure. The brutal realities of industrialized warfare left no room for heroes, however, and most of these young artists and intellectuals quickly became disillusioned. During the 1920s they spat out their revulsion in a host of war novels such as Ernest Hemingway's *A Farewell to Arms* (1929) and Erich Maria Remarque's *All Quiet on the Western Front* (1929), works overflowing with images of meaningless death and suffering.

Postwar writers lamented the decline of western society. A retired German school teacher named Oswald Spengler (1880–1936) made headlines when he published *The Decline of the West* (1918–1922). In this work, which might have been seen as an obituary of civilization, Spengler proposed that all societies pass through a life cycle of growth and decay comparable to the biological cycle of living organisms. His analysis of the history of western Europe led him to conclude that European society had entered the final stage of its existence. All that remained was irreversible decline, marked by imperialism and warfare. Spengler's gloomy predictions provided a kind of comfort to those who sought to rationalize their postwar despair, as did his conviction that all the nations of the world were equally doomed. In England the shock of war caused the historian Arnold J. Toynbee (1889–1975) to begin his twelve-volume classic, *A Study of History* (1934–1961), that sought to discover how societies develop through time. In this monumental comparative study Toynbee analyzes the genesis, growth, and disintegration of twenty-six societies.

Religious Uncertainty

Theologians joined the chorus of despair. In 1919 Karl Barth (1886–1968), widely recognized as one of the most notable modern Christian theologians, published a religious bombshell titled *Epistle to the Romans*. In his work Barth sharply attacked the liberal Christian theology that had embraced the idea of progress—that is, the tendency of European thinkers to believe in limitless improvement—as the realization of God's purpose. Other Christians joined the fray, reminding a generation of optimists that Christ's kingdom is not of this world. The Augustinian, Lutheran, and Calvinist message of original sin—the depravity of human nature—fell on receptive ears, as many Christians refused to accept the idea that contemporary human society was in any way a realization of God's purpose. The Russian orthodox thinker Niokolai Berdiaev (1874–1948) summed up these sentiments succinctly: "Man's historical experience has been one of steady failure, and there are no grounds for supposing it will be ever anything else."

Attacks on Progress

The Great War destroyed long-cherished beliefs such as belief in the universality of human progress. Many idols of nineteenth-century progress came under attack, especially science and technology. The scientists' dream of leading humanity to a beneficial conquest of nature seemed to have gone awry, for scientists had spent the war making poisonous gas and high explosives. Democracy was another fallen idol. The idea that people should have a voice in selecting the leaders of their government enjoyed widespread support in European societies. By the early twentieth century, the removal of property and educational restrictions on the right to vote had resulted in universal male suffrage in most societies. In the years following the Great War, most European governments extended the franchise to women as well. Taken together, these developments led to an unprecedented degree of political participation as millions of people voted in elections and referendums. But many intellectuals abhorred what they viewed as a weak political system that championed the tyranny of the average person. Because they viewed democracy as a product of decay and as lacking in positive values, many people idealized elite rule. In Germany a whole school of conservatives lamented the "rule of inferiors." Common people, too, all too often viewed democracy as a decaying political system because they associated it with corrupt and ineffective party politics. However, antidemocratic strains were not confined to Germany. The widely read essay "Revolt of the Masses" (1930) by the Spanish philosopher José Ortega y Gasset (1883–1955) warned readers about the masses who were destined to destroy the highest achievements of western society. In 1926 the renowned British economist John Maynard Keynes (1883–1946) lectured on the "End of Laissez-Faire," although he was not sure what would replace old-fashioned capitalism.

Revolutions in Physics and Psychology

The postwar decade witnessed a revolution in physics that transformed the character of science. Albert Einstein (1879–1955) struck the first blow with his theory of general relativity (1906), showing that there is no single spatial and chronological framework in the universe. According to the theory, it no longer made sense to speak of space and time as absolutes, for the measurement of these two categories always varies with the motion of the observer. That is, space and time are relative to the person measuring them. To the layperson such notions—usually expressed in incomprehensible mathematical formulas—seemed to suggest that science had reached the limits of what could be known with certainty. A commonsense universe had vanished, to be replaced by a radically new one in which reality or truth was merely a set of mental constructs.

The Uncertainty Principle

One of the best known faces of the twentieth century,

Albert Einstein was the symbol of the revolution in physics.

• Corbis-Bettmann

More disquieting even than Einstein's discoveries was the theory formulated by Werner Heisenberg (1901–1976), who in 1927 published a paper, "About the Quantum-Theoretical Reinterpretation of Kinetic and Mechanical Relationships," which established the "uncertainty principle." According to Heisenberg, it is impossible to specify simultaneously both the position and the velocity of a subatomic particle. The more accurately one determines the position of an electron, in other words, the less precisely one can determine its velocity, and vice versa. In essence, scientists cannot observe the behavior of electrons objectively, because the very act of observation interferes with them. The indeterminacy of the atomic universe demanded that the exact calculations of classical physics be replaced by probability calculations.

It quickly became evident that the uncertainty principle had important implications beyond physics. It also carried broader philosophical ramifications. Heisenberg's theory called into question established notions of truth and seemed to violate the fundamental law of cause and effect. Likewise, objectivity as it had always been understood was no longer a valid concept, because the observer was always part of the process under observation. Accordingly, any observer—an anthropologist studying another society, for instance—had to be alert to the fact that his or her very presence became an integral part of the study.

Equally unsettling as the advances in physics were developments in psychology that challenged established concepts of morality and values. In an indeterminate universe governed by relativity, the one remaining fixed point was the human psyche. But the insights of Sigmund Freud (1856–1939) proved disturbing as well. Beginning in 1896, the medical doctor from Vienna embarked on research that focused on psychological rather than physiological explanations of mental disorders. Through his clinical observations of patients, Freud identified a conflict between conscious and unconscious mental processes that lay at the root of neurotic behavior. This conflict, moreover, suggested to him the existence of a repressive mechanism that keeps painful memories or threatening events away from the conscious mind. Freud believed that dreams held the key to the deepest recesses of the human psyche. Using the free associations of patients to guide him in the interpretation of dreams, he identified sexual drives and fantasies as the most important source of repression. For example, Freud claimed to have discovered a so-called Oedipus complex in which male children develop an erotic attachment to their mother and hostility toward their father.

Freud's Psychoanalytic Theory

From dreams Freud proceeded to analyze literature, religion, politics, and virtually every other type of human endeavor, seeking always to identify the manifestations of the repressed conscious. He was convinced that his theory, known as *psychoanalysis,* provided the keys to understanding all human behavior. In the end Freudian doctrines not only shaped the psychiatric profession but also established a powerful presence in literature and the arts. During the 1920s novelists, poets, and painters acknowledged Freud's influence, as they focused on the inner world—the hidden depths of memory and emotion—of their characters. The creators of imaginative literature used Freud's bold emphasis on sexuality as a tool for the interpretation and understanding of human behavior.

Experimentation in Art and Architecture

The roots of modern painting go back to nineteenth-century French avant-garde artists who became preoccupied with how a subject should be painted. The common denominator among the various schools was disdain for realism and concern for freedom of expression. The aversion to visual realism was heightened by the spread of photography. When everyone could create naturalistic landscapes or portraits with a camera, it made little sense for artists to do so laboriously with paint and brush. Thus modern painters began to think of canvas not as a reproduction of reality, but rather as an end in itself. The purpose of a painting was not to mirror reality, but to create it.

By the beginning of the twentieth century, the possibilities inherent in this new aesthetic led to the emergence of a bewildering variety of pictorial schools, all of which promised an entirely new art. Regardless of whether they called themselves *les fauves* ("wild beasts"), expressionists, cubists, abstractionists, dadaists, or surrealists, artists generally agreed on a program "to abolish the sovereignty of appearance." Paintings no longer depicted recognizable objects from the everyday world, and beauty was expressed in pure color or shape. Some painters sought to express feelings and emotions through violent distortion of forms and the use of explosive colors; others, influenced by Freudian psychology, tried to tap the subconscious mind to communicate an inner vision or a dream.

The artistic heritages of Asian, Pacific, and African societies fertilized various strains of modern painting. Nineteenth-century Japanese prints, for example, influenced French impressionists like Edgar Degas (1834–1917), whose study of them led him to experiment with visual angles and asymmetrical compositions. The deliberate violation of perspective by Japanese painters and their stress on the flat, two-dimensional surface of the picture, as well as their habit of placing figures off center and their use of primary colors, encouraged European artists to take similar liberties with realism. In a revolt against rational society, the Postimpressionist painter Paul Gauguin (1848–1903) fled to central America and Tahiti. He was inspired by the "primitive" art he found there, claiming that it held a sense of wonder that "civilized" people no longer possessed. In Germany a group of young artists known as the "Bridge" made a point of regularly visiting the local ethnographic museum to be inspired by the boldness and power of indigenous art. The early works of Pablo Picasso (1881–1973), the leading proponent of cubism, displayed the influence of African art forms.

By the third decade of the twentieth century, it was nearly impossible to generalize about the history of modern painting. All artists were acknowledged to have a right to their own reality, and generally accepted standards that distinguished between "good" and "bad" art disappeared.

Modern Architecture

Paul Gauguin. *Nafea Faa Ipoipo* ("When are you to be married?"; 1892). Gauguin sought the spiritual meaning for his art in the islands of the South Pacific. This painting of two Tahitian women revealed his debt to impressionism, but also showed his own innovations: strong outlines, flat colors, and flattened forms.

● Rudolf Staechelin Family Foundation, Basel. Photo courtesy Kimbell Museum. Photo by Michael Bodycomb.

During the first decades of the twentieth century, architecture too underwent a revolutionary transformation as designers deliberately set out to create a completely different building style that broke with old forms and traditions.

Pablo Picasso's *Les Demoiselles d' Avignon* (1907) was the first of what would be called Cubist works. This image had a profound impact on subsequent art. ● *Les Demoiselles d'Avignon*. By Pablo Picasso. Paris (June–July 1907). Oil on canvas, 8′ × 7′8″. The Museum of Modern Art, New York. Acquired through the Lillie P. Bliss Bequest. Photograph © 2000 The Museum of Modern Art, New York. © 1999 Estate of Pablo Picasso/Artists Rights Society (ARS), New York

The modern movement in architecture coalesced with the opening of the *Bauhaus,* an institution that brought together architects, designers, and painters from several countries. Located first in Weimar and then Dessau, Germany, the Bauhaus was a community of innovators bent on creating a building style and interior designs that were uniquely suited to the urban and industrial landscape of the twentieth century.

The first director of the Bauhaus was Walter Gropius (1883–1969), and his theory of design became the guiding principle first of the Bauhaus and subsequently of modern architecture in general. To Gropius, design was functional, based on a marriage between engineering and art. The buildings Gropius designed featured simplicity of shape and extensive use of glass and always embodied the new doctrine that form must follow function. The second director of the Bauhaus, Ludwig Mies

Designed by Walter Gropius in 1925, this building introduced the functional international style that dominated for the next half century.   •   Erik Bohr/AKG London

von der Rohe (1886–1969), exerted an equally profound influence on modern architecture. He experimented with steel frames around which he stretched non-load-bearing walls of glass. His designs became the basis for the ubiquitous glass-box skyscraper that first adorned cities like Chicago and New York and later dominated the skylines of most major cities.

The style initiated by the Bauhaus architects, termed the international style, gradually prevailed after 1930 because its functionalism was well suited to the construction of large apartment and office complexes. The work of the world-famous Swiss-French architect Le Corbusier (Charles Édouard Jeanneret, 1887–1965) proved the broad appeal of the new architecture. At the request of Jawaharlal Nehru (1889–1964), India's first prime minister, Le Corbusier laid out the new capital city of the Punjab, Chandigarh, and designed for it three modern concrete government buildings. Governments and businesses eagerly embraced the new style, but the public never quite warmed to the glass box, a cold and impersonal structure that seemed to overwhelm the individual.

 ## GLOBAL DEPRESSION AND EUROPEAN DICTATORSHIPS

After the horrors and debilitating upheavals of the Great War, much of the world yearned for a return to normality and prosperity. By the early 1920s the efforts of governments and businesses to rebuild damaged economies seemed to bear fruit.

Prosperity, however, was short-lived. In 1929 the world plunged into an economic depression that was so long lasting, so severe, and so global that it has become known as the Great Depression. The old capitalist system of trade and finance had effectively collapsed, and until a new system took its place after 1945, a return to worldwide prosperity could not occur.

Amid the gloom and despair, some voices proclaimed the promise of a better tomorrow. Marxists believed that capitalist society was on its deathbed, yet they had faith that a new and better system based on rule by the proletariat was being born out of the ashes of the Russian empire. Others, uncomfortable with the abolition of private property and the "dictatorship of the proletariat," found solace in activist political movements that claimed to have an alternative formula for the reconstruction of society. Among these, the National Socialist German Workers Party figured most prominently. The Nazis claimed to promote a distinct alternative to socialism while still offering revolutionary answers to the problems that seemed to defy solution by traditional liberal democratic means.

The Great Depression

By the middle of the 1920s, some semblance of economic normality had returned, and most countries seemed on the way to economic recovery. Industrial productivity had returned to prewar levels as businesses repaired the damages the war had inflicted on industrial plants, equipment, and transportation facilities. But this prosperity was fragile, perhaps even false, and many serious problems and dislocations remained in the international economy.

The economic recovery and well-being of Europe, for example, were tied to a tangled financial system that involved war debts among the Allies, reparations paid by Germany and Austria, and the flow of U.S. funds to Europe. In essence, the governments of Austria and Germany relied on U.S. loans and investment capital to finance reparation payments to France and England. The French and British governments, in turn, depended on these reparation payments to pay off loans taken out in the United States during the Great War. By the summer of 1928, U.S. lenders and investors started to withdraw capital from Europe, placing an intolerable strain on the financial system.

Economic Problems

There were other problems as well. Improvements in industrial processes reduced worldwide demand for certain raw materials, causing an increase in supplies and a drop in prices. Technological advances in the production of automobile tires, for instance, permitted the use of reclaimed rubber. The resulting glut of natural rubber had devastating consequences for the economies of the Dutch East Indies, Ceylon, and Malaysia, all of which relied on the export of rubber. Similarly, the increased use of oil undermined the coal industry, the emergence of synthetics hurt the cotton industry, and the growing adoption of artificial nitrogen virtually ruined the nitrate industry of Chile.

One of the nagging weaknesses of the global economy in the 1920s was the depressed state of agriculture, the result of overproduction and falling prices. During the Great War, when Europe's agricultural output declined significantly, farmers in the United States, Canada, Argentina, and Australia expanded their own production. At the end of the war, European farmers resumed their agricultural activity, thereby contributing to worldwide surpluses. Above-average global harvests between 1925 and 1929 aggravated the situation. As production increased, demand declined, and prices collapsed throughout the world. By 1929 the price of a bushel of wheat was at its lowest level in four hundred years, and farmers everywhere became impoverished. The reduced income of farm families contributed to high inventories of manufactured goods, which in turn caused businesses to cut back production and to lay off workers.

The Crash of 1929

The United States enjoyed a boom after the Great War: industrial wages were high, and production and consumption increased. Many people in the United States invested their earnings and savings in speculative ventures, particularly the buying of stock on margin—putting up as little as 3 percent of a stock's price in cash and borrowing the remainder from brokers and banks or by mortgaging their homes. By October 1929 hints of a worldwide economic slowdown and warnings from experts that stock prices were overvalued prompted investors to pull out of the market. On Black Thursday (24 October), a wave of panic selling on the New York Stock Exchange caused stock prices to plummet. Investors who had overextended themselves in a frenzy of speculative stock purchases watched in agony. Thousands of people, from poor widows to industrial tycoons, lost their life savings, and by the end of the day eleven financiers had committed suicide. The crisis deepened when lenders called in loans, thereby forcing still more investors to sell their securities at any price.

Economic Contraction Spreads

In the wake of this financial chaos came a drastic decrease in business activity, wages, and employment. Consumer demand no longer sufficed to purchase all the goods that businesses produced, and when businesses realized that they could not sell their inventories, they responded with cutbacks in production and additional layoffs. With so many people unemployed or underemployed, demand plummeted still further, causing more business failures and soaring unemployment. In 1930 the slump deepened, and by 1932 industrial production had fallen to half its 1929 level. National income had dropped by roughly half. Forty-four percent of U.S. banks were out of business, and the deposits of millions of people had disappeared. Because much of the world's prosperity depended on the export of U.S. capital and the strength of U.S. import markets, the contraction of the U.S. economy created a ripple effect that circled the globe.

With the notable exception of the Soviet Union, whose economy was essentially isolated from the international marketplace, most societies experienced economic difficulties throughout the 1930s. Although the severity of the economic contraction varied in intensity, virtually every industrialized society saw its economy shrivel. Nations that relied

Migrant Mother, Nipomo California, 1936, a famous image of the Great Depression by Dorothea Lange. • Library of Congress

on exports of manufactured goods to pay for imported fuel and food—Germany and Japan in particular—suffered the most. The depression also spread unevenly to primary producing economies in Latin America, Africa, and Asia. Hardest hit were countries that depended on the export of a few primary products—agricultural goods, such as coffee, sugar, and cotton, and raw materials, such as minerals, ores, and rubber.

Industrial Economies

U.S. investors, shaken by the collapse of stock prices, tried to raise money by calling in loans and liquidating investments, and Wall Street banks refused to extend short-term loans as they became due. Banking houses in Austria and Germany became vulnerable to collapse, for they had been major recipients of U.S. loans. Devastated by the loss of U.S. capital, the German economy experienced a precipitous economic slide that by 1932 resulted in 35 percent unemployment and a 50 percent decrease in industrial production. As the German economy ground to a virtual halt, the rest of Europe—which was closely integrated with the German economy—sputtered and stalled. Although Germany had lost the Great War, it had remained a leading economic power throughout the postwar years. Because no military engagements took place on German soil, the national economy—its natural resources, infrastructure, and productive capacity—had been spared the physical destruction that seriously disrupted the economies of other lands such as France or Russia. Germany did not escape the ravages of the depression. The situation in Europe deteriorated further when businesses, desperate to raise capital by exporting goods to the United States, found that U.S. markets had virtually disappeared behind tariff walls. Foreign trade fell sharply between 1929 and 1932, causing further losses in manufacturing, employment, and per capita income. Because of its great dependence on the U.S. market, the Japanese economy felt the depression's effects almost immediately. Unemployment in export-oriented sectors of the economy skyrocketed as companies cut back on production.

Primary Producing Economies

Through their global trade connections, industrialized nations transmitted the economic crisis throughout the world. Because they exported agricultural products or raw materials, whose prices declined rapidly after 1929, most Latin American states were vulnerable to the effects of the depression. The prices of sugar from the Carribean, coffee from Brazil and Colombia, wheat and beef from Argentina, tin from Bolivia, nitrates from Chile, and many other products fell sharply. Attempts by producers to raise prices by holding supplies off the market—(Brazilians, for example, set fire to coffee beans or used them in the construction of highways)—failed, and throughout Latin America unemployment rates increased rapidly.

A different situation existed in Africa, for almost the entire continent was under colonial rule, and colonies had no choice but to follow the dictates of their colonizers. African colonies thus were a principal source of agricultural products, ores, and minerals for their European masters. As international markets for primary products shrank under the impact of the depression, European companies that controlled the export of African products suffered accordingly. Africans who produced the commodities destined for export had to contend with high unemployment. Many areas of colonial Africa, however, remained unaffected by the global slump, because their products were not tied to the international economy.

The global economic downturn and depressed markets affected some agricultural economies only slightly, if at all. For example, China's large agrarian economy and small industrial sector were integrated into the world market to only a limited extent. Thus, although Chinese trade in silk and tea declined markedly during the depression, foreign trade made up only a small and relatively insignificant part of the domestic economy. China's large domestic markets—not dependence on foreign trade—dictated the direction of its economy. Another area that did not suffer particularly from the Great Depression was the Philippines, a colony of the United States. The important sugar-producing sector of the Philippine economy, which employed some six million workers, benefited from a protected market in the United States.

Economic Nationalism

The Great Depression destroyed the international financial and commercial network of the capitalist economies. As international cooperation broke down, governments turned to their own resources and began to practice economic nationalism. By imposing tariff barriers, import quotas and import prohibitions, politicians hoped to achieve autarchy, or economic self-sufficiency. In an age of global interdependence, such goals remained unobtainable, and economic nationalism invariably backfired. Each new measure designed to restrict imports provoked retaliation by other nations whose interests were affected. After the U.S. Congress passed the Smoot-Hawley Tariff in 1930, which raised duties on most manufactured products to prohibitive levels, the governments of dozens of other nations immediately retaliated by raising tariffs on imports of U.S. products. The result was a sharp drop in international trade. Instead of higher levels of production and income, economic nationalism yielded the opposite. Between 1929 and 1932 world production declined by 38 percent and trade dropped by more than 66 percent.

Despair and Government Action

By 1933 unemployment in industrial societies reached thirty million, more than five times higher than in 1929. Men lost their jobs because of economic contraction, and a combination of economic trends and deliberate government policy caused women to lose theirs as well. Unemployment initially affected women less directly than men because employers preferred women workers who were paid two-thirds or three-quarters the wages of men doing the same work. But before long, governments enacted policies to reduce female employment, especially for married women. The notion that a woman's place was in the home was widespread. Thus in 1931 a British royal commission on unemployment insurance declared that "in the case of married women as a class, industrial employment cannot be regarded as the normal condition." More candid yet was the French Nobel Prize-winning physician Charles Richet (1850–1935), who insisted that removing women from the workforce would not only solve the problem of male unemployment but also increase the nation's dangerously low birthrate.

Personal Suffering

The Great Depression caused enormous personal suffering. The stark, gloomy statistics documenting the failure of economies the world over do not convey the anguish and despair of those who lost their jobs, savings, and homes, and often their dignity and hope as well. For millions of people the struggle for food, clothing, and shelter grew desperate. Shantytowns appeared overnight in urban areas, and breadlines stretched for blocks. Marriage, childbearing, and divorce rates declined, but suicide rates rose. The acute physical and social problems of those at the bottom of the economic ladder often magnified social divisions and class hatreds. Workers and farmers especially came to despise the wealthy, who, despite their own reduced incomes, remained shielded from the worst impact of the economic downturn and continued to enjoy a comfortable lifestyle. Adolescents completing their schooling faced an almost nonexistent job market.

That the Great Depression deflated not only economies but also hope was especially noticeable in the literature of the period. Writers castigated the social and political order, calling repeatedly for a more just society. The U.S. writer John Steinbeck

(1902–1968) chillingly captured both the official heartlessness and the rising political anger inspired by the depression. In *The Grapes of Wrath* (1939), the Joad family, prototypical "Okies," migrated from Oklahoma to California to escape the Dust Bowl. In describing their journey Steinbeck commented on the U.S. government's policy of "planned scarcity," in which surplus crops were destroyed in order to raise prices while citizens starved. In one of the novel's most famous passages, Steinbeck portrayed the nation's rising political anguish:

Human faces of the Great Depression: children bathing in the Ozark Mountains, Missouri, 1940.   •   Library of Congress

> The people come with nets to fish for potatoes in the river and the guards hold them back; they come in rattling cars to get the dumped oranges, but the kerosene is sprayed. And they stand still and watch potatoes float by, listen to the screaming pigs being killed in a ditch and covered with quicklime, watch the mountains of oranges slop down to a putrefying ooze; and in the eyes of the people there is the failure; and in the eyes of the hungry there is a growing wrath. In the souls of the people the grapes of wrath are filling and growing heavy, growing heavy for the vintage.

Economic Experimentation

Classical economic thought (see chapter 29) held that capitalism was a self-correcting system that operated best when left to its own devices. Governments responded to the economic crisis in one of two ways. Initially, most governments did nothing, hoping against all odds that the crisis would resolve itself. When the misery spawned by the depression sparked calls for action, some governments assumed more active roles, pursuing deflationary measures by balancing national budgets and curtailing public spending. In either case, rather than lifting national economies out of the doldrums, the classical prescriptions for economic ills actually worsened the depression's impact and intensified the plight of millions of people. Far from self-correcting, capitalism seemed to be dying. Many called for a fundamental revision of economic thought.

John Maynard Keynes, the most influential economist of the twentieth century, offered a novel solution. His seminal work, *The General Theory of Employment, Interest, and Money* (1936), was his answer to the central problem of the depression— that millions of people who were willing to work could not find employment. To Keynes the fundamental cause of the depression was not excessive supply, but rather, inadequate demand. Accordingly, he urged governments to play an active role and stimulate the economy by increasing the money supply, thereby lowering interest

Keynes

rates and encouraging investment. He also advised governments to undertake public works projects to provide jobs and redistribute incomes through tax policy. Such intervention would result in reduced unemployment and increased consumer demand, both of which would lead to economic revival. These measures were necessary even if they caused governments to run deficits and maintain unbalanced budgets.

The New Deal   Although Keynes's theories did not become influential with policy makers until after World War II, the administration of U.S. president Franklin Delano Roosevelt (1882–1945) anticipated his ideas. Roosevelt took aggressive steps to reinflate the economy and ease the worst of the suffering caused by the depression. His proposals for dealing with the national calamity included legislation designed to prevent the collapse of the banking system, provide jobs and farm subsidies, give workers the right to organize and bargain collectively, guarantee minimum wages, and provide social security in old age. This program of sweeping economic and social reforms was called the New Deal. Its fundamental premise, that the federal government was justified in intervening to protect the social and economic welfare of the people, represented a major shift in U.S. government policy and started a trend toward social reform legislation that continued long after the depression years.

Japanese and   But ultimately it was more the massive military spending during World War II,
German Approaches   which ended the Great Depression in the United States and elsewhere, than it was the specific programs of the New Deal or similar approaches. Notable exceptions were Japan and Germany. Although the Japanese government had initially taken a passive stance, widespread social unrest and violence, including the assassination of the prime minister, convinced Japan's leaders to intervene aggressively in the economy. A combination of measures that included public works, relief programs for rural areas, incentives and subsidies for selected industries, devaluation of the currency, and the holding down of wages to promote exports—with painful results for Japanese workers—stimulated economic recovery by 1931. In Germany, Adolf Hitler's government also intervened forcefully in the economy after 1933. Large public works projects such as the construction of the famed Autobahn (a network of high-speed roads) quickly brought unemployment under control, and by the end of the decade the German economy actually had to cope with labor shortages. Deficit spending, much of it directed toward military preparation, went a long way toward increasing industrial production as well. By the mid-1930s the economic recovery of Germany was well on its way.

From Lenin to Stalin

In 1917 V. I. Lenin and his fellow Bolsheviks had taken power in the name of the Russian working class. But communist victory did not bring peace and stability to the lands of the former Russian empire. After seizing power, Lenin and his supporters had to defend the world's first "dictatorship of the proletariat" against numerous enemies, including dissident socialists, anti-Bolshevik officers and troops, peasant bands, and foreign military forces.

Civil War   Opposition to the Bolshevik Party—by now calling itself the Russian Communist Party—erupted into a civil war that lasted from 1918 to 1920. Operating out of its new capital in Moscow, Lenin's government began a policy of crushing all opposition. The communists began the Red Terror campaign in which suspected anticommunists known as Whites were arrested, tried, and executed. The secret police killed some two hundred thousand opponents of the regime. In July 1918 the Bolsheviks executed Tsar Nicholas II and his entire family, including several children. The peasantry, although hostile to the communists, largely supported them, fearing that a victory by the Whites would result in the return of the monarchy. However, foreign military intervention supported White resistance to the communist takeover. Russia's withdrawal from the Great War as well as anticommunist sentiment inflamed Russia's former allies, who sent troops and supplies to aid White forces. Although their numbers were negligible, the foreigners' presence sometimes had the effect of bonding otherwise hostile groups to the Reds. Poorly organized and without widespread support, the Whites were defeated by the Red Army in 1920. Estimates place the number of lives lost in the civil war at ten million, with many more people dying from disease and starvation than from the actual fighting. The political system that emerged from the civil war bore the imprint of political oppression, which played a significant role in the later development of the Soviet state.

War Communism

The new rulers of Russia had no real plans to transform the economy, but in the course of the civil war they embarked on a hasty and unplanned course of nationalization, a policy known as war communism. After officially annulling private property, the Bolshevik government assumed control or ownership of banks, industry, and other privately held commercial properties. Landed estates and the holdings of monasteries and churches became national property, although the Bolsheviks explicitly exempted the holdings of poor peasants from confiscation. The abolition of private trade was unpopular, and when the party seized crops from peasants to feed people in the cities, the peasants cut back their production. By 1920 industrial production had fallen to about one-tenth of its prewar level and agricultural output to about half its prewar level.

In 1921, as the Reds consolidated their military victories, Lenin faced the daunting prospect of rebuilding a society that had been at war since 1914. The workers, in whose name he had taken power, were on strike. Other problems included depopulated cities, destroyed factories, and an army that demobilized soldiers faster than the workforce could absorb them. Lenin and the party tried to take strict control of the country by crushing workers' strikes, peasant rebellions, and a sailors' revolt. Yet Lenin recognized the need to make peace with those whose skills would rekindle industrial production. Faced with economic paralysis, in the spring of 1921 he decided on a radical reversal of war communism.

The New Economic Policy

Demonstrating his pragmatism and willingness to compromise, Lenin implemented the New Economic Policy (NEP), which temporarily restored the market economy and some private enterprise in Russia. Large industries, banks, and transportation and communications facilities remained under state control, but the government returned small-scale industries (those with fewer than twenty workers) to private ownership. The government also allowed peasants to sell their surpluses at free market prices. Other features of the NEP included a vigorous program of electrification and the establishment of technical schools to train technicians and engineers. Lenin did not live to see the success of the NEP. After suffering three paralytic strokes, he died in 1924. His death was followed by a bitter struggle for power among the Bolshevik leaders.

Socialism in One Country

Many old Bolsheviks continued to argue for a permanent or continuous revolution, asserting that socialism in Russia would fail if socialism did not move from a national to an international stage. Others in the Politburo, the central governing body of the

Communist Party, favored establishing socialism in one country alone, thus repudiating the role of the Union of Soviet Socialist Republics (1922) as torchbearer of worldwide socialist revolution. Joseph Stalin (1879–1953), who served in the unglamourous bureaucratic position of general secretary, promoted the idea of socialism in one country. A Georgian by birth, an Orthodox seminarian by training, and a Russian nationalist by conviction, Stalin indicated his unified resolve to gain power in his surname, which meant "man of steel." His revolutionary past entailed more banditry than theory. Speaking Russian with a heavy accent, he had been an intellectual misfit among the Bolshevik elite. However, by 1928, Stalin had lived up to his name and had completely triumphed over his rivals in the party through murders and purges, clearing the way for an unchallenged dictatorship of the Soviet Union.

First Five-Year Plan

Stalin decided to replace Lenin's NEP with an ambitious plan for rapid economic development known as the First Five-Year Plan. The basic aims of this and subsequent five-year plans, first implemented in 1929, were to transform the Soviet Union from a predominantly agricultural country to a leading industrial power. The First Five-Year Plan set targets for increased productivity in all spheres of the economy but emphasized heavy industry—especially steel and machinery—at the expense of consumer goods. Through Gosplan, the central state planning agency, Stalin and the party attempted to coordinate resources and the labor force on an unprecedented scale. As the rest of the world teetered on the edge of economic collapse, this blueprint for maximum centralization of the entire national economy offered a bold alternative to market capitalism. Stalin repeatedly stressed the urgency of this monumental endeavor, telling his people, "We are 50 to 100 years behind the advanced countries. Either we do it, or we shall go under."

Collectivization of Agriculture

Integral to the drive for industrialization was the collectivization of agriculture. The Soviet state expropriated privately owned land to create collective or cooperative farm units whose profits were shared by all the farmers. The logic of communist ideology demanded the abolition of private property and market choices, but more practical considerations also played a role. Stalin and his regime viewed collectivization as a means of increasing the efficiency of agricultural production and ensuring that industrial workers would be fed. Collectivization was enforced most ruthlessly against *kulaks*—relatively wealthy peasants who had risen to prosperity during the NEP but accounted for only 3 to 5 percent of the peasantry.

In some places outraged peasants reacted to the government's program by slaughtering more than 50 percent of their livestock and burning their crops. Millions of farmers left the land and migrated to cities in search of work, thereby further taxing the limited supplies of housing, food, and utilities. Unable to meet production quotas, peasants often starved to death on the very land they once owned. When Stalin called a halt to collectivization in 1931, proclaiming the policy makers "dizzy with success," half of the farms in the Soviet Union had been collectivized. Estimates of the cost in number of peasant lives lost have fluctuated wildly, but even the most cautious place it at three million.

The First Five-Year Plan set unrealistically high production targets. Even so, the Soviet leadership proclaimed success after only four years. The Soviet Union industrialized under Stalin, even though the emphasis on building heavy industry first and consumer industries later meant that citizens had to postpone the gratifications of industrialization. Thus before refrigerators, radios, or automobiles became available, the government constructed steel works and hydroelectric plants. The scarcity or

Men and women drive tractors out of one of the Soviet Union's Machine Tractor Stations to work fields where mechanization had been a rare sight.   •   Karl Liebknecht/Sovfoto

nonexistence of consumer goods was to some degree balanced by full employment, low-cost utilities, and—when available—cheap housing and food. Set against the collapse of the U.S. stock market and the depression-ridden capitalist world, the ability of a centrally planned economy to create more jobs than workers could fill made it appear a viable and even attractive alternative.

The Great Purge

Nevertheless, the results of Stalin's five-year plan generated controversy as the Communist Party prepared for its seventeenth congress in 1934, the self-proclaimed "Congress of Victors." The disaster of collectivization and the ruthlessness with which it was carried out had raised doubts about Stalin's administration. Although themes of unity and reconciliation prevailed, Stalin learned of a plan to bring more pluralism back into leadership. The Congress of Victors became the "Congress of Victims" as Stalin incited a civil war within the party that was climaxed by highly publicized trials of former Bolshevik elites for treason and by a purge of two-thirds of the delegates. Between 1935 and 1938 Stalin removed from posts of authority all people who were suspected of opposition, including two-thirds of the members of the 1934 Central Committee and more than half of the army's high-ranking officers. The victims faced either outright execution or long-term suffering in labor camps. In 1939 eight million Soviet citizens were in labor camps, and three million were already dead as a result of the "cleansing," as Stalin's supporters termed this process.

The outside world watched the events unfolding within the Soviet Union with a mixture of contempt, fear, and admiration. Most observers recognized that the political and social upheavals that had transformed the former Russian empire were of worldwide importance. The establishment of the world's first dictatorship of the proletariat not only challenged the values and institutions of liberal society everywhere but also seemed to demonstrate the viability of communism as a social and political system.

German National Socialism

While socialism was transforming the former Russian empire, another political force swept across Europe after 1919. Fascism, an authoritarian political movement that sought to create a viable society by subordinating individuals to the service of the state, developed as a reaction against the social and political changes wrought by the Great War and the spread of socialism. Its name was derived from the *fasces,* an ancient Roman symbol of authority consisting of a bundle of rods strapped together around an axe. Fascism emphasized an extreme form of nationalism, but its appeal crossed national boundaries and affected to some degree all European societies. The term *fascism* was first used by Benito Mussolini (1883–1945), who gained control of the Italian government in 1922 and established a one-party dictatorship. Allying himself and his party with business and landlord interests and the military, *Il Duce* (the leader) crushed labor unions, prohibited strikes, and silenced all political opposition. The most notorious variant of fascism, however, developed in Germany under the Nazi party and its leader of Adolf Hitler (1889–1945).

Adolf Hitler   Hitler did not seem well cast for his later role as national hero, conqueror of most of Europe, and arbiter of the fate of millions. Born on 20 April 1889 in the small village of Braunau, Austria, Adolf Hitler grew up in a middle-class family with an indulgent mother who pampered him and a hot-tempered father who sternly disapproved of his son's poor performance in school. Arrogant and ill-tempered, Hitler left school at the age of sixteen without having graduated. In 1907 he went to Vienna, where he dreamed of becoming an artist. Denied admission to the Academy of Fine Arts, a frustrated Hitler supported himself with odd jobs.

During his five years in Vienna, he learned to hate Jews and Marxists, whom he thought had formed an evil union with the goal to destroy the world. He despised liberalism and democracy as well, and in cheap cafes he directed political harangues at anyone who would listen. Hitler moved to Munich, Germany, in 1913 and volunteered for the German army in the following year after the outbreak of the Great War. He served with great distinction in the war, but he found his true mission in life only after the war and amidst the disappointment at Germany's defeat. He came into contact with an obscure political party sympathetic to his ideas. In 1921 he became chairman of the party now known as the National Socialist German Workers' Party.

The Nazi Party   National Socialism (the Nazi movement) made its first major appearance in 1923 when party members and Adolf Hitler attempted to overthrow the democratic Weimar Republic that had replaced the German empire in 1919. The revolt quickly fizzled under the gunfire of police units; Hitler was jailed, and the Nazi movement and its leader descended into obscurity. When Hitler emerged from prison in 1924, he resolved to use new tactics. Realizing the futility of armed insurrection, he reorganized his movement and launched it on a "path of legality." Hitler and his followers were determined to gain power legally through the ballot box and, once successful, to discard the very instrument of their success.

The Struggle for Power   National Socialism made rapid gains after 1929 because it had broad appeal. Hitler attracted disillusioned people who felt alienated from society and frightened by the specter of socialist revolution. A growing number of people blamed the young German democracy for Germany's misfortunes: a humiliating peace treaty—the Treaty of Versailles—that identified Germany as responsible for the Great War and assigned reparation payments to the Allies; the hyperinflation of the early 1920s that wiped out the savings of the middle class; the suffering brought on by the Great Depression; and the seemingly unending and bitter infighting among the nation's major political parties. Adolf Hitler promised an end to all this by creating a new order that would lead to greatness for Germany. By stressing racial doctrines, particularly anti-semitism, the Nazis added a unique and frightening twist to their ideology. Although the Nazis avoided class divisions by recruiting followers from all strata of society, National Socialism in the main appealed to the members of the lower-middle classes: ruined shopkeepers and artisans, impoverished farmers, discharged white-collar workers, and disenchanted students.

The impact of the Great Depression and political infighting led to bloody street battles, shaking the foundations of Germany's fragile young democracy. The leaders of the nation's democratic and liberal parties groped for solutions to mounting unemployment but were hindered by lack of consensus and the public's loss of faith in the democratic system. The electorate became radicalized. Fewer and fewer Germans were willing to defend a parliamentary system they considered ineffective and corrupt. Between 1930 and 1932, the Nazi Party became the single largest party in parliament, and the reactionary and feeble president, Paul von Hindenburg (1847–1934), decided to offer Hitler the chancellorship. Promising to gain a majority in the next elections, Hitler lost little time in transforming the dying republic into a single-party dictatorship. He promised a German *Reich*, or empire, that would endure for a thousand years.

Consolidation of Power

Under the guise of a state of national emergency, the Nazis used all available means to impose their rule. They began by eliminating all working-class and liberal opposition. The Nazis not only suppressed the German communist and socialist parties but also abrogated virtually all constitutional and civil rights. Subsequently, Hitler and his government outlawed all other political parties, made it a crime to create a new party, and made the National Socialist Party the only legal party. Between 1933 and 1935 the regime replaced Germany's federal structure with a highly centralized state that eliminated the autonomy previously exercised by state and municipal governments. The National Socialist state then guided the destruction of trade unions and the elimination of collective bargaining, subsequently prohibiting strikes and lockouts. The Nazis also purged the judiciary

"Mother and Child" was the slogan on this poster, idealizing and encouraging motherhood. The background conveys the Nazi predilection for the wholesome country life, a dream that clashed with the urban reality of German society. • AKG London

and the civil service, took control of all police forces, and removed enemies of the regime—both real and imagined—through incarceration or murder.

The Role of Women

The worldwide upheavals taking place in this era affected women as well as men, although the status of women in this era of revolutionary change depended on where they lived. While Shanfei in China found more opportunities open to her, women in Nazi Germany did not. In Nazi ideology men and women inhabited distinct and separate spheres, with women relegated primarily to the roles of wife and mother. The new regime exerted considerable effort to mesh ideology with reality. Alarmed by declining birthrates, the Nazis launched a campaign to increase births. Through tax credits, special child allowances, and marriage loans, the authorities tried to encourage marriage— and, they hoped, procreation—among young people. Legal experts rewrote divorce laws so that a husband could get a divorce decree solely on the ground that he considered his wife sterile. At the same time, the regime outlawed abortions, closed birth control centers, restricted birth control devices, and made it difficult to obtain information about family planning. The Nazis also became enamored with a relatively inexpensive form of propaganda: pronatalist (to increase births) propaganda. They set in motion a veritable cult of motherhood. Annually on 12 August—the birth date of Hitler's mother—women who bore many children received the Honor Cross of the German Mother in three classes: bronze for those with more than four children, silver for those with more than six, and gold for those with more than eight. By August 1939 some three million women carried this prestigious award, which many Germans cynically called the "rabbit decoration." In the long term, however, any efforts by the Nazis to increase the fecundity of German women failed, and the birthrate remained below replacement level. German families were simply unwilling to change their reproductive preferences, which called for fewer children.

Anti-Semitism

The quantity of offspring was not the only concern of the new rulers, who were positively obsessed with "quality" as well. Anti-Semitism, or prejudice against Jews, was the hallmark of National Socialist ideology, and immediately after coming to power in 1933 the Nazis initiated systematic measures to suppress Germany's Jewish population. Although Nazi anti-Semitism was based on biological racial theories dating to the nineteenth century, government authorities used religious descent to determine who was a Jew. A flood of discriminatory laws and directives designed to humiliate, impoverish, and segregate Jews from the rest of society followed. In 1935 the notorious Nuremberg Laws deprived German Jews of their citizenship and prohibited marriage and sexual intercourse between Jews and other Germans. The Nazi party, in cooperation with government agencies, banks, and businesses took steps to eliminate Jews from economic life and expropriate their wealth. Jewish civil servants lost their jobs, and Jewish lawyers and doctors

A Nazi "racial expert" measures the racial purity of a German with a caliper. • Hulton Getty/Tony Stone Images

lost their gentile, or non-Jewish, clients. Party authorities also supervised the liquidation of Jewish-owned businesses or arranged for their purchase—at much less than their true value—by companies owned or operated by gentiles.

The official goal of the Nazi regime was Jewish emigration. Throughout the 1930s thousands of Jews left Germany, depriving the nation of many of its leading intellectuals, scientists, and artists. The exodus gained urgency after what came to be known "the night of broken glass" (*Kristallnacht*). During the night of 9–10 November 1938, the Nazis arranged for the destruction of thousands of Jewish stores, the burning of all synagogues, and the murder of more than one hundred Jews throughout Germany and Austria. This *pogrom* (a Yiddish term for devastation) was a signal that the position of Jews in Hitler's Reich was about to deteriorate dramatically. Although they had difficulty finding refuge, roughly 250,000 Jews left Germany by 1938. Those staying behind, especially the poor and the elderly, contemplated an uncertain destiny.

MEIN KAMPF

* * *

Mein Kampf (My Struggle) was the title of a book written by Adolf Hitler in which he presented his political views. Crudely written and turgid in style, it became the bible of the Nazi movement and the blueprint for the Third Reich. Hitler's basic theme was racial. He believed that a titanic struggle between a superior Aryan race and inferior non-Aryan races—including most notably Jews—determined the course of history. Originally, the term Aryan designated a language group, not a mythological breed of people.

So humans invariably wander about the garden of nature, convinced that they know and understand everything, yet with few exceptions are blind to one of the fundamental principles Nature uses in her work: the intrinsic segregation of the species of every living thing on the earth.

Any cross-breeding between two not completely equal beings will result in a product that is in between the level of the two parents. That means that the offspring will be superior to the parent who is at a biologically lower level of being but inferior to the parent at a higher level. This means the offspring will be overcome in the struggle for existence against those at the higher level. Such matings go against the will of Nature for the higher breeding of life.

As little as nature approves the mating of higher and lower individuals, she approves even less the blending of higher races with lower ones; for indeed otherwise her previous work toward higher development perhaps over hundreds of thousands of years might be rendered useless with one blow. If this were not the case, progressive development would stop and even deteriora-

tion might set in. . . . All the great civilizations of the past died out because contamination of their blood caused them to become decadent.

. . . What we see before us today as human culture, all the yields of art, science, and technology, are almost exclusively the creative product of the Aryans. Indeed this fact alone leads to the not unfounded conclusion that the Aryan alone is the founder of the higher type of humanity, and further that he represents the prototype of what we understand by the word: MAN.

The Jew provides the greatest contrast to the Aryan.

Since the Jew—for reasons I will deal with shortly—never had a civilization of his own, others have always provided the foundations of his intellectual labors. His intellect has always developed by the use of those cultural achievements he has found ready at hand around him. Never has it happened the other way around.

He stops at nothing, and his vileness becomes so monstrous that no one should be surprised if among our people the hateful figure of the Jew is taken as the personification of the devil and the symbol of evil. . . .

SOURCE: Adolf Hitler. *Mein Kampf.* Boston: Houghton Mifflin, 1939, pp. 390–414.

STRUGGLES FOR NATIONAL IDENTITY IN ASIA

The Paris peace settlement had barely altered the prewar colonial holdings of Europeans, yet indirectly the Great War affected relations between Asian peoples and the imperial powers. In the decades following the Great War, nationalism developed into a powerful political force in Asia, especially in India and China, where growing numbers of people were influenced by the idea of self-determination of nations that was one of the legacies of the Paris Peace Conference. Achieving the twin ideals of independence from foreign powers and national unity became a dream of intellectuals and a goal of new political leaders. Even as foreign control was being rejected, Asian leaders availed themselves of European ideologies such as nationalism and socialism. But in their search for new identities untainted by the dependent past, the Asians either transformed or adapted these ideologies to fit indigenous traditions.

Both Indian and Chinese society underwent a prolonged period of disorder and struggle until a new order emerged. In India the quest for national identity focused on gaining independence from British rule, a pursuit that was complicated by sectarian differences between Hindus and Muslims. The Chinese path to national identity was fraught with foreign and civil war as two principal groups—the Nationalist and Communist Parties—contended for power. Deeply divided by ideologies, both parties opposed foreign domination, rejected the old Confucian order, and sought a unified Chinese state.

India's Quest for Independence

By the end of the nineteenth century, Indian nationalism began to threaten the British empire's hold on India. The construction of a vast railway network across India to facilitate the export of raw materials contributed to the idea of national unity by bringing the people of the subcontinent within easy reach of one another. Moreover, because it was impossible for a small group of foreigners to control and administer such a vast country, the British had created an elite of educated Indian administrators to help in this task. A European system of education familiarized the local middle-class intelligentsia with the political and social values of European society. The values of democracy, individual freedom, and equality, however, were the antithesis of empire and promoted nationalist movements.

Indian National Congress   Of all the associations dedicated to the struggle against British rule, the greatest and most influential was the Indian National Congress, founded in 1885. This organization, which enlisted the support of many prominent Hindus and Muslims, at first stressed collaboration with the British to bring self-rule to India, but after the Great War the congress pursued this goal in opposition to the British. The formation of the Muslim League, established in 1906, with the encouragement of the British government, added a new current into the movement for national liberation. Both organizations were dedicated to achieving independence for India, but members of the Muslim League increasingly worried that Hindu oppression and continued subjugation of India's substantial Muslim minority might replace British rule.

During the Great War large numbers of Indians—both Hindus and Muslims—rallied to the British cause, and initially nationalist movements remained inactive. But as the war led to scarcities of goods and food, social discontent increasingly focused on the British colonizer. Indian nationalists also drew encouragement from ideas emanating from Washington, D.C., and St. Petersburg. They read Woodrow

Wilson's Fourteen Points, which called for national self-determination, and V. I. Lenin's appeal for a united struggle by proletarians and colonized peoples. The British government responded to the upsurge of nationalist activity that came in the wake of the peace settlement with a series of repressive measures that precipitated a wave of violence and disorder throughout the Indian subcontinent.

Into this turmoil stepped Mohandas Karamchand Gandhi (1869–1948), one of the most remarkable and charismatic leaders of the twentieth century. Gandhi grew up in a prosperous and pious Hindu household, married at thirteen, and left his home town in 1888 to study law in London. In 1893 he went to South Africa to accept a position with an Indian firm, and there he quickly became involved in organizing the local Indian community against a system of racial segregation, which made Indians second-class citizens. During the twenty-five years he spent in South Africa, Gandhi embraced a moral philosophy of tolerance and nonviolence (*ahimsa*) and developed the technique of passive resistance that he called *satyagraha* ("truth and firmness"). His belief in the virtue of simple living led him to renounce material possessions, dress in the garb of a simple Indian peasant, and become a vegetarian. He renounced sex—testing his willpower by chastely sleeping with various comely young women—and extolled the virtues of a daily saltwater enema. He also spent an hour each morning in careful study of the Bhagavad Gita (Sanskrit for "The Lord's Song"), one of the most sacred writings of Hinduism, which he regarded as a spiritual dictionary.

Mohandas K. Gandhi

Returning to India in 1915, Gandhi became active in Indian politics. He succeeded in transforming the Indian National Congress from an elitist body of anglicized gentlemen into a mass organization that became an effective instrument of Indian nationalism. While the reform program of the congress appeared remote from the needs of common people, Gandhi spoke in a language that they could understand. His unique mixture of spiritual intensity and political activism appealed to a broad section of the Indian population, and in the eyes of many he quickly achieved the stature of a political and spiritual leader, their Mahatma, or "great soul." Although he was himself a member of the merchant caste, Gandhi was determined to eradicate the injustices of the caste system. He fought especially hard to improve the status of the lowest classes of society, the casteless Untouchables, whom he called *harijans* ("children of God"). Under Gandhi's leadership the congress launched two mass movements: the Non-Cooperation Movement of 1920–1922 and the Civil Disobedience Movement of 1930. Convinced that economic self-sufficiency was a prerequisite for self-government, Gandhi called on the Indian people to boycott British goods and return to wearing rough homespun cotton clothing. He disagreed with those who wanted India to industrialize, advocating instead manual labor and the revival of rural cottage industries. Gandhi furthermore admonished his people to boycott institutions operated by the British in India such as schools, offices, and courts.

Despite Gandhi's admonitions against the use of force, violence often accompanied the protest movement. The British retaliated with arrests. That the British authorities could react brutally had already been shown in 1919 in the city of Amritsar in Punjab, where colonial troops freely used their rifles to disperse an unarmed crowd, thereby killing 379 demonstrators. In 1997, on the fiftieth anniversary of India's independence, the British monarch Elizabeth II visited the site of the massacre. Sidestepping demands for an official apology, she referred to the massacre merely as a "distressing"episode in relations between Britain and India.

When repressive measures failed to quell the movement for self-rule, the British offered a political compromise. After years of hesitation and deliberation, the British parliament enacted the Government of India Act, which gave India the institutions of a self-governing state. The legislation allowed for the establishment of autonomous

The India Act

legislative bodies in the provinces of British India, the creation of a bicameral (two-chambered) national legislature, and the formation of an executive arm under the control of the British government. Upon the urging of Gandhi, the majority of Indians approved the measure, which went into effect in 1937.

The India Act proved unworkable, however, because India's six hundred nominally sovereign princes refused to cooperate and Muslims feared that Hindus would dominate the national legislature. Muhammad Ali Jinnah (1876–1948), an eloquent and brilliant lawyer who headed the Muslim League, warned that a unified India represented nothing less than a threat to the Muslim faith and its Indian community. In place of one India, he proposed two states, one of which would be the "land of the pure," or Pakistan. Jinnah's proposal reflected an uncomfortable reality, namely, that society in India was split by hostility between Hindus and Muslims, making national unification an increasingly illusory goal.

China's Search for Order

As Shanfei's life story suggested, during the first half of the twentieth century China was in a state of almost continual revolutionary upheaval. The conflict's origins dated from the nineteenth century, when the Chinese empire came under relentless pressure from imperialist powers that rushed in to fill the vacuum created by China's internal political disintegration (see chapter 37). As revolutionary and nationalist uprisings gained widespread support, a revolution in 1911 forced the emperor Xuantong, still a child (also known as Puyi), to abdicate. The Qing empire fell with relative ease. Dr. Sun Yatsen (1866–1925), a leading opponent of the old regime, proclaimed a Chinese Republic in 1912 and briefly assumed the office of president. The dynasty was dead, but there remained the problems of how to bury it and what to put in its place.

The Republic   The revolution of 1911 did not establish a stable government. Indeed, the republic soon plunged into a state of political anarchy and economic disintegration marked by the rule of warlords, disaffected generals from the old imperial Chinese army, and their troops. While the central government in Beijing ran the post office and a few other services, the warlords established themselves as provincial or regional rulers. Because the warlords were responsible for the neglect of irrigation projects crucial to the survival of farmers, for the revival of the opium trade, which they protected, and for the decline of crucial economic investment, they contributed to the deterioration of Chinese society. They never founded a new dynasty, nor did they create even the semblance of a stable central state. Yet warlords were just one symbol of the disintegration of the political order. The fragmented relationship between native authority and foreign powers was another. Since the nineteenth century, a collection of treaties, known in China as the unequal treaties, had guided Chinese relations with foreign countries. These treaties had established a network of foreign control over the Chinese economy that effectively prevented economic development. The continued sway of unequal treaties and other concessions permitted foreigners to intervene in Chinese society. Foreigners did not control the state, but through their privileges they impaired its sovereignty.

Chinese Nationalism   After the Great War, nationalist sentiment developed rapidly in China. Youths and intellectuals, who in the previous decade had looked to Europe and the United States for models and ideals for the reform of China, eagerly anticipated the results of the 1919 Peace Conference in Paris. They expected the U.S. government to support the termination of the treaty system and the restoration of full Chinese sovereignty. These hopes were shattered, however, when the peacemakers approved increasing Japanese interference in China. This decision gave rise to the May Fourth

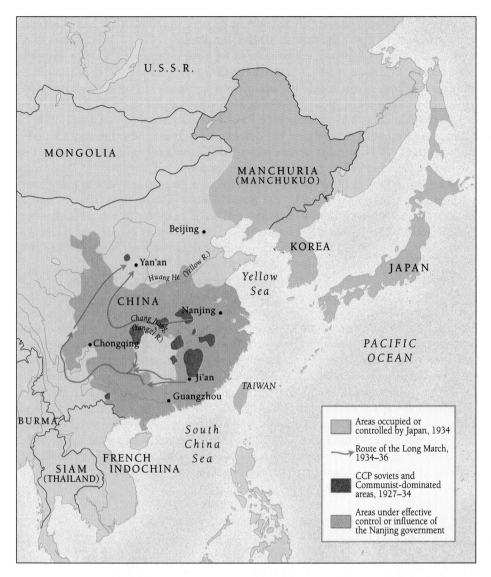

MAP [35.1]

The struggle for control in China.

Movement. Spearheaded by students and intellectuals in China's urban areas, the movement galvanized the country, and all classes of Chinese protested against foreign, especially Japanese, interference. In speeches, newspapers, and novels, the movement's leaders pledged themselves to rid China of imperialism and reestablish national unity. Student leaders like Shanfei rallied their comrades to the cause.

Disillusioned by the cynical self-interest of the United States and the European powers, some Chinese became interested in Marxist thought as modified by Lenin (see chapter 34) and the social and economic experiments under way in the Soviet Union. The anti-imperialist rhetoric of the Soviet leadership struck a responsive chord, and in 1921 the Chinese Communist Party (CCP) was organized in Shanghai. Among its early members was Mao Zedong (1893–1975), a former teacher and librarian who viewed a Marxist-inspired social revolution as the cure for China's problems. Mao's political radicalism extended to the issue of women's equality, which he and other communists championed. As Shanfei's personal experience suggested, Chinese communists believed in divorce, opposed arranged marriages, and campaigned against the practice of foot binding.

The most prominent nationalist leader at the time, Sun Yatsen, did not share the communists' enthusiasm for a dictatorship of the proletariat and the triumph of communism. Sun's basic ideology, summarized in his *Three Principles of the People,* called for elimination of special privileges for foreigners, national reunification, economic development, and a democratic republican government based on universal suffrage. To realize these goals, he was determined to bring the entire country under the control of his Nationalist People's Party, or *Guomindang.* In 1923 members of the small CCP began to augment the ranks of the Guomindang and by 1926 made up one-third of the Guomindang's membership. Both organizations availed themselves of the assistance offered by the Soviet Union. Under the doctrine of V. I. Lenin's democratic centralism—stressing centralized party control by a highly disciplined group of professional revolutionaries—Soviet advisors helped reorganize the Guomindang and the CCP into effective political organizations. In the process, the Soviets bestowed upon China the basis of a new political system.

Civil War   After the death of Sun Yatsen in 1925, the leadership of the Guomindang fell to Jiang Jieshi (Chiang Kai-shek, 1887–1975), a young general who had been trained in the Soviet Union. In contrast to the communists, he did not hold a vision for social revolution that involved the masses of China. Before long Jiang Jieshi launched a political and military offensive, known as the Northern Expedition, that aimed to unify the nation and bring China under Guomindang rule. Toward the end of his successful campaign, in 1927, Jiang Jieshi brutally and unexpectedly turned against his former communist allies, bringing the alliance of convenience between the Guomindang and the CCP to a bloody end. In the following year nationalist forces occupied Beijing, set up a central government in Nanjing, and declared the Guomindang the official government of a unified and sovereign Chinese state. Meanwhile, the badly mauled communists retreated to a remote area of southeastern China, where they tried to reconstitute and reorganize their forces.

Adversaries in the struggle for power in China: at left, Jiang Jieshi (Chiang Kai-shek); at right, Mao Zedong. • UPI/Corbis-Bettmann

The new national government confronted three major problems during the 1930s. First, the nationalists actually controlled only part of China, leaving the remainder of the country in the hands of warlords. Second, by the early 1930s communist revolution was still a major threat. Third, the Guomindang faced increasing Japanese aggression. In dealing with these problems, Jiang Jieshi gave priority to eliminating the CCP and its Red Army. No longer able to ward off the relentless attacks of nationalist forces, the communists took flight in October 1934 to avoid annihilation. Bursting through a military blockade around their bases in Jiangxi province in southeastern China, some eighty-five thousand troops and auxiliary personnel of the Red Army began the legendary Long March, an epic journey of 10,000 kilometers (6,215 miles). After traveling across difficult terrain and fighting for survival against hunger, disease, and Guomindang forces, the marchers arrived in

REPORT ON AN INVESTIGATION OF THE PEASANT MOVEMENT IN HUNAN

• • •

Regarded along with Karl Marx and V. I. Lenin as one of the great theorists of communism, Mao Zedong saw revolutionary potential in the peasantry. After witnessing an uprising of impoverished peasants in his home province in early 1927, he issued a report arguing that peasant discontent was a key force in China and that it deserved communist support. Mao's reliance on the peasantry represented a radical departure from traditional Marxism that counted on industrial workers to establish a dictatorship of the proletariat. The mobilization of peasants made the Chinese experience a viable example for revolution elsewhere, especially in predominantly agrarian societies.

All talk directed against the peasant movement must be speedily set right. All the wrong measures taken by the revolutionary authorities concerning the peasant movement must be speedily changed. Only thus can the future of the revolution be benefitted. For the present upsurge of the peasant movement is a colossal event. In a very short time, in China's central, southern and northern provinces, several hundred million peasants will rise like a mighty storm, like a hurricane, a force so swift and violent that no power, however great, will be able to hold it back. They will smash all the trammels that bind them and rush forward along the road to liberation. They will sweep all the imperialists, warlords, corrupt officials, local tyrants and evil gentry in their graves.

The main targets of attack by the peasants are the local tyrants, the evil gentry and the lawless landlords, but in passing they also hit out against patriarchal ideas and institutions, against the corrupt officials in the cities and against bad practices and customs in the rural areas. In force and momentum the attack is tempestuous; those who bow before it survive and those who resist parish. As a result, the privileges which the feudal landlords enjoyed for thousand of years are being shattered to pieces. Every bit of the dignity and prestige build up by the landlords is being swept into the dust. With the collapse of the power of the landlords, the peasant associations have now become the sole organs of authority and the popular slogan "All power to the peasant associations" has become a reality.

There is revolutionary significance in all the actions which were labeled as "going too far" in this period. To put it bluntly, it is necessary to create terror for a while in every rural area, or otherwise it would be impossible to suppress the activities of the counter-revolutionaries in the countryside or overthrow the authority of the gentry. Proper limits have to be exceeded in order to right a wrong, or else the wrong cannot be righted.

SOURCE: *Selected Works of Mao Tse-Tung,* vol. 1. Peking: Foreign Languages Press, 1977, pp. 23–25, 29.

a remote area of Shaanxi province in northwestern China in October 1935 and established headquarters at Yanan. Although thousands had died in this forced retreat, the Long March inspired many Chinese to join the Communist Party. During the Long March, Mao Zedong emerged as the leader and the principal theoretician of the Chinese communist movement. He came up with a Chinese form of Marxist-Leninism, or Maoism, an ideology grounded in the conviction that peasants rather than urban proletarians were the foundation for a successful revolution. Village power, Mao believed, was critical in a country where most people were peasants.

In the decades after the Great War, European intellectuals questioned and challenged established traditions. While scientists and social thinkers conceived new theories that reshaped human knowledge and perceptions, artists forged a modern aesthetic. In an age of global interdependence, the U.S. stock market crash of 1929 ushered in a period of prolonged economic contraction and social misery that engulfed most of the world. As most of the industrialized world reeled under the impact of the depression, the leadership of the Soviet Union embarked on a state-sponsored program of rapid industrialization. Though causing widespread human suffering, a series of five-year plans transformed the Soviet Union into a major industrial and military power. In Germany the effects of the Great Depression paved the way for the establishment of the Nazi state, which was based on the principle of racial inequality. Although many suffered under the new regime, Jews were the principal victims of the Nazi racial state. Political and social ferment were also visible in Asia, where nationalist movements and leaders forged new national identities free from imperial domination. In both India and China, this process was fraught with violence and setbacks and did not reach fruition until after another world war had come and gone.

CHRONOLOGY

1917	Russian Revolution
1918–1919	Civil war in Russia
1919	May Fourth Movement
1920–1922	Non-Cooperation Movement in India
1921	New Economic Policy
	Founding of Chinese Communist Party
1925	Northern Expedition
1928	First Five-Year Plan
1929	Stock market crash
	Beginning of Great Depression
1930	Civil disobedience movement in India
1933–1945	Hitler is ruler in Germany
1934	Long March
1935	India Act
1937	Japanese invasion of China

FOR FURTHER READING

Jeremy Bernstein. *Einstein*. New York, 1973. This brief and lucid treatment of Einstein's key concepts and ideas is comprehensible to the layperson.

Malcolm Bradbury and James McFarlane, eds. *Modernism, 1890–1930*. Atlantic Highlands, N.J., 1978. A comprehensive survey of the new trends in literature.

Martin Broszat. *The Hitler State. The Foundation and Development of the Internal Structure of the Third Reich*. New York, 1981. An account that does justice to the complexity of the Nazi movement and its rule.

Judith Brown. *Modern India: The Origins of Asian Democracy*. 2nd ed. Oxford, 1994. This survey is a good introduction to the past two hundred years of Indian history.

John K. Fairbank. *China: A New History*. Cambridge, Mass., 1992. A very readable synthesis of Chinese history that also provides a useful guide to scholarship.

Sheila Fitzpatrick. *The Russian Revolution, 1917–1932*. 2nd ed. New York, 1984. This work stands out for the author's ability to make complex processes accessible to the general reader and still instruct the specialist.

George Gamow. *Thirty Years That Shook Physics*. Garden City, N.Y. 1966. A leading physicist engagingly tells the story of modern physics.

Peter Gay. *Freud: A Life for Our Time*. New York, 1988. A balanced biography of one of the most influential social thinkers of the twentieth century.

George Head Hamilton. *Painting and Sculpture in Europe, 1880–1940*. 6th ed. New Haven, 1993. A classic that presents a discerning overview of the subject.

Ian Kershaw. *The Nazi Dictatorship: Problems and Perspectives of Interpretation*. 2nd ed. London, 1989. A superb assessment that also provides the best introduction to the enormous literature on the Third Reich.

Charles Kindleberger. *The World in Depression, 1929–1939*. London, 1973. A sophisticated analysis that focuses on developments in the United States and Europe.

A. J. H. Latham. *The Depression and the Developing World, 1914–1939*. London, 1981. One of the few works that looks beyond the industrialized world to give a global perspective on the subject.

Jim Masselos. *Indian Nationalism*. New Delhi, 1991. A keen work in which the independence struggle takes center stage.

Nikolaus Pevsner. *Pioneers of Modern Design: From William Morris to Walter Gropius*. Rev. ed. New York, 1964. This work chronicles the rise of the international style in architecture.

Richard Pipes. *The Russian Revolution*. New York, 1990. When the Communist Party collapsed in 1991, this sweeping study was quickly translated into Russian and became a national bestseller.

James E. Sheridan. *China in Disintegration: The Republican Era in Chinese History, 1912–1949*. New York, 1975. Best single-volume study on the republican period that traces the rise and fall of the Nationalist party.

NEW CONFLAGRATIONS: WORLD WAR II AND THE EARLY COLD WAR

· · ·

On 6 August 1945, as he listened to the armed services radio on Saipan (a U.S.-controlled island in the north Pacific), U.S. marine Victor Tolley heard the news: the President of the United States announced that a "terrible new weapon" had been deployed against the city of Hiroshima, Japan. Tolley and the other marines rejoiced, realizing that the terrible new weapon—the atomic bomb—might end the war and relieve them of the burden of invading Japan. A few days later Tolley heard that the city of Nagasaki had also been hit with an atomic bomb. He remembered the ominous remarks that accompanied the news of this atomic destruction: radio announcers suggested it might be decades before the cities would be inhabitable.

Imagine Tolley's surprise, then, when a few weeks later, after the Japanese surrender, he and his buddies were assigned to the U.S. occupation forces in Nagasaki. Assured by a superior officer that Nagasaki was "very safe," Tolley lived there for three months, during which he became very familiar with the devastation wrought by the atomic bomb. On his first day in Nagasaki, Tolley investigated the city. As he noted, "It was just like walking into a tomb. There was total silence. You could smell this death all around ya. There was a terrible odor."

Tolley also became acquainted with some of the Japanese survivors in Nagasaki, which proved to be an eye-opening experience. Having seen "young children with sores and burns all over," Tolley, having become separated from his unit, encountered another young child. He and the boy communicated despite the language barrier between them. Tolley showed the child pictures of his wife and two daughters. The Japanese boy excitedly took Tolley home to meet his surviving family, his father and his pregnant sister. Tolley recalled:

> This little kid ran upstairs and brought his father down. A very nice Japanese gentleman. He could speak English. He bowed and said, "We would be honored if you would come upstairs and have some tea with us." I went upstairs in this strange Japanese

Felix Nussbaum, *Self-Portrait with a Jewish Identity Card* (1943). This image captures the artist's fear of discovery as he went into hiding during the Holocaust. Captured in 1944, he and his wife died in Auschwitz concentration camp. ● Kulturgeschichtliches Museum, Osnabrück. VG Bild Kunst, Bonn. Courtesy Auguste Moses-Nussbaum and Shulamith Jaari-Nussbaum

house. I noticed on the mantel a picture of a young Japanese soldier. I asked him, "Is this your son?" He said, "That is my daughter's husband. We don't know if he's alive. We haven't heard." The minute he said that, it dawned on me that they suffered the same as we did. They lost sons and daughters and relatives, and they hurt too.

Before his chance meeting with this Japanese family, Tolley had felt nothing but contempt for the Japanese. He pointed out, "We were trained to kill them. They're our enemy. Look what they did in Pearl Harbor. They asked for it and now we're gonna give it to 'em. That's how I felt until I met this young boy and his family." But after coming face-to-face with his enemies, Tolley saw only their common humanity, their suffering, and their hurt. The lesson he learned was that "these people didn't want to fight us."

The civility that reemerged at the end of the war was little evident during the war years. The war began and ended with Japan. In 1931 Japan invaded Manchuria, thereby ending the post–Great War peace, and the United States concluded hostilities by dropping atomic bombs on Hiroshima and Nagasaki. Between 1931 and 1945 the conflict expanded well beyond east Asia. By 1941 World War II was a truly global war. Hostilities spread from east Asia and the Pacific to Europe, north Africa, and the Atlantic, and large and small nations from North America, Asia, Europe, Africa, and Australia came into close contact for the duration of the war. Beyond its immense geographic scope, World War II exceeded even the Great War (1914–1918) in demonstrating the willingness of societies to make enormous sacrifices in lives and other resources to achieve complete victory. In this total war, contacts with enemies, occupiers, and liberators affected populations around the world. World War II redefined gender roles and relations between colonial peoples and their masters, as women contributed to their nations' war efforts and as colonial peoples exploited the war's weakening of imperial nations. The cold war and the atomic age that began almost as soon as World War II ended complicated the task of recovering economic health and psychological security, but they also brought forth institutions, programs, and policies that promoted global reconstruction. New sets of allies and newly independent nations emerged after the war, signaling that a new global order had arisen.

 ## THE GLOBAL ORIGINS OF WORLD WAR II

In 1941 two major alliances squared off against each other. Japan, Germany, and Italy, along with their conquered territories, formed the Axis powers. The Axis was the name of the alignment between Nazi Germany and Fascist Italy first formed in October 1936, but the term was later used to include Germany's other allies in World War II, especially Japan. The Allied powers included France and its empire; Great Britain and its empire and Commonwealth allies (such as Canada, Australia, and New Zealand); the Soviet Union; China; and the United States and its allies in Latin America. The construction of these grand global alliances took place over the course of the 1930s and early 1940s.

Driven in part by a desire to revise the peace settlements that followed the Great War, and compelled by the economic distress of the worldwide depression, Japan, Italy, and Germany engaged in a campaign of territorial expansion that ultimately broke apart the structure of international cooperation that had kept the world from violence in the 1920s. These revisionist powers, so called because they revised or overthrew the terms of the post–Great War peace, confronted nations that were committed to the international system and to the avoidance of another world war. To expand their global influence, the revisionist nations remilitarized and conquered territories that they deemed central to their needs and to the spread of their imperial control. The Allies acquiesced to the revisionist powers' early aggressive actions, but by the late 1930s and early 1940s the Allies felt compelled to engage the Axis powers in a total war.

Japan's War in Asia and the Pacific

The global conflict opened with Japan's attacks on China in the 1930s: the conquest of Manchuria between 1931 and 1932 was the first step in the revisionist process of expansionism and aggression. After the Great War, Japan had achieved great power status. Political divisions arose within Japan, though, and they became more severe during the depression. Politicians who supported Japan's role in the international, industrial-capitalist system faced increasing opposition from those who were inclined toward a militarist vision of a self-sufficient Japan that would dominate east Asia. The hardships of the depression undermined support for the internationalist position, and the militarists were able to benefit from Japanese militaristic traditions and an unwillingness to be constrained by international cooperation. China's unification, aided by international attempts to reinstate its sovereignty, threatened Japan's economic interests in Manchuria. Manchuria had historically been Chinese territory, but by the twentieth century it had become a sphere of influence where Japan maintained the Manchurian Railroad (built in 1906), retained transit rights, and stationed troops. In 1931 Japan's military forces in Manchuria acted to assert control over the region.

On the night of 18 September 1931, Japanese troops used explosives to blow up a few feet of rail on the Japanese-built South Manchuria Railway just north of Mukden. They accused the Chinese of attacking their railroad. This "Mukden incident" became the pretext for war between Japanese and Chinese troops. Although the civilian government in Japan tried to halt this military incursion, by 1932 Japanese troops controlled all of Manchuria, thereby assuring Japan preeminence and protecting its long-term economic and industrial development of the region. The Japanese established a puppet state called Manchukuo, but in reality Japan had absorbed Manchuria into its empire, challenged the international peace system, and begun a war.

The Mukden Incident

Japanese machine gun patrol in Manchuria, ca 1931. ● Hulton Getty/Liaison

*The Invasion
of China*

Within Japan a see-saw battle continued between supporters and opponents of the aggressive policies adopted in Manchuria, but during the course of the 1930s the militarist position came to dominate, and for the most part civilians lost control of the government and the military. In 1933, after the League of Nations condemned its actions in Manchuria, Japan withdrew from the league and began following an ultranationalist and promilitary policy. The slogan under which Japan pursued expansion in Asia was "Asia for Asians," implying that the Japanese would lead Asian peoples to independence from the despised European imperialists and the international order they dominated. In this struggle for Asian independence, Japan required the region's resources and therefore sought to build a "Greater East Asia Co-Prosperity Sphere." The appeal to Asian independence at first struck a responsive chord, but conquest and brutal occupation made it soon obvious to most that the real agenda was "Asia for the Japanese." Proponents of the Greater East Asia Co-Prosperity Sphere advocated Japan's expansion in Asia and the Pacific while cloaking their territorial and economic designs with the idealism of Asian nationalism.

Seeing territorial control as essential to its survival, Japan launched a full-scale invasion of China in 1937. A battle between Chinese and Japanese troops at the Marco Polo Bridge in Beijing in July 1937 was the opening move in Japan's undeclared war against China. Japanese troops took Beijing and then moved south toward Shanghai and Nanjing, then the capital of China. Japanese naval and air forces bombed Shanghai, killing thousands of civilians, and secured it as a landing area for armies bound for Nanjing. Thus began Japan's control and occupation of large areas of north and east China.

The Japanese invasion of China met with intense international opposition, but by this time Japan had chosen another path—and it was an auspicious time to further its attack on the international system. Other world powers, distracted by depression and military aggression in Europe, could offer little in the way of an effective response to Japanese actions. The government of Japan aligned itself with the other revisionist nations, Germany and Italy, by signing a ten-year military and eco-

A Chinese child crying in the rubble after Japanese bombers devastated Shanghai during the invasion of China. • UPI/Corbis-Bettmann

nomic pact, the Tripartite Pact, in September 1940. It also cleared the way for further empire building in Asia and the Pacific basin by concluding a neutrality pact with the Soviet Union in 1941, thereby precluding hostilities on any other front, especially in Manchuria. Japan did not face determined opposition to its expansion until December 1941, when conflict with the United States created a much broader field of action for Japan and its growing empire.

China under Japanese Occupation

Political instability made China an inviting target, as Japanese military leaders preferred to fight a state that was weakened by internal divisions. During the 1930s Chinese nationalists and communists vied for power, and these internal divisions contributed to the success of Japanese attacks on Manchuria and China. However, in the international system that prevailed in the 1920s and 1930s, a restoration of China's sovereignty seemed possible, especially as Jiang Jieshi, also known as Chiang Kai-shek (1887–1975), battled to unify China under the banner of the Guomindang (Nationalist Party) and concentrated power in Nanjing. When the Japanese invaded Manchuria in 1931, Jiang appealed to the League of Nations, and especially to Great Britain and the United States, to halt Japanese aggression. While China gained the moral high ground in international eyes, little was done to stop aggression. This reaction set the pattern for future responses to the actions of revisionist nations.

Japan's military actions in Manchuria aroused feelings of nationalism among the Chinese, however, and continued to do so as Japanese troops encroached on Mongolia and northern China. Jiang shied away from direct military confrontation with the stronger Japanese forces, but nationalists and communists wanted a stronger response. The United Front of nationalists and communists did not coalesce until the Japanese invaded China in 1937, but even then the coalition did not hold together. Neither the nationalists nor the communists could defeat the Japanese, and as a result China became the first nation to experience the horrors of World War II: brutal warfare against civilians and repressive occupation.

During the invasion of China, Japanese forces used methods of warfare that led to mass death and suffering on a new, almost unimaginable level. Chinese civilians were among the first to feel the effects of aerial bombing of urban centers; the people of Shanghai died in the tens of thousands when Japanese bombers attacked the city to soften Chinese resistance. What became known as the Rape of Nanjing demonstrated the horror of the war as well, as the residents of Nanjing became victims of Japanese troops inflamed by war passion and a sense of racial superiority. Over the course of two months, Japanese soldiers raped seven thousand women, murdered hundreds of thousands of unarmed soldiers and civilians, and burned one-third of the homes in Nanjing. Some four hundred thousand Chinese lost their lives as Japanese soldiers used them for bayonet practice and machine-gunned them into open pits.

The Rape of Nanjing

Despite Japan's campaign of terror and its occupation of much of eastern China, Chinese resistance persisted throughout the war. While Jiang Jieshi kept the Guomindang government alive by moving inland to Chongqing, the Chinese communists carried on guerrilla operations against the Japanese invaders. Lacking any air force or artillery, communist guerrillas staged hit-and-run operations from their mountain bases, sabotaged bridges and railroads, and harassed Japanese troops. The guerrillas did not defeat the Japanese, but they captured the loyalty of many Chinese peasants through their resistance to the Japanese and their moderate policies of land reform. At the end of the war, the communists would be poised to lead China.

Guerrilla War

European Aggression

Like Japan, Italy belonged to the revisionist Axis. Italy's expansionism helped desta-bilize the post–Great War peace and spread World War II to the European conti-nent. Italians had suffered tremendously in World War I. Some six hundred thou-sand Italian soldiers had died, and the national economy never recovered sufficiently for Italy to function as an equal to other European military and economic powers. Many Italians expected far greater recompense and respect than they received at the conclusion of the Great War. Rather than being treated as a real partner in victory by Britain and France, Italy found itself shut out of the divisions of the territorial spoils of war.

Italy   Italians' feelings of disillusionment and discontent promoted the rise of fascist dictator Benito Mussolini (1883–1945). Mussolini beguiled Italians by commiserat-ing with the plight of veterans, vowing to overcome the economic chaos caused by the depression, and promising to bring glory to Italy through the acquisition of ter-ritories that it had been denied after the Great War. Italy's conquest of Ethiopia in 1935 and 1936, when added to the previously annexed Libya, created an overseas empire. Italy also intervened in the Spanish Civil War (1936–1939) on the side of the victorious fascist General Francisco Franco (1892–1975), whose militarists over-threw the republican government, and it annexed Albania in 1939. (Mussolini viewed Albania as a bridgehead for expansion into the Balkans.) The invasion and conquest of Ethiopia in particular infuriated other nations, but as with Japan's inva-sion of Manchuria, the League of Nations and the western democracies offered little effective opposition.

What angered nonrevisionists about Italy's conquest of Ethiopia was not just the broken peace. The excessive use of force against the Ethiopians also rankled. Mus-solini sent an army of 250,000 men, armed with tanks, poison gas, artillery, and air-craft, to conquer the Ethiopians, who were entirely unprepared for the assault. The mechanized troops simply mowed them down. Italy lost 2,000 soldiers while 275,000 Ethiopians lost their lives. Despite its victories in Ethiopia, Italy's prospects for world glory never appeared quite as bright as Japan's, especially since few Italians really wanted to go to war. Throughout the interwar years Italy played a diplomatic game that kept European nations guessing as to its future intentions, but by 1940 it was firmly on the side of the Axis.

Germany   Japan and Italy were the first nations to challenge the post–World War I settle-ments through territorial conquest, but it was Germany that systematically undid the Treaty of Versailles and the fragile peace of the interwar years. Most Germans and their political leaders deeply resented the harsh terms imposed on their nation in 1919. But even the governments of other European nations eventually realized the extreme nature of the Versailles Treaty's terms and turned a blind eye to the revi-sionist actions of Adolf Hitler (1889–1945) and his government.

Hitler came to power in 1933, riding a wave of public discontent with Ger-many's postwar position of powerlessness and the suffering caused by the Great De-pression. Hitler referred to the signing of the 1918 armistice as the "November crime" and blamed it on those he viewed as Germany's internal enemies: Jews, com-munists, and liberals of all sorts. Neighboring European states—Poland, France, Czechoslovakia, Yugoslavia, Hungary, and Austria—also shared in the blame. Hitler's scheme for ridding Germany of its enemies and reasserting its power was remilitarization—which was legally denied to Germany under the Versailles Treaty. Germany's dictator abandoned the peaceful efforts of his predecessors to ease the

The Ethiopian soldiers train with outmoded equipment that proves no match for Italian forces.

● Popperfoto

provisions of the treaty and proceeded unilaterally to destroy it step-by-step. Hitler's aggressive foreign policy helped relieve the German public's feeling of war shame and depression trauma. After withdrawing Germany from the League of Nations in 1933, his government carried out a massive plan to strengthen the German armed forces. Hitler reinstated universal military service in 1935, and in the following year his troops entered the previously demilitarized Rhineland that bordered France. Germany joined with Italy in the Spanish Civil War, where Hitler's troops, especially the air force, honed their skills. In 1938 Hitler began the campaign of expansion that ultimately led to the outbreak of World War II in Europe.

Germany's forced *Anschluss* ("union") with Austria took place in March 1938. Hitler justified this annexation as an attempt to reintegrate all Germans into a single homeland. Europe's major powers, France and Britain, did nothing in response, thereby enhancing Hitler's reputation in the German military and deepening his already deep contempt for the democracies. Soon thereafter, using the same rationale, the Nazis attempted to gain control of the Sudetenland, the western portion of Czechoslovakia. This region was inhabited largely by ethnic Germans, whom Hitler regarded as persecuted minorities. Although the Czech government was willing to make concessions to the Sudeten Germans, Hitler in September 1938 demanded the immediate cession of the Sudetenland to the German *Reich* ("empire"). Against the desires of the Czechoslovak government, the leaders of France and Britain accommodated Hitler and allowed Germany to annex the Sudetenland. Neither the French nor the British were willing to risk a military confrontation with Germany to defend Czechoslovakian territory.

At the Munich Conference held in September 1938, European politicians formulated the policy that came to be known as appeasement. Attended by representatives of Italy, France, Great Britain, and Germany, the meeting revealed how most nations outside the revisionist sphere had decided to deal with territorial expansion by aggressive nations, especially Germany. In conceding gains to Hitler,

Peace for Our Time?

or "appeasing" him, the British and French governments extracted a promise that Hitler would cease further efforts to expand German territorial claims. Their goal was to keep peace in Europe, even if it meant making major concessions. Because the French and British did not want war, they approved the Munich accord. Britain's prime minister Neville Chamberlain (1869–1940) arrived home from Munich to announce that the meeting had achieved "peace for our time." Unprepared for war and distressed by the depression, nations sympathetic to Britain and France also embraced peace as an admirable goal even in the face of aggression by the revisionist nations.

Hitler, however, refused to be bound by the Munich agreement, and in the next year German troops occupied most of Czechoslovakia. As Hitler next began to threaten Poland, it became clear that the policy of appeasement was both a practical and moral failure, which caused Britain and France to abandon it by guaranteeing the security of Poland. By this time Joseph Stalin (1879–1953) had become convinced that British and French leaders were conspiring to deflect German aggression toward the Soviet Union. Despite deep ideological differences that divided communists from Nazis, Stalin accordingly sought an accommodation with the Nazi regime. In August 1939 the foreign ministers of the Soviet Union and Germany signed the Russian-German Treaty of Nonaggression, an agreement that both shocked and outraged the world. The Nazi-Soviet Pact promised neutrality in the event of war with a third party, preventing the possibility of a war on two fronts. Additionally, a secret protocol divided eastern Europe into German and Soviet spheres of influence. Specific terms spelled out German control of western Poland and Lithuania while the Soviet Union gained a free hand in the territories of eastern Poland, eastern Romania, Finland, Estonia, and Latvia. Hitler was ready to conquer Europe.

TOTAL WAR: THE WORLD UNDER FIRE

Two months after the United States became embroiled in World War II, President Franklin Roosevelt (1882–1945) delivered one of his famous radio broadcasts, known as fireside chats. In it he explained the nature of the war: "This war is a new kind of war," he said. "It is warfare in terms of every continent, every island, every sea, every air lane." There was little exaggeration in FDR's analysis. Before World War II was over, almost every nation had participated in it. Battles raged across the vast Pacific and Atlantic Oceans, across Europe and northern Africa, and throughout much of Asia. Every weapon known to humanity was thrown into the war. Even more than the Great War, this was a conflict where entire societies engaged in warfare and mobilized every available material and human resource.

The war between Japan and China had already stretched over eight years when European nations stormed into battle. Between 1939 and 1941 nations both inside and outside of Europe were drawn into the conflict. They included the French and British colonies in Africa, as well as India and the British Dominion allies, Canada, Australia, and New Zealand. Germany's stunning military successes in 1939 and 1940 focused attention on Europe, but after the Soviet Union and the United States entered the war in 1941, the conflict took on global proportions. As the war dragged on, only eleven countries avoided direct involvement: Afghanistan, Greenland, Iceland, Ireland, Mongolia, Portugal, Spain, Sweden, Switzerland, Tibet, and Yemen.

Blitzkrieg: Germany Conquers Europe

During World War II it became common for aggressor nations to avoid overt declarations of war. Instead, the new armed forces relied on surprise, stealth, and swiftness for their conquests. Germany demonstrated the advantages of this strategy in Poland. Nazi forces, banking on their air force's ability to soften resistance and on their *Panzer* ("armored") column's unmatched mobility and speed, Nazi forces moved into Poland unannounced in September 1939. Within a month they subdued its western expanses while the Soviets took the eastern sections in accordance with the Nazi-Soviet Pact. The Germans stunned the world, especially Britain and France, with their *blitzkrieg* ("lightning war") and sudden victory.

While the forces of Britain and France coalesced to defend Europe without yet facing much direct action with Nazi forces, the battle of the Atlantic already raged. This sea confrontation between German *Unterseeboote* ("U-boats" or submarines) and British ship convoys carrying food and war matériel would prove decisive in the European theater of war. The battle of the Atlantic could easily have gone either way—to the German U-boats attempting to cut off Britain's vital imports or to the convoys devised by the British navy to protect its ships from submarine attacks. Although British intelligence had cracked Germany's secret code, advance knowledge of the location of submarines was not always available. Moreover, the U-boats began traveling in "wolf packs" to negate the effectiveness of convoys protected by aircraft and destroyers.

As the sea battle continued, Germany prepared to break through European defenses. In April 1940 the Nazis occupied Denmark and Norway; they then launched a full-scale attack on western Europe. Their offensive against Belgium, France, and the Netherlands began in May, and again the Allies were jolted by *blitzkrieg* tactics. Belgium and the Netherlands fell first, and the French signed an armistice in June. The fall of France convinced Italy's Benito Mussolini that the Germans were winning the war, and it was time to enter the conflict and reap any potential benefits his partnership with the Nazis might offer.

The Fall of France

Adolf Hitler proudly walks through conquered Paris in 1940, with the Eiffel Tower as a backdrop. ● Hulton Getty/Tony Stone Images

Before the battle of France, Hitler had boasted to his staff, "Gentlemen, you are about to witness the most famous victory in history!" Given France's rapid fall, Hitler was not far wrong. Field Marshal Erwin Rommel put it more colorfully: "The war has become practically a lightning Tour de France!" In a moment of exquisite triumph, Hitler had the French sign their armistice in the very railroad car in which the Germans had signed the armistice in 1918. Trying to rescue some Allied troops before the fall of France, the British engineered a retreat at Dunkirk, but it could not hide the bleak failure of the Allied troops. Britain now stood alone against the Nazi forces.

The Battle of Britain

The Germans now launched the battle of Britain, led by its air force, the *Luftwaffe*. They hoped to defeat Britain almost solely through air attacks. "The Blitz," as the British called this air war, rained bombs on heavily populated metropolitan areas, especially London, and killed more than forty thousand British civilians. The Royal Air Force staved off defeat, however, forcing Hitler to abandon plans to invade Britain.

MAP [36.1]

High tide of Axis expansion in Europe and North Africa, 1942–1943.

By the summer of 1941, Hitler's conquests extended to the Balkans, and the battlefront extended to north Africa, where the British fought both the Italians and the Germans. The swastika-bedecked Nazi flag now waved from the streets of Paris to the Acropolis in Athens, and Hitler had succeeded beyond his dreams in his quest to reverse the outcome of World War I. Flush with victory in the spring of 1941, Hitler turned his sights on the Soviet Union. This land was the ultimate Nazi target, from which Jews, Slavs, and Bolsheviks could be expelled or exterminated to create more *Lebensraum* ("living space") for resettled Germans. Believing firmly in the bankruptcy of the Soviet system, Hitler said of Operation Barbarossa, the code name for the June invasion of the Soviet Union, "You only have to kick in the door, and the whole rotten structure will come crashing down."

The Decisive Entry of the Soviet Union and the United States

After his amazing conquests in western Europe, Hitler felt supreme confidence in his troops and his prospects. This may explain his gleeful reaction to the outbreak of war between Japan and the United States in December 1941: "Now it is impossible for us to lose the war: We now have an ally who has never been vanquished in three thousand years." On 11 December 1941, though not compelled to do so by treaty, Hitler declared war on the United States—thus providing the United States with the only reason it needed to declare war on Germany. Winston Churchill (1874–1965), prime minister of Britain, expressed an attitude much contrary to Hitler's, one that ultimately proved right: "So we had won after all!"

Churchill's vast sense of relief at gaining the United States as an ally signaled the great importance that U.S. industrial capacity would bring to bear on the war effort, but the Soviet Union's forced entry into the war turned out to be equally if not more significant in defeating the Nazi forces. With both the Soviet Union and United States in the war, World War II became a more global conflict fought in two vast and interconnected theaters of war, the Eurasian and Asian-Pacific theaters.

During the initial stages of Operation Barbarossa, launched on 22 June 1941, Germany seemed assured of victory. The governments of Hungary, Finland, and Romania all declared war on the Soviet Union and augmented the German invasion force with their own military contingents. Although it was the largest in the world, the Soviet Red Army suffered from a lack of seasoned, dedicated, and innovative officers, largely as a result of the numerous purges and killings carried out by Soviet leader Joseph Stalin before the war. Hitler was counting on a rapid takeover, and the early German offensives made huge territorial advances and captured millions of Soviet soldiers. By December 1941 the Germans had captured the Russian heartland, and Leningrad was under siege. But in December the Soviets gained two new allies: the United States and "General Winter."

Operation Barbarossa

The arrival of winter immediately turned the tide, preventing the Nazis from capturing Moscow. The resulting delay allowed the Soviets to regroup and regain the offensive, however slowly. So sure of victory were the Germans that they had not even bothered to supply their troops with winter clothing and boots. Some one hundred thousand men suffered frostbite, and two thousand of them underwent amputation. The Red Army, in contrast, had prepared for winter and found further comfort as the United States manufactured thirteen million pairs of felt-lined winter boots. Moreover, in the early stages of the war Stalin ordered Soviet industry to relocate to areas away from the front. About 80 percent of firms manufacturing war

Outside Moscow, Soviet women dig antitank trenches against the Nazi onslaught. • Sovfoto

matériel moved to the Ural Mountains between August and October of 1941. As a result, the capacity of Soviet industry outstripped that of German industry. The Soviets also received crucial equipment from their allies, notably trucks from the United States.

This industrial capacity was the key to the Allied victories in both Europe and Asia. The underbelly of Germany's war plan was its economy. The Germans counted on swift victories that would not overtax their industrial base. As victories came more slowly, however, and as Allied powers expanded their war production, the German economy had difficulty matching the Allied effort. In the battle in the Atlantic, for example, it was not until the United States joined the struggle in 1942 that the tide turned in favor of the Allies. Although German submarines sank a total of 2,452 Allied merchant ships and 175 Allied war ships in the course of six years, U.S. naval shipyards simply built more "Liberty Ships" than the Germans could sink. By the end of 1943, sonar, aircraft patrols, and escort aircraft from carriers had finished the U-boat as a strategic threat. German forces also faced bleak prospects as the Soviets began to retake territory. Moscow never fell, and the battle for Stalingrad, which ended in February 1943, marked the first large-scale victory for Soviet forces. Meanwhile British and U.S. forces attacked the Germans first from north Africa and then through Italy. In August the Allies forced Italy to withdraw from the Axis and to join them.

Allied Victory in Europe

The real test came at Normandy, where the British and U.S. forces opened a front in France. On D day, 6 June 1944, British and U.S. troops landed on the French coast of Normandy. Nazi forces now faced a two-pronged pincer attack. Although the fighting was deadly for all sides, the Germans were overwhelmed. With the two fronts collapsing around them and round-the-clock strategic bombing by the United States and Britain that leveled German cities and harried civilians, Nazi resistance faded. A brutal street-by-street battle in Berlin between the Nazis and the Red Army, along with a British and U.S. sweep through western Germany, forced Germany's unconditional surrender on 8 May 1945. A week earlier, on 30 April, as fighting flared right outside his Berlin bunker, Hitler committed suicide, as did many of his Nazi compatriots. He therefore did not live to see the Soviet red flag flying over the Berlin *Reichstag,* Germany's parliament building.

Battles in the Pacific

Even before 1941 the United States had been inching toward greater involvement in the war. After Japan invaded China in 1937, Roosevelt called for a quarantine on aggressors, but his plea fell mostly on deaf ears. However, as war broke out in Europe and tensions with Japan increased, the United States began to take action. In 1939 it instituted a "cash and carry" policy of supplying the British, in which the British paid cash and carried the materials on their own ships. More significant was the Lend-Lease program initiated in 1941, in which the United States "lent" destroyers and other war goods first to the British and then to the Soviets and the Chinese. The United States made diplomatic efforts to curtail Japanese incursions into China but with little success. It insisted that Japan withdraw from China, a demand that the Japanese found unacceptable. The United States then froze Japanese assets in the United States and imposed a tightening embargo on Japan's access to war matériel, especially oil. To Japanese militarists, given the equally unappetizing alternatives of succumbing to U.S. demands or engaging the United States in war, war seemed the lesser of two evils.

Pearl Harbor

The Japanese hoped to knock out American naval capacity in the Pacific with an attack at Pearl Harbor and clear the way for the conquest of southeast Asia and the creation of a defensive Japanese perimeter that would thwart the Allies' ability to strike at Japan's homeland. On 7 December 1941, "the day that will live in infamy," as President Franklin Roosevelt termed it, Japanese pilots took off from aircraft carriers to attack Hawai`i. More than 350 Japanese bombers, fighters, and torpedo planes struck in two waves, sinking or disabling eighteen ships and destroying more than two hundred aircraft. Except for the U.S. aircraft carriers, which were out of the harbor at the time, American naval power in the Pacific was devastated.

Japanese Victories and Allied Recovery

After Pearl Harbor the Japanese swept on to one victory after another. They captured Guam and Wake Island; strengthened their hold on Indochina; and conquered Hong Kong, Singapore, Burma, and much of the Philippines. Moreover, the Japanese navy emerged almost unscathed, with few losses of ships or men. While some Japanese realized the danger of drawing the United States into the war, even the doubters reconsidered their views after the Japanese triumphs in the Pacific and southeast Asia in 1941 and 1942. The most crucial battle, though, centered on Midway (4 June 1942), the last U.S.-controlled island in the Pacific. The United States prevailed there partly because U.S. aircraft carriers had survived the attack on Pearl Harbor.

Although the United States had only a few carriers, it had a secret weapon: a code-breaking operation known as Magic, which enabled a cryptographer monitoring Japanese radio frequencies to discover the plan to attack Midway. On the morning of 4 June, torpedo bombers from the U.S. carrier *Enterprise,* which was located near Midway, attacked the Japanese fleet, sinking three Japanese carriers in one 5-minute strike and a fourth one later in the day. This victory changed the character of the war in the Pacific. Although there was no immediate shift in Japanese fortunes, the Allies took the offensive. They adopted an island-hopping strategy, capturing islands from which they could make direct air assaults on Japan. Deadly, tenacious fighting characterized these battles in which the United States and its allies gradually retook islands in the Marianas and Philippines and then, early in 1945, moved toward areas even more threatening to Japan: Iwo Jima and Okinawa.

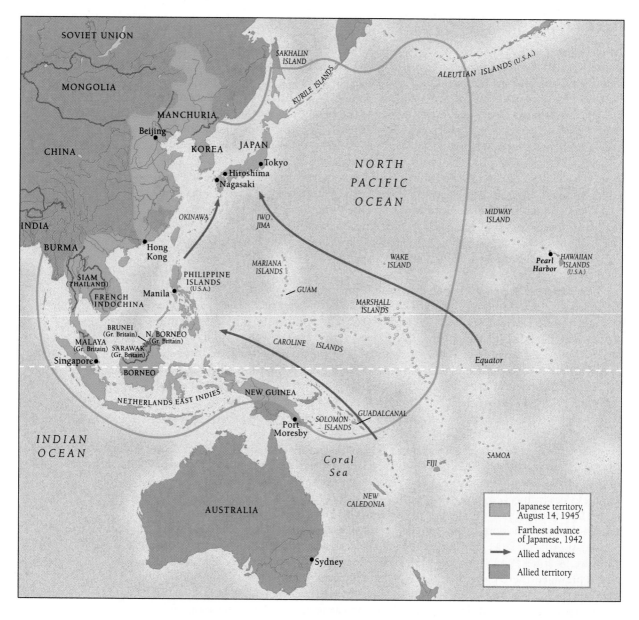

MAP [36.2]

World War II in the Pacific and Asia.

Iwo Jima and Okinawa

The fighting on Iwo Jima and Okinawa was savage. Innovative U.S. amphibious tactics were matched by the vigor and sacrifice of Japanese soldiers and pilots. On Okinawa the Japanese introduced the *kamikaze*—pilots who volunteered to fly planes with just enough fuel to reach an Allied ship and dive-bomb into it. In the two-month battle for Okinawa, the Japanese flew 1,900 kamikaze missions, sinking dozens of ships and killing more than five thousand U.S. soldiers. The kamikaze, and the defense mounted by Japanese forces and the 110,000 Okinawan civilians who died refusing to surrender, convinced many people in the United States that the Japanese would never give up. U.S. forces also engaged in some savagery of their own, however. They pried the gold teeth out of the mouths of dead Japanese soldiers and used flamethrowers to extract Okinawans hiding in caves. As one marine noted, "You developed an attitude of no mercy because they had no mercy on us. It was a no-quarter, savage kind of thing."

View of Nagasaki after the atomic bomb.   •   National Archives

Even as they fought the United States in the Pacific, the Japanese continued to fight in southeast Asia and China, but by 1945 they were on the defensive. Beginning in February 1945, U.S. B-29 bombers subjected the Japanese home islands to massive bombing raids, in which incendiaries ignited firestorms that consumed vast portions of Japanese cities and claimed hundreds of thousands of lives. The final blows came on 6 and 9 August 1945, when the United States used its revolutionary new weapon, the atomic bomb, against the cities of Hiroshima and Nagasaki. The atomic bombs either instantaneously vaporized or slowly killed by radiation poisoning upwards of two hundred thousand people. The Soviet Union had declared war on Japan on 8 August 1945, and this new threat, combined with the devastation caused by the bombs, persuaded Emperor Hirohito (1901–1989) to surrender unconditionally. The Japanese surrendered on 15 August, and the war was officially over on 2 September 1945. Even when Victor Tolley sipped his conciliatory cup of tea with a Nagasaki family, the images of ashen Hiroshima and firebombed Tokyo lingered as reminders of how World War II had brought the war directly home to millions of civilians.

Firebombing and Atomic Bombs

LIFE DURING WARTIME

The widespread bombing of civilian populations during World War II, from its beginning in China to its end in Hiroshima and Nagasaki, meant that there was no safe home front during the war. So, too, did the arrival of often brutal occupation forces in the wake of Japanese and German conquests in Asia and Europe. Strategic bombing slaughtered men, women, and children around the world, and occupation troops forced civilians to labor and die in work and extermination camps. In this total war civilian death tolls far exceeded military casualties. Beside the record of the war's brutality can be placed the contributions of resistance groups battling occupying forces, mobilized women, and survivors of bombings or concentration camps testifying to the horrors of war and the endurance of the human spirit.

The human and material damage of V-1 attacks is visible in the wreckage of a London neighborhood in 1944. ● Imperial War Museum, London

Bombs and More Bombs

Between September 1940 and May 1941, Germans bombarded Britain with high explosives and incendiaries that "blitzed" millions of homes and killed people by the tens of thousands. While city-dwellers learned to take shelter in underground subways and sandbag bunkers, the barrage from the air took a human and psychological toll. A woman serving as an air-raid warden described the chaos and pain: "I offered my services . . . and busied myself finding blankets to cover the five or six mutilated bodies in the street. A small boy, aged about 13, had one leg torn off and was still conscious, though he gave no sign of any pain. . . . Eleven had been killed but a large number were badly injured—an old man staggered down supported by two girls holding a towel to his face; as we laid him on a stretcher the towel dropped, and his face was shockingly cut away by glass."

Flying Bombs   Pulling the dead and injured out of collapsed buildings became a common activity toward the end of the war, when Hitler once more targeted Great Britain for bombardment—this time with "flying bombs," V-1 and V-2 ballistic missiles launched from German-controlled France. One Londoner described the city as "one large, frightened ear" as inhabitants continually listened for the sound of incoming bombs, trying to decide whether or not to seek cover. The V-2 weapons were even more terrifying because their approach was silent. As one woman put it, "The V-2s are absolutely horrifying. They just arrive with an appalling bang and jump one nearly out of one's skin. In the Blitz the noise was fairly continuous, and the V-1s you could hear coming, but these bastards just arrive unannounced."

The point of bombing urban centers filled with civilians was to destroy the enemy country's industrial infrastructure and torment its population. The Allies matched the Axis powers in the efficiency of their strategic bombings in Germany and Japan. By early 1943 Britain's Royal Air Force had committed itself to area bombing in which centers of cities became the targets of nighttime raids. U.S. planes attacked industrial targets in daytime. The British firebombing raid on Dresden in February 1945 literally cooked German men, women, and children in their bomb shelters and was one of the largest massacres of the war: 135,000 people died in the firestorm. The fall of Saipan in July 1944 and the subsequent conquest of Iwo Jima and Okinawa brought the Japanese homeland within easy reach of U.S. strategic bombers. Since high-altitude strikes in daylight had failed to do much damage to industrial sites, military planners changed tactics. The release of napalm firebombs during low-altitude sorties at night met with devastating success. The firebombing of Tokyo in March 1945 destroyed 25 percent of the city's buildings, annihilated approximately one hundred thousand people, and made more than a million homeless. The effects of strategic bombings were less than clear-cut. While the bombings did damage to the infrastructure and in some instances reduced industrial production, they did not destroy civilian morale. The bombings did, however, contribute to psychological confusion and fear.

Strategic Bombing and Atomic Warfare

The psychological impact of losing one's home can be seen in a Japanese reporter's account of his nephew's fate. Kozo, five years old when the war began, had a patriotic, unshakable faith in Japanese victory. All that changed when U.S. bombers leveled his home:

> After his home was burned to the ground during a B-29 raid, destroying almost every familiar material thing that had made up his existence, he told me with great gravity: "We cannot beat the B-29." The psychological effect of the loss of his home went deep. He had been one of the happiest and most carefree of children. He became thoughtful and serious and it was seldom that he laughed. He became ill and died shortly after the war was over. A nervous breakdown, the doctor called it.

The atomic bombings of Hiroshima and Nagasaki, in a light brighter than a thousand suns, not only made irradiated rubble of those cities but killed tens of thousands of people as well. The impact of the atomic bomb continued well after August 1945, debilitating the lives of survivors, who, because of their perceived atomic contamination, also faced discrimination from their fellow citizens.

Occupation, Collaboration, and Resistance

Axis bombardments and invasion were followed by occupation, but the administration imposed on conquered territories by Japanese and German forces varied in character. In territories like Manchukuo, Japanese-controlled China, Burma, and the Philippines, Japanese authorities installed puppet governments that served essentially as agents of Japanese rule. Thailand remained an independent state after it aligned itself with Japan, for which it was rewarded with grants of territory from bordering Laos and Burma. Other conquered territories either were considered too unstable or unreliable for "self-rule" or were deemed strategically too important to be left alone. Thus territories like Indochina (Laos, Cambodia, and Vietnam), Malaya, the Dutch East Indies, Hong Kong, Singapore, Borneo, and New Guinea came under direct military control.

In Europe, Hitler's racist ideology played a large role in determining how occupied territories were administered. As a rule Hitler intended that most areas of

A HIROSHIMA MAIDEN'S TALE

· · ·

Yamaoka Michiko, at fifteen years of age, worked as an operator at a telephone exchange in Hiroshima and attended girls' high school. Many young women had been mobilized for work during World War II, and they viewed even civilian work on telephone exchanges as a means of helping to protect Japan during wartime. On the morning of 6 August 1945, when the first U.S. atomic bomb used in battle devastated Hiroshima, Yamaoka Michiko had just started off for work.

That morning I left the house at about seven forty-five. I heard that the B-29s [U.S. bomber planes] had already gone home. Mom told me, "Watch out, the B-29s might come again." My house was one point three kilometers from the hypocenter [the exact point of the atomic bomb's impact in Hiroshima]. My place of work was five hundred meters from the hypocenter. I walked toward the hypocenter. . . . I heard the faint sound of planes. . . . The planes were tricky. Sometimes they only pretended to leave. I could still hear the very faint sound of planes. . . . I thought, how strange, so I put my right hand above my eyes and looked up to see if I could spot them. The sun was dazzling. That was the moment.

There was no sound. I felt something strong. It was terribly intense. I felt colors. It wasn't heat. You can't really say it was yellow, and it wasn't blue. At that moment I thought I would be the only one who would die. I said to myself, "Goodbye, Mom."

They say temperatures of seven thousand degrees centigrade hit me. You can't really say it washed over me. It's hard to describe. I simply fainted. I remember my body floating in the air. That was probably the blast, but I don't know how far I was blown. When I came to my senses, my surroundings were silent. There was no wind. I saw a threadlike light, so I felt I must be alive. I was under stones. I couldn't move my body. I heard voices crying, "Help! Water!" It was then I realized I wasn't the only one. . . .

"Fire! Run away! Help! Hurry up!" They weren't voices but moans of agony and despair. "I have to get help and shout," I thought. The person who rescued me was Mom, although she herself had been buried under our collapsed house. Mom knew the route I'd been taking. She came, calling out to me. I heard her voice and cried for help. Our surroundings were already starting to burn. Fires burst out from just the light itself. It didn't really drop. It just flashed. . . .

My clothes were burnt and so was my skin. I was in rags. I had braided my hair, but now it was like a lion's mane. There were people, barely breathing, trying to push their intestines back in. People with their legs wrenched off. Without heads. Or with faces burned and swollen out of shape. The scene I saw was a living hell.

Mom didn't say anything when she saw my face and I didn't feel any pain. She just squeezed my hand and told me to run. She was going to rescue my aunt. Large numbers of people were moving away from the flames. My eyes were still able to see, so I made my way toward the mountain, where there was not fire, toward Hijiyama. On this flight I saw a friend of mine from the phone exchange. She'd been inside her house and wasn't burned. I called her name, but she didn't respond. My face was so swollen she couldn't tell who I was. Finally, she recognized my voice. She said, "Miss Yamaoka, you look like a monster!" That's the first time I heard that word. I looked at my hands and saw my own skin was hanging down and the red flesh exposed. I didn't realize my face was swollen up because I was unable to see it. . . .

I spent the next year bedridden. All my hair fell out. When we went to relatives' houses later they wouldn't even let me in because they feared they'd catch the disease. There was neither treatment nor assistance for me. . . . It was just my Mom and me. Keloids [thick scar tissue] covered my face, my neck. I couldn't even move my neck. One eye was hanging down. I was unable to control my drooling because my lip had been burned off. . . .

The Japanese government just told us we weren't the only victims of the war. There was no support or treatment. It was probably harder for my Mom. Once she told me she tried to choke me to death. If a girl had terrible scars, a face you couldn't be born with, I understand that even a mother could want to kill her child. People threw stones at me and called me Monster. That was before I had my many operations.

SOURCE: Yamaoka Michiko. "Eight Hundred Meters from the Hypocenter." In Haruko Taya Cook and Theodore F. Cook. *Japan at War: An Oral History.* New York: The New Press, 1992, pp. 384–387.

western and northern Europe—populated by racially valuable people, according to him—would become part of a Greater Germanic Empire. Accordingly, Denmark retained its elected government and monarchy under German supervision. In Norway and Holland, where governments had gone into exile, the Nazis left the civilian administration intact. Though northern France and the Atlantic coast came under military rule, the so-called Vichy government remained the civilian authority in the unoccupied southeastern part of the country. Named for its locale in central France, the Vichy government provided a prominent place for those French willing to collaborate with Nazi rule. The Nazis made no such special arrangements in eastern Europe and the Balkans, where all conquered territories came under direct military rule as a prelude for harsh occupation, economic exploitation, and German settlement.

Japanese and Germans authorities administered their respective empires for economic gain and proceeded to exploit the resources of the lands under their control for their own benefit regardless of the consequences for the conquered peoples. The occupiers pillaged all forms of economic wealth that could fuel the German and Japanese war machines. The most notorious form of economic exploitation involved the use of slave labor. As the demands of total war stimulated an insatiable appetite for workers, Japanese and German occupation authorities availed themselves of prisoners of war and local populations to help meet labor shortages. In Poland, the Soviet Union, France, Italy, and the Balkan nations, German occupiers forced millions of people to labor in work camps and war industries, and the Japanese did likewise in China and Korea. These slave laborers worked under horrific conditions and received little in the way of sustenance. Many died. Reaction to Japanese and German occupation varied from willing collaboration and mere acquiescence to open resistance.

Exploitation

The majority of people resented occupation forces but usually went on with life as much as possible. This response was especially true in many parts of Japanese-occupied lands in Asia, where local populations found little to resent in the change from one colonial administration to another. In both Asia and Europe, moreover, local notables often joined the governments sponsored by the conquerors because collaboration offered them the means to gain power. In many instances bureaucrats and police forces collaborated because they thought it was better that natives rule than Germans or Japanese. Business people and companies often collaborated simply because they prospered financially from foreign rule. Still other people became collaborators and assisted occupation authorities by turning in friends and neighbors to get even for some past grievances. In western Europe anti-communism motivated Belgians, French, Danish, Dutch, and Norwegians to join units of Hitler's elite military formations, the Waffen SS, creating in the process a multinational army tens of thousands strong. In China several Guomindang generals went over to the Japanese while local landowners and merchants in some regions of China set up substantial trade networks between the occupiers and occupied.

Collaboration

Occupation and exploitation also created an environment for resistance which took various forms. The most dramatic forms of resistance were campaigns of sabotage, armed assaults on occupation forces, and assassinations. Resistance fighters as diverse as Filipino guerrillas and Soviet partisans harassed and disrupted the military and economic activities of the occupiers by blowing up ammunition dumps, destroying communication and transportation facilities, and sabotaging industrial plants. More quietly, other resisters gathered intelligence, hid and protected refugees, or passed on clandestine newspapers. Resistance also comprised simple acts of defiance such as scribbling anti-German graffiti or walking out of bars and restaurants when Japanese

Resistance

soldiers entered. In the Netherlands people associated the royal House of Orange with national independence and defiantly saluted traffic lights when they turned orange.

German and Japanese citizens faced different decisions than conquered peoples when it came to resistance. They had no antiforeign axe to grind, and any form of noncompliance constituted an act of treason that might assist the enemy and lead to defeat. Moreover, many institutions that might have formed the core of resistance in Japan and Germany, such as political parties, labor unions, or churches, were either weak or had been destroyed. As a result there was little or no opposition to the state and its policies in Japan, while in Nazi Germany resistance remained generally sparse and ineffective. The most spectacular act of resistance against the Nazi regime came from a group of officers and civilians who tried to kill Adolf Hitler on 20 July 1944. This plot failed as a bomb explosion killed several bystanders but inflicted only minor injuries on Hitler.

Atrocities   Occupation forces did not hesitate to retaliate when resistance to occupation arose. When in May 1942 members of the Czech resistance assassinated Reinhard Heydrich, the deputy leader of the SS (a Nazi security agency that carried out the most criminal tasks of the regime, including mass murder), the Nazis eliminated the entire village of Lidice as punishment. Six days after Heydrich succumbed to his wounds, SS personnel shot the villages' 179 men on the spot, transported fifty women to a concentration camp where they died, and then burned and dynamited the village to the ground. SS security forces, after examining the surviving ninety children, deemed them racially "pure" and dispersed them throughout Germany to be raised as Germans. Likewise, in the aftermath of the failed attempt on Adolf Hitler's life in 1944, many of the conspirators ended up dying while suspended from meat hooks, a process recorded on film for Hitler. Equally brutal reprisals took place under Japanese rule. After eight hundred forced Chinese laborers escaped from their camp in the small town of Hanaoka, Japan, the townspeople, the local militia, and the police hunted them down. At least fifty of the slave laborers were tortured to death, some beaten as they hung by their thumbs from the ceiling of the village town hall.

Attempts to eradicate resistance movements in many instances merely fanned the flames of rebellion because of the indiscriminate reprisals against civilians. Despite the deadly retaliation meted out to those who resisted occupation, widespread resistance movements grew throughout the war. Life in resistance movements was tenuous at best and entailed great hardship—changing identities, hiding out, and risking capture and death. Nevertheless, the resisters kept alive their nations' hopes for liberation.

The Holocaust

By the end of World War II, the Nazi regime and its accomplices had physically annihilated millions of Jews, Slavs, Gypsies, homosexuals, Jehovah's Witnesses, communists, and others targeted as undesirables. Jews were the primary target of Hitler's racially motivated genocidal policies, and the resulting Holocaust epitomized the tragedy of conquest and occupation in World War II. The Holocaust, the almost complete destruction of European Jews by Nazi Germany, was a human disaster on a scale previously unknown.

The murder of European Jews was preceded by a long history of vilification and persecution of Jews. For centuries Jewish communities had been singled out by

Christian society as a "problem," and by the time the Nazi regime assumed power in 1933, anti-Semitism had contributed significantly to the widespread tolerance for anti-Jewish measures. Marked as outsiders, Jews found few defenders in their societies. Nazi determination to destroy the Jewish population, and Europeans' passive acceptance of anti-Semitism laid the groundwork for genocide. In most war-torn European countries, the social and political forces that might have been expected to rally to the defense of Jews simply did not materialize.

Initially, the Nazi regime encouraged Jewish emigration. While tens of thousands Jews availed themselves of the opportunity to escape from Germany and Austria, many more were unable to do so. Most nations outside the Nazi orbit limited the migration of Jewish refugees. This was especially true if they were impoverished, as most of them were because Nazi authorities had previously appropriated their wealth. This situation worsened as German armies overran one European country after another, bringing an ever-larger number of Jews under Nazi control. At this point Nazi "racial experts" toyed with the idea of deporting Jews to Nisko, a proposed reservation in eastern Poland, or to the island of Madagascar, near Africa. These ideas proved to be not only impractical but also threatening. Concentrating Jews in one area led to the dangerous possibility of creating a separate Jewish state, hardly a solution to the so-called Jewish problem in the Nazi view.

The German occupation of Poland in 1939 and invasion of the Soviet Union in the summer of 1941 gave Hitler an opportunity to solve what he considered the problem of Jews in Germany and throughout Europe. When German armies invaded the Soviet Union in June 1941, the Nazis also dispatched three thousand men in mobile detachments known as *SS Einsatzgruppen* ("action squads") to kill entire populations of Jews, Roma (or Gypsies), and many non-Jewish Slavs in the newly occupied territories. The action squads undertook mass shootings in ditches and ravines that became mass graves. By the end of 1941, the special killing units had killed 1.4 million Jews.

The "Final Solution"

Meanwhile the Nazis hatched plans to extend the "final solution to the Jewish question" to all areas under German control. At the Wannsee Conference on 20 January 1942, leading Nazi bureaucrats agreed to evacuate all Jews from Europe to camps in eastern Poland, where they would be worked to death or outright exterminated. Soon German forces—aided by collaborating authorities in foreign countries—rounded up Jews and then deported them to specially constructed concentration camps in occupied Poland. The victims from nearby Polish ghettos and distant assembly points all across Europe traveled to their destinations by train. On the way the sick and elderly often perished in overcrowded freight cars. The Jewish victims packed into these suffocating railway cars never knew their destinations, but rumors of mass deportations and mass deaths nonetheless spread among Jews remaining at large and among the Allied governmental leaders, who were apparently apathetic to the fate of Jews.

In camps like Kulmhof (Chelmno), Belzec, Majdanek, Sobibòr, Treblinka, and Auschwitz, the "final solution" took on a more organized and technologically sophisticated character. Here, the killers introduced gassing as the most efficient means for mass extermination, though other means of destruction were always retained, such as electrocution, phenol injections, flamethrowers, hand grenades, and machine guns. The largest of the camps was Auschwitz, where at least one million Jews perished. Nazi camp personnel subjected victims from all corners of Europe to industrial work, starvation, medical experiments, and outright extermination. The German commandant of Auschwitz explained proudly how his camp became the

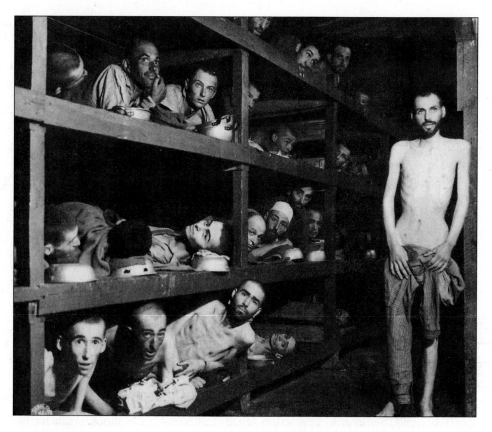

Survivors in the Buchenwald concentration camp upon its liberation by the Allies in 1945.

• National Archives

most efficient at killing Jews: by using the fast-acting crystallized prussic acid Zyklon B as the gassing agent, by enlarging the size of the gas chambers, and by lulling victims into thinking they were simply going through a delousing process. At Auschwitz and elsewhere, the Nazis also constructed large crematories to incinerate the bodies of gassed Jews and hide the evidence of their crimes. This systematic murder of Jews constituted what war crime tribunals later termed a "crime against humanity."

Resistance   The murder of European Jewry was carried out with the help of the latest technology and with the utmost efficiency. For most of the victims, the will to resist had been sapped by prolonged starvation, disease, and mistreatment. Nevertheless, there was fierce Jewish resistance throughout the war. Thousands of Jews joined anti-Nazi partisan groups and resistance movements while others led rebellions in concentration camps or participated in ghetto uprisings from Minsk to Krakow. The best-known uprising took place in the Warsaw ghetto in the spring of 1943. Lacking adequate weapons, some sixty thousand Jews who remained in the ghetto that had once held four hundred thousand rose against their tormentors. It took German security forces using tanks and flamethrowers three weeks to crush the uprising. Despite these and other efforts, 5.7 million Jews perished in the Holocaust.

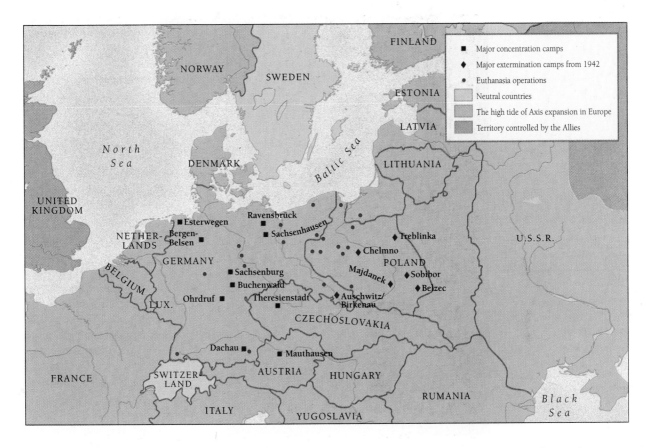

MAP [36.3]

The Holocaust in Europe, 1933–1945.

Women and the War

Observing the extent to which British women mobilized for war, the U.S. ambassador to London noted, "This war, more than any other war in history, is a woman's war." A poster encouraging U.S. women to join the WAVES (Women Appointed for Volunteer Emergency Service in the navy) mirrored the thought "It's A Woman's War Too!" While hundreds of thousands of women in Great Britain and the United States joined the armed forces or entered war industries, women around the world were affected by the war in a variety of ways. A number of nations barred women from engaging in combat or even carrying weapons, including Great Britain and the United States, but Soviet and Chinese women took up arms, as did female members of resistance groups. In fact, women often excelled at resistance work precisely because they were women: they were less suspect in the eyes of occupying security forces and less subject to searches. Nazi forces did not discriminate, though, when rounding up Jews for transport and extermination: Jewish women and girls died alongside Jewish men and boys.

Women's Roles

Women who joined military services or took jobs on factory assembly lines gained an independence and confidence that had previously been denied them, but so too did women who were forced to act as heads of household in the absence of husbands killed or away at war, captured as prisoners of war, or languishing in labor camps. Women's roles changed during the war, often in dramatic ways, but those new roles proved to be temporary. After the war women warriors and workers were expected to return home and assume their traditional roles as wives and mothers.

A WAVE recruitment poster proclaims "It's A Woman's War Too!" • Library of Congress

In the meantime, though, women made the most of their opportunities. In Britain alone, women served as noncombatant pilots, wrestled with the huge balloons and their tethering lines designed to snag Nazi aircraft from the skies, drove ambulances and transport vehicles, and labored in the fields to produce foodstuffs. More than half a million women joined British military services, and approximately 350,000 women did the same in the United States.

Women's experience in war was not always ennobling or empowering. The Japanese army forcibly recruited, conscripted, and dragooned as many as three hundred thousand women aged fourteen to twenty to serve in military brothels called "comfort houses" or "consolation centers." The army presented the women to the troops as a gift from the emperor, and the women came from Japanese colonies such as Korea, Taiwan, and Manchuria, as well as from occupied territo-

Comfort Women   ries in the Philippines and elsewhere in southeast Asia. Fully 80 percent of the women came from Korea.

Once forced into this imperial prostitution service, the "comfort women" had to cater to between twenty and thirty men each day. Stationed in war zones, they often confronted the same risks as soldiers, and many became casualties of war. Others were killed by Japanese soldiers, especially if they tried to escape or contracted venereal diseases. At the end of the war, soldiers massacred large numbers of comfort women to cover up the operation. The impetus behind the establishment of comfort houses for Japanese soldiers came from the horrors of Nanjing, where the mass rape of Chinese women had taken place. In trying to avoid such atrocities, though, the Japanese army only created another horror of war. Comfort women who survived the war experienced deep shame and had to hide their past or face shunning by their own families. They found little comfort or peace after the war.

 ## NEITHER PEACE NOR WAR

The end of World War II produced moving images of peace: Soviet and U.S. soldiers clasping hands in camaraderie at the Elbe River, celebrating their victory over the Nazis; Victor Tolley sharing a quiet bowl of tea with a Japanese boy and his fam-

British women handle a balloon used for defense in the Battle of Britain. • Imperial War Museum, London

ily; Allied bombers transforming into ships of mercy, delivering food and medicine to conquered peoples in Germany and Japan. A sense of common humanity had refused to die even in this deadliest of wars, although further tests of that humanity awaited in the postwar world.

The two strongest powers after World War II, the Soviet Union and the United States, played a central role in shaping, influencing, and rebuilding the postwar world. Each sought to create a world sympathetic to Soviet communist or U.S. capitalist hegemony. The struggle to align postwar nations on one side or the other centered on areas that had been liberated by the Soviet Union and the United States, although ultimately it was not limited to those territories.

The Origins of the Cold War and Postwar Settlements

Although the peoples of victorious nations danced in the streets on Victory in Europe (V-E) Day and Victory in Japan (V-J) Day, they also gazed at a world transformed by war—a world seriously in need of reconstruction and healing. At least sixty million people had perished in World War II. The Soviets lost more than twenty million, only one-third of whom were soldiers; fifteen million Chinese, again mostly civilians, died; Germany and Japan suffered the deaths of four million and two million people, respectively; six million Poles were also dead; and in Great Britain four hundred thousand people died while the United States lost three hundred thousand. The

Holocaust claimed the lives of almost six million European Jews. In Europe and Asia tens of millions of displaced persons further contributed to the difficulty of rebuilding areas destroyed by war.

At the end of the war in Europe, eight million Germans fled across the Elbe River to surrender or to seek refuge in the territories soon to be occupied by Great Britain and the United States. They wanted to avoid capture and presumed torture by the Red Army and Soviet occupiers. The behavior of Soviet troops, who pillaged and raped with abandon in Berlin, did little to alleviate the fears of those facing Soviet occupation. Joining the refugees were twelve million German and Soviet prisoners of war making their way home, along with the survivors of work and death camps and three million refugees from the Balkan lands. This massive population shift put a human face on the political transformations taking place in Europe and around the world.

At the same time, the cold war between the Soviet Union and the United States was beginning. This long-drawn-out conflict (1947–1990) would once again divide global populations, categorizing humans and nations as sympathetic either to the Soviet Union or the United States. The cold war came to define the postwar era as one of political, ideological, and economic hostility between the two superpowers. Cold war hostilities affected nations around the globe, but the rivals usually refrained from armed conflict in Europe, but not in Asia.

The Origins of the Cold War Throughout most of World War II, Hitler had rested some of his hopes for victory on his doubts about the unlikely alliance fighting against him. He believed that the alliance of the communist Soviet Union, imperialist Great Britain, and the unwarlike U.S. democracy would break up over ideological differences. Even when the staunch anticommunist Harry S. Truman (1884–1972) assumed the presidency after Roosevelt's death, however, the Grand Alliance held—at least on the surface. Hitler underestimated the extent to which opposition to his regime could unite such unusual allies. Winston Churchill had made the point in vivid terms when Britain aligned itself with the Soviet Union after the German invasion: "If Hitler invaded Hell, I would at least make favorable reference to the Devil in the House of Commons."

The necessity of defeating the Axis nations glued the Allies together, although there were tensions among them. The Soviets bristled at the delay of the Britain and the United States in opening the second front, and differences of opinion over postwar settlements arose during the wartime conferences held at Yalta (February 1945) and Potsdam (July–August 1945). By the time of the Yalta Conference, the Soviets were 64 kilometers (40 miles) from Berlin, and they controlled so much territory that Churchill and Roosevelt could do little to alter Stalin's plans for eastern Europe. They attempted to convince Stalin to allow democracy in Poland, even having supported their own democratic Polish government in exile, but Stalin's plans for Soviet-occupied nations prevailed. He installed a communist government in Poland and took similar steps elsewhere in eastern Europe, adhering to the Allied principle of occupying and controlling those territories liberated by one's own armed forces.

At Yalta, Stalin ensured that the Red Army's presence would dictate the future of states liberated by the Soviets, and at Potsdam the new U.S. president, Harry S. Truman, initiated the harder-line stance of the United States, confident now that little Soviet aid would be needed to defeat Japan. The successful test of the atomic bomb while Truman was at Potsdam stiffened the president's resolve, and tensions over postwar settlements intensified. Having just fought a brutal war to guarantee the survival of their ways of life, neither the United States nor the Soviet Union would easily forgo the chance to remake occupied territories as either capitalist or communist allies.

In Europe and Asia postwar occupation and territorial divisions reflected both hard postwar realities and the new schism between the Soviet Union and the United States. All that the Allies could agree on was the dismemberment of Axis states and their possessions. The Soviets took over the eastern sections of Germany, and the United States, Britain, and France occupied the western portions. The capital city of Berlin, deep within the Soviet area, remained under the control of all four powers. Because of the rising hostility between the Soviets and their allies, no peace treaty was signed with Germany, and by the late 1940s these haphazard postwar territorial arrangements had solidified into a divided Germany. As Churchill proclaimed in 1946, an "iron curtain" had come down on Europe. Behind that curtain were the nations controlled by the Soviet Union, including East Germany and Poland, while on the other side were the capitalist nations of western Europe. A somewhat similar division occurred in Asia. While the United States alone occupied Japan, Korea remained occupied half by the Soviets and half by the Americans.

Postwar Territorial Division

The enunciation of the Truman Doctrine on 12 March 1947 crystallized the new U.S. perception of a world divided between free and enslaved peoples. Articulated in part in response to crises in Greece and Turkey, where communist movements seemed to threatened democracy as well as western strategic interests, the Truman doctrine starkly drew the battle lines of the cold war. As Truman explained to the U.S. Congress:

The Truman Doctrine

> At the present moment in world history nearly every nation must choose between alternative ways of life. The choice is too often not a free one. One way of life is based upon the will of the majority, and is distinguished by free institutions, representative government, free elections, guarantees of individual liberty, freedom of speech and religion, and freedom from political oppression. The second way of life is based upon the will of a minority forcibly imposed upon the majority. It relies upon terror and repression, a controlled press and radio, fixed elections, and the suppression of personal freedoms. I believe that it must be the policy of the United States to support free peoples who are resisting attempted subjugation by armed minorities or by outside pressures.

The United States then committed itself to an interventionist foreign policy, dedicated to the "containment" of communism, which meant preventing any further expansion of Soviet influence. The United States sent vast sums of money to Greece and Turkey, and the world was polarized into two armed camps, each led by a superpower that provided economic and military aid to nations within its spheres of influence.

Global Reconstruction and the United Nations

As an economic adjunct to the Truman Doctrine, the U.S. government developed a plan to help shore up the destroyed infrastructures of western Europe. The European Recovery Program, commonly called the Marshall Plan after U.S. secretary of state George C. Marshall (1880–1959), proposed to rebuild European economies through cooperation and capitalism, forestalling communist or Soviet influence in the devastated nations of Europe. Proposed in 1947 and funded in 1948, the Marshall Plan provided more than $13 billion to reconstruct western Europe.

The Marshall Plan

Although initially included in the nations invited to participate in the Marshall Plan, the Soviet Union resisted what it saw as capitalist imperialism and countered with a plan for its own satellite nations. The Soviet Union established the Council for Mutual Economic Assistance (COMECON) in 1949, offering increased trade within the Soviet Union and eastern Europe as an alternative to the Marshall Plan. Both the Soviet and U.S. recovery plans for Europe tended to benefit the superpowers either by providing lucrative markets or resources. Yet even these economic programs were cut back as more spending shifted to building up military defenses.

NATO and the
Warsaw Pact

The creation of the U.S.-sponsored North Atlantic Treaty Organization (NATO) and the Soviet-controlled Warsaw Pact signaled the militarization of the cold war. In 1949 the United States established NATO as a regional military alliance against Soviet aggression. The original members included Belgium, Canada, Denmark, France, Great Britain, Iceland, Italy, Luxembourg, the Netherlands, Norway, Portugal, and the United States. The intent of the alliance was to maintain peace in postwar Europe through collective defense. When NATO admitted West Germany and allowed it to rearm in 1955, the Soviets formed the Warsaw Pact as a countermeasure. A military alliance of seven communist European nations, the Warsaw Pact matched the collective defense policies of NATO. Europe's contrasting economic and military alliances were part of postwar global reconstruction, and they gave definition to the early cold war.

The United States and the Soviet Union had become global superpowers as a result of World War II—either through territorial aggrandizement and a massive army, in the case of the Soviet Union, or through tremendous economic prosperity and industrial capacity, in the case of the United States. The dislocation of European and Asian peoples aided the superpowers' quests for world hegemony, but so too did their idealism—however much that idealism cloaked self-interest. Each wanted to guard its preciously won victory by creating alliances and alignments that would support its way of life. The territorial rearrangements of the postwar world, either a direct result of the war or a consequence of the decolonization that followed, gave both superpowers a vast field in which to compete.

The United Nations

Despite their many differences, the superpowers were among the nations that agreed to the creation of the United Nations (UN), a supranational organization dedicated to keeping world peace. The commitment to establish a new international organization derived from Allied cooperation during the war, and in 1944 representatives from China, Great Britain, the Soviet Union, and the United States finalized most of the proposals for the organization at Dumbarton Oaks in Washington, D.C. The final version of the United Nations charter was hammered out by delegates from fifty nations at the United Nations Conference in San Francisco in 1945. The United Nations was dedicated to maintaining international peace and security and promoting friendly relations among the world's nations. It offered an alternative for global reconstruction that was independent of the cold war.

It rapidly became clear, however, that international peace and security eluded both the United Nations and the superpowers. The cold war dominated postwar reconstruction efforts. It remained cold for the most part, characterized by ideological and propaganda campaigns, although certain events came perilously close to warming up the conflict—as when the Chinese communists gained victory over the nationalists in 1949, thereby joining the Soviets as a major communist power. The cold war also became "hot" in places like Korea between 1950 and 1953, and it had the potential to escalate into a war even more destructive than World War II. The Soviet Union broke the U.S. monopoly on the atomic bomb in September 1949, and from that point on the world held its collective breath, for a nuclear war was too horrible to contemplate.

At the end of World War II, it was possible for a U.S. marine to enjoy the hospitality of a Japanese family in Nagasaki, but not for Soviet and U.S. troops to continue embracing in camaraderie. World War II was a total global war that forced violent encounters between peoples and radically altered the political shape of the world. Beginning with Japan and China in 1931, this global conflagration spread to Europe and its empires and to the Pacific Ocean and the rest of Asia. Men, women, and children throughout the world became intimate with war as victims of civilian bombing campaigns, as soldiers and war workers, and as slave laborers and comfort women. When the Allies defeated the Axis powers in 1945, destroying the German and Japanese empires, the world had to rebuild as another war began. The end of the war saw the breakup of the alliance that had defeated Germany and Japan, and within a short time the United States and the Soviet Union and their respective allies squared off against each other in a cold war, a rivalry waged primarily on political, economic, and propaganda fronts. The cold war helped determine the new shape of the world as nations reconstructed under the auspices of either the United States or the Soviet Union, the two superpowers of the postwar era.

CHRONOLOGY

1931	Invasion of Manchuria by Japan
1932	Establishment of Manchukuo
1933–1945	Hitler in power in Germany
1933	Withdrawal of Germany and Japan from the League of Nations
1935	German rearmament
	Invasion of Ethiopia by Italy
1936	Reoccupation of the Rhineland by Germany
1937	Invasion of China by Japan
	The Rape of Nanjing
1938	German *Anschluss* with Austria
	Munich Conference
1939	Nazi-Soviet Pact
	Invasion of Poland by Germany
1940	Fall of France, battle of Britain
1941	German invasion of the Soviet Union
	Attack on Pearl Harbor by Japan
1942	U.S. victory at Midway
1943	Soviet victory at Stalingrad
1944	D day
1945	Capture of Berlin by Soviet forces
	Atomic bombing of Hiroshima and Nagasaki
	Establishment of United Nations
1947	Truman Doctrine
1948	Marshall Plan
1949	Creation of COMECOM
	Establishment of NATO
1950–1953	Korean War
1955	Establishment of Warsaw Pact

FOR FURTHER READING

Gar Alperovitz. *Atomic Diplomacy: Hiroshima and Potsdam,* Rev. ed. New York, 1985. The classic account of the atomic origins of the cold war.

Ian Buruma. *The Wages of Guilt: Memories of War in Germany and Japan.* New York, 1995. A moving account of how societies deal with the war crimes of World War II.

Winston Churchill. *The Second World War,* 6 vols. New York, 1948–1960. An in-depth account of the war from one of the major players in the war.

Haruko Taya Cook and Theodore F. Cook. *Japan at War: An Oral History.* New York, 1992. Views of World War II in the words of the Japanese who witnessed it.

John Dower. *War without Mercy: Race and Power in the Pacific War.* New York, 1986. An insightful and important work on how race influenced the Japanese and U.S. war in the Pacific.

Dwight Eisenhower. *Crusade in Europe.* New York, 1948. An account of the European war from the military point of view of the supreme Allied commander.

Paul Fussell. *Understanding and Behavior in the Second World War.* Oxford, 1989. As in his work on World War I, the author dissects the culture of war in this study.

Margaret Higgonet, Jane Jenson, Sonya Michel, and Margaret Weitz, eds. *Behind the Lines: Gender and the Two World Wars.* New Haven, 1987. A penetrating series of articles on women in both world wars, focusing generally on U.S. and European experiences.

Raul Hilberg. *The Destruction of the European Jews.* New York, 1967. One of the most important works on the Holocaust.

Akira Iriye. *Power and Culture: The Japanese-American War, 1941–1945.* Cambridge, Mass., 1981. An incisive account of the Pacific war by one of the field's leading scholars.

——. *The Origins of the Second World War in Asia and the Pacific.* New York, 1987. Here the author examines the Asian and Pacific origins of the war.

John Keegan. *The Second World War.* New York, 1989. An exhaustive military history.

Charles S. Maier, ed. *The Origins of the Cold War and Contemporary Europe.* New York, 1978. An anthology of essays that concentrates on the relationship of the U.S.-Soviet tension and the social and political development of European nations.

Richard Rhodes. *The Making of the Atomic Bomb.* New York, 1986. An in-depth account of how the atomic bomb was created, with special emphasis on the scientists' role.

Martin Sherwin. *A World Destroyed: The Atomic Bomb and the Grand Alliance.* New York, 1975. A classic study of how the bomb influenced the end of the war.

Sun, You-Li. *China and the Origins of the Pacific War, 1931–1941.* New York, 1993. China takes center stage in the account of the origins of the war.

Studs Terkel. *"The Good War": An Oral History of World War II.* New York, 1984. A valuable collection of oral histories on the war from a U.S. perspective.

Gerhard Weinberg. *A World at Arms: A Global History of World War II.* Cambridge, 1994. An exhaustive look at the war from a global perspective.

LIFE

HOW YOU CAN
SURVIVE
FALLOUT

97 out of 100 people can be saved . . .
Detail plans for building shelters . . .

AND A LETTER
TO YOU FROM
PRESIDENT
KENNEDY

CIVILIAN FALLOUT SUIT

SEPTEMBER 15 · 1961 · 20¢

CHAPTER 37

THE RETREAT FROM EMPIRE IN A BIPOLAR WORLD

• • •

In the summer of 1959, the world was treated to a verbal slugfest—subsequently known as the kitchen debate—between the representatives of the world's two most powerful nations. In July of that year the vice president of the United States, Richard M. Nixon (1913–1994), arrived in Moscow to open the American National Exhibition, a rare display of U.S. goods on Russian soil. Nixon's host, Soviet premier Nikita S. Khrushchev (1894–1971), was in no mood, however, to embrace his guest from the capitalist United States. The U.S. Congress had just passed the "captive nations" resolution, which openly criticized the Soviet Union for mistreating its satellite nations, and Khrushchev was convinced that Nixon's visit to Moscow was timed to humiliate him (Khrushchev) publicly.

Before visiting the exhibit, Khrushchev and Nixon met privately and exchanged heated words about captive nations. According to Nixon's memoirs, the colorful and candid Soviet premier initiated the conversation by remarking: "It stinks like fresh horse shit, and nothing smells worse than that." The equally frank Nixon—aware that Khrushchev had tended pigs in his youth—quickly replied: "There is something that smells worse than horse shit and that is pig shit." Having thus set the mood, Nixon and Khrushchev descended on the exhibit, where they continued their barbed exchange.

The high point of their vocal showdown took place in the kitchen of a U.S. model house built expressly for the exhibit. Without hesitation, Khrushchev mocked the many modern appliances in the kitchen, including a lemon juicer and a built-in dishwasher. In his opinion they epitomized "the capitalist attitude toward women." Besides, Khrushchev argued, the working class could never afford such useless gadgets in the first place. Stung by the criticism, Nixon poked a finger at the chest of the Soviet premier and boisterously declared that any U.S. steel worker could purchase this $14,000 home. What followed was an unrehearsed polemical discourse on communism and capitalism, climaxing with a dispute concerning the relative merits of everything from dishwashers to missiles.

The kitchen debate between Nixon and Khrushchev took place at the height of the cold war and illustrated how deep the rift between the United States of America

In September 1961, *Life* magazine featured a civilian fallout suit on its cover, suggesting the new fashions necessary in the cold war age. • Ralph Morse/Life Magazine, © Time Inc.

Soviet premier Nikita Khrushchev and U.S. vice president Richard Nixon sharing a rare "lighter" moment during the kitchen debate. • Archive Photos

and the Union of Soviet Socialist Republics (USSR) had grown since 1945. The cold war was a strategic struggle that developed after World War II between the United States and its allies on the one hand and the USSR and its allied communist countries on the other. Yet the confrontation was more than an instance of great-power rivalry; it was also a struggle between rival social and economic systems and competing political ideologies. It was this clash between the forces of capitalism and communism that gave rise to a new set of global relationships, shaping the foreign policies, economic systems, and political institutions of nations throughout the world. The cold war signaled a major realignment in international relations and the global balance of power.

The geopolitical and ideological rivalry between the Soviet Union and the United States lasted almost five decades and affected every corner of the world. The cold war was responsible for the formation of military and political alliances, the creation of client states, and an arms race of unprecedented scope. It engendered diplomatic crises, spawned military conflicts, and at times brought the world to the brink of nuclear annihilation. It was a contest in which neither side gave way, yet in the end the United States and Soviet Union always avoided a direct clash of arms, hence the term *cold war*. However devoid of direct military conflict, the cold war nonetheless spurred ideological clashes and led to changing societal and economic practices in the Soviet Union and United States. Societies in this atmosphere could not avoid scrutiny and comparison. Discontented women and African-Americans in U.S. society protested the failings of democratic capitalism while Soviet and east European societies had difficulty matching the increasing wealth and consumerism of western European and U.S. societies.

Like the formation of the cold war world, decolonization—or the relinquishing of colonial possessions—contributed significantly to the global political transformation after World War II. These two developments, the cold war and the end of empire, intertwined to reshape the world in the late twentieth century. The end of empire was one of the most important outcomes of World War II, as dozens of new, independent nations emerged from the British, French, Dutch, Spanish, and Portuguese empires that had been established in the previous century. With two superpowers dedicated to the overthrow of empire, the stage was set for a massive overturning of colonial rule. As cold war animosities deepened, however, the leaders of the Soviet Union and the United States tended to view new nations and struggling nationalist movements through a cold war prism. Emerging nations were often confronted by the demand that they take sides and choose between capitalism and communism. At times this demand compromised their independence, particularly in new nations that were deemed strategically important by the superpowers. Because the pressure exerted by the superpowers included the threat of nuclear weapons, the leaders of newly independent nations had to worry about upsetting the global balance of nuclear terror.

The demands of the cold war, however, could not dim the joy that colonized peoples felt upon gaining independence. No brief treatment of such a broad and variegated process as decolonization can do justice to each individual nation—particularly because more than ninety nations gained independence between the end of World War II and 1980. Nations achieved independence at different times: India and Pakistan became independent nations as early as 1947, Zimbabwe (Southern Rhodesia) as late as 1980. Algerians in North Africa fought a long, hard war against the French for freedom, whereas some peoples in sub-Saharan Africa followed less tortuous routes to independence. Other countries, like Vietnam, became deeply embroiled in the cold war, while others managed to avoid—through neutrality or nonalignment—becoming too perilously enmeshed in that ideological contest. Just as Khrushchev and Nixon debated the relative merits of their systems, so, too, did nations in Asia, Africa, and Latin America as they sought their own paths to freedom and independence in a bipolar world.

THE FORMATION OF A BIPOLAR WORLD

The cold war began at the end of World War II, and its initial arena was war-torn Europe. By the time Nazi Germany surrendered in the spring of 1945, the wartime alliance between the Soviet Union and the United States had already begun to disintegrate. With the advent of peace, the one-time partners increasingly sacrificed cooperation for their own national interests. The competing ideologies of capitalism and communism shaped the postwar aims of the two superpowers. (The term *superpower* came into use during this period to distinguish their supreme global power from the more limited resources of other, merely great powers.) The hostility between these new adversaries resulted in a divided world. First Europe, and Germany in particular, was split into separate blocs and states. Then the cold war became global in scale as the superpowers came into conflict in nations as far afield as Korea and Cuba. The globalization of the cold war also affected the process of decolonization and the development of independent national states. The superpowers competed for allies in Asia, Africa, and Latin America while developing nations considered nonalignment or neutrality a viable choice.

Building the Cold War World

The struggle between the United States and the Soviet Union was not simply a matter of ill will, misunderstandings, and competition for power, although it was all these things, too. It resulted from deep-seated animosities. The commitment to wage the cold war, whose costs were high for both sides, hinged on the belief that the conflict was ultimately a battle between rival—and incompatible—social, political, and economic systems. At the heart of the cold war lay an ideological conflict between capitalism and communism. Ideology mattered profoundly, explaining why political crises occurred so frequently and international tensions remained at a high pitch and why the Soviet Union and the United States were unable to live in peaceful coexistence.

The Contest between Capitalism and Communism

For both sides ideology served as a description and a defense of competing social and economic systems, and ideology promoted idealized versions of the respective strengths of capitalist and communist society. U.S. ideology was committed to liberalism and severe criticism of communism as practiced by the Soviet Union and other regimes. Thus U.S. policy makers were fond of pointing out the communists' disdain for civil liberties and their suppression of civil and religious institutions such as the press, trade unions, opposition parties, and churches. In addition, U.S. ideology promoted capitalism along with property rights and free markets. This version of capitalism was not, however, the laissez-faire capitalism of the nineteenth century, but a new, reformed type of capitalism, one that protected the social and economic rights of citizens by accepting the idea of a welfare state and government intervention in the economy. The sincerity of U.S. rhetoric came under intense scrutiny during the cold war decades, and on some occasions was found wanting, but this criticism did not mean that the United States lacked a true ideological commitment.

After the death of Joseph Stalin in 1953, a refined ideology also emanated from the Soviet Union. Stalin's successor, Nikita Khrushchev, developed a version of communism that inspired generations of reformers in the Soviet Union and eastern Europe. Recognizing that the "historic defects" of communism were a liability in the contest with the United States, Khrushchev offered a reformed communism, one without the terror and intimidation that had characterized the Stalin era. The Soviet premier was also keenly aware of the failure of collectivized agriculture, the overemphasis on heavy industry, and the inefficiencies of central planning. Beyond the relaxation of terror, then, Khrushchev called for a more economically productive type of communism that aimed for balanced growth. Ultimately, he desired nothing more than to give communism the capacity to overtake the capitalist world in the production of material wealth. If the U.S. vision of reformed capitalism sometimes diverged from reality, the same was true of reformed communism. In the long run, however, communism failed to deliver on its major promises—it neither liberated society nor invigorated the economy.

Global Communism and Containment

Responding to what they viewed as a Soviet effort to spread communism throughout the world, U.S. policy makers fashioned the strategy known as containment, a foreign policy that aimed at denying Moscow opportunities to expand its influence. In practice, this strategy meant that U.S. leaders bound the nation to extending military assistance and economic aid to any country that was thought to be in danger of falling prey to communism. They also formed political and military alliances around the world, and they committed themselves to achieving military superiority. The Soviet response to containment evolved into two counterstrategies: support for wars of national liberation or colonial revolution, and attainment of military parity with the United States and its allies. These strategies had important consequences.

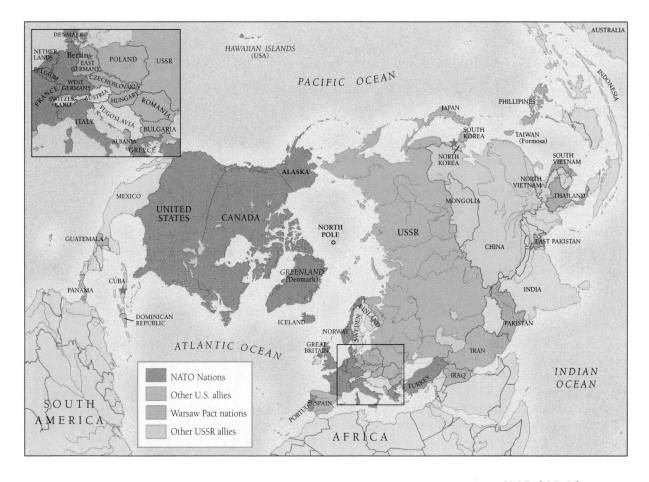

MAP [37.1]

The Cold War, 1949–1962.

The first result was the division of the European continent into competing political, military, and economic blocs—one dependent on the United States and the other subservient to the USSR—separated by what Winston Churchill called an "iron curtain." In essence, both blocs adopted the political institutions, economic systems, and foreign policies of the two superpowers. Thus western European nations tied to the United States embraced parliamentary political systems and capitalist economic structures and adjusted their foreign policies to the U.S. vision of the postwar world. On the other hand, under the watchful eyes of Soviet occupation armies the governments of eastern European states adopted Soviet political and economic institutions and supported Moscow's foreign policy goals. Outside Europe members of the socialist and capitalist blocs often diverged significantly from the political and economic norms of their patrons. Nevertheless, when it suited their needs, both sides in the cold war welcomed regimes that practiced neither democracy nor socialism.

The fault lines of cold war Europe were most visible in Germany. After the collapse of Adolf Hitler's Third Reich, the forces of the United States, the Soviet Union, Britain, and France occupied Germany and its capital, Berlin, both of which they divided up for administrative purposes. As cooperation between the United States and the Soviet Union broke down, the U.S., British, and French zones of

A Divided Germany

NIKITA KHRUSHCHEV ON THE CAPITALIST IRON CURTAIN

• • •

In early 1946 Winston Churchill (1874–1965) delivered his "Iron Curtain" speech, stirring audiences with its image of a Europe firmly and frighteningly divided between communist nations and marking, for some, the beginning of the cold war. Fifteen years after Churchill delivered his speech, Nikita Khrushchev (1894–1971) acknowledged the power of Churchill's imagery by using it in his own speech to the Communist Party Congress. In his 1961 "Report to the Communist Party Congress," Soviet premier Khrushchev blasted capitalism with the same force Churchill had employed in his earlier condemnation of communism.

Comrades! The competition of the two world social systems, the socialist and the capitalist, has been the chief content of the period since the 20th Party Congress [February 1956]. It has become the pivot, the foundation of world development at the present historical stage. Two lines, two historical trends, have manifested themselves more and more clearly in social development. One is the line of social progress, peace and constructive activity. The other is the line of reaction, oppression and war.

In the course of the peaceful competition of the two systems capitalism has suffered a profound moral defeat in the eyes of all peoples. The common people are daily convinced that capitalism is incapable of solving a single one of the urgent problems confronting mankind. It becomes more and more obvious that only on the paths to socialism can a solution to these problems be found. Faith in the capitalist system and the capitalist path of development is dwindling. Monopoly capital, losing its influence, resorts more and more to intimidating and suppressing the masses of the people, to methods of open dictatorship in carrying out its domestic policy and to aggressive acts against other countries. But the masses of the people offer increasing resistance to reaction's acts.

The ruling circles of some imperialist powers have elevated subversive activities against the socialist countries to the level of state policy. With cynical frankness, the United States of America is spending hundreds of millions of dollars on espionage and subversion against socialist countries and organizing so-called "guerilla units," assembling in them criminal elements and cutthroats prepared to undertake the vilest crimes for money. For several successive years the United States has been holding provocational "captive nations weeks." The hired agents of the monopolies call "captive" all those peoples who have liberated themselves from imperialist bondage and taken the path of free development. Truly, imperialist demagogy and hypocrisy know no bounds!

Our society is open to those people who come to us from abroad with open hearts. It is open to honest trade, to scientific, technical and cultural exchanges, to the exchange of truthful information. If it's an iron curtain we're talking about, where it really exists is in the world of capitalism, which, though dubbing itself the "free world," every now and then fearfully slams its gates shut to Soviet people, one moment to our cooks, the next to our chess players. There was a case where one state, which calls itself the "most open," was afraid to let in Soviet dancers. Can they really have feared that Russian folk dancing might shake the foundations of the capitalist world?!

We have long proposed to the capitalist world that we compete not in an arms race but in improving the working people's lives. We are confident that capitalism cannot stand up under that kind of competition! We are confident that in the end all peoples will make the correct choice, will give their preference to the truly free world of communism and turn their backs on the so-called "free world" of capitalism.

SOURCE: From Nikita Khrushchev, "Report to the Communist Party." From *Current Soviet Policies IV,* ed. Charlotte Saikowski and Leo Gruliow, from the translations of *The Current Digest of the Soviet Press.* 1962.

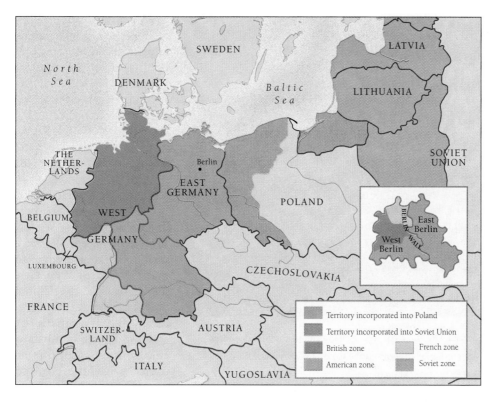

MAP [37.2]
Occupied Germany,
1945–1949.

occupation coalesced to form the Federal Republic of Germany (West Germany) in May 1949. In October the German Democratic Republic (East Germany) emerged out of the Soviet zone of occupation. A similar process repeated itself in Berlin, which was deep within the Soviet zone. The Soviet sector formed East Berlin and became the capital of the new East Germany. The remaining three sectors united to form West Berlin, and the West German capital moved to the small town of Bonn.

By 1961 the communist East German state was hemorrhaging from a steady drain of refugees who preferred life in capitalist West Germany. Between 1949 and 1961 nearly 3.5 million East Germans—many of them young and highly skilled—left their homeland, much to the embarrassment of East Germany's communist leaders. In August 1961 the communists reinforced their fortification along the border between East and West Germany, following the construction of a fortified wall dividing the city of Berlin. The wall, which began as a layer of barbed wire, quickly turned into a barrier several layers deep, replete with watch towers, search lights, antipersonnel mines, and border guards ordered to shoot to kill. Although the erection of the Berlin Wall was an obvious violation of four-power control in Germany, the United States and its British and French partners avoided a direct confrontation with the Soviet Union for fear that the crisis would escalate into a full shooting war. In subsequent years several thousand East Germans escaped to West Germany, often by ingenious means, but several hundred others paid with their lives for attempting to do so. Meanwhile, the Berlin Wall accomplished its purpose of stemming the flow of refugees, though at the cost of shaming a regime that obviously lacked legitimacy among its own people.

Barbed wire and a concrete wall in front of the Brandenburg

Gate in Berlin symbolized the Cold War division of Europe.

● Fritz Henle/Monkmeyer

A central feature of the cold war world was a costly arms race and the terrifying proliferation of nuclear weapons. The struggle between the United States and the Soviet Union led to the creation of two military blocs: the North Atlantic Treaty Organization or NATO (1949), intended to serve as a military counterweight to the Soviet forces in Europe, and the Warsaw Treaty Organization (1955), established as a response to the rearming of West Germany. Because the United States was determined to retain military superiority and the Soviet Union was equally determined to reach parity with the United States, both sides began to

The Nuclear Arms Race   amass enormous arsenals of thermonuclear weapons and develop a multitude of systems for deploying those weapons. It was not until the 1960s that the Soviet Union began to approach parity, and by the end of that decade both sides had achieved what Richard Nixon later called "essential equivalence" in their strategic forces. Thus by 1970 both superpowers had acquired the capacity for mutually assured destruction, or MAD. Yet the balance of terror restrained the contestants and stabilized their relationship, with two important exceptions.

Confrontations in Korea and Cuba

With the unforeseen outbreak of hostilities on the Korean peninsula in the summer of 1950, the focus of the cold war shifted from Europe to east Asia. At the end of World War II, the leaders of the Soviet Union and the United States had partitioned Korea along the thirty-eighth parallel of latitude into a northern Soviet zone and a southern U.S. zone. Because the superpowers were unable to agree on a framework for the reunification of the country, in 1948 they consented to the establishment of two separate Korean states: in the south, the Republic of Korea, with Seoul as its capital and the conservative anticommunist Syngman Rhee (1875–1965) as its president; in the north, the People's Democratic Republic of Korea, with Pyongyang as its capital and the revolutionary communist Kim Il Sung (1912–1995) as its leader. After arming their respective clients—each of which claimed sovereignty over the entire country—U.S. and Soviet troops withdrew.

The Korean War   On the early morning of 25 June 1950, the unstable political situation in Korea came to a head. Determined to unify Korea by force, the Pyongyang regime ordered more than one hundred thousand troops across the thirty-eighth parallel in a surprise attack, quickly pushing back South Korean defenders and capturing Seoul on 27 June. Convinced that the USSR had sanctioned the invasion, the U.S. government lost no time convincing the United Nations to adopt a resolution requesting all member states "to provide the Republic of South Korea with all necessary aid to repel the aggressors." Armed with a UN mandate and supported by token ground forces from twenty countries, the U.S. military went into action. Within two weeks U.S. forces had pushed North Koreans back to the thirty-eighth parallel, thereby fulfilling their mandate. However, sensing an opportunity to unify Korea under a pro-U.S. government, they pushed on into North Korea and within a few weeks had occupied Pyongyang. Subsequent U.S.

In August 1950 U.S. troops marched toward North Korea while South Koreans moved in the opposite direction to escape the fighting. • UPI/Corbis-Bettmann

advances toward the Yalu River on the Chinese border caused the government of the People's Republic of China to issue a warning: The U.S. incursion across the thirty-eighth parallel threatened Chinese national interests and could result in Chinese intervention in the Korean conflict.

When U.S. leaders gave no indication of heeding China's warning, some three hundred thousand Chinese soldiers surged across the Yalu River into North Korea. A combined force of Chinese and North Koreans pushed U.S. forces and their allies back into the south, and the war settled into a protracted stalemate near the original border at the thirty-eighth parallel. After two more years of desultory fighting that raised the number of deaths to three million people—mostly Korean civilians—both sides finally agreed to a cease-fire in July 1953. The failure to conclude a peace treaty ensured that the Korean peninsula would remain in a state of suspended strife that constantly threatened to engulf the region in a new round of hostilities. The war had also intensified the bitterness between north and south, making the prospect for a unified Korea even more remote.

Beyond the human casualties and physical damage it wrought, the Korean conflict also encouraged the globalization of containment. Viewing the North Korean offensive as part of a larger communist conspiracy to conquer the world, the U.S. government

The Globalization of Containment

began to extend military protection and economic aid to the noncommunist governments of Asia. It also entered into a number of security agreements that culminated in the creation of the Southeast Asian Treaty Organization (SEATO), an Asian counterpart of NATO. By 1954 U.S. president Dwight D. Eisenhower (1890–1969), who had contemplated using nuclear weapons in Korea, accepted the famous "domino theory." This strategic theory rationalized worldwide U.S. intervention on the assumption that if one country became communist, neighboring ones would collapse to communism the way a row of dominoes falls sequentially until none remain standing. Subsequent U.S. administrations therefore extended the policy of containment to areas beyond the nation's vital interests and applied it to local or imagined communist threats in Central and South America, Africa, and Asia.

Cuba: Nuclear Flashpoint   The Cuban missile crisis of 1962, which brought the superpowers to the brink of a nuclear exchange, dramatically underscored the risks inherent in extending the cold war throughout the world. The one region that had been entirely off-limits to Soviet influence was the western hemisphere, where U.S. dominance had long been undisputed. Ironically, the cold war confrontation that came closest to unleashing nuclear war took place not at the expected flashpoints in Europe or Asia but on the island of Cuba.

In 1959 a revolutionary movement headed by Fidel Castro Ruz (1926–) overthrew the autocratic Fulgencio Batista y Zaldivar (1901–1973), whose regime had gone to great lengths to maintain the country's traditionally subservient relationship with the United States and especially with the U.S. sugar companies that controlled Cuba's economy. Amid a flurry of rhetorical outbursts against Yankee imperialism, Castro reneged on promises of elections, expropriated foreign properties—most of which were U.S. owned—and killed or exiled thousands of political opponents. The U.S. government promptly retaliated by cutting off Cuban sugar imports to the U.S. market and imposing a severe export embargo of U.S. goods on Cuba.

The severing of ties between Cuba and the United States gave the Soviet Union an unprecedented opportunity to contest the dominant position of the United States in its own hemisphere. Castro's regime gladly accepted a Soviet offer of massive economic aid—including an agreement to purchase half of Cuba's sugar production—and arms shipments. Before long thousands of Soviet technicians, advisors, and diplomatic personnel had arrived in Cuba. In return for the Soviet largesse, Castro declared his support for the USSR's foreign policy. This he did loudly and dramatically on 26 September 1960. Clad in battle fatigues, he delivered a four-and-a-half-hour tirade to the UN General Assembly. In December 1961 he confirmed the U.S. government's worst suspicions when he publicly announced: "I have been a Marxist-Leninist all along, and will remain one until I die."

The Bay of Pigs   Cuba's alignment with the Soviet Union spurred the U.S. government to action. The newly elected President John F. Kennedy (1917–1963) authorized an invasion of Cuba to overthrow Castro and his supporters. In April 1961 a force of 1,500 anti-Castro Cubans—trained, armed, and transported by the Central Intelligence Agency (CIA)—landed on Cuba at a place called the Bay of Pigs. The arrival of the invasion force failed to incite a hoped-for internal uprising, and when the promised American air support failed to appear, the invasion quickly fizzled. Within three days Castro's military had either captured or killed the entire invasion force. The Bay of Pigs fiasco diminished U.S. prestige, especially in Latin America. It may also have encouraged the Soviets to deploy nuclear missiles in Cuba as a deterrent to any future invasion.

Prime Minister Fidel Castro of Cuba addresses a rally. • UPI/Corbis-Bettmann

The Cuban Missile Crisis

On 26 October 1962 the United States learned that Soviet technicians were assembling launch sites for medium-range nuclear missiles on Cuba. The Soviet government had apparently taken this bold step to protect the Castro government, give the USSR greater diplomatic leverage vis-à-vis the United States, undermine U.S. credibility in the region, and gain more influence in Latin America. Whatever the precise motives, the deployment of nuclear missiles that could reach targets in the United States within minutes represented an unacceptable threat to U.S. national security. Under pressure from Congress to deal with the Soviet menace, President Kennedy delivered a public ultimatum, calling on the Soviet leadership to withdraw all missiles from Cuba and stop the arrival of additional nuclear armaments. To back up his demand, Kennedy imposed an air and naval blockade on the island nation that went into effect two days later. The superpowers seemed poised for nuclear confrontation, and for two weeks the world's peoples held their collective breath.

After two weeks, finally realizing the imminent possibility of nuclear war, the Soviet government yielded to the U.S. demands. In return, Khrushchev extracted a pledge from Kennedy to refrain from attempting to overthrow Castro's regime. Despite this concession, it was obvious that the outcome of the Cuban missile crisis represented a major loss of face for the Soviet Union and a cold war victory for the United States. The U.S. secretary of state, Dean Rusk, supplied a pithy assessment of the crisis: "Eyeball to eyeball, they blinked first." The Cuban missile crisis revealed the dangers of the bipolar world, as the world trembled during this crisis, awaiting the apocalypse that potentially lurked behind any superpower confrontation.

The Cold War and Colonial Liberation

Potential nuclear annihilation was not the only danger inherent in the cold war. Superpower influence and interference also threatened the sovereignty of nations gaining their independence after World War II. The United States became the first of the imperial powers to grant independence to a colony after World War II.

The Philippines   The United States had promised to free the Philippines before the war, but that promise was delayed by the war. The United States fulfilled its pledge on 4 July 1946 but did not relinquish all its control and property in the islands. It maintained its strategic military bases at Subic Bay and Clark Field and used its influence to keep in power Filipino politicians who supported U.S. goals. It was no coincidence that a group like the communist-influenced Hukbalahap, famous for fighting both the Japanese and the Filipino landlords who had a stranglehold on land ownership, suffered severe repression in the early postindependence period.

Superpower   This continued exercise of U.S. influence in the Philippines, designed to main-
Influence   tain a noncommunist government friendly to the U.S. interests, suggests one way in which the cold war molded superpower relationships with new nations. Although the immediate postwar years found the superpowers focusing their attention on Europe, the cold war had become global by 1950 with the Chinese communist revolution in 1949 and the Korean War. The superpowers now perceived nations throughout the world as potential military, political, and economic allies. Communist China emerged as a leader in east Asia and demonstrated its status by its deep involvement in the Korean conflict. The Chinese provided the Soviets with a powerful friend, one capable of convincing other independence-seeking nations that it was a model for how to achieve freedom from imperial or colonial control.

While the United States stepped up its policy of containment, the Soviet Union encouraged new nations to reject involvement in the U.S. international system, equating the *Pax Americana* ("American Peace") with imperialism. Soviet leaders pointed to U.S. colonial rule over the Philippines and to U.S. political and economic dominance of numerous nominally independent states in Latin America and the Caribbean, such as Cuba, as examples of this imperialism. The Soviets supported revolutionary communist movements with economic or military aid and promised aid to new nations that agreed to remain neutral or nonaligned. In fact, nonalignment on the part of emerging nations often meant a sympathetic view toward the Soviet Union.

Nonalignment   Leaders of new African and Asian countries first discussed nonalignment at the Bandung Conference. In April 1955 leaders from twenty-three Asian and six African nations met in Bandung, Indonesia, partly to find a "third path," an alternative to choosing between the United States and the Soviet Union. Besides neutrality in the cold war, the Bandung Conference also stressed the struggle against colonialism and racism, and Indonesian president Achmad Sukarno (1901–1970) proudly proclaimed Bandung "the first international conference of coloured peoples in the history of mankind."

India's prime minister, Jawaharlal Nehru (1889–1964), became one of the most impassioned defenders of nonalignment. In a speech made after the Bandung Conference he articulated this point clearly:

> The preservation of peace forms the central aim of India's policy. It is in the pursuit of this policy that we have chosen the path of nonalinement [nonalignment] in any military or like pact of alliance. Nonalinement does not mean passivity of mind or action, lack of faith or conviction. It does not mean submission to what we consider evil. It is a positive and dynamic approach to such problems that confront us. We believe that each country

has not only the right to freedom but also to decide its own policy and way of life. Only thus can true freedom flourish and a people grow according to their own genius.

Bandung was the precursor of the broader Nonaligned Movement, which held occasional meetings so that its members could discuss matters of common interest, particularly their relations with the United States and the Soviet Union. The movement's primary goal was to maintain formal neutrality. However, the Nonaligned Movement suffered from a chronic lack of unity among its members and ultimately failed to present a genuinely united front. Although theoretically nonaligned with either cold war superpower, many member states actually had close ties to one or the other, and this situation caused dissension within the movement. For example, the Philippines and Cuba clearly supported the U.S. and Soviet camps, respectively. Nevertheless, other individual states did avoid becoming pawns in the cold war, and the new nations did succeed in declaring independence from the cold war by announcing the policy of nonalignment.

As the new nations struggled to avoid cold war politics, the superpowers maintained pressure on those nations to join with them. The global competition between the United States and Soviet Union intensified in the 1960s as the superpowers sought to win what U.S. president John F. Kennedy described as "the hearts and minds of the underdeveloped and uncommitted peoples of the world." The superpowers used both military and economic strategies to influence countries that were emerging from colonialism. By the early 1960s, for example, policy makers in Washington tried to extend U.S. influence to developing nations by means of foreign aid programs, which they labeled the Peace Corps and the Alliance for Progress. U.S. economic and technical assistance promoted economic development, and penniless nations and their leaders found such aid attractive. Soviet strategy also involved military, economic, and technical aid but focused on support for wars of national liberation and for established socialist or communist governments. The Soviet approach evoked a response that the U.S. government called counterinsurgency, meaning political and military tactics designed to counter guerrilla warfare. This policy was attractive to regimes that feared insurrection within their borders.

Hearts and Minds

The cold war prolonged western European and U.S. influence and power in developing countries. This outcome was especially true in areas where movements for national liberation or social reform seemed to threaten the perceived balance of power, prompting the U.S. government to prop up authoritarian elites. Superpower intrusions in the developing world also hindered the establishment of democratic political systems. Because local leaders and strongmen often relied on one or the other superpower for aid in building up military or police forces—both of which were all too often used against their own citizens—they had little incentive to accept opposition parties or come to terms with the demands of dissidents. Likewise, they had little incentive to compromise with rival or neighboring states, because each side could rely on the support of either the Soviet Union or the United States.

Despite the many complications posed by the cold war, colonial peoples in Asia and Africa struggled for their freedom—both from colonial rule and from U.S. and Soviet influence. The desire of nations to develop in an atmosphere of peace seemed reasonable, especially since independence itself often led to numerous problems. Independence did not long remain elusive for the nations of Asia, Africa, and Latin America, but peace often did.

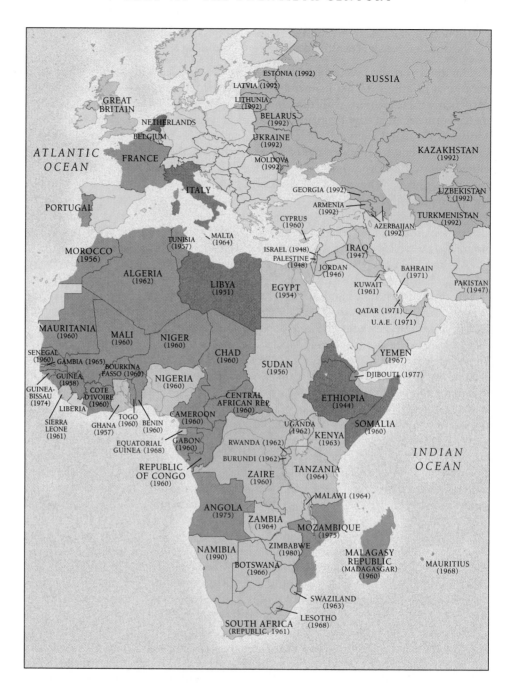

MAP [37.3]

Decolonization.

Cold War Societies

The global political arena after World War II resounded with clashes stemming from both the cold war and decolonization. The conflicts stemming from these dual forces naturally had repercussions in societies around the world. Postwar social transformations demonstrated how domestic policies and international affairs had often become linked, particularly as peoples living in disparate parts of the world discovered commonalities and differences, mutual sympathies and antipathies. Cold

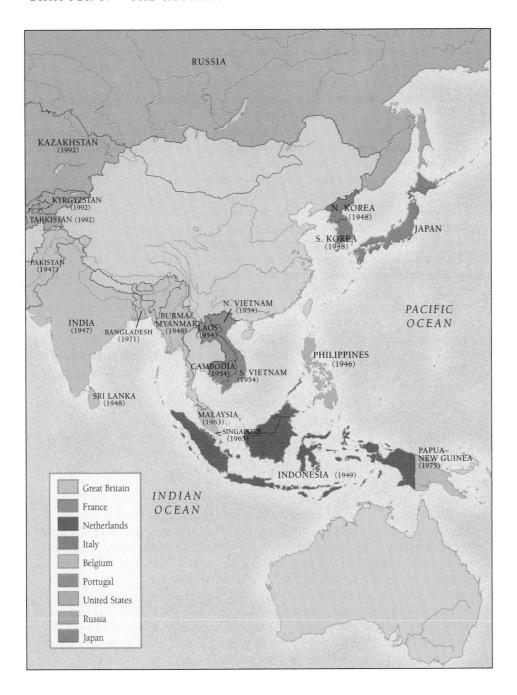

war competition for allies prodded the United States and the Soviet Union to commit their financial resources, military and diplomatic personnel, and goods and services to diverse countries, and those countries experienced firsthand encounters with superpower representatives. Representatives of the superpowers also came face to face with one another for the first time in the late 1950s, and those encounters suggested the extent to which Soviet and U.S. societies also transformed as a result of the cold war and decolonization.

*Domestic
Containment and
Female Liberation*

When Nikita Khrushchev and Richard Nixon squared off in the kitchen debate in Moscow, their argument underscored the importance of women and domesticity as a means of understanding the differences between their respective societies—and by extension, between all capitalist and communist societies. Citizens of the United States, like Nixon, celebrated the wondrous home appliances that made the lives of housewives and mothers so comfortable and that distinguished these U.S. women from their toiling Soviet counterparts. Clinging to the notion that U.S. women best served their families and their nation by staying home and rearing patriotic children, social and political leaders in the United States believed that families provided the best defense against communist infiltration in their nation. Women did not need to work, as they did in the Soviet Union, because their husbands earned enough to support the family in suburban splendor and because a mother's most important job was keeping the family happy and loyal.

Cold war concerns about the spread of communism reached into the domestic sphere, particularly in the United States. Politicians, F.B.I. agents, educators, and social commentators warned of communist spies trying to undermine the institutions of U.S. life, and Senator Joseph McCarthy (1909–1957) became infamous in the early 1950s for his unsuccessful quest to expose communists in the U.S. government. Supporting any radical or liberal cause, or behaving in any odd way, nonetheless subjected citizens of the United States to suspicions about their loyalty. Thousands of citizens—especially those who were or once had been members of the Communist Party—lost their jobs and reputations after being deemed risks to their nation's security. Conformity to a socially sanctioned way of life thus became the norm during the early, most frightening years of the cold war. Staying safely protected in family life meant avoiding suspicion and ignoring some of the more anxious elements of the cold war as waged by the United States—the atomic peril in particular. Some scholars have dubbed this U.S. retreat to the home and family "domestic containment," indicating its similarity to the U.S. foreign policy of the containment of international communism.

While the burden of domestic containment fell on all members of the family, women were most affected by its restraints. Married women in the United States actually worked in larger numbers during the cold war than during World War II, and many began to resent having to feel shame or guilt at not living up to the domestic ideals being showcased on the new and widely viewed television shows that sustained the U.S. public during the cold war. Not all women aspired to be June Cleaver on *Leave It to Beaver* (1957–1963 TV show), and female discontent with postwar domesticity in the United States helped to fuel the modern feminist movement. Aligning themselves to some extent with women in societies like the Soviet Union and taking inspiration from women in Asia and Africa who fought for their independence from the colonial powers—and often won legal equality as a result— U.S. women rejected cold war norms and agitated for their own equal rights.

Building on the dissatisfaction that had surfaced after World War II with their often forcible return to the home from war work, women in European and North American societies expressed a newfound understanding of their oppression at the hands of men. French writer Simone de Beauvoir (1908–1986) wrote *The Second Sex* in 1949, denouncing the second-class status of women. In 1963 U.S. author Betty Friedan (1921–) published *The Feminine Mystique,* laying bare the severe unhappiness of women who presumably enjoyed the best life the cold war United States could provide. Feminists provided just one signal that not all was well within the capitalist orbit, as African-Americans and university students around the world also contested elements of cold war life. When student radicals began to object to U.S. policies in Vietnam, for example, rioting and demonstrating from the mid-1960s to the early 1970s, it became clear that a consensus about cold war policies had broken down. Women activists started to adopt the very language and terms of both Marxism and anticolonialism in their own quest for equality and independence. They referred to women as an "oppressed class" and argued against male "colonization" of female bodies and for "women's liberation." Support for domestic containment, and containment itself, wavered.

Black Nationalism

A cross-fertilization between domestic and foreign policies, and between European, American, and decolonizing societies, took place throughout the early cold war years. This condition was particularly noticeable in regard to black nationalism, be it in the Caribbean, the United States, or the newly emerging states in Africa. The reggae music of Jamaican Bob Marley (1945–1981) spread throughout the world, rallying blacks to the cause. Marley's song, "Get Up Stand Up," although written as a form of resistance to persistent racism and poverty in Jamaica, nonetheless spoke to millions of blacks struggling for their freedom. In his song, Marley urged people to stand up for their rights and to continue fighting for them.

Africans and African-Americans alike had been influenced by the radical ideas of another black nationalist from Jamaica, Marcus Garvey (1887–1940), who advocated that U.S. blacks seek repatriation in Africa. Kwame Nkrumah (1909–1972), who later led Ghana to independence from colonial rule, familiarized himself with the works of Garvey while studying in the United States. Moderate civil rights leaders in the United States who distanced themselves from more radical forms of black nationalism, however, also adopted the ideas and strategies of other nationalist leaders fighting for independence from colonial rule. Dr. Martin Luther King, Jr. (1929–1968), the most prominent of these leaders, relied openly on the Indian leader Mohandas Gandhi's examples of passive nonresistance and boycotting in the struggle to win African-Americans their own equality and independence in the United States.

The Civil Rights Movement

The coinciding of the cold war with the modern civil rights movement in the United States once again shows the links between domestic and foreign policies. The Soviet Union could and did use the appalling conditions of African-Americans to expose the weaknesses of the capitalist system in the United States. In virtually every sphere of life, southern U.S. states institutionalized segregation, a system of laws and customs designed to separate blacks and whites. African-Americans had to contend not only with segregation but also with the loss of voting rights, widespread discrimination, and extra-legal violence. Discrimination was somewhat less pronounced in northern states, where African-Americans could usually vote, but informal segregation practices also influenced northern society. U.S. politicians and lawmakers recognized the adverse propaganda value of this institutionalized racism during the cold war. The U.S. Supreme Court in 1954 ruled segregation in the schools illegal in *Brown v. the Board of Education,* but it was direct action on the part of African-Americans—through the civil rights movement—that brought down segregation and impediments to voting.

The civil rights movement was first and foremost a challenge to segregation. In 1955, when Rosa Parks, an African-American woman living in Montgomery, Alabama, refused to give up her seat on a bus to a white man—as required by law—she accelerated a civil rights revolution that resulted in major advances for blacks in the United States. African-Americans in Montgomery refused to ride city buses until they were desegregated, and the Montgomery bus boycott—led by Martin Luther King—proved the effectiveness of Gandhi's methods. King went on to lead numerous marches and demonstrations and, despite the violence visited on him and his followers, to win major civil rights battles. Until his assassination in 1968, King clung to his dream of black equality in the United States, a nation pressured by both the cold war and African liberation movements to accede rights to its black population.

Cold War Consumerism

The United States fell short in cold war ideological battles in its treatment of African-Americans, but the Soviet Union had difficulty matching the United States and its allies in the provision of material wealth, leisure, and consumer goods. Like women and domesticity, consumerism also became one means of distinguishing communist and capitalist societies. This issue, too, gave bite to the kitchen debate between Nixon and Khrushchev. As the two squabbled over the significance of appliances, it seemed apparent that the Soviet Union and its satellites had achieved success with military and scientific endeavors, but had not provided their people with the stuff of dreams—automobiles, Hollywood movies, record albums, supermarkets, or month-long paid vacations. European and North American peoples had to suffer atomic anxiety and the insecurity of living in the cold war world, but the postwar economic prosperity that stemmed in part from waging the cold war helped relieve some of that pain.

The contrasting economic and social conditions of western and eastern Europe after World War II demonstrated the different lifestyles that emerged in Europe during the cold war. Western European nations experienced what many have termed an economic miracle, recovering swiftly from the war's devastation. Starting with an infusion of $13 billion from the U.S. Marshall Plan between 1948 and 1952, west European government leaders rebuilt their nations by encouraging economic growth and by providing social services that outpaced even the United States—including over time the guarantee of a thirty-day paid vacation. The increased standard of living and consumerism in western Europe was visible in the rapidly growing numbers of Europeans driving the automobiles they could now afford. In 1955 only five million people owned cars in western Europe. By 1963 that figure had jumped to forty-four million.

Peaceful Coexistence

In contrast, eastern European nations experienced less economic growth and enjoyed far fewer consumer items and far less leisure. After the war Stalin imposed Soviet economic planning on governments in east Europe and expected the peoples of both the Soviet Union and eastern Europe to conform to anticapitalist ideological requirements in their cultural productions. Rebellious artists and novelists found themselves silenced or denounced in an exaggerated and reversed form of the McCarthyism (anticommunist repression) that affected government workers, writers, and filmmakers in the United States in the same years. A relaxation of both economic and cultural dictates took place after Stalin's death in 1953 and during most of the years of Khrushchev's leadership in the Soviet Union. With respect to foreign policy, Khrushchev emphasized the possibility of "peaceful coexistence" between different social systems and the achievement of communism by peaceful means. This change in Soviet doctrine reflected the recognition that a nuclear war was more likely to lead to mutual annihilation than to victory. The peaceful coexistence that Khrushchev fostered with the United States appeared to apply to domestic Soviet and eastern European societies as well. There were limits to this Soviet liberalization, though, as Soviet troops cracked down on Hungarian rebels in 1956 and as Soviet novelist Boris Pasternak (1890–1960), author of *Dr. Zhivago,* was not allowed to pick up his Nobel Prize for literature in 1958.

The city of Berlin, divided east and west and deep within East Germany, showcased most stunningly the dual character of western and eastern European societies in the cold war. Between 1948 and 1949 the Soviets had blockaded the roads and railway links to West Berlin in an effort to rid East Germany of this capitalist outpost. The United States and its allies coordinated the Berlin airlift, by which two million West Berliners were provided by air with some of the very consumer items that separated eastern and western Europe: massive food supplies and clothing, enough to make it through the year. The airlift broke the blockade, and West Berlin remained an alluring symbol of the material wealth offered by capitalism.

When in 1961 Nikita Khrushchev approved and East German leaders master-minded the building of the Berlin Wall as a way to halt the outflow of East Germans, Berlin transformed even more clearly into a physical representation of the divisive cold war and its divergent economic and social systems. At the same time, Berlin became the setting for a new genre of fiction that encapsulated other battles waged in the cold war: spy novels. British novels like John Le Carré's *The Spy Who Came in from the Cold* (1963), an international bestseller, invested the wall-divided Berlin with glamour as the preeminent locale for daring adventures of espionage. John Le Carré (1931–), though, also suggested the less glorious ways in which capitalist and communist countries had come to resemble one another—despite their professed ideological differences. By engaging in spying and by allowing their agents to be used and sacrificed for the cause, both sides had forsaken their morality.

Societies in the Soviet Union and the United States may have resembled one another in some ways—in their spying, in their pursuit of nuclear superiority, and in their quest for cold war supremacy—but they also resembled one another in their basic humanity: a fact that may have prevented the ultimate tipping of the balance of terror. A few weeks after the famous kitchen debate, Khrushchev visited the United States and became the first Soviet leader to step foot on U.S. soil. Despite some tense moments, Khrushchev's tour of the United States contributed to a thaw in the cold war, however brief. In his September 1959 travels, which included stops in New York, California, and Iowa, he showed himself to be not only a formidable leader but also a warm and witty man. Television coverage of his trip allowed millions in the United States to see the previously perceived demonic Soviet premier as a human being—understanding his disappointment at not getting to see Disneyland because of security concerns, watching him talk with U.S. farmers, and listening as he thanked his U.S. hosts upon his departure for their hospitality. This one encounter between a Soviet leader and a U.S. audience suggested the ever-shifting possibilities for peace even in the perilous cold war world. The search for peace and security in a bipolar world revamped societies in the Euro-American world and beyond, as that elusive peace involved not only the superpowers and their allies but also the nations seeking their independence from colonial rule.

INDEPENDENCE IN SOUTH, SOUTHWEST, AND SOUTHEAST ASIA

In the wake of World War II, the power of Asian nationalism proved to be irrepressible. New nations emerged throughout Asia, from India and Pakistan in south Asia to diverse Arab nations in southwest Asia and to Vietnam, Cambodia, and Laos in southeast Asia. These lands encountered different conditions in their quests for independence and freedom from imperial control, but everywhere Asian nationalists rallied their people against colonialism and imperialism. Whether fighting against colonial powers that had established formal political and territorial control or against imperial powers, which often exercised a more informal and indirect control, Asians were successful. The result of their efforts, measured in years or decades, was independence and the end of empire in Asia.

India's "Vivisection": Partitioned Independence

In the 1930s Great Britain had granted numerous reforms in response to the tireless campaign of Mohandas Gandhi and the Congress Party. World War II, however, interrupted the gradual trend toward Indian self-rule.

The Coming of Self-Rule   Under the leadership of Winston Churchill, who despised Gandhi and vowed never "to preside over the liquidation of the British empire," measures for home rule were suspended, and India was ordered to support the war effort. British recalcitrance about Indian independence evaporated after the war, however. The British people voted Churchill out of office. His conservative government was replaced with a Labour government more inclined to dismantle the empire. The economic devastation of the war made it unrealistic for Britain to continue bearing the financial burden of empire in India.

The troublesome issue of Muslim separatism grew in importance as the probability of Indian independence became more pronounced, and Muslims increasingly feared their minority status in a free India dominated by Hindus. Muhammad Ali Jinnah (1876–1948), leader of the Muslim League, felt no qualms about fanning such fears, even as Congress Party leaders like Nehru and Gandhi urged all Indians to act and feel as one nation, undivided by what came to be known as communalism—emphasizing religious over national identity. In August 1946, in the midst of negotiations with the British to reach terms regarding independence, the Muslim League called for a Day of

Jawaharlal Nehru (left) and Mohandas K. Gandhi, Hindu leaders of India's independence movement.

• UPI/Corbis-Bettmann

Direct Action, even though the league's leaders knew that Muslim demonstrations would lead to rioting and fighting between Muslims and Hindus. Some six thousand people died in the Great Calcutta Killing that resulted, further fueling communal feeling and adding weight to Jinnah's threat: "The only solution to India's problem is Pakistan."

The idea of partition, the division of India into separate Hindu and Muslim states, violated the most cherished ideals of men like Gandhi and Nehru, who sickened at the prospect and only reluctantly came to accept the notion of a divided but independent India. Gandhi condemned the division of his homeland as "vivisection," using a term that refers to the cutting up of a living body. He avoided the celebrations on 15 August 1947 that accompanied independence for India and Pakistan, glumly prophesying that "rivers of blood" would flow in the wake of partition. His vision came true as the terms of partition were announced and hundreds of thousands of Muslim and Hindu refugees migrated either to Muslim Pakistan (itself divided between parts of Bengal in the east and Punjab in the west) or Hindu India. By mid-1948 an estimated ten million refugees had made the tortuous journey to one or the other state, and between half a million and one million had died in the violence that accompanied those massive human migrations. Gandhi had undertaken a number of measures, including hunger strikes, in the hope of quelling the violence between Muslims and Hindus; he continually urged all Indians and Pakistanis to adhere to the practice of nonviolence. On 30 January 1948 Gandhi became a martyr to his own cause, killed by the violence he so abhorred, when a Hindu extremist shot him.

Partition and Violence

Upon Gandhi's death Nehru announced, "The light has gone out of our lives and there is darkness everywhere." This sentiment expressed the void left by Gandhi's assassination, but efforts to build up the now separate and independent nations of India and Pakistan continued. The continued hostility between migrating Hindus and Muslims spilled over into the enmity between the two states, complicating efforts to build their independent nations. War had already broken out in 1947 over the province of Kashmir, which was claimed by both states, and their continuing hostility made India and Pakistan vulnerable to the pressures of the cold war. When Pakistan lost the battle over Kashmir, it sought an alliance with the United States to strengthen its position. And while Nehru favored a policy of nonalignment, India accepted military aid from the Soviet Union. Partition gave the superpowers a tenuous foothold in South Asia, given Nehru's successful neutrality and his ability to garner economic and military aid from both superpowers.

Conflict between India and Pakistan

Though mired in violence, Indian independence had become a reality with momentous consequences for the entire process of decolonization. India had been the jewel in the crown of the British empire, and its breakaway marked a significant turning point. Just as Gandhi's nonviolent resistance to British rule inspired nationalists around the globe before and after World War II, independence in India and Pakistan further encouraged anti-imperial movements throughout Asia and Africa. Moreover, once India left the British empire, there could be little doubt about the fate of Britain's remaining imperial possessions.

Unlike the Dutch and the French, who at times tenaciously battled to maintain imperial control in Asia, the British recognized that Europeans could not rule in Asia without the cooperation of colonial peoples. Also unlike the Dutch and the French, the British could rely on their own models of decolonization, previously tested in Canada. Like Canada, India and Pakistan gained independence yet retained ties to Britain, becoming Dominion members in the British Commonwealth and even adopting English as their first official language.

Arab National States and the Problem of Palestine

With the exception of Palestine, the Arab states of southwest Asia had little difficulty freeing themselves from the colonial powers of France and Britain by the end of World War II. Even before the war Arab states had agitated for concessions under the mandate system, which had limited Arab nationalist aspirations after the Great War. In fact, Egypt had almost complete autonomy from British rule—an autonomy limited by British military control of the strategic Suez Canal and the oil-rich Persian Gulf.

Arab Independence   After the war, although Syria, Iraq, Lebanon, and Jordan gained complete independence, significant vestiges of imperial rule impeded Arab sovereignty. The battle to rid southwest Asia of these remnants of imperialism took some twists and turns as the superpowers interfered in the region, drawn by its incredible reserves of oil—the lifeblood of the cold war's military-industrial complexes. Throughout, one ambiguous legacy of imperialism—Palestine—absorbed much of the region's energies and emotions.

Palestine   Great Britain served as the mandate power in Palestine after the Great War, and both before and during its mandate it made conflicting promises to the Palestinian Arabs and to the Jews who were migrating to Palestine to establish a secure homeland where they could avoid persecution. With the Balfour Declaration of 1917, the British government committed itself to the support of a homeland for Jews in Palestine, a commitment engendered at least in part by the vibrant Zionist movement that had been growing in Europe since the 1890s. Zionists were dedicated to combating the violent anti-Semitism prevailing in central and eastern Europe by establishing a national Jewish state. The Zionist dream of returning to Palestine, considered the site of the original Jewish homeland, received a boost from the Balfour Declaration and from the Allies' support for it at the Paris Peace Conference (1919). Thus the British were compelled to allow Jewish migration to Palestine under their mandate, but, they also had to allay the fears of those already in possession of the land—the Palestinian Arabs. The British therefore limited the migration and settlement of Jews and promised to protect the Arabs' political and economic rights.

This British attempt to balance the causes of two conflicting groups was unsuccessful, and large-scale violence was prevented only through the use of imperial military forces. To this day the dilemma of how to reconcile the claims of two people who have become staunch foes remains unresolved. Arab Palestinians rejected both British rule and Jewish settlement, seeing both as links in an imperial chain of control. The Jews migrating to Palestine tended to be of European descent, and they threatened Arab interests when they purchased land and established communal farms or *kibbutzim*. The conflict between Arabs and Jews also had a religious dimension, since the Palestinian Muslims perceived the Jews as alien interlopers in their own holy land. In the 1920s and 1930s, Arab resentment against the British and the Jews exploded in anti-Jewish riots and demonstrations. At the same time, European Jews were dangerously under attack. Under the pressure of Nazi persecution, Jews migrated to Palestine in increasing numbers in the 1930s, and Zionists in Palestine began to arm themselves to protect Jewish settlers against Arab reprisals. These conditions exacerbated the already tense situation in Palestine.

At the end of World War II, a battle brewed. As Arab states around Palestine gained their freedom from imperial rule, they developed a pan-Arab nationalism sparked by support for their fellow Arabs in Palestine and opposition to the possibility of a Jewish state there. The Holocaust, along with the British policy of limiting Jewish migration to Palestine after the war, intensified the Jewish commitment to build a state capable of defending the world's remaining Jews—and the tens of thousands of Palestinian Jews who had fought in the British army during the war were seen as potential defenders of the new state.

The Creation of Israel

The British could not adjudicate the competing claims of the Arabs and Jews in Palestine. While the Arabs insisted on complete independence under Arab rule, in 1945 the Jews embarked on a course of violent resistance to the British to compel recognition of Jewish demands for self-rule and open immigration. In effect, the British gave up in 1947, stating that they intended to withdraw from Palestine and turn over the region to the newly created United Nations. Delegates to the UN General Assembly debated the idea of dividing Palestine into two states, one Arab and the other Jewish. Both the United States and the Soviet Union lent their support to this notion, and in November 1947 the General Assembly announced a proposal for the division of Palestine into two distinct states. Arabs both inside and outside Palestine found this solution unacceptable, and in late 1947 civil war broke out. Arab and Jewish troops battled one another as the British completed their withdrawal from Palestine, and in May 1948 the Jews in Palestine proclaimed the creation of the independent state of Israel. This act provoked what turned out to be the first of many Arab-Israeli wars as Egypt, Jordan, Syria, and Iraq declared war on Israel in support of the Palestinian Arabs.

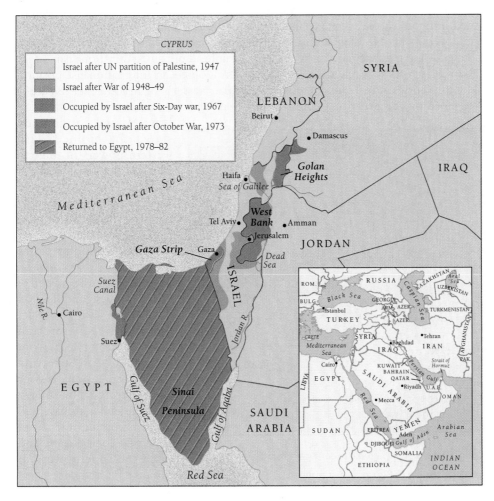

MAP [37.4]
The Arab-Israeli conflict, 1949–1982.

The Arab states, expecting a swift and triumphant victory over the outnumbered Jewish forces, had underestimated the staying power and military skills of the new Israeli military. Arab attacks and campaigns, although boldly fought, were uncoordinated, and the Israelis managed to achieve a stunning victory, gaining territories far larger than those that would have been granted to the Jewish state under the United Nations partition plan. A truce went into effect in early 1949 under UN auspices, and the partition of Palestine resulted. Jerusalem and the Jordan River Valley were divided between the new Israeli state and the Kingdom of Jordan, while Israel controlled the coastal areas of Palestine and the Negev Desert to the Red Sea. During and after the fighting, hundreds of thousands of Palestinian Arabs had fled, first from the war and then from the prospect of life under Jewish political control, and for the surrounding Arab states these refugees served as a symbol of the Arabs' defeat in Palestine and as a spur to the Arab nations' determination to rid their region of the hated presence of Israel.

Egypt and Arab Nationalism

Egyptian military leaders, particularly officers under the leadership of Gamal Abdel Nasser (1918–1970), committed themselves to opposing Israel and taking command of the Arab world. Forsaking constitutional government and democratic principles, they began a political revolution and campaign of state reform through militarism, suppressing the ideological and religious opposition organized by communists and the Muslim Brotherhood. In July 1952 Nasser and other officers staged a bloodless coup that ended the monarchy of King Farouk. After a series of complicated intrigues, Nasser named himself prime minister in 1954 and took control of the government. He then began to labor assiduously to develop Egypt both economically and militarily and make it the fountainhead of pan-Arab nationalism.

In his efforts to strengthen Egypt, Nasser adopted an internationalist position akin to Nehru's nonalignment policy in India. Nasser's neutralism, like Nehru's, was based on the belief that cold war power politics were a new form of imperialism. Nasser condemned states that joined with western powers in military alliances, such as the Baghdad Pact, a British and U.S.–inspired alliance that included Turkey, Iraq, and Iran. Nevertheless, he saw in the new bipolar world opportunities that could be exploited for the advancement of Egypt, and he used his political savvy to extract pledges of economic and military assistance from both the United States and the Soviet Union. Nasser demonstrated how newly independent nations could evade becoming trapped in either ideological camp and force the superpowers to compete for influence.

Gamal Abdel Nasser was president of Egypt from 1954 until his death in 1970. • UPI/Corbis-Bettmann

Nasser also dedicated himself to ridding Egypt and the Arab world of imperial interference, which included destroying the state of Israel—and to this end he gave aid to the Algerians in their war against the French. Nasser did not neglect the remaining imperial presence in his own land: he abolished British military rights to the Suez Canal in 1954. Through such actions, and through his country's antipathy toward Israel, he laid claim to pan-Arab leadership throughout southwest Asia and north Africa.

The Suez Crisis

Nasser sealed his reputation during the Suez crisis, which left him in a dominant position in the Arab world. The crisis erupted in 1956, when Nasser decided to nationalize the Suez Canal and use the money collected from the canal to finance construction of a massive dam of the Nile River at Aswan. When he did not bow to international pressure to provide multinational control for the vital Suez Canal, British, French, and Israeli forces combined to wrest control of the canal away from him. Their military campaign was successful, but they failed miserably on the diplomatic level and tore at the very fabric of the bipolar world system. They had not consulted with the United States, which strongly condemned the attack and forced them to withdraw. The Soviet Union also objected forcefully, thereby gaining a reputation for being a staunch supporter of Arab nationalism. Nasser gained tremendous prestige, and Egypt solidified its position as leader of the charge against imperial holdovers in southwest Asia and north Africa.

Despite Nasser's successes, he did not manage to rid the region of Israel, which was growing stronger with each passing year. More wars would be fought in the decades to come, and peace between the Arab states and Israel seemed not only elusive but at times impossible. While the partition that took place in Palestine appeared to lend itself to manipulation by the superpowers, the region of southwest Asia actually confused, complicated, and undermined elements of bipolarism. The strategic importance of oil dictated that both superpowers would vie for favor in the Arab states, and while the United States became a firm ally of Israel, the Soviet Union also supported Israel's right to exist. The Suez crisis further tangled cold war power politics, since it divided the United States and its allies in western Europe. Southwest Asia, then, proved successful not only at ousting almost all imperial control but also at challenging the bipolar world view.

Nationalist Struggles in Vietnam

Vietnam later became deeply enmeshed in the cold war contest between capitalism and communism, but immediately after World War II it engaged in a struggle to free itself from French colonial control. Vietnam's nationalist communist leader, Ho Chi Minh (1890–1969), had exploited wartime conditions to advance the cause of Vietnamese independence.

After the Japanese conquest of Vietnam, which effectively ended French rule, Ho helped oust the Japanese from Vietnam in the waning days of World War II. He then issued the Vietnamese Declaration of Independence, which was modeled on the U.S. declaration. However, the French, humiliated by their country's easy defeat and occupation by the Nazis, sought to reclaim their world power status and reclaim their imperial possessions.

Fighting the French

Armed with British and U.S. weapons, the French recaptured Saigon and much of southern Vietnam in 1945. Faced with the hostility of the northern nationalist communists, organized as the Viet Minh, the French had to retake the north brutally, bombing Hanoi and Haiphong and killing at least ten thousand civilians. By

Ho Chi Minh, leader of North Vietnam (1945–1969) and one of southeast Asia's most influential communist leaders. • Baldwin H. Ward/Corbis-Bettmann

1947 the French appeared to have secured their power, especially in the cities, but that security proved to be temporary. Much like the Chinese communists in their battles against the Japanese and then against the nationalists in the postwar years, the Vietnamese resistance forces, led by Ho Chi Minh and General Vo Nguyen Giap (1912–), took to the countryside and mounted a campaign of guerrilla warfare. The Vietnamese communists grew increasingly influential in the anti-imperial war, especially after 1949 when communist China sent aid and arms to the Viet Minh. Thus strengthened, they defeated the French at their fortress in Dienbienphu in 1954. The French had to sue for peace at the conference table.

The peace conference, held in Geneva in 1954, determined that Vietnam should be temporarily divided at the seventeenth parallel; North Vietnam

The Geneva Conference and Partial Independence

would be controlled by Ho Chi Minh and the communist forces while South Vietnam remained in the hands of noncommunists. The communist affiliation of Ho and his comrades, along with the globalization of the cold war that accompanied the Korean War, had convinced the United States to lend its support first to the French war effort and then to the government of South Vietnam. U.S. president Dwight Eisenhower applied the domino theory to Vietnam. Violating the terms of the Geneva Agreements, which required elections that would likely have brought Ho to power, South Vietnam's leaders, with U.S. support, avoided elections and instead sought to build a government that would prevent the spread of communism in South Vietnam and elsewhere in Asia. Ngo Dinh Diem (1901–1963), the first president of the Republic of (South) Vietnam, and other South Vietnamese leaders did not garner popular support with the people, however, and growing discontent sparked the spread of guerrilla war in the south.

In 1960 Vietnamese nationalists formed the National Liberation Front (NLF) to fight for freedom from South Vietnamese rule. While Vietnamese from the south made up the majority in this organization, it received direction, aid, weapons, and ultimately troops from the north as well. In turn, the government in the north received economic and military assistance from the Soviet Union and China, and a cold war stalemate ensued.

Cold War Stalemate   Given the lack of popular support for Diem, or for U.S.-style democratic reforms, the nationalist communist attacks against the South Vietnamese government met with continued success. In 1965 President Lyndon Johnson (1908–1973) embarked on a course of action that exponentially increased U.S. involvement in Vietnam. He ordered a bombing campaign against North Vietnam and sent U.S. ground troops to augment the South Vietnamese army. Yet even with the massive firepower and military personnel (reaching more than half a million by 1968), the best the United States and South Vietnam could achieve against the Viet Cong (a name derisively applied to South Vietnamese communists) was a draw. North Vietnam found a stalemate quite acceptable. Vietnamese forces fought for freedom from outside interference of any sort and could show patience while making progress toward independence. They were trapping U.S. troops in a quagmire and a war of attrition typical of successful guerrilla operations against powerful foes. Still, the nationalists' aspirations were thwarted and a long struggle remained. The stalemate in Vietnam dragged on, demonstrating the perils of cold war politics in the age of decolonization—for democrats and communists, for small nations and superpowers.

DECOLONIZATION IN AFRICA

In the 1950s the superpowers' influence intensified. For African lands this situation often meant delays in decolonization. Also complicating the decolonization process were internal divisions in African societies, which undermined attempts to forge national or pan-African identities. Tribal, ethnic, religious, and linguistic divides within and between state boundaries, all of which colonial rulers had exploited, posed a challenge to African leaders, particularly once independence came and the imperial enemy departed. Given the variety of barriers to African independence, from imperial resistance and the cold war to internal tribal conflicts, it should not be surprising that independence came more slowly in Africa than in other regions of the world.

Forcing the French out of North Africa

In Africa as in southeast Asia, the French resisted decolonization. In Algeria the French fought a bloody war that began in 1954, the very year France suffered its defeat at Dienbienphu. Somewhat ironically, while it focused its efforts on Algeria in the 1950s and 1960s, France allowed all of its other territories in Africa to gain independence. In 1956 France granted independence to its colonies in Morocco and Tunisia, and thirteen French colonies in west and equatorial Africa won their independence in 1960, a year that came to be known as "the year of Africa."

France's concessions to its other African colonies illustrated its determination to control Algeria at all costs. The French people expressed differing opinions on the Algerian conflict, being less determined than their government leaders. French settlers demanded that government in Paris defend their cause in north Africa. Some two million French had settled or had been born there by the mid-1940s. The end of World War II, however, marked the beginning of a revitalized nationalist movement in Algeria, fueled by desire for independence from France and freedom from domination by white settlers. The event that touched off the Algerian revolt came in May 1945. French colonial police in the town of Sétif fired shots into an otherwise peaceful demonstration in support of Algerian and Arab nationalism. Algerian rioting and French repression of the disturbances took place in the wake of the incident. In the resulting melee more than eight thousand Algerian Muslims died, along with approximately one hundred French.

France in Africa

The Algerian war of liberation began in 1954 under the command of the Front de Libération Nationale (National Liberation Front, or FLN). The FLN adopted tactics similar to those of nationalist liberation groups in Asia, relying on bases in outlying mountainous areas and resorting to guerrilla warfare. The French did not realize the seriousness of the challenge they faced until 1955, when the FLN moved into more urbanized areas. In an attack on the town of Constantine, the FLN killed

War in Algeria

French paratroopers search for terrorists near Algiers, January 1957.   •   UPI/Corbis-Bettmann

dozens of French settlers. France sent thousands of troops to Algeria to put down the revolution, and by 1958 it had committed half a million soldiers to the war. The war became ugly: Algerians serving with the French had to kill fellow Algerians or be killed by them; Algerian civilians became trapped in the crossfire of war, often accused of and killed for aiding FLN guerrillas; thousands of French soldiers died. By the war's end in 1962, when the Algerians gained independence from France, hundreds of thousands of Algerians had lost their lives.

Frantz Fanon   One ideological legacy for Africa stemmed from Algeria's war of independence. Frantz Fanon (1925–1961) gained fame as an Algerian revolutionary and as an influential proponent of national liberation for colonial peoples through violent revolution. Born in Martinique in the West Indies, Fanon studied psychiatry and medicine in France, went to Algeria to head a hospital's psychiatric department, and then participated in Algeria's battle to free itself from French rule. Fanon furthered his fame and provided ideological support for African nationalism and revolution in his writings. In works like *The Wretched of the Earth* (1961), he urged the use of violence against colonial oppressors as a means of overcoming the racist degradation experienced by peoples in developing or colonial nations outside the Soviet-U.S. sphere. Fanon died just before Algerians achieved independence, but his ideas influenced the independence struggles ongoing in Africa.

Black African Nationalism and Independence

Before and during World War II, nationalism flourished in sub-Saharan Africa. African nationalists celebrated their blackness and Africanness in contrast to their European colonial rulers. Drawing from the pan-African movements that emerged in the United States and the Caribbean, African intellectuals, especially in French-controlled west Africa, established a movement to promote *Négritude* ("Blackness"). Reviving Africa's great traditions and cultures, poets and writers expressed a widely shared pride in Africa.

This celebration of African culture was accompanied by grassroots protests against European imperialism. A new urban African elite slowly began creating the sorts of associations needed to hold demonstrations and fight for independence. Especially widespread, if sporadic, were workers' strikes against oppressive labor practices and the low wages paid by colonial overlords in areas like the Gold Coast and Northern Rhodesia. Some independent Christian churches also provided avenues for anticolonial agitation, as prophets like Simon Kimbangu in the Belgian Congo promised his churchgoers that God would deliver them from imperial control.

Growth of African Nationalism

In the years after World War II, African poets associated with the *Négritude* movement continued to express their attachment to Africanness and encourage Africans to turn away from European culture and colonial rule. Bernard Dadié's poem, "Dry Your Tears, Africa!" illustrated these sentiments:

> Dry your tears, Africa!
> Your children come back to you
> Out of the storms and squalls of fruitless journeys. . . .
>
> Over the gold of the east
> and the purple of the setting sun,
> the peaks of proud mountains
> and the grasslands drenched with light
> They return to you. . . .
>
> And our senses are now opened
> to the splendour of your beauty
> to the smell of your forests
> to the charms of your waters
> to the clearness of your skies
> to the caress of your sun. . . .

The dreams and hopes of African nationalists often had to be placed on hold in the early years after World War II. Often assuming that black Africans were incapable of self-government, imperial powers planned for a slow transition to independence. The presence of white settlers in certain African colonies also complicated the process of decolonization. The politics of the cold war allowed imperial powers to justify oppressive actions in the name of rooting out a subversive communist presence. Despite the delays, however, sub-Saharan states slowly but surely won their independence as each newly independent nation inspired and often aided other lands to win their freedom.

African Independence

Agitation for independence in sub-Saharan Africa took on many forms, both peaceful and violent, and decolonization occurred at a different pace in different nations. Ghana became independent in 1957, but independence came much later to Angola (1975) and Zimbabwe, formerly Southern Rhodesia (1980). Freedom's aftermath often showcased the sorts of divisions and problems that tempered the joy of decolonization. The outbreak of civil war (as in Rwanda, Burundi, and Angola), economic instability, and political and ethnic divisiveness hampered postindependence nation building, but sub-Saharan African states had nonetheless made the break from empire. African nations in many instances symbolized and sealed their severance from imperial control by adopting new names that shunned the memory of European rule and instead drew from the glory of Africa's past empires. Ghana set the pattern, and the map of Africa soon featured similar references to precolonial

African places: Zambia, Malawi, Zimbabwe. As Dadié had predicted, Africans had opened their political senses to the splendor of Africa—past and present.

Freedom and Conflict in Sub-Saharan Africa

Ghana's success in achieving its freedom from British rule in 1957 served as a hallmark in Africa's end of empire. Under the leadership of Kwame Nkrumah, political parties and strategies for mass action took shape. Although the British subjected Nkrumah and other nationalists to jail terms and repressive control, gradually they allowed reforms and negotiated the transfer of power in their Gold Coast colony.

Ghana   After it became independent in 1957, Ghana emboldened and inspired other African nationalist movements. Nkrumah, as a leader of the first sub-Saharan African nation to gain independence from colonial rule, became a persuasive spokesperson for pan-African unity. His ideas, and his stature as an African leader, symbolized the changing times in Africa. In preparation for the 1961 visit of Britain's Queen Elizabeth II (1926–), the people of Ghana erected huge side-by-side posters of the queen and their own leader Nkrumah. These roadside portraits offered a stunning vision of newfound equality and distinctiveness. Ex-colonial rulers, dressed in royal regalia, faced off against new African leaders clothed in traditional African fabrics, the once-dominating white faces matched by the proud black faces.

Kenya and Mau Mau   The process of attaining independence did not always prove as nonviolent as in Ghana. The battle that took place in the British colony of Kenya in east Africa suggests the complexity and difficulty of African decolonization. The situation in Kenya turned tense and violent in a clash between powerful white settlers and nationalists, especially the Kikuyu, one of Kenya's largest ethnic groups. In 1952 a secret Kikuyu society known as Mau Mau embarked on a violent campaign against Europeans and

Roadside portraits of Kwame Nkrumah and Queen Elizabeth II in Accra. The British monarch made a postindependence visit to Ghana in November 1961. • London Daily Express/Archive Photos

KWAME NKRUMAH ON AFRICAN UNITY

• • •

As the leader of the first African nation to gain independence, Kwame Nkrumah (1909–1972) became a respected spokesperson for African unity as a strategy for dealing with decolonization during the cold war. In his book I Speak of Freedom: A Statement of African Ideology *(1961), Nkrumah made an eloquent case for an African solution for the problems of African independence during a global cold war.*

It is clear that we must find an African solution to our problems, and that this can only be found in African unity. Divided we are weak; united, Africa could become one of the greatest forces for good in the world.

Never before have a people had within their grasp so great an opportunity for developing a continent endowed with so much wealth. Individually, the independent states of Africa, some of them potentially rich, others poor, can do little for their people. Together, by mutual help, they can achieve much. But the economic development of the continent must be planned and pursued as a whole. A loose confederation designed only for economic cooperation would not provide the necessary unity of purpose. Only a strong political union can bring about full and effective development of our natural resources for the benefit of our people.

The political situation in Africa today is heartening and at the same time disturbing. It is heartening to see so many new flags hoisted in place of the old; it is disturbing to see so many countries of varying sizes and at different levels of development, weak and, in some cases, almost helpless. If this terrible state of fragmentation is allowed to continue it may well be disastrous for us all.

Critics of African unity often refer to the wide differences in culture, language and ideas in various parts of Africa. This is true, but the essential fact remains that we are all Africans, and have a common interest in the independence of Africa. The difficulties presented by questions of language, culture and different political systems are not insuperable. If the need for political union is agreed by us all, then the will to create it is born; and where there's a will there's a way.

The greatest contribution that Africa can make to the peace of the world is to avoid all the dangers inherent in disunity, by creating a political union which will also by its success, stand as an example to a divided world. A union of African states will project more effectively the African personality. It will command respect from a world that has regard only for size and influence.

We have to prove that greatness is not to be measured in stock piles of atom bombs. I believe strongly and sincerely that with the deep-rooted wisdom and dignity, the innate respect for human lives, the intense humanity that is our heritage, the African race, united under one federal government, will emerge not as just another world bloc to flaunt its wealth and strength, but a Great Power whose greatness is indestructible because it is not built on fear, envy and suspicion, nor won at the expense of others, but founded on hope, trust, friendship and directed to the good of all mankind.

SOURCE: From Kwame Nkrumah, *I Speak of Freedom: A Statement of African Ideology.* New York: Frederick A. Praeger, 1961, x–xii.

alleged traitorous Africans. The settlers controlled the colonial government in Nairobi and refused to see the Mau Mau uprising as a legitimate expression of discontent with colonial rule. Rather, they branded the Kikuyu tribes as radicals bent on a racial struggle for primacy. As one settler put it, "Why the hell can't we fight these apes and worry about the survivors later?" The British government declared a state of emergency in Kenya in 1952 and labeled the Mau Mau as subversives or communists—thereby allowing the British to fight against the red menace, not nationalism, and thus maintain the support of the United States.

Mau Mau suspects in a British internment camp, Nairobi, Kenya.

● Hulton Getty/Liaison

In reality, Mau Mau radicalism and violence had much more to do with nationalist opposition to British land policy and political control in Kenya. The opposition to the British stemmed from their treatment in the 1930s and 1940s, when white settlers pushed the Kikuyu off the most fertile highland farm areas and reduced them to the status of wage slaves, marginal farmers in infertile land areas, or urban refugees in Nairobi. Resistance began in the early 1940s with labor strikes and violent direct action campaigns designed to force or frighten the white settlers off their lands and out of their country. In the 1950s attacks on white settlers and black collaborators escalated, and in 1952 the British established a state of emergency to crush the Mau Mau through jailings and the use of British troops. Unable or unwilling to distinguish Mau Mau radical activism from nonviolent nationalist agitation in Nairobi, the British moved to suppress all such groups. Kenyan nationalist leaders like Jomo Kenyatta (1895–1978) were jailed, and the battle between the Kikuyu and British troops dragged on for three years. Kikuyu who might have supported the Mau Mau struggle were forcibly detained in concentration camps, and as many as ten thousand Kikuyu died fighting the British.

The British crushed the Mau Mau uprising by 1955, but nationalist Kenyans ultimately prevailed. The British resisted the radical white supremacism and political domineering of the settlers in Kenya and instead responded to calls for Kenyan independence. The state of emergency was lifted in 1959, political parties formed, and nationalist leaders like Kenyatta reemerged to lead those parties. By December 1963 Kenya had negotiated its independence.

Despite the difficulties faced by nations in Asia and Africa as they struggled to gain independence from colonial or imperial rule, the first three decades after World War II witnessed the almost complete disintegration of European empires. The politics of the cold war between the Soviet Union and the United States complicated and at times delayed the process of decolonization, but together the cold war and decolonization reshaped the world. The cold war and decolonization also transformed domestic societies throughout the world, inspiring feminism, black nationalism, and a quest for security and contentment in the nuclear age. Competition between capitalism and communism for global allies replaced the previous century's European-dominated scramble for imperial holdings, and dozens of newly free nations emerged from those now-defunct empires. The superpowers and the developing nations faced many challenges, but for the moment they had succeeded in revamping the world's economic and political systems.

CHRONOLOGY

1945	War between France and Vietnam
1946	Independence of Philippines
1947	Independence of India and Pakistan
1948	Establishment of Israel
	First Arab-Israeli War
1949	Division of Germany and Berlin
1950	Outbreak of Korean War
1952	State of emergency in Kenya
1953	End of Korean War
1954	Geneva Conference
	Eisenhower applies domino theory
	Start of Algerian war of independence
1955	Bandung Conference
1956	Suez crisis
1957	Independence of Ghana
1959	Castro comes to power in Cuba
1960	Year of Africa
1961	Bay of Pigs invasion
	Berlin Wall
1962	Independence of Algeria
	Cuban missile crisis
1963	Independence of Kenya
1965	U.S. troops to South Vietnam

FOR FURTHER READING

Franz Ansprenger. *The Dissolution of the Colonial Empires.* New York, 1989. A discerning and thorough treatment of the dismantling of European empires and colonies.

M. E. Chamberlain. *Decolonization: The Fall of European Empires.* Oxford, 1985. A brief but competent summary of the demise of empires.

Michael J. Cohen. *Palestine and the Great Powers 1945–48.* 2nd ed. Princeton, 1992. An evenhanded assessment of the role played by the great powers in the partition of Palestine and the creation of Israel.

John Lewis Gaddis. *Strategies of Containment: A Critical Appraisal of Postwar American National Security Policy.* New York, 1982. Insightful work that traces the U.S. policy of containment from its inception to the late 1970s.

Margot A. Henriksen. *Dr. Strangelove's America: Society and Culture in the Atomic Age.* Berkeley, 1997. Analyzes the crucial role the bomb played in shaping postwar U.S. society.

Akira Iriye. *The Cold War in Asia: A Historical Introduction.* Englewood Cliffs, N.J., 1974. A leading diplomatic historian provides an excellent introduction to the subject.

Madeline Kalb. *The Congo Cables. The Cold War in Africa—From Eisenhower to Kennedy.* New York, 1982. An often neglected aspect of the cold war receives proper attention.

Bruce Kuniholm. *The Origins of the Cold War in the Near East.* Princeton, 1980. Focusing on Greece, Turkey, and Iran, this work dissects great power diplomacy and conflicts.

Walter Lafeber. *America, Russia, and the Cold War, 1945–1992.* 7th ed. New York, 1993. A standard work that emphasizes the corrosive effects the cold war had on democratic values in the United States.

Brian Lapping. *End of Empire.* New York, 1985. The British empire takes center stage in this treatment of decolonization.

Elaine Tyler May. *Homeward Bound: American Families in the Cold War Era*. New York, 1988. An insightful analysis of how the cold war and atomic age affected family and gender roles in U.S. society.

Charles Smith. *Palestine and the Arab-Israeli Conflict*. New York, 1988. A lucid and readable history of the wars between Israel and its Arab adversaries.

William Taubman. *Stalin's America Policy. From Entente to Detente to Cold War*. New York, 1982. An important work that focuses on the Soviet perspective of the cold war.

Stephen Whitfield. *The Culture of the Cold War*. Baltimore, 1991. An in-depth analysis of how the cold war and domestic anticommunism shaped U.S. culture from the 1940s to the early 1960s.

Daniel Yergin. *Shattered Peace. The Origins of the Cold War and the National Security State*. Boston, 1977. An interpretive history that looks at the origins of the cold war and its impact on U.S. political life.

TRANSFORMATION AND CRISIS IN THE CONTEMPORARY WORLD

* * *

On his deathbed in 1994, the chief of the Ndebele tribe in Zimbabwe chose a woman to succeed him, the first time this event had occurred in the tribe's history. Without sons or nephews in his family, he selected his second daughter, Sinqobili Mabhena, to become the next chief. Mabhena, however, faced hostility from members of the tribe who objected to a woman assuming the role of chief. As one Ndebele man exclaimed, "This one is against our culture. We are not going to allow it!" This was an era of transformation and crisis for the Ndebele tribe, a time when the past and the present collided. It took three years for the crisis to be resolved, but in 1997 the tribe installed Mabhena as its first female chief.

The Ndebele people believe that the sacred traditions of their Zulu ancestors are reborn into their chief, and the new chief is a unique recipient of those traditions. Not only is she a woman, but she lives in a city, Bulawayo (Zimbabwe's second city), where she has studied to be a teacher. Her job as chief, while mainly ceremonial, may involve helping her tribe adjust to a new era. In this task she has the support of the Zimbabwe government, which has strived to overcome deep-rooted patriarchy by guaranteeing equal rights for women in its constitution. John Nkomo, minister of local government, welcomes the contemporary influence of a female chief. "You know the world is becoming smaller and smaller every day. So we get these cross-influences, culture, traditions and ways of doing things. We live in one world, one planet." Sinqobili Mabhena put it more simply. With modest pride she proclaimed, "Yes, a woman can do a much better job and I have yet to prove that."

As the first female Zulu chief, Sinqobili Mabhena has had to negotiate her way between the past and the present, and her experiences reflect the new global influences on contemporary African politics. Changing political and economic models of development opened new opportunities and new dangers for societies seeking to define themselves in an era of transformation. Peoples in African villages, eastern European cities, the Asian countryside, and industrial metropolises confronted similar

Diego Rivera, detail from the *History of Mexico*, 1929–1930, fresco, Mexico City, Palacio Nacional.

● Organization of American States

challenges. They lived in one world, but there was no longer only one way to live. World War II and the decolonization that followed it had destroyed the old colonial world. A new global political order arose under the auspisces of the Soviet Union and the United States, but even the bipolar world fractured when the superpowers experienced unexpected setbacks and a political weakening.

Peoples in Europe and Asia strove to gain some measure of control over their societies outside superpower domination. With the exception of China, where Mao Zedong and others fashioned their own notions about building a communist society apart from the Soviet model, these efforts fell short. This was especially true in eastern Europe, where Warsaw Pact tanks crushed dreams of national independence. The superpowers continued to face challenges to their control, though, as evidenced in the Vietnamese victory over the United States and the Afghan victory over the Soviet Union. The superpowers may have dominated the world, but they did not control it. Even the superpowers themselves came to question the benefits of their ideological standoff and began to pursue more conciliatory policies. Their own citizens, especially in the United States, protested cold war policies and created a youthful counterculture that also challenged their societies' institutions and leaders.

Transformations in the contest between capitalism and communism, brought forth by unexpected crises, took place at a time when peoples in the former colonial world labored to build national identities. This situation was true for nations in areas of the world where independence came long ago as well as in areas where peoples achieved independence from colonial or imperial rule only recently. Latin American nations still struggled to achieve political stability free from European and U.S. interference, and South Africans put an end to white rule after decades of political fighting and negotiation. Asian and African lands faced daunting challenges in their pursuit of domestic or regional goals in a rapidly changing world, working to transform their societies in the midst of religious, sectarian, or ethnic crises or neo-imperial or superpower pressures.

Their goals of stability and independence were alternatively aided or impeded by the transformation in the world's balance of power. Some nations that were a part of the colonial world were hindered by periodic financial crises and by dependency on the markets and investment capital of Europe and the United States, while others managed to enter aggressively into the global economy. Nations, like Japan, the four little tigers (Hong Kong, Singapore, South Korea, and Taiwan), and China, foiled both capitalist and communist expectations. The formation of regional cartels and trading blocs also contributed to the transformation in global economic structures, forgoing strictly nationalistic economic goals in favor of regional or global cooperation.

The world was at something of a crossroads. The legacies of colonialism and imperialism continued to influence newly independent and developing countries, just as the cold war exerted restraints on the world's political and economic options. Nevertheless, old arrangements no longer appeared sufficient to guide the destinies of societies in the contemporary world. Societies did not necessarily have to obey the dictates of either U.S. capitalists or Soviet communists; peoples in the decolonized world did not have to bow to the wills of colonial masters; and tribal chiefs did not always have to be men. Sinoqobili Mabhena was not alone in her attempt to mediate the old and the new and to seek different directions in a changing world.

CHALLENGES TO SUPERPOWER HEGEMONY

The global preeminence of the two new superpowers evoked challenges from several quarters. In western Europe, French politicians sought to free their nation from superpower dominance by transforming Europe into an independent strategic bloc. This gambit ultimately failed, although it set the stage for a cautious but more independent political course on the part of other western European nations. Eastern European states also tried to become their own masters, or at least to gain a measure of autonomy from the Soviet Union. Except for Yugoslavia, which resisted Soviet pressure and became a nonaligned state, the nations of the Soviet bloc did not fare well in this endeavor. On several occasions Soviet tanks ruthlessly crushed efforts to leave the Soviet orbit. The leadership of the People's Republic of China mounted the most serious challenge to Soviet hegemony within the communist world. What began as a quarrel over national interests and disagreements concerning ideology grew into an outright schism. Finally, in Vietnam and Afghanistan, respectively, the United States and the Soviet Union suffered serious political and military setbacks that signaled the limits of superpower hegemony.

Western European Defiance

The first direct assault on the bipolar world emanated from France under the leadership of President Charles de Gaulle (1890–1970), who dreamed of a Europe that could act as a third force in world affairs. De Gaulle's pursuit of independence stemmed from dissatisfaction with the international order dictated by leaders in Washington and Moscow. In particular, he regarded the subservience to U.S. authority and unqualified support for U.S. global objectives as intolerable conditions.

France under de Gaulle

As far as de Gaulle and many of his compatriots were concerned, France could never regain great power status—a standing it once held as a great continental and imperial power—if it depended for security on U.S. military protection. Moreover, military dependence carried with it the risk that a nuclear confrontation between the superpowers over issues unrelated to European interests could engulf Europe by virtue of its alliance with the United States. De Gaulle and others also questioned the credibility of the American promise to defend Europe against a Soviet attack by threatening nuclear retaliation against the Soviet Union itself.

De Gaulle pursued independent policies wherever he could. Thus in 1963, despite U.S. disapproval, the French government rejected a partial nuclear test ban treaty that had been signed by the Soviet Union, Great Britain, and the United States and recognized by the communist People's Republic of China. The focus of French policy, however, was disengagement from the U.S.-dominated NATO and the development of an independent nuclear strike force. The latter became a realistic proposition in 1964 when the French detonated their first atomic bomb in the Sahara Desert. Four years later the French military put together a nuclear delivery system consisting of long-range bombers and land- and submarine-based missiles. French military doctrine and capability—the *force de frappe* or nuclear strike force—failed to convince Europeans to leave the protective fold of the United States, however, and by the time de Gaulle left office in 1969 his grand design for France and Europe had all but disappeared. Nevertheless, the vision of a Europe free from superpower domination persisted in a different guise.

CHART 38.1

• • •

MEMBERSHIP GROWTH OF THE EUROPEAN
COMMUNITY (EC)

Country	Year of Admission
Federal Republic of Germany	1958
France	1958
Italy	1958
Belgium	1958
Netherlands	1958
Luxembourg	1958
Great Britain	1973
Ireland	1973
Denmark	1973
Greece	1981
Spain	1986
Portugal	1986
Austria	1995
Finland	1995
Sweden	1995

Membership growth of the European Community.

The European Community

Proponents of European independence redirected their energies to promoting economic growth and integration as the basis for a politically united Europe. In March 1957 representatives of six nations—France, West Germany, Italy, the Netherlands, Belgium, and Luxemburg—took a significant step in this direction by signing the Treaty of Rome, which established the European Economic Community—renamed the European Community (EC) in 1967. At the heart of this new community of nations lay the dismantling of tariffs and other barriers to free trade among member nations. Subsequent treaties creating political institutions such as the Council of Ministers and the European Parliament facilitated the long-range goal of European political integration. The development of a supranational organization dedicated to increasing European economic and political integration culminated in the Maastricht Treaty of 1993, which established the European Union.

Economic integration soon began to pay visible dividends. The EC rapidly evolved into a formidable economic bloc. Within the EC combined gross national product and the standard of living first approached and then surpassed those of the United States. Increasingly, prosperous Europeans questioned the need to synchronize their foreign and defense policies with U.S. global strategies. In essence, the change in the economic relationship between Europe and the United States prompted a change in their political relationships, a change characterized by growing European independence. An illustration of Europe's newly found confidence came during the 1973 Arab-Israeli War, when all members of NATO except Portugal denied landing rights to U.S. planes shipping arms to Israel. U.S. secretary of state Henry Kissinger (1923–) denounced this action as "contemptible" and "jackal-like," to which Willy Brandt (1913–1992), the chancellor of West Germany, confidently rebutted: "Europe has become self-confident and independent enough to regard itself as an equal partner in this relationship. . . . Partnership cannot mean subordination."

Dissent and Intervention in Eastern Europe

There were many challenges to the hegemonic position of the Soviet Union during the cold war decades. The first opposition from within the communist world emanated from Yugoslavia, where a postwar communist regime had come to power without the assistance of the Soviet Union.

Tito's Yugoslavia

This fact along with strong support at home enabled Josip Broz, known as Marshal Tito (1892–1980), to rule the federation of Yugoslavia with an iron hand from 1945 until his death and to assert his nation's independence. Tito's resistance to Soviet control led to a major split with Joseph Stalin (1879–1953), and in 1948 Stalin expelled Yugoslavia from the Soviet bloc. In foreign affairs Tito pursued an independent course that consisted of maintaining good relations with eastern European communist states and establishing strong ties with nonaligned nations.

Developments within the Soviet Union caused more serious changes in eastern Europe. Within three years after Stalin's death in 1953, several communist leaders startled the world when they openly attacked Stalin and questioned his methods of rule. The most vigorous denunciations came from Stalin's successor, Nikita Khrushchev (1894–1971), during a secret speech at the Twentieth Party Congress in February 1956. Khrushchev subsequently embarked on a policy of de-Stalinization, that is, the end of the rule of terror and the partial liberalization of Soviet society. Government officials removed portraits of Stalin from public places, renamed institutions and localities bearing his name, and commissioned historians to rewrite textbooks so as to deflate Stalin's reputation. The de-Stalinization period, which lasted from 1956 to 1964, also brought a "thaw" in government control and resulted in the release of millions of political prisoners. One of these was Alexandr Solzhenitsyn (1919–) who, thanks to Khrushchev's support, was able to publish his novel *One Day in the Life of Ivan Denisovich* (1962), a short and moving description of life in a Siberian forced labor camp. The new political climate in the Soviet Union tempted communist leaders elsewhere to experiment with domestic reforms and seek a degree of independence from Soviet domination.

The Hungarian Challenge

The most serious challenge to Soviet control in eastern Europe came in 1956 from nationalist-minded communists in Hungary. When the communist regime in Hungary embraced the process of de-Stalinization, large numbers of Hungarian citizens demanded democracy and the breaking of ties to Moscow and the Warsaw Pact. In the wake of massive street demonstrations, joined by the Hungarian armed forces, two communist leaders, Imre Nagy (1896–1958) and János Kádár (1912–1989), formed a coalition government that promptly announced its neutrality and withdrawal from the Warsaw Pact. Soviet leaders viewed these moves as a serious threat to their security system. In the late autumn of 1956, Soviet tanks entered Budapest and crushed the Hungarian uprising. Soviet authorities installed Kádár as a dependable communist leader who adhered strictly to a pro-Soviet line of foreign policy and secretly executed Nagy, along with many others who had mistakenly trusted a Soviet promise of safe conduct.

Czech citizens confront Warsaw Pact troops in Prague during the Soviet invasion in the spring of 1968.

● © 1968 Josef Koudelka/Magnum Photos, Inc.

The Prague Spring   Twelve years after the Hungarian tragedy, Soviets again intervened in eastern Europe, this time in Czechoslovakia. In 1968 the Communist Party leader, Alexander Dubček (1921–), launched a "democratic socialist revolution." He supported a liberal movement known as the "Prague Spring" and promised his fellow citizens "socialism with a human face." The Czech's move toward liberal communism aroused fear in the Soviet Union because such ideas could lead to the unraveling of Soviet control in eastern Europe. Intervention by the Soviet army, aided by East German, Bulgarian, and Polish units, brought an end to the Prague Spring. Khrushchev's successor, Leonid Ilyich Brezhnev (1906–1982), justified the invasion of Czechoslovakia by the Doctrine of Limited Sovereignty. This policy, more commonly called the "Brezhnev doctrine," reserved the right to invade any socialist country that was deemed to be threatened by internal or external elements "hostile to socialism." The destruction of the dramatic reform movement in Czechoslovakia served to reassert Soviet control over its satellite nations in eastern Europe and led to tightened controls within the Soviet Union (USSR).

The Chinese-Soviet Rift

Moscow and Beijing drew closer during the early years of the cold war. This relationship was hardly surprising because the leaders of both communist states felt threatened by a common enemy, the United States, which sought to establish anticommunist bastions throughout Asia. Most disconcerting to Soviet and Chinese leadership was the American-sponsored rehabilitation of their former enemy, Japan, as well as client states, South Korea and Taiwan.

Fraternal Cooperation   The Chinese-Soviet partnership that matured during the early 1950s took a distinct form in which Beijing recognized Moscow's undisputed authority in world communism in exchange for Russian military equipment and economic aid. In return Soviet diplomats instigated a campaign in the United Nations to transfer the

Chinese seat in the Security Council from Taiwan to the communist government on the mainland. However, the Soviet tendency to lecture the Chinese on how to construct a socialist society contributed to continuing tension between the two nations.

Before long new cracks appeared in the Soviet-Chinese alliance. From the Chinese perspective Soviet aid programs were far too modest and had too many strings attached. Particularly grating were Soviet demands for territorial concessions, which conjured up memories of similar demands by European powers 150 years earlier. In February 1959, after making Mao Zedong wait for two cold months in Moscow, the Kremlin finally persuaded him to sign a treaty of Friendship, Alliance and Mutual Assistance that recalled the "unequal treaties" of the nineteenth century. Among other things, this pact granted the Soviet Union naval privileges in Port Arthur and economic concessions that were blatantly imperialist in character. In return for these concessions, the Soviets provided China with less economic assistance than noncommunist countries like Egypt and India received. Border clashes in central Asia and Siberia added fuel to the smoldering conflict between the two communist states.

Cracks in the Alliance

By the end of 1964, the rift between the Soviet Union and the People's Republic of China had become embarrassingly public, with both sides engaging in name calling. Because Nikita Khrushchev, fearing nuclear attack, was pursuing a policy of peaceful coexistence with the United States and western Europe at the time, the Chinese government accused the Soviets of being "revisionists," a highly insulting term in the communist vocabulary. The Soviets, for their part, accused the Chinese of being dangerous "left-wing adventurists" because Mao Zedong asserted the inevitability of war with capitalist nations. In addition to name calling, both nations openly competed for influence in Africa and Asia, especially in the nations that had recently gained independence. The fact that the People's Republic had conducted successful nuclear tests in 1964 enhanced its prestige. An unanticipated outcome of the Chinese-Soviet split was that many countries gained an opportunity to pursue a more independent course not only by playing capitalists against communists but also by playing Soviet communists against Chinese communists.

Détente and the Decline of Superpower Influence

By the late 1960s the leaders of the Soviet Union and the United States had agreed on a policy of *détente,* or a reduction in hostility, trying to cool the costly arms race and slow their competition in developing countries. Although détente did not resolve the deep-seated antagonism between the superpowers, it did signal the relaxation of cold war tensions and prompted a new spirit of cooperation.

Between 1972 and 1974 U.S. and Soviet leaders exchanged visits and signed agreements calling for cooperation in areas such as health research, environmental protection, science and technology, space ventures, and expanded cultural exchange programs. However, the spirit of détente was most visible in negotiations designed to reduce the threat posed by strategic nuclear weapons. In 1972 U.S. and Soviet negotiators concluded their Strategic Arms Limitations Talks (SALT) with two agreements and reached another accord in 1979. The two cold war antagonists had cooperated despite the tension caused by the U.S. incursion into Vietnam, Soviet involvement in Angola and other African states, and continued Soviet repression of dissidents in eastern Europe.

An Era of Cooperation

By the early 1980s, however, relations between the superpowers had deteriorated notably. The establishment of full diplomatic relations between the United States and the People's Republic of China in January 1979 and the announcement

The Demise of Détente

in 1981 that the United States would sell weapons to the Chinese military undermined U.S.-Soviet cooperation. The situation was aggravated in December 1979 by Soviet armed intervention to save a Marxist regime in Afghanistan. This action doomed ratification of the most recent SALT agreement by the U.S. Congress and led the U.S. government to impose economic sanctions. The era of détente nonetheless reflected a significant transformation of superpower relations. It coincided with a marked decline in superpower influence, which also changed relations between the superpowers and threatened their standing in the world. First the United States in Vietnam and then the Soviet Union in Afghanistan experienced serious military and political setbacks that undermined their global status.

The U.S. Defeat in Vietnam

Recognizing his country's distaste for the U.S. role in the Vietnam War, President Richard Nixon pledged in 1968 to end the war. Yet his strategy of turning over the war to the South Vietnamese (termed Vietnamization) actually escalated the conflict. Nixon extended the war into Cambodia through bombing and invasion in 1969 and 1970, and he resumed heavy bombing of North Vietnam. At the same time, however, he opened diplomatic channels to the Soviet Union and China, hoping to get them to pressure North Vietnam into a negotiated end to the war. Under these circumstances the continuation of the battle in Vietnam seemed futile. U.S. troops gradually withdrew from the conflict, and in January 1973 the U.S. phase of the Vietnam War ended with the Paris Peace Accords, a complex set of agreements signed by Britain, France, the Soviet Union, the United States, North Vietnam, the National Liberation Front (NFL), and South Vietnam. But although the U.S. presence in Vietnam came to an end, the war did not. Within two years the agreements were torn up as forces from North Vietnam and the NLF continued their struggle to conquer South Vietnam and unite their nation, finally achieving their goals with the military defeat of the South in 1975 and unification in 1976.

The Vietnam War: with her home going up in flames behind her, a Vietnamese woman pleads with a U.S. soldier. ● James Pickerell/Camera Press London/Retna

Soviet Setbacks in Afghanistan

Muslim Afghanistan was a quiet member of the Non-Aligned Movement until 1978, when a pro-Soviet coup drew the republic into the cold war, precipitated foreign intervention, and fomented civil war. Once in power, the leftist People's Democratic Party of Afghanistan (PDPA) wasted little time in introducing radical reforms in education and land and family law. This movement caused a backlash. Especially in rural areas, Islamic religious and ethnic leaders objected both to rapid social change and to the PDPA's brutal methods and called for armed resistance. By the summer of 1979, antigovernment rebels controlled much of the Afghan countryside. At this point the Soviet Union intervened, installing the Marxist Babrak Karmal as president. With the help of Soviet air and land forces and civilian advisors, Karmal tried to establish control over the country. He promised to combine social and economic reform with respect for Islam and Afghan traditions. Nevertheless, the Soviet-backed government remained unpopular, and a national resistance movement spread throughout the country.

For nine years well-equipped Soviet forces fought a brutal but unsuccessful campaign against Afghan mujahideen, or Islamic warriors, who gradually gained control of most of the countryside. Weapons and money from the United States, Saudi Arabia, Iran, Pakistan, and China sustained the mujahideen in their struggle. The Central Intelligence Agency of the United States supplied the decisive weapons in the war: ground-to-air Stinger missiles, which could be used to shoot down heavily armored Soviet helicopters, and thousands of mules to haul supplies from Pakistan.

In 1986 the Soviet leadership replaced the unpopular Karmal with the equally unpopular Muhammad Najibullah, a Soviet favorite who had been in charge of the Afghan secret police. In the same year, the Kremlin also decided to pull its troops out of the costly, unpopular, and unwinnable war. A cease-fire negotiated by the United Nations in 1988 led to a full Soviet withdrawal in 1989. However, the fighting continued as rival ethnic, military, and religious factions prolonged the civil war. In 1996 the Taliban, an organization claiming to be an army of religious students, captured the Afghan capital Kabul after an eleven-month siege, executed Najibullah, and proclaimed Afghanistan a strict Islamist state.

The experiences of the superpowers in Vietnam and Afghanistan demonstrated that they had overextended their influence, involving their military forces in conflicts that did little to further their cold war policies. These forays taxed their nations financially, but more important, they caused dissatisfaction with cold war politics within the superpowers themselves. Internationally, the wars in Vietnam and Afghanistan undermined the prestige of the superpowers and exposed the hollowness of their claims to military superiority.

Cold War Countercultural Protests

While de Gaulle, Brezhnev, and Nixon worked from within their political systems to modify international relations, their citizens and others throughout the world agitated for the abolition of the cold war systems themselves. By 1964 cultural criticism of the cold war and its leaders had clearly influenced the films coming out of Hollywood. The political oppression that had tried to stifle dissent in the United States in the late 1940s and 1950s had lifted by the early 1960s. The 1964 release of Stanley Kubrick's film *Dr. Strangelove or: How I Learned to Stop Worrying and Love the Bomb* was proof positive. The film comedically represented the leaders of the United States and the USSR as insane morons whose irrational policies guaranteed the destruction of all life on earth through nuclear war.

Dr. Strangelove belonged to an era of European and North American cultural ferment that had its roots in the global changes caused by the cold war. Anxiety about nuclear weapons and doubts about cold war policies flourished in the 1960s and 1970s, and the world's youth formed the vanguard in a countercultural revolution that challenged the basic political and cultural precepts of post–World War II societies. Disturbed by their nations' apparent commitment to war and social conformity, European and American students in particular took to the streets or disrupted their universities through massive demonstrations designed to promote peace, end the nuclear arms race and the war in Vietnam, and abolish unfair university rules and restrictions. In the United States students at the University of California at Berkeley formed the Free Speech Movement in 1964 to encourage free political expression on campus; four years later students in France erected barricades in Paris reminiscent of nineteenth-century French revolts.

Student activism suggested the extent to which global youth experienced empowerment in these years, whether in France, the United States, or China, where Red Guard youths controlled much of the Cultural Revolution. This youthful influence also accounted for the worldwide popularity of rock 'n' roll, a new form of musical expression born in the postwar era. Whereas U.S. singer Elvis Presley (1935–1977) shocked parents and attracted the young with his wild rock 'n' roll music and dancing, British groups like the Beatles and the Rolling Stones "invaded" the United States and the world in the 1960s (this phenomenon was called the "British invasion"). Rock 'n' roll in the 1960s and 1970s also underscored the political radicalism of youths disaffected from their states' leaders and policies. The Beatles sang of "Revolution," and the Rolling Stones wrote rock musical odes to a "Street Fighting Man."

Although himself a fan of Elvis Presley, Richard Nixon became a victim of the societal discontentment aroused by the cold war and exploited by the young. In an atmosphere of increased scrutiny of leaders, Nixon's operations in the Vietnam War (bombing and invading Cambodia) and in the Watergate scandal (1972–1974) were exposed by journalists and members of the U.S. Congress. Upset at news leaks to the *New York Times* about his unauthorized bombings in Cambodia, he ordered wiretaps placed on the phone lines of reporters and members of his own staff. This action started the trend toward criminal activities in the Nixon White House that culminated in the scandal surrounding a break-in at the Democratic national headquarters (at the Watergate building) during the 1972 presidential elections.

The burglars were caught, Nixon and his staff attempted to cover up the crimes committed for the president's benefit, and journalistic and congressional investigations ultimately unraveled the criminal links that led to Nixon's resignation in August 1974. Richard Nixon was a prominent leader associated with the cold war throughout his entire political career. He left office in disgrace and reinforced the negative images of politicians featured in films like *Dr. Strangelove* and in the youth movement as a whole. His fate suggested the vulnerability of cold war leaders whose hegemony was contested abroad and at home.

NEW POLITICAL ORIENTATIONS IN THE POSTCOLONIAL ERA

The shifting political fortunes of the superpowers contributed to transformations in the global political order, but so too did the efforts of developing nations to establish new political structures. Political stability, however, proved elusive in the developing nations. The legacies of imperialism, either direct or indirect, hindered the creation of democratic institutions in many parts of the world—not only in recently decolonized nations like those of Africa but also in some of the earliest lands to gain independence, like those of Latin America. Continued interference by the former colonial powers or by more developed nations impeded progress, as did local elites with ties to the colonial powers. The result was an unstable succession of governments, based either on an authoritarian one-party system or on harsh military rule. South Africa and India, however, were able to transform themselves into functioning democracies despite deep racial and religious divides. In Asia and the Islamic world, some governments kept order by relying on tightly centralized rule, as in China, or on religion, as in Iran after the 1979 revolution. Few developing or newly industrialized countries, however, escaped the disruption of war or revolution that also characterized the postcolonial era.

Politics in Latin America

Like other nations in Central and South America, the North American state of Mexico grappled with the conservative legacies of Spanish and Portuguese colonialism, particularly the political and economic power of the landowning elite of European descent. Like the other states of Latin America, Mexico also had to deal with neocolonialism, since the United States intervened militarily when it felt that its interests were threatened and influenced Mexico's economy through investment and full or part ownership of enterprises like the oil industry. In the nineteenth century Latin American states may have looked to the United States as a model of liberal democracy, but by the twentieth century U.S. interference provoked negative reactions. This condition was true in Mexico, particularly after the Mexican War (1846–1848), in which Mexico lost huge chunks of its northern territories to the United States.

Mexicans dedicated to overthrowing both elite rule and foreign economic control fomented a revolution that began in 1910 and lasted into the 1930s. Their demands for land and liberty were institutionalized in the Constitution of 1917, and after that date Mexican presidents designed policies to carry out reform. The constitution stated that the Mexican government owned its subsoil and its products and that the state had the right to redistribute land to village peasants after confiscating it and compensating the landowners. The constitution also incorporated reformist social laws and guaranteed civil liberties. The program of land redistribution that followed the constitution reached its peak during the presidency of Lázaro Cárdenas (1934–1940), when the state returned forty-five million acres to peasants. Cárdenas also took control of the Mexican oil wells away from foreign investors.

Mexico

The reforms enacted by progressive presidential administrations did not continue during the decades following the revolution, and Mexico wavered in its ability to keep U.S. interests at bay. Conservative governments controlled by the Institutional Revolutionary Party (PRI) often ruled harshly and experimented with various economic strategies that either decreased or increased Mexico's dependence on foreign markets and capital. The PRI has come under attack in the 1990s as Mexican peasants in the Chiapas district protested their political oppression. Cuauhtemoc Cárdenas, the son of Lázaro Cárdenas, took on the leadership of an opposition party, the Democratic Revolutionary Party (PDR).

Just as Mexico served as a model for political development in Latin America, Argentina seemed to be a candidate for leadership in South America. It had a reasonably expansive economy based on cattle raising and agriculture, a booming urban life, the beginnings of an industrial base, and a growing middle class in a population composed mostly of migrants from Europe. Given its geographic position far to the south, Argentina remained relatively independent of U.S. control and became a leader in the Latin American struggle against U.S. and European economic and political intervention in the region. A gradual shift to free elections and a sharing of political power beyond that exercised by the landowning elite also emerged. Given the

Argentina

Juan Perón

military's central role in its politics, however, Argentina became a model of a less positive form of political organization: the often brutal and deadly sway of military rulers.

During World War II, nationalistic military leaders gained power in Argentina and established a government controlled by the army. In 1946 Juan Perón (1895–1974), a colonel in the army, was elected president. Although he was a nationalistic militarist, his regime garnered immense popularity among large segments of the Argentine population, partly because he appealed to the more downtrodden Argentines. He promoted a nationalistic populism calling for industrialization, support of the working class, and protection of the economy from foreign control.

However opportunistic Perón may have been, his popularity with the masses was real. His wife, Eva Perón (1919–1952), helped to foster that popularity, as Argentinians warmly embraced their "Evita" (little Eva). She herself had risen from the ranks of the desperately poor. An illegitimate child who migrated to Buenos Aires at the age of fifteen, she found work as a radio soap-opera actress. She met Perón in 1944, and they were married shortly thereafter. Reigning in the Casa Rosada (the "Pink House") as Argentina's first lady from 1946 to 1952, Eva Perón transformed herself into a stunningly beautiful political leader, radiant with dyed gold-blonde hair and clothed in classic designer fashions. While pushing for her husband's political reforms, she also tirelessly ministered to the needs of the poor, often the same *descamisados* or "shirtless ones" who formed the core of her husband's supporters. Endless lines of people came to see her in her offices at the labor ministry—asking for dentures, wedding clothes, medical care, and the like. Eva Perón accommodated these demands and more: she bathed lice-ridden children in her own home, kissed lepers, and created the Eva Perón Foundation to institutionalize and extend such charitable endeavors. When she died of uterine cancer at the age of thirty-three, the nation mourned the tragic passing of a woman who came to be elevated to the status of "Santa Evita."

Some saw Eva Perón not as a saint, but as a grasping social climber and a fascist sympathizer (she had, for example, made an official visit to General Franco's Spain),

Eva Perón waves to adoring *descamisados* in Buenos Aires in 1950.   •   Hulton Getty/Liaison

and her husband as a political opportunist, but after Juan Perón's ouster from office in 1955, support for the Peronist party remained strong. However, with the exception of a brief return to power by Perón in the mid-1970s, brutal military dictators held sway for the next three decades. Military rule took a sinister turn in the late 1970s and early 1980s, when dictators approved the creation of "death squads" that fought a "dirty war" against suspected subversives. Between six thousand and twenty-three thousand people disappeared between 1976 and 1983. Calls for a return to democratic politics increased in the aftermath of the dirty war, demands that were intensified by economic disasters and the growth of the poor classes.

The political models and options open to states in Latin America were rather diverse, including the establishment of communist and socialist regimes in lands like Cuba and Nicaragua, but in many nations the landowning elites that had gained power during the colonial era were able to maintain their dominant position. This situation resulted in societies that were badly split between the few rich, backed by the United States, and the masses of the poor. It was difficult to govern such societies without either keeping the elite in power or promoting revolution on behalf of the poor. Thus, although political security has often eluded the Latin American nations, these industrializing societies continue to seek stability and independence from foreign interference.

War and Peace in Sub-Saharan Africa

The optimism that arose in Africa after World War II faded over time. There seemed little prospect for widespread political stability in sub-Saharan Africa. A large number of unsettling coups replaced the civilians running newly independent states with military leaders. As in Latin America, this condition largely reflected the impact of colonialism: European powers carved Africa into territories whose boundaries were artificial conveniences that did not correspond to economic or ethnic divisions. As a result, achieving national unity was difficult, especially because there were numerous conflicts between tribes within states. Political institutions foundered, and the grinding poverty in which most African peoples lived increased tensions and made the absence of adequate administration and welfare programs more glaring. Poverty also prevented nations from accumulating the capital that could have contributed to a sound political and economic infrastructure.

The Aftermath of Decolonization

The Organization of African Unity (OAU), created in 1963 by thirty-two member states, recognized some of these problems and attempted to prevent conflicts that could lead to intervention by former colonial powers. The artificial boundaries of African states, while acknowledged as problematic, were nonetheless held inviolable by the OAU in order to prevent disputes over boundaries. Pan-African unity was also promoted, at least by the faction headed by Kwame Nkhrumah (1909–1972), as another way for African states to resist interference and domination by foreign powers. But while national borders have generally held, unity has not: African nations have been unable to avoid internal conflicts. Nkhrumah, the former president of Ghana, is a case in point: he was overthrown in 1966, and Ghanaians tore down the statues and photographs that celebrated his leadership. Thus in Ghana as in many other sub-Saharan states politics evolved into dictatorial one-party rule, with party leaders forgoing multiparty elections in the name of ending political divisiveness. Several African nations fell prey to military rule. South Africa managed in part to solve its political crisis and discord, providing a model for multiethnic African transformation even as ethnic violence flared.

South Africa   As elsewhere in Africa, the presence of large numbers of white settlers in South Africa had long delayed the arrival of black freedom. The state of South Africa had gained independence from Britain by 1910, but its black population, though a majority, remained dispossessed and disenfranchised. Anticolonial agitation thus was significantly different in South Africa than in the rest of sub-Saharan Africa: it was a struggle against internal colonialism, against an oppressive white regime that denied basic human and civil rights to tens of millions of South Africans.

The ability of whites to resist majority rule had its roots in the South African economy, the strongest on the continent. This strength had two sources: extraction of minerals and industrial development, which had received a huge boost during World War II. The growth of the industrial sector opened many jobs to blacks, creating the possibility of a change in their status. Along with black activism and calls for serious political reform after World War II, these changes struck into the hearts of white South Africans. In 1948 the Afrikaner National Party, which was dedicated to quashing any move toward black independence, came to power. Under the National Party the government instituted a harsh new set of laws designed to control the restive black population; these new laws constituted the system known as *apartheid* or "separateness."

Apartheid   The system of apartheid asserted white supremacy and institutionalized the racial segregation that had been established in the years before 1948. The government designated approximately 87 percent of South Africa's territory for white residents. Remaining areas were designated as homelands for black and colored citizens. Nonwhites were classified according to a variety of ethnic identifications—colored or mixed-race peoples, Indians, and "Bantu," which in turn was subdivided into numerous distinct tribal affiliations (for example, Zulu, Xhosa, Sotho). As other imperial powers had done in Africa, white South Africans divided the black and colored population in the name of preventing the rise of unified liberation movements. The apartheid system, complex and varied in its composition, evolved into a system designed to keep blacks in a position of political, social, and economic subordination.

However divided the nonwhite population might be, these dispossessed peoples all found in apartheid an impetus for resistance to white rule. The African National Congress (ANC), formed in 1912, gained new young leaders like Nelson Mandela (1918–), who inspired direct action campaigns to protest apartheid. In 1955 the ANC published its Freedom Charter, which proclaimed the ideal of multiracial democratic rule for South Africa. As its goals directly challenged white rule, the ANC and all black activists in South Africa faced severe repression. The government declared all of its opponents communists and escalated its actions against black activists. Protests increased in 1960, the so-called year of Africa, and on 21 March 1960 white police gunned down black demonstrators in Sharpeville, near Johannesburg. Sixty-nine blacks died and almost two hundred were wounded. Sharpeville instituted a new era of radical activism.

When the white regime banned black organizations like the ANC and jailed their adherents, international opposition to white South African rule grew. Newly freed nations in Asia and Africa called for UN sanctions against South Africa, and in 1961 South Africa declared itself a republic, withdrawing from the British Commonwealth. Some leaders of the ANC began to see the necessity of armed resistance, but in 1963 government forces captured the leaders of ANC's military unit, including Nelson Mandela. The court sentenced them to life in prison, and Mandela and others became symbols of oppressive white rule. Protests against the system persisted in the 1970s and 1980s, spurred especially by student activism and a new black-consciousness movement. The combined effects of massive black agitation and a powerful international antiapartheid boycott eventually led to reform and a growing recognition that if it was to survive, South Africa had to change.

When F. W. de Klerk (1936–) became president of South Africa in 1989, he and the National Party began to dismantle the apartheid system. De Klerk released Mandela from jail in 1990, legalized the ANC, and worked with Mandela and the ANC to negotiate the end of white minority rule. Collaborating and cooperating, the National Party, the ANC, and other African political groups created a new constitution and in April 1994 held elections that were open to people of all races. The ANC won overwhelmingly, and Mandela became the first black president of South Africa. In 1963, at the trial that ended in his jail sentence, Mandela had proclaimed, "I have cherished the ideal of a democratic and free society in which all persons live together in harmony and with equal opportunities. It is an ideal which I hope to live for and to achieve. But if needs be, it is an ideal for which I am prepared to die." Mandela lived to see his ideal fulfilled. In 1994, as president, he proclaimed his nation "free at last."

The End of Apartheid

Outside South Africa political stability remained difficult to achieve. The fleeting character of African political identity and stability can be seen in the history of the land once known as the Belgian Congo, which was reconfigured as Zaire in 1971 and renamed the Democratic Republic of the Congo in 1997. Mobutu Sese Seko (1930–1997) took power in 1965 by having Zaire's first prime minister, Patrice Lumumba (1925–1961), killed in a military coup. Lumumba was a Maoist Marxist, and the U.S. Central Intelligence Agency (CIA) supported Mobutu's coup. Mobutu thereafter received support from the United States and other European democracies that hoped to quell subversive uprisings. With international backing and financial support, Mobutu ruled Zaire in dictatorial fashion, using his power to amass personal fortunes for himself, his family, and his allies but devastating Zaire's economy. One observer termed Mobutu and his cronies "a vampire elite," as they plundered one of the richest African nations.

The Democratic Republic of the Congo

Mobutu's full adopted name, Mobutu Sese Seko Kuku Ngbendu Wa Za Banga, means "the all-powerful warrior who, by his endurance and will to win, goes from conquest to conquest, leaving fire in his wake." Mobutu endured until 1997, when he was ousted by Laurent Kabila. Having earlier called Zaire "a fabrication of the dictator," Kabila changed the nation's name to the Democratic Republic of the Congo. Kabila's first concern was stability, which translated into vast personal power for himself as president, head of the military, and head of state. Kabila promised that this stage was a transition phase, preparatory to a democratic and stable Republic of Congo. However, just a year after his revolution, in 1998 Kabila came under attack by rebels in the Congo aided by the governments of some neighboring states.

The assumption of political power by military dictators, united in the Mobutu reign in Zaire, demonstrated one form of African political development. Different directions in African politics appeared in Laurent Kabila's overthrow of Mobutu. The fact that Nelson Mandela, president of the multiracial South African government, negotiated a cease-fire between Kabila and Mobutu in the last month of the civil war also pointed to a new leadership role for South Africa. South Africa's experiment with democracy in a land of diverse ethnic groups serves as a model for a continent otherwise splintered by hundreds of tribal and ethnic identities.

Islamic Resurgence in Southwest Asia and North Africa

The geographic convergence of the Arab and Muslim worlds in southwest Asia and north Africa encouraged the development of Arab nationalism in states of those regions that gained independence in the years after World War II. Whether in Libya, Algeria, or Egypt in north Africa or in Syria, Saudi Arabia, or Iraq in southwest Asia, visions of Arab nationalism, linked to the religious force of Islam, dazzled nations that wished to fend off European and U.S. influence. In North Africa Egypt's Gamal Abdel Nasser (1918–1970) provided the leadership for this Arab nationalism, and Arab-Muslim opposition to the state of Israel held the dream together.

Muslim Revival and Arab Disunity

The hopes attached to pan-Arab unity did not materialize. Although Arab lands shared a common language and religion, divisions were frequent and alliances shifted over time. The cold war split the Arab-Muslim world as some states allied themselves with the United States while others associated with the Soviet Union. Some also shifted between the two, as Egypt did when it left the Soviet orbit for the U.S. sphere in 1976. Governments in these nations included military dictatorships, monarchies, and Islamist revolutionary regimes. Religious divisions also complicated the attainment of Arab unity, as Sunni and Shi'ite Muslims followed divergent theologies and foreign policies.

In southwest Asia peace seemed a distant prospect for decades, given the political turmoil caused by the presence of Israel in the midst of Arab-Islamic states, many of which allied themselves with the Soviet Union as Israel became a staunch ally of the United States. Israel soundly defeated Egypt and Syria in the 1967 Arab-Israeli War and in the 1973 Arab-Israeli, or Yom Kippur, War, so named by Israel because the Arab attack took place on the major Jewish holy day of Yom Kippur in 1973. These conflicts greatly intensified the tensions in the region. But the wars also ultimately led to a long series of peace negotiations. Anwar Sadat (1918–1981), who replaced Nasser as Egypt's president, masterminded the Yom Kippur surprise attack on Israel, but he also facilitated the peace process. The United States helped negotiate the peace. In 1976 Sadat renounced his nation's friendship treaty with the Soviet Union, and in 1977 he traveled to Israel in an attempt to break a deadlock in the negotiations. Between 1978 and 1980 the leaders of Egypt and Israel signed peace treaties.

Sadat was assassinated in 1981 by opponents of his policies toward Israel, and the Arab states along with the Palestinian Liberation Organization (PLO) worked to isolate Egypt. The PLO, the political organization that served as a government in exile for Palestinians displaced from Israel, had been created in 1964 under the leadership of Yasser Arafat (1929–) to promote Palestinian rights. Despite more violence by both Israelis and Palestinians, in the 1990s even these implacable foes moved to end hostilities. In 1993 and 1995 Arafat and Israeli prime minister Yitzhak Rabin (1922–1996) signed peace treaties that advanced the notion of limited Palestinian self-rule in Israeli-occupied territories. The assassination of Rabin in 1994 by a Jewish extremist, who opposed the peace agreements, and other hurdles blocked the peace process. But cracks had appeared in Arab-Muslim solidarity, and there was still hope for a peaceful resolution of the long-running conflict between Israel and the Palestinians.

The Iranian Revolution

The Arab-Muslim world may have been divided on a number of issues, but the revolution that took place in Iran in 1979 demonstrated the power of Islam as a means of staving off secular foreign influences. Islamist influences penetrated Iran during the lengthy regime of Shah Mohammed Reza Pahlavi (1919–1980), whom the CIA had helped bring to power in 1953. The vast sums of money that poured in from Iran's oil industry helped finance industrialization, and the United States pro-

Iranians show their devotion to the Ayatollah Khomeini at his funeral in 1989.   •   Alexandra Avakian/
Woodfin Camp

vided the military equipment that enabled Iran to become a bastion of anticommunism in the region. In the late 1970s, however, opposition to the shah's government coalesced. Shi'ite Muslims despised the shah's secular regime, Iranian small businesses detested the influence of U.S. corporations on the economy, and leftist politicians rejected the Shah's repressive policies. The shah fled the country in early 1979 as the revolution gained force, and power was captured by the Islamist movement under the direction of Ayatollah Ruhollah Khomeini (1900–1989).

The revolution took on a strongly anti-U.S. cast, partly because the shah was allowed to travel to the United States for medical treatment. In retaliation Shi'ite militants captured sixty-nine hostages at the U.S. embassy in Tehran, fifty-five of whom remained captives until 1981. In the meantime Iranian leaders shut down U.S. military bases and confiscated U.S.-owned economic ventures. This Islamic power play against a developed nation like the United States inspired other Muslims to undertake terrorist actions. The resurgent Islam of Iran did not lead to a new era of solidarity, however. Iranian Islam was the minority sect Shi'ite Islam, and one of Iran's neighbors, Iraq, attempted to take advantage of the revolution to invade Iran.

The Iran-Iraq War

By the late 1970s Iraq had built up a formidable military machine, largely owing to oil revenues and the efforts of Saddam Hussein (1937–), who became president of Iraq in 1979. Hussein launched his attack on Iran in 1980, believing that victory would be swift and perhaps hoping to become the new leader of a revived pan-Arab nationalism. (Iran is Muslim in religion, but not ethnically Arab, as are Iraq, Kuwait, and Saudi Arabia.) Although they were initially successful, Iraqi troops faced a determined counterattack by Iranian forces, and the conflict became a war of attrition that did not end until 1988.

The Iran-Iraq War killed as many as one million soldiers. In Iran the human devastation is still visible, if not openly acknowledged, in a nation that permits little dissent from Islamist orthodoxy. Young people are showing signs of a growing discontent, caused both by the war and by the rigors of a revolution that also killed

AYATOLLAH KHOMEINI'S "MESSAGE TO THE PILGRIMS"

• • •

On 13 September 1980, Ayatollah Ruhollah Khomeini (1900–1989) delivered a fiery speech called the "Message to the Pilgrims." In his speech he urged the Muslim world to unite against the superpowers and all foreign influences, especially those stemming from the United States. Khomeini personified the vital Islamist revival of the contemporary era and suggested how Islam could serve as a counterforce to the power and influence of global powerhouses like the United States.

Muslims the world over who believe in the truth of Islam, arise and gather beneath the banner of *tauhid* [divine unity] and the teachings of Islam! Repel the treacherous superpowers from your countries and your abundant resources. Restore the glory of Islam, and abandon your selfish disputes and differences, for you possess everything! Rely on the culture of Islam, resist Western imitation, and stand on your own feet. Attack those intellectuals who are infatuated with the West and the East, and recover your true identity. Realize that intellectuals in the pay of foreigners have inflicted disaster upon their people and countries. As long as you remain disunited and fail to place your reliance in true Islam, you will continue to suffer what you have suffered already. We are now in an age when the masses act as the guides to the intellectuals and are rescuing them from abasement and humiliation by the East and the West. For today is the day that the masses of the people are on the move; they are the guides to those who previously sought to be the guides themselves.

Know that your moral power will overcome all other powers. With a population of almost one billion and with infinite sources of wealth, you can defeat all the powers. Aid God's cause so that He may aid you. Great ocean of Muslims, arise and defeat the enemies of humanity. If you turn to God and follow the heavenly teachings, God Almighty and His vast hosts will be with you.

America is the number-one enemy of the deprived and oppressed people of the world. There is no crime America will not commit in order to maintain its political, economic, cultural, and military domination of those parts of the world where it predominates. . . . Iran has tried to sever all its relations with this Great Satan and it is for this reason that it now finds wars imposed upon it. America has urged Iraq to spill the blood of our young men, and it has compelled the countries that are subject to its influence to boycott us economically in the hope of defeating us. Unfortunately, most Asian countries are also hostile to us. Let the Muslim nations be aware that Iran is a country effective at war with America, and that our martyrs—the brave young men of our army and the Revolutionary Guards—are defending Iran and the Islam we hold dear against America. . . . Were we to compromise with America and the other superpowers, we would not suffer these misfortunes. But our nation is no longer ready to submit to humiliation and abjection; it prefers a bloody death to a life of shame. We are ready to be killed and we have made a covenant with God to follow the path of our leader, the Lord of the Martyrs.

SOURCE: Hamid Algar, ed. and trans. *Islam and Revolution: Writings and Declarations of Imam Khomeini.* Berkeley: Mizan Press, 1981, pp. 304–306.

thousands. Signs of recovery and a relaxation of Islamist strictness appeared in Iran in the late 1990s, but the devastation from war also remained visible. In contrast to Iranians, their lives altered and diminished by revolution and war, Iraqis continued on a militant course. Two years after the end of the Iran-Iraq War, Hussein's troops invaded Kuwait (1990) and incited the Gulf War (1991), which again pitted Arab and Muslim nations against each other. Hussein again suffered defeat, creating further hardship for Iraqis and much of a divided southwest Asia.

Communism and Democracy in Asia

Except for Japan and India, the developing nations in south, southeast, and east Asia adopted some form of authoritarian or militarist political system, and many of them followed a communist or socialist path of political development. Under Mao Zedong (1893–1976) China served as a guide and inspiration for those countries seeking a means of political development distinct from the ways of their previous colonial masters.

Mao reunified China for the first time since the collapse of the Qing dynasty, transforming European communist ideology into a distinctly Chinese communism. After 1949 he embarked on programs designed to accelerate development in China and to distinguish Chinese communism from Soviet communism. The Great Leap Forward (1958–1961) and the Great Proletarian Cultural Revolution (1966–1976) were far-reaching policies that nonetheless hampered the very political and economic development that Mao so urgently sought.

Mao's China

Mao envisioned his Great Leap Forward as a way to overtake the industrial production of more developed nations, and to this end he worked to collectivize all land and to manage all business and industrial enterprises collectively as well. Private ownership was abolished, and farming and industry became largely rural and communal. The Great Leap Forward—or "great leap backward" as some have dubbed it—failed. Most disastrous was its impact on agricultural production in China: the peasants, recalcitrant and exhausted, did not meet quotas, and a series of bad harvests also contributed to one of the deadliest famines in history. Rather than face reality, Mao blamed the sparrows for the bad harvests, accusing these counterrevolutionaries of eating too much grain. He ordered tens of millions of peasants to kill the feathered menaces, leaving insects free to consume what was left of the crops. Between 1959 and 1962 as many as twenty million Chinese may have died of starvation and malnutrition in this crisis.

In 1966 Mao tried again to mobilize the Chinese and reignite the revolutionary spirit, with the inauguration of the Great Proletarian Cultural Revolution. Designed to root out the revisionism Mao perceived

The Cultural Revolution

A 1966 poster shows Mao Zedong inspiring the people to launch the Great Proletarian Cultural Revolution. • Sovfoto/Eastfoto

in Chinese life, especially among Communist Party leaders and others in positions of authority, the Cultural Revolution subjected millions of people to humiliation, persecution, and death. The elite—intellectuals, teachers, professionals, managers, and anyone associated with foreign or bourgeois values—constituted the major targets of the Red Guards, youthful zealots empowered to cleanse Chinese society of opponents to Mao's rule. Victims were beaten and killed, jailed, or sent to corrective labor camps or to toil in the countryside. The Cultural Revolution, which cost China years of stable development and gutted its educational system, did not die down until after Mao's death in 1976. It fell to one of Mao's heirs, Deng Xiaoping, to heal the nation.

Deng's Revolution   Although he was a colleague of Mao, Deng Xiaoping (1904–1997) suffered the same fate as millions of others during the Cultural Revolution: he had to recant criticisms of Mao, identify himself as a petit-bourgeois intellectual, and labor in a tractor-repair factory. After a radical faction failed to maintain the Cultural Revolution after Mao's death, China began to recover from the turmoil. Deng came to power in 1981, and the 1980s are often referred to as the years of "Deng's Revolution." Deng moderated Mao's commitment to Chinese self-sufficiency and isolation and engineered China's entry into the international financial and trading system, a move that was facilitated by the normalization of relations between China and the United States in the 1970s.

The student democracy movement in Tiananmen Square, Beijing, June 1989. • Forrest Anderson/Liaison International

To push the economic development of China, Deng opened the nation to the very influences that had been so suspect under Mao—foreign, capitalist values. His actions included sending tens of thousands of Chinese students to foreign universities so as to rebuild the professional, intellectual, and managerial elite needed for modern development. These students were exposed to the democratic societies of the Euro-American world. When they staged pro-democracy demonstrations in Beijing's Tiananmen Square in 1989, Deng, whose experiences in the Cultural Revolution made him wary of zealous revolutionary movements, approved a bloody crackdown. Not surprisingly, Deng faced hostile world opinion after crushing the student movement. The issue facing China as it entered the global economy was how (or whether) to reap economic benefits without compromising its identity and its authoritarian political system. This issue gained added weight as Hong Kong, under British administration since the 1840s and in the throes of its own democracy movement, reverted to Chinese control in 1997.

The flourishing of democracy in India stands in stark contrast to the political trends not just in developing nations in Asia but throughout the world. While other nations turned to dictators, military rule, or authoritarian systems, India maintained its political stability and its democratic system after gaining independence in 1947. Even when faced with the crises that shook other developing nations—ethnic and religious conflict, wars, poverty, and overpopulation—India remained committed to free elections and a critical press. Its first postindependence prime minister, Jawaharlal Nehru (1889–1964), guided his nation to democratic rule.

Indian Democracy

In 1966 Indira Gandhi (1917–1984), Nehru's daughter (and no relation to Mahatma Gandhi), became leader of the Congress Party. She served as prime minister of India in 1966–1977 and 1980–1984 and under her leadership India embarked on the "green revolution" that increased agricultural yields for India's eight hundred million people. Although the new agricultural policies tended to aid wealthier farmers, the masses of peasant farmers fell deeper into poverty. Beyond the poverty that drove Indians to demonstrations of dissatisfaction with Gandhi's government, India was beset by other troubles: overpopulation and continuing sectarian conflicts.

These problems prompted Indira Gandhi to take stringent action to maintain control. To quell growing opposition to her government, she declared a "national emergency" (1975–1977) that suspended democratic processes. She used her powers under the emergency to forward one of India's most needed social reforms, birth control, but rather than persuading or tempting Indians to control the size of their families (offering gifts of money for those who got vasectomies, for example), the government engaged in repressive birth control policies, including involuntary sterilization. A record eight million sterilization operations were performed in 1976–1977. The riots that ensued, and the fear of castration among men who might be forced to undergo vasectomies, added to Gandhi's woes.

When Indira Gandhi allowed elections to be held in 1977, Indians voted against her because of her abrogation of democratic principles and her harsh birth control policies. She returned to power in 1980, however, and again faced great difficulty keeping the state of India together in the face of religious, ethnic, and secessionist movements. One such movement was an uprising by Sikhs

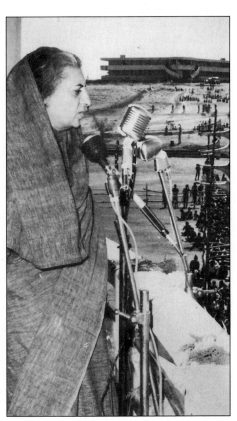

Indira Gandhi delivers a speech in 1972.

• Corbis-Bettmann

who wanted greater autonomy in the Punjab region. The Sikhs, representing perhaps 2 percent of India's population, practiced a religion that was an offshoot of Hinduism, and they had a separate identity and a history of militarism and self-rule—symbolized by their distinctive long hair and headdresses. Unable or unwilling to compromise in view of the large number of groups agitating for a similar degree of autonomy, Indira Gandhi ordered the army to attack the sacred Golden Temple in Amristar, which had harbored armed Sikh extremists. In retaliation, two of her Sikh bodyguards—hired for their martial skills—assassinated her a few months later in 1984.

Indira Gandhi's son Rajiv Gandhi (1944–1991) took over the leadership of India in 1985 and offered reconciliation to the Sikhs. He was assassinated by a terrorist in 1991 while attempting to win back the office he had lost in 1989. Despite these setbacks, however, Nehru's heirs maintained democracy in India and continued to work on the problems plaguing Indian development—overpopulation, poverty, and sectarian division.

GLOBAL ECONOMIC EXPERIMENTS

Many of the political transformations of the postcolonial era were tied to economic well-being—or the lack of it. This point holds true for the developing lands working to establish sound political and economic structures as well as for the superpowers whose economic and political dominance decreased as other industrialized or industrializing nations began to challenge their financial power. Transformations in global trade relations, in the form of regional cartels and trade alliances, also undermined the economic status quo by forging new power blocs to participate in global economic competition. While many former colonies experienced financial crises and continuing dependence on European and U.S. capital, other nations, such as Japan and China, industrialized and competed with established economic powerhouses in the global economy. Cartels like the Organization of Petroleum Exporting Countries (OPEC) and trading blocs like the EC likewise unsettled the old way of doing business, setting the stage for a new world economic order no longer controlled by any single power.

Dependence in Latin America and Africa

The mid-twentieth century seemed promising for economic health and well-being in Latin America, as nations in that region experienced sustained economic growth through expanded export trade and diversification of foreign markets. Exports included manufactured goods as well as the traditional export commodities of minerals and foodstuffs (for example, sugar, fruits, and coffee).

Latin America   Economic growth and industrialization attracted foreign investment and promoted further expansion. The global recession of the 1970s and 1980s, however, halted that expansion. Latin American states had incurred huge foreign debts, and commodity prices fell during the recession, reducing export profits so much that it became almost impossible to pay the interest on those debts. The recession and the debt crisis hit Latin America hard, and renegotiating debt payments to the developed nations opened the region to efforts to influence their economic policies. Latin American peoples have continued to finance their economic development through European and U.S. capital, thus maintaining ties to global markets and money, and their economies are strong enough to limit the effects of dependency.

Unlike the industrialized, developed lands of Latin America, most African nations are less developed countries (LDCs)—countries that have the world's lowest per capita incomes and little industrial development. Africa contains 10 percent of the world's population but accounts for only 1 percent of its industrial output. By the mid-1980s only seven African nations had per capita incomes of $1,000 or more, and the continent had the world's highest number of low-income states. Africa is rich in mineral resources, raw materials, and agricultural products, but it lacks the capital, technology, foreign markets, and managerial class necessary to exploit its natural wealth. An ever-growing population compounds Africa's economic woes. Sub-Saharan Africa has one of the highest rates of population growth in the world—between 2.5 and 3 percent per year.

African Dependency

Africa's economic prospects after decolonization were not always so bleak, and they may improve in coming decades. The postwar period saw growing demand for Africa's commodity exports, and many African nations developed or continued financial links with ex-colonial powers to finance economic development. After the 1970s, however, nations in Africa and Latin America faced the same crises: huge foreign debts, falling commodity prices, and rising import costs. Africa's burdens were complicated by droughts, famines, and agricultural production that could not keep pace with population growth. Leaders of African nations were among the strongest supporters of the New International Economic Order (NIEO), which had been called for by a coalition of developing nations. These states sought a more just allocation of global wealth, especially by guaranteeing prices and markets for commodities. Nevertheless, African states have continued to attempt wider integration into the global economy, despite the dependency this move often entails.

While the political and economic optimism that accompanied decolonization has dimmed in Africa, some bright spots remain on the horizon. African nations are many and diverse, and they do not all suffer the same economic or political fate. The multiracial government in South Africa serves as a symbol of the political possibilities in Africa and as a capitalist model for economic development, given its high level of industrial production and economic growth. While the populations of African states continue to grow, so do hopes for a new generation of economic solutions that can promote the health and welfare of those populations.

Economic Growth in Asia

While the strength of the industrialized lands of Europe and the United States often appeared undiminished in their economic relationships with societies in Latin America and Africa, Asian nations embarked on a path of economic development that allowed them to compete with European and U.S. economies. Just as the recovery of western European economies following World War II contributed to a decline of U.S. influence in European politics, so did the similar process that unfolded in east Asia, where Japan developed into an impressive economic power. As it had done with defeated Germany, the U.S. government viewed Japan as a counterweight to Soviet and Chinese communism and actively encouraged the island nation's economic recovery.

U.S. policies jumpstarted Japan's economic revival after its defeat in 1945, and by 1949 the Japanese economy had already attained its prewar level of productivity. As western European countries had benefited from the Marshall plan, so Japan benefited from direct U.S. financial aid ($2 billion), investment, and the timely abandonment of war reparations. In addition, there were no restrictions on the entry of Japanese products into the U.S. market. The United States, in its role as Japan's

Japan

military protector, contributed to long-term economic growth as well. Because a 1952 mutual defense treaty stipulated that Japan could never spend more than 1 percent of its gross national product on defense, Japan's postwar leaders channeled the nation's savings into economic development. U.S. purchases of supplies for use in the Korean War also stimulated an economic boom in Japan. By the mid-1950s the people of Japan enjoyed the highest standard of living in all of Asia.

U.S. aid, investments, and protection were not, however, the sole or even the principal determinant of Japan's economic "miracle." U.S. policies had laid the foundation for indigenous ingenuity and development. At first sight Japan's economy was ill equipped for intensive economic growth. Japan had lost its overseas empire and was hampered by a large population and a lack of natural resources. Japan's economic planners sidestepped many of these disadvantages by promoting an economic policy that emphasized export-oriented growth supported by low wages. The large and mostly compliant work force, willing to endure working conditions and wages considered intolerable by organized labor in western Europe and the United States, gave Japanese employers a competitive edge over international rivals. Although Japanese industries had to pay for the import of most raw materials, the low cost of Japanese labor assured the production of goods that were cheap enough to compete on the basis of price.

At first the Japanese economy churned out labor-intensive manufactured goods such as textiles, iron, and steel slated for export to markets with high labor costs, particularly the United States. During the 1960s Japanese companies used their profits to switch to more capital-intensive manufacturing, producing radios, television sets, motorcycles, and automobiles. In the following decade Japanese corporations took advantage of a highly trained and educated work force and shifted their economic resources toward technology-intensive products such as random access memory chips, liquid crystal displays, and CD-ROM drives. By this time the label "Made in Japan," once associated with cheap manufactured goods, signified state-of-the-art products of the highest quality.

Japan's economic prowess, like that of the EC, did not lead directly to a global realignment, for U.S. diplomatic and military influence remained strong. Yet Japan's economic achievements gave its banks, corporations, and government an increasingly prominent voice in global affairs. Although the Japanese role in world affairs remained to be defined precisely, neither the European imperial powers of the past nor the U.S. colossus of the present could dictate Japan's position in the world. Equally significant, the Japanese success story served as an inspiration for other Asian countries.

The Little Tigers   The earliest and most successful imitators of the Japanese model for economic development were Hong Kong, Singapore, South Korea, and Taiwan. Their remarkable and rapid growth rates earned them the sobriquet of the "four little tigers," and by the 1980s these newly industrializing countries (NICs) had become major economic powers. Like Japan, all four countries suffered from a shortage of capital, lacked natural resources, and had to cope with overpopulation. But like Japan a generation earlier, they transformed apparent disadvantages into advantages through a program of export-driven industrialization. By the 1990s the four little tigers were no longer simply imitators of Japan, but had become serious competitors. As soon as new Japanese products had carved out market niches, corporations based in the four little tigers moved in and undercut the original item with their own cheaper versions.

China provides yet another economic success story. As noted earlier Deng's rev- *Deng's China*
olution had much to do with China's economic expansion. Under his leadership
China industrialized and entered the international financial and trading system. It
shifted from heavy to light industry, turned to export-oriented production, and allowed limited free market operations and private ownership of property. In reality,
China is divided into two economic zones: the vast rural interior, which has remained largely untouched by this economic revolution, and the coastal zones, which
are centers of economic development. As Hong Kong became integrated into this
coastal zone of development, China's power in the region and the world increased.

Global Trade Relations

In the rapidly changing global economy, groups of nations entered into economic
alliances designed to achieve advantages and greater strength for their partners in
the competitive global economy. One of the earliest and most successful of such alliances was the Organization of Petroleum Exporting Countries (OPEC), a producer cartel, established in 1960 by the oil-producing states of Iran, Iraq, Kuwait,
Saudi Arabia, and Venezuela and later joined by Qatar, Libya, Indonesia, Abu
Dhabi, Algeria, Nigeria, Ecuador, and Gabon.

The mostly Arab and Muslim member states of OPEC sought to raise the price *OPEC*
of oil through cooperation, but OPEC demonstrated during the Arab-Israeli War of
1973 that cooperation had political as well as economic potential. The cartel ordered an embargo on oil shipments to the United States, Israel's ally, and quadru-
pled the price of oil between 1973 and 1975. The huge increase in the cost of petroleum triggered a global economic downturn, as did a curtailment of oil exports in
the later 1970s. OPEC's policies therefore contributed to the global recession and
debt crisis that hurt many developing nations, but its members—also developing
nations—demonstrated how the alliance could exert control over the developed
world and its financial system. OPEC's influence diminished in the 1980s and 1990s
as a result of overproduction and dissension among its members over the Iran-Iraq
War and the Gulf War.

While some alliances, like OPEC, worked to control production and prices, *GATT*
other nations lobbied for the abolition of all restrictions on free trade. The call for
free trade appealed to nations with fully developed and industrialized economies, especially the United States. U.S. politicians and business leaders wanted to establish
an international trading system that suited their interests, and pushed for the elimination of restrictive trading practices that stood in the way of free trade. The main
vehicle for the promotion of unrestricted global trade was the General Agreement
on Tariffs and Trade (GATT), which was signed by the representatives of twenty-
three noncommunist nations in 1947. GATT members held a series of negotiations
with the intent of removing or loosening barriers to free trade. After the round of
negotiations that ended in 1994, the member nations of GATT (now totaling 123)
signed an agreement to establish the World Trade Organization (WTO), which took
over the activities of GATT in 1995. World trade between 1948 and 1966 grew by
6.6 percent annually and by 9.2 percent between 1966 and 1977. Although trade
slowed in the 1980s, by 1990 world trade (exports and imports) exceeded six tril-
lion U.S. dollars, roughly double the figure for 1980.

Promoting free trade meant acknowledging global economic interdependence; *Regional Trading*
no single economic power could fully control global trade and commerce. In more *Alliances*

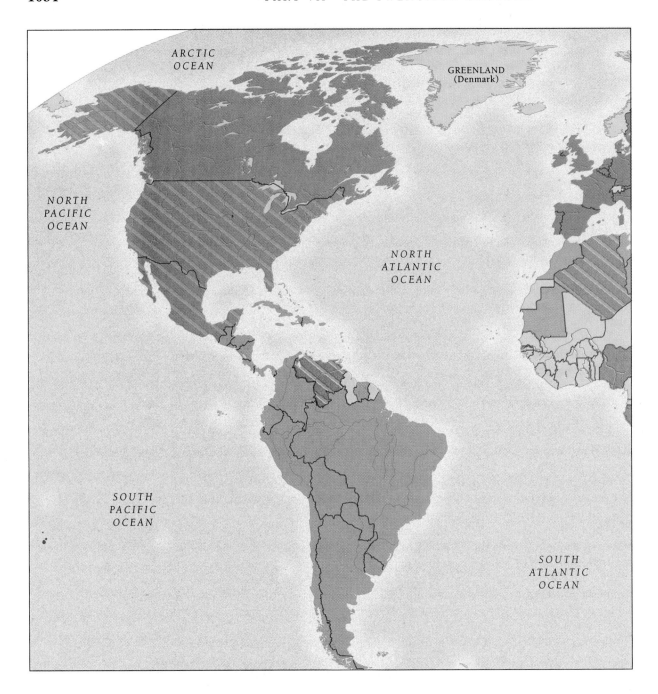

MAP [38.1]

International organizations.

practical terms, promotion of free trade has occurred in regional trading alliances that take advantage of shared political and economic interests to promote trade among member nations and increase their economic growth and political strength.

One of the oldest organizations of this type is the Association of Southeast Asian Nations or ASEAN. Established in 1967 by the foreign ministers of Thailand, Malaysia, Singapore, Indonesia, and the Philippines, its principle objectives were to accelerate economic progress and promote political stability in southeast Asia.

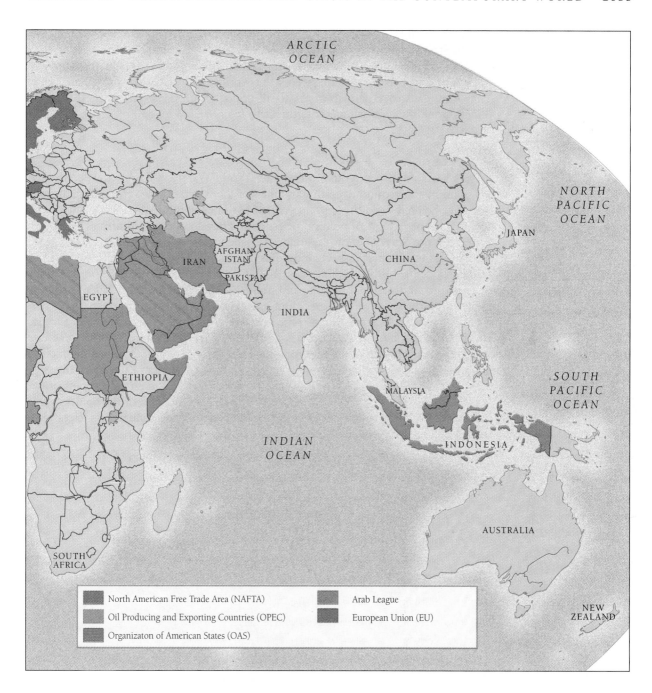

North American Free Trade Area (NAFTA)

Oil Producing and Exporting Countries (OPEC)

Organizaton of American States (OAS)

Arab League

European Union (EU)

Originally conceived as a bulwark against the spread of communism in the region, the economic focus of ASEAN came into sharper relief after it signed cooperative agreements with Japan in 1977 and the European Community in 1980. In 1992 member states agreed to establish a free-trade zone and to cut tariffs on industrial goods over a fifteen-year period. Equally as old, and representing the largest of these regional trading blocs, is the European Union (EU, 1993), the successor to the EC. Through economic and political cooperation, the EU—and the EC before it—has been able to distance itself from the influence of the United States. The United States entered its own regional alliance, approving the North American Free Trade Agreement (NAFTA) with Canada and Mexico in 1993. NAFTA, which went into effect in 1994, constitutes the world's second-largest free-trade zone. There are plans to expand NAFTA to all noncommunist nations in the Americas, underscoring the increasing commitment to regional and global free trade.

In the years immediately before and after World War II, a few nations controlled the political and economic destiny of much of the world. However, with the demise of colonial empires and the shifting political fortunes of the United States and Soviet Union, no one pattern of political or economic development held firm. The United States and the Soviet Union experienced challenges to their hegemony, from both outside and inside their respective borders. Although their bipolar world survived, it no longer defined global politics as it had in the past. The former colonial nations struggled to find national identity and political stability in a world that was still influenced by the legacies of imperialism and in lands often torn by ethnic and religious strife. Most societies found some measure of security even in an era of turmoil and change. Economic transformations undercut nationalistic economic practices and initiated a new era of global economic interaction. Old expectations dimmed in importance; like Sinoqobili Mabhena becoming the first woman Zulu chief, the peoples of the world had to establish new places for themselves in an era of transformation and crisis. It was a task made more challenging by the end of the cold war and the collapse of communism and by the increasing interconnectedness of societies.

CHRONOLOGY

1910	Start of Mexican Revolution
1946–1955	Rule of Juan and Eva Perón in Argentina
1947	GATT
1948	Beginning of apartheid in South Africa
1949	Establishment of People's Republic of China
1956	Uprising in Hungary
1958	Great Leap Forward in China
1959	Sino-Soviet Friendship Treaty
1960	Establishment of OPEC
1963	Founding of Organization of African Unity
1964	Sino-Soviet rift
1966–1976	Great Proletarian Cultural Revolution in China
1967	Arab-Israeli War Establishment of ASEAN Establishment of European Community
1968	Prague Spring
1972	Beginning of détente

1973	Arab-Israeli War Start of Arab oil embargo U.S. defeat in Vietnam
1974	Beginning of global economic recession
1975–1977	State of emergency declared by Indira Gandhi
1976	Death of Mao Zedong
1979	Revolution in Iran
1980	Deng Xiaoping in power in China Beginning of debt crisis
1980–1988	Iran-Iraq War
1983	Assassination of Indira Gandhi
1987	Start of Palestinian uprising
1989	Death of Ayatollah Khomeini Tiananmen Square demonstrations Withdrawal of Soviets from Afghanistan
1990	Invasion of Kuwait by Iraq
1991	Gulf War
1993	Establishment of NAFTA
1994	Hutu genocidal slaughter of Tutsis in Rwanda Election of Nelson Mandela in South Africa
1997	Transfer of British Hong Kong to People's Republic of China End of Mobutu reign in Zaire

FOR FURTHER READING

Leonard Blussé et al., eds. *History and Underdevelopment: Essays on Underdevelopment and European Expansion in Asia and Africa.* Leiden, 1980. Critical essays on a controversial topic.

Mark Borthwick, ed. *Pacific Century: The Emergence of Modern Pacific Asia.* Boulder, 1992. An excellent source for an overview of southeast and east Asia.

David Calleo. *Beyond American Hegemony: The Future of the Western Alliance.* New York, 1987. A broad treatment of Europe during and after the cold war.

Basil Davidson. *The Black Man's Burden: Africa and the Curse of the Nation State.* New York, 1992. This critical postindependence account emphasizes the shortcomings of nationalism and the national state.

R. N. Gwynne. *New Horizons? Third World Industrialization in an International Framework.* New York, 1990. Examines diverse forms of industrialization in the developing world.

Robert Hardgrave Jr. and Stanley A. Hardgrave. *India: Government and Politics in a Developing Nation.* 4th ed. San Diego, 1986. Indian postindependence politics are at the center of this work.

Benjamin Keen. *Latin American Civilization: History and Society, 1492 to the Present.* 6th ed. Boulder, 1996. A series of primary documents with accompanying historical analysis, with a progressive or leftist interpretation.

Phyllis M. Martin and Patrick O'Meara, eds. *Africa.* 3rd ed. Bloomington, 1995. An insightful collection of articles addressing the cultural, social, economic, and political development of Africa.

Mark Mathabane. *Kaffir Boys: The True Story of a Black Youth's Coming of Age in Apartheid South Africa.* New York, 1986. A gripping real-life story.

Roy A. Medvedev and Zhores A. Medvedev. *Khrushchev: The Years in Power.* New York, 1976. One of the more insightful accounts of Khrushchev and de-Stalinization.

Robert A. Mortimer. *The Third World Coalition in International Politics.* New York, 1980. Surveys the political evolution of the nonaligned world.

Bernard D. Nassiter. *Global Struggle for More: Third World Conflicts with the Rich Nations.* New York, 1986. Summarizes the economic problems of developing societies.

Don Peretz. *The Middle East Today.* 4th ed. New York, 1988. Thorough survey of contemporary history of the various countries of southwest Asia and north Africa.

Thomas E. Skidmore and Peter H. Smith. *Modern Latin America*. New York, 1992. Excellent overview covering the region from 1880s to 1980s, supported by an extensive bibliography.

Derek W. Unwin. *The Community of Europe: A History of European Integration since 1945*. London, 1991. Sweeping treatment of the coming together of western European nations.

Jeffrey N. Wasserstrom and Elizabeth J. Perry, eds. *Popular Protest and Political Culture in Modern China*. 2nd ed. Boulder, 1994. Scholars from various disciplines take a critical look at contemporary China in this collection of essays.

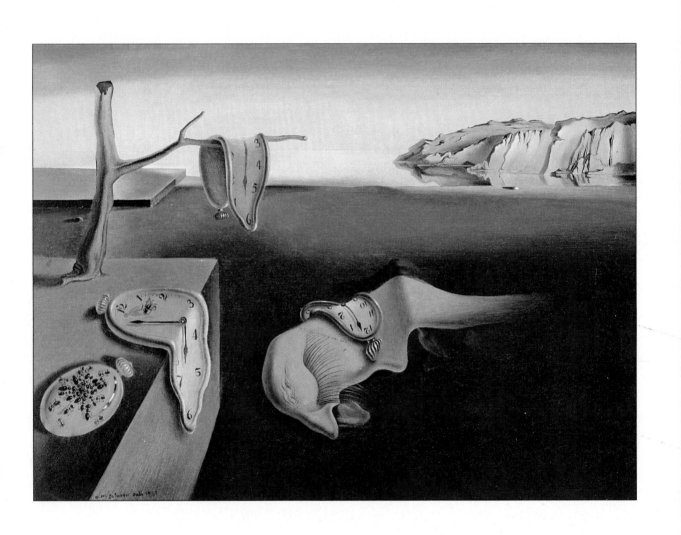

CHAPTER 39

A WORLD WITHOUT BORDERS

· · ·

On 9 November 1989, Kristina Matschat felt both excitement and tension in the night air of Berlin. She had joined thousands of other East Germans at Checkpoint Charlie, one of the most famous crossing points in the Berlin Wall. Anticipating that some momentous event was soon to occur at the Wall, that the Wall might indeed come down that very night, she also shivered in fear at the proximity of the *Volkspolizei* ("people's police")—the same officers who since 1961 had gunned down East Germans attempting to scale the Wall and escape to freedom in West Berlin. She had worn running shoes in case she needed to sprint away if shooting broke out or tanks rumbled through East Berlin to prevent the destruction of the Wall.

She remembered that "everybody was full of fear—but also full of hope." Bitter memories flooded her consciousness as she recalled not being allowed to study what she wanted in school, not being able to speak freely of her discontent in case her friends were government spies, and not being able to locate disgruntled colleagues whom the government had condemned as "unwanted elements." Her hope overcame her fears, though, as she began to chant with her fellow compatriots, "Tear the wall down! Open the gates!" She could see that on the other side of the Wall that massive crowds of West Berliners had gathered to join their demonstration. Thrilled by this open protest against the most salient symbol of the cold war, she was nonetheless psychologically unprepared for victory when it came. Just before midnight East German soldiers suddenly began not only opening gates in the Wall but also gently helping East Germans crossing to the West, often for the first time in their lives. Her near disbelief at the swift downfall of Berlin's decades-old barricade registered in the word she heard shouted over and over again by those passing through the Wall: *Wahnsinn* ("craziness").

Kristina Matschat remained at the Wall until 3:00 or 4:00 a.m., celebrating with the hundreds of thousands of other Berliners who now mingled, drinking champagne and dancing on top of the Wall. While celebrating the fall of the barbed wire and mortar structure, she became aware of the significance of a world without borders: "Suddenly we were seeing the West for the first time, the forbidden Berlin we

Salvador Dali, *The Persistence of Memory,* (1931). A leading surrealist, Dali declared that his ambition was to "systemize confusion." • *The Persistence of Memory,* 1931. By Salvador Dail. Oil on canvas, 9½″ × 13″. The Museum of Modern Art, New York. Given anonymously. Photograph © 2000 The Museum of Modern Art, New York. © 1999 Fundacion Gala-Salvador Dali/Artists Rights Society (ARS), New York

had only seen on TV or heard about from friends. When we came home at dawn, I felt free for the first time in my life. I had never been happier." The fall of the Berlin Wall brought down one of the world's most notorious borders and symbolized the breaching of all sorts of boundaries in the contemporary world. The death of communist regimes in eastern and central Europe and in the Soviet Union marked the end of the cold war, and the geographic, political, and ideological divisions of the bipolar world evaporated within an amazingly short period. As old political borders shifted and the iron curtain lifted, new if uncertain political opportunities arose.

Along with the end of the cold war, many other forces were at work to create a new, more open world. Although certain national and communist borders changed only at the end of the cold war, cultural and technological developments since World War II steadily broke down the distances between countries and peoples. Cultural integration resulted from the never-ending stream of ideas, information, and values spreading from one society to another. Consumer goods, popular culture, television, computers, and the Internet all spread outward from advanced capitalist and industrialized nations, particularly Europe and the United States, and other societies had to come to terms with this breakdown of cultural and technological barriers. Cultural traditions from Europe and the United States were challenged as often as they were accepted, as most the world's peoples attempted to blend foreign cultural practices with their own.

The world's peoples themselves underwent changes in a world with fewer barriers. Women struggled to close the divide between the sexes, at times fighting for equal economic, social, and political rights and at other times abiding by gender expectations while waiting for new opportunities to improve their condition. As populations grew at often alarming rates, women spent much of their time at the traditional female task of child rearing, but both women and men embarked on migrations when their societies could no longer adequately support their growing populations. They moved to the cities or to other nations either to escape suffering or to seek new fortunes.

The populations moving around the globe revealed the diminishing significance of national boundary lines, but they also posed problems that could not be solved by any one state acting alone. International organizations like the United Nations acknowledged that global problems needed global solutions, underscoring anew the tenuousness of borders in the contemporary world. Not everyone experienced the ecstasy Kristina Matschat felt at the Berlin Wall when that most restrictive border disappeared, but global interconnectedness made it more difficult to maintain boundaries among the peoples and countries of the world.

THE END OF THE COLD WAR

The destruction of the Berlin Wall signaled the collapse of the Soviet Union–backed regime responsible for its construction. The cold war was coming to its end. Between 1989 and 1990, through a series of mostly nonviolent revolutions, the peoples of eastern and central Europe regained their independence, instituted democratic forms of government, and adopted market-based economies.

The collapse of communist regimes in Europe was the direct consequence of interrelated economic and political developments. The economic weakness of the communist regimes in eastern and central Europe and the Soviet Union became so apparent as to require reforms. The policies espoused by Soviet leader Mikhail S. Gorbachev

(1931–), who came to power in 1985, represented an effort to address this economic deterioration, but they also unleashed a tidal wave of revolution that brought down governments from Czechoslovakia to the Soviet Union itself. As communism unraveled throughout eastern and central Europe, Gorbachev desperately tried to save the Soviet Union from disintegration by restructuring the economy and liberalizing society. Caught between the rising tide of radical reforms and the opposition of entrenched interests, however, there was little he could do but watch as events unfolded beyond his control. By the time the Soviet Union collapsed in 1991, the Soviet vision of socialism had ceased to inspire either fear or emulation. The cold war system of states and alliances had become irrelevant to international relations.

Revolutions in Eastern and Central Europe

The inability to connect communism with nationalism had left communist regimes vulnerable throughout eastern and central Europe. Those regimes had been born in Moscow, transplanted by the Soviet army, and then shored up by tanks and bayonets. To most of eastern and central Europeans, the Soviet-imposed governments lacked legitimacy from the beginning, and despite the efforts of local communist leaders, the regimes never became firmly established.

For a while it seemed possible that Stalin's "friendly governments" might succeed in establishing rapport with indigenous populations. By the end of World War II, conservative political parties had lost credibility because they had not supported democracy in the interwar period and subsequently aided the Nazis during the war. Conversely, left-wing parties had acquired a solid record of opposition to authoritarian regimes in general and Nazi rule in particular. As for the Soviet Union, its prestige was high after the war because it had played a major role in defeating fascism and liberating eastern and central Europe from Nazi rule.

Moscow's Legacies

Emanating from the Soviet Union itself was the hope that reform might push the regimes of eastern and central Europe toward less harsh and more enlightened communist rule. Nikita Khrushchev's denunciation of the Stalin era and his vision of a more prosperous and humane communism inspired a generation of reformers in both the Soviet Union and Europe. The brutal Soviet interventions in 1956 (Hungary) and 1968 (Czechoslovakia), however, dashed the aspirations and dreams of reformers. By the early 1970s intellectuals and dissidents had abandoned all hope for a humane socialism. The Polish intellectual Leszek Kolakowski echoed the sentiments of many when he bitterly complained in 1971 that "the dead and by now also grotesque creature called Marxist-Leninism still hangs at the necks of the rulers like a hopeless tumor."

Despite economic stagnation and obvious signs of discontent, the rulers of eastern and central Europe were too reluctant to confront the challenge and restructure their ailing systems. It remained for a new Soviet leader, Mikhail S. Gorbachev, to unleash the forces that would result in the disappearance of the Soviet empire in Europe. By the time Gorbachev visited East Berlin in 1989 on the fortieth anniversary of the German Democratic Republic, he had committed himself to a restructuring of the Soviet Union and to unilateral withdrawal from the cold war. In public interviews he surprised his grim-faced hosts with the announcement that the Brezhnev Doctrine was no longer in force and that from then on each country would be responsible for its own destiny. As one observer put it, the "Sinatra doctrine" ("I did it my way") replaced the Brezhnev Doctrine. The new Soviet orientation led in rapid succession to the collapse or overthrow of regimes in Poland, Bulgaria, Hungary, Czechoslovakia, Romania, and East Germany.

Gorbachev's Impact

*Revolutions
in Eastern Europe*

Polish demonstrators raise a placard with Mikhail Gorbachev's photograph, illustrating the impact of his reforms on the collapse of communism in Europe. • Georges Merillon/Liaison International

The end of communism came first in Poland, where Solidarity—a combined trade union and nationalist movement—put pressure on the crumbling rule of the Communist Party. The Polish government legalized the previously banned Solidarity movement and agreed to multiparty elections in 1989 and 1990. The voters favored Solidarity candidates, and Lech Walesa (1943–), the movement's leader, became president of Poland. In Bulgaria popular unrest forced Todor Zhivkov (1911–), eastern Europe's longest surviving communist dictator, to resign in November 1989. Two months later a national assembly began dismantling the communist state. Hungarians tore down the Soviet-style political system during 1988 and 1989. In 1990 they held free elections and launched their nation on the rocky path toward democracy and a market economy.

The demise of communism continued elsewhere in eastern Europe. In Czechoslovakia a "velvet revolution" swept communists out of office and restored democracy by 1990. The term *velvet revolution* derived from the fact that aside from the initial suppression of mass demonstrations, little violence was associated with the transfer of power in societies formerly ruled by an iron fist. The communist leadership simply stood by and watched events take their course. In 1993 disagreements over the time frame for shifting to a market economy led to a "velvet divorce," breaking Czechoslovakia into two new nations, the Czech Republic and Slovakia. In Rumania, by contrast, the regime of dictator Nicolae Ceauşescu (1918–1989) refused to acknowledge the necessity of reform. In 1989 Securitate, a brutal secret police force, savagely repressed demonstrations, setting off a national uprising that ended within four days and left Ceauşescu and his wife dead.

East Germany had long been a staunchly communist Soviet satellite. Its aging leader Erich Honecker (1912–1994) openly objected to Gorbachev's ideas and clung to Stalinist policies. When he showed genuine bewilderment at the fact that East German citizens fled the country by the thousands through openings in the iron curtain in Hungary and Czechoslovakia, his own party removed him from power. It was too late for anything other than radical changes, and when the East

German regime decided to open the Berlin Wall to intra-German traffic on 9 November 1989, the end of the German Democratic Republic was in sight. In 1990 the two Germanies, divided by the cold war, formed a united nation.

The Collapse of the Soviet Union

The desire to concentrate attention and resources on urgent matters at home motivated Gorbachev's decision to disengage his nation from the cold war and its military and diplomatic extensions. When he came to power in 1985, Gorbachev was keenly aware of the need for reform of the economy and liberalization of Soviet society, although he never intended to abolish the existing political and economic system. Yet it

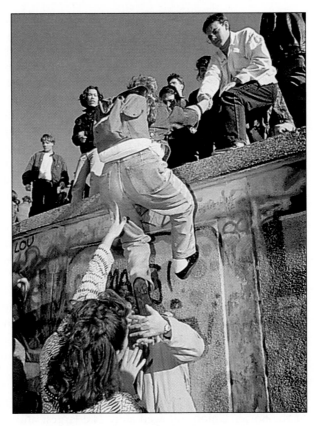

Berliners climb the Wall after it fell on 9 November 1989.

• © 1989 Tom Stoddart/Katz Pictures/Woodfin Camp

proved impossible to fix parts of the system without undermining the whole. The desire of the Communist Party to control every aspect of the system precluded partial reforms.

Gorbachev's reform efforts focused on the ailing economy. Antiquated industrial plants, obsolete technologies, and inefficient government control of production resulted in shoddy and outmoded products. The diversion of crucial resources to the military made it impossible to produce enough consumer goods—regardless of their quality. The failure of state and collective farms to feed the population compelled the Soviet government to import grains from the United States, Canada, and elsewhere. By 1990 the government had imposed rationing to cope with the scarcity of essential consumer goods and food. Economic stagnation in turn contributed to the decline of the Soviet standard of living. Ominous statistics documented the disintegration of the state-sponsored health care system: infant mortality increased while life expectancy decreased. Funding of the educational system dropped precipitously, and pollution threatened to engulf the entire country. Demoralization affected ever larger numbers of Soviet citizens as divorce rates climbed, corruption intensified, and alcoholism became widespread.

Gorbachev's Reforms

Under the slogan of *uskorenie,* or "acceleration," Gorbachev tried to shock the economy out of its coma. Yet the old methods of boosting production and productivity through bureaucratic exhortation and harassment paid few dividends; in fact, they called attention to the drawbacks of centralized economic control. Gorbachev then contemplated different kinds of reform, using the term *perestroika,* or "restructuring," to describe his efforts to decentralize the economy. To make perestroika work, the Soviet leader linked it to *glasnost,* a term that referred to the opening of Soviet society to public criticism and admission of past mistakes.

Perestroika and Glasnost

Perestroika proved more difficult to implement than Gorbachev had imagined, and glasnost unleashed a torrent of criticism that shook the Soviet state to its foundations. When Gorbachev began pushing economic decentralization, the profit motive and the cost-accounting methods he instituted engendered the hostility of those whose privileged positions depended on the old system. Many of Gorbachev's comrades and certain factions of the military not only objected to perestroika but also worked to undermine or destroy it. Glasnost also turned out to be a two-edged sword as it opened the door to public criticism of party leaders and Soviet institutions in a way that would have been unimaginable only a short time earlier. While discontent with Soviet life burst into the open, long-repressed ethnic and nationalist sentiments bubbled to the surface, posing a threat to the multiethnic Soviet state. Only half of the 285 million Soviet citizens were Russian. The other half included numerous ethnic minorities, most of which had never fully reconciled themselves to Soviet dominance.

By the summer of 1990, Gorbachev's reforms had spent themselves. As industrial and agricultural production continued their downward slide against a backdrop of skyrocketing inflation, the Soviet economy began to disintegrate. Inspired by the end of the Soviet empire in eastern and central Europe, many minorities now began to contemplate secession from the Soviet Union. The Baltic peoples—Estonians, Latvians, and Lithuanians—were first into the fray, declaring their independence in August 1991. In the following months the remaining twelve republics of the Soviet Union followed suit. The largest and most prominent of the Soviet republics, the Russian Soviet Federated Socialist Republic, and its recently elected president Boris N. Yeltsin (1931–), led the drive for independence. Soviet leaders vacillated between threats of repression and promises of better treatment, but neither option could stop the movement for independence.

Collapse

Although the pace of reform was neither quick nor thorough enough for some, others convinced themselves that they had already gone too far. While Gorbachev was vacationing in the Crimea in August 1991, a group of conspirators—including discontented party functionaries, disillusioned KGB (secret police) officials, and dissatisfied military officers—decided to seize power. Gorbachev's former friend and ally, the flamboyant Boris Yeltsin, crushed the coup with the help of loyal Red Army units. Gorbachev emerged unscathed from house arrest, but his political career had ended. He watched from the sidelines as Yeltsin dismantled the Communist party and pushed the country toward market-oriented economic reforms. As the Soviet system disintegrated, several of its constituent regions moved toward independence. On 25 December 1991 the Soviet flag fluttered for the last time atop the Kremlin, and by the last day of that year the Union of Soviet Socialist Republics had ceased to exist.

Toward an Uncertain Future

In many ways the cold war had provided comfort to the world—however cold that comfort seemed at the time. World War II had left most of the major imperialist, fascist, and militarist nations in shambles, and the United States and the Soviet Union had stepped into what could have been an uncomfortable vacuum in global leadership. Perilous and controlling it may have been, but the cold war that resulted from the ideological contest between the superpowers had ordered and defined the world for almost fifty years. The cold war had also shaped how the nations and peoples of the world perceived themselves—as good capitalists fighting evil communists, as progressive socialists battling regressive capitalists, or as nonaligned peoples striving to follow their own paths. While these perceptions placed constraints on the choices open to them, particularly given the control exerted by the United States and the USSR at the peak of their power, the choices nonetheless were familiar. At the end of the cold war, those easy choices had disappeared. The stunning impact of the end of the cold war thus reverberated both in policy-making circles and on the streets.

The most immediate and obvious loss that accompanied the end of the cold war involved the alliance systems built by the two former superpowers. At one time critics of the cold war routinely denounced military alliances like NATO or the Warsaw Pact for promoting an expensive arms race and for constantly threatening to transform local conflicts into nuclear confrontations between the superpowers. After the end of the cold war, it became fashionable to praise the same alliances for their ability to manage rather than to escalate such conflicts. Moreover, many observers praised the cold war system for providing peace and security around the world, despite the nuclear balance of terror. The loss of deterrence against global disorder and violence was matched by a corresponding lack of certainty regarding the future and by a declining sense of purpose in an era no longer characterized by ideological struggle.

A Future without Divisions

The disappearance of communist regimes in eastern Europe, the dissolution of the Soviet Union, and the increasing market orientation of the People's Republic of China virtually guaranteed the diminishing popularity of the communist model. To be sure, a few states, such as Cuba and North Korea, clung to communism. But their economies teetered on the edge of collapse, and without the support once furnished by the Soviet Union, their long-term viability as communist regimes was doubtful. The end of the cold war suggested the possibility of a radical shift in power relations, a global realignment that marked a new era of world history devoid of the categories embraced during the cold war.

CROSS-CULTURAL EXCHANGES AND GLOBAL COMMUNICATIONS

The fall of the Berlin Wall and the end of the cold war brought down the most obvious political barriers of the post–World War II world. Long before then, however, cultural and technological developments had started a similar process of breaching boundaries. By showcasing the consumer goods of capitalist societies and spreading news of each new chapter in the fall of communism, television, in fact, had helped spur the revolutions that ended the cold war. As Kristina Matschat testified, before the Berlin Wall fell she had seen West Berlin only on television. One of the first products of the global consumer culture imbibed by East Germans was Coca-Cola, served to them by store owners in West Berlin.

Like trade and business organizations, cultural practices have also become globalized, thriving on a continuous flow of information, ideas, tastes, and values. At the turn of the twentieth century, local traditions—commonly derived from gender, social class, or religious affiliation—still determined the cultural identity of the vast

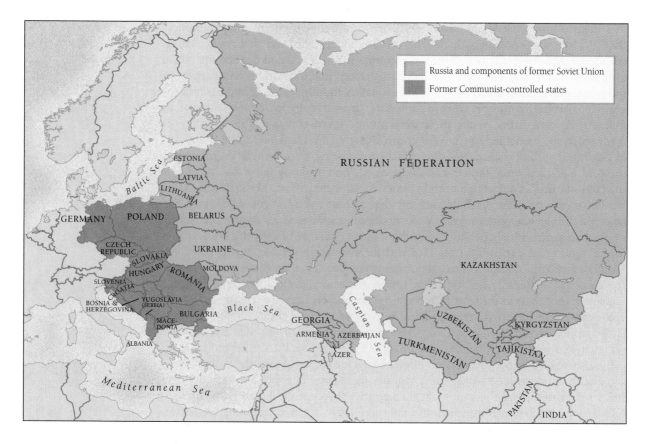

MAP [39.1]

The collapse of the Soviet Union and European communist regimes.

majority of people. At the end of the twentieth century, thanks in part to advances in technology and communications, information and cultural practices were becoming truly global. Their impact was summarized in a jingle popularized by the Walt Disney corporation during the 1964–65 World's Fair in New York City: "It's a small world after all."

Global Barbie

In October 1996 the Associated Press flashed a news story over its wires (and onto the Internet, through CNN Interactive) with the headline: "Iran's Answer to Barbie." The story described the creation of the Sara doll, who would fight American cultural influences as embodied in the Barbie dolls on store shelves in Tehran. Sara's creator clearly meant the doll to compete with Barbie while promoting the chaste dress and pure values expected of Islamic girls and women. Sara is clothed in long flowing robes and head coverings. She and her brother doll, Dara (an Islamic cleric), pose a stark contrast to the plastic couple from the United States, Barbie and Ken, who show no shame in exposing their bodies and premarital relationship to the world. The cultural gulf between Sara and Dara and Barbie and Ken was intentional; according to Majid Ghaderi, the designer of the dolls and the director of Iran's Institute for the Intellectual Development of Children and Young Adults, "Barbie is an American woman who never wants to get pregnant and have babies. She never wants to look old, and this contradicts our culture."

Ghaderi viewed Barbie as a metaphor for unwanted cultural dominance: "Barbie is like a Trojan Horse. Inside it, it carries Western cultural influences, such as makeup and indecent clothes. Once it enters our society, it dumps these influences on our children." Whether Sara will effectively counter Barbie in Iran is still an open question, but the influence of Islamic clerics on Iranian notions of feminism is apparent. Shopkeepers in Tehran do not expect the doll to do well against Barbie but generally support the idea behind Sara. As one merchant said, "I myself believe that Barbie dolls are not good for our children, although they are beautiful." Feminists might chafe at the idea of Barbie representing a type of emancipated woman that is not welcome in the Islamic world. Iranian Muslims equate women's liberation with not getting pregnant, staying young and wearing makeup and little else. They associate it with a plastic figurine whose impossibly ideal dimensions have given women fits. However, Barbie does serve as one symbol of the U.S. cultural products that are swamping global markets. And Iran's Sara demonstrates how countries have attempted to maintain their own cultural traditions.

Sara versus Barbie in Iran

That Iranian officials perceived Barbie as a Trojan horse bringing in foreign, feminist values—and created the traditional Sara doll to oppose Barbie's influence— suggests how strongly some societies strive counteract foreign cultural influences. At the same time, however, the U.S. cultural system adapted to the demands and sensibilities of the world, modifying its products to conform to indigenous expectations. When Mattel Corporation wanted to market Barbie in Japan, it had to adjust to Japanese cultural sensibilities. Japanese girls preferred Licca, a doe-eyed, brunette, younger doll. They found Barbie's eyes scary, her smile too aggressively toothy, and her attitude too much of a professional woman on the go. Because Barbie challenged Japanese notions of a less-emancipated femininity, Mattel reformed Barbie: she was marketed in family settings, with stroller and children, and she had a rounder face, bigger eyes, a closed mouth, and less shockingly blonde hair. Barbie sales increased. As the manager at a major Japanese toy company concluded: "I don't think their doll is considered American like before. Now there are kids who play with Licca and Barbie together. It's a borderless era."

Barbie in Japan

Consumption and Cultural Interaction

New communications media have tied the world together and have promoted a global cultural integration whose hallmark is consumption. Beginning in the eighteenth century, industrialization and the subsequent rise in per capita income gave birth to a type of society in which the consumption of goods and services satisfied wants and desires rather than needs or necessities. While the desire to consume is hardly novel, the modern consumer culture means more than simple consumption. It implies that consumers want more than they need and that the items they consume take on symbolic value. Consumption, in other words, has become a means of self-expression as well as a source for personal identity and social differentiation. The peculiar shape of this consumer culture resulted from two seemingly contradictory trends: a tendency toward homogenization of cultural products and heightened awareness of local tastes and values.

Critics sometimes refer to the homogenizing aspect of global culture as the "Americanization" or "McDonaldization" of the world. These terms suggest that the consumer culture that developed in the United States during the mid-twentieth century has been exported throughout the world, principally through advertising. Thus it is no accident that young people clad in blue jeans and T-shirts hum the same Michael Jackson lyrics in San Francisco, Sarajevo, and Beijing. Still, nothing symbolizes the global marketing of U.S. mass culture more than the spread of its food and beverage products. While Pepsi and Coca-Cola fight battles over the few places on earth that their beverages have not yet dominated, fast-food restaurants such as Burger King, McDonalds, and Pizza Hut sell their standardized foods throughout the world. The closing of many bistros and cafes in France, for instance, is the result of more French people opting for fashionable fast food instead of taking the time for more traditional and lengthy lunches. So successful has the global spread of U.S. mass culture been that it seems to threaten local or indigenous cultures everywhere.

The export of U.S. products and services is not the sole determinant of global cultural practices, however, as we have seen in the case of Barbie. Because the contemporary consumer culture stresses minute differences between products and encourages consumers to make purchase decisions based on brand names, designed to evoke particular tastes, fashion, or lifestyle, it also fosters differentiation. Indeed, global marketing often emphasizes the local or indigenous value of a product. Genuinely Australian products, such as Drizabone wet-weather gear and Foster's Lager, have become international commodities precisely because they are Australian in origin. Likewise, young upwardly mobile consumers continue to prefer Rolex watches from Switzerland, Armani clothes from Italy, miniature electronics from Japan, and Perrier mineral water from France.

Pan-American Culture

The experiences in the Americas demonstrate that U.S. patterns of cultural consumption have not simply dominated the globe without competition or critical evaluation. For example, as she was dying, the Argentine political and cultural icon Eva Perón is reputed to have said, "I will return and I will be millions." Her prophecy has come true in the images of her that continually appear around the world, and especially in the Americas. In Buenos Aires, city housing projects are named after her, a new Argentine film about her life played in 1996, and her face appears on souvenir T-shirts sold in the streets. In an Argentine supper club, the show's cast members sing "Don't Cry for Me, Argentina" as their grand finale, and audiences rise to their feet applauding. The song is from the musical *Evita* by Sir Andrew Lloyd Webber and Tim Rice, which was first performed in London and subsequently became a hit on Broadway (1979). While Argentine performers sing a Euro-American song, their Evita has become an icon in the United States and Europe, not only in the musical but also in the 1996 film *Evita* starring Madonna.

Although Latin American critics often decry the spell cast by North American popular culture on Latin American audiences, Evita-mania has indicated that the sharing or imposing of cultural practices is a two-way phenomenon. A recent trend in Latin America is Music Television (MTV) Latino, perceived by many as another case of foreign cultural intrusion, where Latin video deejays speak "Spanglish" or "Chequenos" ("check us out"), mixing Spanish and English. Yet whereas Latin Americans once had called for protection against such alien influence, by the 1990s many had relaxed their guard. They see evidence of increased cultural sharing among Latin societies, noting that MTV and cable television have come to serve as a means of communication and unity by making the nations of Latin America more aware of one another. While the sheer dominance and size of the U.S. entertainment-technology industry keeps cultural sharing lopsided, cultural dominance is also limited by those societies' ability to blend and absorb a variety of foreign and indigenous practices.

The Age of Access

Throughout history technological advances such as in shipbuilding provided the means to dissolve boundaries between localities and peoples and thus allowed cultural transmission to take place. Today virtually instantaneous electronic communications have dissolved time and space. Contemporary observers have labeled our era the age of access. Communication by radio, telephone, television, fax machine, and networked computers has spawned a global village that has swept away the social, economic, and political isolation of the past. However, because it takes capital to purchase the necessary equipment, maintain and upgrade it, and train people to use it, many societies find it difficult to plug into the global village. The existing gulf between the "connected" and "unconnected" has the potential therefore to become one border in a world without borders.

This new world of global interconnectedness is not without its detractors. Critics have charged, for instance, that mass media are a vehicle for cultural imperialism because most electronic media and the messages they carry emanate from advanced capitalist societies. A specific consequence is that English is becoming the primary language of global communications systems, effectively restricting vernacular languages to a niche status.

Preeminence of the English Language

The Internet only reinforces the contemporary fact that English has become the universal tongue of the twentieth century. As a result of British conquest or colonialism, subjugated people the world over had been compelled to learn English and become at least bilingual, speaking their own languages along with those of the conqueror. In more recent times many people have voluntarily adopted the language of a politically and economically preeminent English-speaking society, especially the United States. In this fashion English has almost become a universal language, enjoying acceptance in scientific, diplomatic, and commercial circles. However understandable, English-language dominance on the Internet rankles some users. Xia Hong, a manager for an Internet access provider in Shanghai, articulates this concern:

> There's no question about it: the Internet is an information colony. From the moment you go online, you're confronted with English hegemony. It's not merely a matter of making the Nét convenient for users in non-English-speaking countries. People have to face the fact that English speakers are not the whole world. What's the big deal about them, anyway? Our ideal is to create an exclusively Chinese-language network. It will be a Nét that has Chinese characteristics, one that is an information superhighway for the masses.

Such sentiments apparently reflect the thinking of Chinese political leaders, for authorities are currently going to great lengths to ensure that China and its communications system do not become a spiritual colony of capitalist powers like the United States. Accordingly, officials of China's Public Security Bureau—an agency that concerns itself with crimes ranging from murder to cultural espionage—are trying to contain the influence of the Internet by erecting around China a so-called *fanghuo qiang,* or "firewall" (a direct translation from the English). The more prevailing and popular phrase for it is *wangguan*—literally "net wall"—a name that invokes many centuries of Chinese efforts to repulse foreign invaders. However, because the original Great Wall had limited success, the fate of its digital successor remains an open question.

Some societies have managed to adapt European and U.S. technology to meet their own needs while opposing cultural interference. Television, for example, has

Adaptations of Technology

A citizen of Kuwait lugs a television through streets filled with European and U.S. consumer products. From tennis shoes to automobiles to English-language signs, cultural interpenetration is occurring around the globe. • © Bruno Barbey/Magnum Photos

been used to promote state building around the world, since most television industries are state-controlled. In Zaire, for example, the first television picture residents saw each day was of Mobutu Sese Seko. He especially liked to materialize in segments that pictured him walking on clouds—a miraculous vision of his unearthly power. The revolution in electronic communications has been rigidly controlled in societies, including Vietnam and Iraq, where authorities limit access to foreign servers on the Internet.

They thus harness the power of technology for their own purposes while avoiding cultural interference.

 ## CROSSING BOUNDARIES

Human populations also underwent radical transformations. Peoples throughout the world challenged gender definitions and embarked on large-scale migrations. Women in Europe, the United States, China, and the Soviet Union gained greater equality with men, partly by advocating women's liberation and a nonbiological or culturally defined understanding of gender. Elsewhere, women continued to follow their societies' dictates for acceptable female behavior, although extraordinary circumstances propelled some women to prominence even in countries that resisted the feminist revolution.

Both women and men also experienced either forced or voluntary migrations and in the process helped to create an increasingly borderless world. By the end of the twentieth century, many traditional areas of state responsibility—whether pertaining to population policies, health concerns, or environmental issues—needed to be coordinated on an intergovernmental level. Global problems demanded global solutions, and together they compelled the governments of individual states to surrender some of their sovereignty to larger international organizations such as the United Nations.

Women's Traditions and Feminist Challenges

The status of women began changing after World War II. Women gained more economic, political, social, and sexual rights in highly industrialized states than in developing nations, but nowhere have they achieved full equality with men. While women have increasingly challenged cultural norms requiring their subordination to men and confinement in the family, attainment of basic rights for women has been slow. Agitation for gender equality is often linked to women's access to employ-

Women belonging to the U.S. feminist group the National Organization for Women (NOW) march for equal rights in Washington, D.C., in 1992. • Brad Markel/Liaison International

ment, and the industrialized nations have the largest percentage of working women. Women constitute 40 to 50 percent of the workforce in industrial societies, compared to only 20 percent in developing countries. In Islamic societies 10 percent or less of the workforce is composed of women. In all countries women work primarily in low-paying jobs designated as female—that is, teaching, service, and clerical jobs. Forty percent of all farmers are women, many at the subsistence level. Rural African women, for example, do most of the continent's subsistence farming and produce more than 70 percent of Africa's food. Whether they are industrial, service, or agricultural workers, women earn less than men earn for the same work and are generally kept out of the highest paid professional careers.

The discrimination women faced in the workplace was a major stimulus for the feminist movement in industrialized nations. Women in most of these nations had gained the right to vote after the Great War, but they found that political rights did not guarantee economic or sexual equality. After World War II, when more and more women went to work, women started to protest job discrimination, pay differentials between women and men, and their lack of legal equality. In the 1960s these complaints expanded into a full-blown feminist movement that critiqued all aspects of gender inequality. In the United States, for example, the civil rights movement that demanded equality for African-Americans influenced the women's movement and provided a training ground for women activists.

Feminism and Equal Rights

Women started to expose the ways in which a biologically determined understanding of gender led to their oppression. In addition to demanding equality in the workplace, women demanded full control over their bodies and their reproductive systems. Access to birth control and abortion became as essential to women's liberation as economic equality and independence. Only with birth control measures

A poster advertising China's one-child family rule. • J-P Laffont/Sygma

would women be able to determine whether or when to have children and thus avoid the notion that "biology is destiny." The U.S. Civil Rights Act of 1964 prohibited discrimination on the basis of both race and sex, and the introduction of the birth control pill in the 1960s and legal protection of abortion in the 1970s provided a measure of sexual freedom. The gender equality that an Equal Rights Amendment (ERA) would have secured never materialized, however, as the amendment failed to achieve ratification before the 1982 deadline.

Gender Equality   Some socialist or communist societies transformed their legal systems to ensure
in China   basic equality. Legally, the position of women most closely matched that of men in communist or formerly communist countries like the Soviet Union, Cuba, and China. "Women hold up half the sky," Mao Zedong had declared, and this eloquent acknowledgment of women's role translated into a commitment to fairness. The communist dedication to women's rights led to improvement in the legal status of Chinese women once the communists gained power in China. In 1950 communist leaders passed the so-called marriage law, which declared a "new democratic marriage system, which is based on free choice of partners, on monogamy, on equal rights for both sexes, and on protection of the lawful interests of women and children." The law abolished patriarchal practices like child betrothal and upheld equal rights for men and women in the areas of work, property ownership, and inheritance.

Critics argue that despite such laws China's women have never gained true equality. Certainly few women have gained high status in the Communist Party's leadership. And while most women in China have full-time jobs outside the home, they do not receive wages equal to those of men. They do most of the work at home as well. Nevertheless, they are able to enter most professions, although most Chinese women engage in menial work. Long-standing Confucian values continue to degrade the status of women, especially in rural areas. Parents almost universally prefer boys over girls. One unintended consequence of China's population policies, which limits couples to one child, is the mysterious statistical disappearance of a

Education offers hope for the future of Muslim and Arab women. • Francois Perri/Cosmos/
Woodfin Camp

large number of baby girls. Demographers estimate that annually more than one-
half million female births go unrecorded in government statistics. Although no one
can with certainty account for the "missing" girls, some population experts speculate
that a continued strong preference for male children causes parents to send baby
girls away for adoption or to be raised secretly, or in some cases to single them out
for infanticide.

Although girls and women in industrial and communist nations are guaranteed   *Domesticity*
basic if not fully equal legal rights, and are educated in roughly the same numbers as   *and Abuse*
boys and men, women in other areas of the world have long been denied access to
education. Expected to stay at home, girls and women have high illiteracy rates in
these societies. In Arab and Muslim lands, women are twice as likely as men to be illiterate, and in some places nine of ten women are illiterate. This situation is beginning to change. Fifty years ago most women in these societies were illiterate, but in
the last twenty years girls have begun to catch up with boys in education.

The same cannot be said for girls and women in India. In the 1980s only 25 percent of Indian women were literate, and women remained largely confined to the
home. The percentage of women in the workforce declined to 12 percent, and the
birth rate remained high despite birth control measures. This condition has ensured
a life of domesticity for many Indian women. The issue that has most dramatically illustrated the perilous status of women in south Asia, though, is the prevalence of

dowry deaths. What makes the birth of girl children in India so burdensome is the custom of paying dowries (gifts of money or goods) to the husband and his family upon a woman's marriage, a requirement that is difficult for many Indian families to meet. If the husband and his family perceive the dowry as inadequate, if the husband wants a new wife without returning his first wife's dowry, or even if the wife has simply annoyed the husband or her in-laws, the wife is doused with kerosene and set on fire—so that her death can be explained as a cooking accident. Some seven hundred official cases of dowry deaths were reported in Delhi alone in 1983.

This form of domestic abuse has not been restricted to India and Hindu women, but has spread through south Asia. In Pakistan more than five hundred husbands set fire to their wives between 1994 and 1997. The motives for burnings go beyond dowry, as husbands have set fire to wives who overcooked or oversalted the men's food. The victims themselves, some of whom survive, voice perhaps the saddest aspect of this treatment: resignation to their fate. One Pakistani survivor noted, "It's my fate. From childhood, I have seen nothing but suffering." These attitudes may be changing, though, as Indian and Pakistani women activists challenge these practices and establish shelters for women threatened with burning.

Women Leaders   Around the world most women have the right to vote. They do not, however, exert political power commensurate with their numbers. Some women have nonetheless attained high political offices or impressive leadership positions. The same south Asia that revealed so many continued barriers to women's rights on a day-to-day basis also elevated numerous women to positions of power, breaking down other political barriers. Indira Gandhi (1917–1984) and Benazir Bhuto (1953–) led India and Pakistan as effective politicians, having been raised by fathers who themselves were prominent in politics. In 1994 Chandrika Bandaranaike Kumaratunga (1945–) became the first female president of Sri Lanka. Both of her parents had previously served as prime ministers, her mother Sirimavo Bandaranaike (1916–) became the first elected woman prime minister in 1960. As president, Kumaratunga appointed her mother to serve a third term as prime minister.

In Myanmar (formerly Burma), Daw Aung San Suu Kyi (1945–) has emerged as a leader, again deriving her political authority from her father Aung San, assassinated in 1947. Assuming the leadership of the democracy after her return from exile in 1988, Suu Kyi called for a nonviolent revolution against Myanmar's "fascist government." The government placed her under house arrest from 1989 to 1995, during which time she created a new political institution, the "gateside meeting," speaking to her followers from behind the gates of her home. In the 1990 elections Suu Kyi and her party won a landslide victory, but they were not allowed to come to power. Awarded the Nobel Peace Prize for her efforts in 1991, she could not accept the award personally because she was under house arrest.

Women demonstrated their leadership abilities in a variety of ways. They became highly visible political figures, as in south Asia, or they more anonymously joined organizations or participated in activities designed to further the cause of women's rights. The United Nations launched a Decade for Women program in 1975, and since then global conferences on the status of women have been held regularly, attracting large crowds. Even in Iran, where the Islamic revolution severely limited opportunities for women, internal forces could radically transform the image and role of women. Today revolutionary patrols walk the streets of Tehran making sure that women conform to the society's rule of dress and behavior, but during the war with Iraq, Iranian women themselves became revolutionary, picking up guns and receiving weapons training. They protected their national borders while defying gender boundaries.

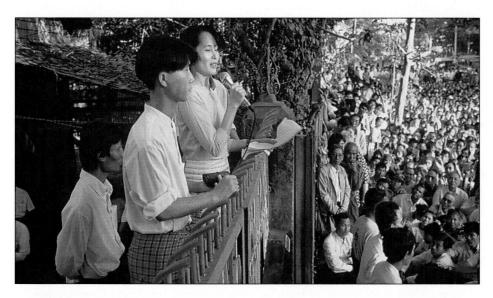

Opposition leader and Nobel Prize winner Aung Saul Suu Kyi at one of her "gateside meetings" in Rangoon, Burma. • Jan Banning/LAIF/Impact Visuals

Population Pressures

The twentieth century has been accompanied by vast population increases. As the result of advances in agriculture, industry, science, medicine, and social organization, the world experienced a fivefold population increase over a period of three hundred years: from 500 million people in 1650 to 2.5 billion in 1950. After World War II the widespread and successful use of vaccines, antibiotics, and insecticides, along with improvements in water supplies and increased agricultural yields, caused a dramatic decline in worldwide death rates. The rapid decline in mortality among people who also maintained high levels of fertility led to explosive population growth in many areas of Asia and Africa. In some developing nations population growth now exceeds 3.1 percent, a rate that assures the doubling of the population within twenty-three years. In 1994 roughly 5.5 billion people shared the planet, and the population division of the United Nations has estimated that the earth's population will stabilize around 11.6 billion in 2200. Although fertility rates have been falling fast in the last two decades, 100 million people are joining the world's total population each year. More importantly, unless fertility declines to replacement levels, that is, two children per woman, the world's population would grow forever. If present fertility rates continue, for example, an unimaginable 700 billion people could inhabit the planet in 2150.

This situation raises the question, How many people can the earth support? That is, what is the earth's carrying capacity? The exact carrying capacity of the planet is, of course, a matter of debate, but by many measures the earth seems to strain already to support the current population. Scientists and concerned citizens have become increasingly convinced that human society cannot infinitely expand beyond the physical limits of the earth and its resources. Beginning in 1967 a group of international economists and scientists—dubbed the Club of Rome—attempted to specify the limits of both economic and population growth in relation to the capacity of the planet to support them. Praised by some as the conscience of the world and

The Planet's Carrying Capacity

THE EARTH IN DEFICIT

• • •

During the last few decades scholarly and popular writers have sounded warnings about the environmental perils posed by technological and industrial advances. In 1985 Thomas Berry, a Christian theologian and committed environmentalist, penned one of the more eloquent statements condemning the contemporary economic practices that led to the ravaging of the earth. The on-going depletion of the earth's resources remains a pressing problem, and Berry's warning has yet to be fully heeded by the majority of the planet's peoples.

In the natural world there exists an amazing richness of life expression in the ever-renewing cycle of the seasons. There is a minimum of entropy. The inflow of energy and the outflow are such that the process is sustainable over an indefinite period of time—so long as the human process is integral with these processes of nature, so long is the human economy sustainable into the future. The difficulty comes when the industrial mode of our economy disrupts the natural processes, when human technologies are destructive of earth technologies. In such a situation the productivity of the natural world and its life systems is diminished. When nature goes into deficit, then we go into deficit. . . .

The earth deficit is the real deficit, the ultimate deficit, the deficit so absolute in some of its major consequences as to be beyond adjustment from any source in heaven or earth. Since the earth system is the ultimate guarantor of all deficits, a failure here is a failure of last resort. Neither economic viability nor improvement in life conditions for the poor can be realized in such circumstances. They can only worsen, especially when we consider rising population levels throughout the developing world.

This deficit in its extreme expression is not only a resource deficit but the death of a living process, not simply the death of *a* living process but of *the* living process—a living process which exists, so far as we know, only on the planet earth. This is what makes our problems definitively different from those of any other generation of whatever ethnic, cultural, political or religious tradition or of any other historical period. For the first time we are determining the destinies of the earth in a comprehensive and irreversible manner. The immediate danger is not *possible* nuclear war but *actual* industrial plundering.

Economics has invaded the earth itself. Our industrial economy is closing down the planet in the most basic modes of its functioning. The air, the water, the soil are already in a degraded condition. Forests are dying on every continent. The seas are endangered. Aquatic life forms in lakes and streams and in the seas are contaminated. The rain is acid. . . . While it is unlikely that we could ever extinguish life in an absolute manner, we are eliminating species at a rate never before known in historic time and in a manner never known in biological time.

Thus the mythic drive to control our world continues, even though so much is known about the earth, its limited resources, the interdependence of life systems, the delicate balance of its ecosystems, the consequences of disturbing the atmospheric conditions, of contaminating the air, the soil, the waterways and the seas, the limited quantity of fossil fuels in the earth, the inherent danger of chemicals discharged into natural surroundings. Although much of this has been known for generations, neither the study nor the commercial-industrial practise of economics has shown any capacity to break free from the mythic commitment to progress, or any awareness that we are in reality creating wasteworld rather than wonderworld. This mythic commitment to continuing economic growth is such that none of our major newspapers or newsweeklies considers having a regular ecological section, equivalent to sports or business or arts or entertainment, although the ecological issues are more important than any of these, more important than the daily national and international political news. The real history that is being made is interspecies and human-earth history, not inter-nation history. Our real threat is from the retaliatory powers of the abused earth, not from other nations.

SOURCE: Thomas Berry, "Wonderworld as Wasteworld: The Earth in Deficit," *Cross Currents,* Winter 1985/86, 35:408–410.

decried by others as being excessively negative, the Club issued a report in 1972 with the subtitle "The Limits to Growth." Because the world's physical resources are in finite supply, the Club of Rome concluded, any transgression of these limits would be calamitous. Less than two decades later, 1500 scientists, including ninety-nine Nobel laureates and representatives from a dozen of the world's most prestigious academies, signed a document entitled "Warning to Humanity" (1992). The report sounded a clear alarm, stating that "human beings and the natural world are on a collision course . . . [that] may so alter the living world that it will be unable to sustain life in the manner that we know."

The problem is not simply one of depleting nonrenewable resources or expanding populations. The prodigious growth of the human population is at the root of many environmental problems. As people are born, pollution levels increase, more habitats and animal and plant species disappear, and more natural resources are consumed. In recent decades two environmental issues have taken center stage: biodiversity and global warming. *Environmental Impact*

Biodiversity relates to the maintenance of multiple species of plants and animals. The most serious threat to biodiversity emerged from the destruction of natural habitats in the wake of urbanization, extension of agricultural activity, and exploitation of mineral and timber resources. Extinction currently threatens some 4,500 animal species. Global warming refers to a rise in global temperature, which carries potentially dire consequences for humanity. Atmospheric pollution causes global warming because the emission of so-called greenhouse gases prevents solar heat from escaping from the earth's atmosphere.

Like the glass panes in a greenhouse, hydrocarbon emissions from automobiles, carbon dioxide emissions from burning fossil fuel, and methane emitted from the stool of farm animals trap heat within the atmosphere, leading to a rise in global temperatures. Even a seemingly modest rise of one to three degrees Celsius in the temperature of the atmosphere might have serious consequences, such as a rise in sea levels that would completely inundate low-lying islands and coastal areas on all continents. In the ancient Japanese capital of Koyto, at a conference dedicated to pressing environmental problems, the delegates of 159 countries agreed in 1997 to cut greenhouse gas emissions blamed for global warming. Although the conference delegates agreed that developed nations should cut the emissions of carbon dioxide and other dangerous gases, the conference did not require developing countries—some of them major polluters, like India and China—to reduce their emissions at all.

For decades the issue of population control was highly politicized. Political leaders in developing countries, for example, charged representatives of industrialized countries with racism when they raised concerns regarding overpopulation. Industrialized nations were also accused of trying to safeguard their outrageous consumption patterns of the world's nonrenewal resources. Some leaders, such as Mexico's Luis Echeverria, went so far as to promote pronatalist measures (to increase births), urging his fellow citizens to have numerous children. The problems caused by rapid population growth eventually convinced many governments to take action to control fertility. By this time the old but pervasive notion that a large population is a source of national power had given way to the idea that the best way to promote the health and well-being of a population is to control its growth. *Population*

As death rates have declined persistently throughout the world during the latter part of this century, reducing birth rates became a central concern of many governments, and to date some eighty countries have adopted birth control programs. The United Nations and two of its specialized agencies, the World Health Organization

TABLE 39.1

• • •

POPULATION FOR MAJOR AREAS OF THE WORLD, 1900–1998

Major Area	1900	1950	1998	2050
Asia	947	1402	3585	5268
Africa	133	221	749	1766
Europe	408	547	729	628
Latin America	74	167	504	809
North America	82	172	305	392
Oceania	6	13	30	46
World (total)	1650	2521	5901	8909

SOURCE: United Nations, *World Population Prospects: The 1998 Revisions.*

(WHO) and the UN Fund for Population Activities, have aided many countries in organizing and promoting family-planning programs. However, the availability and promotion of contraceptives does not guarantee effective control of fertility. Whereas China has, however stringently, significantly reduced its population growth rate and some Latin American societies have also seen a decline in their birth rates, people in other societies have resisted efforts to reduce birth rates. In some instances resistance stems from both religious and political motives. In India, for example, the Hindu emphasis on fertility has impeded birth control efforts. Thus global efforts to prevent excessive population growth have had mixed results.

Migration

Migration, the movement of people from one place to another, is as old as humanity and has shaped the formation and identity of societies throughout the world. The massive influx of outsiders has transformed the ethnic, linguistic, and cultural composition of indigenous populations. With the advent of industrialization during the eighteenth century, population experts distinguished between two types of migration: internal migration and external or international migration. Internal migration describes the flow of people from rural to urban areas within one society, whereas external migration describes the movement of people across long distances and international borders. Both types of migration result from "push" or "pull" factors, or a combination of both. Lack of resources such as land or adequate food supplies, population pressure, religious or political persecution, or discriminatory practices aimed at ethnic minorities push people to move. Conversely, opportunities for better employment, the availability of arable land, or better services such as health care and education pull people to new locations. In the most general sense, migration is caused by differences, and because differences among societies are widening, the potential for migration has increased.

Internal Migration   The largest human migrations today are rural-urban flows. During the last half century, these internal migrations have led to rapid urbanization in much of the world. Today the most highly urbanized societies are those of western and northern Europe, Australia, New Zealand, and temperate South America and North America.

TABLE 39.2

• • •

WORLD'S URBAN AREAS OF 10 MILLION OR MORE INHABITANTS IN 1996

Rank	Urban Area	Country	Population (thousands)
1	Tokyo	Japan	27,242
2	Mexico City	Mexico	16,908
3	São Paulo	Brazil	16,792
4	New York	United States	16,390
5	Bombay	India	15,725
6	Shanghai	China	13,659
7	Los Angeles	United States	12,576
8	Calcutta	India	12,118
9	Buenos Aires	Argentina	11,931
10	Seoul	Republic of Korea	11,768
11	Beijing	China	11,414
12	Lagos	Nigeria	10,878
13	Osaka	Japan	10,618
14	Delhi	India	10,298
15	Rio de Janeiro	Brazil	10,264
16	Karachi	Pakistan	10,119

SOURCE: United Nations, *World Population Prospects: The 1998 Revisions.*

In these societies the proportion of people living in urban areas exceeds 75 percent; in some, as in Germany, it exceeds 85 percent. (A more recent phenomenon visible in developed countries is a reverse migration, from the city to the country.) The societies of tropical Latin America are in an intermediate stage of urbanization, with 50 to 65 percent of the population living in cities. In many countries in Africa and Asia, the process of urbanization has just begun. While most people still resides in rural areas, the rate of urbanization is very high.

Urbanization has proved to be a difficult and challenging transformation for rural folk who have chosen or been forced to adjust to a new way of life. In Latin America, Africa, and south Asia, large numbers of people have migrated to metropolitan areas in search of relief from rural poverty. Once in the cities, though, they often find themselves equally destitute. Life is bleak in the slums outside Bombay; in the shanty towns around Kinshasa or Nairobi; and in the *barriadas,* barrios, and *villas miserias* of Lima, Mexico City, and Buenos Aires. More than ten million people cram the environs of cities like Calcutta, Cairo, and Mexico City, straining those cities' resources. The few services originally available to the slum dwellers—potable water, electricity, and medical care—have diminished with the continuous influx of new people. Among the unemployed or underemployed, disease runs rampant, and many suffer from malnutrition.

External Migration   A combination of voluntary and forced international migrations has transformed the human landscape, especially during the past five hundred years. Between the sixteenth and twentieth centuries, more than sixty million European migrants, for example, colonized the Americas, Australia, Oceania, and the northern half of Asia. Between 1820 and 1980, in the course of the Atlantic migration, thirty-seven million migrants of European descent made their home in the United States alone. Slave migrations supplemented these voluntary movements of people. Between the sixteenth and nineteenth centuries, slave traders consigned about twelve million Africans to the Americas, though many died in the appalling conditions of the Atlantic voyages.

During World War II the Nazi regime initiated the largest mass expulsions of the twentieth century, deporting eight million persons to forced-labor sites and extermination camps. Following the war, the Soviet regime expelled some ten million ethnic Germans from eastern and central Europe and transported them back to Germany. The largest migrations in the second half of the twentieth century have consisted of refugees fleeing war. For example, the 1947 partition of the Indian subcontinent into two independent states resulted in the exchange of six million Hindus from Pakistan and seven million Muslims from India. More recently, three million to four million refugees have fled war-torn Afghanistan during the 1980s.

Many of these migrants left their home countries because they wanted to escape the ravages of war, but economic inequities between societies have caused most international migration. That is, people leave their country of birth in search of better jobs and more readily available health care, educational opportunities, and other services provided by the new society. Thus most contemporary mass migrations involve movement from developing countries to industrialized ones. Since 1960 some thirteen million "guest workers" from southern Europe, Turkey, and northern Africa have taken up permanent residence in western Europe, and more than ten million permanent migrants—mostly from Mexico—have been admitted to the United States. Foreigners currently make up more than half of the working population in the oil-producing countries of southwest Asia. Approximately 130 million people

Afghan refugees fled Iran in 1986, joining the ranks of the hundreds of thousands of forced displaced persons in the contemporary world.

• A. Hollmann/United Nations High Commissioner for Refugees

currently live outside their country of citizenship, collectively constituting a "nation of migrants" equivalent in size to Japan, the world's eighth most-populous nation.

International mass migrations have accelerated and broadened the scope of cross-cultural interaction. After their arrival on foreign shores, migrants established cultural and ethnic communities that maintained their social customs and native languages. The sounds of foreign languages, as well as the presence of ethnic foods, arts, and music, have transformed especially large cities into multicultural environments. But while the arrival of migrants has enriched societies in many ways, it has also sparked resentment and conflict. People in host countries often believe that foreigners and their ways of life undermine national identity, especially if defined in terms of language and other cultural characteristics. Beyond that, many citizens of host societies view migrants, who are often willing to work for low wages and not join labor unions, as competitors for jobs. When unemployment rates climb, there is a tendency to look for scapegoats, and all too frequently the blame falls on migrants. In many countries governments have come under pressure to restrict immigration or even expel foreign residents. Moreover, xenophobia, or an unreasonable fear of foreigners, has sometimes produced violence and racial tension, as when skinheads (shaved-head youths) in England assaulted members of ethnic minority groups or when neo-Nazis in Germany bombed the community centers of Turkish workers. Thus while migrants are reshaping the world outside their home countries, international mass migration poses challenges both to the migrants themselves and to the host society.

Migrant Communities

Cross-Cultural Travelers

A more recent and transient form of migration is tourism. Although travelers have established cultural links between societies since the beginning of recorded history, travel for a long time took place mainly in connection with military conquest, religious pilgrimage, trade, or diplomacy. If more people did not take to travel, it was because most had little incentive to leave their homes, especially when transport was slow, expensive, and inconvenient. So risky was travel that most people regarded travelers as either very courageous or very foolish.

Industrial society gave birth to mass tourism by providing both safer and faster transport and by institutionalizing two modern features of social life—leisure and travel. By the mid-nineteenth century, tourism—travel for recreation or study—had become a growing industry in western Europe and the United States. In England, Thomas Cook (1808–1892) established the first travel agency, bearing his name and offering first guided tours of Europe in the 1850s and subsequently of the United States. For the more independent-minded travelers, his agency arranged travel and hotel accommodations. In Germany, Karl Baedeker (1801–1859) and his son exploited the economic potential of tourism. They established a publishing firm that specialized in travel guides that were popular not only in their original German editions but also in French and English translations.

Mass Tourism

In the early and mid 1800s, it became fashionable in Europe for the affluent to vacation, often for extended periods, and then later in the century working people began to copy the fashions of the wealthy. Working-class families took to the road during holidays to escape the grimy drudgery of the industrial city, and in the process created working-class pleasure zones such as seaside resort in Britain, Coney Island in the United States, or Varna at the Black Sea. People journeyed for pleasure, engaging in activities they normally did not do, such as breathing fresh air, wearing oddly colorful clothes, or taking long walks for no reason at all. By the twentieth century leisure travel took on added symbolic value when travelers could show off the special

Effects of Mass Tourism

clothes required for their journeys, such as ski apparel or bikinis. Others established that they had traveled through changes in their physical appearance, which could include varying degrees of sunburn or a leg encased in plaster. After World War II companies created the packaged tour, which enabled millions of tourists to swarm across the world. Today middle-class tourists, "new age" travelers, and "eco" tourists—often weighted down by duty-free goods—busily crisscross the entire planet in their search for rarely visited sites. At the dawn of the next millennium, the tourism business is poised to become the single largest industry on the planet.

The cultural impact of mass tourism has had several dimensions. The global scope of contemporary tourism reflects the degree to which modern travelers view the world as a single space, without geographic or even political boundaries. Tourism also exposes travelers to cultural variations, thereby confirming the validity and diversity of local traditions. Finally, those who are the objects of the tourists' gaze frequently compare and contrast their own cultural practices and values to those of the visitors, which sometimes has led to the revival and transformation of indigenous cultural traditions. One such place is Toraja in the Celebes, where tourists go to witness local death ceremonies. Their arrival has prompted the "ritual inflation" of elaborate death ceremonies, organized for people whose death once would have been a relatively minor event. But the more tourists that locals can attract, the greater the honor for the village. Moreover, the presence of tourists has also led to a revival of local crafts, such as woodcarving, weaving, and the building of houses in traditional ways.

International Organizations

Although the world's nations and peoples are becoming increasingly interdependent, governments still operate on the basis of the territorially delimited state. Because global economic and cultural interdependence demands that political activity focus on cross-societal concerns and solutions, nations are under pressure to surrender portions of their sovereignty. Moreover, as national borders become less important in the face of new economic and cultural connections, the effectiveness of national governments has declined. The widespread recognition that the national state is ill equipped to handle problems of a global magnitude has led to an increase in the number of organizations dedicated to solving global problems through international coordination and action. Often categorized as nongovernmental international organizations and governmental international organizations (NGOs), these institutions are important because they have the potential to tackle problems that do not respect territorial boundaries and are beyond the reach of national governments.

Nongovernmental Organizations

Contemporary efforts at global cooperation have antecedents in the past. A prototypical NGO is the Red Cross, an international humanitarian agency. Founded on the initiative of the Swiss philanthropist Jean Henri Dunant (1828–1910), this agency was originally dedicated to alleviating the sufferings of wounded soldiers, prisoners of war, and civilians in time of war. In 1864 the representatives of twelve nations signed the first Geneva Convention, which laid down the rules for the treatment of the wounded and the protection of medical personnel and hospitals. The convention adopted the red cross as a symbol of neutral aid. (Most Muslim countries use a red crescent.) Later protocols—signed by most nations—revised and amended the original principles enunciated in the first Geneva Convention to include protection for noncombatants as well. The Red Cross ultimately extended its mission to peacetime, rendering medical aid and other help for victims of natural disasters such as floods, earthquakes, and famines.

An especially prominent contemporary NGO is Greenpeace founded in 1970, an environmental organization dedicated to the preservation of the earth's natural resources and its diverse animal and plant life. In their pursuit of a green and peaceful world, Greenpeace activists have gained international notoriety and fame for their daring exploits, which are calculated to attract media attention to environmental concerns. With the world watching, Greenpeace members in small rubber rafts have disrupted whaling expeditions by placing themselves between the whales and the hunters' harpoons. On other occasions Greenpeace has convinced major news networks to broadcast disturbing pictures of the slaughter of baby harp seals. After getting the attention of the media, Greenpeace activists worked to prevent further slaughter by spraying red paint on the seals, making their fur worthless for commercial purposes.

The Greenpeace flagship, *Rainbow Warrior,* launched in 1989 and named for a Native American prophecy that predicted a rainbow warrior would save the earth from disaster. • Jean Louis Cholet/ Liaison International

The United Nations

The premier international governmental organization is the United Nations, which superseded the League of Nations (1920–1946). This association of sovereign nations attempts to find solutions to global problems and to deal with virtually any matter of concern to humanity. Unlike a national parliament, the UN does not legislate. Yet in its meeting rooms and corridors, representatives of the vast majority of the world's countries have a voice and a vote in shaping the international community of nations.

Under its charter a principal purpose of the UN is "to maintain international peace and security." Cynics are quick to point to the UN's apparent inability to achieve this goal, citing as evidence the eight-year war between Iraq and Iran, the civil war in Somalia, and the many years of bloodshed in Afghanistan. However flawed its role as an international peacemaker and a forum for conflict resolution, the UN has compiled an enviable record with respect to another role defined in its charter, namely, "to achieve international cooperation in solving international problems of an economic, social, cultural, or humanitarian character." Quietly and without attracting attention from the news media, the specialized agencies of the UN have achieved numerous successes. For example, in 1980 the World Health Organization proclaimed the worldwide eradication of smallpox as a result of its thirteen-year-old global program. On other fronts UN efforts resulted in a 50 percent decrease in child mortality in developing countries since 1960, an increase in female literacy rates in developing countries from 36 percent in 1970 to 56 percent in 1990, and safe drinking water for 1.3 billion people living in rural areas of the world.

Given the present level of global interaction, international coordination is a necessity. Collaboration within and between international organizations has often left much to be desired. Meetings, talks, and consultations have frequently deteriorated into arguments. At the height of the cold war, this situation hampered progress in finding solutions to crucial problems. Contentious issues have sometimes paralyzed the UN and its affiliated organizations, as societies at different stages of economic development have pursued sometimes conflicting social and political goals. Cultural diversity continues to make it difficult for people to speak a common language. Despite the shortcomings of international organizations, however, for the present they represent the closest thing humanity has to a global system of governance that can help the world's peoples meet the challenges of international problems.

The new relevance of international organizations and the increasing irrelevance of national boundaries signified the arrival of a world without borders. The end of the cold war dramatically altered global political alignments and opened up the possibility of new, less divisive models for international relations. Technological and cultural developments likewise combined to break down barriers and create a "global village" that connected diverse peoples. Although many societies resisted cultural influences from Europe and the United States, the prevalence of communications technology and cultural diffusion made interaction inevitable. Women's efforts to achieve greater equality with men also collided with cultural traditions; but, while many barriers, to women's liberation remain, others have fallen. The global movement of human populations crisscrossed boundaries, both internal and external, and contributed to global problems that could be solved only through international cooperation. In the borderless world of contemporary times, nothing less is acceptable.

CHRONOLOGY

1950	Chinese marriage law World population at 2.5 billion
1960	Introduction of the birth control pill
1961–1989	Berlin Wall
1964	U.S. Civil Rights Act
1967	Establishment of the Club of Rome
1975	Declaration of the Decade of Women by the U.N.
1982	Defeat of the Equal Rights Amendment in the United States
1989–1990	End of communism in east and central Europe
1990	Reunification of Germany
1991	Collapse of the Soviet Union End of the cold war Nobel Peace Prize awarded to Aung San Suu Kyi
1992	First Earth Summit
1994	World population at 5.5 billion

FOR FURTHER READING

André Burguière et. al. *A History of the Family,* Vol. 2: *The Impact of Modernity,* Cambridge, Mass., 1996. A collection of in-depth articles on modern families in different parts of the world.

Joel E. Cohen. *How Many People Can the Earth Support?* New York, 1997. The author treads were few demographers dare to go.

John Bellamy Foster. *The Vulnerable Planet: A Short Economic History of the Environment.* New York, 1994. Sympathetic account of technological and environmental change.

Margaret Jean Hay and Sharon Stichter. *African Women South of the Sahara.* Boston, 1984. An analysis of social and economic change and how it affected African women in the twentieth century.

Nikki R. Keddie and Beth Baron, eds. *Women in Middle Eastern History: Shifting Boundaries in Sex and Gender.* New Haven, 1992. A sensitive selection of articles by the leading scholars in the field.

Joanna Liddle and Rama Doshi. *Daughters of Independence: Gender, Caste, and Class in India.* New Delhi, 1986. The Indian caste system, British colonial rule, and class structure provide the backdrop for this work on the contemporary women's movement.

Charles S. Maier. *Dissolution: The Crisis of Communism and the End of East Germany.* Princeton, 1997. Not an easy read, but a very scholarly and insightful analysis of how and why the country fell apart and disappeared.

Michael Mandelbaum. *The Dawn of Peace in Europe.* New York, 1997. An elegant work focusing on the central question of continental security.

Julian L Simon. *Population Matters: People Resources, Environment and Immigration.* New Brunswick, N.J. 1990. Broad and general treatment of demographic, environmental, and economic problems.

Malcom Waters. *Globalization.* New York, 1995. Framed by sociological theory, this crisp, to-the-point guide covers globalization and its consequences.

Wang Gungwu, ed. *Global History and Migrations.* Boulder, 1997. A fine collection of essays on topics that range from the Atlantic slave trade to diasporas and their relationship to the nation-state.

Margery Wolfe. *Revolution Postponed: Women in Contemporary China.* New Haven, 1985. Explores one of the more problematic legacies of the Chinese Revolution.

PRONUNCIATION KEY

. . .

AH—a sound, as in Car, father
IH—short i sound, as in fit, his, or mirror
OO—long o sound, as in ooze, tool, crew
UH—short u sound, as in up, cut, color
A—short a sound, as in asp, fat, parrot
EE—long e sound, as in even, meet, money
OH—long o sound, as on open, go, tone
EH—short e sound, as in ten, elf, berry
AY—long a sound, as in ape, date, play
EYE—long i sound, as in ice, high, bite
OW—dipthong o sound, as in cow,
    how, bow
AW—dipthong a sound, as in awful,
    paw, law

NOTE ON EMPHASIS: syllables in capital letters receive the accent. If there is no syllable in capitals, that means that all syllables get equal accent, almost like two separate single syllable words.

Ab al-Hamid II (AHB ahl·HAH·mihd)
Abbasid (ah·BAH·sihd)
Abu al-Abbas (ah·BOO uhl ah·BAHS)
Abu Bakr (ah·BOO BAHK·uhr)
Abyssinia (AB·uh·SIHN·nee·uh)
Achaemenids (ah·KEE·muh·nids)
Addis Ababa (AD·ihs AB·uh·buh)
Aegean (ih·JEE·uhn)
Aeneas (ih·NEE·uhs)
Aeschylus (ES·kuh·luhs)
Ahimsa (uh·HIM·suh)
Ahmosis (AH·moh·sis)
Ahura Mazda (uh·HOOR·uh MAHZ·duh)
Akbar (AHK·bahr)
Akhenaten (AH·ken·AH·tuhn)
Akkadian (uh·KAY·DEE·uhn)
Al-Andalus (al·ANN·duh·luhs)
Al Bakri (al·BAHK·ree)
Albigensians (AL·bih·jehn·see·uhns)
Alboquerque, Afonso d' (d'AHL·boh·kehr·kee, ah·FON·zoh)
Allah (AH·lah)
Amenhotep (ah·muhn·HOH·tehp)

Amon-Re (AH·muhn RAY)
Amundsen, Roald (AH·moond·sehn, ROH·ahld)
Anatolia (ANN·uh·toh·lee·uh)
Ancien Regime (ann·SEE·ehn ray·JEEM)
Ankor (AHN·kohr)
Ankor Wat (AHN·kohr WAHTT)
Ankor Thom (AHN·kohr TAHM)
Angra Mainyu (AHNG·ruh MINE·Yoo)
Anschluss (AHN·schloos)
Antigonid (ann·TIHG·uh·nihd)
Antigonus (ann·TIHG·uh·noos)
Anyang (AHN·YAHNG)
Apartheid (ah·PAHR·teyed)
Aquinas, Thomas (ah·KWEYE·nuhs, TOM·uhs)
Aquitaine (Eleanor of) (AK·wih·tayn)
Aramaic (ar·uh·MAY·ik)
Arawaks (AR·ah·wahks)
Aresta (AR·ehs·tuh)
Arianism (AR·ee·uhn·iz·uhm)
Arikamedu (AR·ee·kah·may·doo)
Aristophanes (ar·uh·STAWF·uh·neez)
Aristotelean (ar·ihs·toh·TEEL·ee·uhn)
Aristotle (AIR·ih·staw·tuhl)
Arius (AHR·ee·uhs)
Armenian (AHR·mee·nee·an)
Artha (AR·thah)
Arthashastra (AR·thah·sha·strah)
Aryans (AIR·ee·anns)
Ascetics (uh·SET·icks)
Ashoka (ah·SHOH·kah)
Assyrians (uh·SEAR·ee·uhns)
Astrakhan (AH·strah·kahn)
Aten (AHT·uhn)
Audiencias (AW·dee·ehn·see·uhs)
Aung San Suu Kyi (AWNG SAHN SOO KEY)
Aurangzeb (ohr·AHNG·zehb)
Australopithecus (ah·strah·loh·PITH·uh·kuhs)
Avvakum (AH·vah·koom)
Aztalan (AHZ·tuh·lahn)

Babur (BAH·boor)
Babylon (BAB·ih·lawn)
Bacchus (BAHK·uhs)
Bactria (BAHK·tree·uh)
Bakufu (bah·KOO·foo)
Balboa, Vasco Nunez de (BAL·boh·uh, VAHS·koh NOO·nehz deh)
Bantu (BAN·too)
Batista y Zaldivar, Fulgencio (BAH·tees·tah ee zahl·dih·vahr, FOOL·jehn·see·ah)
Bauhaus (BOW·hows)
Bedouin (BEHD·oh·ihn)
Beijing (BAY·jihng)
Benazir Bhuto (BEHN·ah·zeer BOO·toh)
Benefice (BEN·uh·fihs)
Bengali (ben·GAH·lee)
Besalarius (BEHS·ah·lahr·ee·uhs)
Bhagavad Gita (BUG·uh·vahd GEE·tuh)
Bhakti (BOHK·tee)
Boddhisatvas (BOH·dih·SAT·vuhs)
Bolivar, Simon (BOH·lih·vahr, see·mohn)
Bolshevik (BOHL·shih·vehk)
Boucher, Guillaume (BOO·shay, gee·ohm)
Boyars (BOY·ahrs)
Brahmins (BRAH·minz)
Brezhnev, Leonid Ilyich (BREHJ·nehv, LAY·oh·nihd EE·lee·ihch)
Brhadaranyaka (BRAHD·ahr·ahn·yah·kah)
Brunelleschi, Filippo (BROON·ehl·EHS·kee, FIHL·lee·poh)
Bubonic Plague (boo·BON·ihk PLAYG)
Buddha (BOO·duh)
Buddhism (BOO·diz'm)
Bugunda (boo·GUHN·dah)
Bukhara (boo·KAHR·uh)
Bukka (BOO·kuh)
Bulghar (BUHL·gahr)
Bunraku (boon·RAH·koo)
Bushido (BOH·shee·DOH)
Buonarotti, Michaelangelo (BON·uh·rah·tee, mik·uh·LAHN·juh·loh)
Byzantine (BIHZ·ann·teen)
Byzantium (bih·ZANN·tee·uhm)

Caesarea (SEHZ·ah·REE·uh)
Cahokia (kuh·HOH·kee·uh)
Caliph (KAL·ihf)
Cambyses (kam·BEYE·seez)
Capetian (cah·PEE·shuhn)
Carolingians (kahr·uh·LIN·jihns)
Castillo, Bernal Diaz del (kahs·TEE·lyoh, ber·nahl DEE·ahz dehl)
Castizos (kah·STEET·zohs)
Catal Huyuk (cha·TAHL hoo·YOOK)
Caucusus (KAW·cuh·suhs)
Caudillos (KAW·dee·ohs)
Cayuga (KEYE·yoo·guh)
Ceres (SIHR·eez)
Ceylon (SAY·lohn)
Chalcedon (KAL·seh·dohn)
Chamorro (KAH·mohr·oh)
Chan Bahlum (CHAHN BAH·lahm)
Chanchan (Chahn·chahn)
Chandogya (CHANN·dawg·yah)
Chandragupta maurya (CHAHN·drah·goop·tuh MOHR·yah)
Chang'an (CHAHNG AHN)
Charlemagne (SHAHR·luh·MANE)
Chichen Itza (CHEE·chehn eet·SAH)
Cicero (SIS·uh·roh)
Circumnavigation (SIHR·cuhm·nav·ih·GAY·shuhn)
Cixi (TSEE·SHEE)
Coen, Jan Pieterszoon (KOHN, YAHN PEE·tehrs·zoon)
Confucian(s) (kuhn·FYOO·shuhn(s)
Confucius (kuhn·FYOO·shuhs)
Conquistadores (kohn·KEE·stah·dohr·ayz)
Copernicus, Nicolaus (coh·PUR·nih·kuhs, NIH·koh·luhs)
Coptic (KOP·tik)
Coromandel (KOHR·oh·mahn·dehl)
Corpus iuris civilis (KOR·puhs yoor·uhs sih·VEE·lihs)
Cortes, Hernan (kohr·TEHZ, HER·nahn)
Cossacks (KAW·sacks)
Creole (KREE·ohl)
Criollos (kree·OH·lohs)
Cro-Magnon (CROW MAG·nuhn)
Croesus (KREE·suhs)
Ctesiphon (tehs·IH·phawn)
Cuneiform (Kyoo·NEE·uh·form)
Cybele (SIHB·eh·luh)
Cyrillic (sih·RIHL·ihk)
Cyrus (SY·ruhs)

Da Gama, Vasco (dah GAH·mah, VAH·skoh)
Da Vaca, Cabeza (duh VAH·kuh, kah·BAY·zah)
Dahomey (dah·HOH·mee)
Daimyo (DEYEM·yoh)
Damascus (duh·MAS·kuhs)
Daodejing (DOW·DAY·JIHNG)
Daoism (DOW·i'zm)
Daoists (DOW·ists)
Dardanelles (dahr·dehn·EHLZ)
Darius (duh·REYE·uhs)
Deccan (DEK·uhn)
Degas, Edgar (day·GAH, ehd·gahr)
Deism (DEE·iz'm)
Delphi (DEL·feye)
Demeter (duh·MEE·tuhr)
Demotic (deh·MAH·tihk)
Deng Xiaoping (DEHNG show·PIHNG)
Dharma (DAHR·muh)
Dhimmi (dihm·mee)
Dias, Bartholomew (DEE·ahz, bar·TAWL·oh·mew)
Diaz, Porfirio (DEE·ahz., pohr·feer·ee·oh)
Dienbienphu (DEE·ehn·BEE·ehn·FOO)
Diocletian (DEYE·oh·CLEE·shun)
Dionysus (DEYE·oh·NEYE·suhs)
Dom Henrique (dawm on·REE·kay)
Donotello (DON·uh·tell·oh)
Dravidians (druh·VIHD·ee·uhns)
Dubcek, Alexander (DOOB·chehk, AL·ehks·ann·der)

Ecrasez l'infame (ay·crah·ZAY lahn·FAHM)
Einsatzgruppen (EYEN·sahtz·groo·pehn)
Encomenderos (ehn·KOH·mee·ehn·deher·ohs)
Encomienda (ehn·KOH·mee·ehn·dah)
Engentio (ehn·GEHN·see·oh)
Entente (ahn·TAHNT)
Ephesus (EHF·ih·suhs)
Epictetus (EHP·ihk·TEE·tuhs)
Epicurians (ehp·ih·kyoo·REE·uhns)
Equiano, Olaudah (EH·kwee·ah·noh, OH·low·dah)
Erasmus, Desiderius (ih·RAZ·muhs, dehs·ih·DEER·ee·uhs)
Etruscans (ih·TRUHS·kuhns)
Eucharist (YOO·kuh·rihst)
Eunuchs (YOO·nihks)

Euphrates (yoo·PHRAY·teez)
Euripides (yoo·RIP·ih·deez)

Farsi (FAHR·see)
Fatehpur Sikri (FAH·tah·per SEEK·ree)
Fauves, Les (FOHV, LAY)
Feudalism (fyoo·duh·lizm)
Fief (FEEF)
Filial piety (FIHL·ee·uhl PEYE·eh·tee)
Fourier, Charles (FOOR·ee·ay, CHAHRLS)
Freud, Sigmund (FROYD, SIHG·moond)
Fu Hao (FOO HOW)
Fulani (foo·LAH·nee)
Funan (foo NANN)

Galileo Galilei (gal·ih·LAY·oh gal·ih·LAY·ee)
Gallipoli (gal·IH·poh·lee)
Gandhara (gahn·DAHR·ah)
Gandhi, Mohandas (GAHN·dee, moh·HAHN·duhs)
Ganges (GAHN·jeez)
Gansu (GAHN·soo)
Garibaldi, Giuseppe (GAHR·ih·bahl·dee, JEE·oo·seh·pee)
Gathas (GATH·uhs)
Gauchos (GOW·chohz)
Gaugemela (Gow·guh·MEE·luh)
Gauguin, Paul (goh·GANN, pawl)
Gens de couleur (jehn deh koo·lur)
Ghana (GAH·nuh)
Ghazi (GAH·zee)
Ghaznarids (GAHZ·nah·rihds)
Gilgamesh (GIL·gah·mesh)
Giza (GEE·zuh)
Gizilbash (gih·ZIHL·bahsh)
Glasnost (GLAHS·nohst)
Gobineau (GOH·bih·now)
Golondrinas (GOH·lohn·dree·nahs)
Gorbachev, Mikhail (GOHR·bah·chehv, MEE·kayl)
Gouges, Olympe de (GOOJ, oh·lymp deh)
Gropius, Walter (GROH·pee·uhs, wahl·tur)
Guadalupe (GWAH·dah·loo·pay)
Guanahani (GWAH·nah·hah·nee)
Guanches (GWAHN·chehs)
Guangdong (GWANG·dahng)
Guiscard, Robert (GEES·car)
Gujarat (goo·juh·RAHT)
Guomintang (GWOH·mihn·dahng)

Hacienda (HAH·see·ehn·dah)

Hagia Sophia (HAY·jee·uh SOH·fee·uh)

Haiti (HAY·tee)

Haitian (HAY·shuhn)

Hajj (HAHJ)

Hammurabi (hahm·uh·RAH·bee)

Han (HAHN)

Han Feizi (HAHN feye·tsee)

Han Wudei (HAHN wu·DEYE)

Hangzhou (HAHNG·joh)

Hanseatic (HAN·see·AT·ihk)

Haoma (how·muh)

Harappa (hah·RAP·puh)

Harun al–Rashid (hah·ROON al·rah·SHEED)

Hatshepsut (hat·SHEP·soot)

Heian (HI·ahn)

Heliopolis (hee·lee·OP·uh·luhs)

Helots (HELL·uhts)

Henan (HEH·NAHN)

Heresy (HEHR·uh·see)

Herodotus (heh·ROHD·uh·tus)

Heisenberg, Werner (HEYE·sehn·behrg, VER·ner)

Hernandez, Jose (hehr·NANN·dehz, HOH·zay)

Hidalgo, Guadalupe (hih·DAHL·goh, gwah·dah·LOO·pay)

Hidalgo, Miguel de (hee·DAHL·goh, mee·GWEHL)

Hieroglyphics (heye·ruh·GLIPH·iks)

Himalayas (HIM·uh·lay·uhs)

Hinayana (HEE·nah·yah·nuh)

Hispaniola (HISS·pann·yoh·lah)

Hittites (HIT·eyets)

Ho Chi Minh (HOH CHEE MIHN)

Hominids (HAWM·ih·nihds)

Homo Erectus (HOH·MOH ee·REHK·tuhs)

Homo Sapiens (HOH·MOH SAY·pee·uhns)

Hongwu (HAWNG·WOO)

Hong Xiuquan (HAWNG·shoo·KWAHN)

Hormuz (hohr·MOOZ)

Huangchao (HWAHNG·CHOW)

Huari (HWAHR·ee)

Huitzilopochtli (wee·tsee·loh·pockt·lee)

Hulegu (HOO·luh·goo)

Hurrem Sultana (HOO·rehm SOOL·tah·nah)

Hussein, Saddam (HOO·sayn, sah·DAHM)

Hwang He (hwang hwee)

Hyksos (HICK·sohs)

Ibn Battuta (IB·uhn ba·TOO·tuh)

Ibn Rushd (IB·uhn RUSH·uhd)

Iconoclasts (eye·KAHN·oh·klasts)

Ieyasu (ee·YAH·soo)

Ihara Saikaku (ee·HAH·rah seye·KAH·koo)

Iliad (ILL·ee·uhd)

Ilkan Ghazan (EEL·kahn gah·ZAHN)

Ilkahnate (EEL·kahn·ate)

Inquisition (IHN·kwih·zih·shuhn)

Investiture (ihn·VEHST·tih·tyoor)

Ionian (eye·OH·nee·uhn)

Iroquois (EAR·uh·kwoi)

Istanbul (IHS·tahn·bool)

Ito Hirobumi (EE·toh HEE·roh·BOO·mee)

Iturbide, Augustin de (EE·tur·bee·deh, AH·guhs·tihn deh)

Itzcoatl (EET·zuh·koh·aht'l)

Jahangir (YA·hahn·geer)

Jains (JEYENS)

Janissaries (JAN·ih·sayr·ees)

Jiang Jieshi (Chiang Kai-shek) (JANG·JIH·shee (CHANG KEYE·shek)

Jizya (JIHZ·yuh)

Juarez, Benito (WAHR·ehz, behn·EE·toh)

Jurchen (JUHR·chen)

Ka'ba (KAH·buh)

Kabuki (kah·BOO·kee)

Kalinga (kah·LEENG·uh)

Kama (kah·mah)

Kamakura (kah·mah·KOO·rah)

Kamikaze (KAH·mih·kah·zee)

Kanesh (KAHN·esh)

Kang Yuwei (KAHNG yoo·WAY)

Kangxi (KAHNG·jee)

Kanun (KAH·noon)

Kara- kiri (kah·rah·KIHR·ee)

Karakorum (Kahr·uh·KOHR·uhm)

Karma (KAHR·mah)

Kashgar (KASH·gahr)

Kashmir (KASH·meer)

Kazan (kah·ZAHN)

Khadija (ka·DEE·juh)

Khan (KAHN)

Khanbaliq (KAHN·bah·LEEK)

Khmelnitsky, Bogdan (KAH·mehl·neet·skee, BOHG·dahn)

Khmers (K'mehrs)

Khomeini, Ayatollah Ruhollah (KOH·may·nee, EYE·ah·toh·lah ROO·hohl·lah)

Kubilai Khan (KOO·buh·leye KAHN)

Khufu (KOO·FOO)

Khurasan (kor·uh·SAHN)

Khwarazm Shah (KWAH·RAZ·uhm shah)

Khyber Pass (KEYE·bihr pass)

Kim Il Sung (KIHM ihl SOONG)

Knossos (NAHS·suhs)

Krushchev, Nikita (KROOZ·chehf, nih·KEE·tah)

Kong Fuzi (kahng foo·tsee)

Kshatriyas (KSHAHT·ree·uhs)

Kumiss (KOO·mihs)

Lagash (luh·GAHSH)

Lamaist (LAH·muh·ihst)

Lamu (LAH·moo)

Laozi (LOW·tseh)

Lascaux (lah·SKOH)

Latifundia (LAT·ih·FOON·dee·uh)

Lebensraum (LAY·behnz·rowm)

Legazpi, Miguel Lopez de (LEH·gahz·pee, MEE·gwehl LOH·pehz deh)

Levee en Masse (leh·VEE on MASS)

Lex talionis (lehks tah·lee·oh·nihs)

Li (LEE)

Liang Qichao (LEE·ahng CHEE·CHOW)

Loyola, Ignatius (loy·OH·luh, ihg·NAY·shuhs)

Luba (LOO·bah)

Lunda (LOON·dah)

Luoyang (LWOH·yahng)

Macedonia (MAS·ih·doh·nee·uh)

Machismo (mah·KEEZ·moh)

Madrasas (MAH·drahs·uhs)

Magadha (MAH·gah·duh)

Magyars (MAH·jahrs)

Magellan, Ferdinand (mah·GEHL·uhn, FER·dih·nand)

Mahabharata (mah·hah·BAH·rah·tah)

Mahayana (mah·huh·YAH·nuh)

Mahmud (MAH·muhd)

Malagasy (mal·uh·GAHS·ee)

Malayan (muh·LAY·ehn)

Mali (MAH·lee)

Malindi (mah·LIHN·dee)

Maluku (mah·LOO·koo)

Mani (mah·nee)

Manichaeism (man·ih·KEE·iz'm)

Mansa Musa (mahn·suh MOO·suh)

Mao Zedong (MOW·tsay·dawng)

Maodun (mow·duhn)

Maori (MAY·oh·ree)

Manzikert (MANZ·ih·kuhrt)

Marduk (MAR·dook)

Mare nostrum (MAH·ray NOH·struhm)

Mariana (MEHR·ee·AHN·uh)

Marquesas (mahr·KAY·suhs)

Masaccio (muh·SAHT·choh)

Marseillaise (MAHR·say·ehz)

Marseilles (mahr·SAY)

Maruitania (MORE·ih·tay·nee·uh)

Masai (mah·SEYE)

Mauryan (more·ee·ahn)

Maya (MAH·yuh)

Mazzini, Giuseppi (mah·ZEE·nee, JEE·oo·seh·pee)

Mbanza (m'BAHN·zah)

Medes (meeds)

Megasthenes (meg·ASS·thehn·ees)

Mehmed (MEH·mehd)

Meiji (MAY·jee)

Mekong (MAY·kahn)

Melaka (may·LAH·kah)

Mencius (MEN·shuhs)

Mendicants (MEN·dih·cants)

Menes (MEE·neez)

Mesopotamia (mehs·uh·poh·TAY·mee·uh)

Mestizo (mehs·TEE·zoh)

Metis (meh·TEEZ)

Minamoto (mih·nah·MOH·toh)

Minerva (mih·NERV·uh)

Minoan (mih·NOH·uhn)

Minos (MIHN·ohs)

Missi dominici (mihs·see doh·mee·nee·chee)

Mithraism (MITH·rah·iz'm)

Mizuno Tadakuni (mih·ZOO·noh TAH·dah·KOO·nee)

Moche (MOK)

Mochica (moh·CHEE·kuh)

Mogadishu (MOH·guh·DEE·shoo)

Mohammed Ali Jinnah (MOH·hah·mehd AH·lee JIH·nah)

Mohenjo-daro (moh·hen·joh·DAHR·oh)

Moltke (MOHLT·kee)

Mombasa (mom·BAH·sah)

Monotheists (MAW·noh·thee·ihsts)

Montesquieu (MAWN·tehs·skyoo)

Montezuma (MAHN·teh·zoo·muh)

Motecuzoma II (MOH·the·koo·ZOH·mah)

Mozambique (MOH·zam·beek)

Mughals (MOO·guhls)

Muhammad (muh·HAH·mehd)

Mulattoes (moo·LAH·tohs)

Mumtaz Mahal (MOOM·tazh mah·HAHL)

Murasaki Shikibu (MUR·ah·sah·kee shee·KEE·boo)

Muromachi (MRI·oh·MAH·chee)

Mussolini, Benito (MOO·soh·lee·nee, BEHN·ee·toh)

Muziris (mu·ZEE·rees)

Mycenaean (meye·seh·NEE·uhn)

Nahuatl (NAH·waht'l)

Nanjing (NAHN·jing)

Napata (nah·PAY·tuh)

Nasser, Gamal Abdel (NASS·ahr, GAH·mahl AHB·dehl)

Navajo (NAH·vuh·hoh)

Ndongo (n'DAWN·goh)

Neandertal (nee·ANN·duhr·thawl)

Nebuchadnezzar (NAB·oo·kuhd·nehz·uhr)

Negritude (NEH·grih·tood)

Nehru, Jawaharlal (NAY·roo, YAH·wah·hahr·lahl)

Neolithic (NEE·oh·lihth·ihk)

Nestorian (neh·STOHR·ee·uhn)

Nestorius (neh·STOHR·ee·uhs)

Ngo Dinh Diem (n'GOH DIHN dee·EHM)

Ngola (n'GOH·lah)

Niani (NYAH·nee)

Nicaea (neye·see·uh)

Nikon (NEYE·kon)

Nirvana (nuhr·VAH·nuh)

Novgorod (NOHV·goh·rod)

Nubia (NOO·bee·uh)

Nurhaci (nur·HAH·chee)

Nzinga (n'ZIHN·gah)

Odysseus (oh·DIHS·see·uhs)

Olduvai Gorge (awl·DOO·veye Gorj)

Omar Khayyam (OH·mahr KEYE·yahm)

Oneida (oh·NEYE·duh)

Onondaga (on·uhn·dah·gyuh)

Oprichniki (oh·PREEK·nee·kee)

Oprichnina (oh·PREEK·nee·nah)

Osiris (oh·SEYE·rihs)

Osmanlis (ahz·MAN·lees)

Palenque (pah·LENG·kee)

Paleolithic (PAY·lee·oh·lith·ihk)

Pantheon (pan·thee·on)

Parsis (pahr·SEES)

Parthians (PAHR·thee·uhns)

Pasargadae (pah·sahr·gah·dee)

Pater familias (PAH·tur fuh·MEE·lee·ahs)

Patriarch (PAY·tree·ahrk)

Pax Romana (pahks roh·MAH·nah)

Peloponnesus (pehl·oh·puh·nee·suhs)

Peninsulares (pehn·IHN·soo·LAH·rayz)

Perestroika (PAYR·eh·stroy·kuh)

Pericles (PEHR·ih·klees)

Persepolis (pehr·SEHP·uh·lihs)

Petrarcha, Francesco (PEE·trahr·kuh, frahn·CHESS·koh)

Pharaohs (FARE·ohs)

Philosophes (PHIHL·oh·sohfs)

Phoenician (fih·NEE·shuhn)

Picasso, Pablo (pih·KAH·soh, PAHB·loh)

Pizarro, Francisco (pih·ZAH·roh, fran·SIHS·koh)

Plato (PLAY·toh)

Plebians (plih·BEE·uhns)

Poleis (poh·LAYS)

Polis (POH·lihs)

Popul Vuh (paw·pawl vuh)

Prakrit (PRAH·kriht)

Procopius (proh·KOH·pee·uhs)

Ptolemaic (TAWL·oh·may·ihk)

Ptolemy (TAWL·oh·mee)

Pueblo (PWEHB·loh)

Pugachev (POO·gah·chehv)

Punic Wars (PYOO·nihk)

Punjab (POON·jahb)

Qanat (kah·NAHT)

Qi (chee)

Qianlong (CHIHN·lawng)

Qin (chihn)

Qing (chihng)

Qinghai (chihng·heye)

Quetzalcoatl (keht·sahl·koh·AHT 'l)

Quilon (KEE·lahn)

Quinto (KWIHN·toh)

Quipu (KEE·poo)

Quran (koo·RAHN)

Rabban Sauma (RAH·BAHN sou·mah)

Rabin, Yitzhak (RAH·been, EET·sahk)

Raja (rah·jah)

Ramayana (rah·mah·yah·nah)

Ramisht of Siraf (rah·MEESHT of see·RAHF)

Re (RAH)

Realpolitik (ree·EHL·paw·lee·teek)

Reconquista (ray·kohn·KEE·stah)

Remus (REE·muhs)

Repartimento (reh·PAHR·tih·mehn·toh)

Ricci, Matteo (REE·CHEE, mah·TAY·oh)

Richelieu (REE·shih·lyoo)

Riel, Louis (REE·ehl, LOO·ee)

Robespierre (ROHBS·pee·air)

Roi soleil, Le (rwah soh·LAY, lih)

Romanov (ROH·mah·nahv)

Romulus (RAWM·yoo·luhs)

Rosas, Juan Manuel de (ROH·sahs, WAHN man·WEHL deh)

Rubaiyat (ROO·bee·aht)

Sadat, Anwar (SAH·daht, AHN·wahr)

Safavid (SAH·fah·vihd)

Safi al-Din (SAH·fee ahl·DIHN)

Salah al-Din (sah·lah ahl·DIHN)

Saljuqs (sahl·JYOOKS)

Samarkand (SAM·uhr·kand)

Samsara (sahm·SAH·ruh)

Samundra Gupta (sah·MUHN·drah GOOP·tah)

Samurai (SAM·uhr·eye)

Sanscrit (san·skriht)

Santa Ana, Antonio Lopez de (SAN·tah ANN·ah, ANN·toh·nee·oh LOH·pehz deh)

Santiago de Compestela (SAHN·tee·ah·goh dih COHM·pohs·stehl·lah)

Sao Jorge de Mina (SOW YOR·gay deh MEE·nah)

Sao Tome (SOW·TOH·may)

Sardis (SAHR·dees)

Sargon of Akkad (SAHR·gone of AHK·KAHD)

Sasanids (suh·SAH·nids)

Sati (SOO·TEE)

Satyagraha (SAH·tyah·GRAH·hah)

Satraps (SAY·traps)

Satrapy (SAY·trap·ee)

Schlieffen (SCHLEE·fehn)

Seleucids (sih·LOO·sihds)

Seleucus (sih·LOO·suhs)

Selim (SAY·lihm)

Semitic (suh·miht·ihk)

Sengoku (sehn·GOH·koo)

Shah Abbas (SHAH·ah·BAHS)

Shah Ismail (SHAH·IHS·may·ehl)

Shah Jahan (SHAH jah·HAHN)

Shamanism (SHAH·mah·niz'm)

Shang (shahng)

Shangdu (Shahng·doo)

Shanghai (Shahng·heye)

Shankara (SHAHN·kah·rah)

Shari'a (shah·REE·ahn)

Shia (SHEE·ah)

Shiism (SHEE·i'zm)

Shiite (SHEE·eyet)

Shinto (SHIHN·toh)

Shiva (SHEE·vuh)

Shudras (SHOO·druhs)

Sichuan (SEHCH·WAHN)

Siddhartha Gautama (sih·DHAR·tuh GOW·tah·mah)

Sikhs (SIHKS)

Sind (SIHND)

Sinhalese (sihn·huh·LEEZ)

Socrates (SAWK·ruh·tees)

Sophocles (SOPH·uh·klees)

Song (SOHNG)

Srivijaya (sree·VIH·juh·yuh)

Stoics (STOH·ihks)

strabo (TRAY·boo)

Sui (SWEE)

Sui Yangdi (SWEE yahng·dee)

Sulla, Lucius Cornelius (SOO·luh, LOO·shus kohr·nee·lee·uhs)

Suleyman (SOO·lee·mahn)

Sumerians (soo·MEHR·ee·uhns)

Sun Yatsen (SUHN yeht·sehn)

Sundiata (soon·JAH·tuh)

Sunni (SOON·nee)

Sunni Ali (SOO·nee AH·lee)

Swahili (swah·HEE·lee)

Syncretic (sihn·KREH·tihk)

Syngman Rhee (SIHNG·mahn REE)

Taino (TEYE·noh)

Taiping (TEYE·pihng)

Taklamakan (TAH·kluh·muh·KAHN)

Tamerlane (TAM·uhr·layn)

Tang (TAHNG)

Tang Taizong (TAHNG TEYE·zohng)

Tanis (TAH·nihs)

Tarim (TAH·reem)

Tarsus (TAHR·suhs)

Temujin (TEM·oo·chin)

Tenochtitlan (teh·NOCH·tee·tlahn)

Teotihuacan (tay·uh·tee·wah·KAHN)

Terra Nullius (TEHR·rah NOO·lee·uhs)

Theodora (thee·oh·DOHR·ah)

Theodosius (thee·oh·DOH·shuhs)

Tiahuanaco (tee·uh·wuh·NAH·koh)

Tian (TEE·ehn)

Tian Shan (TEE·ehn SHAHN)

Tiberius (teye·BEER·ee·uhs)

Tigris (TEYE·grihs)

Tikal (tee·KAHL)

Timur-i lang (tee·MOOR·yee LAHNG)

Tokugawa (TOH·koo·GAH·wah)

Trezibond (TREHZ·ih·bahnd)

Tughril Beg (TUUG·rahl behg)

Turkistan (TURH·kee·shtahn)

Turpan (TUHR·pahn)

Tuthmosis (tuhth·MOH·sihs)

Tsar (ZAHR)

Turkana (tur·KAH·nah)

Uddalaka (YOO·dah·lah·kah)

Uighurs (WEE·goors)

Ulaanbaatar (OO·lahn·bah·tahr)

Umayyad (oo·MEYE·ahd)

Umma (UM·mah)

Upanishads (oo·PAHN·ee·shahds)

Ur (oor)

Urdu (OOR·doo)

Uruk (OO·rook)

Utopian (yoo·TOH·pee·ahn)

Uzbek (OOZ·behk)

Vaishyas (VEYES·yuhs)

Varna (VAHR·nuh)

Vaqueros (vah·KEHR·ohs)

Vedas (VAY·duhs)

Venta, La (VEHN·tuh, lah)

Veracruz (VEHR·uh·crooz)

Vernacular (ver·NA·kyoo·lar)

Versailles (vehr·SEYE)

Vesta (VEHS·tah)

Vijayanagar (vee·juh·yah·NAH·gahr)

Vishnu (VIHSH·noo)

Visigoths (vih·sih·gahths)

Vodou (voh·DOW)

Volk (FOHLK)
Volksgeist (FOHLKS·geyest)
Volta do mar (VOHL·tah doh MAHR)
Voltaire (vohl·TAIR)

Walesa, Lech (WAH·lehn·sah, LEHK)
Wanli (wahn·LEE)
Wei (WAY)
Witte, Sergei (VIHT·tee SAYR·gay)
Wu Ding (woo dihng)
Wuwei (woo·WAY)

Xi'an (SHEE·ahn)
Xia (shyah)

Xianyang (SHYAHN·YAHNG)
Xiao (SHYAH·ow)
Xinjiang (shin·jyahng)
Xuanzang (shoo·WAHN·ZAHNG)

Yahweh (YAH·way)
Yangshao (YAHNG·show)
Yangzi (YAHNG·zuh)
Yongle (YAWNG·leh)
Yu (yoo)
Yuan (yoo·AHN)
Yucatan (yoo·kuh·TAN)
Yurts (yuhrts)

Zaibatsu (zeye·BAHT·soo)
Zaire (zah·EER)

Zambesi (ZAM·BEE·zee)
Zambos (ZAHM·bohs)
Zamudio, Adela (ZAH·moo·dee·oh, ah·DEH·lah)
Zanzibar (ZAN·zih·bahr)
Zarathustra (zar·uh·THOO·struh)
Zheng He (JUNG HEH)
Zhou (JOH)
Zhu Xi (choo·SHEE)
Ziggurats (ZIG·uh·rahts)
Zimbabwe (zihm·BAHB·way)
Zmestvov (ZEHMST·voh)
Zoroastrianism (zohr·oh·ASS·tree·ahn·iz'm)
Zoroastrians (zohr·oh·ASS·tree·ahns)

CREDITS

. . .

TEXT

Chapter 22

Alfonso di Alboquerque, *Commentaries of the Great Alfonso Dalboquerque,* 4 vols., trans. by Walter de Gray Birch (London: Hakluyt Society, 1875–84), 1:105, 112–114 .

Chapter 23

Adam Smith, *An Inquiry into the Nature and Causes of the Wealth of Nations* (Edinburgh, 1863), pp 198–200.

Chapter 24

Bernardino de Sahagun, Florentine Codex: General History of the Things of New Spain, 13 vols., trans. by Charles E. Dibble and Arthur J.O. Anderson. Copyright 1982. Reprinted by permission of the University of Utah Press and the School of American Research.

Chapter 25

Olaudah Equiano, *The Interesting Narrative of the Life of Olaudah Equiano, or Gustavus Vassa, The African, Written by Himself,* 2 vols. (London, 1979).

Chapter 26

J.O.P. Brand, *Annals and Memoirs of the Court of Peking* (Boston: Houghton Mifflin, 1914), pp 325–31.

Chapter 27

Babur, *The Babur-nama in English (Memoirs of Babur),* trans. by Annette Susannah Beveridge (London: Luzac, 1922).

Chapter 28

Jakob Staehlin von Storcksburg, *Original Anecdotes of Peter the Great* (London: J. Murray, 1788), pp 190–98.

Chapter 30

Karl Marx and Friedrich Engels, *Manifesto of the Communist Party.* Trans. by Samuel Moore. London: W. Reeves, 1888.

Chapter 31

Simon Bolivar, *Selected Works of Bolivar,* Compiled by Vincente Lecuna, ed. by Harold A. Bierck, Jr., trans. by Lewis Bertrand (New York: Colonial Press, 1951) 1:175–76, 181–83.
From: *Been in the Storm too Long* by Leon F. Litwack. Copyright © 1979 by Leon F. Litwack. Reprinted by permission of Alfred A. Knopf, Inc.

Chapter 32

From Rondo Cameron, editor, *Civilization Since Waterloo: A Book of Source Readings,* (Harlan Davidson, 1971), pp 245–246, Copyright © 1971 by Harlan Davidson, Inc. Reprinted by permission.
Dun J. Li, *China in Transition* (International Thompson Publishers).

Chapter 33

Rudyard Kipling, "The White Man's Burden," *McClure's Magazine* 12:4 (1899): 290–291.

Chapter 34

Edmund Blunden, ed. *The Poems of Wilfred Owen.* London: Chattus & Windus, 1933.
From: V. I. Lenin, *The State and Revolution.* Copyright 1973. Reprinted by permission of Foregin Languages Press.

Chapter 35

Excerpts from *Mein Kampf* by Adolf Hitler, translated by Ralph Manheim. Copyright (c) 1939, 1943 by Houghton Mifflin Company. Reprinted by permission of Houghton Mifflin Company, and Random House UK, Ltd. all rights reserved.
From: *Selected Works of Mao Tse-Tung, Volume I.* Copyright © 1977. Reprinted by permission of Foreign Languages Press.

Chapter 36

Yamaoka Michiko, "Eight Hundred Meters From the Hypocenter." In Haruko Taya Cook and Theodore F. Cook, *Japan at War: An Oral History* (The New Press, 1992), 384–287. In Stuart B. Schwartz, et. al. *The Global Experience: Readings in World History, II* (New York: McGraw-Hill, 1998), 247–251.

Chapter 37

Reprinted by permission of the Social Science Research Council.
From: Kwame Nkrumah, *I Speak of Freedom: A Statement of African Ideology* (New York: Praeger, 1961).

Chapter 38

From: Hamid Algar, ed. and trans., *Islam and Revolution: Writings and Declarations of Imam Khomeini* (Berkeley: Mizan Press 1981), pp 304–306. In Phillip F. Riley, et. al., *The Global Experience,* Second Edition, Volume II (Upper Saddle River: Prentice Hall, 1992), p. 300.

Chapter 39

From: Thomas Berry, "Wonderland as Wasteland: The Earth in Deficit," *Cross Currents,* Winter 1985, pp 408–410, 412. Copyright 1985. Reprinted by permission.

INDEX

· · ·

Note: entries printed in **boldface** type and followed by a small **f** refer to figures, by a small **m** to maps, and by a small **t** to tables.